BARRON'S

How to Prepare for the

High School

Equivalency Examination

by **Murray Rockowitz**

Member, Board of Examiners, Board of Education, New York City
Licensed academic high school principal
Former principal, John Philip Sousa Jr. High School, New York City
Former Chairman, English Department, Charles Evans Hughes High School, New York City

Samuel C. Brownstein

Former Chairman, Biology Department
Wingate High School, Brooklyn, New York

Max Peters

Former Chairman, Mathematics Department
Wingate High School, Brooklyn, New York

Special Science Editor

Maurice Bleifeld

Principal of Martin Van Buren High School, Queens Village, New York

THIRD REVISED EDITION

BARRON'S Educational Series, Inc. Woodbury, New York

Que 40 gm comes 120 gm / 3 ml.

Step 1:
look @ the problem - see what
you have (gm - gm - ml -) (If only 1
of something you know answer will
be: in this case mL.)

Step 2:
Set the problem up. Keep Alike on top
and alike on bottom.

$$\frac{40 \text{ gm}}{x \text{ mL}} = \frac{120 \text{ gm}}{3 \text{ mL}}$$

Step 3:
Convert
$$x \frac{mL}{40 \text{ gm}} = \frac{3 \text{ mL}}{120 \text{ gm}}$$

Step 4:
Cross multiply to get x by itself.

$$\frac{x \text{ ml}}{40 \text{ gm}} = \frac{3 \text{ ml} \times 40 \text{ gm}}{120 \text{ gm}} =$$

$$\frac{3 \text{ ml} \times 40 = 120 \text{ ml}}{120} \text{ over}$$

$$= 1 \text{ mL}.$$

Contents

Contents

Contents

PART THREE

CHAPTER 8

Test A

Contents

Preface

The Revised Edition

This revised, enlarged edition appears as a result of the success of the first edition and incorporates the suggestions made by teachers and students who have used the book. Serious minded students requested additional practice material. We have therefore added three sample High School Equivalency Tests. Teachers found the glossary of scientific terms and the vocabulary of literature most valuable. In this edition we have expanded this concept to include the social sciences and also have added the definition of 1100 words that all high school graduates should know.

To the Reader

"Until recently, all we asked of a job applicant was that he be able to sign his name and find his way to the time clock. Now he's got to have a high school diploma." These words of an electronics manufacturer are a warning to the student and jobseeker of today.

- IF   you want an interesting job—one that does not lead to a dead end;
- IF   you want to be accepted in a good company's apprenticeship program;
- IF   you want to advance on the job to technician or troubleshooting levels from a one-operation task;
- IF   you want to continue your studies at a technical school;
- IF   you want to get a technical or junior professional Civil Service position;
- IF   you want to be accepted in a specialized assignment in the Armed Forces;

You Must Have a High School Diploma

If you have not yet completed high school, this book will help you earn that precious diploma by passing a High School Equivalency Examination. Nearly all states have programs that enable you to do this.

To Help You

We have carefully analyzed all existing state programs and the examinations that are most widely used.

We have carefully prepared materials that provide
— explanations of key ideas
— concise summaries of each topic
— thorough drill exercises
— realistic practice tests.

All you need add is the determination to use these materials according to the schedule we have suggested. If you do, you will gain the confidence and knowledge you need to pass the High School Equivalency Examination and earn your high school diploma.

To the Instructor

If you are using this book in a class preparing for the High School Equivalency Examination, please note that

— all the necessary background materials have been included;
— after every principle are found appropriate illustrations;
— after each topic and subtopic there are plentiful drill exercises;
— sample reading selections have been thoroughly analyzed;
— answers for all exercises have been included and, in many cases, there are explanations for the correct answer given.

You will *not* have to go to any other sources for additional materials. We have included more than enough practice and drill for any student in your class who seeks the High School Equivalency Diploma.

Acknowledgments

We should like to express our gratitude to the various officials of the State Departments of Education who cooperated by giving us the details of their high school equivalency programs.

We are also indebted to Scholastic Magazines, Inc. for their kind permission to reproduce material from *Science World* and *Senior Science*. These passages formed the basis for original questions on the interpretation of science materials.

Murray Rockowitz
Samuel C. Brownstein
Max Peters
Maurice Bleifeld

Dress Rehearsal

Do you want to have a preview of the experience of taking an examination similar to the High School Equivalency Examination to:

(1) find out if you are ready?

(2) find out those areas which you need to study most intensely in the final weeks before you actually take the test?

If so, send us the form on page 357 with a fee of $10

We will send you an examination to help you do just this. Complete the examination. Return your answers to us. We will send you your scores with an indication of your probable success on the actual examination and suggestions for intensive study.

1

The Scope of the High School Equivalency Examination

ITS IMPORTANCE TO YOU

To an adult who has not completed the formal requirements for a high school diploma, the High School Equivalency Testing Program is a golden opportunity to gain this diploma without returning to school. With this diploma, you will be able to qualify for civil service positions, enroll in special training and education programs of the armed forces, take part in many job training courses and union apprenticeship programs, and even gain admission to one of many colleges that recognize the high school equivalency diploma. As *Business Week* recently reported, in an article headed "Today's hiring rule: no diploma, no job," today the high school diploma has become the minimum requirement for many basic industrial jobs. Even in companies where the lack of a diploma is not a bar to employment, personnel men agree it is a bar to advancement.

If you have not completed high school, bear in mind that one-half of the U.S. citizens 25 or older have not been graduated from high school. Also, government statistics tell us that, within the 18–25 age bracket, more than 7 million lack a high school diploma.

This book will prepare you for the high school equivalency test and help you earn this valuable diploma.

The G E D Testing Program

Let us examine the General Educational Development Testing Program (High School Equivalency Examination). Each part of the Test Battery is described so that the content and format will be familiar to you as you prepare for the tests. In addition, sample questions for each test follow the description. Use these questions for diagnosis of your weaknesses and plan an effective and efficient program of study with the help of the chapters that follow.

THE FIVE TEST AREAS

Test 1. Correctness and Effectiveness of Expression

This test emphasizes correct spelling, punctuation, capitalization, and grammatical usage. It also requires ability to choose correct words and phrases, and to organize and express ideas.

Test 2. Interpretation of Reading Materials in the Social Studies

In this test passages from the field of social studies at the high school level are presented. It requires background information in American History, Civics, and World History. The questions that follow each passage measure ability to comprehend and interpret the content of the passage.

Test 3. Interpretation of Reading Materials in the Natural Sciences

This test consists of passages from the field of natural sciences at the level of the General Science course usually given in the ninth grade. A series of questions follow each passage which test ability to comprehend and interpret the content of the passage, and to apply the information to scientific topics, laws, generalizations, and developments.

Test 4. Interpretation of Literary Materials

This test consists of passages, both prose and verse, from American and English literature. The questions measure ability to comprehend and interpret the content of the passage, figures of speech, sentence structure and meaning, and to recognize mood and purpose.

Test 5. General Mathematical Ability

This examination requires a knowledge of whole numbers, fractions, and decimals and the ability to apply them to problems. It includes questions on interpretation of data from graphs, number series, as well as common areas in general mathematics. Problems include practical situations such as insurance, installment buying, taxes, investments, simple home construction and repair projects. Some questions in elementary algebra and plane geometry are also included.

HOW THE TESTS ARE MARKED

The tests are marked by machine. In tests corrected by machine, a usual device is to ask you to blacken (fill in with pencil) on the answer sheet the double dotted lines of the correct answer choice. (1–5 for example or a–e). To familiarize you with the technique, an example is printed below. Most of the practice exercises in this book also employ this technique.

EXAMPLE: Underline the *one* misspelled word in the following numbered group and blacken the appropriate space in the answer column.

1. (1) refinement (2) goverment (3) adamant (4) grievous (5) grammar   (1) 1 2 3 4 5

Since the second word is misspelled, you would indicate that fact by filling in the second space (marked 2) in the answer column.

SAMPLE TESTS

TEST **1**

Correctness and Effectiveness of Expression

Part 1 Spelling

Directions: Choose the *one* misspelled word in each of the following numbered groups, underline it, then blacken its space in the answer column at the right.

1. (1) design   (2) pleurisy   (3) naptha   (4) liquor   (5) describe   **1.** 1 2 3 4 5

2. (1) logical   (2) parenthesis   (3) zephyr   (4) counterfiet   (5) receipt   **2.** 1 2 3 4 5

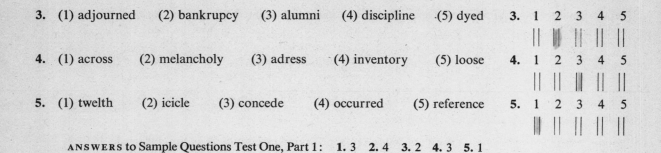

3. (1) adjourned (2) bankrupcy (3) alumni (4) discipline (5) dyed

4. (1) across (2) melancholy (3) adress (4) inventory (5) loose

5. (1) twelth (2) icicle (3) concede (4) occurred (5) reference

ANSWERS to Sample Questions Test One, Part 1: **1.** 3 **2.** 4 **3.** 2 **4.** 3 **5.** 1

Part 2 Correct Usage and Grammar

Directions: The 20 questions that follow the paragraph below are designed to test your appreciation of correct usage and effective expression in English. The paragraph is presented first in full so that you may read it through for sense. Disregard the errors you find, as you will be asked to correct them in the questions that follow.

The paragraph is then presented sentence by sentence, with portions underlined and numbered. At the right of this material you will find numbers corresponding to those below the underlined portions, each followed by five alternatives numbered 1 to 5. In some cases the usage in the underlined portion is correct. In other cases it requires correction. In every case, the usage in the alternative numbered 1 is the same as that in the original paragraph and is followed by four other possible usages. Choose the usage you consider best in each case and blacken its space in the answer column at the right.

When this war is over, no nation will either be isolated in war or peace. Each will be within trading distance of all the others and will be able to strike them. Every nation will be most as dependent on the rest for the maintainance of peace as is any of our own American states on all the others. The world that we have known was a world made up of individual nations, each of which had the priviledge of doing about as they pleased without being embarassed by outside interference. That world has dissolved before the impact of an invention, the airplane has done to our world what gunpowder did to the feudal world. Whether the coming century will be a period of further tragedy of one of peace and progress depend very largely on the wisdom and skill with which the present generation adjusts their thinking to the problems immediately at hand. Examining the principal movements sweeping through the world, it can be seen that they are being accelerated by the war. There is undoubtedly many of these whose courses will be affected for good or ill by the settlements that will follow the war. The United States will share the responsibility of these settlements with Russia, England and China. The influence of the United States, however, will be great. This country is likely to emerge from the war stronger than any other nation. Having benefitted by the absence of actual hostilities on our own soil, we shall probably be less exhausted than our allies and better able than them to help restore the devastated areas. However many mistakes have been made in our past, the tradition of America, not only the champion of freedom but also fair play, still lives among millions who can see light and hope scarcely nowhere else.

When this war is over, no nation will either be
isolated in war or peace.
       1

1. (1) either be isolated in war or peace
   (2) be either isolated in war or peace
   (3) be isolated in neither war nor peace
   (4) be isolated either in war or in peace
   (5) be isolated neither in war or peace

1. 1 2 3 4 5

Each will be
 2

2. (1) Each (2) It (3) Some (4) They (5) A nation

2. 1 2 3 4 5

within trading distance of all the others and
                3
will be able to strike them.

3. (1) within trading distance of all the others and will be able to strike them (2) near enough to trade with and strike all the others (3) trading and striking the others (4) within trading and striking distance of all the others (5) able to strike and trade with all the others

3. 1 2 3 4 5

Every nation will be most as dependent on
                       4

4. (1) most (2) wholly (3) much (4) mostly (5) almost

4. 1 2 3 4 5

the rest for the maintainance of peace as is
                  5
any of our own American states on all the
others. The world that we have known was

5. (1) maintainance (2) maintainence (3) maintenence (4) maintenance (5) maintanence

5. 1 2 3 4 5

a world made up of individual nations, each
                              6

6. (1) nations, each (2) nations. Each (3) nations: each (4) nations; each (5) nations each

6. 1 2 3 4 5

of which had the priviledge of doing about as
                  7

7. (1) priviledge (2) priveledge (3) privelege (4) privalege (5) privilege

7. 1 2 3 4 5

they pleased without being
 8

8. (1) they (2) it (3) they individually (4) he (5) the nations

8. 1 2 3 4 5

embarassed by outside interference. That
 9
world has dissolved before the impact of an

9. (1) embarassed (2) embarrassed (3) embaressed (4) embarrased (5) embarressed

9. 1 2 3 4 5

invention, the airplane has done to our world
    10
what gunpowder did to the feudal world.
Whether the coming century will be a period of further tragedy or one of peace and

10. (1) invention, the (2) invention but the (3) invention: the (4) invention. The (5) invention and the

10. 1 2 3 4 5

progress depend very largely on the wisdom
         11
and skill with which the present generation

11. (1) depend (2) will have depended (3) depends (4) depended (5) shall depend

11. 1 2 3 4 5

adjusts their thinking to the problems im-
    12
mediately at hand.

12. (1) adjusts their (2) adjust there (3) adjusts its (4) adjust our (5) adjust it's

12. 1 2 3 4 5

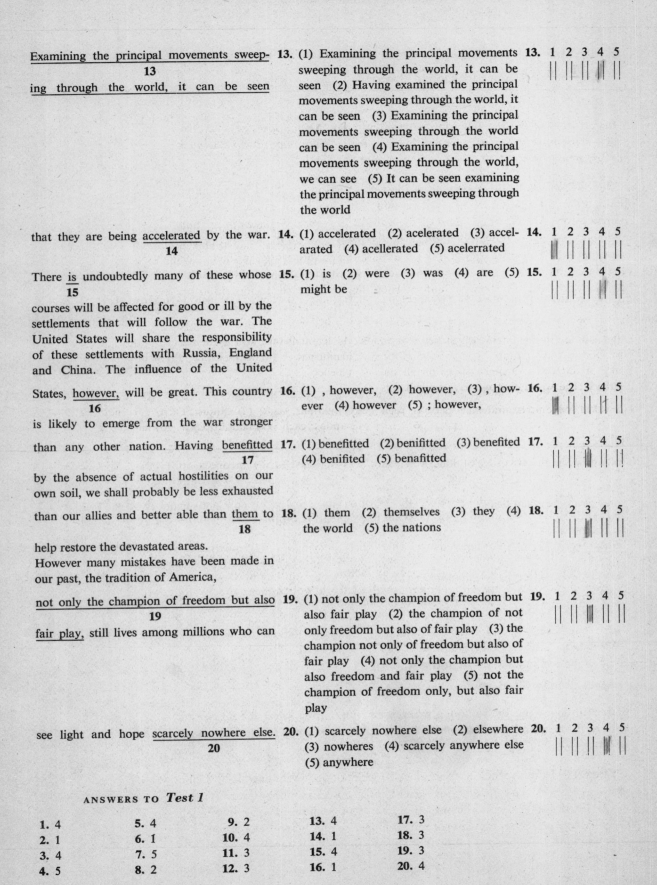

Examining the principal movements sweep-
                    13
ing through the world, it can be seen

13. (1) Examining the principal movements sweeping through the world, it can be seen (2) Having examined the principal movements sweeping through the world, it can be seen (3) Examining the principal movements sweeping through the world can be seen (4) Examining the principal movements sweeping through the world, we can see (5) It can be seen examining the principal movements sweeping through the world

13. 1 2 3 4 5

that they are being accelerated by the war.
                              14

14. (1) accelerated (2) acelerated (3) accelarated (4) acellerated (5) acelerrated

14. 1 2 3 4 5

There is undoubtedly many of these whose
        15
courses will be affected for good or ill by the settlements that will follow the war. The United States will share the responsibility of these settlements with Russia, England and China. The influence of the United

15. (1) is (2) were (3) was (4) are (5) might be

15. 1 2 3 4 5

States, however, will be great. This country
        16
is likely to emerge from the war stronger

16. (1) , however, (2) however, (3) , however (4) however (5) ; however,

16. 1 2 3 4 5

than any other nation. Having benefitted
                            17
by the absence of actual hostilities on our own soil, we shall probably be less exhausted

17. (1) benefitted (2) benifitted (3) benefited (4) benifited (5) benafitted

17. 1 2 3 4 5

than our allies and better able than them to
                                18
help restore the devastated areas.
However many mistakes have been made in our past, the tradition of America,

18. (1) them (2) themselves (3) they (4) the world (5) the nations

18. 1 2 3 4 5

not only the champion of freedom but also
                    19
fair play, still lives among millions who can

19. (1) not only the champion of freedom but also fair play (2) the champion of not only freedom but also of fair play (3) the champion not only of freedom but also of fair play (4) not only the champion but also freedom and fair play (5) not the champion of freedom only, but also fair play

19. 1 2 3 4 5

see light and hope scarcely nowhere else.
                        20

20. (1) scarcely nowhere else (2) elsewhere (3) nowheres (4) scarcely anywhere else (5) anywhere

20. 1 2 3 4 5

ANSWERS TO *Test 1*

1. 4	5. 4	9. 2	13. 4	17. 3
2. 1	6. 1	10. 4	14. 1	18. 3
3. 4	7. 5	11. 3	15. 4	19. 3
4. 5	8. 2	12. 3	16. 1	20. 4

TEST **2**

Interpretation of Reading Materials
in the Social Studies

Directions: **Read the following passage carefully. Then select the answer to each of the numbered questions which in your opinion best completes the statement or question.**

Since 1750, about the beginning of the Age of Steam, the earth's population has not been an evolutionary phenomenon with biological causes. Yet there was an evolution—it took place in the world's economic organization. Thus, 1,500,000,000 more human beings can now remain alive on the earth's surface, can support themselves by working for others who in turn work for them. This extraordinary tripling of human population in six short generations is explained by the speeded-up economic unification which took place during the same period. Thus most of us are now kept alive by this vast cooperative unified world society. Goods are the great travelers over the earth's surface, far more than human beings. Endlessly streams of goods crisscross, as on Martian canals, with hardly an inhabited spot on the globe unvisited.

1. The title below that best expresses the ideas of this passage is:
    (1) Modern Phenomena　(2) The Age of Steam　(3) Increasing Population　(5) Our Greatest Travelers　(5) Our Economic Interdependence

    1.　1　2　3　4　5

2. A generation is considered to be
    (1) 20 years　(2) 25 years　(3) 33 years　(4) 40 years　(5) dependent on the average age at marriage

    2.　1　2　3　4　5

3. The writer considers trade necessary for
    (1) travel　(2) democracy　(3) political unity　(4) self-preservation　(5) the theory of evolution

    3.　1　2　3　4　5

4. The basic change which led to the greatly increased population concerns
    (1) new explorations　(2) economic factors　(3) biological factors　(4) an increase in travel　(5) the growth of world government

    4.　1　2　3　4　5

TEST **3**

Interpretation of Reading Materials
in Natural Sciences

Directions: **Read the following passage carefully. Then select the answer to each of the numbered questions which in your opinion best completes the statement or question.**

Over 500 Bedouin men, all more than 30 years of age, were examined. Only one case of coronary thrombosis—a clot in a coronary artery—was found. Although Bedouins rarely eat meat or eggs—both common sources of animal fat in American diets—they do eat milk and cheese and butter. These, too, are common sources of animal fat in the United States. Thus, the Bedouin diet is not especially low in fat. What, then, was responsible for the low incidence of coronary thrombosis among these semi-nomads of the desert? The important factor might be the weight of the Bedouins; few Bedouins ever get fat.

In contrast, obesity (overweight) is considered to be one of the major health problems in the United States. Many Americans become obese when they maintain the eating patterns established in their more active youth. Most people become less active as they grow older. At the same time, the metabolic rate— the rate at which the body's tissues use food—tends to decline with age. But if our food intake remains constant as we grow older and the amount of food used up by our bodies declines, there can be only one result: fat accumulation.

Senior Science 3/24/65

5. A source of fat in the Bedouin diet is
   (1) eggs (2) meat (3) dairy products (4) vegetables (5) olive oil

6. The fact that coronary thrombosis occurs more frequently in the United States is possibly linked to
   (1) extravagance in food marketing (2) youth (3) obesity (4) our national diet (5) increase in metabolic rate

7. The health problem in the United States discussed in this passage, is
   (1) vitamin deficiency (2) obesity (3) metabolic disturbances (4) heart murmur (5) senility

8. Older people often become overweight because
   (1) their activity usually decreases (2) the metabolic rate declines (3) eating habits are not modified (4) all of the above (5) none of the above

9. A characteristic of Bedouins discussed in the passages is that they
   (1) abstain from animal fats (2) are naturally obese (3) have a lower metabolism as they grow old (4) are prone to coronary thrombosis (5) seldom suffer from obesity

10. According to this passage the chief cause of overweight is
    (1) nomadic living conditions (2) basal metabolism (3) source of animal fat (4) overeating (5) source of vegetable fat

11. Coronary thrombosis is best described as
    (1) the rate at which the tissues of the body use food (2) an underweight condition (3) blockage in the coronary artery due to a clot (4) an overweight condition (5) failure of the blood to clot

TEST **4**
Interpretation of Literary Materials

Directions: **Read the following passage carefully. Then select the answer to each of the numbered questions which in your opinion best completes the statement or question.**

As we know the short story today it is largely a product of the nineteenth and twentieth centuries and its development parallels the rapid development of industrialism in America. We have been a busy people, busy principally in evolving a production system supremely efficient. Railroads and factories have blossomed almost overnight; mines and oil fields have been discovered and exploited; mechanical inventions by the thousands have been made and perfected. Speed has been an essential element in our endeavors, and it has affected our lives, our very natures. Leisurely reading has been, for most Americans, impossible. As with our meals, we have grabbed bits of reading standing up, cafeteria style, and gulped down cups of sentiment on the run. We have had to read while hanging on to a strap in a swaying trolley car or in a rushing subway or while tending to a clamoring telephone switchboard. Our popular magazine has been our literary automat and its stories have often been no more substantial than sandwiches.

12. The title below that best expresses the ideas of this paragraph is:
(1) "Quick-lunch" Literature   (2) Life in the Machine Age   (3) Culture in Modern Life   (4) Reading while Traveling   (5) The Development of Industrialism

12.   1   2   3   4   5

13. The short story today owes its popularity to its
(1) settings   (2) plots   (3) style   (4) length   (5) characters

13.   1   2   3   4   5

14. The short story has developed because of Americans'
(1) reactions against the classics   (2) need for reassurance   (3) lack of culture   (4) lack of education   (5) taste for speed

14.   1   2   3   4   5

15. From this selection one would assume that the author's attitude toward short stories is one of
(1) approval   (2) indifference   (3) amusement   (4) curiosity   (5) regret

15.   1   2   3   4   5

ANSWERS TO *Tests 2, 3 and 4*

1. 5	6. 3	11. 3
2. 1	7. 2	12. 1
3. 4	8. 4	13. 4
4. 2	9. 5	14. 5
5. 3	10. 4	15. 5

TEST **5**

General Mathematical Ability

Directions: **Work out the following problems reducing each answer to its simplest form. Then select the correct answer and blacken the corresponding space in the answer column.**

1. When Mr. Brown bought his car he paid $500 down and agreed to pay 36 monthly installments of $75 each. Mr. Brown's total payment for the car was
(1) $2,700   (2) $1,800   (3) $3,100   (4) $3,200   (5) $8,000

1.   1   2   3   4   5

2. On a map, 1 inch represents 280 miles. If the distance between New York City and Chicago is $3\frac{3}{8}$ inches on the map, the actual distance between New York City and Chicago, in miles, is
(1) 630   (2) 945   (3) 700   (4) 900   (5) 798

2.   1   2   3   4   5

3. At a sale, a coat which had sold for $65 was marked down 15%. The sale price of the coat was
   (1) $9.75   (2) $56.25   (3) $50   (4) $55.25   (5) $54.25

3. 1 2 3 4 5

4. Mr. Duncan's house was assessed for $12,500. His town tax rate was $2.34 per $100 of valuation. Mr. Duncan's town tax was
   (1) $272.50   (2) $359.00   (3) $292.50   (4) $29.25   (5) $302.50

4. 1 2 3 4 5

5. The outside dimensions of a pool are 50 feet by 30 feet. A cement walk 4 feet wide is built around the inside of the pool. The area of the cement walk is
   (1) 1,196 sq. ft.   (2) 1,500 sq. ft.
   (3) 1,300 sq. ft.   (4) 1,320 sq. ft.
   (5) 576 sq. ft.

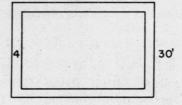

5. 1 2 3 4 5

6. One acute angle of a right triangle is twice the size of a second angle. The number of degrees in the smallest angle of the triangle is
   (1) 40   (2) 90   (3) 30   (4) 80   (5) 60

6. 1 2 3 4 5

7. The table below gives the yearly premium on each $1,000 of life insurance for each of two policies at different ages of the insured.

7. 1 2 3 4 5

AGE	STRAIGHT LIFE PREMIUM PER $1,000	20-PAYMENT LIFE PREMIUM PER $1,000
20	$16.03	$27.24
25	18.74	29.05
30	21.39	32.78
35	25.18	36.39
40	29.84	40.03

   Mr. Evans is 25 years old. He wishes to purchase a $5,000 life insurance policy. The difference in annual premium between a 20-payment life policy and a straight life policy is
   (1) $10.31   (2) $.31   (3) $51.55   (4) $50.55   (5) $47.79

8. According to some building standards a single house should not take up more than 30% of the area of the lot on which it is built. If a lot is 60 feet by 120 feet which of the following house dimensions does *not* meet the standard?
   (1) 40' by 50'   (2) 35' by 60'   (3) 40' by 40'   (4) 45' by 40'   (5) 35' by 65'

8. 1 2 3 4 5

9. A man 6 feet tall casts a shadow 5 feet long. At the same time, the height of a building which casts a shadow 30 feet long is
   (1) 25 ft.   (2) 60 ft.   (3) 36 ft.   (4) 40 ft.   (5) 27½ ft.

9. 1 2 3 4 5

10. On a motor trip Mr. Avery drove for two hours at the rate of 50 miles per hour. For the balance of the trip, which took three hours, he was on a parkway and drove at the rate of 60 miles per hour. His average driving speed for the entire trip was
    (1) 55 miles per hour   (2) 56 miles per hour   (3) 58 miles per hour
    (4) 53 miles per hour   (5) 54 miles per hour

10. 1 2 3 4 5

11. The inside dimensions of a truck are $9' \times 6' \times 3'$, as shown in the diagram. The number of truckloads needed to cart 567 cubic feet of sand is

(1) $3\frac{1}{2}$ (2) $5\frac{1}{4}$ (3) 7 (4) $31\frac{1}{2}$ (5) 9

11. 1 2 3 4 5

12. A formula for finding the number of hours a child should sleep is

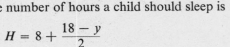

$$H = 8 + \frac{18 - y}{2}$$

In this formula,

H = the number of hours a child should sleep
y = the age of the child in years

According to this formula, a child 10 years of age should sleep

(1) 10 hours (2) 9 hours (3) 11 hours (4) 12 hours (5) 8 hours

12. 1 2 3 4 5

13. The graph below shows the receipts and expenditures for a certain town for the years shown. The shaded bars indicate receipts and the hollow bars indicate expenditures.

13. 1 2 3 4 5

COMPARISON BETWEEN RECEIPTS AND EXPENDITURES

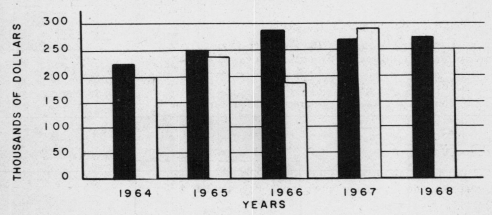

The year in which the town received $100,000 more than it spent was

(1) 1964 (2) 1965 (3) 1966 (4) 1967 (5) 1968

14. The mileage meter on Mr. Crane's car read 6,537.4 miles when he left on a trip. At the end of the trip the reading was 7,964.2 miles. If Mr. Crane used 82 gallons of gasoline on the trip, the number of miles covered for each gallon of gasoline used was

(1) 18 (2) 18.4 (3) 17.2 (4) 17.4 (5) 16.3

14. 1 2 3 4 5

15. Mr. Evans borrowed $6,400 from his bank for a year. The bank charged interest at the rate of $6\frac{1}{2}\%$ per year. The amount of interest that Mr. Evans had to pay was

(1) $4,160 (2) $416 (3) $704 (4) $70.40 (5) $316

15. 1 2 3 4 5

ANSWERS TO *Test 5*

1. 4	**6.** 3	**11.** 1
2. 2	**7.** 3	**12.** 4
3. 4	**8.** 5	**13.** 3
4. 3	**9.** 3	**14.** 4
5. 5	**10.** 2	**15.** 2

ANSWERS TO *Test 5 Explained*

1. ans. 4 Mr. Brown paid $500 + (36 \times 75) = 500 + 2,700 = \$3,200$.

2. ans. 2 To obtain the actual distance between New York and Chicago we multiply $280 \times 3\frac{3}{8}$.

$$280 \times 3\frac{3}{8}$$

$$280 \times \frac{27}{8}$$

$$\overset{35}{\cancel{280}} \times \frac{27}{\underset{1}{\cancel{8}}}$$

$$35 \times 27 = 945 \text{ miles}$$

3. ans. 4 We write 15% as .15.

$$65 \times .15 = \$9.75$$
$$\$65.00 - \$9.75 = \$55.25$$

4. ans. 3 There are 125 hundreds in 12,500.

$$\text{Tax} = 125 \times 2.34 = \$292.50.$$

5. ans. 5 The area of the cement walk is found by subtracting the area of the inner rectangle from the area of the outer rectangle.

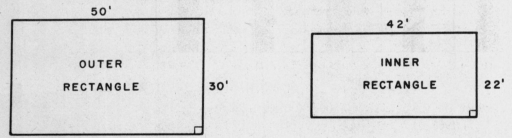

Note that the length of the inner rectangle is obtained from the length of the outer rectangle by subtracting two widths of the walk. That is, $50' - 2 \times 4 = 42'$. Similarly, the width of the inner rectangle is obtained from the width of the outer rectangle by subtracting two widths of the walk. That is, $30' - 2 \times 4 = 22'$.

$$\text{Area of outer rectangle} = 50' \times 30' = 1,500 \text{ sq. ft.}$$
$$\text{Area of inner rectangle} = 42' \times 22' = 924 \text{ sq. ft.}$$
$$1,500' - 924' = 576 \text{ sq. ft.}$$

6. ans. 3 The sum of the angles of a triangle is 180°. A right angle contains 90°. This leaves 90° for the sum of the other two angles.

Let x = the number of degrees in the smaller acute angle.
Let $2x$ = the number of degrees in the larger acute angle.

$$x + 2x = 90$$
$$3x = 90$$
$$x = 30$$

7. ans. 3 The annual premium on a $5,000 20-payment life policy at age 25 is
5 × $29.05 = $145.25.

The annual premium on a $5,000 straight life policy at age 25 is 5 × $18.74 =
$93.70.

The difference is $145.25 − $93.70 = $51.55.

8. ans. 5 The area of the lot is 60′ × 120′ = 7,200 sq. ft. 30% of this area =
.3(7,200) = 2,160 sq. ft.

The 35′ by 65′ lot contains 35 × 65 = 2,275 sq. ft.

The 35′ by 65′ lot does not meet the standard.

9. ans. 3 The ratio of the man to his shadow is the same as the ratio of a building
to its shadow at any given time during the day.

Let x = the height of the building.

The ratio of the man to his shadow is $\frac{6}{5}$.

The ratio of the building to its shadow is $\frac{x}{30}$.

Thus,
$$\frac{6}{5} = \frac{x}{30}$$
$$5x = 6 \times 30$$
$$5x = 180$$
$$x = \frac{180}{5} = 36$$

10. ans. 2 In order to obtain the average driving speed for the entire trip we must
divide total distance covered by the total time of the trip.

Distance of first part of trip   = 2 × 50 = 100 miles
Distance of second part of trip = 3 × 60 = 180 miles
Total distance   = 280 miles

Total time of the trip = 2 + 3 = 5 hours
Average speed of the trip = $\frac{280}{5}$ = 56 miles per hour

11. ans. 1 The volume of the box shown in the diagram is obtained by using the
formula $V = l \times w \times h$, where

V = volume
l = length
w = width
h = height

The volume of this box is 9 × 6 × 3 = 162 cubic feet. Thus, each truckload will
cart 162 cubic feet. To find the number of truckloads needed we divide 567 by 162

$$\begin{array}{r} 3.5 \\ 162\overline{)567.0} \\ 486 \\ \hline 81\,0 \\ 81\,0 \\ \hline \end{array}$$

The number of truckloads needed is 3.5, or $3\frac{1}{2}$.

12. ans. 4 To find the number of hours of sleep needed in this case we replace Y by 10
and compute the value of H.

$$H = 8 + \frac{18 - 10}{2}$$

$$H = 8 + \frac{8}{2}$$

$$H = 8 + 4 = 12$$

13. ans. 3 An examination of the graph shows that in 1966 the town received $100,000 more than it spent.

14. ans. 4

$$\begin{array}{r} 7,964.2 \\ -6,537.4 \\ \hline 1,426.8 \end{array}$$

Mr. Crane covered 1426.8 miles on the trip. To find the number of miles covered for each gallon of gasoline used we divide 1,426.8 by 82.

$$\begin{array}{r} 17.4 \\ 82\overline{)1,426.8} \\ \underline{82} \\ 606 \\ \underline{574} \\ 32\,8 \\ \underline{32\,8} \end{array}$$

Mr. Crane covered 17.4 miles for each gallon of gasoline used.

15. ans. 2 To find the interest we use the formula

$$I = P \times R \times T$$

where I = interest

　　　P = principal, or amount of money borrowed

　　　T = time, in years

$$I = 6,400 \times \frac{6\frac{1}{2}}{100} \times 1$$

$$I = 6,400 \times \frac{13}{200} \times 1$$

$$I = \overset{32}{\cancel{6,400}} \times \frac{13}{\cancel{200}}$$

$$I = 32 \times 13 = \$416$$

How to Use Your Results on the Sample Tests

You have now taken tests which sample your ability in the areas tested on the high school equivalency examination.

It is important that you analyze your mistakes and discover your own strengths and weaknesses. Most people like to avoid those areas in which they are weakest because they feel a sense of frustration in studying those subjects. You must be realistic and face up to the fact that most of your study should be directed to your own weaknesses. If you missed three or more of the spelling exercises, spelling is one of your weaknesses. If you did not score at least 12 out of 20 on the correct usage and grammar then you are weak in that area. If you did not achieve at least six out of ten on tests 2, 3, and 4 then your major problem is reading and interpreting the written page. It is important that you be honest with yourself. If you are, the help that this book provides will enable you to enter the examination with confidence and with a feeling that you will be successful.

HOW THIS BOOK CAN HELP YOU

The material in this book was carefully prepared specifically for this test. The authors, acclaimed as master teachers, have incorporated in this book their many years of experience in teaching high school students not only subject matter but effective study methods. They have enlisted the cooperation of experts in the choice of study material and method of presentation. This book along with a good dictionary on your desk is all you need to prepare for the test.

Since the states vary in their requirements and testing schedules, you should consult Chapter 2 to find out the information which applies to your state. Do not hasten to apply for the test prematurely. Take full advantage of the study material in this book. With the many opportunities presented for testing and self-evaluation, you will know when you are prepared to take the test and pass it.

However, if your local school has classes you can attend to prepare you for this examination, by all means take advantage of them, if you can. You will find this book a valuable supplement to your class-room work—and teachers of those classes will find the material well suited to class needs. If you are in an area where the TV classes preparing students for the G.E.D. tests are shown, see as many of them as you can. You can't be too well prepared!

SOME HINTS ON STUDYING

Capitalize on your maturity. People like yourself too often overemphasize their reasons for leaving school, the gap of long years since they attended school, and their inability to concentrate as well as young students. Instead, think positively! Since *you* have decided to study for this test, half the battle is over. You have demonstrated a *desire* to learn. Educators call this motivation and regard this as the first step toward success. Take advantage of your maturity. Now you understand the need for the proper study habits which we will outline for you. You will be more able to visualize a situation which may be part of a problem or a question. Young students have great difficulty in handling life situations. Actually you never stopped learning after you left school. You read newspapers; you followed political events; you traveled; you conversed with people; you took sides on issues; you listened to the radio, watched television programs and went to the movies. These experiences added to your educational background.

Let us consider rules for successful study.

1. PHYSICAL CONDITIONS. Find a quiet place. Have no distractions—noise or music. Do not work in an overheated room.

2. TIMING. You will learn faster and remember longer if you study in several short sessions rather than in one long session. Do not attempt to study for an entire weekend. Fatigue will set in after a few hours. It is wiser to spend some time each day rather than to "cram" your work into one or two days.

3. SCHEDULE FOR STUDY. A study schedule must be workable, realistic, practical and above all suited to you and your other obligations. Decide which days and hours you can spare for study. Make a schedule and stick to it.

4. USING ODD MOMENTS. Put spare time and wasted moments to work. Riding in the bus or train may be a good time to memorize troublesome spelling words, to study rules of grammar or definitions of newly acquired terms.

5. EFFICIENCY. Most people find that learning occurs faster in the early part of the day. Perhaps you can work into your schedule some study before your day's work begins or the mornings of weekends. Certainly you should not schedule yourself for study in the later hours of the evening.

6. REVIEW PERIODS. On certain days, plan to review. Take stock of yourself in these study periods. Check up on yourself. This will serve at least two purposes. It will definitely reinforce the learning and the gratification of knowing that you have acquired new material will stimulate you to go on to learn more.

7. WRITE WHILE YOU LEARN. Wherever possible write what you are studying. Spelling can best be learned by writing. Get into the habit of writing down key ideas of the passages you read. It will focus attention on your learning. It will avoid distractions that may cause your mind to wander. It will give you an opportunity to check up on yourself. Also, educators believe that the more senses employed in studying the more effective is the learning.

8. READ, READ, READ. The best way to improve reading comprehension is by practicing reading. You will find that a great part of the test involves interpretation of reading material (social studies, literature, and science). As a matter of fact, the mathematics test also involves interpretation of words and symbols. Read your newspaper very carefully. Make it a habit to read the editorials. If possible, engage a member of your family or a friend in frequent discussions of ideas presented in your newspaper. Of course, this book has specific reading exercises on the various phases of the test. But remember there is no substitute for general reading.

9. THE DICTIONARY. The most important single book in addition to this one which can help you prepare for the High School Equivalency Examination is the dictionary. It is important for you to have one nearby as you study. A suggested very inexpensive dictionary is the pocket-size paperback edition of Webster's New World Dictionary of the American Language published by Popular Library, Inc.

WHAT YOU MUST KNOW TO BE ABLE TO USE THE DICTIONARY

1. *You must know how to alphabetize.*
These words are taken from the page of a widely used dictionary.

> fuel
> fugitive
> fugue
> Fuhrer
> fulcrum
> fulfill
> fulgent
> full
> fullback

All these words begin with "fu . . . " and, to locate *fugue*, your eye must be able to pick out "fug" as coming between "fue" and "Fuh" on the page.

2. *You must know how to use guide words.*
All dictionaries have two words at the top of each page. All words on that page come alphabetically between the words given. For example, on the page mentioned above, the guide words are "fuel" and "funny." You can locate the word "funeral" a lot faster if your eye moves over the two guide words at the top of the page ("funeral" comes between "fuel" and "funny") rather than all the words on that page.
Try your hand at these.
Guide words are "heartache" and "hedge." Which of these words are found on that page? Hebrew; height; heathen; headquarters; heaven; heckle; helicopter; heavy.

3. *You must know certain abbreviations.*

Most dictionaries give you a list of the abbreviations they use on the page or pages immediately preceding the *first* page of definitions. The abbreviations, for the most part, concern grammatical parts of speech (v., verb) and countries where words originated (Scot., Scottish).

4. *You must know how to choose the suitable definition.*

Take this dictionary entry as an example.

"sheer, adj. 1. very thin; transparent: said of textiles. 2. absolute; downright: as, *sheer* folly. 3. extremely steep."

It is obvious that the three definitions have no relationship to one another. You must match one of the definitions to the phrase, clause, or sentence in which the word appears. Try to choose the suitable definition for each of the following sentences:

    1. She wore *sheer* stockings.
    2. He fell over the *sheer* cliff.
    3. They spoke *sheer* nonsense.

WHAT THE DICTIONARY CAN DO FOR YOU

1. *It can help you with spelling.*

You find that you have to use the word "embar?as?ed" in some writing you are doing. You're not sure of the spelling. Are there two *r*'s or one? Two *s*'s or one? Your dictionary has the answer. Check it and you won't be embarrassed.

In addition, your dictionary will help you to divide the word into syllables. You note that the word is broken up as follows: em bar rassed. You now know where to put the hyphen when you come to the end of a line of writing and you must break up the word.

2. *It can help you with meaning.*

You find that you cannot understand a passage you are reading because you do not know the meaning of a key work. Let us take, for example, a passage in biology which uses the word *nucleus* again and again. Your dictionary will list all the meanings of the word in order of the frequency in which they are used, the most frequent first, the least frequent last. The dictionary we have been referring to lists four meanings, the fourth definition reading "4. in *biology*, the central mass of protoplasm in a cell." You now can make sense of the paragraph or selection you are reading.

3. *It can help you with pronunciation.*

You find you have to use the name of the city, Detroit, in a talk you are giving. You are not sure where the accent falls. Is it on the first syllable– De– or on the second– troit? You look up the name in the dictionary and find next to the word the markings (di-troit′) and you know that the name of the city is accented on the second syllable. By the way, the key to the sounds represented by these markings (called diacritical marks) is generally found on the bottom of the page.

4. *It can help you with grammar.*

You find you have to use the past tense of the verb *to lie* meaning "to be in a reclining position." You look up the word and you find -*v.i.*—the part of speech is a verb, intransitive, as well as the principal parts (LAY, LAIN, LYING). You now know that the sentence you want to use should read "I lay under the tree for four hours."

You can also find the plural for some very troublesome nouns. Is it *heros* or *heroes*? The dictionary leaves no doubt. It indicates (*pl.* -ROES).

5. *It can help you with usage*.

You find that you'd like to use the word *cop* meaning "policeman" in a formal letter you are writing to a city official. Your dictionary indicates (Slang) before the definition of *cop* so you know that good form does not allow you to use the word as you had wanted.

You find you want to use the word *girl* in the sense of sweetheart—"introducing my girl to my parents." You check the dictionary and you find (Colloq.) before the definition. This means you may use the word when speaking but it is not advisable that you use it in formal writing. A word of caution. Dictionaries often disagree on levels of usage. What may be *Slang* to one is *Colloquial* to another. What is *Colloquial* to one may be completely acceptable to another. Always be certain to check a good dictionary and be guided by it.

6. *It can help you build your vocabulary by providing the origin of words and indicating word families*. You check the word *telescope*. You learn it comes from the Greek *tele* meaning *far off* and *scope* meaning *to view*. You notice that other words on the page use the combining form *tele:* telecast; telegram; telegraph; telephone; telephoto; teletype; television. You have learned a whole family of words. In addition, you can add the family of *scope* words: horoscope, kinescope, microscope, periscope, and just plain scope.

7. *It can help you with information on literature and social studies*.

You can find references to mythology (Midas) and to literature (Hamlet). You can find place names in geography (New York) and in history (Valley Forge). You can find references to Biblical names (Babel). You can find the meaning of such well-known phrases as "auld lang syne."

Specific Study Suggestions. There are special study techniques for the various subject areas. You will be alerted to these in the special sections.

HOW TO HANDLE READING COMPREHENSION PASSAGES

As you will note, three-fifths of the High School Equivalency Examination is actually a test of reading. Here are some tips for better reading comprehension with particular reference to the kinds of questions you will encounter on these tests:

1. Read the passage first for the main idea.
2. Underline significant phrases and ideas.
3. Read *each* question carefully.
4. Look out for words that *change* or *qualify* the meaning of a question or statement: *not*, *never*, *always*, *wholly*, etc. Know what is meant by *implies*, *states*, *denies*, *suggests*, *believes*, etc. Correct answers often depend on such words.
5. If the passage has more than one paragraph, look for answers in *all* parts of the reading selection. Questions do not necessarily follow the order of the material in the selection.
6. Answer the questions you *know* first. Then, if time permits, go back to those you don't know.
7. Unless you are told that credit will be deducted for *wrong* answers, try to answer every question.
8. Base your answers only on the passage you have read—*unless otherwise directed*.

THREE FINAL TIPS FOR SUCCESS

1 BE PREPARED: Don't hasten to apply for the examination prematurely. Make certain that you are adequately prepared to be successful by testing yourself with the exercises and tests in this book. It is far better to postpone taking the examination until such time when success can reasonably be expected than to go into the test at an earlier date trusting to good fortune. Though many states have arrangements for retesting after a waiting period, the notice of failure is an unpleasant experience and may discourage you from further success. Last minute cramming seldom leads to success. It is advisable to extend preparation for the test over a long period of time.

2 BE RELAXED: It is highly desirable to relax the night before the test. A good night's sleep will put the body in a better condition to think logically. Walk into the room with confidence. Arrive early. If you have the opportunity to choose a seat, pick one that has adequate light. Avoid last-minute discussions on questions and answers with frantic applicants. Relax.

3 BE SMART: During the actual testing period, be sure to read the questions carefully. If you encounter a difficult question, don't be discouraged. A successful applicant need not answer all questions correctly. Perhaps in such situations you can eliminate some of the choices as unreasonable, contradictory, or entirely incorrect. A shrewd analysis of a question often leads to choosing the correct answer.

WHEN YOU TAKE THE EXAMINATION

To Guess or Not to Guess

Four or five possible answers are given to each question. It is foolish to guess if you have no idea of the answer to the question. The chances are only one in four or five. Similarly, if you are certain that only one answer is wrong, it is still wise to avoid guessing because the odds are very much against you.

Only if you can definitely eliminate two of the possible answers should you attempt to guess. Not only are your chances better, but you probably know enough about the question to make a reasoned choice since you have already eliminated several of the possible answers.

There is a tendency on the part of some people who take examinations to give up on a question. Don't. If necessary, read the question several times; eliminate as many answers as possible; then leave the question and come back to it later. DON'T SPEND TOO MUCH TIME ON ANY SINGLE QUESTION, especially a mathematics problem. While you are working on the answers to other questions, your mind is subconsciously "thinking" about the question you have left for later consideration. When you come back to it, there is a good chance you might see the question in a new light and it will seem very much easier to you.

For the Left-Handed

Many schools have seats with arms for writing on the left side. Ask for one if it is available.
If not, it is generally better to place the question paper to the right and to mark your answers on the answer sheet which is placed nearer your left hand.

A SUGGESTED SCHEDULE

Do not be overwhelmed by the task of preparing for the high school equivalency test. To help you budget your time, a specific schedule is suggested on the basis of 30 home study sessions, between an hour and a half and two hours for each session. If you follow this plan you will not be guilty of "hopping" from one subject to another with the constant fear that you are neglecting a particular subject area. If, for personal reasons, you cannot devote this length of time to one session, you will find it relatively easy to divide the work into 60 sessions. In any case, if you follow the pattern and check off the tasks you accomplish, you will be prepared to walk into the examination room with confidence.

Session I Read *Hints for Studying* in Chapter 1. Plan a schedule for study. Do Test 1 in Chapter 1.

Session II Do Sample Tests 2, 3, 4, 5 of Chapter 1. Correct your answers. Analyze your errors.

Session III Study *The Basic Hundred* in the spelling section. Review *Whole Numbers* and fundamental operations in mathematics.

Session IV Study *The Vocabulary of Grammar and Usage*. Review fractions. Study Selections 1 and 2 in Social Studies.

Session V Study *Sentence Structure*. Study *How to Read and Interpret Literature Materials*. Study the sample passages.

Session VI Study *Agreement of Subject and Verb*, and *Agreement of Pronoun and Antecedent*. Study sample selection in Natural Sciences. Analyze answers.

Session VII Study spelling list—*Two Hundred Often Used Easy Words*. Study Literary Selections 1 and 2. Study Social Studies Selections 3 and 4.

Session VIII Study Literary Selections 3 and 4. Study Social Studies Selections 5 and 6.

Session IX Review troublesome spelling words. Study *decimals, percent, insurance* . Do practice exercises.

Session X Study Natural Science Selections 1–8. Study *investments* and *taxation*. Do practice exercises.

Session XI Study spelling list *Three Hundred and Twenty-Five More Frequently Used Words*. Study Social Studies Selections 7 and 8.

Session XII Study *Case of Nouns and Pronouns*. Review spelling words. Check errors in mathematics exercises.

Session XIII Study Literary Selections 5 and 6. Study Social Studies Selections 9 and 10. Review grammar and usage.

Session XIV Study Natural Science Selections 9–12. Review *Arithmetic*.

Session XV Take practice test in spelling—*Two Hundred Practice Questions in Spelling*. Study misspelled words. Study Social Studies Selections 11 and 12. Study Literary Selection 7.

Session XVI Study Social Studies Selections 13 and 14. Study Science Selections 13 and 14. Study and do practice exercise in *Algebra*.

Session XVII Do *First Hundred Practice Questions in Spelling*. Study *Algebra* .

Session XVIII Finish *Second One Hundred Practice Questions in Spelling*. Study Literary Selections 8 and 9. Study *Troublesome Verbs*. Study *Algebra*.

Session XIX Study Science Selections 15, 16, and 17. Study Literary Selections 10, 11, and 12. Study Social Studies Selections 15, and 16.

Session XX Complete study of *Algebra* and practice exercises. Study *Troublesome Adjectives and Adverbs*.

Session XXI   Study Literary Selections 13 and 14. Study Social Studies Selections 17, 18, and 19. Start Geometry exercises.

Session XXII   Study Science Selections 18, 19, and 20. Study Literary Selections 13 and 14. Study Social Studies Selections 20 and 21.

Session XXIII   Complete study of *Geometry* and do practice exercises. Analyze errors committed. Study *Confusing Constructions*.

Session XXIV   Study *Preferred Modern Usage*. Do exercise—*Word Hunt*. Study Literary Selections 15 and 16.

Session XXV   Study *graphs* and do practice exercises. Analyze errors committed. Study Science Selections 21, 22, 23, 24.

Session XXVI   Review *measures* and do practice exercises. Analyze errors committed. Study Literary Selections 17 and 18.

Session XXVII   Study *Basic Rules of Punctuation* and *Basic Rules of Capitalization*. Do Test 1—General Mathematics Ability.

Session XXVIII   Study Literary Selections 19 and 20. Do Test 2 and 3—General Mathematics Ability. Analyze errors committed.

Session XXIX   Do Practice Exercises in Correctness of Expression—Group 1, 2, and 3. Do Test 4—General Mathematics Ability. Study Science Selections 25–28.

Session XXX   Do Practice Examination in Correctness of Expression. Do Test 5—General Mathematics Ability. Analyze errors committed.

> A WORD ABOUT TIME: Don't try to learn everything or take every test in one gulp. Go at your own speed and in your own way. A book can't be completely flexible—but we urge you to be flexible in using this book to suit your individual needs. If you need review in math but feel pretty confident about English, concentrate on the math. If you want to try the exams first and skip a study section, do it. Remember that High School Equivalency Tests are given frequently. Remember that you can take one test at a time—or two, or three, or all five. Remember, especially, that if you fail one test, you can take another . . . and another. But you probably will take just one test in each of the five parts—and pass the first time! That's what this book aims to help you to do.

PRACTICE FOR READING SKILLS

The most important skill in getting ready for and taking the High School Equivalency Examination tests is the ability to understand what you read. For explanation and practice you should use Barron's book, Preparation for the High School Equivalency Examination—Reading Interpretation Tests, by Eugene J. Farley. It tells how to prepare for and how to pass the High School Equivalency tests. Skills of reading, especially in relation to social studies, sciences, and literature, are emphasized. There are many passages and questions like those on the High School Equivalency Examination. Complete information is given on how to take the test and how to gain a high school equivalency certificate in each state, commonwealth, or territory.

2

Qualifications by States

In this chapter you will find a summary of the various state programs for the issuance of High School Equivalency certificates and diplomas. The information was gathered from questionnaires answered by Adult Education Directors, Superintendents of Public Instruction and Commissioners of State Boards of Education. The information includes general qualifications, residence and age requirements, minimum required scores on the Tests of General Educational Development; provisions for retesting, and fees involved. Also, a specific address is furnished for obtaining further details and application forms.

A sample application form is also given for your convenience. This one is used by New York State. Other states have similar forms.

STATE PROGRAMS

ALABAMA   The State Certificate of High School Equivalency is granted by the State Department of Education and may be used as a basis for admission to the colleges of the state. *General Qualifications:* Applicants must be 20 years of age but those 19 years of age who have been out of school at least one year may take the test. However, the certificate is not granted to anyone less than 20 years old. Residence in the state for one year immediately preceding the date of application is required. However, former residents who attended school at least one year in the state are eligible. *Test Requirements:* The applicant must pass the General Educational Development Test with a standard score of not less than 35 on each part of the test OR with an average of not less than 45 on the battery of GED tests. *Testing Fees:* The charge for the complete battery of five tests is $7.50. For retest a fee of $2.00 is charged for each part. Personnel of the Armed Forces take the test under the supervision of appropriate officers without charge. *Retesting:* A waiting period of six months is required except where proof is submitted that intensive study was completed for at least six weeks.

FURTHER DETAILS: Division of Secondary Education, State Department of Education, Montgomery 36104.

ALASKA   The Commissioner of Education of the state is authorized to issue a special diploma marked "By Examination," if the applicant meets certain requirements. *General Qualifications:* An applicant 19 years of age or above who is a bona fide resident of the state or a serviceman at least 18 years old, stationed in the state, is eligible for the special high school diploma. Under no circumstances is a diploma granted ahead of time the applicant would have received it had the applicant remained in school. *Test Requirements:* Scores on the General Educational Development Test must be in the 50th percentile or above. *Fees:* None. *Retesting:* After additional study, tests may be retaken after a waiting period of six months. In the case of members of the Armed Forces re-take tests are allowed according to USAFI regulations. *Additional Requirements:* A transcript of all high school courses must be submitted. Servicemen or veterans must submit an official record of military service and experience. In addition an autobiography of about 300 words is required.

FURTHER DETAILS: Commissioner of Education, 326 Alaska Office Building, Juneau 99801.

ARIZONA   The State Board of Education awards High School Equivalency Certificates on the basis of the General Educational Development Test battery. *General Qualifications:* To be eligible for the equivalency certificate an applicant must be at least 19 years of age. However, the test may be taken at age 18 for military recruitment purposes, but in that case the certificate is issued after the applicant reaches age 19. Also, the test may be taken at age 17 to establish tenth grade level of equivalency for the use of the Barber and Cosmotology Board. *Test Requirements:* An applicant must score at least 35 on each of the Tests of General Educational Development and an average score of 45 on each of the five tests. For tenth grade equivalency the required minimum is 31 with an average of 39. *Additional Requirements:* An applicant cannot obtain a twelfth grade equivalency certificate before such time as he would have graduated from high school by normal attendance. *Testing Fees:* A fee of $10.00 payable to GED Testing Center is charged. A fee of $2.00 per test is made for retesting. *Retesting:* After a waiting period of 30 days, one retake is allowed for each test, provided written evidence of additional tutoring or study is submitted.

FURTHER DETAILS: State Department of Public Instruction, GED Division, Capitol Building, Suite 165, Phoenix 85007.

ARKANSAS   The State Department of Education issues a Certificate of Equivalency of High School Graduation under certain conditions. *General Qualifications:* The applicant must be at least 20 years old, out of school six months or more. He must have completed 120 hours of instruction in an approved General Adult Education class. Exceptions are made when an employer receives special permission from the Assistant Commissioner for Instructional Services, by stating that he will employ the applicant if he passes the GED tests. *Test Requirements:* An applicant must make a minimum standard score of 40 on each of the five parts of the Tests of General Educational Development OR an average standard score of 50 on the entire battery of GED tests. *Veterans:* State residents, at least 20 years of age, with Honorable Discharge after at least 90 days of service are eligible. They must attain the same minimum scores on the GED tests as other applicants.

FURTHER DETAILS: Associate Commissioner for Instructional Services, State Department of Education, Little Rock 72201.

CALIFORNIA   The awarding of diplomas from high school is the legal responsibility of the various school districts. *Veterans:* A veteran who entered the military service of the United States while a student in the twelfth grade and has satisfactorily completed the first half of the work of the twelfth grade is granted a high school diploma. A veteran who was honorably discharged from the Armed

Forces may receive a diploma by meeting the following conditions: (1) He must have entered active service after September 16, 1940 and served for at least 90 days. (2) He must have completed the Tests of General Educational Development and attained an average standard score of at least 45 on the five tests and at least a standard score of 35 on each of the five tests. (3) He must meet the state requirement of United States history and United States constitution.

FURTHER DETAILS: Department of Education, 721 Capitol Mall, Sacramento 95814.

COLORADO The Colorado Department of Education grants a Certificate of Equivalency on the basis of the results of the General Educational Development Tests. *General Requirements:* Applicant must be a resident of the state for at least 6 months, must be at least 20 years old, and the test must be taken after the class of which the applicant was a member has been graduated from high school. *Veterans:* Military personnel are eligible if they have resided in the state for at least six months prior to entering the Armed Forces and are still in the service at the time of application for the Certificate. Veterans are eligible provided they entered the Armed Forces while residents of the state and have returned to the state upon discharge from the service or have made application for the Certificate within six months after discharge from the service. *Testing Fees:* A charge of $7.50 is made by the agency administering the battery of five tests and a charge of $2.00 for the administration of each single test. *Test Requirements:* A score of at least 35 must be achieved on each of the five tests with an average standard score of 45 or above on the battery of the five tests. *Retesting:* If an applicant fails any one of the tests or fails to attain the required average for the five tests, he may apply for another test after a six month waiting period. Evidence that additional preparation for the test has been made is required. However, the applicant must complete all parts, including retests, within a two-year period.

FURTHER DETAILS: Colorado State Board of Education, Denver 80203.

CONNECTICUT The State Department of Education issues State High School Diplomas on the basis of examination and certain requirements. *General Qualifications:* An applicant must be at least 18 years of age, a state resident for at least six months, must be out of school for at least one academic year, and the class of which he was a member must already have been graduated from high school. *Test Requirements:* Application to take the Tests of General Educational Development must be made in person before a designated official of a local school system or at the State Office Building in Hartford. To qualify for the State High School Diploma a Standard Score of at least 35 on each of the five parts AND an average Standard Score of at least 45 must be attained. *Retesting:* After a waiting period of at least six months an applicant may retake the parts not passed. *Testing Fees:* No fee is required of veterans who have been honorably discharged from service. Also exempt from fees are members of the Armed Forces. Others are required to pay $3.00 for the first examination, $2.00 for a retest, if necessary, and $2.00 for the State High School Diploma when earned and desired.

FURTHER DETAILS: Bureau of Higher and Adult Education, State Department of Education, Hartford 06115.

DELAWARE There is no state program for issuance of a high school equivalency diploma or certificate. A statewide high school extension program is available.

FURTHER DETAILS: Delaware Extension Program, P.O. Box 697, Dover 19901.

DISTRICT OF COLUMBIA The District of Columbia issues High School Equivalency Certificates to residents over 21 years of age who have attained an average score of 45 or more on the General Educational Development Tests. *General Qualifications:* Candidates must be at least 21 years of age; an applicant between the ages of 19 and 21 who has not been enrolled in a regular day school during the 24 month period immediately preceding the date of application may be granted a waiver of the 21 year age requirement at the discretion of the Chief Examiner. An applicant must be a resident of the District of Columbia for the 12 months immediately preceding date of application except in the case of a non-resident whose last schooling was received in the District of Columbia. *Test Requirements:* Candidates must attain a minimum standard score of at least 35 or above on each of the five tests and an average standard score of 45 on all five tests. *Testing Fees:* A fee of $5.00 is charged which includes issuance of credential.

FURTHER DETAILS: Board of Examiners, Webster Administration Annex #4, Washington 20001.

FLORIDA The State Department of Education has the authority to issue State High School Equivalency Diplomas to qualified applicants. *General Qualifications:* Candidates must be at least 20 years of age except that this requirement may be waived in cases of inmates of correctional or penal institutions. The residence requirement may be met by living in the state for at least one year or owning a home or business in the state at the time of application. Candidates must have high school credit in American History and in addition either Government or Civics. This requirement may also be met by passing an examination in these subjects. *Test Requirements:* Candidates must attain a minimum standard score of at least 40 on each of the five Tests of General Educational Development AND an average standard score of 45 or above on all five of the tests. *Retesting:* Candidates who fail to attain the required minimum scores on their initial testing may retake the tests ofter a period of at least six months has elapsed. The candidate who fails one or two of the five tests may retake only the tests failed. Those who fail three or more of the five tests must retake the entire battery. The waiting period may be reduced to not less than three months ONLY in cases where an applicant fails to make the required scores on not more than two tests, or where he passes all five tests but does not attain the required overall average score. In all cases where the waiting time is reduced, the candidate must pursue an intensive course of study under a qualified teacher. *Testing Fees:* A fee of $7.50 is required and in retesting a fee of $2.00 for each part is payable to the local testing agent at the time of the retesting. *Veterans:* Veterans may claim credit for tests of GED taken while in service. State veterans confined to Veteran Administration Hospitals may take these tests under the supervision of the proper hospital authorities.

FURTHER DETAILS: Adult and Veteran Education, Department of Education, Tallahassee 32304.

GEORGIA The State Department of Education issues a High School Equivalency Certificate to adults on the basis of the Tests of General Educational Development. High schools are authorized to issue regular diplomas to service personnel and veterans on the basis of the GED tests and other requirements. *General Qualifications:* The applicant must be at least 20 years old and either a bona fide resident of the state or have attended school in the state. *Test Requirements:* A standard score of 35 or above on each of the tests of GED and an average standard score of 45 on all five tests is required. *Testing Fees:* Fees are determined locally but do not exceed $5.00. *Veterans:* Principals of high schools may issue regular diplomas to service personnel and veterans who have completed at least four units of high school work at the high school where the diploma is requested. In addition they must attain the required scores on the GED tests.

FURTHER DETAILS: Division of Administrative Leadership Services, State Department of Education, Atlanta 30334.

HAWAII The Adult Education Branch of the Department of Education issues a High School Certificate to applicants who meet certain specified requirements. *General Qualifications:* An applicant must be at least 18 years old and his high school class must have graduated. Even if all requirements are met, at least one semester must elapse between the time the regular high school class was graduated and the issuance of the certificate. Residence requirements include living in the state or attendance in an adult educational community school in the state for at least one semester where at least one-half credit in the secondary field was earned. *Test Requirements:* A standard score of at least 35 on each of the five parts of the Tests of General Educational Development and an average standard score of 45 on all five tests is required. *Testing Fees:* The charge at VTS agencies is $7.50 plus a $1.00 screening fee.

FURTHER DETAILS: Administrator, Adult Education Branch, Department of Education, 1106 Koko Head Avenue, Honolulu 96816.

IDAHO The State Department of Education issues an Equivalency Certificate to adults who meet certain requirements. *General Qualifications:* The applicant must be at least 20 years old and must be a bona fide resident of the state for at least six months preceding the application. *Test Requirements:* An applicant must attain a standard score of at least 45 on each of the five parts of the Tests of General Educational Development. *Additional Requirement:* A one-semester course in American Government is required. This course must include United States Constitution, and principles of state or local government. *Testing Fees:* The fees are set by the GED testing agency. A charge of $2.00 is made for the issuance of the certificate. However, the $2.00 fee is waived for service personnel and veterans.

FURTHER DETAILS: Director of Secondary Education, Department of Education, 206 Statehouse, Boise 83702.

ILLINOIS The Superintendent of Public Instruction has the authority to issue High School Equivalency Certificates. *General Qualifications:* An adult of at least 21 years who has maintained residence in the state for at least one year immediately preceding the date of filing the application is eligible. *Test Requirements:* An applicant must make a standard score of 35 or above on each of the five Tests of General Educational Development AND a total standard score of at least 225 on the entire battery of GED tests. An applicant must take the battery of tests in two days since not more than three tests may be completed in one day. *Additional Requirements:* An applicant must pass an examination on

American patriotism and the principles of representative government as enunciated in the American Declaration of Independence, the Constitution of the United States of America, the Constitution of the State of Illinois and the proper use and display of the American Flag, as provided by Section 27-3 of the School Code. *Testing Fees:* A charge of $5.00 is made for taking the tests. This accompanies the application. An additional fee of $5.00 is charged for the issuance of the High School Equivalency Certificate upon request of the County Superintendent. *Retesting:* An applicant who fails to make the required scores on the GED tests may ask to be retested on the entire battery or the test failed. A year waiting period is required before re-examination unless the applicant presents to the County Super- intendent evidence of having completed a formal program of studies related to the tests to be retaken. A request to the County Superintendent for a re-examination accompanied by official evidence of such instruction is sufficient. Applicants must pay the $5.00 fee for such retests. An applicant who fails the Constitution Examination will be permitted to review the subject and subsequently be retested. If he fails the retest he must wait one year for re-examination unless he presents evidence of completion of formal instruction to the County Superintendent. *Veterans:* Servicemen and veterans over 21 years of age who have previously passed the GED tests may claim credit for these tests.

FURTHER DETAILS: Office of the Superintendent of Public Instruction, Supervisor, High School Equivalency Testing Program, Springfield 62706.

INDIANA   High schools may grant an Achievement Test Certificate to resident adults who are 21 years of age or over who have passed the General Educational Development Tests. *Test Require- ments:* An average of 45 on all five tests and at least a score of 35 on each test is required for the High School Equivalency Diploma. *Testing Fees:* Testing at official GED agencies is $5.00 per battery; $1.00 per single test.

FURTHER DETAILS: Department of Public Instruction, 227 State House, Indianapolis 46204.

IOWA   The State Superintendent is authorized to issue a High School Equivalency Certificate to adults meeting the necessary requirements. *General Qualifications:* The applicant must have resided in the state for at least one year prior to filing for the certificate. He may not apply until one year after his class has been graduated. *Test Requirements:* The Test of General Educational Development is admin- istered at an approved testing center after the application is processed. The minimum standard score is 40 on each of the five parts of the GED and the minimum average on all five parts is 45. *Testing Fees:* A fee of $5.00 is charged with the application and an additional $5.00 fee is required for the issuance of the High School Equivalency Certificate. *Retesting:* After a waiting period of one year from the last testing date, an applicant may apply for a retest. However, by furnishing proof that intensive instruction was completed in the areas of weakness, an applicant is permitted to be retested sooner. The fee for the retest is $5.00.

FURTHER DETAILS: State Department of Public Instruction, Section of Adult Education, State Office Building, Des Moines 50319.

KANSAS   The State Department of Public Instruction issues a High School Equivalency Diploma to adult residents who have met certain conditions. *General Qualifications:* In order to qualify for the equivalency diploma, one must be 20 years of age, have lived in the state for at least one year or have taken his last formal schooling from an institution in the state. *Test Requirements:* A standard score of at least 35 must be achieved on each part of the Tests of General Educational Development and an average of 45 on all five parts.

FURTHER DETAILS: Director of Adult Education, State Department of Public Instruction, Topeka 66612.

KENTUCKY The Director of Adult Education of the State Department authorizes a local Board of Education to issue a High School Equivalency Certificate to qualified adults. *General Qualifications:* An applicant must be at least 21 years of age, or at least 18 years old, out of school for at least one year, and have completed the equivalent of one semester's work in an organized course of instruction. Applicants must be civilian residents for at least six months, or former residents who attended school in Kentucky, or confined to a health or correctional institution in the state. *Test Requirements:* After receiving the approval of the applicant's district school superintendent, the applicant may take the Tests of General Educational Development. A standard score of 35 or above on each of the five parts of this test AND an average of 45 on all five parts are required. *Testing Fees:* The fees for administering the GED test vary at testing centers. *Retesting:* A minimum of thirty days must elapse between the first test and a retest.

FURTHER DETAILS: Superintendent of Public Instruction, Department of Education, Frankfort 40601.

LOUISIANA The State Superintendent of the Department of Education issues a High School Equivalency Certificate to adults who complete the requirements of the Adult Education Program in the state. *General Qualifications:* The applicant must be a resident of the state. *Test Requirements:* The Tests of General Educational Development are administered through GED Testing Centers. Minimum required scores are 35 on each of the battery of five tests OR an average of 45 on all of the parts. *Testing Fees:* No charge at parish GED agencies.

FURTHER DETAILS: Director of Secondary Education, Department of Education, Baton Rouge 70804.

MAINE The Commissioner of Education issues High School Equivalency Certificates to adults who meet certain requirements. *General Qualifications:* A veteran or serviceman is eligible if his high school class has graduated and he is a bona fide Maine resident, or for six months immediately preceding application he has lived in Maine or has been stationed at a military installation in Maine. A civilian applicant is eligible if he is 21 or older and is a bona fide resident of Maine or has lived in Maine for six months immediately prior to applying. By special regulation a girl aged 19–20 who is enlisting in military service may take the tests if her high school class has graduated and if she has met all other requirements for enlistment. *Test Requirements:* The minimum scores on the Tests of Educational Development include a score of 35 or above in each of the five tests and a total of 225 for the five tests. *Testing Fees:* Veterans are not required to pay an examination fee. Others pay $5.00 which is mailed with the application. *Retesting:* A person failing to meet certificate standards in a first examination may apply for a retest after four months provided application is accompanied by evidence of additional preparatory study. Further retesting will be permitted after one year and considerable more preparation.

FURTHER DETAILS: Secretary, High School Equivalency Program, Bureau of Secondary Education, State Department of Education, 400 State Office Building, Augusta 04330.

MARYLAND A Maryland Certificate of High School Equivalency is issued on the basis of the scores on the General Educational Development Tests. *General Qualifications:* An applicant must be at least 19 years of age and must have lived in the state for at least one year. *Test Requirements:* An average score of 50 with no individual score under 40, or at least 45 in each part of the examination. *Alternate Plan:* If an applicant lacks one or two units of the sixteen required for graduation, he may earn a Certificate of High School Equivalency by passing tests in individual subjects. *Testing Fees:* No charge.

FURTHER DETAILS: Maryland State Department of Education, 301 West Preston Street, Baltimore 21201.

MASSACHUSETTS The State High School Equivalency Certificate is awarded on the basis of the identical sixteen units required for a local high school diploma. The certificate is not awarded on the basis of the General Educational Development Test alone. *General Qualifications:* Residents and nonresidents of the state who last attended school in the state are eligible provided they have not received a high school diploma. Candidates must be at least 20 years of age. They must have written consent of the principal of the last day school attended. If the last school attended was not a secondary school they must receive the approval of the local high school principal or the superintendent of schools in the town of residence. *Requirements:* The applicant must submit a transcript of all his previous high school work. The applicant must take the GED tests. His record is evaluated and a Supervisor is assigned with whom the applicant confers and the subjects needed to complete the requirements for the certificate are announced. *Fees:* The following charges are made: $5.00 for filing the original application, $5.00 for the administration of the GED tests, $5.00 for preparing the certificate when all requirements have been met, and $1.00 for an end-of-course examination or a re-take of an individual part of the GED test. Veterans, inmates of state hospitals or federal hospitals located in the state, blind persons, and senior citizens are exempt from any of these fees.

FURTHER DETAILS: State High School Equivalency Certificate Program, Division of University Extension, 200 Newbury Street, Boston 02116.

MICHIGAN There are 28 approved local testing centers where the Test of General Educational Development is administered. Test results may be used by local school districts toward high school graduation credit. The Department of Public Instruction suggests a pattern for granting credit. *General Qualifications:* Students participating in this program must be at least 21 years of age and state residents. *Test Requirements:* An average Standard Score of 45 or more in the GED tests must be attained to receive credit toward a high school diploma. Maximum credit of 25 semester periods in English may be attained by receiving a passing score in Test I (Correctness and Effectiveness of Expression) and a maximum of 15 semester periods may be received in elective credit-Literature for Test IV (Interpretation of Literary Materials). Test I may not be used to satisfy the American Literature requirement. For Test II (Interpretation of Reading Materials in the Social Studies) an applicant may receive credit for

15 semester periods in social science. However this cannot be used to satisfy the United States History or the United States Government requirements. A maximum of 30 semester periods may be granted in the Mathematics-Science requirements by passing Test III (Interpretation of Reading Materials in the Natural Sciences) and Test V (General Mathematics Ability). Test III alone may earn credit of 20 semester periods but cannot be used to satisfy the laboratory science requirement. Test V alone may earn credit of 20 semester periods but cannot be used in lieu of algebra, geometry or trigonometry.

FURTHER DETAILS: Superintendent of Public Instruction, Department of Education, Lansing 48902.

MINNESOTA   The local secondary schools may issue equivalency certificates to individuals on the basis of the successful completion of the Tests of General Educational Development. *General Qualifications:* The GED tests are administered to residents of the state who are 20 years of age or older, or 19 years of age with the full approval of the local school authorities. A resident of the state is defined as an individual who has resided in the state for six months prior to taking the GED tests. *Test Requirements:* Applicants must obtain standard scores of 35 or more on each individual GED test and an average of at least 45 on all five parts. *Testing Fees:* The cost of taking the battery of five tests is $10.00 in most of the sixteen bonded testing centers.

FURTHER DETAILS: Director Secondary Education, Department of Education, Centennial Office Building, St. Paul 55101.

MISSISSIPPI   The State Department of Education may issue a Certificate of High School Equivalence to residents who meet certain conditions. *General Qualifications:* The applicant must be a resident of the state for at least one year. The minimum age requirement of 20 years is waived in the case of those who are at least 18 years old and have completed 40 hours of instruction in an adult high school equivalency course. *Test Requirements:* An applicant must attain a score of not less than 40 on each of the five parts of the Tests of General Educational Development OR an average of 45 on the entire test. *Retesting:* Unsuccessful candidates are eligible to take the GED tests again after a waiting period of six months. *Veterans:* Military personnel and veterans may claim credit for the GED tests already taken outside the state.

FURTHER DETAILS: Division of Instruction, Department of Education, Jackson 39205.

MISSOURI   A State Certificate of High School Equivalence is issued by the State Department of Education on the basis of certain conditions of eligibility. *General Qualifications:* An applicant must give proof of residence in the state for at least one year and must be at least 20 years of age. Members of the Armed Forces are eligible provided they were residents of the state at the time of entering the services. *Test Requirements:* A standard score of at least 43 in each of the parts of the Tests of General Educational Development and an average of not less than 48 on all five parts is required. *Testing Fees:* A fee of $5.00 must be paid by the applicant who wishes to take GED tests at a State Testing Center. A fee of $2.00 is charged if the GED tests are taken through USAFI. No fee is required for patients or inmates of state institutions and veterans' hospitals. *Retesting:* An applicant who fails to qualify for the certificate on his first attempt may be approved for a second and third attempt, but only if a minimum of six months has elapsed since the previous attempt. Application and fee are required each time tests are taken.

FURTHER DETAILS: Director of General Supervision, State Department of Education, Jefferson City 65102.

MONTANA   The State Superintendent of Public Instruction issues High School Equivalency Certificates to qualified adults. *General Qualifications:* The applicant must be at least 19 years of age at the time he takes the Tests of General Educational Development. Legal residence in the state is required. However regular employment in the state, or assignment by military authority to a station in the state is acceptable. *Test Requirements:* An applicant must attain a standard score of 35 or above on each of the five tests AND an average standard score of 45 on all five Tests of General Educational Development. *Other Requirements:* A knowledge of the principles of American Government is required. This may be fulfilled by submitting credit for such a course in an accredited high school or by special examination administered at testing service agencies in the state. *Testing Fees:* A charge of $4.00 is made by the administration of the GED tests. This fee includes the administration of the American Government examination to those applicants who must take this special one-hour test. A fee of $1.00 is charged for the administration of the American Government examination when it is not taken with the GED tests. *Retesting:* A waiting period of one month is required before applicants may retake the American Government examination and/or any part of the Tests of General Educational Development. A waiting period of three months is required for any subsequent retest on the Tests of General Educational Development and/or the American Government examination. *Veterans:* Veterans or service personnel may receive credit for the GED tests taken in the service.

FURTHER DETAILS: High School Supervisor, Superintendent of Public Instruction, Helena 59601.

NEBRASKA   The State Department of Education issues a Certificate of High School Equivalency when an applicant meets certain conditions. *General Qualifications:* An applicant must be at least 21 years of age, and have spent the last period of high school attendance in a high school in the state. He must also give evidence of having completed a minimum of two years of regular high school work. *Test Requirements:* An applicant must attain a standard score of 45 or above in each of the five parts of the Test of General Educational Development OR an average standard score of 50 on all five parts. *Military Service:* An applicant can be granted a certificate on the basis of achievements in approved tests, military training, work experience, and educational training in Service Schools or Institutes. *Testing Fees:* Approved GED Testing Centers usually charge $5.00 except at Omaha and Ralston where a $10.00 fee is required.

FURTHER DETAILS: State Director, Guidance Services, State Capitol, Lincoln 68509.

NEVADA   High Schools are authorized to grant diplomas to qualified adults. *General Qualifications:* The applicant must be at least 21 years of age, a bona fide resident of the state, who has earned at least eight units, including credits in American History and Civics. *Test Requirements:* An applicant must attain a standard score of at least 35 on each of the five parts of the Tests of General Educational Development AND an average of 45 or above on all parts. *Testing Fees:* A fee of $5.00 is made for administering the tests to nonservice personnel or nonveterans.

FURTHER DETAILS: State Department of Education, Carson City 89701.

NEW HAMPSHIRE A High School Equivalency Certificate by the State Department of Education of New Hampshire on the basis of the results of the General Educational Development Test is issued. *General Requirements:* The applicant must be a resident of the state or must submit evidence that the last school attended must have been in the state and must have been in attendance for a complete school year. *Age:* The applicant must be 19 years of age or prove that the last class in which he was a member has been graduated. *Testing Fees:* A fee of $5.00 is required with application. A fee of $2.00 is required of applicants who wish to receive a certificate on the basis of tests previously taken. *Test Requirements:* A standard score of 35 or above on each of the five tests AND a total standard score of 225 or above on all five tests are required. Veterans who have taken the test while in service and nonveteran adults who have taken the tests at authorized GED testing agencies may apply for a certificate.

FURTHER DETAILS: Department of Education, State House Annex, Concord 03301.

NEW JERSEY The Commissioner of Education is authorized to issue a High School Equivalent Certificate to non-high school graduates who meet certain requirements. One of these plans includes a procedure involving the General Educational Development Tests. *General Qualifications:* A candidate must submit proof that he is at least twenty years of age and a resident of the state. *Testing Fees:* A fee of $5.00 must accompany the application and an additional $5.00 fee is required for the issuance of the certificate. *Test Requirements:* A candidate must attain an average standard score of at least 45 with no standard score less than 35 on any one of the five parts of the test. *Retesting:* If an applicant has scored the required average of 45 but has a score of less than 35 in any of the parts of the battery of tests, he is required to retake only the test or tests where his score is less than 35. A fee of $5.00 is required for any retesting. A waiting period of one year may be required. However, a retest may be given earlier if the applicant submits proof of having completed a program of studies relating to the subject matter of the tests to be taken. *Veterans:* Armed Forces personnel and veterans may complete the GED tests while in service. The minimum scores are similar to those required of other residents. *Alternate Plans:* A certificate may be secured by passing examinations in subject areas for which the applicant has not received credit in high school. Also, veterans or applicants over 24 years of age may receive a certificate by examination at college for readiness for admission and admission to an accredited college on the basis of passing standard aptitude tests.

FURTHER DETAILS: Department of Education, 225 West State Street, Trenton 08625.

NEW MEXICO The State Department of Education issues a High School Equivalency Certificate to adults who have met certain requirements. *General Qualifications:* An applicant, who is at least 18 years old and has successfully completed a special vocational school program, or who is in military service, is eligible. Other applicants must also be at least 18 years old, and the high school class of which they were members must have graduated before they can qualify. All applicants must show proof of age and evidence of at least one year's residence in the state. *Test Requirements:* A standard score of at least 40 on each of the five parts of the Tests of General Educational Development is required. In addition the applicant must achieve an average of 50 on all five parts. *Testing Fees:* A $3.00 fee is optional with the approved testing agency.

FURTHER DETAILS: Division of Adult Basic Education, State Department of Education, Santa Fe 87501.

NEW YORK A High School Equivalency Diploma is issued to adult residents who demonstrate their educational growth. *General Qualifications:* An applicant must be at least 21 years of age except in cases where an eighteen year old has not been enrolled in a regular high school for at least two years. Also, a woman at least 18 years of age is eligible for the Testing Program if she needs the test scores for enlistment in the Women's Armed Forces. Other applicants under 21 but at least 18 years of age may be tested by submitting proof that the test scores are needed for further educational training. Legal residence in the state is required except in cases where military personnel are assigned to duty in the state or are Job Corps Trainees assigned to centers in the state. *Test Requirements:* A score of 35 on each of the five parts of the Tests of General Educational Development AND at least a total of 225 on all five parts in the battery is required for the issuance of the High School Equivalency Diploma. *Testing Fees:* An applicant must pay a $6.00 fee to the local high school official or to an examiner for the Equivalency Testing Program. *Retesting:* After a period of one year an applicant may retake the GED tests. A fee of $6.00 is charged for the retesting. The applicant must take the entire battery of tests at each retesting, even if satisfactory scores were obtained previously in some parts of the test. *Veterans:* Successful scores on the GED Tests while in service are accepted.

FURTHER DETAILS: High School Equivalency Program, State Education Department, Albany 12224.

A Word about Preparation: No one is ever *too well prepared* for the High School Equivalency Examination. Besides using this book for individual study there are two ways in which you can be sure that you're properly and completely prepared:

(1) Attend a class at your local or community school—if there is a class designed to prepare you for this examination. If not, how about trying to interest the educational leaders in starting one? Your state department of education will help.

(2) If you are in the area where lessons preparing people for the High School Equivalency Examination are given on T.V., try to watch as many as possible.

NORTH CAROLINA The State Department of Public Instruction issues a High School Equivalency Certificate to adults who have met certain requirements. *General Qualifications:* An applicant must be at least 21 years of age, a resident of the state for at least one year, and must have a definite vocational or educational purpose. A person at least 19 years of age may take the required test with the permission of the local superintendent of schools. *Test Requirements:* The passing mark on the Tests of General Educational Development is a total score of 225 points with no single test below a score of 35. *Retesting:* Part or all of the GED tests may be taken after a six months' waiting period. *Testing Fees:* A charge of $10.00 is payable to the testing center at the time the tests are taken. The cost for retests is $2.00 per test. *Veterans:* Active military service personnel may take the test and use a special Defense Department form.

FURTHER DETAILS: State Superintendent of Public Instruction, Raleigh 27602.

NORTH DAKOTA The State Department of Public Instruction issues a State High School General Achievement Certificate to qualified adult residents who meet prescribed requirements. *General Qualifications:* A certificate is not issued to anyone under 21 years of age. An applicant must be a bona fide resident of the state with a recommendation for a certificate from the superintendent or principal of the last school attended. *Testing Fees:* The fees vary from $5.00 to $7.50 according to the GED agency. *Test Requirements:* A standard score of 40 or above on each of the five parts of the Tests of General Educational Development OR an average standard score of at least 50 on all five tests. *Veterans:* Veterans must have honorable discharge. Scores are acceptable from the United States Armed Forces Institute, directors of Veteran Administration Hospitals, and in some cases from the GED Testing Service.

FURTHER DETAILS: Director of Secondary Education, State Department of Public Instruction, Bismarck 58502.

OHIO   The State Department of Education may issue a Statement of High School Equivalence on the basis of the General Educational Development Tests. *General Qualifications:* An applicant must be at least 21 years at the time he applies, and must have resided in the state for at least six months. *Test Requirements:* A standard score of at least 40 on each of the five parts of the Tests of General Educational Development and an average standard score of 48 on all five tests is required. *Fees:* The fee for test administration varies from one Testing Center to another. A fee of $5.00 must accompany each completed application. *Retesting:* An applicant who fails to qualify for the Statement of High School Equivalence on his first attempt may be approved for a second attempt after a minimum of six months has elapsed since the previous attempt. An applicant who is re-examined may not be required to take all five subtests. He must take those tests which he previously failed. If the applicant needs only to raise his average score, he may take one or more of the five subtests.

FURTHER DETAILS: State Supervisor, Ohio Testing Services, Division of Guidance and Testing, State Department of Education, 751 Northwest Boulevard, Columbus 43212.

OKLAHOMA   The Division of Instruction of the State Department of Education has the authority to issue a Certificate of High School Equivalency to qualified adults. *General Qualifications:* An applicant must be a bona fide resident of the state and must submit proof that he is more than 21 years of age. *Test Requirements:* A standard score of 35 or above on each of the parts of the Tests of General Educational Development and an average of 45 on all five parts is required. *Testing Fees:* A fee is charged by the authorized testing agency. This varies from one agency to another. It is payable at the time the tests are taken. *Retesting:* An applicant who fails to qualify for the certificate on his or her first attempt may be approved for a second and third attempt, but only if a minimum of six months has elapsed since the previous attempt. Application is required each time tests are taken.

FURTHER DETAILS: Division of Instruction, State Department of Education, Oklahoma City 73105.

OREGON   The State Department of Education issues a Certificate of Equivalency to adult residents who meet certain requirements: *General Qualifications:* An applicant must be a bona fide resident of the state or has had his last formal school attendance in the state. He must be at least 21 years of age except in hardship cases with the approval of the Superintendent of Public Instruction. *Test Requirements:* A standard score of at least 40 on each of the five parts of the Tests of General Educational Development is required. *Testing Fees:* The fees at the various GED agencies vary. *Retesting:* In case of failure to achieve a satisfactory score an applicant may take a retest after a six months' waiting period. No more than two retests are permitted an applicant.

FURTHER DETAILS: Director, Secondary Education, State Department of Education, Public Service Building, Salem 97310.

PENNSYLVANIA   The Department of Public Instruction issues a Commonwealth Secondary School Diploma to qualified residents and a certificate to nonresidents. *General Qualifications:* To qualify as a resident, the applicant must have resided in the state for at least three months prior to making application for the tests. For service personnel, residence is defined as living in the state for at least three months prior to entry into military service. An applicant must be more than 18 years old and must show that the class of which he was a member has already been graduated. Exception to this rule is made where an applicant has attended an approved summer high school in order to accelerate. *Testing Fees:* The fee for the General Educational Development Test is paid when the applicant appears for the examination at the testing center. The fees are $5.00 except at Philadelphia and Waynesburg, where it is $10.00, and at Bradford where the fee is $8.00. *Test Requirements:* A total standard score of 225 with no single standard score of less than 35 on the Tests of General Educational Development is required. *Retesting:* A twelve month waiting period is required for candidates who fail the GED test and wish to be retested. However, this waiting period may be reduced at the discretion of the Division of Testing upon filing of evidence of additional preparation in the areas of deficiency following the original testing.

FURTHER DETAILS: Department of Public Instruction, Box 911, Harrisburg 17126.

RHODE ISLAND   The Department of Education issues a Senior High School Equivalency Diploma to qualified applicants. *General Qualifications:* The Tests of General-Educational Development may be taken by residents of the state or military personnel assigned to an installation in the state. An applicant must have done half of his schooling in the state and must wait six months after his high school class has graduated. *Test Requirements:* The tests are given every two months. It takes three evenings (approximately ten hours) to complete the tests. (A standard score of 43 or above on Tests 1 and 3 and a standard score of 44 or above on Tests 2 and 4, and of 42 or above on Test 5 are required; an average standard score of 50 is also admissible.) *Retesting:* An applicant who has failed any of the five parts of the GED may re-take those parts. There is no fee for retesting. *Fees:* A fee of $3.00 is charged for the administration of the test and the issuance of the diploma.

FURTHER DETAILS: Division of Adult Education, State Department of Education, Roger Williams Building, Providence 02908.

SOUTH CAROLINA   The State Department of Education administers the High School Certificate examination. *General Qualifications:* An applicant must be a resident or a former resident whose last school attendance was in the state. He must be at least 19 years of age on the day of the examination. Exception is made in extreme hardship cases where the individual is more than 17 years old but not yet 19 years of age. *Veterans:* An applicant in military service at the time of application who has resided in the state over a six month period prior to entering military service is eligible for the test. Veterans are eligible if they have resided in the state over continuous periods immediately prior to induction and immediately after military service for a total of at least six months. *Test Requirements:* The passing mark is in terms of a required total score on the several tests, so that persons who are weak in one or another field can frequently reach the passing total by attaining high scores in fields in which they are better prepared. The required passing mark is an average standard score of 47 on all five tests. *Retesting:* A candidate who fails to attain the passing mark on the first trial may take the examination a second time as early as it is offered, but six months must elapse after a second trial before a third trial and between subsequent trials. The fee of $10.00 must be paid for each repeat examination.

FURTHER DETAILS: High School Certificate Examiner, 937 Main Street, Columbia 29201.

SOUTH DAKOTA The State Department of Public Instruction issues a Certificate of Attainment as a high school equivalency certificate to adults who meet certain requirements: *General Qualifications:* The applicant must be a resident of the state or received his last formal education in the state. He must be at least 19 years old and out of school for at least one year. *Test Requirements:* The applicant must have received a standard score of 35 on each of the five parts of the General Educational Development Test OR have an average score of 45. *Fees:* A processing fee of $1.00 is required of persons taking the test at any place other than a South Dakota Civilian Testing Center. Applicants who take the GED test at one of the South Dakota Testing Centers pay a fee of $5.00 at the time the test is administered.

FURTHER DETAILS: Director of Secondary Education, State Department of Public Instruction, Pierre 57501.

TENNESSEE The State Department of Education issues an Equivalency Diploma to adults who meet certain requirements. *General Qualifications:* An applicant must be at least 21 years of age, a bona fide resident of the state or must have had his last schooling in the state. Application is made to the principal of the high school last attended or the principal of the high school located in, or nearest to, the community in which the applicant lives. *Test Requirements:* The minimum average standard score of not less than 50 is required on all five parts of the Tests of General Educational Development. *Testing Fees:* At GED official agencies the fee is a maximum of $5.00.

FURTHER DETAILS: Director, Adult Education, State Department of Education, Nashville 37219.

TEXAS The Texas Education Agency of the State Department of Education issues a Certificate of High School Equivalency to qualified candidates. *General Qualifications:* The applicant must be at least 21 years of age or a member of the Armed Forces stationed at a Texas base. Application for the equivalency certificate is made to the Texas Education Agency in Austin. No special application is required. *Test Requirements:* A standard score of 40 or above on each of the five parts of the Tests of General Educational Development OR an average standard score of 45 on all five parts is required. *Testing Fees:* These vary with the testing center.

FURTHER DETAILS: Division of Instruction, Texas Education Agency, Austin 78711.

UTAH The State Board of Education issues a high school diploma to adults who may earn a total of five units of credit toward graduation on the basis of test scores. *General Qualifications:* The applicant who seeks credit through results of the Tests of General Educational Development must be at least

21 years of age. *Test Requirements:* In order to receive five units of credit the applicant must achieve an average standard score of 50 or higher on the entire battery of GED with no score below 45 on any of the parts of the examination. *Military Service:* A maximum of three units may be granted for basic training. This credit may be credited as military science, first aid, and health.

FURTHER DETAILS: Division of Special Educational Services, 1400 University Club Building, 136 East South Temple, Salt Lake City 84111.

VERMONT A Certificate of High School Equivalency is granted to eligible adults. *General Qualifications:* An applicant must submit evidence of legal residence in the state and of the attainment of age 20 or more. The Commissioner of Education may grant an exception to the age requirement when an applicant is able to present credentials showing eligibility for military service. *Test Requirements:* To receive a state Secondary School Equivalence Certificate an applicant must be recommended by the high school principal after receiving satisfactory scores on the Tests of General Educational Development. The required scores are an average standard score of 45 on all five tests and no score less than 35 on each of the five parts. *Testing Fees:* A fee of $5.00 must be paid at the testing center.

FURTHER DETAILS: Secretary, Division of Instructional Services, State Department of Education, Montpelier 05602.

VIRGINIA The State Board of Education permits local school administrators to issue Certificates of General Educational Development to applicants who fulfill certain requirements. *General Qualifications:* An applicant must be at least 20 years of age. Under certain conditions the age requirement may be lowered but not for acceleration of graduation. He must be a resident of the state for at least one year prior to applying for testing and must reside in the school division through which he is making application. In addition, an applicant must have earned at least 8 high school units exclusive of health and physical education. Applicants who are 21 years of age who have not earned 8 units of high school credit may be permitted to take the battery of tests. *Test Requirements:* An applicant must attain a score of at least 40 on each of the five parts of the Tests of General Educational Development. *Retesting:* An applicant who fails to achieve a passing score on any one of the tests may be given an opportunity for retesting provided he can present satisfactory evidence of further study. *Servicemen:* An applicant must have last attended a high school in the state prior to entering the Armed Forces. Age and completion of high school credits is similar to the requirements of other applicants. A minimum standard score of 40 on each of the USAFI Tests of General Educational Development is required. Courses in Service Schools and Institutes are acceptable.

FURTHER DETAILS: Supervisor of Adult Education, State Board of Education, Richmond 23219.

WASHINGTON The State Department of Public Instruction issues a Certificate of Educational Competence to adult residents who have not completed high school but who meet prescribed requirements. *General Qualifications:* The applicant must be a bona fide resident of the state over 21 years of age, although exception is made in special cases. *Testing Fees:* A fee of $7.50 is charged. *Test Requirements:* A standard score of 35 or above on each of the five parts of the General Educational

Development Tests and an average score of at least 45 on all five parts are required. *Retesting:* An applicant who has failed to achieve a minimum test score may apply for a re-test at the discretion of the testing official. *Veterans:* Test scores are accepted as official from official GED agencies, the United Armed Forces Institute, and directors of Veterans Administration hospitals.

FURTHER DETAILS: Superintendent of Public Instruction, P.O. Box 527, Olympia 98501.

WEST VIRGINIA The State Department of Education may issue a State High School Equivalency Diploma to adult residents if they meet certain requirements. *General Qualifications:* Bona fide residents of the state or those who have last attended school in the state are eligible if they are at least 21 years of age. *Test Requirements:* A standard score of 35 or above on each of the Tests of General Educational Development OR an average standard score of 45 on all five tests is required. For admission to the State colleges, applicants without the regular high school diploma must attain a score of 40 on each of the GED tests. *Testing Fees:* The payment varies with the local official GED agency.

FURTHER DETAILS: Assistant State Superintendent in Charge of Instruction and Curriculum, State Department of Education, Capitol Building, Charleston 25305.

WISCONSIN Scores of the Tests of General Educational Development are not recognized as acceptable for issuing high school diplomas or equivalency certificates. The State Superintendent of Public Instruction may grant persons declarations of equivalency of high school graduation if in his judgment they have presented satisfactory evidence of having completed a recognized high school course of study or its equivalent. He may establish the standards by which high school graduation equivalency may be determined. Such standards may consist of evidence of high school courses completed in high schools recognized by the proper authorities as accredited, results of examinations given by or at the request of the State Superintendent, successful completion of correspondence study courses by acceptable correspondence study schools, course credits received in schools meeting the approval of the State Superintendent, or by other standards established by him.

WYOMING The State Superintendent of Public Instruction issues a High School Equivalency Certificate to applicants with satisfactory scores on the Tests of General Educational Development who have met the State Board requirements. *General Qualifications:* Candidates must be legal residents of the state for at least one year or have previously attended school in the state or be members of the Armed Forces or dependents of a member of the Armed Forces stationed in the state. An applicant must be at least 21 years of age or be at least 20 years of age in the case of veterans. In addition the applicant may be asked to obtain a written statement for the need of the test from a prospective employer, school official, or military recruiting officer. *Testing Fees:* A fee of $10.00 is charged for taking the test and where necessary, a charge for retesting of $2.00 per test, *Test Requirements:* An average standard score of not less than 45 on the five parts of the GED tests and a score of not less than 35 on any one of the five parts are required. *Retesting:* A waiting period of six months is required before retesting may be authorized except where special instruction has been completed.

FURTHER DETAILS: State Department of Education, Cheyenne 82001.

APPLICATION FOR STATE HIGH SCHOOL EQUIVALENCY DIPLOMA

(Applicant must sign application in presence of school official. <u>School official will mail application with proper fee to official testing center.</u>) Applicant must answer all questions.

For use of Albany office only

PERSONAL INFORMATION

1. Name [*Last, first, middle*] : (Please print.)
   Mr.
   Miss
   Mrs.

2. I desire to be tested in the month of

3. Legal residence [*No., street, city, State, zip code*] : (Please print.)

4. Telephone number:

5. Height:

7. Color of eyes:

6. Weight:

8. Color of hair:

9. Check one:
   ☐ Nonveteran   ☐ Veteran   ☐ Now a member of Armed Forces

10. Date of birth:
    Month—   Day—   Year—

11. Place of birth [*City or town, State*]

12. Are you 21 years of age or over?   ☐ Yes   ☐ No
    (If No, complete 12*a*, 12*b*, 12*c*, and 12*d*.)

12*a*. Circle highest grade completed: 1, 2, 3, 4, 5, 6, 7, 8, 9, 10, 11

12*b*. Date withdrew from full-time enrollment in school: *Month*—   *Day* —   *Year* —

12*c*. Name of school last attended full-time :......

12*d*. Address of school last attended full-time :......

TESTING DATA

13. Have you previously taken the High School Equivalency Examination (GED Tests) at an official testing center of the New York State Education Department? ☐ Yes ☐ No

    If yes, where? 1...... When?......
               [*Location of center*]   [*Month*]   [*Year*]

    2...... When?......
               [*Location of center*]   [*Month*]   [*Year*]

    (If you have taken the High School Equivalency Examination more than once, list the most recent examination first. Failure to comply with the retesting regulations, as outlined on the reverse side of this application, will invalidate the examination of the applicant.)

14. Are you applying for the High School Equivalency Diploma on the basis of USAFI GED Tests taken in service? ☐ Yes   ☐ No

    If yes, where?...... When?...... *Service Serial No......
               [*Station*]   [*Month*]   [*Year*]

15. Are you applying for the High School Equivalency Diploma on the basis of the USAFI GED Tests taken at a civilian center of the GED Testing Service located outside of New York State? ☐ Yes   ☐ No

    If yes, where?...... When?......
                         [*Month*]   [*Year*]

16. Are you applying for the High School Equivalency Diploma so you may qualify for further education or training? ☐ Yes   ☐ No

CERTIFICATION

I hereby apply to the Regents of the State of New York for a New York State High School Equivalency Diploma. I certify that I have not been issued a New York State Regents High School Diploma and that the above statements are true to the best of my knowledge. I certify also that I am a permanent resident of New York State or am submitting with this application a Certificate for Nonresidents (Form DET 603C). My fee of $6 is attached.

......
[*Signature of applicant*]

I certify that I have inspected this application and find the information is accurate to the best of my knowledge and that the applicant is qualified as a candidate for the High School Equivalency Diploma. The applicant's signature was affixed in my presence.

Date......

......
[*Signature of school principal or counselor*]**

County of......

......
[*Official title*]

......
[*School address*]

* Veterans and members of the Armed Forces applying on the basis of tests taken in service must provide their service serial number. Failure to do so will result in the return of the application.

** If the applicant is a member of the armed services, the term "school principal or counselor" may be interpreted to mean a commissioned officer of his unit. Veterans must have application signed by school principal or notary.

DET-603(8-66) E

X4623-Ag66-30,000(51896)*

3

The Test of Correctness and Effectiveness of Expression

The Test of Correctness and Effectiveness of Expression is designed to find out what you know about spelling, punctuation and capitalization, correct grammar, sentence structure, and usage.

HOW THIS CHAPTER CAN HELP YOU

To help you prepare for this test, we have four review sections: (1) complete preparation for spelling—lists of most frequently misspelled words, spelling rules, hints for improving your spelling; (2) a Dictionary of the Vocabulary of Grammar and Usage which explains concisely but completely every aspect of grammar you will be expected to know, with examples to illustrate each item; (3) a carefully selected vocabulary list of 1100 words with definitions of 300 useful nouns, 300 useful verbs, and 500 adjectives; (4) an analysis of all the kinds of errors people make in sentence structure, agreement of verb and subject, agreement of pronoun and antecedent, case of nouns and pronouns, tenses and forms of verbs, the use of adverbs and adjectives, difficult constructions, frequently confused words, punctuation, and capitalization.

A WORD OF ADVICE: Get the habit of referring to the Vocabulary of Grammar and Usage or to the sections explaining specific errors or spelling rules whenever you are uncertain about a point of grammar or a word in the practice exercises and examinations that follow the review material.

A WORD ABOUT REVIEW: Don't be alarmed at all the review material in this chapter. We've included much more than you will probably need simply because we didn't want to omit anything that might be useful to you. Remember that the High School Equivalency Tests examine background, not classroom or book learning. They test the kind of information you've acquired from reading newspapers and magazines, from T.V. and radio, from working at a job or running a home. They test experience and common sense. The review section simply organizes knowledge in this field, reminds you of some things you may have forgotten, fills in some gaps you may have in your background.

TIME TO STUDY:

THE SPELLING TEST

Correct spelling is included in the test which measures correctness and effectiveness of expression. Usually 20 words are given in groups of 4 and you are asked to select the misspelled word.

If you are one of the thousands of people in the United States who simply can't spell, take heart. You needn't be. Modern educational research has made the job of becoming a good speller a lot easier than it used to be. We now know which words are used most frequently in print. In fact, the words on these lists, if thoroughly mastered, will prepare you to spell correctly approximately *two-thirds* of the words you need.

The Basic Hundred

The first list contains 100 basic words that all students should know thoroughly.

ache	done	making	there
again	don't	many	they
always	early	meant	though
among	easy	minute	through
answer	enough	much	tired
any	every	none	tonight
been	February	often	too
beginning	forty	once	trouble
believe	friend	piece	truly
blue	grammar	raise	Tuesday
break	guess	read	two
built	half	ready	used
business	having	said	very
busy	hear	Saturday	wear
buy	heard	says	Wednesday
can't	here	seems	week
choose	hoarse	separate	where
color	hour	shoes	whether
coming	instead	since	which
cough	just	some	whole
could	knew	straight	women
country	know	sugar	won't
dear	laid	sure	would
doctor	loose	tear	write
does	lose	their	writing

How do you go about studying this list? One way involves the following steps.

1. Fold a sheet of paper into three parts holding the paper lengthwise.
2. Fold the left third of the paper over so that it covers the center part.
3. Look at the word, noticing the difficult spot or spots. Say it aloud carefully.
4. Look at the word again, spelling it aloud by syllables. We'll help you with the problem of dividing words into syllables later on.
5. Spell the word aloud by syllables again, without looking at it this time.

6. Look at the word a third time, copying the letters on the folded part of the paper while you say them aloud by syllables.

7. Turn the fold back, this time writing the letters on the right-hand part of the paper while you again say them aloud by syllables.

8. Fold the left third of the paper over again so that you can compare the word you originally copied with the word you wrote from memory. If it is spelled correctly, turn the fold back and write the word twice more, being careful to spell the word aloud by syllables each time. If you made an error, the word will require more study, particularly of the letter or syllable you misspelled.

The second word list contains two hundred words which are somewhat more difficult than the basic hundred but are still rated "Easy" by those who test spelling ability. After you have mastered the Basic Hundred, turn to this list. We've tried to help you by italicizing the letters or parts of the words which cause difficulty.

200 Often Used Easy Words

ab*s*ence	clo*th*	everybody	l*y*ing
accept	clo*the*s	eviden*tly*	maga*zine*
ac*c*ident	cloud	ex*cell*ent	me*re*ly
ad*dr*ess	coarse	expen*s*e	min*utes*
adjourn	collar	exp*erie*nce	mov*a*ble
advi*c*e	common	extreme*ly*	ne*i*ther
advi*s*e	conc*eal*	fa*tigue*	never*th*e*less*
airp*lane*	confident	form*erly*	nick*el*
a*ll*owed	con*quer*	for*th*	n*ie*ce
a*l*most	corner	for*ward*	ni*ne*ty
a*l*ready	c*ou*rse	f*our*teen	ni*n*th
a*l*together	crowd	f*our*th	o'clock
*A*merican	c*ur*tain	fu*ture*	*off*icer
am*ou*nt	cust*o*mer	general*ly*	op*e*rate
a*nn*ual	decided	gen*ius*	ow*i*ng
an*x*ious	delivery	gen*tle*men	p*ai*d
ar*ou*nd	destroy	good-bye	par*t*ner
ar*ou*sed	determ*ine*	*g*uard	pa*ss*ed
a*rr*ival	device	hand*le*	pa*st*
arti*cle*	dictator	hand*ful*	*per*form
a*s*ked	didn't	hand*some*	*per*haps
a*th*letic	di*ff*erent	hasn't	perm*a*nent
atta*cked*	dining	h*eight*	plan*ning*
a*tt*ention	discu*ss*ed	ho*p*ing	politi*cs*
*au*thor	di*v*ided	hund*red*	po*ss*ible
be*c*au*s*e	doesn't	hungry	pre*s*ence
be*fore*	dro*pp*ed	hurr*y*ing	proba*bly*
bra*k*es	d*ue*	interesting	prom*ptly*
breath*e*	d*y*ing	invi*t*ation	promin*en*t
careful*	*ear*liest	it*s*	proved
carr*y*ing	ea*s*ily	it's	*p*urpose
cer*t*ain	e*ff*ect	j*ea*lous	quar*ter*
chang*i*ng	eigh*th*	lad*ies*	qu*i*et
ch*ief*	elim*i*nate	la*ter*	qu*ite*
chi*l*dren	*E*nglish	la*tt*er	qui*zz*es
choi*c*e	en*tire*ly	led	reali*z*e
cho*s*en	enve*lope*	library	real*ly*
clim*b*ed	etc.	lo*s*ing	rec*ei*pt

received
recognize
reference
safety
salary
sandwich
scarcely
secretary
sentence
shining
shriek
speech

stopped
stories
strength
stretched
strictly
striking
studying
succeed
success
summer
surely
surround

terrible
than
they're
those
threw
thorough
together
toward
tries
twelfth
until
unusual

useful
varied
wasn't
weather
weird
welfare
whose
wonderful
wouldn't
written
you're
yours

The third list contains 325 additional words that are somewhat more difficult and which occur frequently in print. Each appears on several well-known spelling lists of words often misspelled by high school students. Each appears regularly on examinations. You will find that the 625 words on these three lists will solve most of your spelling problems.

325 More Frequently Used Words

absolutely
accidentally
accommodate
accordance
accordingly
accurately
achievement
acknowledge
acquainted
acquired
across
actually
additional
adequate
advertisement
advisable
affectionately
agreement
aisle
allege
all right
amateur
angle
apparatus
apparently
appearance
application
appreciate
approaching
approval
approximately
arctic
argument
arrangements
ascertain
assistance

association
attaching
attendance
audience
available
aviator
awkward
balance
beautiful
beggar
benefited
bicycle
Britain
bulletin
bureau
buried
cafeteria
calendar
campaign
candidate
capital
capitol
captain
career
carriage
ceiling
celebrity
cemetery
changeable
chaos
character
chocolate
circumstances
college
colonel
column

commission
committee
communication
community
comparative
competition
completely
complement
compliment
concerning
connection
conscience
conscious
conscientious
consequently
consideration
continually
controlled
convenience
coolly
correspondence
council
consul
courageous
courteous
courtesy
criticism
crucial
deceive
decision
decisively
definite
dependent
descent
description
desert

desirable
despair
desperate
dessert
develop
difficulty
disappeared
disappointed
disastrous
discipline
disease
disposition
dissatisfied
division
doubt
duly
efficiency
eligible
embarrass
eminent
endeavor
enemies
emphasize
environment
equipment
equipped
especially
essentially
examination
exceedingly
except
excitement
exercise
exhausted
existence
explanation

extension
familiar
fascinating
finally
financial
forcibly
forehead
foreign
foresee
freight
fugitive
fundamental
further
government
grateful
grievance
guarantee
guardian
harassed
heroes
hospital
humorous
hurriedly
identity
imaginary
immediately
incidentally
indefinitely
independence
individual
influential
ingenious
inoculate
inquiry
intelligence
interfere
interrupt
jewelry
judgment
kindergarten
knowledge
laboratory
legible
length
lieutenant

lightning
literature
livelihood
loneliness
loveliness
maintenance
marriage
material
mathematics
meanness
medicine
memorandum
merchandise
miniature
minimum
miracle
mischievous
misspelled
mortgage
mournful
murmur
muscle
mutual
mysterious
naturally
necessary
noticeable
oblige
obstacle
occasion
occurred
omitted
opinion
opportunity
organization
origin
original
pamphlet
parallel
particular
pastime
patience
perfectly
personally
personnel

persuading
physically
pleasant
portrayed
possesses
possibility
practically
preceding
preference
preferred
prejudice
preparations
principal
principle
privilege
procedure
proceeded
professional
professor
prophecy
prophesy
psychology
pursuing
quantity
quarreling
recommend
referee
referred
refugee
regretting
relevant
relieve
religious
remedy
remittance
repetition
replying
representative
requirements
reservoir
resistance
resources
respectability
response
restaurant
rhyme

rhythm
ridiculous
sacrifice
satisfactory
scene
schedule
seize
sergeant
severely
siege
similar
sincerely
skiing
sophomore
specified
specimen
stationary
stationery
stomach
suddenness
sufficient
suggestion
superintendent
surprise
suspense
sympathy
technical
temperature
temporary
tendency
therefore
tobacco
tragedy
transferred
typical
unnecessary
unusually
valuable
vegetable
village
villain
weight
wholly
woman
yield

Most Frequently Made Errors

To help you study these lists, modern research has identified the errors which are made most frequently. *Over sixty per cent of all spelling errors* are caused by either *leaving out a letter* that belongs in a word *or substituting one letter for another* (usually because of incorrect pronunciation of the word). An example of a word misspelled because a letter is left out is the word "recognize." Many students mispronounce the word by leaving out the "g"; they also, therefore, leave out the "g" when they spell the word. An example of a word misspelled because one letter is substituted for another is the word "congratulations"

Many students mispronounce the word by substituting the voiced "d" sound for the unvoiced "t" sound; they also, therefore, substitute a "d" for the "t" when they spell the word. Other words which are misspelled because of the omission or substitution of letters are:

accident*a*lly	envi*r*onment	lib*r*ary	su*r*prise
ar*c*tic	e*s*cape	par*t*ner	tempe*r*ature
can*d*idate	February	pos*t*pone	tragedy
choc*o*late	gover*n*ment	pre*j*udice	tremen*d*ous
di*ph*theria	labo*r*atory	prob*a*bly	us*u*ally

Over twenty per cent of all errors are caused by either *adding letters to a word* or *reversing two letters within the word.* An example of a word to which a letter is added is the word "equipment." Some people incorrectly pronounce the word with a "t" after the "p." As a result, they add a "t" to the word when they spell it. An example of a reversal of letters within the word is the simple word "doesn't." Very often, the letters "e" and "s" are reversed and the student spells the word incorrectly—"dosen't." Other words which are misspelled because of the addition or reversal of letters are:

aspara*gus*	(*not* gras)
athletics	(*no* e after the *th*)
barbarous	(*no* i after the second *ba*)
chimney	(*no* i after the *m*)
disastrous	(*no* e after the *t*)
hun*dred*	(*not* derd)
in*tro*duce	(*not* ter)
lightning	(*no* e after the *t*)
mischievous	(*no* i after the *v*)
mo*dern*	(*not* dren)
*per*cent	(*not* pre)
*per*formance	(*not* pre)
*per*spire	(*not* pre)
*pro*duce	(*not* per)
*pro*fession	(*not* per)
*pro*nounce	(*not* per)
*pro*tect	(*not* per)
remembrance	(*no* e after the *b*)
se*cre*tary	(*not* er)
umbrella	(*no* e after the *b*)

The next most common error is the confusion of two words having the *same pronunciation* but *different spellings and meanings.* These are called *homonyms.* In this humorous sentence—"A doctor must have lots of patients (patience)"—there is no way of our knowing which word the speaker means if the sentence is spoken. Therefore, we don't know how to spell the word. The words "patients" and "patience" are homonyms.

Forty of the most frequently used groups of homonyms follow. Be certain to check the meaning of each word in each group so that you can figure out the spelling from the meaning of the word as it is used in a sentence.

air; ere; heir	groan; grown	pair; pare; pear	steal; steel
ate; eight	hear; here	peace; piece	straight; strait
blew; blue	him; hymn	principal;	some; sum
bough; bow	hole; whole	principle	son; sun
brake; break	hour; our	read; red	their; there;
buy; by	knew; new	right; write	they're
cent; scent; sent	know; no	road; rode	threw; through
coarse; course	lead; led	sew; so; sow	to; too; two
for; four	mail; male	scene; seen	way; weigh
forth; fourth	meat; meet	stationary;	wood; would
grate; great	pail; pale	stationery	

You now know the five most frequent types of spelling errors.

How to Become a Good Speller

There are three things you can do to help eliminate these errors and to equip yourself with the skills you will need to become a good speller.

1. *Learn how to syllabicate.* Knowing how to syllabicate—divide a word into syllables—will help you avoid many kinds of errors. This skill is particularly helpful with words of more than average length. Here are some simple rules that will help you syllabicate properly.

RULE 1. When a word has more than one vowel sound, it is broken into parts or syllables.

EXAMPLE: stre*ng*th (one syllable); m*e* / t*a*l (two syllables)

RULE 2. Every syllable contains a sounded vowel or pair of vowels sounded as one vowel (digraph).

EXAMPLE: g*o* / *i*ng (sounded vowel in each syllable); br*ea*k / *ou*t (pairs of vowels sounded as one vowel in each syllable)

RULE 3. Sometimes a sounded vowel forms a syllable by itself.

EXAMPLE: *a* / gain

RULE 4. Double consonants usually are separated.

EXAMPLE: mit / ten; pos / ses / ses

RULE 5. A consonant between two vowels usually is joined to the vowel that follows it.

EXAMPLE: lo / cal; fi / nal

RULE 6. When the suffix "ed" is added to a word ending in "d" or "t," it forms a separate syllable.

EXAMPLE: add / ed

Applying these rules to the words listed earlier will help you avoid many of the common types of errors, particularly in the omission and addition of letters.

> EXAMPLES: ath / le / tics
> chim / ney
> um / brel / la
> ac / ci / den / tal / ly

2. *Learn the correct pronunciation of the word you must spell.* Mispronunciation is known to be one of the most common causes of misspelling. Your best ally in learning the pronunciation of a word is the dictionary. Knowing the correct pronunciation will help you attack successfully such words as:

> Feb / ru / a / ry   (the first "r" is often not pronounced)
> gov / ern / ment   (the first "n" is often not pronounced)
> choc / o / late   (the second "o" is often not pronounced)

3. *Learn the thirteen most helpful spelling rules and how to apply them.*
Each rule is given with an example of how it is applied to the words you will need to spell.

RULE 1. Plurals of most nouns are formed by adding "s" to the singular.

> EXAMPLE: house, houses

RULE 2. When the noun ends in s, x, ch, or sh, the plural generally is formed by adding "es."

> EXAMPLES: gas, gases; box, boxes; witch, witches; dish, dishes

RULE 3. Plural of a noun ending in "y" preceded by a consonant is formed by changing the "y" to "i" and adding "es." Nouns ending in "y" following a vowel do not change "y" to "i" except for words ending in quy (soliloquy, soliloquies)

> EXAMPLES: lady, ladies; toy, toys

RULE 4. A word ending in "y" and following a consonant usually changes the "y" to "i" before a suffix unless the suffix begins with "i." A word that ends in a "y" preceded by a vowel usually keeps the "y" when a suffix is added.

> EXAMPLES: beauty, beautiful; try, trying

RULE 5. A word that ends in silent "e" generally keeps the "e" when a suffix beginning with a consonant is added. A word that ends in silent "e" generally drops the "e" when a suffix beginning with a vowel is added.

> EXAMPLES: care, careful; believe, believable; move, moving; safe, safest

RULE 6. (This rule consists of exceptions to Rule 5.) Words ending in "ce" and "ge" keep the letter "e" before "able" and "ous."

> EXAMPLES: notice, noticeable; change, changeable; courage, courageous

RULE 7. A one-syllable word that ends in one consonant following a short vowel generally doubles the consonant before a suffix that begins with a vowel.

EXAMPLES: big, biggest; thin, thinner

RULE 8. A word of more than one syllable that ends in one consonant following one short vowel generally doubles the final consonant before a suffix beginning with a vowel *if* the accent is on the last syllable.

EXAMPLES: omit, omitted; regret, regretting; allot, allotted. *But* offer, offered.

RULE 9. The letter "i" is generally used before "e" except after "c." (*Note:* There are many exceptions to this rule: either, neither; neighbor, weigh; leisure, etc.)

EXAMPLES: believe, receive

RULE 10. An apostrophe is used to show that a letter has been omitted in a contraction.

EXAMPLES: it is, it's; they are, they're

RULE 11. An abbreviation is always followed by a period.

EXAMPLE: etc.

RULE 12. Nouns of Latin origin ending in "us" become "i" in the plural; those ending in "a" become "ae" in the plural; those ending in "um" become "a" in the plural; those ending in "is" become "es" in the plural.

EXAMPLES: radius, radii; formula, formulae; medium, media; axis, axes

RULE 13. The suffix "ful" is spelled with a single "l."

EXAMPLES: helpful; tablespoonful

NOTE: **The word "full" itself is the only exception.**

200 Practice Questions in Spelling

Directions: **In each of the following groups of words choose the misspelled word and rewrite that word correctly spelled.**

1. aknowledge, immensely, quantities, postponed   1._____

2. approval, calendar, fourty, balloon   2._____

3. asending, benefit, disappear, obsolete   3._____

4. sandwhich, colloquial, squeamish, complimentary   4._____

5. utterance, dissect, legendary, ancesters **5.**_____

6. laboratory, gardner, phase, skeleton **6.**_____

7. independence, affirmative, responcibility, luscious **7.**_____

8. perjury, maritime, humilliate, physique **8.**_____

9. glacial, eventual, sincerity, feindish **9.**_____

10. deceased, villian, antenna, liability **10.**_____

11. perform, apologize, occasion, acheive **11.**_____

12. appreciate, forhead, dual, withholding **12.**_____

13. accumulate, endeavor, labratory, interruption **13.**_____

14. agreeable, arrouse, conscience, psychology **14.**_____

15. antagonize, reguardless, treacherous, unsanitary **15.**_____

16. symbilize, neutrality, optimistic, noticeable **16.**_____

17. prarie, recruiting, breathe, nourishment **17.**_____

18. complexion, pitifully, metropolitain, accuracy **18.**_____

19. appraisel, remnant, facet, nobly **19.**_____

20. propaganda, interpreted, triumphant, efficently **20.**_____

21. delegate, capacity, foriegner, spokesmen **21.**_____

22. society, disguise, fullfilling, personnel **22.**_____

23. uncontrollable, furthermore, edible, paticularly **23.**_____

24. congenial, soliloquy, proceedure, especially **24.**_____

25. mathematician, partisipate, retroactive, befriended **25.**_____

26. cylinder, arguement, sympathetic, gingham **26.**_____

27. stepfather, conclusivly, commodity, intercede **27.**_____

28. siege, almanac, lisence, manageable **28.**_____

29. franchise, alliteration, plaintiff, disobediant **29.**_____

30. chaufeur, specialty, sacrilege, pulleys **30.**_____

31. elliminate, appendix, luxuries, mountainous **31.**_____

32. rewritting, triangular, women's, identity   32._____

33. capacity, axiom, kindred, tomatoe   33._____

34. cemetary, pneumonia, slaughter, temperature   34._____

35. loses, conservatory, orniment, technique   35._____

36. benefactor, referendum, discription, inadequate   36._____

37. abusive, practicle, threshold, contestant   37._____

38. cordially, fictitous, priority, nuisance   38._____

39. facinate, vicinity, bisect, inaugural   39._____

40. hundreths, grasshopper, popularize, maintenance   40._____

41. fulfilled, representative, parallell, congratulate   41._____

42. heros, nevertheless, corridor, unanimous   42._____

43. inherent, fiscal, illiterate, atheletics   43._____

44. occured, dismissal, fiery, boulevard   44._____

45. bankruptcy, overwhelmed, ingriedients, conqueror   45._____

46. chronicle, immagination, surname, amiable   46._____

47. meanness, boycott, visible, privalege   47._____

48. distruction, lightning, appealing, accompanying   48._____

49. existance, sophomore, premise, millionaire   49._____

50. satelite, pneumatic, conspiracy, misapprehend   50._____

51. historical, managment, successfully, calendar   51._____

52. communicate, foreign, conciet, development   52._____

53. deferment, appearence, vehicle, preamble   53._____

54. acquitted, undeceided, criticism, wariness   54._____

55. glistening, predicament, fervent, lazyness   55._____

56. muscle, errosion, extravagant, frostbitten   56._____

57. inverted, financial, respectibility, personnel   57._____

58. miscelaneous, transparent, businesslike, subtlety   58._____

59. proprietor, circumstantial, hypocrisy, economicly 59._____

60. generousity, keenest, seafaring, bronchial 60._____

61. disappointment, jubilant, tarriff, immigrant 61._____

62. census, ridiculous, finally, miniature 62._____

63. absolutly, interpretation, nuclear, precipice 63._____

64. contrivance, amunition, surrounded, exaggerate 64._____

65. pioneers, concrete, humane, loyality 65._____

66. antiquity, respectively, domicile, surgury 66._____

67. maintenance, enviroment, proceed, temperament 67._____

68. excapade, colossal, unveiling, tubular 68._____

69. forty-fourth, peculiarty, drought, platoon 69._____

70. canvassed, neighborhood, excellence, polititian 70._____

71. contagious, transfered, summarize, serviceable 71._____

72. wilderness, diameter, lubricate, excercise 72._____

73. favoritism, offensive, scissors, approachs 73._____

74. sluice, ajacent, columnist, shrubbery 74._____

75. survival, inquirey, lightning, mutually 75._____

76. clientele, diagnosis, antisipate, competence 76._____

77. interferred, anonymous, supremacy, pollution 77._____

78. electricity, liesure, disposable, emigrant 78._____

79. juvenile, species, adversly, allegiance 79._____

80. congradulate, hilarious, recommendation, incriminate 80._____

81. reciever, mattress, diamond, gladdened 81._____

82. plurallity, warrant, quotient, upholstery 82._____

83. rhythmic, monotonous, annulment, inocence 83._____

84. commercial, scarsely, sheaves, precipice 84._____

85. unnoticed, preying, murdured, witnessed 85._____

86. glossary, posioned, remittance, thoroughly 86._____

87. insignifigant, sarcasm, bizarre, feasible 87._____

88. digit, milestone, furlough, obsticles 88._____

89. divisible, metropolitan, unduely, egotism 39._____

90. hygienic, livlihood, tragedy, jewelry 90._____

91. advertising, peircing, recommend, convertible 91._____

92. transparent, survivor, attendence, partnership 92._____

93. reverence, bulletin, tremendous, idenity 93._____

94. competetor, medicine, creditable, jamboree 94._____

95. expence, minstrel, cruising, feudal 95._____

96. boundry, municipal, omission, brakeman 96._____

97. fraudulent, allergy, linoleum, preformance 97._____

98. celebraty, coefficient, bodyguard, meteorites 98._____

99. anniversary, conspicous, argumentative, preceding 99._____

100. disciple, suicidal, pamplet, equipment 100._____

101. utensil, audiance, stricken, excitement 101._____

102. coarsely, cafateria, curtained, despise 102._____

103. larceny, explination, coincidence, celery 103._____

104. inadequate, abbreviation, thorough, hopeing 104._____

105. legislator, visibility, gaurantee, absence 105._____

106. insignificant, preliminary, chronicle, consentrate 106._____

107. physiology, illegal, wierd, boredom 107._____

108. seizing, serialize, accomodation, vaccinate 108._____

109. mortality, bureaucracy, parliamentry, collegiate 109._____

110. macaroni, picknicking, condescend, judiciary 110._____

111. prosperity, ourselves, ajustment, pharmacy 111._____

112. scenery, pleasurable, dizziness, couragous 112._____

113. defiance, manufacturer, alleviate, umberella   113._____

114. saboteur, iresponsible, superintendency, gruesome   114._____

115. analyze, artical, household, stamina   115._____

116. comedian, alcohol, wresling, prudence   116._____

117. wearisome, compitent, sympathetic, pneumatic   117._____

118. twelth, derelict, alkali, virus   118._____

119. agregate, fatality, necessity, glacial   119._____

120. autocratic, phenomenal, capitalism, preforated   120._____

121. abyss, imature, corruption, predicament   121._____

122. ethical, dittoed, embargoes, preperation   122._____

123. brittle, weasel, prepaid, pianoes   123._____

124. arrangement, visulize, extravagant, suffrage   124._____

125. interveiw, query, rubbish, appraisal   125._____

126. battery, challange, succumbing, mortgage   126._____

127. contemporary, negotiation, seized, sponser   127._____

128. referree, vengeance, testament, anchorage   128._____

129. beautify, registrar, prefabracate, commodity   129._____

130. specifically, embarrasment, colleague, humorist   130._____

131. argueing, contagious, knives, shepherd   131._____

132. civillian, primeval, trigonometry, bewitches   132._____

133. thousandth, unreleived, vengeful, obituary   133._____

134. dissapprove, apologetic, truancy, statuesque   134._____

135. cadence, millinery, lonliness, burglarize   135._____

136. perpetuate, familiar, mannerism, ajournment   136._____

137. publicity, bureaucracy, patriarch, sacrafice   137._____

138. righteous, wiry, critisize, usefulness   138._____

139. loosely, breakage, symtom, bridle   139._____

140. vindictive, transferable, preliminary, obstinite 140._____

141. obtuse, writhe, foreword, rebelion 141._____

142. cylindar, audible, sojourn, uniqueness 142._____

143. barbarous, trajic, sensible, labeling 143._____

144. hosiery, juvenile, missionary, imformation 144._____

145. vertue, unusual, extravagance, nonessential 145._____

146. alienate, nonsensical, novelty, prevalant 146._____

147. potassium, aprehension, celluloid, adjustment 147._____

148. severity, antholigy, auditor, reverent 148._____

149. senility, lavender, iceing, prodigal 149._____

150. sincerely, affidavit, stubbornness, integrety 150._____

151. correspondence, precipice, reconize, supervisory 151._____

152. imovable, cubicle, headache, exemption 152._____

153. promoter, weild, ostrich, planned 153._____

154. clarify, playright, glossary, officially 154._____

155. stetistical, feigned, hygienic, analyzing 155._____

156. permanent, replica, twentieth, discriptive 156._____

157. alledge, stationery, sociability, molasses 157._____

158. repititious, intercede, assimilate, congratulatory 158._____

159. sedative, fiscal, truthfullness, transit 159._____

160. disiplinary, judiciary, linguist, gymnastics 160._____

161. ilegally, masquerade, spinach, supersede 161._____

162. assignment, medecine, equality, ammunition 162._____

163. secratarial, immediately, treachery, preferred 163._____

164. abreviate, strategy, thoroughfare, dissolve 164._____

165. scandalous, encouragment, merciless, assortment 165._____

166. exquisite, agravate, complexion, emphasis 166._____

167. unschedualed, analysis, homogenized, approximately **167.**_____

168. extension, converse, language, occassion **168.**_____

169. condemnation, grandeur, outragious, aspirin **169.**_____

170. compliance, potential, unmanagable, constraint **170.**_____

171. missunderstood, career, artificially, acquired **171.**_____

172. apprentices, decision, oppresion, familiar **172.**_____

173. annoyance, themselves, convenient, beseiged **173.**_____

174. evasion, indiffrent, suffuse, quizzical **174.**_____

175. extension, embellish, humerous, worrisome **175.**_____

176. curiosity, sincerety, extraordinary, persuasive **176.**_____

177. maneuver, resistance, tolerance, benificial **177.**_____

178. grotesque, gaiety, vineger, processional **178.**_____

179. protectorate, delinquint, ratified, legendary **179.**_____

180. delegation, injunction, senitorial, alkali **180.**_____

181. simultaneous, celestial, epoch, appartment **181.**_____

182. surgeon, structeral, systematic, pitiable **182.**_____

183. diameter, symphony, fertilizer, anouncement **183.**_____

184. volanteer, diseased, rejoicing, merger **184.**_____

185. documentary, suffrage, boycoted, strategy **185.**_____

186. apparently, strengthened, desperse, catapult **116.**_____

187. acquaintance, physics, indefinate, artificial **187.**_____

188. reconciliation, incorrigible, sectarian, vigilence **188.**_____

189. congenital, rearangement, summation, guttural **189.**_____

190. likelihood, grudging, pyramid, rightous **190.**_____

191. villiage, despair, hereditary, conscience **191.**_____

192. preservation, revelation, chassis, temperture **192.**_____

193. orphanned, nondescript, malicious, diminutive **193.**_____

194. marionette, exhilaration, literaly, analytical   194._____

195. uncompromising, artifice, vacinate, strident   195._____

196. calories, carnaval, prescribe, syllabus   196._____

197. substantial, goddesses, derisive, approximitly   197._____

198. condenser, usefulness, unvieling, hustling   198._____

199. whereabouts, cocksure, billiard, calous   199._____

200. contemptous, reaffirm, mileage, itinerary   200._____

A WORD ABOUT TESTS: Do you consider yourself a person who "goes to pieces" on tests? Cheer up! Psychologists claim that more than ninety per cent of us think we don't perform well on tests *of any kind*. Nobody likes tests. But more than 80% of the people who have taken the High School Equivalency Tests in the New York area, for example, have passed them. They must be doing something right. And so can you—with the right attitude and careful preparation.

ANSWERS TO *Practice Questions in Spelling*

1. acknowledge
2. forty
3. ascending
4. sandwich
5. ancestors
6. gardener
7. responsibility
8. humiliate
9. fiendish
10. villain
11. achieve
12. forehead
13. laboratory
14. arouse
15. regardless
16. symbolize
17. prairie
18. metropolitan
19. appraisal
20. efficiently
21. foreigner
22. fulfilling
23. particularly
24. procedure
25. participate
26. argument
27. conclusively
28. license
29. disobedient
30. chauffeur
31. eliminate
32. rewriting
33. tomato
34. cemetery
35. ornament
36. description
37. practical
38. fictitious
39. fascinate
40. hundredths
41. parallel
42. heroes
43. athletics
44. occurred
45. ingredients
46. imagination
47. privilege
48. destruction
49. existence
50. satellite
51. management
52. conceit
53. appearance
54. undecided
55. laziness
56. erosion
57. respectability
58. miscellaneous
59. economically
60. generosity
61. tariff
62. finally
63. absolutely
64. ammunition
65. loyalty
66. surgery
67. environment
68. escapade
69. peculiarity
70. politician
71. transferred
72. exercise
73. approaches
74. adjacent
75. inquiry
76. anticipate
77. interfered
78. leisure
79. adversely
80. congratulate
81. receiver
82. plurality
83. innocence
84. scarcely
85. murdered
86. poisoned
87. insignificant
88. obstacles
89. unduly
90. livelihood
91. piercing
92. attendance
93. identity
94. competitor
95. expense
96. boundary
97. performance
98. celebrity
99. conspicuous
100. pamphlet
101. audience
102. cafeteria
103. explanation
104. hoping
105. guarantee
106. concentrate
107. weird
108. accommo-
      dation
109. parliamentary
110. picnicking
111. adjustment
112. courageous
113. umbrella
114. irresponsible
115. article

116. wrestling	138. criticize	161. illegally	181. apartment
117. competent	139. symptom	162. medicine	182. structural
118. twelfth	140. obstinate	163. secretarial	183. announce- ment
119. aggregate	141. rebellion	164. abbreviate	184. volunteer
120. perforated	142. cylinder	165. encourage- ment	185. boycotted
121. immature	143. tragic	166. aggravate	186. disperse
122. preparation	144. information	167. unscheduled	187. indefinite
123. pianos	145. virtue	168. occasion	188. vigilance
124. visualize	146. prevalent	169. outrageous	189. rearrange- ment
125. interview	147. apprehension	170. unmanage- able	190. righteous
126. challenge	148. anthology	171. misunder- stood	191. village
127. sponsor	149. icing	172. oppression	192. temperature
128. referee	150. integrity	173. besieged	193. orphaned
129. prefabricate	151. recognize	174. indifferent	194. literally
130. embarrass- ment	152. immovable	175. humorous	195. vaccinate
131. arguing	153. wield	176. sincerity	196. carnival
132. civilian	154. playwright	177. beneficial	197. approxi- mately
133. unrelieved	155. statistical	178. vinegar	198. unveiling
134. disapprove	156. descriptive	179. delinquent	199. callous
135. loneliness	157. allege	180. senatorial	200. contemptuous
136. adjournment	158. repetitious		
137. sacrifice	159. truthfulness		
	160. disciplinary		

> *What's your score?*

_____right, _____wrong

Excellent	181–200
Good	161–180
Fair	140–160

If you scored lower, turn back to the section giving the rules that can help to make you a good speller. Then try the test again, possibly having someone dictate to you the words you missed.

WORD HUNT

This exercise is designed to test your ability to detect errors in spelling. While this is not the format of the spelling questions on the High School Equivalency Test, it will serve to check your spelling skill.

Directions: In each group of four sentences one sentence does *not* contain any misspelled word. In the line below each numbered question write the *letter* preceding the sentence which contains *no* misspelled word. Underline the misspelled words in the other 3 sentences. Next to the letter identifying your choice of the correct answer, write *all* the misspelled words in the other sentences, spelling them correctly.

EXAMPLE:

a. It is quite discouraging to meet a customer who has finally decided to purchase an article and suddenly <u>anounces</u> that she doesn't have enough money with her.

b. A cloud of doubt surrounds the excellent speech of the candidate because of his youth.

c. You can <u>elimanate</u> the necessity of a letter by enclosing a note with the gift.

d. <u>Its</u> summer and they're ready for anything save serious work.

b. announces eliminate It's

1. a. The weight of the choclate was plainly marked on the wrapper.
   b. The need for comunication among the various members of the team was emphasized.
   c. The boy was taught how to candle eggs so that he could seperate the good from the bad.
   d. In the desert, one doesn't worry about the dessert.

   1.

2. a. It may be all right to be <u>absolutly</u> certain that one's answers are correct but verification of the details is always in order.
   b. The <u>amature</u>, with an eye toward success in his work, may tend to pay more attention to detail.
   c. Without rhyme or reason you may suddenly decide that there is altogether too much money spent on a particular article of clothing such as shoes.
   d. Styles in clothes are <u>changeing</u> but this may be due to the fact that we Americans are anxious to keep up with our neighbors.

   2.

3. a. The heroes of medicine may be found among the patients in the hospital and with the test tubes in the labratory.
   b. To entirely eliminate crime and poverty would make the futur generation a happy one.
   c. It is quite difficult to realize that the libary must be a place of quiet.
   d. The success of his speech was due to the care with which his secretary worked over each sentence.

   3.

4. a. The author held the interest of his readers by his humerous references to commonplace situations.
   b. Considerable doubt was raised about the imediate improvement of the environment of the slums.
   c. As the bride walked down the aisle all eyes turned toward the veil.
   d. As the curtain rose, the audience gave courteous atention to the actors.

   4.

5. a. The tendency to give the <u>vilain</u> a minor part must be accepted as standard procedure.
   b. The permanent planning committee served without salary.
   c. Circumstances beyond the control of the editor caused the <u>criticsm</u> of the article in the magazine.
   d. <u>Repitition</u> and constant drill made the typist a champion.

   5.

6. a. Wouldn't it be wonderful if the committee gave every consideration to the problem at hand?

    b. Essentially, preparing for an examination is a job to be done and with consciencious effort success could be expected.

    c. The beggar was buried in his serious financial problems and gave no consideration to his disease.

    d. To embarass a young college student, ask him what advice he would give to a genius.

    6. _____

7. a. The existance of a single dark cloud in the sky is of no concern to the aviator.

    b. Everybody discused the magazine article on politics before Election Day.

    c. The enemies of the dictator were conscious of his schemes.

    d. The difficulty came from the poor description of the suspect as reported by the frightined woman.

    7. _____

8. a. The purpose of the kindergarten is not so much aquiring knowledge as it is learning to do things and learning to live with others.

    b. The knowledge of the essentials of grammer together with correct spelling habits make for good English.

    c. The guarantee of good service was ommited from the contract.

    d. The professor gave his opinion about politics daily.

    8. _____

9. a. We found it exceedingly difficult to obtain additional funds to pay for the advertisment.

    b. A dependant is a financial burden except at the time when income taxes are due.

    c. The expense involved in obtaining a college education will definately be investigated.

    d. The cafeteria displayed practically all items on the menu.

    9. _____

10. a. It is ridiculous to buy merchandise simply because it is advertised as a sacrifice sale.

    b. Purchasing furs and jewelry require considerible judgment.

    c. It came as a great suprise to find out how much tobacco was consumed by teenagers.

    d. The ocassion was one that called for sympathy.

    10. _____

11. a. The automobile tragedy involved injuries to the forhead, stomach and limbs.

    b. The quarelling sophomores attracted the attention of the upperclassmen.

    c. The scene of the first act showed the medicine man giving the fundamentals of healthful living.

    d. At the begining of the story the character of the hero was questionable.

    11. _____

12. a. The principle of self-preservation was not evident when the mother made the sacrafice to save the child.
   b. It's entirely up to the host to see to it that everybody is happy.
   c. It was a cold day in Febuary when the brakes failed.
   d. Almost every dyeing man would like to postpone the inevitable.

   12.————————————————————

13. a. Do not accept the excuse that we all are entitled to an ocasional accident.
   b. Generally speaking, the amount of money spent annually on food is constant.
   c. The arrival of the children at the school gates on the first day after the summer vacation is an intresting sight.
   d. The scientist asked his assistant to develope more care in handling expensive equipment.

   13.————————————————————

14. a. The murmur of the heartbeat had perfect rhythm.
   b. It takes a good teacher to recognize weakness in mathamatics but it takes a superior teacher to recommend a cure.
   c. It is a miracle how they obtained such a large morgage for the house.
   d. His tendency to give imaginary accounts of his feats was noticable.

   14.————————————————————

15. a. The principal discussed the requirements for graduation.
   b. The privelege of voting is taken for granted by so many.
   c. The term schedule included psycology and geology.
   d. Their first quarrel occured on the day after their marriage.

   15.————————————————————

16. a. The financial wizard acquainted with the methods of buisness quickly became aware of the questionable habits of one of his partners.
   b. The advertisement made us conscious of the steps saved by the installation of an extension telephone.
   c. The dificulty with many candidates is that they regard a platform as a means of getting into office.
   d. The bicicyle is a most efficient vehicle for getting around the college campus.

   16.————————————————————

17. a. The hungry student welcomes the invitation to dinner even if it means delaying his homework.
   b. In using the equipment it is recomended by the manufacturer that one be acquainted with the catalog description of the various parts.
   c. The twelth sentence in the paragraph made reference to the courageous colonel.
   d. It is possible that a sandwich will suffise for lunch but not for dinner.

   17.————————————————————

18. a. The absense of the guard at the gate made it possible for some of the visitors to go close to the airplane.

  b. The handsome young gentleman of forteen often seems ready to go forth and meet the problems of the world.

  c. The effect of the eighth grade teacher on the children was noticeable at the end of the school year.

  d. The coarse of the river could be followed from the height of the mountain to the depth of the valley.

    18.——————————————————

19. a. Essentially the excitment of the audience was caused by the arrival of the celebrity.

  b. The description of the details of the accident was open to criticism.

  c. It is hard to beleive that the handsome young man with an excellent school record was unhappy on the campus.

  d. It's quite an achievment to be able to maintain good discipline in a class of bright young children.

    19.——————————————————

ANSWERS TO *Practice Questions in Word Hunt*

1   d   chocolate, communication, separate
2   c   absolutely, amateur, changing
3   d   laboratory, future, library
4   c   humorous, immediate, attention
5   b   villain, criticism, repetition
6   a   conscientious, financial, embarrass
7   c   existence, discussed, frightened
8   d   acquiring, grammar, omitted
9   d   advertisement, dependent, definitely
10   a   considerable, surprise, occasion
11   c   forehead, quarreling, beginning
12   b   sacrifice, February, dying
13   b   occasional, interesting, develop
14   a   mathematics, mortgage, noticeable
15   a   privilege, psychology, occurred
16   b   business, difficulty, bicycle
17   a   recommended, twelfth, suffice
18   c   absence, fourteen, course
19   b   excitement, believe, achievement

TIME TO STUDY:

THE TEST OF GRAMMAR
AND USAGE

This is the part of the examination that causes many students the most concern. With careful preparation you can substitute confidence for concern. The Vocabulary of Grammar and Usage which follows will give you the meaning of all the terms of usage and grammar and an illustrative example for each.

The words defined here are those which are most frequently used in grammar and usage. They are to be studied in conjunction with the summary of grammar and usage contained in this book. Develop the habit of referring to this list any time you are in doubt about a point of grammar or usage.

The Vocabulary of Grammar and Usage

ACTIVE VERB   A verb is active when its subject is the doer of the action the verb is indicating. (The batter *hit* the ball.)

ADJECTIVE   A part of speech which helps describe a noun or pronoun by giving it a more exact meaning. (*big* house; *many* friends; *this* pencil)

ADJECTIVE CLAUSE   A group of words having a subject and a predicate which is unable to stand alone and which helps describe a noun or pronoun by giving it a more exact meaning. (the pen *which has red ink;* the food *I like*—"that" or "which" is understood)

ADVERB   A part of speech which helps describe a verb, an adjective, or another adverb by giving it a more exact meaning. (walks *slowly; very* pretty)

ADVERBIAL CLAUSE   A group of words having a subject and a predicate which is unable to stand alone and which helps describe a verb, an adjective, or another adverb by giving it a more exact meaning. (He played *although he had a broken leg;* She was prettier *than I had imagined;* He was *so* busy *that he didn't answer.*)

AGREEMENT   This refers to parts of a sentence which are alike in gender, number, and person such as a subject and its verb and a pronoun and its antecedent. (*I* stud*y; He* stud*ies;* The *dog* wagged *its* tail.)

ANTECEDENT   Noun which is replaced with a pronoun. (EVERYONE will please remove *his* hat. WALKING is *what* I like to do most.)

ANTONYM   Word that is opposite in meaning to another word. (happy, sad)

APPOSITION   Condition describing two nouns, next to each other in a sentence, which are equivalent in meaning. (my brother, Joe; Mrs. Brown, the secretary)

ARTICLE   Special kind of adjective which refers to these three words: the, a, an. (*the* book; *a* house; *an* egg)

AUXILIARY VERB   Verb which helps another word show tense or voice. (I *would have* forgotten. She *had* left.)

CASE   Form of a noun or pronoun which shows its relation to the other words in a sentence. *Nominative* case of pronouns has the forms I, you, he, she, we, they, who, and is used as the subject of a verb or as a predicate noun. (*They* go. It is *we.*) *Possessive* case shows possession. In nouns, it is formed with the apostrophe: (Frank's). Possessive pronouns include mine, yours, his, hers, its, ours, theirs, whose.

> NOTE: **There are no apostrophes in any possessive pronoun.**

Objective case of pronouns has the forms me, you, him, her, us, them, whom, and is used as object of a verb, object of a preposition, subject or object of an infinitive. (They hit *him.* They gave it to *him.* I want *him* to go. I want to hit *him.*)

CLAUSE   Group of words in a sentence which contains a subject and a predicate. *Independent* clauses can stand alone. (He played well.) *Dependent* clauses, adverb, adjective, or noun clauses, cannot stand alone. (He played well *although he was hurt.* The book *which I read* was very interesting. *That he recovered* was a miracle.)

CLICHE   An expression used so often that it loses effectiveness. ("bigger and better"; "let's put our shoulders to the wheel")

COMMON NOUN   Noun which refers to a group of persons, places, or things and not to any individual person, place, or thing. (pupils; states; schools)

COMPARISON   Change of form in adjectives and adverbs to show increase in amount or quality. (strong, strong*er*, strong*est;* good, bett*er*, be*st*). *Comparative* refers to a greater degree in quality or quantity of one item with respect to another. (smarter of the two). *Superlative* refers to a greater degree in quality or quantity of one item with respect to two or more other items. (larg*est* of the three).

COMPLEX SENTENCE   Sentence which has one independent clause and at least one dependent clause. (We are happy *that you came.*)

COMPLIMENTARY CLOSE   That part of a letter just before the signature where the writer takes polite leave of the reader. (In formal letters, "Yours truly,"; in informal letters, "Cordially,")

COMPOUND-COMPLEX SENTENCE   Sentence which has two independent clauses and at least one dependent clause. (Joe sang and Joan played the song which she had been studying.)

COMPOUND PREDICATE   Two or more predicates usually joined by "and" or "or." (He goes to school by day and works at night.)

COMPOUND SENTENCE   Sentence which has two independent clauses. (*Joe sang* and *Joan played the piano*.)

COMPOUND SUBJECT   Two or more subjects that take the same verb. (*Frank* and *I* will come.)

CONJUNCTION   Part of speech which connects words, phrases or clauses. (bread *and* butter; "to be *or* not to be"; She came *when* I left.)

CONNOTATION   The suggested meaning of a word beyond the specific meaning it conveys. (He was warned by the flashing red signal. Red is a color which has the connotation of danger.)

CONSONANT   Letter other than *a, e, i, o, u* (which are considered vowels) or *y* (which is considered a semi-vowel).

CONTEXT   Other words with which a given word is associated in a sentence and which determine the meaning of that word. (sheer *nonsense;* sheer *cliff;* sheer *stockings*)

DASH   Punctuation mark which shows a pause or break in a sentence. (He may not come—but why should I worry?)

DECLARATIVE SENTENCE   Sentence which makes a statement. (Sue loves Joe.)

DENOTATION   Direct specific meaning of a word. (Red as a color rather than as a sign of danger or, when capitalized, as a Communist)

DICTION   Effectiveness with which words are chosen by a writer or speaker to express his thoughts.

DIRECT OBJECT   Noun or pronoun which receives the action of the verb. (Joe struck *him.* Give *it* to Frank.)

DIRECT QUOTATION   Use of the exact words of the speaker. (The teacher said, "Do your homework.")

EUPHEMISM   Roundabout expression used instead of a more direct one which might have too harsh an effect on the reader or listener. ("short of funds" instead of "bankrupt")

FIRST PERSON   Pronoun and verb forms which refer to the person speaking. (*I, we; my, our; me, us; am, are*)

FUTURE TENSE   Time of verb which shows a happening yet to take place. (He will retire next year.)

GENDER   Classification of nouns and pronouns into three groups: masculine, feminine and neuter. A *masculine* pronoun is *he;* a *feminine* pronoun is *she;* a pronoun in the *neuter* gender is *it.*

GERUND   Verb form ending in "ing" which is used as a noun. It can be used as a subject (*Walking* is fun) or as an object (I hate *walking*).

GLOSSARY   Listing of difficult or unusual words occurring in a book with their definitions. It is usually found in the back of the book.

HEADING   In an informal letter, this contains the address of the sender and the date the letter is written. In a formal letter, this contains the date the letter is written since the address is on the letterhead.

HOMONYM   Word with the same sound but different spelling and meaning from another word. (to, too, two; pear, pair, pare)

HYPHEN   Mark (-) used to join compound words (two-thirds), join certain prefixes to words (ex-president) or to separate words into syllables (Eng-lish).

IDIOM   Group of words which, taken together, has a different meaning from the individual words used separately. (once upon a time)

IMPERATIVE SENTENCE   A sentence which gives a command. The subject is "you" although it may not be stated. (Study hard for your test.)

INDEFINITE ARTICLE   Refers to "a" and "an."

INDIRECT OBJECT   Word that shows, without any preposition, to whom or for whom the action in the sentence is taking place. (He gave *me* a pen.)

INDIRECT QUOTATION   Quotation which does not use the exact words of the speaker. (The candidate said (that) he would accept the nomination.)

INFINITIVE   Verb form which is usually indicated by "to" before the verb. Sometimes the "to" is understood. (I want *to go;* He made me *laugh.*)

INSIDE ADDRESS   Name and address of the person to whom the letter is written.

INTERJECTION   Independent word which expresses strong feeling. (ah!; oh!; alas!)

INTERROGATIVE ADJECTIVE   Adjective which is used before a noun in a question. (*Which* boy came? *What* book did you read?)

INTERROGATIVE ADVERB   Adverb which is usually used at the beginning of a question. (*When* did you come? *Where* did you eat?)

INTERROGATIVE PRONOUN   Pronoun which is usually used at the beginning of a question. (*Who* came? *Whom* did you see?)

INTERROGATIVE SENTENCE   Sentence that asks a question. (Did he leave?)

INTRANSITIVE VERB   Verb that has no object. (He *stands*. I *sit*.)

MODIFIER   Word or group of words which help describe another word or group of words by giving a more exact meaning. See ADJECTIVE, ADJECTIVE CLAUSE, ADVERB, ADVERBIAL CLAUSE.

NOMINATIVE ABSOLUTE   Independent group of words containing a noun and a participle which are included as part of a sentence. (*The sun shining*, we left for the park.)

NOMINATIVE CASE   Case of the subject or predicate noun in a sentence. (*Frank* is *president*.)

NOUN   Part of speech which is the name of a person, place, or thing. (George Washington, New York, toy)

NOUN CLAUSE   Group of words having a subject and a predicate which is unable to stand alone and which is either the subject or object in a sentence. (*That Washington was our first president* is a fact; He knew *that Washington was our first president*.)

NUMBER   Change in the form of a noun, pronoun, adjective, or verb to show whether there is one (SINGULAR) or more than one (PLURAL). (man, men; he, they; this, these; is, are)

OBJECT   Noun or pronoun which shows the person or thing acted upon by the verb. (She brought the *book;* I hate *her*.)

OBJECTIVE CASE   Form of the noun or pronoun which shows it is the person or thing which receives the action. (I hit *him*.)

OBJECT OF THE PREPOSITION   Noun or pronoun which follows a preposition and which is controlled by it. (with *me;* between *you* and *me;* among *him* and *them*)

PARALLELISM   Two parts of a sentence which have equal importance and are given the same form (and therefore the same importance) in the sentence. (He eats *both* MEAT *and* VEGETABLES; *Not only* THE RELATIVES were invited *but also* THE FRIENDS.)

PARTICIPLE   Form of a verb which is used both as an adjective and as part of a verb. (the *sleeping* child; am *going*). PRESENT PARTICIPLE, going; PAST

PARTICIPLE, gone; PERFECT PARTICIPLE, having gone.

PART OF SPEECH   One of eight categories into which words in a sentence are assigned: NOUN, PRONOUN, VERB, ADJECTIVE, ADVERB, PREPOSITION, CONJUNCTION, INTERJECTION.

PASSIVE   Form of verb which is used when the subject of the sentence receives the action. (The watch *was given* to Joe; The man *was laid* to rest.)

PAST TENSE   Time of verb which shows that an action has been completed. (He *went;* We *did go*.)

PAST PERFECT TENSE   Time of verb which shows that an action had been completed in the past before another completed action. (The train *had left* when I arrived.)

PERSON   Form of pronoun or verb which tells that a person (or persons) is speaking or is doing the action (FIRST PERSON), a person (or persons) is being spoken to or is doing the action (SECOND PERSON), a person (or persons) spoken about is doing the action (THIRD PERSON). (*We* left for home; *You* stayed here; *They* arrived late.)

PHRASE   Group of words without a subject and predicate, usually introduced by a preposition, which has a use in a sentence like that of a noun, adjective, or adverb. (*In the park* is where I like to sit; Jeanie *with the light brown hair;* He ran *to first base*.)

PLURAL   Form of noun, pronoun, adjective, or verb which indicates that more than one person, place or thing is being spoken about in the sentence. (boys, they, these, are)

POSSESSIVE   Form of noun or pronoun which shows that something belongs to it. (*girl's* pencil; *ladies'* hats; *its* paw)

PREDICATE   Part of the sentence which tells something about the subject (what the subject does, what is done to the subject, or what is true about the subject). (The boy *went home quickly*.)

PREDICATE ADJECTIVE   Adjective in the predicate which describes the subject by giving it a more exact meaning. (He is *honest*.)

PREDICATE NOUN   Noun in the predicate which is the same in meaning as the subject and can sometimes be interchanged with it. (He is *president*. She became an *actress*.)

PREFIX   Part added to the beginning of a word which adds to or changes its meaning. (*im*possible; *ex-*president; *re*view; *pre*fix)

PREPOSITION   Part of speech which shows the relationship between a noun or pronoun which it controls (and which is its object) and some other word in the sentence. (Mary went TO the *library*.)

PRESENT PERFECT TENSE   Time of verb which shows an action which started in the past and is continuing or has just been completed in the present. (It requires the use of an auxiliary verb in the present tense and the past participle.) (He *has been* our friend for years.)

PRESENT TENSE   Time of verb which shows an action which is going on now at present. There are three forms of the verb—he *says*, he *is saying*, he *does say*.

PRINCIPAL PARTS OF THE VERB   Three parts which include verb forms in the present tense, past tense, and the past participle. (go, went, gone; walk, walked, walked)

PRONOUN   Part of speech which is used in place of a noun. (John came. *He* was welcome.) The four main kinds of pronouns are: DEMONSTRATIVE (this, that; these, those); PERSONAL (I, you, he, she, it, we, they); POSSESSIVE (mine, yours, his, hers, ours, theirs); RELATIVE (that, what, who, which)

PROPER NOUN   Noun that refers to an individual person, place or thing. (George Washington, New York City, City Hall)

REDUNDANCY   Use of unnecessary words. (cooperate together; return back).

REFLEXIVE PRONOUN   Pronoun which accompanies a noun in the same sentence and refers back to it. (The president *himself* was there. She dressed *herself* quickly.)

ROOT   Basic part of a word without prefixes or suffixes which gives the main meaning of the word. ("cred"—believe; with prefix "in" and suffix "ible"—"in *cred* ible"—unbelievable)

RUN-ON (or COMMA FAULT) SENTENCE   Two sentences which are made into one by mistake. They are separated either by a comma or by no punctuation at all. (Wrong: Joe is class president, he is my friend. Correct: Joe is class president. He is my friend.)

SALUTATION   Part of a letter where the writer greets the reader. It usually is "Dear Sir:" in formal letters or "Dear *name of friend*," in informal letters.

SENTENCE   Group of words containing a subject and a predicate and expressing an independently complete thought. (*He* CAME EARLY.) Three chief kinds of sentences are: DECLARATIVE (makes a statement); INTERROGATIVE (asks a question); IMPERATIVE (gives a command)

SENTENCE FRAGMENT   Group of words which may contain a subject and a predicate but which fails to express a complete thought and is, by error, punctuated as if it did. (Wrong: Hoping to hear from you. Correct: I am hoping to hear from you.)

SIMPLE SENTENCE   Sentence which contains no dependent clauses and only one independent clause. (The sun shone all day.)

SINGULAR   Form of noun, pronoun, adjective, or verb which refers to one person, place, or thing in a sentence. (boy, he, this, is)

SUBJECT   Part of the sentence which does the action or is spoken about. (*He* hit the ball. *The watch* was given to the man.)

SUBJECT OF AN INFINITIVE   Noun or pronoun in the objective case which does the action indicated by the infinitive. (I want *him* to go.)

SUFFIX   Part added to the ending of a word which adds to or changes its meaning. (hand*ful*; quick*ly*; act*or*)

SYLLABICATION   Division into syllables. (Eng-lish)

SYLLABLE   Smallest group of sounds consisting of a vowel sound and one or more consonant sounds which are pronounced as a unit. (con-so-nant)

SYNONYM   Word that is very similar in meaning to another word. (happy—glad)

TENSE   Time of an action indicated by the verb as PRESENT, PAST, FUTURE, PAST PERFECT, etc. These are the most widely used tenses in English.

TRANSITIVE VERB   Verb which can take an object of the action it indicates. (He *hit* the ball.) An INTRANSITIVE VERB has no object. (He *was lying* in bed.)

USAGE   Actual use of language by the people at large. GOOD USAGE is the actual use of language by educated persons and persons in positions of importance. Good usage is constantly subject to the changes made in the use of language by these persons.

VERB   Part of speech which indicates the action carried out by the subject or which tells something about the subject. (He *hit* the ball. She *was* in the garden.)

VOICE   Form of the verb which shows whether the subject is doing the action (ACTIVE VOICE) or is receiving the action (PASSIVE VOICE). (He *hit* the boy. He *was hit* by the boy.)

VOWEL   Letters representing the sounds *a, e, i, o, u.* The letter *y* is considered a semi-vowel as in "slowly."

A BASIC 1100 WORD VOCABULARY

To help you build your vocabulary, we have selected 1100 words which every high school graduate should know. They are grouped into lists of nouns, verbs, and adjectives. You should use these lists and the definitions together with a good dictionary such as *Webster's New World Dictionary of the American Language*. (See page 16 for hints on using the dictionary.) For each word, we have provided a definition which is most widely used but is often far removed from the first or literal meaning. You may wish to study other meanings of each word. We have also provided many words, sentences or phrases to show you how the particular word should be used.

TIME TO STUDY:

---

300 Useful Nouns

ACCESS   (means of) approach or admittance (e.g. to records)

ACCORD   agreement

ADAGE   proverb (As "Better late than never")

AFFLUENCE   abundance; wealth (e.g. age of _____)

AGENDA   list of things to be done or discussed (e.g. at a meeting)

ALACRITY   brisk willingness (e.g. agreed with _____)

ALIAS   assumed name (e.g. Fred Henry, _____John Doe)

ANIMOSITY   great hatred (e.g. towards strangers)

ANTHOLOGY   collection of writings or other creative work such as songs

APATHY   indifference (e.g. towards poverty)

APEX   the highest point (e.g. _____ of a triangle)

ATLAS   book of maps

AUDACITY   boldness

AVARICE   greed for wealth

AWE   feeling of respect and wonder (e.g. in _____ of someone's power)

BEACON   guiding light (e.g. of knowledge)

BENEDICTION   blessing

BIGOTRY   unwillingness to allow others to have different opinions and beliefs from one's own

BLEMISH   defect (e.g. on one's record)

BONDAGE   slavery

BOON   benefit (e.g. a _____ to business)

BRAWL   noisy fight

BREVITY   shortness

BROCHURE   pamphlet (e.g. a travel _____)

BULWARK   strong protection (e.g. a _____ against corruption)

CALIBER   quality (e.g. a person of high _____)

CAMOUFLAGE   disguise, usually in war, by changing the appearance of persons or materiel

CASTE   social class or distinction

CATASTROPHE   sudden disaster (e.g. an earthquake)

CHAGRIN   feeling of deep disappointment

CHRONICLE   historical record

CLAMOR   uproar

CLEMENCY   mercy (e.g. toward a prisoner)

CONDOLENCE   expression of sympathy (e.g. extended _____ to a bereaved)

CONNOISSEUR   expert judge (e.g. of paintings, food)

CONSENSUS   general agreement

CONTEXT   words or ideas just before or after a given word or idea (e.g. meaning of a word in a given _____)

CRITERION   standard of judgment (e.g. good or poor by this _____)

CRUX   the essential point (e.g. the _____ of the matter)

CYNIC   one who doubts the good intentions of others

DATA   known facts (e.g. _____ were found through research)

DEARTH   scarcity (e.g. of talent)

DEBACLE   general defeat (e.g. in a battle)

DEBUT   first appearance before an audience (e.g. actor, pianist)

DELUGE   great flood (e.g. rain or, in a special sense, mail)

DEPOT   warehouse

DESTINY   predetermined fate (e.g. it was his _____ to)

DETRIMENT   damage or loss (e.g. it was to his _____)

DIAGNOSIS   determining the nature of a disease or a situation

DICTION   manner in which words are used in writing and speech (e.g. the radio announcer's _____ was excellent)

DILEMMA   situation requiring a choice between two unpleasant courses of action (e.g. he was in a _____)

DIN   loud continuing noise

DIRECTIVE   a general order (e.g. from an executive or military commander)

DISCORD   disagreement

DISCREPANCY   inconsistency (e.g. in accounts, in testimony)

DISCRETION   freedom of choice (e.g. he was given _____ to spend the money as he saw fit)

DISSENT   difference of opinion (e.g. from a decision)

DROUGHT   long spell of dry weather

EGOTIST   one who judges everything only as it affects his own interest; a self-centered person

ELITE   choice part (e.g. of society)

ENTERPRISE   an important project

ENVIRONMENT   surrounding influences or conditions

EPITOME   typical representation (e.g. she was the _____ of beauty)

EPOCH   period of time identified by an important person or event (e.g. the _____ of space flight)

ERA   period of time marked by an important person or event (e.g. the Napoleonic _____)

ESSENCE   basic nature (e.g. of the matter)

ETIQUETTE   rules of social behavior which are generally accepted

EXCERPT   passage from a book or a document

EXODUS   departure, usually of large numbers

FACET   side or aspect (e.g. of a problem)

FACSIMILE   exact copy

FALLACY   mistaken idea; reasoning which contains an error

FANTASY   imagination (e.g. he indulged in _____)

FEUD   continued deadly hatred (e.g. between two families)

FIASCO   complete humiliating failure

FIEND   inhumanly cruel person

FINALE   last part or performance

FLAIR   natural talent (e.g. for sports)

FLAW   defect

FOCUS   central point (e.g. of attention)

FOE   enemy

FORMAT   physical appearance or arrangement (e.g. of a book)

FORTE   one's strong point (e.g. school grades)

FORTITUDE   steady courage (e.g. when in trouble)

FORUM   a gathering for the discussion of public issues

FOYER   entrance hall (e.g. to a building or dwelling)

FRAUD   deliberate deception

FRICTION   rubbing of the surface of one thing against the surface of another

FUNCTION   purpose served by a person, object, or organization

FUROR   outburst of excitement (e.g. over a discovery)

GAMUT   the whole range (e.g. of experiences)

GAZETTEER   geographical dictionary, usually accompanying an atlas

GENESIS   origin (e.g. of a plan)

GHETTO   section of a city where members of a particular group (formerly religious, now racial) live

GIST   essential content (e.g. of a speech or an article)

GLUTTON   one who overeats or who indulges in anything to excess

GRIEVANCE   complaint made against someone responsible for a situation believed to be unjust

HAVOC   great damage and destruction (e.g. wreak _____ on)

HAZARD   danger

HERITAGE   inheritance either of real wealth or of a tradition

HOAX   deliberate attempt to trick someone either seriously or as a joke

HORDE   crowd

HORIZON   limit (of knowledge, experience, or ambition)

HUE   shade of color

HYSTERIA   wild emotional outburst

IDIOM   expression peculiar to a language which has a different meaning from the words which make it up) (e.g. hit the road)

ILLUSION   idea or impression different from reality

IMAGE   likeness or reflected impression of a person or object

IMPETUS   moving force

INCENTIVE   spur or motive to do something (e.g. profit _____)

INCUMBENT   present holder of an office

INFIRMITY   physical defect

INFLUX   flowing in (e.g. of money into banks, tourists into a country)

INFRACTION   violation of a rule or a law

INITIATIVE   desire or ability to make the first step in carrying out some action (often a new plan or idea)

INNOVATION   introduction of a new idea or method

INTEGRITY   moral and intellectual honesty and uprightness

INTERIM   meantime (e.g. in the _____)

INTERLUDE   period of time between two events (e.g. _____ between the acts of a play)

INTRIGUE   secret plot

INTUITION   knowledge through instinct rather than thought

IOTA   very small amount

ITINERARY   route followed on a trip, actual or planned

JEOPARDY   risk of harm (e.g. put into _____)

KEYNOTE   main theme (e.g. He sounded the _____ of the convention)

LARCENY   theft (e.g. They couldn't decide whether it was grand or petty _____)

LAYMAN   one who is not a member of a particular profession (e.g. from the point of view of a _____)

LEGACY   material or spiritual inheritance (e.g. _____ from a parent)

LEGEND   story or stories passed on from generation to generation and often considered to be true

LEGION   large number

LIAISON   contact between two or more groups (e.g. _____ between headquarters and field units)

LORE   body of traditional knowledge (e.g. nature _____)

MALADY   disease (e.g. incurable _____)

MANEUVER   skillful move (e.g. a clever _____)

MANIA   abnormal absorption (e.g. She had a _____ for clothes.)

MARATHON   contest requiring endurance

MAVERICK   one who acts independently rather than according to an organizational pattern

MAXIM   saying which provides a rule of conduct (e.g. Look before you leap)

MEDIUM   means of communication (e.g. _____ of radio)

MEMENTO   object which serves as a reminder (e.g. a _____ of the war)

METROPOLIS   main city of a state or region (or any large city)

MILIEU   surroundings

MORALE   state of mind as it affects possible future action (e.g. The troops had good _____)

MORES   well-established customs (e.g. the _____ of a society)

MULTITUDE   a large number

MYRIAD   a large number of varied people or things

MYTH   a story which is a traditional explanation of some occurrence, usually in nature (e.g. the _____ of Atlas holding up the heavens)

NICHE   a suitable and desirable place (e.g. He found his _____ in the business organization)

NOMAD   wanderer

NOSTALGIA   desire to return to past experiences or associations

OASIS   a place which provides relief from the usual conditions (e.g. an _____ of peace in a troubled world)

OBLIVION   place or condition in which one is completely forgotten

ODYSSEY   long journey

OMEN   something which is believed to predict a future event (e.g. an evil _____)

OPTIMUM   the best possible quantity or quality (e.g. He participated to the _____)

OVATION   enthusiastic reception usually accompanied by generous applause (e.g. He received a tumultuous _____)

OVERSIGHT   failure to include something through carelessness (e.g. His name was omitted because of an _____.)

OVERTURE   first step which is intended to lead to others in either action or discussion (e.g. He made a peace _____,)

PAGEANT   public spectacle in the form of a stage performance or a parade (e.g. a historical _____)

PANACEA something considered a cure for all diseases or problems

PANORAMA a clear view of a very broad area

PARADOX statement of a truth which appears to contradict itself (e.g. a 20-year-old who had only five birthdays because he was born on February 29).

PASTIME way of spending leisure time (e.g. He took up golf as a _____)

PAUCITY scarcity (e.g. a _____ of nuclear scientists)

PAUPER very poor person

PEER an equal as to age, social standing, ability or other feature

PHENOMENON a natural occurrence such as the tides

PHOBIA fear of something which is so great as to be unreasonable (e.g. _____ against cats)

PHYSIQUE build (of the human body)

PILGRIMAGE long trip to some place worthy of respect or devotion

PINNACLE highest point (e.g. the _____ of power)

PITFALL trap

PITTANCE very small sum of money (e.g. He survived on a _____)

PLATEAU area of level land located at a height

PLIGHT condition, usually unfavorable (e.g. the sorry _____ of the refugees)

POISE calm and controlled manner of behavior (e.g. He showed _____ in difficult situations.)

POPULACE the common people

POSTERITY future generations (e.g. leave a peaceful world to our _____)

PRECEDENT event or regulation which serves as an example or provides the basis for approval of a later action (e.g. set a _____)

PREDICAMENT unpleasant situation from which it is difficult to free oneself (e.g. He found himself in a _____).

PREFACE introductory statement to a book or speech

PRELUDE something which is preliminary to some act or work which is more important

PREMISE statement from which a conclusion is logically drawn (e.g. Granted the _____ that . . . , we may conclude . . .)

PREMIUM amount added to the usual payment or charge (e.g. He paid a _____ for the seats)

PRESTIGE respect achieved through rank, achievement, or reputation

PRETEXT reason given as a cover up for the true purpose of an action (e.g. He gave as a _____ for stealing it, his sentimental attachment to the ring)

PRIORITY something which comes before others in importance (e.g. He gave _____ to his studies)

PROCESS step by step system for accomplishing some purpose (e.g. the _____ of legislation)

PROSPECT outlook for the future (e.g. the _____ of peace)

PROVISO requirement that something be done, usually made in writing

PROWESS superior ability (e.g. _____ in athletics)

PROXIMITY nearness

PSEUDONYM assumed name, usually by an author (e.g. Mark Twain, _____ of Samuel Clemens)

PUN play on words depending on two different meanings or sounds of the same word (e.g. Whether life is worth living depends on the *liver*)

QUALM uneasy doubt about some action (e.g. He had a _____ about running for office.)

QUANDARY uncertainty over a choice between two courses of action (e.g. He was in a _____ between the careers of law or medicine.)

QUERY question

QUEST   search (e.g. _____ for knowledge)

RAPPORT   harmonious relationship (e.g. _____ between teacher and pupil)

RARITY   something not commonly found (e.g. A talent like his is a _____.)

REFUGE   place to which one can go for protection (e.g. He found _____ in the church.)

REMNANT   remaining part (e.g. _____ of the troops)

REMORSE   deep feeling of guilt for some bad act (e.g. He felt _____ at having insulted his friend.)

RENDEZVOUS   a meeting or a place for meeting

RENOWN   fame (e.g. an actor of great _____)

REPAST   meal

REPLICA   an exact copy (e.g. _____ of a painting)

REPRIMAND   severe criitcism in the form of a scolding (e.g. He received a _____ from his superior.)

REPRISAL   return of something in kind (e.g. _____ for an injury—"An eye for an eye")

RESIDUE   remainder

RESOURCES   assets, either material or spiritual, which are available for use

RESPITE   temporary break which brings relief (e.g. _____ from work)

RESUMÉ   summary

REVERENCE   feeling of great respect (e.g. _____ for life)

ROBOT   one who acts mechanically or like a mechanical man

ROSTER   list of names (e.g. _____ of guests)

SABOTAGE   deliberate damage to vital services of production and supply, usually to those of an enemy in wartime

SAGA   long tale, usually of heroic deeds

SALUTATION   greeting, written or spoken (e.g. The _____ of a letter may be "Dear Sir.")

SANCTION   approval, usually by proper authority

SARCASM   use of cutting remarks

SATIRE   attack upon evil or foolish behavior by showing it to be ridiculous

SCAPEGOAT   someone who is blamed for the bad deeds of others

SCENT   distinctive smell

SCOPE   entire area of action or thought (e.g. the _____ of the plan)

SCROLL   roll of paper or parchment containing writing

SECT   group of people having the same beliefs, usually religious

SEGMENT   part or section of a whole (e.g. _____ of a population)

SEMBLANCE   outward appearance (e.g. He gave the _____ of a scholar.)

SEQUEL   something that follows from what happened or was written before (e.g. _____ to a novel)

SHAM   false imitation (e.g. His devotion was a _____ of true love.)

SHEAF   bundle either of grain or of papers

SHEEN   luster (e.g. of furniture)

SILHOUETTE   outline drawing in black

SITE   location of an object or an action (e.g. original _____ of a building)

SLANDER   untruth spoken or spread about someone which damages his reputation

SLOGAN   motto which is associated with an action or a cause (e.g. Pike's Peak or Bust!)

SLOPE   slant (e.g. _____ of a line)

SNARE   trap

SOLACE   comfort (e.g. She found _____ in work.)

SPONSOR   one who endorses and supports a person or an activity

SPUR   something which moves one to act (e.g. a _____ to sacrifice)

STAMINA   ability to fight off physical difficulties such as fatigue

STATURE   height reached physically or morally (e.g. a man of great _____)

STATUS   standing, social or professional

STIGMA   mark of disgrace

STIMULUS   any encouragement to act

STRATEGY   skillful planning and execution (e.g. the _____ in a battle)

STRIFE   conflict (e.g. _____ between labor and management)

SUMMIT   the highest point (e.g. the _____ of his career)

SUPPLEMENT   amount added to complete something (e.g. _____ to a budget)

SURVEY   broad study of a topic (e.g. a _____ of employment)

SUSPENSE   tenseness brought about by uncertainty as to what will happen

SYMBOL   something which is used to stand for something else (e.g. Uncle Sam is a _____ of the United States)

SYMPTOM   indication of something (e.g. _____ of disease)

SYNOPSIS   brief summary

TACT   ability to say and do the right thing socially

TACTICS   skillful actions to achieve some purpose (e.g. The _____ he used to win were unfair.)

TALLY   record of a score or an account (e.g. the _____ of the receipts)

TANG   strong taste or flavor

TECHNIQUE   method or skill in doing work (e.g. the _____ of an artist)

TEMPERAMENT   natural disposition, often to act in a contrary manner (e.g. He displayed a changeable _____)

TEMPO   pace of activity (e.g. The _____ of life is increasing)

TENSION   mental or emotional strain (e.g. He was under great _____)

THEME   topic of a written work or a talk

THRESHOLD   the starting point (e.g. the _____ of a career)

THRIFT   ability to save money (e.g. He became wealthy because of _____.)

TINT   a shade of color

TOKEN   sign which stands for some object or feeling (e.g. a _____ of esteem)

TONIC   something which is a source of energy or vigor

TRADITION   customs and beliefs which are received by one generation from another

TRAIT   distinguishing feature (e.g. _____ of character)

TRANSITION   movement from one situation to another (e.g. _____ from dictatorship to democracy)

TRIBUNAL   place of judgment such as a court

TRIBUTE   showing of respect or gratitude (e.g. He paid a _____ to his parents.)

TURMOIL   disturbance (e.g. great _____ at the meeting)

TUTOR   a private teacher

TYCOON   wealthy and powerful businessman

ULTIMATUM   a final ("Take it or Leave it") offer

UNREST   restless dissatisfaction

UPHEAVAL   sudden overthrow, often violent

USAGE   established practice or custom

UTENSIL   implement which is of use (e.g. a kitchen _____)

UTOPIA   ideal place or society

VALOR   courage

VENTURE   something involving risk

VICINITY   neighborhood

VICTOR   winner

VIGOR   vitality

VIM   energy

VOW   solemn pledge

WAGER   bet

WHIM   sudden notion or desire

WOE   great sorrow (e.g. He brought _____ to his friends.)

WRATH   intense anger (e.g. He poured his _____ on his enemies)

ZEAL   eager desire

ZENITH   the highest point

ZEST   keen enthusiasm (e.g. _____ for competition)

300 Useful Verbs

ABHOR   hate

ABSOLVE   free from guilt (e.g. for a crime)

ACCEDE   agree to (e.g. a request)

ACCELERATE   speed up

ACCOST   go up and speak to

ADHERE   give support to (e.g. a cause)

ADJOURN   put off to a later time (e.g. a meeting)

ADVOCATE   act in support of (e.g. revolution)

ALLAY   calm (e.g. fears)

ALLEGE   claim

ALLOT   assign (e.g. a share)

ALLUDE   refer to (e.g. a book)

ALTER   change

ASSENT   agree

ATONE   make up for (e.g. a sin)

AUGMENT   add to

AVERT   prevent

BAFFLE   puzzle

BAN   forbid

BAR   exclude

BEFALL   happen to

BERATE   scold

BESEECH   plead

BESTOW   grant (used with on or upon)

CEDE   give up (e.g. territory)

CENSURE   blame

CHAR   scorch

CHASTISE   punish

CHIDE   scold

CITE   mention in order to prove something

COERCE   force

COLLABORATE   work with someone

COMMEND   praise

COMPLY   act in answer to (e.g. a request)

CONCEDE   admit that something is true (e.g. an argument)

CONCUR   agree

CONSTRICT   squeeze

CULL   pick out

CURTAIL   cut short or reduce

DEDUCE   make a conclusion from given facts

DEEM   consider

DEFER   postpone

DEFRAY   pay (e.g. the costs)

DELETE   remove or erase (e.g. a word)

DELVE   investigate

DEPLETE   use up

DEPLORE   be sorry about

DEPRIVE   keep someone from having or getting something

DESPISE   scorn

DETAIN   delay temporarily

DETECT   uncover something that is not obvious

DETER   keep someone from doing something

DETEST   hate

DETRACT   take away from

DEVOUR   eat up greedily

DIGRESS   depart from the subject under consideration

DILUTE   weaken by adding something less strong to the original (e.g. a mixture)

DISBURSE   pay out

DISCERN   make out clearly (e.g. a pattern)

DISDAIN   look down on with scorn

DISINTEGRATE   fall apart

DISMAY   dishearten

DISPEL   drive away

DISPERSE   scatter

DISRUPT   break up

DISTORT   present incorrectly (e.g. facts)

DIVERGE   go in different directions

DIVERT   turn from a course (e.g. a stream)

DIVULGE   reveal

DON   put on (e.g. clothing)

EFFACE   blot out

EFFECT   bring about

EJECT   throw out

ELATE   make happy

EMIT   give forth (e.g. sounds)

ENCOUNTER   meet

ENCROACH   intrude on (e.g. property)

ENDEAVOR   try

ENDOW   provide with (e.g. a desirable quality)

ENHANCE   increase the value of

ENSUE   follow as a result

ENTREAT   plead

ERR   make a mistake

ERUPT   break out

ESTEEM   value

EVADE   avoid or escape from someone or something

EVICT   expel

EXALT   raise to greater heights

EXCEED   surpass

EXPEDITE   speed up the handling of

EXPLOIT   take advantage of a situation or a person

EXTOL   praise highly

FALTER   stumble

FAMISH   starve

FEIGN   pretend

FLAUNT   show off

FLOURISH   thrive

FLOUT   defy mockingly

FOIL   prevent

FORGO   do without

FORSAKE   abandon

FRUSTRATE   prevent someone from achieving something

GAUGE   estimate

HARASS   disturb constantly

HEAVE   lift and throw

HEED   pay attention to (e.g. advice)

HINDER   keep back

HOVER   hang in the air above a certain spot

HURL   throw with force

IGNITE   set fire to

IMMERSE   plunge into a liquid

IMPAIR   damage

IMPEDE   stand in the way of

IMPLY   suggest

INCITE   arouse

INCUR   bring upon oneself (e.g. criticism)

INDUCE   persuade

INDULGE   satisfy (e.g. a desire)

INFER   come to a conclusion based on something known

INHIBIT   restrain

INSTIGATE   spur to action

INSTILL   put a feeling into someone gradually (e.g. fear)

INTERCEPT   interrupt something (or someone) which is on its way

INTERROGATE   question

INTIMIDATE   frighten by making threats

INVOKE   call upon

IRK   annoy

JAR   shake up (e.g. as in a collision)

JEER   poke fun at (e.g. as by sarcastic remarks)

LAMENT   feel sorrow for

LAUNCH   set in motion

LOOM   appear in a threatening manner

LOP   cut off

LURE   tempt

LURK   remain hidden

MAGNIFY   make larger

MAIM   cripple

MIMIC   imitate

MOCK   ridicule

MOLEST   bother

NARRATE   tell (e.g. a story)

NAVIGATE   steer (e.g. a ship)

NEGATE   deny

ORIENT   adjust oneself or someone to a situation

OUST   expel

PARCH   make dry

PEER   look closely

PEND   remain undecided

PERFECT   complete

PERPLEX   puzzle

PERSEVERE   continue on a course of action despite difficulties

PERTAIN   have reference to

PERTURB   upset to a great extent

PERUSE   read carefully

PINE   long for

PLACATE   make calm

PONDER   think through thoroughly

PRECLUDE   prevent something from happening

PRESCRIBE   order (e.g. for use or as a course of action)

PRESUME   take for granted

PREVAIL   win out over

PROBE   investigate thoroughly

PROCURE   obtain

PROFESS   claim with doubtful sincerity

PROSPER   be successful

PROTRUDE   project

PROVOKE   arouse to action out of irritation

PRY   look closely into

QUELL   subdue

RAVAGE   ruin

REBATE   give back, usually part of an amount paid

REBUFF   repulse

REBUKE   disapprove sharply

RECEDE   move backward

RECOMPENSE   repay

RECONCILE   bring together by settling differences

RECOUP   make up for (e.g. something lost)

RECTIFY   correct

RECUR   happen again

REDEEM   buy back; make good a promise

REFRAIN   keep from

REFUTE   prove false

REIMBURSE   pay back

REITERATE   repeat

REJECT   refuse to take

RELINQUISH   give up

REMINISCE   recall past happenings

REMIT   send (e.g. money)

REMUNERATE   pay for work done

RENOUNCE   give up (e.g. a claim)

RENOVATE   restore (e.g. a house)

REPENT   feel regret for (e.g. a sin)

REPLENISH   make full again

REPOSE   rest

REPRESS   hold back (e.g. a feeling)

REPROACH   blame

REPUDIATE   refuse to recognize

REPULSE   drive back (e.g. an attack)

RESCIND   cancel (e.g. a rule or regulation)

RESPIRE   breathe

RESTRAIN   hold back

RETAIN   keep

RETALIATE   return in kind (e.g. a blow for a blow)

RETARD   delay

RETORT   answer sharply

RETRACT   take back (e.g. something said)

RETRIEVE   get back

REVERE   have deep respect for

REVERT   go back to a former condition

REVOKE   withdraw (e.g. a law)

RUPTURE   break

SALVAGE   save something out of a disaster such as fire

SCALD   burn painfully with steam or hot liquid

SCAN   look at closely

SCOFF   mock

SCORN   treat with contempt

SCOUR   clean thoroughly; move about widely in a search

SCOWL   make an angry look

SECLUDE   keep away from other people

SEEP   ooze

SEETHE   boil

SEVER   divide

SHEAR   cut with a sharp instrument

SHED   throw off (e.g. clothing)

SHIRK   seek to avoid (e.g. duty or work)

SHRIVEL   contract and wrinkle

SHUN   avoid

SHUNT   turn aside

SIFT   sort out through careful examination (e.g. evidence)

SIGNIFY   mean

SINGE   burn slightly

SKIM   read over quickly

SMITE   hit hard

SMOLDER   burn or give off smoke after the fire is out

SNARL   tangle

SOAR   fly high in the air

SOJOURN   live temporarily in a place

SOLICIT   plead for (e.g. help)

SPURN   reject scornfully

STARTLE   surprise

STIFLE   suppress (e.g. feelings)

STREW   scatter

STRIVE   try hard

STUN   daze

SUBSIDE   lessen in activity

SUBSIST   continue to live with difficulty

SUCCUMB   yield to

SUFFICE   be enough

SUPPRESS   put down (e.g. a revolt)

SURGE   increase suddenly

SURMOUNT   overcome (e.g. an obstacle)

SUSTAIN   support

SWARM   move in great numbers

SWAY   move back and forth

TAMPER   meddle with

TARNISH   discolor

TAUNT   reproach mockingly

THAW   melt

THRASH   defeat thoroughly

THRIVE   prosper

THROB   beat insistently

THROTTLE   choke

THRUST   push forcefully and suddenly

THWART   prevent someone from achieving something

TINGE   color slightly

TORMENT   afflict with pain

TRANSFORM   change the appearance of

TRANSMIT   send along

TRANSPIRE   come to light

TRAVERSE   cross over

TRUDGE   walk with difficulty

UNDERGO   experience

UNDO   return to condition before something was done

USURP   seize power illegally

UTILIZE   make use of

UTTER   speak

VACATE   make empty

VANQUISH   conquer

VARY   change

VEND   sell

VERGE   be on the point of

VERIFY   prove the truth of

VEX   annoy

VIBRATE   move back and forth

VIOLATE   break (e.g. a law)

VOUCH   guarantee

WAIVE   give up (e.g. a right or privilege)

WANE   decrease in strength

WARP   twist out of shape

WAVER   sway back and forth

WHET   sharpen

WIELD   put to use (e.g. power or a tool such as a club)

WILT   become limp

WITHER   dry up (e.g. a flower)

WITHSTAND   hold out against (e.g. pressure)

WREST   pull violently

WRING   force out by squeezing

WRITHE   twist and turn about

YEARN   long for

YIELD   give up

500 Useful Adjectives

ACRID sharp to taste or smell (e.g. odor)

ADAMANT unyielding

ADEPT skilled

ADROIT skillful

AESTHETIC having to do with beauty

AGILE nimble

AMBIDEXTROUS equally skilled at using both hands

AMENABLE disposed to follow (e.g. advice)

AMIABLE friendly

APT suitable

AQUATIC living in or practiced on water

ARDENT passionate

ARROGANT overly proud

ARTICULATE able to express oneself clearly (e.g. a person)

ASTUTE shrewd

AUSPICIOUS favorable (e.g. circumstances)

AUSTERE harsh

AUTHENTIC genuine

AUXILIARY helping

BARREN unfruitful

BIZARRE strange

BLAND gentle

BLATANT overly loud

BOISTEROUS rambunctious

BRUSQUE rudely brief

CALLOUS unfeeling

CANDID honest

CASUAL offhand

CHIC stylish

CHRONIC continuing over a long period of time

CIVIC municipal

CIVIL courteous

COGENT convincing (e.g. argument)

COHERENT clearly holding together

COLLOQUIAL conversational

COLOSSAL huge

COMPATIBLE capable of getting along together

COMPLACENT satisfied with oneself

CONCISE brief but complete

COPIOUS plentiful

CRAFTY sly

CREDIBLE believable

CREDULOUS given to believing anything too easily

CUMBERSOME bulky

CURSORY done quickly but only on the surface (e.g. an examination)

CURT rudely brief

DEFT skillful

DEFUNCT dead

DEMURE overly modest

DEROGATORY belittling

DESOLATE lonely

DESPONDENT depressed

DESTITUTE poverty-stricken

DETERGENT cleansing

DEVIOUS indirect

DEVOID completely free of (e.g. feeling)

DEVOUT very religious

DIFFIDENT shy

DIMINUTIVE tiny

DIRE dreadful

DISCREET careful

DISCRETE distinctly separate

DISINTERESTED impartial

DISMAL gloomy

DISTRAUGHT driven to distraction

DIVERSE varied

DOCILE easily led

DOGMATIC stubbornly positive (e.g. opinion)

DOMESTIC having to do with the home

DOMINANT ruling

DORMANT sleeping

DRASTIC extreme (e.g. changes)

DREARY gloomy

DUBIOUS doubtful

DURABLE lasting

DYNAMIC energetic

EARNEST intensely serious

EBONY black

ECCENTRIC peculiar (e.g. behavior)

EDIBLE fit to be eaten

EERIE weird

ELEGANT tastefully fine

ELOQUENT powerfully fluent in writing or speech

ELUSIVE hard to get hold of

EMINENT distinguished (e.g. author)

EPIC heroic in size

ERRATIC not regular

ETERNAL everlasting

ETHNIC having to do with race

EXORBITANT unreasonable (e.g. price)

EXOTIC foreign

EXPEDIENT suitable in a given situation but not necessarily correct

EXPLICIT clearly indicated

EXQUISITE extremely beautiful

EXTEMPORANEOUS spoken or accomplished with little preparation

EXTENSIVE broad

EXTINCT no longer existing

EXTRANEOUS having nothing to do with the subject at hand

FANATIC extremely emotionally enthusiastic

FEASIBLE possible to carry out (e.g. a plan)

FEEBLE weak

FERTILE productive

FERVENT warmly felt

FESTIVE in the spirit of a holiday (e.g. celebration)

FICKLE changeable

FLAGRANT noticeably bad (e.g. violation)

FLEET   swift

FLIMSY   not strong (e.g. platform)

FLUENT   smooth (e.g. speech)

FORLORN   hopeless

FORMIDABLE   fear-inspiring because of size or strength (e.g. enemy)

FRAGILE   easily broken

FRAIL   delicate

FRANK   outspoken

FRATERNAL   brotherly

FRIGID   extremely cold

FRUGAL   thrifty

FUTILE   useless

GALA   festive

GALLANT   courteously brave (e.g. conduct)

GAUDY   tastelessly showy

GAUNT   overly thin and weary-looking

GENIAL   kindly

GERMANE   pertinent

GHASTLY   frightful (e.g. appearance)

GIGANTIC   huge

GLIB   fluent but insincere

GLUM   gloomy

GORY   bloody

GRAPHIC   vividly realistic

GRATIS   free

GRIEVOUS   causing sorrow

GRIM   sternly forbidding (e.g. future)

GROSS   glaringly bad (e.g. injustice)

GROTESQUE   distorted in appearance

GRUESOME   horrifying

GULLIBLE   easily fooled

GUTTURAL   throaty (e.g. sound)

HAGGARD   worn-looking

HALE   healthy

HAPHAZARD   chance

HARDY   having endurance

HARSH   disagreeably rough

HAUGHTY   overly proud

HEARTY   friendly (e.g. welcome)

HECTIC   feverish

HEINOUS   outrageous (e.g. crime)

HIDEOUS   extremely ugly

HILARIOUS   very gay

HOMOGENEOUS   of like kind (e.g. group)

HORRENDOUS   horrible

HOSTILE   unfriendly (e.g. unwelcome)

HUMANE   merciful

HUMBLE   modest

HUMID   damp

ILLICIT   illegal

IMMACULATE   spotlessly clean

IMMENSE   very large

IMMINENT   about to happen (e.g. storm)

IMPARTIAL   unbiased

IMPERATIVE   necessary

IMPERTINENT   rude

IMPETUOUS   acting on impulse

IMPLICIT   implied

IMPROMPTU   without any preparation (e.g. remarks)

IMPUDENT   rudely bold

INANE   silly

INCENDIARY   causing fire (e.g. bomb)

INCESSANT   uninterrupted

INCLEMENT   rough (e.g. weather)

INCOGNITO   with real identity hidden

INCOHERENT   not clearly connected

INDELIBLE   unable to be erased

INDIFFERENT   showing no interest

INDIGENT   poor

INDIGNANT   very angry

INDISPENSABLE   absolutely necessary

INDUSTRIOUS   hard-working

INEPT   ineffective

INFALLIBLE   unable to make a mistake

INFAMOUS   having a bad reputation

INFINITE   endless

INFINITESIMAL   very very small

INFLEXIBLE   unbending

INGENIOUS   clever

INGENUOUS   naturally simple

INHERENT   existing in someone or something

INNATE   inborn

INNOCUOUS   harmless

INSIPID   uninteresting (e.g. conversation)

INSOLENT   boldly rude

INTEGRAL   essential to the whole

INTENSIVE   thorough (e.g. study)

INTERMITTENT   starting and stopping (e.g. rain)

INTOLERANT   unwilling or unable to respect others or their beliefs

INTRICATE   complicated

INVINCIBLE   unable to be conquered

IRATE   angry

IRRATIONAL   unreasonable

JOVIAL   good-humored

JUBILANT   joyous

JUDICIOUS   showing good judgment (e.g. decision)

LABORIOUS   demanding a lot of work

LANK   tall and thin

LATENT   hidden (e.g. talent)

LAUDABLE   worthy of praise

LAVISH   extremely generous (e.g. praise)

LAX   loose (e.g. discipline)

LEGIBLE   easily read (e.g. print)

LEGITIMATE   lawful (e.g. claim)

LETHAL   fatal

LISTLESS   lacking in spirit

LITERAL following the exact words or intended meaning of the original (e.g. translation)

LITERATE educated to the point of being able to read and write (e.g. person)

LIVID discolored by a bruise (e.g. flesh)

LOATH reluctant

LOFTY very high

LOQUACIOUS talkative

LUCID clear

LUCRATIVE profitable (e.g. business)

LUDICROUS ridiculous

LURID shockingly sensational (e.g. story)

LUSTY vigorous

MAJESTIC grand (e.g. building)

MALICIOUS spiteful

MALIGNANT harmful

MAMMOTH gigantic

MANDATORY required

MANIFEST evident

MANUAL done by the hands (e.g. labor)

MARINE of the sea (e.g. life)

MARTIAL warlike

MASSIVE bulky and heavy

MEAGER scanty

MENIAL lowly (e.g. task)

MERCENARY working only for financial gain (e.g. soldier)

METICULOUS extremely careful

MILITANT aggressive

MOBILE movable (e.g. home)

MOOT debatable (e.g. question)

MORBID unhealthily gloomy

MUTUAL reciprocal (e.g. admiration)

NAIVE innocently simple

NAUSEOUS disgusting

NAUTICAL having to do with ships and sailing

NEGLIGENT neglectful

NEUROTIC describing the behavior of a person suffering from an emotional disorder

NIMBLE moving quickly and easily

NOCTURNAL of the night (e.g. animal)

NOMINAL small in comparison with service or value received (e.g. fee)

NONCHALANT casual and unexcited

NOTABLE important (e.g. person)

NOTORIOUS well-known in an unfavorable way (e.g. criminal)

NULL having no effect

OBESE overly fat

OBJECTIVE free from prejudice (e.g. analysis)

OBLIQUE indirectly indicated (e.g. suggestion)

OBNOXIOUS extremely unpleasant (e.g. behavior)

OBSOLETE out-of-date (e.g. machine)

OBSTINATE stubborn

OMINOUS threatening (e.g. clouds)

ONEROUS burdensome (e.g. task)

OPPORTUNE timely

OPULENT wealthy

ORNATE   elaborately decorated

ORTHODOX   usually approved (e.g. religious beliefs)

OSTENSIBLE   apparent

OUTRIGHT   complete

OVERT   open

PALTRY   insignificant (e.g. sum of money)

PARAMOUNT   chief (e.g. importance)

PASSIVE   not active (e.g. participation)

PATENT   obvious

PATHETIC   pitiful

PEDESTRIAN   unimaginative (e.g. ideas)

PEEVISH   irritable

PENITENT   repentant

PENSIVE   thoughtful

PERENNIAL   lasting for a long time (e.g. problem)

PERILOUS   dangerous

PERTINENT   relevant

PETTY   relatively unimportant

PICAYUNE   petty

PIOUS   devoutly religious

PLACID   calm (e.g. waters)

PLAUSIBLE   apparently true (e.g. argument)

PLIABLE   flexible

POIGNANT   keenly painful to the emotions

POMPOUS   self-important (e.g. person)

PORTABLE   capable of being carried (e.g. radio)

POSTHUMOUS   taking place after a person's death (e.g. award)

POTENT   powerful (e.g. drug)

POTENTIAL   possible (e.g. greatness)

PRACTICABLE   capable of being done (e.g. plan)

PRAGMATIC   practical

PRECARIOUS   risky

PRECISE   exact

PRECOCIOUS   advanced to a level earlier than is to be expected (e.g. child)

PREDOMINANT   prevailing

PREPOSTEROUS   ridiculous

PREVALENT   widespread

PRIMARY   fundamental (e.g. reason)

PRIME   first in importance or quality

PRIMITIVE   crude (e.g. tools)

PRIOR   previous (e.g. appointment)

PRODIGIOUS   extraordinary in size or amount (e.g. effort)

PROFICIENT   skilled

PROFUSE   abundantly given (e.g. praise)

PROLIFIC   producing large amounts (e.g. author)

PRONE   disposed to (e.g. accident)

PROSAIC   ordinary

PROSTRATE   laid low (e.g. by grief)

PROVINCIAL   narrow (e.g. view of a matter)

PRUDENT   discreet (e.g. advice)

PUGNACIOUS   quarrelsome (e.g. person)

PUNGENT   sharp to taste or smell (e.g. odor)

PUNITIVE   inflicting punishment (e.g. action)

PUNY   small in size or strength (e.g. effort)

PUTRID   rotten

QUAINT   pleasantly odd (e.g. custom)

RADIANT   brightly shining

RAMPANT   spreading unchecked (e.g. violence)

RANCID   having the bad taste or smell of stale food (e.g. butter)

RANDOM   decided by chance (e.g. choice)

RANK   complete (e.g. incompetency)

RASH   reckless

RAUCOUS   harsh (e.g. sound)

RAVENOUS   extremely hungry

REFLEX   of an involuntary response (e.g. action)

REGAL   royal

RELENTLESS   persistent (e.g. chase)

RELEVANT   pertinent

REMISS   careless (e.g. in one's duty)

REMOTE   far distant (e.g. time or place)

REPLETE   filled (e.g. with thrills)

REPUGNANT   extremely distasteful

REPULSIVE   disgusting

REPUTABLE   respectable (e.g. doctor)

RESIGNED   submitting passively to (e.g. one's fate)

RESOLUTE   firmly determined

RESONANT   resounding (e.g. sound)

RESTIVE   restless (e.g. pupils)

RETICENT   speaking little (e.g. child)

RIGID   stiff

ROBUST   strong and healthy

ROWDY   rough and disorderly (e.g. mob)

RUGGED   rough

RUSTIC   of the country (e.g. life)

RUTHLESS   pitiless (e.g. dictator)

SAGE   wise (e.g. advice)

SALIENT   prominent (e.g. points)

SALUTARY   healthful (e.g. climate)

SANE   mentally sound

SANGUINARY   bloody

SANGUINE   cheerfully hopeful

SCANTY   meager

SCHOLASTIC   having to do with school and education (e.g. record)

SCRAWNY   thin

SCRUPULOUS   careful and honest (e.g. accounting)

SECRETIVE   given to secrecy

SECULAR   not religious (e.g. education)

SEDATE   dignified

SERENE   calm

SHEER   very thin (e.g. stockings); utter (e.g. nonsense)

SHIFTLESS   lazy

SHIFTY   tricky

SHODDY   inferior in quality (e.g. material)

SHREWD   clever in one's dealings (e.g. businessman)

SIMULTANEOUS   happening at the same time (e.g. events)

SINGULAR   remarkable; strange (e.g. behavior)

SINISTER   threatening evil

SKEPTICAL   showing doubt (e.g. attitude)

SLACK   not busy (e.g. business season); loose (e.g. rope)

SLEEK   smooth and glossy (e.g. appearance)

SLENDER   small in size or amount (e.g. contribution)

SLOVENLY   untidy

SLUGGISH   slow-moving

SMUG   self-satisfied

SNUG   comfortable

SOBER   serious

SOLEMN   grave (e.g. occasion)

SOLITARY   lone

SOMBER   dark and gloomy (e.g. outlook)

SOPHISTICATED   wise in the ways of the world

SORDID   wretched (e.g. condition)

SPARSE   thinly scattered

SPIRITED   lively

SPIRITUAL   of the spirit or soul

SPONTANEOUS   happening as a result of natural impulse (e.g. reaction)

SPORADIC   happening at irregular times (e.g. shooting)

SPRY   nimble

STACCATO   with breaks between successive sounds

STAGNANT   dirty from lack of movement (e.g. water)

STALWART   robust

STAUNCH   firm (e.g. friend)

STARK   bleak (e.g. outlook)

STATELY   dignified

STATIC   stationary

STATIONARY   not moving

STEADFAST   firm

STERN   severe (e.g. look)

STOCKY   short and heavily built

STODGY   uninteresting

STOICAL   unmoved emotionally

STOUT   fat; firm (e.g. resistance)

STRAIGHTFORWARD   honest (e.g. answer)

STRENUOUS   demanding great energy (e.g. exercise)

STUPENDOUS   amazing (e.g. effort)

STURDY   strongly built

SUAVE   smoothly polite (e.g. manner)

SUBLIME   inspiring admiration because of noble quality (e.g. music)

SUBSIDIARY   of less importance (e.g. rank)

SUBSTANTIAL   of considerable numbers or size

SUBTLE   suggested delicately (e.g. hint)

SULLEN   resentful

SULTRY   extremely hot and humid (e.g. weather)

SUMPTUOUS   costly (e.g. meal)

SUNDRY   various

SUPERB   of a high degree of excellence

SUPERFICIAL   not going beyond the obvious (e.g. examination)

SUPERFLUOUS   beyond what is needed

SUPERLATIVE   superior to all others (e.g. performance)

SUPPLE   limber (e.g. body)

SURLY   offensively rude

SUSCEPTIBLE easily affected by (e.g. colds)

SWARTHY dark-skinned

TACIT not openly said but implied (e.g. approval)

TANGIBLE capable of being touched; actual (e.g. results)

TARDY late (e.g. student)

TART having a sharp taste (e.g. food)

TAUT tightly stretched (e.g. rope)

TEDIOUS long and tiresome (e.g. study)

TEMPERATE moderate (e.g. climate)

TENACIOUS holding fast (e.g. grip)

TENTATIVE for a temporary period of trial (e.g. agreement)

TEPID lukewarm (e.g. water)

TERMINAL concluding

TERSE brief but expressing a good deal (e.g. comment)

THANKLESS unappreciated (e.g. task)

TIDY neat (e.g. appearance)

TIMELESS eternal (e.g. beauty)

TIMELY happening at a desirable time (e.g. arrival)

TIMID shy

TIRESOME tiring

TITANIC of enormous size or strength

TORRID intensely hot

TRANQUIL calm (e.g. waters)

TRANSIENT passing away after a brief time

TRIFLING of little importance

TRITE ordinary (e.g. remark)

TRIVIAL insignificant

TURBULENT agitated

ULTIMATE final (e.g. conclusion)

UNANIMOUS in complete agreement (e.g. decision)

UNASSUMING modest

UNCANNY unnatural (e.g. accuracy)

UNCONDITIONAL absolute (e.g. surrender)

UNCOUTH crude and clumsy (e.g. adolescent)

UNDAUNTED not discouraged

UNDERHAND sly

UNDULY overly (e.g. concerned)

UNEASY disturbed

UNGAINLY awkward (e.g. youth)

UNIQUE only one of its kind (e.g. specimen)

UNKEMPT not combed

UNRULY disorderly (e.g. crowd)

UNSCATHED uninjured

UNWIELDY clumsy to use, usually because of size (e.g. implement)

UPRIGHT honest (e.g. citizen)

UTMOST most extreme (e.g. in distance, height or size)

UTTER complete (e.g. failure)

VAIN futile (e.g. attempt); conceited (e.g. person)

VALIANT brave

VALID (legally) sound (e.g. argument)

VAST very large in extent or size (e.g. distances)

VEHEMENT violent in feeling (e.g. protest)

VERBATIM word for word (e.g. report)

VERSATILE able to perform many tasks well (e.g. athlete)

VIGILANT   watchful (e.g. sentry)

VILE   highly disgusting (e.g. conduct)

VISIBLE   able to be seen (e.g. object)

VITAL   essential (e.g. contribution)

VIVACIOUS   lively

VIVID   bright (e.g. color)

VOID   not binding legally (e.g. contract)

VOLUMINOUS   very great in size (e.g. writings)

VORACIOUS   greedy for food (e.g. appetite)

VULNERABLE   open to attack (e.g. position)

WARY   cautious

WEARY   tired

WEE   very small

WEIGHTY   important (e.g. decision)

WHOLESOME   causing a feeling of well-being (e.g. entertainment)

WILY   cunning (e.g. magician)

WISHFUL   showing desire that something be so (e.g. thinking)

WITTY   amusingly clever (e.g. remark)

WORDY   using too many words (e.g. reply)

WORLDLY   enjoying the pleasures and experiences of this world (e.g. person)

WORTHY   deserving (e.g. choice)

WRETCHED   miserable

THE 10 ''PROBLEM'' AREAS IN ENGLISH GRAMMAR AND USAGE

Perhaps you never thought about it, but the truth is that most of the errors in written English can be found in only 10 areas—plus spelling, of course, which has been discussed previously.

The following descriptions of the 10 "problem areas" in English grammar and usage (1) indicate and analyze the kinds of mistakes commonly made in each area; (2) give ways of correcting them; (3) give sufficient practice material after each section so that you can be confident of your mastery of each principle.

Area 1 Sentence Structure

A sentence may be defined as a group of words having a subject and a predicate and expressing a complete thought. Each sentence should be separated from the sentence which follows it by some form of end punctuation such as a period, a question mark, or an exclamation point. In one important group of errors, the student fails to separate two or more sentences by using the proper end (or terminal) punctuation, either using no punctuation at all or incorrectly using a comma. This group of errors is called by the general term-RUN-ON SENTENCE. Here are frequently made errors and the ways they may be corrected.

TYPES OF RUN-ON SENTENCES

1. Cause and effect relationship incorrectly expressed

WRONG: Joe was elected class president$_x$ he is very popular.

CORRECT: Joe was elected class president *because* he is very popular.

> EXPLANATION: Each—Joe was elected class president—and—he is very popular—is an independent sentence. The two sentences have been run together because there is no end punctuation between them. This error can be corrected by simply placing a period between the two sentences. A better way to correct this error is to look for a relationship between the two sentences. The first sentence—Joe was elected president—happened because of the second, the fact that—he is very popular; the first sentence is a result of the second.

It is, therefore, possible to join the two sentences using the conjunction, *because*. Joe was elected president *because* he is very popular.

Another similar error which is frequently made is the incorrect use of an adverb instead of a conjunction. (See THE VOCABULARY OF GRAMMAR AND USAGE for definitions of these words.)

WRONG: Joe is very popular$_x$ therefore he was elected president.

WRONG: Joe is very popular$_x$ so he was elected president.

To correct this type of error, *you must substitute a conjunction* for the adverbs "therefore" and "so" or you must break the wrong run-on sentence at the point marked$_x$ with either a period or semicolon.

CORRECT: Joe is very popular. Therefore, he was elected president.

CORRECT: Joe is very popular; therefore, he was elected president.

CORRECT: Joe is very popular and, as a result, he was elected president.

IMPORTANT NOTE: **The next three types of run-on sentences all involve finding the relationship between two run-on sentences. Use the same reasoning that was used in correcting the first type of error we have just identified.**

2. Result incorrectly related to the cause

WRONG: Joe worked hard$_x$ he was bound to succeed.

WRONG: Joe worked hard$_x$ consequently he was bound to succeed.

CORRECT: Joe worked *so* hard *that* he was bound to succeed.

CORRECT: Joe worked hard. *Consequently,* he was bound to succeed.

CORRECT: Since Joe worked hard, he was bound to succeed.

3. Opposite idea incorrectly connected to the idea it apparently contradicts

WRONG: Joe disliked English$_x$ he got a good mark anyhow.

CORRECT: Joe disliked English *but* he got a good mark anyhow.

WRONG: Joe disliked English$_x$ nevertheless he got a good mark.

CORRECT: Joe disliked English. *Nevertheless,* he got a good mark.

CORRECT: Although Joe disliked English, he got a good mark.

WRONG: Joe disliked English$_x$ however he got a good mark.

CORRECT: Joe disliked English. *However,* he got a good mark.

4. Additional idea incorrectly connected to the idea to which it is added

WRONG: Joe is excellent in mathematics$_x$ he is also good in English.

CORRECT: Joe is excellent in mathematics *and* he is also good in English.

WRONG: Joe is excellent in mathematics$_x$ furthermore he is good in English.

WRONG: Joe is excellent in mathematics$_x$ besides he is good in English.

CORRECT: Joe is excellent in mathematics. *Furthermore,* he is good in English.

CORRECT: Joe is excellent in mathematics. He is *also* good in English.

CORRECT: Joe is excellent in mathematics. Besides, he is good in English.

IMPORTANT NOTE: **The next type of error is different from those we have identified thus far.**

5. Descriptive (adjective) clause incorrectly connected to the word (noun) described

WRONG: Joe is always imitating the coach, he respects him greatly.

CORRECT: Joe is always imitating the coach *whom* he respects greatly.

In the above example, "coach" is the word (noun) described and "whom he respects greatly" is the descriptive clause.

The following type of error also presents a new kind of problem.

6. Two different sentences incorrectly run together because there is a change in the kind of sentence

WRONG: Did Joe win$_x$ he was the best candidate.

CORRECT: Did Joe win? He was the best candidate.

EXPLANATION: **"Did Joe win?" is an interrogative sentence. "He was the best candidate" is a declarative sentence. Often students combine, in error, the question and the answer given to it.**

The final type of run-on sentence error is a bit complicated because it also involves punctuation of quotations. (Refer to the Basic Rules of Punctuation.)

7. Two different sentences run together improperly because there is a divided quotation

WRONG: "Joe won," he said, "I thought he was the best runner."

CORRECT: "Joe won," he said. "I thought he was the best runner."

CORRECT: "Joe won." He said, "I thought he was the best runner."

In another important group of errors, the student does not complete even one sentence. You will remember that a sentence was defined as a group of words having a subject and a predicate and expressing a complete thought. In the kind of error called a SENTENCE FRAGMENT, either the subject is left out so that you have a predicate standing by itself (example—Wish you were here.) or a part of the predicate is broken off from the sentence and made to stand by itself. (example—Walking down the street.)

TYPES OF SENTENCE FRAGMENTS

1. Subject of the sentence is improperly left out.

WRONG: Having a wonderful time. Wish you were here.

CORRECT: *I* am having a wonderful time. *I* wish you were here.

In each case, without the subject it is impossible to know *who* is doing the action indicated in the predicate.

2. Parts of a compound predicate are improperly made independent.

WRONG: Joe studied hard. Passed all his tests and was graduated.

CORRECT: Joe studied hard, passed all his tests and was graduated.

Note that "studied hard," "passed all his tests," and "was graduated" are all parts of the predicate and they all tell us something about Joe.

3. Part of the predicate, *a clause*, is incorrectly detached from the sentence to which it belongs and is made independent.

WRONG: Joe got a good mark in English. Although he doesn't like the subject. (*Adverbial clause*)

CORRECT: Joe got a good mark in English, although he doesn't like the subject.

WRONG: Joe has an English teacher. Whom he likes very much. (*Adjective clause*)

CORRECT: Joe has an English teacher whom he likes very much.

4. Part of the predicate, *a phrase*, is incorrectly detached from the sentence to which it belongs and is made independent.

WRONG: Joe got up early. To go to school. (*Infinitive phrase*)

CORRECT: Joe got up early to go to school.

WRONG: Joe worked hard. Studying his lessons. (*Participial phrase*)

CORRECT: Joe worked hard studying his lessons.

WRONG: Walking down the street. Joe thought about his job. (*Participial phrase*)

CORRECT: Walking down the street, Joe thought about his job.

> IMPORTANT NOTE: Both the clause and the phrase can be detached at both the *beginning* and the *end* of the sentence.

WRONG: Joe went to the movies. With his friend.

WRONG: Joe enjoyed himself. At the movies.

CORRECT: Joe went to the movies with his friend.

CORRECT: Joe enjoyed himself at the movies.

5. **Part of the predicate, one or more nouns in *apposition* with a noun in the predicate, are incorrectly detached from the sentence to which they belong and are made independent.**

WRONG: Joe enjoys all sports. Baseball, football and swimming.

CORRECT: Joe enjoys all sports: baseball, football and swimming.

> IMPORTANT NOTE: The colon is used to introduce the listing which follows. See Basic Rules of Punctuation.

WRONG: Joe admires the captain of the team. Ron Jones.

CORRECT: Joe admires the captain of the team, Ron Jones.

6. **Part of the predicate, one or more nouns in a series, is incorrectly detached from the sentence to which it belongs and is made independent.**

WRONG: Joe has excelled in his studies. Also in sports and extracurricular activities.

CORRECT: Joe has excelled in his studies, in sports, and in extracurricular activities.

TIME TO PRACTICE:

Test your knowledge of sentence structure by working on the following exercises. All the kinds of errors identified above are included with some correct sentences thrown in to keep you on your toes.

Directions: **If the sentence is correct, write "correct" on the line below it. If there is an error in sentence structure, rewrite the sentence correctly on the line below it.**

1. I like all flavors of ice cream. Vanilla, chocolate, and strawberry.

_____

2. Since Dad came back, Things have quieted down around the house.

_____

3. Frank didn't like baseball games, he came with us because he liked our company.

_____

4. Will you come to my party? I'd be delighted to have you meet my friends.

_____

5. Sylvia has many interests. Playing the piano, sewing her own clothes, painting landscapes, and taking long hikes.

_____

6. His friend's father was very rich, he retired at an early age.

_____

7. The club planned its finances carefully they were able to make ends meet.

_____

8. He studied very hard therefore he got a good mark.

_____

9. He worked for an employer who was very demanding.

_____

10. We have a full program of camping activities. Including sports, hikes, and cook-outs.

_____

11. Ed is outstanding in French in addition, he excels in mathematics.

_____

12. Sally was chosen queen of the festival she was the prettiest contestant.

_____

13. "Don't work too hard," Frances pleaded, "you have to think of your health."

_____

14. Am out of funds, Can't pay my bills. Send check as soon as possible.

_____

15. He did all his homework, finished all his chores, and went to sleep.

_____

16. John brought along all his equipment. Also some food and drink.

_____

17. Surveying the situation. He decided not to take part in the plan.

_____

18. There were two reasons why he did not want to go he was tired and he had a lot to do at home.

_____

19. Flying in a jet plane, skiing on mountain slopes, and scuba diving in deep water all appealed to him.

_____

20. I don't like artichokes also I don't go for spinach and broccoli.

_____

A WORD ABOUT REVIEW: **Don't be alarmed at all the review material in this chapter. We've included much more than you will probably need simply because we didn't want to omit anything that might be useful to you. Remember** that the High School Equivalency Tests examine background, not classroom or book learning. They test the kind of information you've acquired from reading newspapers and magazines, from T.V. and radio, from working at a job or running a home. They test experience and common sense. The review section simply organizes knowledge in this field, reminds you of some things you may have forgotten, fills in some gaps you may have in your background.

TIME TO STUDY:

Area 2   Agreement of Subject and Verb

A frequently made error is the failure to provide agreement between subject and verb.

This is the basic rule: THE VERB MUST AGREE WITH ITS SUBJECT IN NUMBER AND IN PERSON. If the subject is singular (there is only one person or thing spoken about), the verb must be *singular*. If the subject is plural (there is more than one person or thing spoken about), the verb must be *plural*. This is called agreement in *number*. In addition, the verb must agree with the subject in *person*. For example, it is correct to say "I study" but you must say "he studies." "I study" is in the first person; "he studies" is in the third person. See the VOCABULARY OF GRAMMAR AND USAGE for a more complete definition of "person."

There are two difficulties to be overcome.

1. WHAT IS THE SUBJECT?

Ask yourself, "What is spoken about?" Ordinarily you should have no trouble. Sometimes, however, the subject and the verb are separated by a number of intervening words. Example: Joe, despite the fact that many of his friends were absent, was elected president. (Joe is still the subject—singular.)

The intervening words may contain a plural. Example: Joe, together with all his friends, came in. (Joe is still the subject—singular.)

2. IS THE SUBJECT SINGULAR OR PLURAL?

EXAMPLE: A box of chocolates *is* on the table. (*Box* is singular and the subject.)

Most of the time *pronouns* will be involved. The following pronouns are all singular: anybody, anyone, each, either, everybody, everyone, neither, nobody, no one, one, somebody, and someone.

At other times, pronouns will be involved which, depending upon the meaning of the sentence, can be either *singular* or *plural*. These include any, all, more, and some.

When a subject has more than one part and the parts are connected by *and* or a word or groups of words similar in meaning to *and*, it is considered a *compound subject* and is plural.

EXAMPLE: Joe *and* his friend *are* here.

A compound subject can consist of more than one group of words, of more than one phrase, or one clause.

EXAMPLE: To study hard, to play hard, to enjoy life are desirable aims.

EXAMPLE: His outstanding contribution to school athletics, his service as class officer, and his excellent scholastic record make him qualified for the position of president.

Sometimes the subject comes *after* the verb. It is still the subject and may be singular or plural.

> EXAMPLE: Pasted in the upper right-hand corner of the envelope were two three-cent stamps. (*Stamps* is the subject, even though it is the last word in the sentence. The verb is plural because the subject, *stamps*, is plural.)

> EXCEPTION: **When a compound subject consists of two singular subjects connected by either-or, neither-nor, it is considered a singular subject.**

> EXAMPLE: Neither Joe nor his friend *is* here.

Remember another basic rule. Agreement is always with the number of the part of the subject nearest the verb.

> EXAMPLE: Neither Joe nor I *am* voting for Frank.

SOME SPECIAL PROBLEMS

We have touched on the problems of words intervening between the subject and verb, of pronouns singular and plural, of compound subjects and of subjects appearing after the verb. We pointed out the exception of the either-or, neither-nor subject. Now let us turn to some additional special problems.

1. Agreement of subject and certain irregular verbs.

> WRONG: It don't matter.
> CORRECT: It doesn't matter.

> EXPLANATION: **The addition of the negative contraction, n't, should not result in an error you would not make if the n't were omitted. You would never say, "It do matter." You would say, "It does matter."**

> WRONG: Was you there?
> CORRECT: Were you there?

> EXPLANATION: **Sometimes the reversal of subject and verb in a question causes an error that would not be made in a declarative sentence.**

2. Use of singular or plural after "there" at the opening of a sentence.

> WRONG: There's many ways to skin a cat.
> CORRECT: There are many ways to skin a cat.

The form of "is" or "are" depends on the *noun or pronoun that follows* the verb.

3. Subjects that are plural in form but singular in meaning.

Just because a noun ends in "s" doesn't make it plural. Here are some nouns that end in "s" which generally have singular meanings:

economics	measles	news
mathematics	mumps	politics

4. Subjects that are singular in form but plural in meaning.

Despite what you might think, these subjects take a *singular* verb since the group involved is thought of as a single unit. Examples of such words are:

army	crowd	orchestra
class	group	team
club		

> EXAMPLE: The crowd *was* dispersed by the police.

TIME TO PRACTICE:

Directions: For each of the following, correct the error in agreement *or* identify the sentence as being correct.

21. A box of new materials are in the cabinet.
     is

---

22. The leader of the flock, as well as most of his followers, has jumped the fence.

---

23. There's several ways to solve that problem.
     are

---

24. The kind of books they read show their taste in literature.
     shows

---

25. I believe that *Hamlet* is the greatest of all the plays that has ever been written. (Clue: what noun is closest to each verb?)
     have

---

26. People's efficiency are seriously affected by illness and worry.
     is

---

27. Politics makes strange bedfellows.

---

28. There is sometimes only one course possible.

---

29. Here, Mr. Chairman, is all the reports of the executive committee.
     are

---

30. The most important feature of the series of swimming lessons were the large number of strokes taught.
     was

TIME TO STUDY:

Area 3   *Agreement of Pronoun and Antecedent*

Another frequently made error is the failure to provide agreement between a pronoun and the noun it is replacing, its *antecedent*.

This is the basic rule:

A PRONOUN MUST AGREE WITH ITS ANTECEDENT IN NUMBER, PERSON, AND GENDER. If the antecedent is singular, the pronoun replacing it is singular.

      EXAMPLE: Joe does *his* homework.

The pronoun "his" takes the place of "Joe." Joe is singular (one person); therefore, the pronoun is singular.

If the antecedent is masculine, the pronoun replacing it is masculine. If the antecedent is feminine, the pronoun is feminine.

      EXAMPLE: Susan does *her* homework.

Finally, both Joe and Susan are in the third person; therefore, the pronouns replacing each must be in the third person—his, her.

There is one main difficulty to overcome.

What is the antecedent?

Sometimes it is not easy to determine what noun the pronoun is replacing. The antecedent may be separated from the pronoun which takes its place by a number of words or a phrase.

      EXAMPLE: Joe is a *boy* who does *his* work. ("boy"—antecedent; "his"—pronoun)

      EXAMPLE: *One* of the boys who walked to school was late to *his* class. ("one"—antecedent; "his"—pronoun)

The same procedure should be used to determine the number of the pronoun when it replaces a compound subject.

      EXAMPLE: *Joe and* his *friend* brought *their* books.

      IMPORTANT NOTE: **When either-or, neither-nor is used, the pronoun is considered to replace a singular subject.**

      EXAMPLE: *Neither* Joe *nor* his friend brought *his* book.

SOME SPECIAL PROBLEMS

1. Pronouns which appear to be plural but are in fact singular.

Some pronouns appear to refer to more than one person, but they never refer to more than one person *at a time*.

These include:

anybody	either
anyone	neither
each	no one
every	somebody
everyone	someone

It may sound a little strange to you but the following sentence is correct.

EXAMPLE: Every student must do *his* homework every day.

2. Pronouns which refer to nouns that appear to be plural, but are singular in form.

These require a verb in the singular.

EXAMPLE: The team continued *its* winning streak.

3. Pronoun with indefinite antecedents.

The antecedent must be clear or the sentence rephrased.

WRONG: Frank told Joe to take *his* books to school.

To whom does "his" refer? to Frank or to Joe? The sentence must be rewritten to clear up this confusion.

CORRECT: Frank told Joe to take Frank's books to school for him.

Or better:

CORRECT: Frank said to Joe: "Take my books to school for me."

TIME TO PRACTICE:

Directions: For each of the following, correct the error in agreement *or* identify the sentence as being correct.

31. The teacher said, "I'm happy to note that everybody in the class knows their work."

_____ *his* _____

32. The John Adams Chess Club decided to revise their constitution.

_____ *its* _____

33. The policeman told the pedestrian to pick up his hat.

_____ *My* _____

34. The teacher said, "Let every student who knows the answer raise his hand."

_____

35. One of the most highly respected citizens of our town gave their approval to our project.

_____ *his* _____

Area 4   Case of Nouns and Pronouns

In English, the form of a noun rarely changes because of its case (its relation to the other words in the sentence).

EXAMPLE: Frank hit Joe.
EXAMPLE: Joe hit Frank.

In the first sentence, Frank is the subject in the *nominative case*. In the second, Frank is the object in the *objective case*. Yet, in both examples, the form of the noun, Frank, has not changed. Only in the *possessive case* does the form of most nouns change.

EXAMPLE: Frank's friend went away.

Nearly all pronouns have different forms in the nominative, objective, and possessive cases. Here is a convenient table of these forms:

NOMINATIVE CASE (for subjects)	POSSESSIVE CASE	OBJECTIVE CASE (for objects)
I	my, mine	me
you	your, yours	you
he	his	him
she	her, hers	her
it	its	it
we	our, ours	us
they	their, theirs	them
who	whose	whom
whoever	—	whomever

You will note that only the pronoun forms *you* and *it* do not change when their case changes from nominative to objective or vice versa. With these tables in mind, let us turn to the basic rules for the case of pronouns.

1. The subject of a verb, noun or pronoun, is in the nominative case. This is true whether the subject is singular or compound.

WRONG: Me and Frank are good friends.
CORRECT: Frank and *I* are good friends.

2. A predicate pronoun is in the nominative case.
   Even though it may not sound right, the following example is correct.

EXAMPLE: They thought that the visitor was *he*.

The same is true for the plural.

EXAMPLE: Frank and Joe knocked on the door. "It is *they*," Sue said.

3. Pronouns in apposition with nouns in the nominative case are also in the nominative case.

EXAMPLE: The two contestants, she and I, were tied for first place.

4. The object of a verb, noun or pronoun, is in the objective case. This is true whether the object is singular or compound.

EXAMPLE: They applauded him and her.

EXAMPLE: Did they face Frank and us in the contest?

5. The object of a preposition is in the objective case. This is true whether the object is singular or compound.

EXAMPLE: Everyone but *her* did his homework.

EXAMPLE: Between *you* and *me*, Sue is my best friend.

6. Pronouns in apposition with nouns in the objective case are also in the objective case.

> EXAMPLE: They gave the prizes to the *winners, her and me*.

> EXAMPLE: For *us amateurs*, it is fun to watch professionals perform.

7. The subject of an infinitive is in the objective case.

> EXAMPLE: We asked *him* to go.

The same is true for the object of an infinitive.

> EXAMPLE: We wanted him to ask *them* to come along.

8. Nouns in the possessive case *always* require an apostrophe to indicate possession.

> EXAMPLE: Sue's hat is very becoming.

> EXAMPLE: The boys' sweaters were very attractive.

Pronouns in the possessive case *never* have an apostrophe.

> EXAMPLE: The dog wagged *its* tail.

> EXAMPLE: We have met the enemy and they are *ours*.

> EXAMPLE: She has *hers;* they have *theirs*.

SOME SPECIAL PROBLEMS

As you have realized by now, the case of pronouns is one of the most troublesome topics in the study of English. After you have mastered these eight rules, turn to these three tricky problems.

1. The case of pronouns coming after a comparison involving *than* or *as*.

> EXAMPLE: Joe received more votes than *I*.

The problem of deciding the case, and therefore the form, of the pronoun is complicated by the fact that the verb following "I" is understood.

> EXAMPLE: Joe received more votes than I (did).

This is, therefore, a special instance of Rule 1—The subject of a verb is in the nominative case. This rule is true even if the verb is understood.

2. The case of the relative pronoun (see VOCABULARY OF GRAMMAR AND USAGE) *who* or *whom*.

The rule to remember here is to determine whether the relative pronoun is the subject or the object in its clause.

> EXAMPLE: *Who* do you think *was elected* president?

Don't be fooled by the words which come between the subject and the verb. "Who" is the subject of "was elected" and is, therefore, in the nominative case.

> EXAMPLE: *Whom did you invite* to the party?

"Whom" is the object of "you did invite" and is, therefore, in the objective case.
The same rule applies to "whoever" and "whomever."

> EXAMPLE: Give the book to *whoever asks* for it.

"Whoever" is the subject of "asks" and is in the nominative case.

　　EXAMPLE: He impressed whomever he approached.

"Whomever" is the object of "he approached" and is in the objective case.

3. The case of pronouns coming before verbs ending in "ing" and used as nouns.

　　EXAMPLE: I do not object to *his* going with me.

"Going" is a verb ending in "ing" and used as a noun—object of the preposition "to." This is a fine point but it often appears on tests. Here are several more examples:

　　EXAMPLE: Fatigue was the cause of *Frank's* falling asleep at the wheel.

　　EXAMPLE: *My* going to school daily helped my work.

　　EXAMPLE: The television program interfered with *Sue's* and *Joe's* doing their homework.

TIME TO PRACTICE:

Directions: **For each of the following, correct the error in the case of the pronoun *or* identify the sentence as being correct.**

36. This is the story of a girl who's father was a doctor.

_____ *Whose* _____

37. He voted against whoever favored that proposal.

_____

38. We have no room in the car for suitcases as large as yours.

_____

39. If you will describe its color, perhaps we can find it.

_____

40. Whom do you believe is the most capable?

_____ *who* _____

41. When the dance was held, all came except her.

_____

42. Are you willing to allow we boys to form a cooking class?

_____ *us* _____

43. Such a comment about anyone whom we know to be thoughtful is unfair.

_____

44. The only girls who have won prizes in the contest are you and I.

_____

45. Yes, my brother can do this work as well as me.

_____*I*_____

46. The boy's being older influenced the judges in his favor.

_____

47. All the pupils except George and she plan to order the book.

_____*her*_____

48. If I were she, I'd accept such an attractive invitation.

_____

49. I fear that it is you who are mistaken.

_____

50. Mother would not let Mary and I attend the hockey game.

_____*me*_____

51. I'm not certain that your's is the best solution.

_____*yours*_____

52. It was us girls who swept the gym floor after the dance.

_____*we*_____

53. The money found on the stairs proved to be neither John's nor our's.

_____*Ours*_____

54. The committee consisted of John, Henry, Tom, and I.

_____*prep.*_____*me*_____

55. The letters were intended for we two only.

_____*prep. take object*_____*us.*_____

TIME TO STUDY:

Area 5   Troublesome Verbs

The verb, the part of the sentence which indicates the action carried out by the subject, also indicates *when* the action was carried out. It does so by its tense.

The most widely used tenses are the present, the past, and the future. For most regular verbs, the form of the verb in these tenses is easy to recognize.

I live in New York now. (present tense)

I lived in New York last year. (past tense)

I shall live in New York next year. (future tense)

Two additional tenses, less frequently used, sometimes cause difficulty.

I have lived in New York for five years. (present perfect tense)

I had lived in New York before moving to Boston. (past perfect tense)

Both these tenses require the use of a helping verb (have, had) and the verb's past participle (lived). The principal parts of the *regular* verb to live are:

live   lived (past)   have lived (past participle)

Many of the difficulties you have with verbs are with the *irregular* verbs. These change form in either the past or the past participle or both. The most frequent error is the use of the wrong part of the verb, most often the use of the past participle for the simple past.

WRONG: I seen him do it.

CORRECT: I saw him do it.

WRONG: I done it.

CORRECT: I did it.

WRONG: I laid under the tree for an hour.

CORRECT: I lay under the tree for an hour.

To avoid these errors in tense and in use of the principal parts of irregular verbs, study these forty-nine most frequently confused verbs.

Frequently Used Irregular Verbs

Verb	Past	Present Perfect Tense
be	I was	I have been
beat	I beat	I have beaten
become	I became	I have become
begin	I began	I have begun
bite	I bit	I have bitten
blow	I blew	I have blown
break	I broke	I have broken
bring	I brought	I have brought
buy	I bought	I have bought
catch	I caught	I have caught
choose	I chose	I have chosen
come	I came	I have come
dig	I dug	I have dug
do	I did	I have done
draw	I drew	I have drawn
drink	I drank	I have drunk
eat	I ate	I have eaten
fall	I fell	I have fallen
fly	I flew	I have flown
freeze	I froze	I have frozen
get	I got	I have got or I have gotten

give	I gave	I have given
go	I went	I have gone
grow	I grew	I have grown
have	I had	I have had
know	I knew	I have known
lay	I laid (place)	I have laid
lead	I led	I have led
lie	I lay (recline)	I have lain
lose	I lost	I have lost
make	I made	I have made
ride	I rode	I have ridden
ring	I rang	I have rung
rise	I rose	I have risen
run	I ran	I have run
say	I said	I have said
see	I saw	I have seen
shake	I shook	I have shaken
sink	I sank	I have sunk
speak	I spoke	I have spoken
swim	I swam	I have swum
swing	I swung	I have swung
take	I took	I have taken
teach	I taught	I have taught
tear	I tore	I have torn
think	I thought	I have thought
throw	I threw	I have thrown
win	I won	I have won
write	I wrote	I have written

50 Other Irregular Verbs That Can Cause Trouble

Verb	Past Tense	Present Perfect Tense
arise	I arose	I have arisen
awake	I awaked, awoke	I have awaked, awoke
bear	I bore	I have borne, born
bend	I bent	I have bent
bind	I bound	I have bound
build	I built	I have built
creep	I crept	I have crept
deal	I dealt	I have dealt
dive	I dived, dove	I have dived
drive	I drove	I have driven
drown	I drowned	I have drowned
feed	I fed	I have fed
feel	I felt	I have felt
fight	I fought	I have fought
find	I found	I have found
flee	I fled	I have fled
forget	I forgot	I have forgotten
forgive	I forgave	I have forgiven
hang (an object)	I hung	I have hung
hang (a person)	I hanged	I have hanged
hide	I hid	I have hidden

hold	I held	I have held
kneel	I knelt	I have knelt
leave	I left	I have left
lend	I lent	I have lent
meet	I met	I have met
mistake	I mistook	I have mistaken
pay	I paid	I have paid
prove	I proved	I have proved or
		I have proven
seek	I sought	I have sought
sell	I sold	I have sold
send	I sent	I have sent
sew	I sewed	I have sewed or
		I have sewn
shine	I shone	I have shone
shrink	I shrank	I have shrunk
sing	I sang	I have sung
slay	I slew	I have slain
slide	I slid	I have slid
sleep	I slept	I have slept
spend	I spent	I have spent
spring	I sprang	I have sprung
steal	I stole	I have stolen
strike	I struck	I have struck
swear	I swore	I have sworn
sweep	I swept	I have swept
swing	I swung	I have swung
wake	I waked or woke	I have waked or
		I have woken
wear	I wore	I have worn
weep	I wept	I have wept
wind	I wound	I have wound

SOME SPECIAL PROBLEMS

The irregular verbs you have just studied present difficulties when used in simple sentences. Even more difficult are complex sentences (see VOCABULARY OF GRAMMAR AND USAGE). In these, you have to figure out the time (or tense) relationship between the verbs in the two clauses.

1. What is the proper sequence of tenses for verbs in the main and dependent clauses of a complex sentence?

   Let us start with some easy ones.

   EXAMPLE: I *gain* weight when I *eat* too much.

   The verbs in both clauses are in the present tense.

   EXAMPLE: The audience *applauded* when the soloist *finished*.

   The verbs in both clauses are in the past tense.
   Sometimes the verbs in each clause are in different tenses.

   EXAMPLE: I *shall leave* when he *comes*.

   The main clause contains a verb in the future tense; the dependent clause has a verb in the present tense. This is one of the more frequently used sequences of tenses.

   EXAMPLE: I *believe* that he *studied* for the examination.

The main clause contains a verb in the present tense; the dependent clause has a verb in the past tense.

The next two sequences are the most difficult of all.

Study this sentence.

EXAMPLE: I *played* my first concert after I *had studied* the piano for three years.

The verb in the main clause is in the past tense; the verb in the dependent clause has a verb in the past perfect tense. Why? Because the action in the dependent clause (the studying) had taken place *before* the action in the main clause. The sequence is, therefore, this: Main clause—past tense; dependent clause—past perfect tense.

The second sequence is found in this sentence.

EXAMPLE: Joe *would have been elected* president if he *had received* my vote.

The verb in the main clause is in the past conditional tense; the verb in the dependent clause is in the past perfect case.

IMPORTANT NOTE: Never use the past conditional tense in a dependent clause starting with "if." "If he would have been there, . . ." is wrong. It must read, "If he *had been there* . . ."

Here is a special case. Study it carefully.

EXAMPLE: He *wanted* to go before dark.

Sometimes the sentence is written incorrectly as, "He wanted to have gone before dark." This is wrong, because, according to the meaning of the sentence, he hasn't left yet. Therefore the present tense of the infinitive (see VOCABULARY OF GRAMMAR AND USAGE)—in this sentence, to go—must be used.

2. The special case of an assumption which isn't true.

The technical term for the type of error we are going to try to avoid next is the failure to use the subjunctive in a condition contrary to fact. The problem becomes clear if you study this example.

EXAMPLE: If I *were* Joe, *I'd accept* the offer.

The verb, "*were*," is in the subjunctive mood because it isn't true that "I" and "Joe" are one and the same person. It is only an assumption that isn't true; it's an "if" that is contrary to fact.

This is probably the one form in which you will meet this special problem. Here's another example:

EXAMPLE: They *would vote* for her if only she *were* older.

3. The problem of verbs performing the same function in a sentence and keeping the same form.

Here again there is a technical term for the type of error which is made. It is called the failure to use parallel structure.

WRONG: Joe likes *swimming, fishing*, and, if he has the time, *to take* a long walk.

The sentence tells us of three things Joe likes. Two are gerunds (verbs used as nouns in the -ing form)—swimming, fishing. The third is suddenly changed to an infinitive—to take. Verbs having the same function should have the same form. They would then be parallel in structure. The sentence should read

CORRECT: Joe likes *swimming, fishing*, and, if he has the time, *taking* a long walk.

TIME TO PRACTICE:

Directions: For each of the following, correct the error involving the verb *or* identify the sentence as being correct.

56.   If only we had began before it was too late!

  _____ *begun* _____

57.   We were not allowed to skate on the pond until the ice had froze to a depth of ten inches.

  _____ *frozen* _____

58.   Overnight the river had raised another foot.

  _____ *risen* _____

59.   Mary, aren't you suppose to take part in the assembly program?

  _____ *supposed* _____

60.   If you had been more patient you might not have tore it.

  _____ *torn* _____

61.   We intended to have gone before Tuesday.

  _____ *go* _____

62.   The general lead his troops into battle.

  _____ *led* _____

63.   I am living in New York for five years now.

  _____ *have lived* _____

64.   He was a good student, but he was very clumsy in athletics.

  _____

65.   They took part in baseball games, in swimming contests, and in learning about golf.

  _____ *lessons* _____

66.   He lay quiet for over an hour.

  _____

67.   If he was my friend, I should lend him the money.

  _____ *were* _____ *would* _____

68.   If Joe would have received the letter, he would have come promptly.

  _____

69. Frank had already swum a mile when I jumped into the pool.

_____

70. When I first saw the car, its steering wheel was broke.

_____ _broken_ _____

TIME TO STUDY:

Area 6 Troublesome Adjectives and Adverbs

Most of the time, it is easy to decide whether an adjective or an adverb is required in a given sentence. The adjective is used to describe a noun or pronoun.

> EXAMPLE: He wore a _dark_ hat.

The adverb is used to modify a verb, adjective or another adverb.

> EXAMPLE: He played _very poorly_. (_poorly_ modifies _played; very_ modifies poorly)

There are times, however, when adjectives and adverbs can be confused. The confusion can be caused by the kind of verb in the sentence. If the verb is not an action verb or if the verb describes a condition, then an adjective rather than an adverb must follow it. Why? Because the adjective really modifies the subject and not the verb. Here are some examples.

> EXAMPLE: He looks _sick_. (_sick_ describes _he_)

> EXAMPLE: I feel _good_. (_good_ describes _I_)

> EXAMPLE: The fruit tastes _sweet_. (_sweet_ describes _fruit_)

Other widely used verbs that do not depict action are seem, become, smell, grow, sound, be (am, is, are, was, were, has been).

The confusion can also be caused by the form of the adjective or the adverb. Some words have the same form for both adjective and adverb. These include fast, slow, deep, long, ill, sharp.

> EXAMPLE: He worked very fast.

> EXAMPLE: He cut deep into the skin.

SOME SPECIAL PROBLEMS

1. Adjectives indicate the degree to which they describe nouns. They do this in one of two ways: either the adverb more or most is placed before the adjective or the form of the adjective changes to _____er or _____est.

   > EXAMPLE: He was _more quiet_ than she.

   > EXAMPLE: He was _quieter_ than she.

   > EXAMPLE: He was the _most friendly_ person there.

   > EXAMPLE: He was the _friendliest_ person there.

What is the problem? It is that you must use the "more" or _____er form where two and only two persons are involved. Similarly, you must use the "most" or _____est form where three or more persons are involved.

EXAMPLE: He was the *shyer* of the two.

EXAMPLE: He was the *most shy* among the three of them.

2. Another problem is the use of two negative adverbs in the same sentence, or a negative adverb and a negative adjective in the same sentence. This is incorrect. Here are some examples.

WRONG: He *hadn't scarcely* a friend. (Two negative adverbs—n't and scarcely)

CORRECT: He *had scarcely* a friend.

WRONG: He *doesn't do no* work. (A negative adverb—n't and a negative adjective—no)

CORRECT: He doesn't do *any* work.

TIME TO PRACTICE:

Directions: For each of the following correct the error in the use of the adverb or adjective or identify the sentence as correct.

71.   He had an unbelievable large capacity for food.

_____

72.   A person who works as efficient as John deserves high praise.

_____

73.   The magician used his hands so skillful that the audience was completely mystified.

_____

74.   "Don't you think that the old building would have served just as good?"

_____

75.   Food prepared in this manner tastes more deliciously.

_____

76.   Johnson has scarcely no equal as a quarterback.

_____

77.   It was the worse storm that the inhabitants of the island could remember.

_____

78.   Frank was the least prepared of the two who took the examination.

_____

79.   He hadn't hardly any friends.

_____

80.   Because he couldn't go, he felt bad.

_____

TIME TO STUDY:

Area 7   Confusing Constructions

Very often, there is confusion in meaning because the writer has failed to state clearly what he wanted to communicate to the reader. Let us turn to the most common of these kinds of confusing constructions.

1. This is the case of the *misplaced modifier*. (See VOCABULARY OF GRAMMAR AND USAGE.) Just compare these two sentences.

   EXAMPLE: Jane hurt herself while driving *badly*.

   EXAMPLE: Jane hurt herself *badly* while driving.

In the first example, "badly" is the modifier of "driving."
In the second example, "badly" is the modifier of "hurt."
The meaning is completely changed by the placement of the modifier.
Here is another pair of sentences.

   EXAMPLE: The fire was extinguished by the firemen before any damage was done.

   EXAMPLE: The fire was put out before any damage was done by the firemen.

It is nearly certain that the writer meant to indicate that the fire was put out before any damage was done. Yet the second sentence, because of the misplaced modifier ("by the firemen") completely confuses the meaning.
You will not fall victim to this kind of confusing construction if you remember this rule: Always place the modifier near the word it is modifying (or describing). The modifier may be a single word ("badly") or a group of words ("by the firemen").

2. This is the case of the *dangling modifier*.
   It is important, when starting sentences with a phrase, to make certain that it modifies the noun you intend it to modify. Note the following confusing sentences.

WRONG: Standing on the corner, the car passed me by.
WRONG: Walking around in the zoo, the gorilla caught my eye.
WRONG: At ten, my parents took me on a trip to California.

In the first sentence, "standing" is the dangling modifier. As a result, the way the sentence reads it is the car which is standing on the corner.

CORRECT: Standing on the corner, I was passed by the car.

In the second sentence, "walking" is the dangling modifier. As a result, it appears as though the gorilla were walking around the zoo.

CORRECT: As I walked around the zoo, I saw the gorilla.

In the third sentence, it is not clear who was ten, the parents or I. The phrase, "at ten," does not have a noun it clearly modifies.

CORRECT: When I was ten, my parents took me on a trip to California.

You will avoid this error if you remember this rule: An introductory phrase should be followed immediately by the word it modifies.

TIME TO PRACTICE:

Directions: For each of the following correct the faulty construction or identify the sentence as correct.

81. Getting up to bat, the pitcher threw me a fast ball.

_____

82. Frank and Jane were almost engaged for two years.

_____

83. While shaving quickly, he cut himself with the razor.

_____

84. The animal was taken to the veterinarian with a broken leg.

_____

85. After walking for three hours in the sun, the drink was most welcome.

_____

TIME TO STUDY:

Area 8   Preferred Modern Usage

In this section, we shall turn to a variety of mistakes which go contrary to accepted use of the English language by educated people.

Let us consider first twenty pairs of words which are frequently confused.

ACCEPT, EXCEPT

Accept is most frequently used as a verb meaning to receive something or to agree to something.

> EXAMPLE: He was chosen to *accept* the gift.

Except is most frequently used as a preposition meaning leaving out. The use of "except" as a verb meaning to leave out is rare.

> EXAMPLE: Everyone came *except* him.

AFFECT, EFFECT

Affect is most frequently used as a verb meaning to influence.

> EXAMPLE: Climate and topography *affect* the life of people everywhere.

Effect is most frequently used as a noun meaning result.

> EXAMPLE: The war had a far-reaching *effect* on the entire people.

The use of effect as a verb meaning "to bring about" is rare.

AGGRAVATE, IRRITATE

The verb aggravate means to make worse.

EXAMPLE: Constant rubbing tended to *aggravate* the already painful wound.

The verb irritate means to annoy.

EXAMPLE: The behavior of the child *irritated* all the guests.

In general, a person is irritated; a situation or a condition is aggravated.

ALLUSION, ILLUSION

An allusion is an indirect reference to something, often a literary work or a literary character.

EXAMPLE: He made an *allusion* to herculean efforts of the leader.

An illusion is a wrong idea or a misconception.

EXAMPLE: The loser continued under the *illusion* that he won the contest.

ALREADY, ALL READY

Already is an adverb of time meaning previously.

EXAMPLE: When I arrived, he had *already* left.

All ready means exactly what the two words indicate—all prepared.

EXAMPLE: When I arrived, I found them *all ready* for the meeting.

ALTOGETHER, ALL TOGETHER

Altogether is an adverb of degree meaning completely.

EXAMPLE: He was *altogether* unprepared for the assignment.

All together means exactly what the two words indicate—all the persons in a group.

EXAMPLE: We found the team *all together* in the locker room.

AMONG, BETWEEN

Among is used when more than two persons or things are involved.

EXAMPLE: Frank, Joe, and Ed shared the expenses *among* them.

Between is used when only two persons or things are involved.

EXAMPLE: Jane and Joan shared the expenses *between* them.

You needn't be concerned with the rare exceptions to these rules.

AMOUNT, NUMBER

Amount is used for things or ideas which cannot be counted.

EXAMPLE: Sue displayed a large *amount* of intelligence at the meeting.

Amount is usually followed by a singular noun—money, talent, courage.
Number is used for things which can be counted.

EXAMPLE: The *number* of accidents this year is greater than we thought.

Compare these two sentences.

EXAMPLE: I needed a large *amount* of money.

EXAMPLE: I needed a large *number* of dollars to pay my bills.

In the first sentence, the word "money" is thought of as a single unit.

In the second, the word "dollars" is thought of as individual items which can be counted.

AS, LIKE

Only "as" can introduce a clause. "Like" cannot serve as a conjunction to introduce a clause. It is most frequently used as a preposition meaning "similar to."

WRONG: This cereal tastes good like a cereal should.

CORRECT: This cereal tastes good as a cereal should.

CORRECT: He wanted everyone to be like him.

BESIDE, BESIDES

Beside means at the side of.

EXAMPLE: He came over to sit *beside* me.

Besides means in addition.

EXAMPLE: There were nine others present *besides* Joe.

BRING, TAKE

Bring is used when the movement in the sentence is towards the speaker or the writer.

EXAMPLE: *Bring* the pencils to me, please.

Take is used when the movement in the sentence is away from the speaker or the writer.

EXAMPLE: *Take* these books to the principal's office.

CAN, MAY

Can is used to indicate the knowledge or ability to do something.

EXAMPLE: I *can* tie a slip knot.

May is used when permission is sought to do something, most frequently in the form of a question.

EXAMPLE: *May* I have the car tonight?

FEWER, LESS

The correct use of these words follows the same rules as those indicated for amount and number. Fewer is used for things which can be counted.

EXAMPLE: The number of accidents this year is *fewer* than we thought.

Less is used for things or ideas which cannot be counted.

EXAMPLE: We enjoyed *less* freedom this year than last.

Note that less is usually followed by a singular noun, fewer by a plural noun.

IMPLY, INFER

Imply is used to indicate that the speaker or the writer is making a hint or suggestion.

EXAMPLE: I mean to *imply* that he didn't get the job done.

Infer is used to indicate the hint or suggestion made by the speaker was taken by the audience which drew a conclusion from it.

EXAMPLE: I *infer* from your remarks that he was lazy.

IN, INTO

In is used to indicate that something is already at a place.

   EXAMPLE: The dog is *in* the living room.

Into is used to indicate that someone or something is moving from the outside to the inside of a place.

   EXAMPLE: The dog dashed *into* the living room from the kitchen.

LEARN, TEACH

Learn is used to indicate that knowledge or behavior is being acquired.

   EXAMPLE: He tried to *learn* how to speak softly.

Teach is used to indicate that knowledge or behavior is being provided.

   EXAMPLE: I tried to *teach* him how to speak softly.

LIABLE, LIKELY

Likely is used to indicate the probability that something will happen.

   EXAMPLE: He is *likely* to receive the medal.

Liable is used in two ways. It can indicate legal responsibility.

   EXAMPLE: If you drive too quickly, you are *liable* to a fine.

It can also indicate an undesirable possibility.

   EXAMPLE: If you don't study, you are *liable* to fail the course.

MYSELF, ME

Myself may be used properly in one of two ways. It can be used for emphasis.

   EXAMPLE: I *myself* will attend to this matter.

It can be used as the object of an action verb with "I" as the subject.

   EXAMPLE: I hit *myself* in the hand.

Never use "myself" when "I" or "me" should be used.

WRONG: He gave the awards to Frank and myself.
CORRECT: He gave the awards to Frank and me.
WRONG: Frank and myself will get the awards.
CORRECT: Frank and I will get the awards.

PRINCIPAL, PRINCIPLE

Principal may be used in two ways. It can denote the head of a school.

   EXAMPLE: The *principal* addressed the teachers and parents.

It can be used as an adjective meaning "the main" or "the most important."

   EXAMPLE: He was the *principal* speaker at the graduation exercises.

Principle may be used to indicate a law or rule of conduct.

   EXAMPLE: We are dedicated to the *principle* that all men are created equal.

QUITE, QUIET

Quite may be used as an adverb meaning "completely" or "very."

EXAMPLE: He was *quite* angry when he lost the game.

Quiet may be used only as an adjective meaning "still" or "calm."

EXAMPLE: After his fit of temper, he became *quiet*.

Now let us turn our attention to ten important DON'T's.

DON'T use the expression "being that."
  Use instead a conjunction such as "because" or "since."

  WRONG: Being that he was first, he won the prize.
  CORRECT: Since he was first, he won the prize.

DON'T use the expressions "could of," "should of," or "would of."
  Use instead the correct expressions for which these aural distortions are the incorrect substitutions.

  WRONG: He could of been the winner if he had tried.
  CORRECT: He could have been the winner if he had tried.

DON'T use the expression "different than."
  Use instead "different from."

  WRONG: Playing baseball is different than playing softball.
  CORRECT: Playing baseball is different from playing softball.

NOTE: Here are some other frequently misused idioms involving prepositions.

  WRONG: May I borrow a dollar off you?
  CORRECT: May I borrow a dollar from you?
  WRONG: Come over our house for a party.
  CORRECT: Come to our house for a party.

DON'T use "don't" in the third person singular.
  Use "doesn't" since it is the contraction of "does not."

  WRONG: He don't belong here. (This can also be—He do not belong here.)
  CORRECT: He doesn't belong here.

DON'T use "due to" as part of an adverbial phrase.
  Use "due to" as an adjective which modifies or is the predicate adjective referring back to a noun.

  WRONG: Due to overeating, he was heavy.
  CORRECT: His heaviness was due to overeating.
  WRONG: He was late due to the traffic.
  CORRECT: He was late because of the traffic.

DON'T use the expression "had ought."
  Use "ought" alone since it expresses obligation or duty without the need for any other word.

  WRONG: I had ought to write to my parents.
  CORRECT: I ought to write to my parents.

DON'T use an article after the expressions "kind of" and "sort of."

  WRONG: He's not the kind of a person I like.
  CORRECT: He's not the kind of person I like.

DON'T use the expression "the reason is because."

Use "the reason is that" since the words "reason" and "because" both have similar meanings. A reason is indeed a cause.

WRONG: The reason he left is because he did not get a raise.

CORRECT: The reason he left is that he did not get a raise.

DON'T use extra words such as "this *here*" and "that *there*" where you can avoid them.

Omit all unnecessary words. Here are several examples with the words to be omitted indicated.

WRONG: He left after the conclusion of the game.

WRONG: The consensus of opinion was that he was correct.

WRONG: They decided to continue on to Chicago.

WRONG: If we cooperate together, we shall succeed.

WRONG: Let us divide up the assignment.

WRONG: I enclose the check herewith.

WRONG: I like books, magazines, and et cetera.

WRONG: I found it inside of the house.

WRONG: He knocked it off of the table.

WRONG: This is more preferable to that.

WRONG: I'll see you at 2 P.M. in the afternoon.

WRONG: Refer this back to a committee.

WRONG: Return this back to whom it belongs.

WRONG: This here book is better than that there one.

WRONG: My father, he doesn't believe in allowances.

DON'T use "who's" when you want to use "whose."

"Whose" should be used to show possession. "Who's" is a contraction of "who is."

WRONG: I know who's book this is.

CORRECT: I know whose book this is.

Let us conclude this section with some fine distinctions between five pairs of words.

CONTINUAL, CONTINUOUS

"Continual" refers to something which is repeated often with stops in between. "Continuous" refers to something which goes on without interruption.

EXAMPLE: The game was *continually* interrupted by showers.

EXAMPLE: The sun shone *continuously* for eight hours.

DISINTERESTED, UNINTERESTED

"Disinterested" refers to someone who has nothing to gain personally from a particular activity. He may be very much interested (concerned) in the matter. "Uninterested" refers to someone who is lacking interest or concern in an activity.

EXAMPLE: The umpire was a *disinterested* participant in the game.

EXAMPLE: The students were *uninterested* in the work of the class.

HANGED, HUNG

"Hanged" refers to a specific kind of execution which has taken place.

"Hung" refers to something which has been suspended from an object.

> EXAMPLE: The murderer was *hanged*.

> EXAMPLE: The picture was *hung* on the hook attached to the wall.

HEALTHY, HEALTHFUL

"Healthy" refers to a condition of people. "Healthful" refers to anything which helps to produce or maintain health.

> EXAMPLE: The doctor found the patient to be *healthy*.

> EXAMPLE: The doctor recommended lots of *healthful* exercise.

PRACTICAL, PRACTICABLE

"Practical" refers to something which can be made to serve a useful purpose. "Practicable" refers to something which can be made to operate but which may not be practical.

> EXAMPLE: He found it *practicable* to extract gold from ocean water but the costs involved made the whole procedure not a *practical* one.

TIME TO PRACTICE:

Directions: For each of the following, correct the error in usage or identify the sentence as correct. Write the answer on the line below.

86. If people had helped Burns, he might of become a greater poet.

_____

87. When the teacher spoke, the room became very quite.

_____

88. The actors were all ready to perform long before the curtain went up.

_____

89. Irregardless of what you believe, your answer is incorrect.

_____

90. The teacher explained the principal of refrigeration.

_____

91. Try to find one that is shorter then this one.

_____

92. Being that he was the best qualified person, he received the job.

_____

93. Although he had excepted the invitation, John failed to attend.

_____

94. He is one of those persons which deserve great credit for courage.

_____

95. What have been the principal affects of the serum?

_____

96. I am not all together in agreement with the author's point of view.

_____

97. I believe that you had ought to study harder.

_____

98. Who's money is this on the desk?

_____

99. The number of votes cast in the election was very small.

_____

100. John, where is the party at?

_____

101. Do like I tell you.

_____

102. If he continues to work hard, he's liable to become president.

_____

103. There were less persons present at the second meeting than at the first.

_____

104. The teacher came to sit besides me.

_____

105. Due to the bad weather, the game was postponed.

_____

TIME TO STUDY:

Area 9   Basic Rules of Punctuation

Rules will be given for each of the major punctuation marks.

THE PERIOD

1. The period is used after a sentence which makes a statement.

   EXAMPLE: He arrived on time.

2. The period is used after a sentence which gives a command.

   EXAMPLE: Sit up straight.

3. The period is used after most abbreviations.

   EXAMPLE: Mr., lb., A.M., etc.

THE QUESTION MARK

The question mark is used after a sentence which asks a question.

   EXAMPLE: Did you like the game?

THE EXCLAMATION MARK

The exclamation mark is used after a sentence which emphasizes a command or which conveys strong feeling.

   EXAMPLE: Stop writing immediately!

   EXAMPLE: What a pleasant surprise!

THE COMMA

1. The comma is used to separate words that indicate the person to whom a remark is addressed.

   EXAMPLE: John, please come here.

   EXAMPLE: Who, John, do you think will come?

2. The comma is used to separate words that are in apposition with a noun, that is, that add information about the noun.

   EXAMPLE: Nancy, my secretary, is very efficient.

3. The comma is used to set off expressions or phrases which are inserted in the sentence and which interrupt the normal word order.

   EXAMPLE: Notre Dame, in my opinion, will win the championship.

   EXAMPLE: Joan, on the other hand, disagrees with us.

4. The comma is used after introductory phrases and clauses, particularly when they are long or when the meaning may be temporarily confused if the comma is omitted.

EXAMPLE: When the dog jumped up, Joe's parents became frightened.

EXAMPLE: After a long but exciting trip through the Alps, Joe returned tired but happy.

EXAMPLE: Springing into action, the police caught the bandit.

5. The comma is used to separate independent clauses of a compound sentence joined by a conjunction such as *and, but, for, nor, or, so,* or *yet.*

EXAMPLE: Joe decided to attend the game, but I remained at home.

NOTE: **Rules 4 and 5 do not apply to short introductory phrases and clauses and short independent clauses.**

EXAMPLE: Joe returned but I remained.

EXAMPLE: After the game we left for home.

6. The comma is omitted before the first item and after the last, if there is no confusion in meaning.

EXAMPLE: For breakfast he had juice, ham and eggs, and coffee.

EXAMPLE: The box contained books, toys, games and tools.

7. The comma is used before the text of a quotation.

EXAMPLE: The teacher said, "Return to your seats."

In a divided quotation, commas are used to set off the speaker.

EXAMPLE: "Return to your seats," said the teacher, "so we may continue the lesson."

8. The comma is used to set off clauses and phrases which are not essential to the meaning of the sentence.

EXAMPLE: Joan, who was seated beside me, left early.

(The clause, "who was seated beside me," is not essential to the sentence which, without it, would read, "Joan left early.")

NOTE: **No commas are needed if the clause or phrase is essential to the meaning intended by the speaker or writer.**

EXAMPLE: The students who studied hard passed the test.

(The clause, "who studied hard," is essential since only those students who studied hard passed. Without this clause the meaning intended by the writer—that the others who did not study hard failed—would not be clear to the reader.)

The comma also has a number of uses which are the result of custom. They include:

9. The comma is used after the salutation in a friendly letter.

EXAMPLE: Dear Dad,

10. The comma is used after the complimentary close in all letters.

EXAMPLE: Very truly yours,

11. The comma is used between the day of the month and the year in writing a date.

EXAMPLE: May 24, 1919

12. The comma is used between the city and state in writing an address.

EXAMPLE: Brooklyn, New York 11201

Two cautions:

Do *not* use a comma between a subject and its verb when the verb immediately follows the subject.

EXAMPLE: The boys on the team celebrated their victory.

Do *not* use a comma to separate parts of a compound predicate.

EXAMPLE: They wanted to have a good dinner and see a play.

THE SEMICOLON

1. The semicolon is used to separate independent clauses in a sentence, generally when the clauses are short.

EXAMPLE: I came; I saw; I conquered.

2. The semicolon is used to separate items in a series when these items contain commas.

EXAMPLE: The guests included Mr. Justice Warren, Chief Justice of the Supreme Court; Mr. Dean Rusk, Secretary of State; and Mr. David Bruce, Ambassador to Great Britain.

THE COLON

1. The colon is used to introduce a series or a list of items.

EXAMPLE: These items were included on the shopping list: fruit, vegetables, meat, fish and ice cream.

2. The colon is used before a restatement, an illustration or an explanation of the main idea of the sentence.

EXAMPLE: I have but one rule of conduct: do unto others as you would be done by.

3. The colon is used after the salutation of a business letter.

EXAMPLE: Dear Sir:

THE APOSTROPHE

1. The apostrophe is used to indicate possession.

In general, to make a singular noun possessive, add an apostrophe and "s" ('s) to words not ending in "s."

To make a plural noun possessive, add an apostrophe if the plural noun ends in "s." If it does not end in "s," add an apostrophe and "s."

EXAMPLES: boy's hat; ladies' hats; men's coats.

A WORD OF WARNING: First form the plural of the noun; child—children. Then add the apostrophe to make the possessive—children's.

ANOTHER CAUTION: Do *not* break up a word by using the apostrophe. The apostrophe can be added only at the end of a word.

WRONG: ladie's hats

CORRECT: ladies' hats

2. The apostrophe is used to indicate that one or more letters have been omitted in a contraction.

EXAMPLE: He didn't come.

3. The apostrophe is used to indicate the plural of letters or numbers.

EXAMPLE: There are 4 s's in Mississippi.

QUOTATION MARKS

1. Quotation marks are used to indicate the titles of works that are part of a book. Note: The titles of whole books are underlined to indicate that the title should be italicized when what is written is printed.

EXAMPLE: "Trees" is a poem by Joyce Kilmer.

2. Quotation marks are used to set off a direct quotation of the speaker or the writer. Note: Only his words may be used.

EXAMPLE: Nathan Hale said: "I regret that I have but one life to give for my country."

Indirect quotations, quotations which do not use the exact words of the speaker or writer, do *not* require quotation marks.

EXAMPLE: The boy said that he would be late.

Compare this with the direct quotation.

EXAMPLE: The boy said, "I will be late."

TIME TO PRACTICE:

Directions: **Correct the punctuation of the following sentences or identify them as correct. Write the answers on the line below.**

106. The Smiths have several 4's in the number of their car license.

_____

107. Mr. Carter expects to sell childrens shoes.

_____

108. We have no room in the car for suitcases as large as yours.

_____

109. If you will describe its color, perhaps we can find it.

_____

110. I'm not certain that your's is the best solution.

_____

111. "The Spy" is a novel by James Fenimore Cooper.

_____

112. I was told to buy, beets, carrots, tomatoes and celery.

_____

113. "Don't go" said Dad, "until I get back."

_____

114. I should not go, I cannot go, I will not go.

_____

115. After the group had convened John and Frank showed up.

_____

TIME TO STUDY:

Area 10 _Basic Rules of Capitalization_

1. Capitalize the first word of a sentence.

EXAMPLE: We went to the theatre.

2. Capitalize the first word of a direct quotation.

EXAMPLE: He said, "Don't give up."

3. Capitalize the first word of a line of poetry.

EXAMPLE: "Poems are made by fools like me . . ."

4. Capitalize proper nouns (names of specific persons, places, or things).

EXAMPLE: Winston Churchill; Mr. James Jones

EXAMPLE: New York City; Main Street; City Hall

5. Capitalize proper adjectives (adjectives formed from proper nouns).

EXAMPLE: American; Shakespearean

6. Capitalize names of specific organizations or institutions.

EXAMPLE: Sousa Junior High School; Columbia University; American Red Cross; Federal Bureau of Investigation

7. Capitalize days of the week, months of the year and holidays.

EXAMPLE: Sunday; June; Thanksgiving

NOTE: Do _not_ capitalize seasons such as winter.

8. Capitalize languages.

> EXAMPLE: French; Hebrew

> NOTE: **Languages are the *only* school subjects which are capitalized.**

> EXAMPLE: I study English, French, biology, mathematics and social studies.

9. Capitalize races and religions.

> EXAMPLE: Negro; Christian

10. Capitalize references to the Deity and to titles of holy books.

> EXAMPLE: the Almighty; the Old Testament; the Koran

11. Capitalize titles of people when they are followed by a name, being careful to capitalize both the title and the name.

> EXAMPLE: President Lyndon Johnson; Dr. Schweitzer

> NOTE: **If a specific person is meant, the name may, at times, be omitted.**

> EXAMPLE: The Premier attended the meeting of Parliament.

12. Capitalize titles of works of literature, art and music.

> EXAMPLE: War and Peace (note that articles, short prepositions and conjunctions like "and" are not capitalized in titles); American Gothic; Beethoven's Fifth Symphony

13. The pronoun "I" is capitalized at all times.

14. Sections of the country are capitalized but directions are not.

> EXAMPLE: I lived in the South for five years.

> EXAMPLE: I walked one mile south to the school.

TIME TO PRACTICE:

Directions: **Supply the necessary capitals or change those that are incorrect. Write the correct form on the line below each sentence.**

116. I attend junior high school.

_____

117. The American indian is confined largely to the reservation.

_____

118. He failed Chemistry and French but passed English and Social Studies.

_____

119.   He was elected president of his class.

_____

120.   He read the story by Poe entitled "Murders In The Rue Morgue."

_____

121.   He lived two miles North of Broadway.

_____

122.   My favorite book is the bible.

_____

123.   His son was a member of the Boy Scouts of America.

_____

124.   The senator believed in jacksonian democracy.

_____

125.   He lived on Twenty-first Street.

_____

ANSWERS TO *Questions in Correctness of Expression*

SENTENCE STRUCTURE

1. I like all flavors of ice cream: vanilla, chocolate and strawberry.
2. Since Dad came back, things have quieted down around the house.
3. Although Frank didn't like baseball games, he came with us because he liked our company.
4. Will you come to my party? I'd be delighted to have you meet my friends.
5. Sylvia has many interests: playing the piano, sewing her own clothes, painting landscapes and taking long hikes.
6. His friend's father was very rich; consequently, he retired at an early age.
7. Because the club planned its finances carefully, they were able to make ends meet.
8. He studied very hard; therefore, he got a good mark.
9. Correct
10. We have a full program of camping activities including sports, hikes and cook-outs.
11. Ed is outstanding in French. In addition, he excels in mathematics.
12. Sally was chosen queen of the festival because she was the prettiest contestant.
13. "Don't work too hard," Frances pleaded. "You have to think of your health."
14. I am out of funds so I can't pay my bills. Send a check as soon as possible.
15. Correct
16. John brought along all his equipment and also some food and drink.
17. Surveying the situation, he decided not to take part in the plan.
18. There were two reasons why he did not want to go: he was tired and he had a lot to do at home.
19. Correct
20. I don't like artichokes, spinach, and broccoli.

AGREEMENT OF SUBJECT AND VERB

21. A box of new materials is in the cabinet.
22. Correct
23. There are several ways to solve that problem.
24. The kind of books they read shows their taste in literature.
25. I believe that *Hamlet* is the greatest of all the plays that have ever been written.
26. People's efficiency is seriously affected by illness and worry.
27. Correct
28. Correct
29. Here, Mr. Chairman, are all the reports of the executive committee.
30. The most important feature of the series of swimming lessons was the large number of strokes taught.

AGREEMENT OF PRONOUN AND ANTECEDENT

31. The teacher said, "I'm happy to note that everybody in the class knows his work."
32. The John Adams Chess Club decided to revise its constitution.
33. The policeman said to the pedestrian, "Pick up your (my) hat."
34. Correct
35. One of the most highly respected citizens of our town gave his approval to our project.

CASES OF PRONOUNS

36. This is the story of a girl whose father was a doctor.
37. Correct
38. Correct
39. Correct
40. Who do you believe is the most capable?
41. Correct
42. Are you willing to allow us boys to form a cooking class?
43. Correct
44. Correct
45. Yes, my brother can do this work as well as I.
46. Correct
47. All the pupils except George and her plan to order the book.
48. Correct
49. Correct
50. Mother would not let Mary and me attend the hockey game.
51. I'm not certain that yours is the best solution.
52. It was we girls who swept the gym floor after the dance.
53. The money found on the stairs proved to be neither John's nor ours.
54. The committee consisted of John, Henry, Tom and me.
55. The letters were intended for us two only.

TROUBLESOME VERBS

56. If only we had begun before it was too late!
57. We were not allowed to skate on the pond until the ice had frozen to a depth of ten inches.
58. Overnight the river had risen another foot.
59. Mary, aren't you supposed to take part in the assembly program?
60. If you had been more patient, you might not have torn it.
61. We intended to go before Tuesday.

62. The general led his troops into battle.
63. I have been living in New York for five years now.
64. He was a good student, but he was a clumsy athlete.
65. They took part in baseball games, in swimming contests, and in a golf lesson.
66. Correct
67. If he were my friend, I should lend him the money.
68. If Joe had received the letter, he would have come promptly.
69. Correct
70. When I first saw the car, its steering wheel was broken.

ADJECTIVES AND ADVERBS

71. He had an unbelievably large capacity for food.
72. A person who works as efficiently as John deserves high praise.
73. The magician used his hands so skillfully that the audience was completely mystified.
74. "Don't you think that the old building would have served just as well?"
75. Food prepared in this manner tastes more delicious.
76. Johnson has scarcely any equal as a quarterback.
77. It was the worst storm that the inhabitants of the island could remember.
78. Frank was the less prepared of the two who took the examination.
79. He had hardly any friends.
80. Correct

CONFUSING CONSTRUCTIONS

81. When I got up to bat, the pitcher threw me a fast ball.
82. Frank and Jane were engaged for almost two years.
83. Correct
84. The animal with a broken leg was taken to the veterinarian.
85. After walking for three hours in the sun, I found the drink most welcome.

USAGE

86. If people had helped Burns, he might have become a greater poet.
87. When the teacher spoke, the room became very quiet.
88. Correct
89. Regardless of what you believe, your answer is incorrect.
90. The teacher explained the principle of refrigeration.
91. Try to find one that is shorter than this one.
92. Since he was the best qualified person, he received the job.
93. Although he had accepted the invitation, John failed to attend.
94. He is one of those persons who deserve great credit for courage.
95. What have been the principal effects of the serum?
96. I am not altogether in agreement with the author's point of view.
97. I believe that you ought to study harder.
98. Whose money is this on the desk?
99. Correct
100. John, where is the party?
101. Do as I tell you.
102. If he continues to work hard, he's likely to become president.
103. There were fewer persons present at the second meeting than at the first.
104. The teacher came to sit beside me.
105. Because of the bad weather, the game was postponed.

PUNCTUATION

106. Correct
107. Mr. Carter expects to sell children's shoes.
108. Correct
109. Correct
110. I'm not certain that yours is the best solution.
111. *The Spy* is a novel by James Fenimore Cooper.
112. I was told to buy beets, carrots, tomatoes and celery.
113. "Don't go," said Dad, "until I get back."
114. I should not go; I cannot go; I will not go.
115. After the group had convened, John and Frank showed up.

CAPITALIZATION

116. Correct
117. The American Indian is confined largely to the reservation.
118. He failed chemistry and French but passed English and social studies.
119. Correct
120. He read the story by Poe entitled "Murders in the Rue Morgue."
121. He lived two miles north of Broadway.
122. My favorite book is the Bible.
123. Correct
124. The senator believed in Jacksonian democracy.
125. Correct

What's your score?	_____right, _____wrong
	Excellent 111–125
	Good 96–110
	Fair 80–95

If you scored low, perhaps you need more review in one or more areas. To help you analyse your own weaknesses, the areas to which specific test sentences relate. Turn back and reread the explanations and examples. Then when you progress to the three tests that follow, see how much higher you will score.

PRACTICE IN CORRECTNESS OF EXPRESSION

Each of the 3 practice tests and the one practice examination which follow examine your ability to recognize correct and proper expression.

Practice Test 1

Directions: **Each of the following sentences contains an underlined expression. Below each sentence are four suggested answers. Underline the answer you consider correct. Then blacken the space under the number at the right which corresponds to the answer you have chosen.**

1. A sight to inspire fear <u>are wild animals on the lose.</u>
    (1) Correct as is   (2) are wild animals on the loose   (3) is wild animals on the loose   (4) is wild animals on the lose

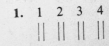

2. For many years, the settlers <u>had been seeking to worship as they please.</u>
(1) Correct as is   (2) had been seeking to worship as they pleased   (3) sought to worship as they please   (4) sought to have worshiped as they pleased

2. 1 2 3 4
   || || || ||

3. The girls stated that the dresses were <u>their's.</u>
(1) Correct as is   (2) there's   (3) theirs   (4) theirs'

3. 1 2 3 4
   || || || ||

4. <u>Please fellows</u> don't drop the ball.
(1) Correct as is   (2) Please, fellows   (3) Please fellows;   (4) Please, fellows,

4. 1 2 3 4
   || || || ||

5. Your sweater <u>has laid</u> on the floor for a week.
(1) Correct as is   (2) has been laying   (3) has been lying   (4) laid

5. 1 2 3 4
   || || || ||

6. I wonder whether <u>you're sure that scheme of yours'</u> will work.
(1) Correct as is   (2) your sure that scheme of your's   (3) you're sure that scheme of yours   (4) your sure that scheme of yours

6. 1 2 3 4
   || || || ||

7. Please let <u>her and me</u> do it.
(1) Correct as is   (2) she and I   (3) she and me   (4) her and I

7. 1 2 3 4
   || || || ||

8. I expected him to be angry <u>and to scold</u> her.
(1) Correct as is   (2) and that he would scold   (3) ; and that he would scold   (4) , and to scold

8. 1 2 3 4
   || || || ||

9. Knowing little about algebra, <u>it was difficult to solve the equation.</u>
(1) Correct as is   (2) the equation was difficult to solve.   (3) the solution to the equation was difficult to find.   (4) I found it difficult to solve the equation.

9. 1 2 3 4
   || || || ||

10. He <u>worked more diligent</u> now that he had become vice president of the company.
(1) Correct as is   (2) works more diligent   (3) works more diligently   (4) worked more diligently

10. 1 2 3 4
    || || || ||

11. <u>Flinging himself at the barricade he</u> pounded on it furiously.
(1) Correct as is   (2) Flinging himself at the barricade, he   (3) Flinging himself at the barricade—he   (4) Flinging himself at the barricade; he

11. 1 2 3 4
    || || || ||

12. When he <u>begun to give us advise,</u> we stopped listening.
(1) Correct as is   (2) began to give us advise   (3) begun to give us advice   (4) began to give us advice

12. 1 2 3 4
    || || || ||

13. John was the only one of the boys <u>whom as you know was</u> not eligible.
(1) Correct as is   (2) who as you know were   (3) whom as you know were   (4) who as you know was

13. 1 2 3 4
    || || || ||

14. Why <u>was Jane and he</u> permitted to go?
(1) Correct as is   (2) was Jane and him   (3) were Jane and he   (4) were Jane and him

14. 1 2 3 4
    || || || ||

15. <u>Take courage Tom:</u> we all make mistakes.
(1) Correct as is   (2) Take courage Tom—we   (3) Take courage, Tom; we   (4) Take courage, Tom we

15. 1 2 3 4
    || || || ||

16. Henderson, the president of the class and <u>who is also captain of the team,</u> will lead the rally.
(1) Correct as is   (2) since he is captain of the team   (3) captain of the team   (4) also being captain of the team

16. 1 2 3 4
  || || || ||

17. Our car has always <u>run good</u> on that kind of gasoline.
(1) Correct as is   (2) run well   (3) ran good   (4) ran well

17. 1 2 3 4
  || || || ||

18. There was a serious difference of opinion <u>among her and I.</u>
(1) Correct as is   (2) among she and I   (3) between her and I   (4) between her and me

18. 1 2 3 4
  || || || ||

19. "This is most unusual," said <u>Helen, "the</u> mailman has never been this late before."
(1) Correct as is   (2) Helen, "The   (3) Helen. "The   (4) Helen; "The

19. 1 2 3 4
  || || || ||

20. The three main characters in the story are Johnny Hobart, a <u>teenager, his mother a widow, and</u> the local druggist.
(1) Correct as is   (2) teenager; his mother, a widow; and   (3) teenager; his mother a widow; and   (4) teenager, his mother, a widow and

20. 1 2 3 4
  || || || ||

21. How much <u>has food costs raised</u> during the past year?
(1) Correct as is   (2) have food costs rose   (3) have food costs risen   (4) has food costs risen

21. 1 2 3 4
  || || || ||

22. "Will you come <u>too" she pleaded?</u>
(1) Correct as is   (2) too,?" she pleaded.   (3) too?" she pleaded.   (4) too," she pleaded?

22. 1 2 3 4
  || || || ||

23. If he <u>would have drank</u> more milk, his health would have been better.
(1) Correct as is   (2) would drink   (3) had drank   (4) had drunk

23. 1 2 3 4
  || || || ||

24. Jack had <u>no sooner laid down and fallen asleep when</u> the alarm sounded.
(1) Correct as is   (2) no sooner lain down and fallen asleep than   (3) no sooner lay down and fell asleep when   (4) no sooner laid down and fell asleep than

24. 1 2 3 4
  || || || ||

25. Jackson is <u>one of the few Sophomores, who has</u> ever made the varsity team.
(1) Correct as is   (2) one of the few Sophomores, who have   (3) one of the few sophomores, who has   (4) one of the few sophomores who have

25. 1 2 3 4
  || || || ||

26. The general<u>, with all his soldiers, was</u> captured.
(1) Correct as is   (2) , with all his soldier's were   (3) , with all his soldiers; was   (4) ' with all his soldiers, was

26. 1 2 3 4
  || || || ||

27. He is the <u>boy who's</u> poster was chosen for the contest.
(1) Correct as is   (2) boy, whose   (3) boy whose   (4) boy, who's

27. 1 2 3 4
  || || || ||

28. Humbled by the loss of prestige, <u>his plans changed.</u>
(1) Correct as is   (2) a change in his plans occurred.   (3) his plans were changed.   (4) he changed his plans.

28. 1 2 3 4
  || || || ||

29. We were not surprised at <u>him loosing</u> his way.
(1) Correct as is   (2) his losing   (3) him for loosing   (4) his loosing

29. 1 2 3 4
  || || || ||

30. The prize money is to be divided <u>among you and I.</u>
    (1) Correct as is   (2) among you and me   (3) between you and me   (4) between you and I

30.   1   2   3   4
      || || || ||

A WORD ABOUT TESTS: Do you consider yourself a person who "goes to pieces" on tests? Cheer up! Psychologists claim that more than ninety per cent of us think we don't perform well on tests *of any kind*. Nobody likes tests. But more than 80% of the people who have taken the High School Equivalency Tests in the New York area, for example, have passed them. They must be doing something right. And so can you, with the right attitude and careful preparation.

Practice Test 2

Directions: In each of the following sets of sentences, only one sentence contains an error in grammar, usage, spelling, punctuation, etc. Underline the sentence that is *incorrect*. Then blacken the space under the number at the right which corresponds to the answer you have chosen.

31. (1) I don't like it here; I'd rather go home.   (2) I wish I were in college now.   (3) Will you loan me two dollars until tomorrow?   (4) We were enthusiastic about his plans.   (5) Where have you been?

31.   1   2   3   4   5
      || || || || ||

32. (1) With that kind of a government, dictatorship is a potential danger.   (2) The murderer was hanged at dawn.   (3) This should teach you the value of money.   (4) Bread is a healthful part of our diet.   (5) Who is there?

32.   1   2   3   4   5
      || || || || ||

33. (1) Will you vote for whomever I support?   (2) Give it to whoever you feel deserves it.   (3) He invited whoever was interested in photography to join the Camera Club.   (4) How can you trust a man whom everyone knows has a prison record?   (5) Am I late?

33.   1   2   3   4   5
      || || || || ||

34. (1) Next term, I shall study English, Spanish, mathematics, and American history.   (2) I expect to be graduated from High School next year.   (3) Please call for me at eight P.M.   (4) He went south during the winter.   (5) I went home early.

34.   1   2   3   4   5
      || || || || ||

35. (1) This book has been lying on the table.   (2) Because I was tired, I lay down for a rest.   (3) It is obvious that these bricks were laid by an amateur bricklayer.   (4) Laying down on the job is not my idea of loyalty to the employer.   (5) The floor was not laid properly.

35.   1   2   3   4   5
      || || || || ||

36. (1) My favorite studies were Latin and science.   (2) The committee made its report.   (3) To get your work done promptly is better than leaving it until the last minute.   (4) That's what he would do if he were governor.   (5) He said that his chosen colors were red and blue.

36.   1   2   3   4   5
      || || || || ||

37. (1) Punish whoever disobeys orders.   (2) Come here, Henry; and sit with me.   (3) Has either of them his notebook?   (4) He talked as if he meant it.   (5) You did well; therefore you should be rewarded.

37.   1   2   3   4   5
      || || || || ||

38. (1) Many of us students were called to work.   (2) He shot the albatross with a crossbow.   (3) A house that is set on a hill is conspicuous.   (4) The wooden beams had raised slowly about a foot and then had settled back into place.   (5) Whom do you want to go with you?

38.   1   2   3   4   5
      || || || || ||

39. (1) He does not drive as he should.   (2) I can't hardly wait for the holidays.   (3) I like it less well than last week's.   (4) You were troubled by his coming.   (5) I don't know but that you are correct.

39. 1 2 3 4 5

40. (1) He was angry with both of us, her and me.   (2) When one enters the town, they see big crowds.   (3) They laid the tools on the ground every night.   (4) He is the only one of my friends who has written.   (5) He asked for a raise in wages.

40. 1 2 3 4 5

41. (1) None came with his excuse.   (2) Walking down the street, a house comes into view.   (3) "Never!" shouted the boy.   (4) Both are masters of their subject.   (5) His advice was to drive slowly.

41. 1 2 3 4 5

42. (1) There is both beef and lamb on the market.   (2) Either beans or beets are enough with potatoes.   (3) Where does your mother buy bananas?   (4) Dinners at the new restaurant are excellent.   (5) Each was rewarded according to his deeds.

42. 1 2 3 4 5

43. (1) Accordingly, we must prepare the food.   (2) The work, moreover, must be done today.   (3) Nevertheless, we must first have dinner.   (4) I always chose the most liveliest of the ponies.   (5) At six o'clock tomorrow the job will have been completed.

43. 1 2 3 4 5

44. (1) If their willing, let's all go together.   (2) Theirs was the last boat in.   (3) No doubt there's plenty to do.   (4) Tom and Dick sent their suits to the tailor's.   (5) In our group there were ten different beliefs.

44. 1 2 3 4 5

45. (1) We shall soon have completed ten sets.   (2) It might be safer to leave the door locked.   (3) Hadn't you ought to take your sister?   (4) If you should ask him, he would help you.   (5) He writes as if he were tired.

45. 1 2 3 4 5

46. (1) Not one of the three is worth buying.   (2) Bonbons taste sweeter than chocolates.   (3) Who ate more, Sally or he?   (4) I have eaten only three pieces.   (5) You yourself should learn to dance before you try to learn others.

46. 1 2 3 4 5

47. (1) There is no more butter, Anne.   (2) Each horse ran it's best.   (3) Elsie's mother's hat is very becoming.   (4) Without a quorum, the meeting could not proceed.   (5) Because of bad weather, he remained.

47. 1 2 3 4 5

48. (1) It surely was she who should have spoken first.   (2) It never occurred to us girls to enter.   (3) Those men need not have stood in line.   (4) The principal sent word for Ralph and I to come to his office.   (5) Can you, my dear, recall Sue's address?

48. 1 2 3 4 5

49. (1) Whom does Mrs Lee think wrote the poem?   (2) Who did your mother say were there?   (3) Whom did he refer to?   (4) Who do you believe will vote for it?   (5) Who was told to go?

49. 1 2 3 4 5

50. (1) The wind blew the roof off the garage.   (2) He had not drank all his coffee before the alarm sounded.   (3) A few cattle were lost on the range.   (4) We were through before you began.   (5) My favorite study has always been mathematics.

50. 1 2 3 4 5

51. (1) The audience took their seats promptly. (2) Each boy and girl must finish his examination this morning. (3) Every person turned their eyes toward the door. (4) Everyone has his own opinion. (5) The club nominated its officers by secret ballot.

52. (1) I can do that more easily than you. (2) This kind of weather is more healthful. (3) Pick out the really important points. (4) Because of his aggressive nature, he only plays the hardest games. (5) He pleaded with me to let him go.

51. 1   2   3   4   5

52. 1   2   3   4   5

53. (1) It is I who am mistaken. (2) Is it John or Susie who stand at the head of the class? (3) He is one of those who always do their lessons. (4) He is a man on whom I can depend in time of trouble. (5) Had he known who it was, he would have come.

53. 1   2   3   4   5

54. (1) Somebody has forgotten his umbrella. (2) Please let Joe and me use the car. (3) We thought the author to be he. (4) Whoever they send will be welcome. (5) They thought the intruders were we.

54. 1   2   3   4   5

55. (1) If I had known that you were coming, I should have met you. (2) All the girls but her were at the game. (3) I expected to have heard the concert before the present time. (4) Walter would not have said it if he had thought it would make her unhappy. (5) I have always believed that cork is the best material for insulation.

55. 1   2   3   4   5

56. (1) Their contributions amounted to the no insignificant sum of ten thousand dollars. (2) None of them was there. (3) Ten dollars is the amount I agreed to pay. (4) Fewer than one hundred persons assembled. (5) Exactly what many others have done and are doing, Frank did.

56. 1   2   3   4   5

57. (1) Neither Jane or her sister has arrived. (2) Either Richard or his brother is going to drive. (3) Refilling storage batteries is the work of the youngest employee. (4) Helen has to lie still for two weeks. (5) Mother lay down for an hour yesterday.

57. 1   2   3   4   5

58. (1) He is not the man whom you saw entering the house. (2) He asked why I wouldn't come. (3) This is the cow whose horns are the longest. (4) Helen, this is a man I met on the train one day last February. (5) He greeted every foreign representative which came to the conference.

58. 1   2   3   4   5

59. (1) You, but not I, are invited. (2) Guy's technique of service and return is masterly. (3) Please pass me one of the books that are lying on the table. (4) Mathematics is my most difficult subject. (5) Unable to agree on a plan of organization, the class has departed in several directions.

59. 1   2   3   4   5

60. (1) He spoke to Gertrude and to me of the seriousness of the occasion. (2) They seem to have decided to invite everyone except you and I. (3) Your attitude is insulting to me who am your friend. (4) He wished to know who our representative was. (5) You may tell whomsoever you wish.

60. 1   2   3   4   5

61. (1) All things considered, he did unusually well. (2) The poor boy takes everything too seriously. (3) Our club sent two delegates, Ruth and I, to Oswego. (4) I like him better than her. (5) His eccentricities continually made good newspaper copy.

61. 1   2   3   4   5

62. (1) If we except Benton, no one in the club foresaw the changes. (2) The two-year-old rosebushes are loaded with buds—and beetles! (3) Though the pitcher had been broken by the cat, Teena was furious. (4) Virginia got the cake recipe off of her grandmother. (5) Neither one of the twins was able to get a summer vacation.

62. 1 2 3 4 5
|| || || || ||

63. (1) "What do you wish?" he asked, "may I help you?" (2) Whose gloves are these? (3) Has he drunk all the orange juice? (4) It was he who spoke to the manager of the store. (5) Mary prefers this kind of evening dress.

63. 1 2 3 4 5
|| || || || ||

64. (1) Charles himself said it before the assembled peers of the realm. (2) The wind stirred the rose petals laying on the floor. (3) The storm beat hard on the frozen windowpanes. (4) Worn out by the days of exposure and storm, the sailor clung pitifully to the puny raft. (5) The day afterward he thought more kindly of the matter.

64. 1 2 3 4 5
|| || || || ||

65. (1) Between you and me, I think Henry is wrong. (2) This is the more interesting of the two books. (3) This is the most carefully written letter of all. (4) During the opening course I read not only four plays but also three historical novels. (5) This assortment of candies, nuts, and fruits are excellent.

65. 1 2 3 4 5
|| || || || ||

66. (1) According to your report card, you are not so clever as he. (2) If he had kept his eyes open, he would not have fallen into that trap. (3) We were certain that the horse had broken it's leg. (4) The troop of scouts and the leader are headed for the North Woods. (5) I knew it to be him by the knock at the door.

66. 1 2 3 4 5
|| || || || ||

67. (1) Being one of the earliest spring flowers, we welcome the crocus. (2) The cold running water became colder as time sped on. (3) Those boys need not have stood in line for lunch. (4) Can you, my friend, donate ten dollars to the cause? (5) Because it's a borrowed umbrella, return it in the morning.

67. 1 2 3 4 5
|| || || || ||

68. (1) If Walter would have planted earlier in the spring, the rosebushes would have survived. (2) The flowers smell overpoweringly sweet. (3) There are three *e*'s in *dependent*. (4) May I be excused at the end of the test? (5) Carl has three brothers-in-law.

68. 1 2 3 4 5
|| || || || ||

69. (1) We have bought neither the lumber nor the tools for the job. (2) Jefferson was re-elected despite certain powerful opposition. (3) The Misses Jackson were invited to the dance. (4) The letter is neither theirs nor yours. (5) The retail price for those items are far beyond the wholesale quotations.

69. 1 2 3 4 5
|| || || || ||

70. (1) To find peace of mind is to gain treasure beyond price. (2) Fred is cheerful, carefree; his brother is morose. (3) Whoever fails to understand the strategic importance of the Arctic fails to understand modern geography. (4) They came promptly at 8 o'clock on August 7, 1949, without prior notification. (5) Every one tried their best to guess the answer, but no one succeeded.

70. 1 2 3 4 5
|| || || || ||

Practice Test 3

Directions: In each of the sentences which follow, certain portions are underlined and numbered. On the right hand side of the page are suggested several ways
of writing or punctuating each underlined portion or several positions in which to
place it in the sentence. Choose the answer which you consider correct or which
sounds best and indicate on the dotted lines at the right the number of your choice.

Today she is wearing a <u>different dress than</u>
                       71

the one she wore yesterday.

71. (1) different dress than   (2) different dress from   (3) different dress
to

71. . . . .

<u>Being that</u> he is <u>that kind of a boy,</u> we
 72   73

cannot expect too much from him.

72. (1) Being that   (2) Being as   (3)
Since

73. (1) that kind of boy   (2) that kind
of a boy

72. . . . .

73. . . . .

He divided the candy <u>between</u> John, Mary
                   74

and <u>I.</u>
   75

74. (1) among   (2) between

75. (1) me   (2) I   (3) myself

74. . . . .

75. . . . .

"Why did you buy <u>that,</u>" he <u>asked,</u> "we
              76   77

have too many knick-knacks <u>now.</u>"
                      78

76. (1) that,"   (2) that?"   (3) that."
77. (1) asked, "we   (2) asked? "we   (3)
asked. "We   (4) asked. "we
78. (1) now.   (2) now?"   (3) now."   (4)
now"?   (5) now".

76. . . . .
77. . . . .

78. . . . .

<u>There are many</u> people <u>who</u> are now look-
    79   80

for apartments.

79. (1) There are many   (2) Many
80. (1) who   (2) OMIT

79. . . . .
80. . . . .

If <u>I were</u> president, I would repeal that
    81

law.

81. (1) I were   (2) I was

81. . . . .

That medicine did not <u>effect</u> me <u>like</u> the
                 82   83

doctor told me it would.

82. (1) effect   (2) affect   (3) effects
83. (1) like   (2) as

82. . . . .
83. . . . .

<u>I have not and</u> will not ever give you any
    84

grounds for complaint.

84. (1) OMIT   (2) have not and   (3)
have not given and

84. . . . .

This is a book <u>where</u> most of the char-
          85

acters die.

85. (1) where   (2) in which   (3) that
has

85. . . . .

<u>At the age of twelve,</u> my aunt took me
      86

to Europe.

86. (1) At the age of twelve,   (2) Being
I was twelve years old   (3) When I
was twelve years old,   (4) When I
was twelve years old

86. . . . .

Neither Jack nor Bill <u>has reported</u> to the
                        87
doctor.

87. (1) has reported   (2) have reported

87. . . . .

He cared little for <u>those</u> kind of books.
                        88

88. (1) those   (2) these   (3) that

88. . . . .

He told me, <u>who is</u> chairman, to talk
           89
about <u>Mary</u> coming late to meetings.
      90

89. (1) who is   (2) who am

90. (1) Mary   (2) Mary's   (3) Marys

89. . . . .

90. . . . .

He was tired and dirty, <u>in addition,</u> he
                      91
was penniless.

91. (1) , in addition,   (2) . in addition
     (3) ; in addition   (4) ; in addition,

91. . . . .

I discovered I <u>only</u> remembered half of
           92
my assignment.

92. (1) Place before "discovered"   (2)
Place before "half"   (3) Leave
were it is

92. . . . .

<u>Who</u> do you want to be?
 93

93. (1) Who   (2) Whom

93. . . . .

<u>Who</u> did you expect the captain to be?
 94

94. (1) Who   (2) Whom

94. . . . .

He <u>ought to</u> have spoken to me before
    95
this.

95. (1) ought to   (2) had ought to   (3)
should of

95. . . . .

The book fell from my arm <u>going to</u>
                        96
<u>school.</u>

96. (1) Leave as is   (2) Put at beginning
(3) while I was going to school.

96. . . . .

Everybody likes to think <u>they are</u> doing
                        97
<u>their</u> best.
 98

97. (1) they are   (2) he is

98. (1) their   (2) his

97. . . . .

98. . . . .

We <u>can but</u> pardon the culprit.
   99

99. (1) can but   (2) can help but   (3)
cannot help but

99. . . . .

She was very cordial to my sister and
<u>myself.</u>
 100

100. (1) myself,   (2) me.

100. . . . .

ANSWERS TO *Practice Tests 1, 2, and 3 in Correctness of Expression*

1. 3	**11.** 2	**21.** 3	**31.** 3	**41.** 2	**51.** 3	**61.** 3	**71.** 2	**81.** 1	**91.** 4
2. 2	**12.** 4	**22.** 3	**32.** 1	**42.** 1	**52.** 4	**62.** 4	**72.** 3	**82.** 2	**92.** 2
3. 3	**13.** 4	**23.** 4	**33.** 4	**43.** 4	**53.** 2	**63.** 1	**73.** 1	**83.** 2	**93.** 1
4. 4	**14.** 3	**24.** 2	**34.** 2	**44.** 1	**54.** 3	**64.** 2	**74.** 1	**84.** 3	**94.** 2
5. 3	**15.** 3	**25.** 4	**35.** 4	**45.** 3	**55.** 3	**65.** 5	**75.** 1	**85.** 2	**95.** 1
6. 3	**16.** 3	**26.** 1	**36.** 3	**46.** 5	**56.** 1	**66.** 3	**76.** 2	**86.** 3	**96.** 3
7. 1	**17.** 2	**27.** 3	**37.** 2	**47.** 2	**57.** 1	**67.** 1	**77.** 3	**87.** 1	**97.** 2
8. 1	**18.** 4	**28.** 4	**38.** 4	**48.** 4	**58.** 5	**68.** 1	**78.** 3	**88.** 3	**98.** 2
9. 4	**19.** 3	**29.** 2	**39.** 2	**49.** 1	**59.** 5	**69.** 5	**79.** 2	**89.** 2	**99.** 1
10. 4	**20.** 2	**30.** 3	**40.** 2	**50.** 2	**60.** 2	**70.** 5	**80.** 2	**90.** 2	**100.** 2

What's your score?

_____right, _____wrong

Excellent   91–100
Good   81–90
Fair   70–80

If you didn't make out as well as you hoped, don't get discouraged. Try to find out *why* you failed. Were you careless? Perhaps you need to review once again the areas on punctuation or sentence structure or other points of grammar. The High School Equivalency Test in Correctness of Expression is one *you* are going to pass. We can help—but the essential factor is your determination and your use of these materials.

Practice Examination

Directions: Below is a paragraph in which words or groups of words have been underlined. For each underlined and numbered section there are five suggested answers. Choose the one you consider correct and indicate on the dotted lines at the right the number of your choice.

The process by which the community <u>influence the actions of its members</u> is
1
known as social control.

1. (1) influence the actions of its members (2) influences the actions of its members (3) had influenced the actions of its members (4) influences the actions of their members (5) will influence the actions of its members

1. ....

Imitation <u>which</u> takes place when the ac-
2
tion of one individual awakens the im-

2. (1) which (2) , which (3) —which (4) that (5) what

2. ....

pulse in <u>each other</u> to attempt the same
3
thing, is one of the means by which society gains this control. When the child

3. (1) each other (2) some other (3) one other (4) another (5) one another

3. ....

acts as other members of this group <u>acts,</u>
4
he receives their approval.

4. (1) acts (2) act (3) has acted (4) will act (5) will have acted

4. ....

There <u>is</u> also adults who seem almost
5
equally imitative. Advertisers of luxuries are careful to convey the idea that important persons use and indorse the merchandise concerned, for most folk will do their utmost to follow the example of

5. (1) is (2) are (3) was (4) were (5) will be

5. ....

those <u>whom</u> they think are the best peo-
6
ple. Akin to imitation as a means of social control is suggestion. The child is taught

6. (1) whom (2) what (3) which (4) who (5) that which

6. ....

to think and feel as <u>do</u> the adults of his community.   7

7. (1) do (2) does (3) had (4) may (5) might

7. ....

He is <u>neither encouraged to be critical or to examine</u> all the evidence for his
<u>   8   </u>
opinions.

8. (1) neither encouraged to be critical or to examine   (2) neither encouraged to be critical nor to examine   (3) either encouraged to be critical or to examine   (4) encouraged either to be critical nor to examine   (5) not encouraged either to be critical or to examine

8. . . . .

To be sure, there would be <u>scarcely no</u>
<u>   9   </u>
time left for other things

9. (1) scarcely no   (2) hardly no   (3) scarcely any   (4) enough   (5) but only

9. . . . .

if school children <u>would have been</u> ex-
<u>   10   </u>

10. (1) would have been   (2) should have been   (3) would have   (4) were   (5) will be

10. . . . .

pected <u>to have considered</u> all sides of
<u>   11   </u>
every matter on which they hold opinions.

11. (1) to have considered   (2) to be considered   (3) to consider   (4) to have been considered   (5) and have considered

11. . . . .

It is possible, <u>however</u> and probably very
<u>   12   </u>
desirable, for pupils of high school age to learn that the point of view accepted in their community is not the only one, and that many widely held opinions may be mistaken. The way in which suggestion operates is illustrated by advertising methods.

12. (1) , however   (2) however,   (3) ; however,   (4) however   (5) , however,

12. . . . .

<u>Depending on skillful suggestion, argument is seldom used in advertising.</u> The
<u>   13   </u>
words accompanying the picture do not seek to convince the reason but only to intensify the suggestion.
Some persons are more susceptible to suggestion than others. The ignorant person is more easily moved to action by suggestion than he who is well educated,

13. (1) Depending on skillful suggestion, argument is seldom used in advertising.   (2) Argument is seldom used by advertisers, who depend instead on skillful suggestion.   (3) Skillful suggestion is depended on by advertisers instead of argument.   (4) Suggestion, which is more skillful, is used in place of argument by advertisers.   (5) Instead of suggestion, depending on argument is used by skillful advertisers.

13. . . . .

<u>education developing</u> the habit of criti-
<u>   14   </u>
cizing what is read and heard. Whoever would think clearly, freeing himself from emotion and prejudice, must beware of the influence of the crowd or mob. A crowd is a group of people in a highly suggestible condition, each stimulating the feelings of the others until an intense uniform emotion has control of the group. Such a crowd may become irresponsible

14. (1) , education developing   (2) , education developed by   (3) , for education develops   (4) . Education will develop   (5) Education developing

14. . . . .

and anonymous, <u>and whose</u> activity may
　　　　　　　　15
lead in any direction. The educated person ought to be beyond reach of this kind

of appeal, <u>no</u> one may be said to have a
　　　　　16
real individuality who, at the mercy of the

suggestions of others, <u>allow themselves</u> to
　　　　　　　　　　17
succumb to "crowd-mindedness."

15. (1) and whose　(2) whose　(3) and
its　(4) and the　(5) and the crowd's

16. (1) , no　(2) : no　(3) —no　(4) . No
(5) omit punctuation

17. (1) allow themselves　　(2) allows
themselves　(3) allow himself　(4)
allows himself　(5) allow ourselves

15. . . . .

16. . . . .

17. . . . .

ANSWERS TO *Practice Examination*

1. 2	**5.** 2	**9.** 3	**13.** 2
2. 2	**6.** 4	**10.** 4	**14.** 3
3. 4	**7.** 1	**11.** 3	**15.** 3
4. 2	**8.** 5	**12.** 5	**16.** 4
			17. 4

What's your score?

_____right, _____wrong

Excellent　　　15–17
Good　　　　　13–14
Fair　　　　　　10–12

If your score is unsatisfactory on the last two tests, perhaps the form has confused you. Actually they are similar to, although a bit more difficult than, other practice exercises you have already done in which you are asked to decide on the correct way to write underlined portions. The only difference is that in this case it is in paragraph form. If some principle or point of grammar is still causing you trouble, go back to that section and really learn it! A good way to test yourself again on this section, since it is not too long, would be to have someone dictate it to you. Then you can check your results against the correct answer to be sure of your mastery of this examination.

4

The Test of Interpretation of Literary Materials

The Test of Interpretation of Literary Materials is a reading test in which the emphasis is on your ability to understand and interpret passages of both prose and verse from American and English literature. You will want to review the hints for better reading comprehension given in Chapter 1. For the test on Interpretation of Literary Materials you must demonstrate an ability to answer not only questions on the content of the passage in question but to know (1) how to explain figurative language; (2) what the meaning is of sentences with difficult or unusual constructions; and (3) how to determine the mood and purpose of the author.

HOW THIS SECTION CAN HELP YOU

To help you acquire this special ability we have included a full list of words used frequently in discussing literature. You are not expected to know *all* of these, but it will help you considerably to have a knowledge of many of them. Use the Vocabulary of Literature dictionary for reference when you are in doubt about a question involving literary terms.

Another helpful feature is a careful, question-by-question analysis of a prose selection and a poem preceding the practice exercises. Read these analyses carefully; try to follow the suggested procedures when you prepare to answer the questions on the practice selections. In time you will find that you will sharpen your ability to understand exactly *what each question means and how it should be answered.*

TIME TO STUDY:

THE VOCABULARY OF LITERATURE

The words defined here are those which are most frequently used in discussing literature. They are to be used in conjunction with the literature reading passages contained in this book. Get the habit of referring to this list as you read the passages that follow.

ACCENT   The emphasis given to a syllable or syllables of a word. Accent is used primarily with reference to poetry. This term is also used for the mark which shows this emphasis. (′)

ALLEGORY   Presentation in concrete terms of an abstract idea or series of abstract ideas. In *Pilgrim's Progress*, Christian proceeds via Vanity Fair to the Celestial City.

ALLITERATION   The repetition of the same consonant sound at the beginning of two or more words in close proximity. An example is "The fair *b*reeze *b*lew, the white *f*oam *f*lew . . ."

ALLUSION   Offhand reference to a famous figure or event in literature or history. "He opened a Pandora's box."

ANAPEST   A poetic foot consisting of three syllables with two unaccented syllables followed by an accented one. ("to the store")

ANTITHESIS   Strong contrast in ideas. ". . . wretches hang that jury-men may dine."

APHORISM   Brief statement of an idea or guide to conduct. "Honesty is the best policy."

APOSTROPHE   Words addressed to someone or something absent as if it were present. ". . . sail on, O Ship of State!"

AUTOBIOGRAPHY   Story of a person's life written by himself. (Franklin's *Autobiography*)

BALLAD   Verse form which presents in simple story form a single dramatic or exciting episode and stresses such feelings as love, courage, patriotism and loyalty. ("Sir Patrick Spens")

BIOGRAPHY   Story of a person's life written by someone else. (Boswell's *Life of Johnson*)

BLANK VERSE   Unrhymed lines, ten syllables each, whose second, fourth, sixth, eighth, tenth syllables are accented. (The lines consist of five iambs and are in iambic pentameter. An example is "Was this the face that launched a thousand ships . . .")

CLIMAX   High point in the telling of a story, be it in fictional, poetic, or dramatic form. (An example is the appearance of Banquo's ghost in "Macbeth.")

COMEDY   Light form of drama which tries to amuse and/or instruct us and which ends happily. ("All's Well That Ends Well")

COUPLET   Two lines of verse which rhyme and tend to form an independent thought. ("Hope springs eternal in the human breast: Man never is, but always to be, blest.")

DACTYL   Poetic foot consisting of one accented syllable followed by two unaccented syllables. ("Rising and . . .")

DENOUEMENT   Final unraveling of the plot in a play or novel. Included is an explanation of all the complications and mysteries of the plot.

DIALOGUE   Conversation between people in a play.

DIDACTIC VERSE   Verse whose main purpose is to teach a moral lesson. ("Ode to Duty")

ELEGY   Lyric poem expressing a poet's ideas concerning death. (Gray's "Elegy Written in a Country Churchyard")

ENJAMBEMENT   Continuing of a sentence from one line or couplet into the next without a stop at the end of the line. This is also known as a RUN-ON LINE. (" 'Tis the majority In this, as all, prevails.")

ENVOY   Concluding stanza added to certain forms of poems, usually a French verse form called a Ballade.

EPIC   Long poem which tells a story about noble people and their adventures centering around one character who is the hero. The poem is usually closely tied to a single country and serves a patriotic purpose. (Greece—"The Iliad"; Rome—"The Aeneid")

EPIGRAM   A short poem with a witty or satirical point. This term also refers to a brief saying. An example is "Man proposes but God disposes."

EPITHET   Adjective which effectively identifies a significant quality of the noun it describes. (Alexander the *Great*)

ESSAY   Prose writing which can be recognized by its incomplete treatment of any topic no matter how unimportant and by its approach—formal (containing an analysis with a moral) or informal (revealing the personality of the author through his humor, bias, and style). Formal: Bacon, "Of Friendship"; informal: Lamb, "A Dissertation on Roast Pig"

FIGURE OF SPEECH   Expression used to appeal to the reader's emotions and imagination by presenting words in unusual meaning or context. ("My love's like a red, red rose")

FOOT Certain number of syllables making up a unit in a verse of poetry. The four main kinds are the iamb, the trochee, the anapest, and the dactyl—each defined separately.

FREE VERSE Verse that has an irregular pattern of meter and has a variety of rhythmical effects. Stanza form is irregular and rhyme is usually absent. An example is "Chicago" by Carl Sandburg.

HEXAMETER A line of six metrical feet.

HYPERBOLE Figure of speech used by a writer who purposely wants to exaggerate. (An example is "rivers of blood.")

IAMBIC PENTAMETER Line of ten syllables divided into five feet, each composed of one unaccented and one accented syllable, in that order. An IAMB is a foot of two syllables, the first unaccented, the second accented.

IMAGE A figure of speech, especially a simile or a metaphor. See the definitions of those terms.

INVERSION Reversal of the normal order of words in a sentence. (An example is "A king of men am I.")

IRONY Figure of speech in which the writer or speaker uses words meaning the exact opposite of what he really thinks. (In "Julius Caesar," Antony attacks Brutus with the words, "Brutus is an honorable man.")

LIMERICK Jingle in verse containing five lines, with lines 1, 2, and 5 rhyming and lines 3 and 4 rhyming.

LYRIC Short poem expressing deep emotion in highly melodic and imaginative verse. An example is "The Daffodils."

MEDIAL RHYME Rhyme occurring within a line. An example is "Once upon a midnight *dreary*, while I pondered weak and *weary* . . ."

METAPHOR Figure of speech which compares two things or a person and a thing by using a quality of one applied to the other. "Like" or "as" is omitted. ("All the world's a stage.")

METER Rhythm resulting from the repetition of one of several kinds of poetic feet. (See Iamb, Trochee, Anapest, and Dactyl)

METONYMY A figure of speech using a commonly associated word to describe the object. ("He likes Shakespeare." In reality, he likes Shakespeare's plays.)

MYTH Story of unknown origin, religious in character, which tries to interpret the natural world, usually in terms of supernatural events. (Example—the story of Atlas)

NARRATIVE A story of events or experiences, true or fictitious. A poem may be narrative as "The Rime of the Ancient Mariner."

NOVEL Lengthy prose story dealing with imaginary characters and settings which creates the illusion of real life. (Scott's *Ivanhoe*)

OCTET The first eight lines of a sonnet, particularly the Italian sonnet, which generally state the theme of the poem. (See Milton's sonnets)

ODE Lyric poem of particularly serious purpose written in language which is dignified and inspired. (Keats' "Ode to a Grecian Urn")

ONOMATOPOEIA Use of words whose sounds resemble and/or suggest their meaning. (e.g. buzz; hiss)

PARADOX A statement which seems contradictory but which may, in fact, be true. (In "The Pirates of Penzance," the hero had only five birthdays although he was 21 years old. He was born on February 29th of a leap year!)

PARODY Writing which pokes fun at a serious work by using exaggeration or broad humor in an imitation of the serious work.

PATHETIC FALLACY An expression that gives human feelings to natural or inhuman things. Example: "The waves danced with glee."

PERSONIFICATION Figure of speech where an idea or a thing is given human qualities. ("Death, be not proud . . .")

POEM Literature which has any or all of the following qualities to a high degree: deep emotion; highly imaginative language with figures of speech; distinctive rhythm; compression of thought; use of the familiar in a symbolic sense; some kind of rhyme scheme; words which mean more than they apparently say.

QUATRAIN A stanza of four lines.

REFRAIN A word or group of words repeated regularly in a poem, usually at the end of a stanza. ("Nevermore" from "The Raven")

REPETITION The restating of a phrase or line for emphasis. An example is
"And miles to go before I sleep
And miles to go before I sleep."

RHYME   In poetry, agreement in the final sounds of two or more words at the ends of lines. (June, moon; crunch on, luncheon)

RHYTHM   In poetry and certain kinds of prose, patterns of stress or accent in the units which make up the verse or sentence.

SARCASM   A figure of speech which is harsh in tone and expresses meaning by use of the opposite. ("Excellent" said when a mistake is made.)

SATIRE   Work which makes fun of a person, an idea, or a social custom or institution by stressing its foolishness or lack of reasonableness. (Swift's *Gulliver's Travels*)

SCANNING   Division of a verse into feet by finding the accents to determine its meter. ("I think that I shall never see"— ⌣ ′ ⌣ ′ ⌣ ′ ⌣′—verse contains four iambs)

SESTET   The last six lines of a sonnet, generally making comment on the theme set in the first eight lines.

SHORT STORY   Short prose narrative dealing with imaginary characters usually in a single setting, often relating a single incident, and striving for a single effect such as terror. (Poe's "The Pit and the Pendulum")

SIMILE   Figure of speech in which two things essentially unlike are compared with *like* or *as* being used to make the comparison. (". . . a poem lovely as a tree")

SOLILOQUY   Speech of a character in a play uttered when he is alone on the stage and in which he informs the audience of his thoughts or of knowledge it needs to follow the action of the play. (Hamlet's "To be or not to be . . .")

SONNET   A form of poetry consisting of fourteen verses in which two aspects of an idea are presented. In the ITALIAN OR PETRARCHAN SONNET, the first aspect of the idea or theme is presented in the first eight lines which rhyme a b b a a b b a; the second aspect of the idea or commentary on the theme is presented in the second six lines which rhyme (in various combinations) c d e c d e. The first eight lines are the OCTET; the second six lines the SESTET. In the SHAKESPEAREAN SONNET, the first aspect is presented in the first twelve lines which rhyme a b a b c d c d e f e f; the second aspect is presented in the last two lines which rhyme g g.

STANZA   A unit in a poem, similar to a paragraph in a piece of prose writing.

SYMBOL   An object that represents ideas, either psychological, philosophical, social, or religious. The cross represents Christianity; the Star of David is the symbol of Judaism.

SYNECHDOCHE   A figure of speech that uses the part to stand for the whole. ("All *hands* perished when the ship sank.")

TETRAMETER   A line of verse consisting of four feet.

TRAGEDY   Form of drama which has any or all of the following qualities: conflict of character that ends in disaster; person of great and noble character who meets his downfall because of his own weakness; drama that appeals to our emotions of pity and fear. (Example—"Othello")

TROCHEE   A poetic foot, consisting of two syllables, with an accented syllable preceding an unaccented syllable. ("Glory . . .)

HOW TO READ AND INTERPRET LITERARY MATERIALS

This part of the examination is a test of your ability to read and interpret literary materials. These selections are drawn from world literature, both prose and poetry. Regular reading skill is necessary plus a group of special skills—the ability to interpret figures of speech (see the special vocabulary of literary terms), the ability to figure out unusual word meanings from the sentences in which they appear, the ability to deal with involved sentences and sentence structure of earlier centuries, and the ability to recognize the mood of a selection and the purpose for which it was written.

The emphasis is often on interpretation rather than on literal meaning. The questions on the reading selections may contain such terms as "we may most safely conclude," "the author implies," "the author suggests," "the author's chief purpose," and "the author's attitude towards _____ is," and other similar terms. As a result, the reading selections we have chosen for you will proceed from the more familiar skills of reading for the main idea ("the title that best expresses the ideas of this passage"), reading for details, deriving the meaning of words from their context, and word attack methods to the more subtle and difficult skills of drawing conclusions and inferences, forecasting results, determining attitudes, identifying purpose, and determining the tone of a selection.

Let us interpret two selections together before you proceed to the others on your own.

SAMPLE PASSAGES WITH ANALYSES

Selection 1

1   The light carriage swished through the layers of fallen leaves upon
2   the terrace. In places, they lay so thick that they half covered the stone
3   balusters and reached the knees of Diana's stag. But the trees were bare;
4   only here and there a single golden leaf trembled high upon the black twigs.
5   Following the curve of the road, Boris's carriage came straight upon the
6   main terrace and the house, majestic as the Sphinx herself in the sunset.
7   The light of the setting sun seemed to have soaked into the dull masses
8   of stone. They reddened and glowed with it until the whole place became
9   a mysterious, a glorified abode, in which the tall windows shone like a
10   row of evening stars.
11   Boris got out of the britska in front of the mighty stone stairs
12   and walked toward them, feeling for his letter. Nothing stirred in the
13   house. It was like walking into a cathedral. "And," he thought, "by the
14   time that I get into that carriage once more, what will everything be
15   like to me?"

QUESTION 1

The title below that expresses the main idea of this passage is:

1. The Lure of Autumn
2. Sphinx in the Sunset
3. A Mysterious Cathedral
4. A Terrifying Surprise
5. An Important Visit

ANALYSIS

Ans. 1 cannot be correct. Going back to the passage, we find on line three that "the trees were bare; only here and there a single golden leaf trembled high upon the black twigs." This and a reference to "layers of fallen leaves" in line 1 are the only indications of season. And "the lure" of attraction of the season is not even mentioned. We reject this because it is only the setting for the main idea of the selection and background detail at best. It is not the _main_ idea.
Ans. 2 and 3 are incorrect for similar reasons. In each case, a _detail_ has been picked out of the selection and offered as the _main_ idea. Ans. 2 is taken from line 6 where the house is compared to a Sphinx. Ans. 3 is a combination of words taken from lines 9 and 13, both also involving a comparison—this time of the house with a cathedral.

Ans. 4 is completely incorrect. There is no surprise, nor is the selection's mood one of terror. There is anticipation of something about to happen rather than something surprising which has happened.

Ans. 5 is the correct choice. Boris has come to the house and, as he enters, he wonders what changes may take place for him as a result of his visit. To Boris, this will be "an important visit."

QUESTION 2

From the description of the house, we may most safely conclude that the house

1. is sometimes used as a place of worship
2. is owned by a wealthy family
3. was designed by Egyptian architects
4. is constructed of modern brick
5. is a dark, cold-looking structure

1. 1 2 3 4 5
    ‖ ‖ ‖ ‖ ‖

ANALYSIS

Ans. 1 and 3 are both incorrect, again for similar reasons. Each is based on a figure used in the passage, the implied comparison between the house and a cathedral and the stated comparison of the house to the Sphinx. These are comparisons in the mind of the writer.

Ans. 4 is incorrect because it flatly contradicts the passage. The house is built of stone.

Ans. 5 is incorrect because it, too, contradicts the selection. The stone is not dark; it glows with the light of the setting sun.

Ans. 2 is correct. We can conclude that the house is owned by a wealthy family because there are several terraces, the stone stairs are "mighty," the windows are tall, and there are "masses of stone." Of the possibilities offered, this is the one "we may most safely conclude" is correct.

QUESTION 3

This story probably takes place in

1. the British Isles
2. the Far East
3. eastern Europe
4. southern United States
5. the Mediterranean

1. 1 2 3 4 5
    ‖ ‖ ‖ ‖ ‖

ANALYSIS

Ans. 3 is correct. This question calls on you to draw an inference. The chief character is named Boris, a Russian name. He gets out of a britska, and, even if you don't know that it is a kind of open carriage used in eastern Europe, the word suggests a conveyance that immediately eliminates the possibilities of "the British Isles" and "southern United States." It is safe to conclude because of the name, Boris, that the story "probably takes place in eastern Europe."

QUESTION 4

We may most safely conclude that Boris has come to the house in order to

1. secure a job
2. find out about his future
3. join his friends for the holidays
4. attend a hunting party
5. visit his old family home

ANALYSIS

The purpose of the question is to see whether you can determine the purpose of Boris' visit from the *evidence given*. While answers 1, 3, and 4 may possibly be correct, there is *no evidence* in the passage that they are.

Ans. 5 must be considered along with Answer 2. If the selection ended just before the final sentence, the two choices would be equally correct. But Boris is not merely making a visit. The question he asks himself in the final sentence makes it clear that the visit promises to change his future. Therefore, Answer 2 is the better of the two.

QUESTION 5

In this passage, which atmosphere does the author attempt to create?

1. pleasant anticipation
2. quiet peace
3. carefree gaiety
4. unrelieved despair
5. vague uncertainty

ANALYSIS

Usually this type of question can be quite difficult. It involves not only locating details but deciding the feeling that the author wishes these details to create in you, the reader.

Answers 1, 3 and 4 are inadequate. They involve some indication of Boris' feelings—of pleasure, of gaiety, of despair. But the passage contains no such indications.

Answer 5 and Answer 2 remain possibilities. While "quiet peace" could describe the situation, "vague uncertainty" is clearly superior as the answer. The whole place became "mysterious." Boris feels for his letter, the contents of which we are forced to guess. The uncertainty is climaxed by Boris' question which asks, in effect, "What will become of me?"

QUESTION 6

From this passage, which inference can most safely be drawn?

1. The house was topped by a lofty tower.
2. Boris is tired from his journey.
3. There is only one terrace before the house is reached.
4. The most imposing feature of the house is the door.
5. Boris intends to stay at the house for only a short time.

ANALYSIS

This question again calls for an inference, a conclusion which you, the reader, must draw from the facts which are presented.

Answers 1, 2, and 4 cannot be based on any facts in the passage. No tower is mentioned. Neither is the door. And Boris' feelings are not described. Answer 3 contradicts the facts in the passage. One terrace is mentioned in line 2 and a main terrace is mentioned in line 6. Clearly there are two terraces.

Answer 5 is correct because it represents the inference which "can most safely be drawn." Boris mentions getting back into the carriage. From this *fact* in the passage, we can *infer* that he intends to stay at the house for only a short time.

SUMMARY

What have we learned thus far from our study of this passage with respect to skills of interpretation?

1. READ THE SELECTION CAREFULLY.

2. IN SELECTING A TITLE THAT EXPRESSES THE MAIN IDEA, GO BACK TO THE SELECTION CONSTANTLY. ARRIVE AT THE CORRECT ANSWER BY A PROCESS OF ELIMINATION. Eliminate the possibilities which are clearly incorrect. Usually one will fall into this category. Eliminate the possibilities which are based on minor details. One or two of these will be given. From the remaining choices, you must select the one that expresses the main rather than the subordinate idea.

3. IN DRAWING INFERENCES, FIND THE CLUES IN THE PASSAGE FROM WHICH YOU CAN DRAW THE PROPER CONCLUSION. The clue may be a name, a place, an adjective, an object, an unusual word. You may have to reread the selection a few times before you locate the clue or the two details which can be linked to make a clue.

4. IN DETERMINING PURPOSE, ASK YOURSELF WHY THE AUTHOR WROTE THE PASSAGE, WHAT HE WANTED YOU, THE READER, TO UNDERSTAND OR FEEL. After you have read the passage several times, try to define the TOTAL IMPRESSION you get from your reading. The purposes of authors at various times may be to inform, to arouse anger, to poke fun at, to evoke pity, to amuse, and to urge to action, among others. Which of these predominates?

5. IN DETERMINING MOOD, TRY TO FIND WORDS WHICH CREATE EITHER AN ATMOSPHERE OR EVOKE AN EMOTION. This is related to the author's purpose but may not necessarily be his main purpose. There are two main guides to determining atmosphere: SELECTION OF DETAILS and USE OF ADJECTIVES AND ADVERBS.

Having derived these general guidelines from a study of our first passage, let us turn to a second.

Selection 2.

OPPORTUNITY

—Edward Rowland Sill

1 This I beheld, or dreamed it in a dream:—
2 There spread a cloud of dust along a plain;
3 And underneath the cloud, or in it, raged
4 A furious battle, and men yelled, and swords

5   Shocked upon swords and shields. A prince's banner
6   Wavered, then staggered backward, hemmed by foes.
7   A craven hung along the battle's edge,
8   And thought, "Had I a sword of keener steel—
9   That blue blade that the king's son bears—but this
10 Blunt thing!" he snapped and flung it from his hand,
11 And lowering crept away and left the field.
12 Then came the king's son, wounded, sore bestead,
13 And weaponless, and saw the broken sword,
14 Hilt-buried in the dry and trodden sand,
15 And ran and snatched it, and with battle-shout
16 Lifted afresh he hewed his enemy down,
17 And saved a great cause that heroic day.

QUESTION 1

The main purpose of the poem is to
1. tell what happened in a dream
2. relate an act of cowardice
3. applaud an act of bravery
4. teach a lesson in conduct
5. tell an interesting story

1.   1   2   3   4   5
     ‖   ‖   ‖   ‖   ‖

ANALYSIS

The question is difficult because it is possible to accept all the possible answers as being purposes of the author. Closer examination of the five choices shows that there can be only one *main* purpose among those listed.

Answers 1 and 5 are too general. Although the author does both of these—tell what happened in a dream and tell an interesting story—the question of why he did these is still unanswered.

Answers 2 and 3 are more specific. It is true that there are both acts of cowardice and bravery in the poem, but we still have to ask ourselves, "What is the point of the action in the poem?" Neither of these possibilities answers that question.

Answer 4 is correct because it focuses on the main purpose of the poem. Why did the poet write the poem? To teach us a lesson in conduct. What lesson? The lesson that, regardless of our station in life, we must make our own opportunities with the resources we have at hand.

QUESTION 2

The most logical words to continue the quotation on line 8 are
1. ". . . I could defend myself better."
2. ". . . but I cannot have the blue blade."
3. ". . . I could safely escape."
4. ". . . I could help defeat the enemy."
5. ". . . but what good would it do."

1.   1   2   3   4   5
     ‖   ‖   ‖   ‖   ‖

ANALYSIS

Answers 1 and 3 are not logical because we are told that the craven did get away and leave the field (line 11).

Answer 2 does not answer the question "What would he do?" Nor does Answer 5.

Answer 4 is correct because it logically follows from the incomplete thought, "Had I a sword of keener steel, I could help defeat the enemy." We know that these words are merely a "sour grapes" thought of the coward, but they are the "most logical" words to continue the quotation.

QUESTION 3

The word "craven" as used in this poem means a person who is best described as

1. envious
2. desirous
3. cowardly
4. traitorous
5. angry

ANALYSIS

We can rule out Answer 4 since there is no betrayal or treason mentioned. Answer 5 is not justified by the action in the poem, for, although the "craven" snaps the sword, there is no one he is angry with.

Both Answers 1 and 2 are not the best because they might describe the individual who desires the prince's blade and envies him his possession of it, but does so as an excuse for inaction.

Answer 3 is the best description because the "craven" hangs along the edge of the battle and creeps away, both actions of a cowardly person.

QUESTION 4

The poet speeds the action of the poem by effective use of enjambement (run-on lines) in all of the following EXCEPT

1. lines 3 and 4
2. lines 4 and 5
3. lines 5 and 6
4. lines 9 and 10
5. lines 10 and 11

ANALYSIS

Since this question involves the use of a literary term, you should consult THE VOCABULARY OF LITERATURE. There you find this definition of "enjambement"—"continuing on of a sentence from one line or couplet into the next without a stop at the end of the line."

Applying this definition to the lines mentioned in choices 1, 2, 3, 4, we note that line 3 runs into line 4 without a stop at the end of the line—"raged a furious battle." The same is true for lines 4 and 5—"swords shocked upon swords." Lines 5 and 6 are also an example of the enjambement or run-on line —"A prince's banner wavered." Finally, line 9 runs into line 10—"this blunt thing."

The correct answer: the lines where the poet does *not* use this poetic device are lines 10 and 11. There is punctuation at the end of line 10, a comma which forces us to pause, making it impossible for us to run ahead to line 11 unless we do so. This is contrary to the definition which indicates continuing "without a stop at the end of the line." Therefore, the correct answer is 5.

QUESTION 5

The most perfect line of iambic pentameter among the following is line

1. one
2. two
3. five
4. six
5. fourteen

1. 1 2 3 4 5
‖ ‖ ‖ ‖ ‖

ANALYSIS

This question, as will many of the questions dealing with literature, calls for special information. If you consult the LITERATURE VOCABULARY in this book, you will find the following definition of "iambic pentameter":

"Line of ten syllables divided into five feet, each composed of one unaccented and one accented syllable, in that order." Example:

"Wăs thís thĕ fáce thăt láunchĕd ă thóusănd shíps"

Checking the lines indicated, we find that four of the lines indicated have accented first syllables: lines one, five, six, and fourteen. Only line 2 follows strictly the definition of "iambic pentameter"

Thĕre spréad ă clóud ŏf dúst ălóng ă pláin

The correct answer of the most perfect line of iambic pentameter is Answer 2.

TIME TO PRACTICE:

---

20 SELECTIONS

Directions: **Read each of the following selections carefully. After each selection there are questions to be answered or statements to be completed. Select the best answer and underline it. Then blacken the appropriate space in the answer column to the right.**

Selection 1.

Yet the fact remains that as enthusiasm for Shakespearean drama has increased, the tendency has been steadily away from realism and spectacle and steadily toward a rediscovery of the Shakespearean play in conditions resembling its first staging. It has, for instance, been realized that the alternation of scenes— swift scenes following the major crises, gay scenes switching the mood from sadness, comedy breaking in on dire tragedy—enormously enhances the emotional effect of the whole play. Shakespeare wrote his plays to be acted at a single stretch. The alternation of scene and mood is like the orchestration of a symphony, the climaxes carefully prepared in subsidiary themes, the tension heightened or relaxed, the movement quickened or slowed to suit the general rhythm of the drama. It follows that Shakespeare cannot be successfully confined on a stage within a picture-frame set statically fixed throughout the three-quarters of an hour allotted to each act. The stage must be one on which the quick succession of scenes and rapid alternation of moods is technically possible.

1. The title below that best expresses the ideas of this passage is:
   (1) Shortening Shakespeare's Plays   (2) Modern Trends in Stage Design
   (3) Decline of the Picture-frame Set   (4) Appropriate Shakespearean Staging   (5) Revival of Interest in Shakespeare

   1.   1   2   3   4   5

2. The emotional effect in Shakespeare's plays results from
   (1) tension   (2) realism   (3) contrasts   (4) mood music   (5) elaborate spectacles

   2.   1   2   3   4   5

3. Certain scenes in a Shakespearean play are written to
   (1) provide a musical theme   (2) decrease production costs   (3) provide relief for the actors   (4) contribute to a desired effect   (5) show Shakespeare's versatility

   3.   1   2   3   4   5

Selection 2

Sir Walter Scott, the prince of prose romancers, should be reckoned among the great benefactors of mankind. Of the works of prose in the nineteenth century which have contributed to human happiness on the universal scale, the Waverley Novels hold a place by virtue of their millions of readers; and now, coming into the hands of the fourth generation, they are still one of the principal effective contemporary possessions of the English race in literature. Criticism, which sooner or later assails all works of great fame, has the most trifling effect upon them; they are invulnerable in the hearts of the people. They contain so much humanity in its plain style; they disclose such romantic scenes, such a stir of gallantry, such a high behavior, in connection with events and personages otherwise memorable; and they are, besides, so colored with the hues of the mind arising from local association, imaginative legend, historic glamor and the sense of the presence of fine action, that their reception by the heart is spontaneous.

4. The title below that best expresses the ideas of this passage is:
   (1) Sir Walter Scott, Newest Prince of Prose Writers   (2) Sir Walter Scott, First-ranking Literary Critic   (3) The Appeal of the Waverly Novels
   (4) The Characters in Scott's Novels   (5) The Criticism of Scott as a Novelist

   4.   1   2   3   4   5

5. The Waverley Novels appeal because of
   (1) the high rank of the characters   (2) their idealism and romanticism   (3) the timeliness of the period treated   (4) the historical accuracy of characters and events   (5) the absolute reliability of facts about famous places

   5.   1   2   3   4   5

Selection 3

It is no longer needful to labor Dickens' power as a portrayer of modern society nor the seriousness of his "criticism of life." But we are still learning to appreciate his supreme attainment as an artist. Richnesses of poetic imagery, modulations of emotional tone, subtleties of implication, complex unities of structure, intensities of psychological insight, a panoply of achievement, mount up to overwhelming triumph. Though contemporary readers perhaps still feel somewhat queasy about Dickens' sentiment, his comedy and his drama sweep all before them. Even his elaborate and multistranded plots are now seen as great symphonic compositions driving forward through theme and variation to the resolving chords on which they close.

6. The title below that best expresses the ideas of this passage is:
    (1) Dickens—a Portrayer of Modern Society   (2) Dickens as a Critic of His Times   (3) The Appeals of Dickens   (4) Psychological Insight   (5) A Weakness of Dickens

7. According to the passage, readers most recently have begun to appreciate Dickens'
    (1) feeling for culture   (2) criticisms of life   (3) rhythms   (4) literary references   (5) literary craftsmanship

8. The author suggests that Dickens was
    (1) a prophet   (2) a musician   (3) a playwright   (4) a wealthy man   (5) an artist

9. According to the passage, the endings of Dickens' works are most probably characterized by
    (1) frequent use of comic relief   (2) unexpected developments   (3) visually effective symbols   (4) a lack of sense of completion   (5) dramatic power

10. In which sentence is the main idea of this passage started?
    (1) first   (2) second   (3) third   (4) fourth   (5) fifth

Selection 4

Somewhere between 1860 and 1890, the dominant emphasis in American literature was radically changed. But it is obvious that this change was not necessarily a matter of conscious concern to all writers. In fact, many writers may seem to have been actually unaware of the shifting emphasis. Moreover, it is not possible to trace the steady march of the realistic emphasis from its first feeble notes to its dominant trumpet-note of unquestioned leadership. The progress of realism is, to change the figure, rather that of a small stream, receiving accessions from its tributaries at unequal points along its course, its progress now and then balked by the sand bars of opposition or the diffusing marshes of error and compromise. Again, it is apparent that any attempt to classify rigidly, as romanticists or realists, the writers of this period is doomed to failure, since it is not by virtue of the writer's conscious espousal of the romantic or realistic creed that he does much of his best work, but by virtue of that writer's sincere surrender to the atmosphere of the subject.

11. The title that best expresses the ideas of this passage is:
    (1) Classifying American Writers   (2) Leaders in American Fiction (3) The Sincerity of Writers (4) The Values of Realism (5) The Rise of Realism

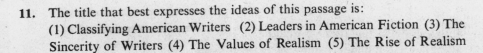

12. Which characteristic of writers does the author praise?
(1) their ability to compromise   (2) their allegiance to a "school"   (3) their opposition to change   (4) their awareness of literary trends   (5) their intellectual honesty

13. As used in the last sentence, *by virtue of* most nearly means
(1) in spite of   (2) by rejection of   (3) because of moral excellence   (4) through the force of   (5) connection with

14. In this passage, which statement does the author make about realism?
(1) It is too strong a force in current literature.   (2) It is to be preferred to romanticism.   (3) Its advocates are vitally concerned with its progress.
(4) Its origins are obscure.   (5) Its writers are very skillful.

15. One may infer from reading this selection that its author
(1) favors a return to realism in writing   (2) has little knowledge of the romantic movement in American literature   (3) views literature from a broad perspective   (4) is annoyed by the inconsistent approaches of American writers to their subjects   (5) finds American writers very easy to classify

Selection 5

For though the terms are often confused, obscurity is not at all the same thing as unintelligibility. Obscurity is what happens when a writer undertakes a theme and method for which the reader is not sufficiently prepared. Unintelligibility is what happens when the writer undertakes a theme and method for which he himself is not sufficiently prepared.

A good creation is an enlarging experience, and the act of enlargement must require the reader to extend himself. Only the thoroughly familiar—which is to say, the already encompassed—may reasonably be expected to be immediately clear. True, the surface of a poem may seem deceptively clear, thus leading the careless reader to settle for an easy first-response as the true total. But even in work of such surface clarity as Frost's, it will be a foolish reader indeed who permits himself the illusion that one easy reading will reveal all of the poem. In this sense, indeed, there can be no great poetry without obscurity.

16. The title that best expresses the ideas of this passage is:
(1) Enlarging Experience   (2) The Cult of Unintelligibility   (3) The Clarity of Robert Frost's Poems   (4) The Familiar in Poetry   (5) The Careful Writer

17. The author defines obscurity and unintelligibility in order to
(1) show his knowledge of literature   (2) please the reader   (3) set the stage for what follows   (4) clarify his own thinking   (5) defend unintelligibility

18. According to this selection, good poetry
(1) has surface clarity   (2) has figurative language   (3) confuses the reader
(4) requires more than one reading   (5) can be appreciated only by college students

19. Which quality would the author of this passage expect in a poet?
(1) sense of humor   (2) skill in rhyming   (3) use of the direct approach
(4) surface clarity   (5) knowledge of subject

20. The author of this selection implies that
(1) the understanding of literature requires effort   (2) most readers of literature read carelessly   (3) most modern poems are unintelligible   (4) obscure poems are inevitably great poems   (5) familiar poems are the most popular

21. As used in the passage, the word "encompassed" (line 8) most nearly means
(1) guided   (2) expected   (3) encountered   (4) described   (5) revised

Selection 6

A humorous remark or situation is, moreover, always a pleasure. We can go back to it and laugh at it again and again. One does not tire of the Pickwick Papers, or of Jacob's stories, any more than the child tires of a nursery tale which he knows by heart. Humor is a feeling and feelings can be revived. But wit, being an intellectual and not an emotional impression, suffers by repetition. A witticism is really an item of knowledge. Wit, again, is distinctly a gregarious quality; whereas humor may abide in the breast of a hermit. Those who live by themselves almost always have a dry humor. Wit is a city, humor a country, product. Wit is the accomplishment of persons who are busy with ideas; it is the fruit of intellectual cultivation and abounds in coffeehouses, in salons, and in literary clubs. But humor is the gift of those who are concerned with persons rather than ideas, and it flourishes chiefly in the middle and lower classes.

22. The title that best expresses the ideas of this passage is:
(1) Humorous Books   (2) Why Wit Pleases   (3) Wit and Humor   (4) Intelligence Versus Emotions   (5) A Feeling for Humor

23. According to the passage, a humorous story
(1) soon becomes monotonous   (2) bears repeating   (3) is popular with literary groups   (4) must be shared with others   (5) reveals the intelligence of the narrator

24. According to the passage, to be witty one needs to have
(1) solitude   (2) deep feelings   (3) a childlike attitude   (4) a mentally active life   (5) a pleasant disposition

25. It is probable that the paragraph preceding this one discussed the
(1) Pickwick Papers   (2) characteristics of literature   (3) characteristics of human nature   (4) characteristics of humor   (5) nature of human feelings

26. Which expression applies to humor?
(1) city-bred   (2) timeless   (3) idea-centered   (4) intellectual in appeal   (5) capitalistic in appeal

Selection 7

Parody is a selective joy. We are told by eminent psychologists that its charm lies in identification; the audience aligns itself with the parodist and feels superior to the celebrity who is the target—cutting him down to size, as it were. Yet you may have noticed that persons who are amused when they see intellectuals parodied are not always quite so hilarious when they see tycoons parodied as Babbitts. Even Voltaire, who lampooned everything, was rather annoyed at parodies of his own works.

In Steinese it might be put this way: one man's parody is another man's desecration is another man's exposure of pomposity is another man's envious imitation is another man's satire.

And the operative phrase, in a different sense, is "another man's"; for parody, we must never forget, is a parasite. It draws its vitality from someone else's looks or style or general body of work. It bores from within—the better to bring laughter out.

27. The title that best expresses the ideas of this passage is:
    (1) Another Man's Parody   (2) The Psychologist and the Parodist   (3) A Plea for Parody   (4) Parody—an Ancient Literary Form   (5) The Nature of Parody

28. It can be inferred that who would least likely be amused by the story of Babbitt?
    (1) a businessman   (2) an actor   (3) a scientist   (4) a philosopher   (5) an author

29. As used in this passage, the word "lampooned" (line 6) most nearly means   (1) envied   (2) suspected   (3) disapproved of   (4) ridiculed   (5) selected

30. According to the passage, parody is most likely to lack appeal for the
    (1) psychologist   (2) audience   (3) intellectual   (4) satirist   (5) victim

31. The author classes parody as a parasite because parody
    (1) lacks vitality   (2) cannot exist by itself   (3) is basically cruel   (4) is difficult to destroy   (5) is easily overlooked

32. The author's chief purpose in the second paragraph is to
    (1) prove that he is familiar with his subject   (2) write a parody of the style of Stein   (3) illustrate the power of parody to expose human weakness   (4) show that parody may be viewed in different ways by different people   (5) help the reader identify various kinds of parody

Selection 8

We still have, in short, all the weapons in the arsenal of satire: the rapier of wit, the broadsword of invective, the stiletto of parody, the Damoclean swords of sarcasm and irony. Their cutting edges are bright and sharp; they glisten with barbs guaranteed to stick and stay stuck in the thickest hide, or stab the most inflated Polonius in the arras. Yet though they hang well-oiled and ready to our hands, we tend to use them separately and gingerly. We are afraid of hurting someone's feelings or of being hurt in a return bout. We tremble at the prospect of treading on someone's moral corns. We are too full of the milque-toast of human kindness. We always see the Other Side of the Case, always remember that our Victim may have a Mom who loves him, always fear that we may be setting him back a few hundred hours in his psychiatric progress toward the Terrestrial City of Perfect Readjustment. Oh, yes. We poke and pry a bit. We pin an errant butterfly to a board or two. But for real lessons in the ungentlest of the arts we must turn back to the older masters.

33. The title below that best expresses the main idea of the passage is:
(1) Idle weapons (2) The well-adjusted person (3) Writing and psychiatry (4) Lessons and past masters (5) The advantages of satire

34. According to the passage, we avoid using satire because we
(1) are afraid of it (2) do not understand it (3) feel inferior to the older masters (4) are not inquisitive (5) are too uneducated in its use

35. As used in the passage, the word "gingerly" (line 6) most nearly means
(1) insincerely (2) effectively (3) clumsily (4) carefully (5) unhappily

36. Which device does the author *not* use in the passage?
(1) literary allusions (2) metaphor (3) anecdotes (4) sarcasm (5) wit

37. The passage suggests that modern man chiefly aspires to
(1) a sense of security (2) a feeling of aggressiveness (3) material wealth (4) freedom from hunger (5) protection from satire

38. The tone of the latter part of the passage is one of
(1) outraged dignity (2) quiet irony (3) grudging distrust (4) calm resignation (5) happy abandon

39. The passage suggests that Polonius (line 5) was
(1) sensitive (2) religious (3) tough (4) greedy (5) egotistical

40. The passage suggests that "invective" (line 2) is
(1) thin (2) obvious (3) gentle (4) careless (5) subtle

41. In this passage the author seems concerned that we
(1) do not have certain weapons available to us (2) pin butterflies to boards (3) are too considerate of our fellow man (4) do not appreciate art (5) regard satire as unnecessary

42. The "ungentlest of the arts" is
(1) satire (2) irony (3) sarcasm (4) wit (5) parody

	1	2	3	4	5
33.	‖	‖	‖	‖	‖
34.	‖	‖	‖	‖	‖
35.	‖	‖	‖	‖	‖
36.	‖	‖	‖	‖	‖
37.	‖	‖	‖	‖	‖
38.	‖	‖	‖	‖	‖
39.	‖	‖	‖	‖	‖
40.	‖	‖	‖	‖	‖
41.	‖	‖	‖	‖	‖
42.	‖	‖	‖	‖	‖

Selection 9

Gather ye rosebuds while ye may;
  Old Time is still a-flying;
And this same flower that smiles to-day
  To-morrow will be dying.

The glorious lamp of heaven, the sun,   5
  The higher he's a-getting,
The sooner will his race be run,
  And nearer he's to setting.

That age is best which is the first,
  When youth and blood are warmer;   10
But being spent, the worse and worst
  Times still succeed the former.

Then be not coy, but use your time,
   And while ye may, go marry;
For, having lost but once your prime,   15
   You may forever tarry.

                                             —Robert Herrick

43. The advice given by the poet is to   43. 1 2 3 4 5
     (1) enjoy the present   (2) prepare for the future   (3) remember your
     youth   (4) maintain a careful approach to life   (5) look ahead to old age

44. The reasons given for his "counsel" by the poet include *all* the following   44. 1 2 3 4 5
     EXCEPT
     (1) Things in nature die with age.   (2) Youth is the best time of life.   (3)
     Every day must come to a close.   (4) Shyness may result in spinsterhood.
     (5) The best in life lies in the future.

45. Examples of personification are found in   45. 1 2 3 4 5
     (1) lines 2 and 3   (2) lines 2 and 9   (3) lines 5 and 9   (4) lines 9 and
     10   (5) lines 11 and 12

46. Metaphors are found in   46. 1 2 3 4 5
     (1) lines 1 and 9   (2) lines 5 and 7   (3) lines 7 and 8   (4) lines 11 and 12
     (5) lines 13 and 15

47. The tone of the poem may best be described as   47. 1 2 3 4 5
     (1) sarcastic   (2) ironic   (3) resentful   (4) casual   (5) formal

     Selection 10

I deny not, but that it is of greatest concernment in the Church and Commonwealth, to have a vigilant eye how books demean themselves as well as men;
and thereafter to confine, imprison, and do sharpest justice on them as male-
factors; for books are not absolutely dead things, but do contain a potency of
life in them to be as active as that soul was whose progeny they are; nay, they
do preserve as in a vial the purest efficacy and extraction of that living intellect
that bred them. (2) I know they are as lively, and as vigorously productive, as
those fabulous dragon's teeth; and being sown up and down, may chance to
spring up armed men. (3) And yet, on the other hand, unless wariness be used, as
good almost kill a man as kill a good book: Who kills a man kills a reasonable
creature, God's image; but he who destroys a good book, kills reason itself,
kills the image of God, as it were in the eye. (4) Many a man lives a burden to
the earth; but a good book is the precious life-blood of a master-spirit, em-
balmed and treasured up on purpose to a life beyond life. (5) 'Tis true, no age
can restore a life, whereof perhaps there is no great loss; and revolutions of
ages do not oft recover the loss of a rejected truth, for the want of which whole
nations fare the worse.
(6) We should be wary therefore what persecution we raise against the living
labors of public men, how we spill that seasoned life of man, preserved and
stored up in books; since we see a kind of homicide may be thus committed,
sometimes a martyrdom, and if it extend to the whole impression, a kind of
massacre; whereof the execution ends not in the slaying of an elemental life,
but strikes at that ethereal and fifth essence, the breath of reason itself, slays
an immortality rather than a life.

                                             —John Milton

48. The main purpose of the passage is to warn against the evils of
(1) homicide (2) revolution (3) armed men (4) books (5) censorship

49. The main idea is contained in sentence
(1) one (2) three (3) four (4) five (5) six

50. The "potency of life" referred to in the first sentence was given by
(1) the author (2) the reader (3) future generations (4) the church (5) the commonwealth

51. The persecution Milton argues against is compared to *all* of the following EXCEPT
(1) homicide (2) execution (3) massacre (4) war (5) killing eternal life

52. Milton claims that those who persecute "the living labors of public men" commit a crime against
(1) the church (2) the commonwealth (3) God (4) their fellow men (5) reason

Selection 11

Death, be not proud, though some have called thee
Mighty and dreadful, for thou art not so:
For those whom thou think'st thou dost overthrow
Die not, poor Death, nor yet canst thou kill me.
From rest and sleep, which but thy pictures be,   5
Much pleasure; then from thee much more must flow;
And soonest our best men with thee do go,
Rest of their bones, and soul's delivery.
Thou'rt slave to Fate, Chance, kings, and desperate men,
And dost with poison, war, and sickness dwell,   10
And poppy or charms can make us sleep as well
And better than thy stroke. Why swell'st thou then?
One short sleep past, we wake eternally,
And death shall be no more. Death, thou shalt die!

—John Donne

53. The attitude of the poet toward death is best characterized as one of
(1) resignation (2) acceptance (3) defiance (4) indifference (5) fear

54. Evidence that the poet is a devout person is found in line
(1) one (2) four (3) six (4) nine (5) thirteen

55. The form of the poem is that of
(1) an Elizabethan sonnet (2) an English sonnet (3) an Italian sonnet
(4) a Shakespearean sonnet (5) a Spenserian sonnet

56. The figures of speech that run throughout the poem are
(1) apostrophe and personification (2) apostrophe and metaphor (3) personification and simile (4) personification and hyperbole (5) simile and metaphor

57. The title of this 17th century poem was used in this century as the title of
(1) a poem by Robert Frost (2) a novel by John Steinbeck (3) a play by Arthur Miller (4) a biography by John Gunther (5) a short story by O. Henry

Selection 12

Besides, our histories of six thousand moons make no mention of any other regions, than the two great empires of Lilliput and Blefuscu. Which two mighty powers have, as I was going to tell you, been engaged in a most obstinate war for six and thirty moons past. It began upon the following occasion. It is allowed on all hands, that the primitive way of breaking eggs before we eat them, was upon the larger end: but his present Majesty's grandfather, while he was a boy, going to eat an egg, and breaking it according to the ancient practice, happened to cut one of his fingers. Whereupon the Emperor his father published an edict, commanding all his subjects, upon great penalties, to break the smaller end of their eggs. The people so highly resented this law, that our histories tell us there have been six rebellions raised on that account; wherein one Emperor lost his life, and another his crown. These civil commotions were constantly fomented by the monarchs of Blefuscu; and when they were quelled, the exiles always fled for refuge to that empire. It is computed that eleven thousand persons have, at several times, suffered death, rather than submit to break their eggs at the smaller end. Many hundred large volumes have been published upon this controversy: but the books of the Big-Endians have been long forbidden, and the whole party rendered incapable by law of holding employments. During the course of these troubles, the Emperors of Blefuscu did frequently expostulate by their ambassadors, accusing us of making a schism in religion, by offending against a fundamental doctrine of our great prophet Lustrog, in the fifty-fourth chapter of the *Brundecral* (which is their Alcoran). This, however, is thought to be a mere strain upon the text: for the words are these; *That all true believers shall break their eggs at the convenient end:* and which is the convenient end seems, in my humble opinion, to be left to every man's conscience, or at least in the power of the chief magistrate to determine. Now the Big-Endian exiles have found so much credit in the Emperor of Blefuscu's court, and so much private assistance and encouragement from their party here at home, that a bloody war hath been carried on between the two empires for six and thirty moons with various success; during which time we have lost forty capital ships, and a much greater number of smaller vessels, together with thirty thousand of our best seamen and soldiers; and the damage received by the enemy is reckoned to be somewhat greater than ours. However, they have now equipped a numerous fleet, and are just preparing to make a descent upon us; and his Imperial Majesty, placing great confidence in your valour and strength, hath commanded me to lay this account of his affairs before you.

—Jonathan Swift

58. The chief purpose of the author of this account is to
    (1) give an historical account of the war between Blefuscu and Lilliput
    (2) satirize war   (3) criticize the Emperor of Blefuscu   (4) defend the Big-Endians   (5) attack some customs of mankind

58. 1 2 3 4 5

59. According to the passage, the conflict between Blefuscu and Lilliput arose because of
    (1) religious differences   (2) hatred between the Emperors   (3) the Big-Endian exiles   (4) the monarch of Blefuscu   (5) no reason at all

59. 1 2 3 4 5

60. The true statement among the following is:
(1) The Little-Endians are now in control in Blefuscu   (2) The Big-Endians are now in control in Blefuscu   (3) The Little-Endians are now in control in Lilliput   (4) The Big-Endians are now in control in Lilliput (5) Eggs are broken at the convenient end in both Blefuscu and Lilliput

60. 1   2   3   4   5
     ‖ ‖ ‖ ‖ ‖

61. All of the following are contributing to the obstinate war EXCEPT
(1) the Big-Endian exiles in Blefuscu   (2) the Big-Endians in Lilliput   (3) the monarchs of Blefuscu   (4) the Imperial Majesty of Lilliput   (5) the chief magistrate of Lilliput

61. 1   2   3   4   5
     ‖ ‖ ‖ ‖ ‖

62. The next step in the present war, according to the author, is to be
(1) an invasion of Blefuscu   (2) an invasion of Lilliput   (3) land action on Blefuscu   (4) land action on Lilliput   (5) bloody battles on both islands

62. 1   2   3   4   5
     ‖ ‖ ‖ ‖ ‖

Selection 13

The curfew tolls the knell of parting day,
The lowing herd wind slowly o'er the lea,
The ploughman homeward plods his weary
   way,
And leaves the world to darkness and to me.

Now fades the glimmering landscape on the
   sight,   5
And all the air a solemn stillness holds,
Save where the beetle wheels his droning
   flight,
And drowsy tinklings lull the distant folds:

Save where from yonder ivy-mantled tower
The moping owl does to the moon com-
   plain   10
Of such as, wandering near her secret
   bower,
Molest her ancient solitary reign.

Beneath those rugged elms, that yew-tree's
   shade
Where heaves the turf in many a moldering
   heap,
Each in his narrow cell for ever laid,   15
The rude forefathers of the hamlet sleep.

The breezy call of incense-breathing morn,
The swallow twittering from the straw-
   built shed,
The cock's shrill clarion, or the echoing
   horn,
No more shall rouse them from their lowly
   bed.   20

For them no more the blazing hearth shall
  burn,
Or busy housewife ply her evening care:
No children run to lisp their sire's return,
Or climb his knees the envied kiss to share.

Oft did the harvest to their sickle yield,   25
Their furrow oft the stubborn glebe has
  broke;
How jocund did they drive their team
  afield!
How bowed the woods beneath their sturdy
  stroke!

Let not ambition mock their useful toil,
Their homely joys, and destiny obscure;   30
Nor grandeur hear with a disdainful smile
The short and simple annals of the poor.

The boast of heraldry, the pomp of power,
And all that beauty, all that wealth e'er
  gave
Awaits alike th' inevitable hour:—   35
The paths of glory lead but to the grave.

—Thomas Gray

63. Gray's main purpose in this section of the poem is to
(1) create an attractive rural setting   (2) describe the sorrow of those
who mourn the dead   (3) defend the life of the poor farmers   (4)
deplore the treatment of the poor farmers   (5) criticize the lack of
ambition of the poor farmers

63. 1 2 3 4 5

64. The *incorrectly* matched figure of speech and the line in which it occurs is
(1) alliteration—line 6   (2) onomatopoeia—line 8   (3) metaphor—line 9
(4) apostrophe—line 27   (5) personification—line 29

64. 1 2 3 4 5

65. A word in this passage *not* used in its ordinary meaning is
(1) knell—line 1   (2) complain—line 10   (3) rude—line 16   (4) horn—
line 19   (5) jocund—line 27

65. 1 2 3 4 5

66. Inversion is found in *all* of these lines EXCEPT
(1) 5   (2) 6   (3) 24   (4) 30   (5) 34

66. 1 2 3 4 5

67. This poem giving the poet's meditations on death may be considered
(1) a ballad   (2) an elegy   (3) a eulogy   (4) a monologue   (5) an ode

67. 1 2 3 4 5

Selection 14

She dwelt among the untrodden ways
  Beside the springs of Dove,
A Maid whom there were none to praise
  And very few to love;

A violet by a mossy stone   5
  Half hidden from the eye!
—Fair as a star, when only one
  Is shining in the sky.

She lived unknown, and few could know
  When Lucy ceased to be;   10
But she is in her grave, and, oh,
  The difference to me!

              —William Wordsworth

68. The emotion which is strongest in the poem is
    (1) nostalgia (2) love (3) grief (4) modesty (5) gratitude

69. Lucy's character is best brought out by the word
    (1) fair (2) untrodden (3) maid (4) violet (5) unknown

70. The diction (use of words) in the poem is characterized by
    (1) extreme simplicity   (2) deliberate vagueness   (3) flowery adjectives
    (4) unexpected contexts (5) archaic meanings

71. An example of euphemism is found in line
    (1) 3 (2) 6 (3) 8 (4) 10 (5) 12

72. An example of a simile is found in line
    (1) 5 (2) 7 (3) 9 (4) 11 (5) 12

	1	2	3	4	5
68.	‖	‖	‖	‖	‖
69.	‖	‖	‖	‖	‖
70.	‖	‖	‖	‖	‖
71.	‖	‖	‖	‖	‖
72.	‖	‖	‖	‖	‖

Selection 15

I wander'd lonely as a cloud
That floats on high o'er vales and hills,
When all at once I saw a crowd,
A host of golden daffodils,
Beside the lake, beneath the trees,   5
Fluttering and dancing in the breeze.

Continuous as the stars that shine
And twinkle on the Milky Way,
They stretch'd in never-ending line
Along the margin of a bay: 10
Ten thousand saw I at a glance
Tossing their heads in sprightly dance.

The waves beside them danced, but they
Out-did the sparkling waves in glee:—
A Poet could not but be gay   15
In such a jocund company!
I gazed—and gazed—but little thought
What wealth the show to me had brought;

For oft, when on my couch I lie
In vacant or in pensive mood,   20

They flash upon that inward eye
Which is the bliss of solitude;
And then my heart with pleasure fills,
And dances with the daffodils.

—William Wordsworth

73. The emotion expressed in this poem is
(1) sympathy   (2) nostalgia   (3) regret   (4) serenity   (5) joy

73.   1   2   3   4   5

74. The poet relives his experience by
(1) returning to the scene in person   (2) recollecting it in thought   (3) seeing pictures he had taken   (4) discussing it with company   (5) sharing it with others

74.   1   2   3   4   5

75. Similes are found in lines
(1) one and four   (2) one and seven   (3) four and seven   (4) seven and eleven   (5) seven and thirteen

75.   1   2   3   4   5

76. Line 11 contains an example of
(1) apostrophe   (2) hyperbole   (3) metaphor   (4) metonymy   (5) synecdoche

76.   1   2   3   4   5

77. An example of the pathetic fallacy is found in lines
(1) one and two   (2) seven and eight   (3) thirteen and fourteen   (4) seventeen and eighteen   (5) twenty-three and twenty-four

77.   1   2   3   4   5

Selection 16

(1) Rip Van Winkle, however, was one of those happy mortals, of foolish, well-oiled dispositions, who take the world easy, eat white bread or brown, which ever can be got with least thought or trouble, and would rather starve on a penny than work for a pound. (2) If left to himself, he would have whistled life away, in perfect contentment; but his wife kept continually dinning in his ears about his idleness, his carelessness, and the ruin he was bringing on his family. (3) Morning, noon, and night, her tongue was incessantly going, and everything he said or did was sure to produce a torrent of household eloquence. (4) Rip had but one way of replying to all lectures of the kind, and that, by frequent use, had grown into a habit. (5) He shrugged his shoulders, shook his head, cast up his eyes, but said nothing. (6) This, however, always provoked a fresh volley from his wife, so that he was fain to draw off his forces, and take to the outside of the house—the only side which, in truth, belongs to a henpecked husband.

Rip's sole domestic adherent was his dog Wolf, who was as much henpecked as his master; for Dame Van Winkle regarded them as companions in idleness, and even looked upon Wolf with an evil eye as the cause of his master's going so often astray. True it is, in all points of spirit befitting an honorable dog, he was as courageous an animal as ever scoured the woods—but what courage can withstand the ever-doing and all-besetting terrors of a woman's tongue? The moment Wolf entered the house, his crest fell, his tail drooped to the ground, or curled between his legs, he sneaked about with a gallows air, casting many a sidelong glance at Dame Van Winkle, and at the least flourish of a broomstick or ladle, he would fly to the door with yelping precipitation.

Times grew worse and worse with Rip Van Winkle as years of matrimony rolled on; a tart temper never mellows with age, and a sharp tongue is the only edged tool that grows keener with constant use. For a long while he used to console himself, when driven from home, by frequenting a kind of perpetual club of the sages, philosophers, and other idle personages of the village, which held its sessions on a bench before a small inn, designated by a rubicund portrait of His Majesty George the Third. Here they used to sit in the shade through a long, lazy summer's day, talking listlessly over village gossip, or telling endless, sleepy stories about nothing. But it would have been worth any statesman's money to have heard the profound discussions which sometimes took place, when by chance an old newspaper fell into their hands from some passing traveller. How solemnly they would listen to the contents, as drawled out by Derrick Van Brummel, the school-master, a dapper learned little man, who was not to be daunted by the most gigantic word in the dictionary; and how sagely they would deliberate upon public events some months after they had taken place.

The opinions of this junto were completely controlled by Nicholas Vedder, a patriarch of the village and landlord of the inn, at the door of which he took his seat from morning till night, just moving sufficiently to avoid the sun, and keep in the shade of a large tree; so that the neighbors could tell the hour by his movements as accurately as by a sun-dial.

—Washington Irving

78. The story takes place about
(1) 1660   (2) 1770   (3) 1800   (4) 1812   (5) 1848

78. 1   2   3   4   5

79. An example of Irving's sense of humor may be found in sentence
(1) 2   (2) 3   (3) 4   (4) 5   (5) 6

79. 1   2   3   4   5

80. The blame for Rip's conduct was placed by Dame Van Winkle on
(1) Wolf   (2) George the Third   (3) Derrick Van Bummel   (4) Nicholas Vedder   (5) other idle villagers

80. 1   2   3   4   5

81. Rip may be described by *all* of the following adjectives EXCEPT
(1) henpecked   (2) easygoing   (3) happy   (4) complaining   (5) resigned

81. 1   2   3   4   5

82. *All* of these are correctly matched EXCEPT
(1) Dame Van Winkle—sharp-tongued   (2) Derrick Van Bummel—learned   (3) George the Third—ruddy   (4) Wolf—honorable   (5) Nicholas Vedder—restless

82. 1   2   3   4   5

A WORD ABOUT TESTS: Do you consider yourself a person who "goes to pieces" on tests? Cheer up! Psychologists claim that more than ninety per cent of us think we don't perform well on tests *of any kind*. Nobody likes tests. But more than 80% of the people who have taken the High School Equivalency Tests in the New York area, for example, have passed them. They must be doing something right. And so can you—with the right attitude and careful preparation.

Selection 17

We must learn to reawaken and keep ourselves awake, not by mechanical aids, but by an infinite expectation of the dawn, which does not forsake us in our soundest sleep. I know of no more encouraging fact than the unquestionable ability of man to elevate his life by a conscious endeavor. It is something to be able to paint a particular picture, or to carve a statue, and so to make a few objects beautiful; but it is far more glorious to carve and paint the very atmosphere and medium through which we look, which morally we can do. To affect the quality of the day, that is the highest of arts. Every man is tasked to make his life, even in its details, worthy of the contemplation of his most elevated and critical hour. If we refused, or rather used up, such paltry information as we get, the oracles would distinctly inform us how this might be done.

I went to the woods because I wished to live deliberately, to front only the essential facts of life, and see if I could not learn what it had to teach, and not, when I came to die, discover that I had not lived. I did not wish to live what was not life, living is so dear; nor did I wish to practise resignation, unless it was quite necessary. I wanted to live deep and suck out all the marrow of life, to live so sturdily and Spartan-like as to put to rout all that was not life, to cut a broad swath and shave close, to drive life into a corner, and reduce it to its lowest terms, and, if it proved to be mean, why then to get the whole and genuine meanness of it, and publish its meanness to the world; or if it were sublime, to know it by experience, and be able to give a true account of it in my next excursion. For most men, it appears to me, are in a strange uncertainty about it, whether it is of the devil or of God, and have *somewhat hastily* concluded that it is the chief end of man here to 'glorify God and enjoy him forever.'

Still we live meanly, like ants; though the fable tells us that we were long ago changed into men; like pygmies we fight with cranes; it is error upon error, and clout upon clout, and our best virtue has for its occasion a superfluous and evitable wretchedness. Our life is frittered away by detail. An honest man has hardly need to count more than his ten fingers, or in extreme cases he may add his ten toes, and lump the rest. Simplicity, simplicity, simplicity! I say, let your affairs be as two or three, and not a hundred or a thousand; instead of a million count half a dozen, and keep your accounts on your thumb-nail.

—Henry Thoreau

83. The best statement of the reason why Thoreau went to the woods is that he went to
(1) discover that he had not lived   (2) live meanly, like ants   (3) practice resignation   (4) reduce life to its simplest terms   (5) glorify God

83. 1 2 3 4 5
     || || || || ||

84. Thoreau is disturbed by *all* of the following EXCEPT
(1) man's failure to make use of each and every day   (2) man's concern for petty detail   (3) man's uncertainty about the purpose of life   (4) man's ability to lift himself by conscious effort   (5) man's low estimate of himself

84. 1 2 3 4 5
     || || || || ||

85. Thoreau thinks that life should be *all* of the following EXCEPT
(1) Spartan-like   (2) complicated   (3) creative   (4) noble   (5) moral

85. 1 2 3 4 5
     || || || || ||

86. All of the following words as used in this selection are correctly defined EXCEPT
(1) deliberately—unhurriedly   (2) front—confront   (3) swath—space
(4) mean—nasty   (5) frittered—wasted

86. 1 2 3 4 5
     || || || || ||

87. The tone of the selection is
(1) bitter cynicism   (2) moral indignation   (3) flippant humor   (4) quiet resignation   (5) self-congratulation

87. 1 2 3 4 5
     || || || || ||

Selection 18

The House of the Seven Gables, antique as it now looks, was not the first habitation erected by civilized man on precisely the same spot of ground. Pyncheon Street formerly bore the humbler appellation of Maule's Lane, from the name of the original occupant of the soil, before whose cottage-door it was a cowpath. A natural spring of soft and pleasant water—a rare treasure on the sea-girt peninsula, where the Puritan settlement was made—had early induced Matthew Maule to build a hut, shaggy with thatch, at this point, although somewhat too remote from what was then the centre of the village. In the growth of the town, however, after some thirty or forty years, the site covered by this rude hovel had become exceedingly desirable in the eyes of a prominent and powerful personage, who asserted plausible claims to the proprietorship of this, and a large adjacent tract of land, on the strength of a grant from the legislature. Colonel Pyncheon, the claimant, as we gather from whatever traits of him are preserved, was characterized by an iron energy of purpose. Matthew Maule, on the other hand, though an obscure man, was stubborn in the defence of what he considered his right; and, for several years, he succeeded in protecting the acre or two of earth, which, with his own toil, he had hewn out of the primeval forest, to be his garden-ground and homestead. No written record of this dispute is known to be in existence. Our acquaintance with the whole subject is derived chiefly from tradition. It would be bold, therefore, and possibly unjust, to venture a decisive opinion as to its merits; although it appears to have been at least a matter of doubt, whether Colonel Pyncheon's claim were not unduly stretched, in order to make it cover the small metes and bounds of Matthew Maule. What greatly strengthens such a suspicion is the fact that this controversy between two ill-matched antagonists—at a period, moreover, laud it as we may, when personal influence had far more weight than now—remained for years undecided, and came to a close only with the death of the party occupying the disputed soil. The mode of his death, too, affects the mind differently, in our day, from what it did a century and a half ago. It was a death that blasted with strange horror the humble name of the dweller in the cottage, and made it seem almost a religious act to drive the plough over the little area of his habitation, and obliterate his place and memory from among men.

Old Matthew Maule, in a word, was executed for the crime of witchcraft. He was one of the martyrs to that terrible delusion, which should teach us, among its other morals, that the influential classes, and those who take upon themselves to be leaders of the people, are fully liable to all the passionate error that has ever characterized the maddest mob.

—Nathaniel Hawthorne

88. The events described in the passage took place
    (1) 10 years earlier   (2) 50 years earlier   (3) 100 years earlier   (4) 150 years earlier   (5) 250 years earlier

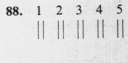

89. In the controversy between Matthew Maule and Colonel Pyncheon, the author
    (1) takes no sides   (2) feels Maule is absolutely right   (3) feels Pyncheon is absolutely right   (4) has doubts about Maule's position   (5) has doubts about Pyncheon's position

90. All of the following are true about Maule's house EXCEPT
(1) he built it himself   (2) it was on a plot of one to two acres   (3) it was located near a spring   (4) it was known as the House of the Seven Gables (5) it was destroyed after his death

90.   1   2   3   4   5
    || || || || ||

91. The author's knowledge of the Maule-Pyncheon dispute is based on
(1) histories of the time   (2) oral tradition   (3) official records   (4) personal acquaintance with the disputants   (5) legal documents

91.   1   2   3   4   5
    || || || || ||

92. The author feels that the witchcraft trials were
(1) brought about by Col. Pyncheon   (2) condoned by the community leaders   (3) justified under any circumstances   (4) justified when they took place   (5) religious acts

92.   1   2   3   4   5
    || || || || ||

Selection 19

It is impossible to conceive of a human creature more wholly desolate and forlorn than Eliza, when she turned her footsteps from Uncle Tom's cabin.

Her husband's sufferings and dangers, and the danger of her child, all blended in her mind, with a confused and stunning sense of the risk she was running, in leaving the only home she had ever known, and cutting loose from the protection of a friend whom she loved and revered. Then there was the parting from every familiar object,—the place where she had grown up, the trees under which she had played, the groves where she had walked many an evening in happier days, by the side of her young husband,—everything, as it lay in the clear, frosty starlight, seemed to speak reproachfully to her, and ask her whither could she go from a home like that?

But stronger than all was maternal love, wrought into a paroxysm of frenzy by the near approach of a fearful danger. Her boy was old enough to have walked by her side, and, in an indifferent case, she would only have led him by the hand; but now the bare thought of putting him out of her arms made her shudder, and she strained him to her bosom with a convulsive grasp, as she went rapidly forward.

The frosty ground creaked beneath her feet, and she trembled at the sound; every quaking leaf and fluttering shadow sent the blood backward to her heart, and quickened her footsteps. She wondered within herself at the strength that seemed to be come upon her; for she felt the weight of her boy as if it had been a feather, and every flutter of fear seemed to increase the supernatural power that bore her on, while from her pale lips burst forth, in frequent ejaculations, the prayer to a Friend above—"Lord, help! Lord, save me!"

If it were *your* Harry, mother, or your Willie, that were going to be torn from you by a brutal trader, to-morrow morning,—if you had seen the man, and heard that the papers were signed and delivered, and you had only from twelve o'clock till morning to make good your escape,—how fast could *you* walk?

                                     —Harriet Beecher Stowe

93. By her question, the author is seeking to evoke *in the reader* the feeling of
(1) despair   (2) indignation   (3) sadness   (4) nostalgia   (5) wonder

93.   1   2   3   4   5
    || || || || ||

94. The imminent danger facing Eliza is
(1) the selling of her husband   (2) the selling of her son   (3) the selling of Uncle Tom   (4) the selling of her friend   (5) her own being sold

95. The "friend" Eliza was leaving was
(1) Harry   (2) Willie   (3) her young husband   (4) her boy   (5) Uncle Tom

96. Eliza was accompanied in her flight by
(1) a friend   (2) her husband   (3) her mother   (4) her son   (5) Uncle Tom

97. All of the following moved Eliza emotionally during her flight EXCEPT
(1) a mother's love   (2) a departure from the familiar   (3) a feeling of risk   (4) a sense of danger   (5) a resignation to her fate

Selection 20

"Don't you know what a feud is?"

"Never heard of it before—tell me about it."

"Well," says Buck, "a feud is this way: A man has a quarrel with another man, and kills him; then that other man's brother kills *him*; then the other brothers, on both sides, goes for one another; then the *cousins* chip in—and by and by everybody's killed off, and there ain't no more feud. But it's kind of slow, and takes a long time."

"Has this one been going on long, Buck?"

"Well, I should *reckon!* It started thirty years ago, or some'ers along there. There was trouble 'bout something, and then a lawsuit to settle it; and the suit went agin one of the men, and so he up and shot the man that won the suit—which he would naturally do, of course. Anybody would."

"What was the trouble about, Buck—land?"

"I reckon maybe—I don't know."

"Well, who done the shooting? Was it a Grangerford or a Shepherdson?"

"Laws, how do *I* know? It was so long ago."

"Don't anybody know?"

"Oh, yes, pa knows, I reckon, and some of the other old people: but they don't know now what the row was about in the first place."

"Has there been many killed, Buck?"

"Yes; right smart chance of funerals. But they don't always kill. Pa's got a few buckshot in him; but he don't mind it 'cuz he don't weigh much, anyway. Bob's been carved up with a bowie, and Tom's been hurt once or twice."

"Has anybody been killed this year, Buck?"

"Yes; we got one and they got one. 'Bout three months ago my cousin Bud, fourteen year old, was riding through the woods on t'other side of the river, and didn't have no weapon with him, which was blame' foolishness, and in a lonesome place he hears a horse a-coming behind him, and sees old Baldy Shepherdson a-linkin' after him with his gun in his hand and his white hair a-flying in the wind; and 'stead of jumping off and taking to the brush, Bud 'lowed he could outrun him; so they had it, nip and tuck, for five mile or more, the old man a-gaining all the time; so at last Bud seen it warn't any use, so he stopped and faced around so as to have the bullet-holes in front, you know, and the old man he rode up and shot him down. But he didn't git much chance to enjoy his luck, for inside of a week our folks laid *him* out."

"I reckon that old man was a coward, Buck."

"I reckon he *warn't* a coward. Not by a blame' sight. There ain't a coward amongst them Shepherdsons—not a one. And there ain't no cowards amongst the Grangerfords either. Why, that old man kep' up his end in a fight one day for half an hour against three Grangerfords, and come out winner. They was all a-horseback; he lit off of his horse and got behind a little wood-pile, and kep' his horse before him to stop the bullets; but the Grangerfords stayed on their horses and capered around the old man, and peppered away at him, and he peppered away at them. Him and his horse went home pretty leaky and crippled, but the Grangerfords had to be *fetched* home—and one of 'em was dead, and another died the next day. No, sir; if a body's out hunting for cowards he don't want to fool any time amongst them Shepherdsons, becuz they don't breed any of that *kind*."

Next Sunday we all went to church, about three mile, everybody a-horseback. The men took their guns along, so did Buck, and kept them between their knees or stood them handy against the wall. The Shepherdsons done the same. It was pretty ornery preaching—all about brotherly love, and such-like tiresomeness; but everybody said it was a good sermon, and they all talked it over going home, and had such a powerful lot to say about faith and good works and free grace and preforeordestination.

—Mark Twain

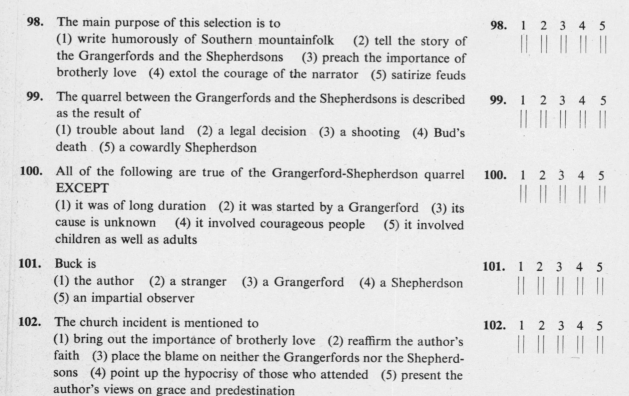

98.   The main purpose of this selection is to
(1) write humorously of Southern mountainfolk   (2) tell the story of the Grangerfords and the Shepherdsons   (3) preach the importance of brotherly love   (4) extol the courage of the narrator   (5) satirize feuds

98.   1   2   3   4   5

99.   The quarrel between the Grangerfords and the Shepherdsons is described as the result of
(1) trouble about land   (2) a legal decision   (3) a shooting   (4) Bud's death   (5) a cowardly Shepherdson

99.   1   2   3   4   5

100.   All of the following are true of the Grangerford-Shepherdson quarrel EXCEPT
(1) it was of long duration   (2) it was started by a Grangerford   (3) its cause is unknown   (4) it involved courageous people   (5) it involved children as well as adults

100.   1   2   3   4   5

101.   Buck is
(1) the author   (2) a stranger   (3) a Grangerford   (4) a Shepherdson   (5) an impartial observer

101.   1   2   3   4   5

102.   The church incident is mentioned to
(1) bring out the importance of brotherly love   (2) reaffirm the author's faith   (3) place the blame on neither the Grangerfords nor the Shepherdsons   (4) point up the hypocrisy of those who attended   (5) present the author's views on grace and predestination

102.   1   2   3   4   5

ANSWERS TO *Reading Selections in Literature*

1. 4	27. 5	53. 3	79. 5
2. 3	28. 1	54. 5	80. 1
3. 4	29. 4	55. 3	81. 4
4. 3	30. 5	56. 1	82. 5
5. 2	31. 2	57. 4	83. 4
6. 3	32. 4	58. 2	84. 4
7. 5	33. 1	59. 3	85. 2
8. 5	34 1	60. 3	86. 4
9. 5	35. 4	61. 5	87. 2
10. 2	36. 3	62. 2	88. 4
11. 5	37. 1	63. 3	89. 5
12. 5	38. 2	64. 4	90. 4
13. 4	39. 5	65. 3	91. 2
14. 4	40. 2	66. 5	92. 2
15. 3	41. 3	67. 2	93. 2
16. 1	42. 1	68. 3	94. 2
17. 3	43. 1	69. 4	95. 5
18. 4	44. 5	70. 1	96. 4
19. 5	45. 1	71. 4	97. 5
20. 1	46. 2	72. 2	98. 5
21. 3	47. 4	73. 5	99. 2
22. 3	48. 5	74. 2	100. 2
23. 2	49. 5	75. 2	101. 3
24. 4	50. 1	76. 2	102. 4
25. 4	51. 4	77. 3	
26. 2	52. 5	78. 2	

What's your score?

_____right, _____wrong

Excellent   90–100
Good   80–89
Fair   65–79

A WORD ABOUT SCORES: If you did well, don't knock it. You're likely to do equally well—or better—on the real test. If you're not satisfied with your score though, don't get discouraged. Try to find out why you failed. Were you careless? Perhaps you need to review the hints on reading comprehension. Did you lack information on some essential point? Turn back to the study section and learn that point. The High School Equivalency Test is one *you* are going to pass. We can help—but the essential factor is your determination and your use of these materials. We're counting on you. We haven't lost a High School Equivalency Diploma candidate yet!

A WORD ABOUT REVIEW: **Don't be alarmed at all the review material in this chapter. We've included much more than you will probably need simply because we didn't want to omit anything that might be useful to you. Remember that the High School Equivalency Tests examine background, not classroom or book learning. They test the kind of information you've acquired from reading newspapers and magazines, from T.V. and radio, from working at a job or running a home. They test experience and common sense. The review section simply organizes knowledge in this field, reminds you of some things you may have forgotten, fills in some gaps you may have in your background.**

For Further Reading

Barron's Preparation for the High School Equivalency Examination—Reading Interpretation Tests, by Eugene J. Farley, provides extensive practice material and drill in this area.

5

The Test of Interpretation of Reading Materials in the Social Studies

To help you prepare for the part of the test which requires that you read passages in the Social Studies, we have prepared three *Selected Vocabulary Lists* totaling 401 words which are widely used in American and world history, government, and economics.

THE VOCABULARY OF SOCIAL STUDIES

CAUTION: You are advised to use the following word lists with care. The words may refer to complex movements in history, complicated governmental procedures, and difficult economic ideas. The definitions which follow have been simplified and, in the simplification, some aspects have been omitted. If the definition is not clear, be certain to consult a dictionary.

American and World History

ABOLITIONIST one who favored abolishing Negro slavery in the United States prior to the Civil War

ABSOLUTISM form of government in which unlimited power is put in the hands of a ruler

AGGRESSION attack by one country on another without any provocation

ANGLICAN refers to the Church of England

ANNEXATION adding of territory to an already existing country or state

APARTHEID policy of racial segregation and discrimination against the blacks followed by the Republic of South Africa

APPEASEMENT policy of giving into the demands of an enemy power in an effort to maintain peace

ARMADA fleet of warships, particularly those sent by Spain against England in 1588

ARMISTICE temporary stopping of war by agreement of both sides before a peace treaty is signed

ARYAN term wrongly used by the Nazis to mean a person of non-Jewish descent

AUTHORITARIANISM policy of complete obedience to the authority of a ruler

AXIS in World War II, the countries who fought against the United States——Nazi Germany, Fascist Italy and Japan

BENELUX term for *Be*lgium, the *Ne*therlands and *Lux*emburg

BLACKLIST a list of people or organizations to avoid in trade or to deny employment to because of government policy or suspected disloyalty

BLOCKADE   action taken to cut off trade and communication with an enemy

BOLSHEVIK   follower of Lenin and member of the Communist party who took part in the Russian Revolution

BOONDOGGLE   spend public money to create unnecessary jobs

BOURGEOISIE   the middle class

BOYCOTT   refuse to deal with a country or an organization for political or economic reasons

BYZANTINE   having to do with the eastern part of the Roman Empire between 330 and 1453; capital at Byzantium or Constantinople

CARPETBAGGER   Northern politician or businessman who went to the South during the Reconstruction Era to take advantage of conditions there

CAVALIER   supporter of Charles I of England against Parliament (1641-1649)

CHARTER   in colonial times, a grant from the English ruler to a person or corporation giving certain rights and privileges of settlement

COLLECTIVE   settlement in the Soviet Union where people work together as a group rather than as individuals

COLONY   settlement in a distant land which remains under control of the country from which its settlers came

COMPROMISE   agreement in which each side gives up some things it wanted

CONCORDAT   agreement between the Pope and a government on matters dealing with the church

CONSERVATION   policies and practices which aim at preservation of natural resources such as forests

COPPERHEAD   a Northerner who sympathized with the South at the time of the Civil War

COUP D'ETAT   sudden overthrow of a government by force

CRUSADES   military expeditions between the 11th and 13th centuries made by Christians to drive the Moslems from the Holy Land

DECREE   an order of a government or a church

DESEGREGATION   removal of separation of races in public places such as schools

DESPOT   a ruler with unlimited powers

DIET   legislative body of some countries such as Japan

DISARMAMENT   reduction in arms and armed forces as a result of agreement between nations

DISCRIMINATION   prejudice in the treatment of one group compared with another in such things as jobs, housing, etc.

DIXIECRAT   Southern Democrat who supported the States' Rights Party in 1948 in the United States

DOCTRINE   a principle or belief or a set of principles or beliefs; sometimes identified with a person, like the Truman doctrine

DOVE   one who is identified as espousing the cause of peace and/or pursuing a conciliatory policy in foreign affairs

DYNASTY   successive series of rulers from the same family

ECCLESIASTICAL   having to do with the church or the clergy

EDICT   official proclamation or decree

EMANCIPATION   the setting free of a slave or anyone in bondage

EMBARGO   official order preventing ships from entering or leaving the ports of a country for the purpose of commerce

EMIGRATION   movement of a person or persons from one country to settle in another

EMIGRE   supporter of the king who fled from France during the French Revolution

EMPIRE   a unit of a group of states, colonies or territories joined together under the rule of one dominant power

ENCYCLICAL   letter from the Pope to the clergy dealing with church affairs and frequently involving church policy

ENLIGHTENMENT an 18th century philosophical movement in Europe which put all accepted beliefs and institutions to the test of reason

ENTAIL strict limitation of the inheritance of an estate to a specific line of heirs

ENTENTE informal, friendly agreement between nations which calls for cooperation in policy or action

ESTATE(S) in feudal times and in pre-Revolutionary France, one of three social classes with political power: clergy, nobility, bourgeoisie

EVOLUTION theory of Darwin which states that plants and animals develop from earlier forms by transmitting variations which help them better to survive

EXCOMMUNICATION church order cutting a person off from all privileges of church membership as a punishment

EXPROPRIATION taking away of property from a private owner in the public interest for public use

EXTRATERRITORIALITY removal from control of the country in which he lives of a foreign person such as a diplomat

FEMINISM movement to win for women rights equal to those of men in political, social and economic areas

FEUDALISM medieval political and economic organization of society (9th to 15th centuries) in Europe in which land held by vassals in return for service to the lord of the manor was worked by serfs

FIEF land held from a lord under feudalism in return for service, said land being able to be handed down to an heir

GENOCIDE systematic killing off of an entire national, racial or cultural group

GOTHIC western European style of achitecture (12th to 16th centuries) which featured pointed arches, steep roofs, etc.

GREENBACK American political party after the Civil War which advocated government paper money as the only money to be used

GUILD in medieval Europe, a group of men in the same trade or craft who joined to protect its members and to maintain standards in the trade

HAWK one who advocates an aggressive and warlike approach to his country's foreign policy

HEGEMONY dominance of one country over others in the same league or in the same geographic area

HEGIRA the flight of Mohammed from Mecca to Medina (622 A.D.)

HELLENIC decribing the civilization and culture of ancient Greece up to the time of Alexander the Great (4th century B.C.)

HELLENISTIC describing the civilization and culture of ancient Greece from the time of Alexander the Great until the 1st century B.C.

HELOT member of the class of serfs in ancient Sparta (Greece) who was neither a slave nor a citizen

HERESY a religious belief opposed to doctrine established by the church

HUGUENOT French Protestant of the 16th or 17th century

HUMANISM intellectual and cultural movement stressing human (as opposed to natural or religious) interests and the study of classical literature which led to the Renaissance

IMMIGRATION movement of a person into a new country to settle there

IMPERIALISM policy of a nation to extend its power by establishing colonies, controlling territories, raw materials, and world markets

INQUISITION court established by the Roman Catholic Church in the 13th century to discover heresy and punish heretics

INTERVENTION interference of one country in the affairs of another

ISLAM Moslem religion whose God is Allah and whose chief prophet is Mohammed

ISOLATIONISM policy of a country which is based on unwillingness to take part in international affairs

MANDATE   authority given by the League of Nations to one nation to administer some territory or geographic region

MANIFESTO   public declaration by a government or any person or persons of intention to act or of action taken

MANOR   under feudalism, a landed estate over which a lord had authority

MARITIME   having to do with the sea, navigation and shipping

MARXISM   doctrine that the state has exploited the masses and that a class struggle will change capitalism into socialism after a period of "dictatorship of the proletariat"

MEDIEVAL   referring to the period in Europe between the 5th and 15th centuries A.D.

MILITARISM   belief that the military should dominate the government and that military efficiency is the ideal of the state

MONARCHY   government where supreme power is placed in a king, queen, or emperor and where such power may be absolute or limited

MONOTHEISM   doctrine that there is only one God

MORATORIUM   legal permission, in an emergency, to delay the payment by one nation of its debt to another

MOSLEM   a believer of Islam and follower of Mohammed

MUCKRAKER   in the late 19th and early 20th centuries, one who, in America, sought to expose corruption by politicians or businessmen

NATIONALISM   doctrine that the interests and security of one's own country are more important than those of other nations or international groups

NAZISM   system in Germany (1933-1945) which controlled all activities of the people, fostered belief in the supremacy of Hitler as Fuhrer and the German people as a master race, and its establishment as the dominant world power

NOBILITY   the class of nobles in a state

NON-AGGRESSION   referring to an agreement between two nations not to attack one another

NULLIFICATION   in the United States, the right of a State to refuse to recognize or enforce a Federal law within its limit which it feels violates its own authority

PACIFISM   belief that conflicts between nations should be settled by peaceful means rather than by war

PACT   an agreement or treaty between nations

PAN-AMERICANISM   belief in political, economic, social and cultural cooperation and understanding between the nations of North, Central and South America

PANIC   in the United States, specific periods in which fear of economic collapse results in wild attempts to convert property, goods, and securities into cash

PARLIAMENT   the legislative body of Great Britain consisting of the House of Lords and the House of Commons

PARTITION   division of a geographic area into two or more countries or into areas annexed to already existing countries

PATRICIAN   in ancient Rome, a member of the nobility

PATROON   in colonial areas under the Dutch, one who held a landed estate

PLEBEIAN   in ancient Rome, a member of the lower class

PLEBISCITE   direct vote of all eligible voters on an important political issue

PRIMOGENITURE   the right of the first-born son to inherit his father's estate

PROHIBITION   in the United States, the period between 1920 and 1933 when the manufacture and sale of alcoholic drinks was forbidden by Federal law.

PROPAGANDA   systematic spread of ideas or doctrines with a view to convincing others of their truth, using repetition and, in some cases, distortion

PROTECTORATE   weaker state protected and in some instances controlled by a stronger state

PROTOCOL   signed document containing points of agreement between nations before a final treaty is negotiated

PROVISIONAL   referring to a government which functions temporarily until a permanent government is established

PURGE   getting rid of persons in a nation or political party who are considered disloyal or who hold views other than those of the majority of the party

PURITAN   Protestant in 16th and 17th century England and America who sought greater reform in the Church of England

QUOTA   the greatest number of persons who may be admitted, as to the United States or to an institution like a college

RATIFICATION   the giving of formal approval, as to a constitution or a treaty

REACTIONARY   extreme conservative, one who opposes progress or liberalism

RECIPROCAL   applying by mutual agreement to both parties or countries concerned, as in trade

RECONSTRUCTION   the period, after the Civil War (1865-1877), during which the Confederate states were controlled by the Federal government and reorganized prior to readmission to the Union

REFORMATION   the religious movement (16th century) that started to reform the Roman Catholic Church and ended in establishing Protestantism

REGIME   political system being administered at a given time

RENAISSANCE   period of revival in learning and the arts in Europe (14th through 16th centuries)

REPARATION   payment by a defeated nation for damages done to persons and property of the victorious country in a war

ROUNDHEAD   supporter of Parliament in the English Civil War (1642-1652)

SANCTIONS   measures taken by a group of nations to force another to stop a violation of international law it is considered to have made

SATELLITE   a small state that is dependent on a larger, more powerful state and must, as a result, keep its policies in line with it

SCALAWAG   Southern white who cooperated with Northern rule during the Reconstruction period

SCHISM   split in a group or institution such as the church which results from a difference of opinion in thought or doctrine

SECTIONALISM   placing of the interests of a section of a country ahead of those of the nation

SEDITION   acts which tend to foment rebellion against the existing government

SELF-DETERMINATION   right of a people to determine its own form of government independently

SERF   under feudalism, a person who worked the land, was bound to it, and went with it to a new owner

SHARECROPPER   farmer who does not own his land but who works it for a share of the crop

SOVEREIGNTY   referring to a state's supreme and independent political authority

STATUS QUO   the existing condition at a given time, as the present political, social and economic order

SUFFRAGETTE   woman who works actively for the right of women to vote

SYNDICALISM   political movement which advocates the use of any direct action, including violence, to bring production and distribution of goods under the control of labor unions

THEOCRACY   government ruled by religious officials on behalf of divine authority

TITHE   tax to support church and clergy (equal to one-tenth of the yearly yield of one's land)

TOLERATION   freedom to hold religious beliefs different from those in authority

TRIPARTITE   agreement or treaty made among three parties or nations

TRIUMVIRATE   government by three men or a group of three parties

TRUSTEESHIP   authority from the United Nations to one country to administer a territory or region

UNIFICATION formation of one state or nation from many smaller units of government, as in the case of Italy (1859-1870)

VASSAL under the feudal system, one who held land and served the lord of the domain in return for his protection

WHIG member of a political party which (a) fa-vored democratic change in England (1697-1832); (b) supported limitation of presidential power and opposed the Democrats in the United States (1836-1856); also a person who supported the American Revolution

ZIONIST supporter of the movement to establish a Jewish national state in Palestine; now, a supporter of the State of Israel

Government

ACT document made into law by a legislative body

ADMINISTRATION term of office of the executive branch of government

AGENCY bureau which administers a governmental function

ALIEN one who owes allegiance to a government or country other than the country in which he resides

ALLEGIANCE duty of a citizen to his government

ALLIANCE formal agreement between nations to achieve a common purpose

AMENDMENT change or revision made in a con-stitution or a law

AMNESTY general pardon to a group of persons freeing them from punishment usually for of-fenses against a government

ANARCHY complete absence of government and law with resulting disorder

APPELLATE court that can receive appeals and re-verse the decisions of lower courts

APPORTIONMENT allotting representatives to a group in proportion to their numbers

APPROPRIATION money made available by formal act of a legislative body for a specific public pur-pose

AT-LARGE Official chosen by all the voters of a particular election district, known as assembly-man-at-large, for example

AUTOCRACY government in which one person has supreme power and is accountable to no one

AUTONOMY self-government

BALLOT refers both to the paper on which a vote is recorded and to the vote itself

BICAMERAL legislature which is made up of two houses, such as a Senate and an Assembly or a Senate and a House of Representatives

BILL preliminary form of a law proposed to a legislative body

BIPARTISAN representing or composed of members of two parties

BLOC combination of legislators or nations which acts as a unit for a common interest or purpose

BOSS politician who controls a political machine and has influence over legislation and appoint-ments to office

BUREAUCRACY government which functions through departments which follow given rules and have varying degrees of authority in the organization

CABINET group of advisers to the head of a coun-try who usually administer a governmental de-partment

CAMPAIGN program of activities designed to elect a candidate to political office

CAUCUS closed meeting of party members to de-cide policy or to select candidates for office

CENSURE reprimand voted by a governmental body of one of its members or of the government or its cabinet

CENTER in politics, a party or group which fol-lows policies between the left (which advocates change) and the right (which opposes it)

CHECKS AND BALANCES system of government which provides for each branch of the government (executive, legislative, and judicial) to have some control over the others

CIVIL SERVICE those in the employ of government who got their positions through open competitive examination on the basis of merit; also the process involved

CLOTURE procedure which results in closing off debate and in bringing up for a vote the matter under discussion

COALITION temporary alliance of countries or parties for action to achieve some purpose

COMMISSION government agency with administrative, judicial or legislative powers

COMMITTEE group chosen by a legislative body to consider a particular law or topic

CONFERENCE meeting of committees from two branches of a legislature to settle differences in a bill they have enacted

CONFIDENCE in politics, a vote of confidence is evidence of legislative support

CONFIRMATION approval by a legislative body of an act or appointment by an executive

CONGRESS the legislature of the United States made up of the Senate and the House of Representatives

CONSERVATIVE person or party which tends to oppose change in government and its institutions; also refers to political parties in Great Britain and the United States

CONVENTION a gathering of members or delegates of a political group for a specific purpose as choosing a candidate for office

DE FACTO GOVERNMENT the actual government whether legal or not

DE JURE GOVERNMENT the legal government

DELEGATE representative to a convention; person empowered to act on behalf of those who choose him

DEMOCRACY government by the people directly or through representatives chosen in free elections

DICTATORSHIP state ruled by one who has absolute power and authority

DISSOLUTION formal dismissal of a legislative body

ELECTION choosing by vote among candidates for public office

ELECTORAL referring to a college or group elected by the voters to formally elect the President and Vice-President of the United States

ELECTORATE those qualified to vote in an election considered as a group

EXECUTIVE that branch of government charged with administering the laws of a nation

FASCISM a system of government in which there is power in the hands of a dictator, suppression of opposition parties, and aggressive nationalism (Italy, 1922-1945)

FEDERAL referring to a system of government in which a constitution divides powers between the central government and such political subdivisions as states

FEDERATION a union of states, cantons, or other groups which are part of a federal system of government

FELONY a major crime such as murder for which the law punishes more severely than any other

FILIBUSTER tactics used by a minority in a legislative body to delay action on a bill in the hope that it will be withdrawn

FRANCHISE either (1) the right to vote or (2) a special right or privilege granted to an individual or group by a government

GERRYMANDER action by the party in power to divide unfairly a voting area in such a way that it will win a majority of the districts

HEARING session of a legislative committee in which evidence is obtained from witnesses bearing on possible legislation

IMPEACH(MENT) bring(ing) charges against a public official for wrong-doing prior to possible trial and removal from office, if a conviction is obtained

INAUGURATION formal induction into office of a public official

INDICTMENT   formal accusation of someone with the commission of a crime, usually after investigation by a grand jury of charges made by a prosecutor

INITIATIVE   the right of a citizen to bring up a matter for legislation, usually by means of a petition signed by a designated number of voters

INJUNCTION   court order preventing a person or a group from taking an action which might be in violation of the law and do irreparable damage to other persons or property

JUDICIAL   having to do with the courts and their functions or with the judges who administer these functions

JUNTA   group which controls a government usually after seizing power by revolution or coup d'état

JURISDICTION   the authority of a government or court to interpret and apply the law

LAW   bill which has been approved by a legislative body and signed by the chief executive; all the rules established by legislation, interpretation of legislation, and authority of a given government or other community

LEFT   members of a legislative body who take more radical and liberal political positions than the others

LEGISLATIVE   having the power to make laws

LEGISLATION   the laws made by a legislative body, such as a Senate

LEGISLATURE   a group of persons having the responsibility and authority to make laws for a nation or a political subdivision of it

LIBERAL   an individual or political party whose beliefs stress protection of political and civil liberties, progressive reform, and the right of an individual to govern himself

LICENSE   formal legal permission to carry on an activity

LOBBY   work to influence legislators to support bills which favor some special group or interest

LOG-ROLLING   agreement between legislators to support bills in which each one has a separate interest ("You vote for mine; I'll vote for yours.")

MACHINE   political organization under the leadership of a boss and his lieutenants which controls party policy and job patronage

MAJORITY   number of votes for a candidate which is greater than the votes for all the other candidates put together; party in a legislative body which commands the largest number of votes

MINORITY   political group which is smaller than the controlling group in a government or legislature; group which does not have the necessary votes to gain control

MISDEMEANOR   a minor offense, usually the breaking of a local law such as loitering

MUNICIPAL   having to do with local government such as that of a city, town or village

MUNICIPALITY   a city or town which has the power to govern itself

NATURALIZE   give the rights of citizenship to a noncitizen or alien

NEUTRALITY   policy of a government which avoids taking sides directly or indirectly in disputes between other nations

NOMINATE   name a candidate for election to public office

OLIGARCHY   government in which power is in the hands of a very few

ORDINANCE   law enacted by local governmental authority

OVERRIDE   action taken by a legislative body to enact a law which has been disapproved (vetoed) by the chief executive of a political unit such as a nation or state

PARDON   official release from (continued) legal punishment for an offense

PARTISAN   a position or vote which follows party policy ("the party line")

PARTY   an organization of persons who work to elect its candidates to political office to further the governmental philosophy and causes in which they believe

PATRONAGE   the power of a political organization or its representative to give political or other jobs to persons who supported that party in an election

PETITION   request for specific legal or judicial action which is initiated and signed by an interested individual or group of individuals

PLANK   one of the items or principles in a party program or platform

PLATFORM   statement of the policies and principles of a political party or its candidate for office

PLURALITY   number of votes by which the winning candidate in an election defeats his nearest opponent

POLL   vote as recorded by a voter; the count of these votes; the place where the votes are cast; questioning of a group of people chosen at random on their views on political and other matters

PORK-BARREL   granting of money by a governmental agency to a locality in order to further the political ends of a party or its local representatives

PRECINCT   subdivision of a town or city which serves as an election unit

PRIMARY   vote by members of a political party to choose candidates for political office or for some other political purpose

PROGRESSIVE   a person or party who stands for moderate political and social change or reform

QUORUM   the minimum number of a legislative body which must be present before it can legally conduct business

RADICAL   a person or party who stands for extreme political and social change or reform

RATIFY   give formal approval to a document such as a treaty or constitution

RECALL   the right of or action taken by vote of the people or by petition to remove a public official from office

REFERENDUM   the principle or practice of submitting to direct popular vote a proposed law or one that has been passed by a legislative body; the right of the people to such a vote

REFORM   political movement designed to correct abuses in government by changes in the law

REGISTRATION   signing up of a person in his election district to enable him to vote

REGULATE   be or bring under control of government or a governmental agency

REPRESENTATIVE   member of a legislative body chosen to act on behalf of those who elected him to represent them

REPRIEVE   postpone the punishment of a person convicted of a crime

REPUBLIC   government in which power remains with all the citizens who are entitled to vote and who elect representatives who act for them and who are responsible to them

RESOLUTION   formal statement of opinion or intention voted by a legislative or other group.

REVIEW   re-examination by higher judicial authority of the proceedings or decision of a lower court

RIGHT   members of a legislative body who hold more conservative views than the other members, opposing change in current practice; that which belongs to an individual by law or tradition, such as the right to free speech

SELF-GOVERNMENT   government of a people by its own members or their representatives instead of by some outside power

SENIORITY   consideration given to length of service in a legislative body in making assignments to important positions or to membership in committees of that body

SPEAKER   public official who presides over a lawmaking body such as the House of Representatives or an assembly

STATUTE   law passed by a legislative body

SUBPOENA   a written order to a person to appear in court or before a legislative body to give evidence

SUBVERSIVE   an act or a person that would tend to overthrow the existing government

SUFFRAGE   the right to vote in political elections or on political matters

SUMMONS   a written order to appear in court to a person who may be involved in or has knowledge of a crime

SURROGATE   judge who acts in place of another

person to see to it that guardians are appointed, wills approved, and estates settled

TARIFF   tax imposed by a country on imported goods (usually to protect manufacturers in that country)

TENURE   length of time a person holds office; his right to hold that office until retirement or death

TESTIFY   present evidence in a court under oath

TICKET   list of candidates nominated for election by a political party

TOTALITARIAN   kind of government in which one political party is in power to the exclusion of all others

TREASON   betrayal of one's country by actively

helping its enemies in their attempt to overthrow it or defeat it in war

TREATY—formal agreement dealing with commerce or policies entered into by two or more nations.

URBAN   having to do with a town or a city

VETO   the act or power of a chief executive to turn down or temporarily prevent from taking effect a bill passed by a legislative body by actually rejecting it or refusing to sign it

VOTE   casting a ballot or taking any other necessary action to express one's choice in an election of a candidate for office or of any proposal for legislative change

WHIP   member of a political party in a legislative body such as Congress whose duty it is to enforce party discipline

Economics

ARBITRATION   attempt to settle or settlement of a dispute, generally between labor and management, by submitting it to a third party designated to decide it after hearing evidence presented by both sides on their own behalf

ASSET   property and resources of all kinds of a person or a corporation

AUTOMATION   in business and industry, the method whereby production and distribution of goods is made to take place automatically by mechanical and electronic rather than human means

BANKRUPTCY   financial condition in which a person or company is found legally unable to pay off the creditors who then may share the assets of the bankrupt person or company

BARGAINING   more properly, collective bargaining, refers to negotiation between representatives of management and labor on wages, hours, working conditions and other benefits

BIMETALLISM   use of two metals (for example, gold and silver) as the legal monetary standard of a country with each in a fixed ratio of value to the other (for example 16:1)

BOND   certificate indicating the obligation of a business or government to pay the holder certain interest or principal plus interest at indicated time or times

BUDGET   statement of an individual, business, or government in which expected incomes are allocated as expenses in designated necessary areas

CAPITALISM   an economic system based on private ownership of the means of production with freedom of private enterprise to earn a profit under free market (competitive) conditions

CARTEL   combination of businesses to establish a national or, more frequently, an international monopoly by limiting competition through such means as price fixing

CENSUS   an official count of the population of a country, (required every ten years in the United States by the constitution.)

CERTIFICATE   a document which shows that someone owns stock, among other purposes, and is entitled to benefits and liabilities of a stockholder

CHECK-OFF   system, usually arranged under collective bargaining, in which the employer deducts union dues from the member's wages and turns them over to the union

CLOSED   describes a shop in which, by agreement, the employer hires only members of a union

COMMERCE   large scale buying and selling of goods usually involving transportation of the goods between cities or countries

COMMODITY   any good that is bought or sold in a commercial transaction

COMPENSATION   payment given to make up for an injury or loss, as to a worker who has been hurt on the job

COMPETITION   in a free enterprise system, the attempt by rival businesses to get customers for the goods they manufacture or distribute

CONCILIATION   in a dispute, the attempt to settle differences between parties (for example, labor and management) in a friendly manner

CONSUMER   one who uses goods or services out of need

CORPORATION   a group of individuals who possess shares and which, as a group, has the privileges and obligations of a single person (for example, to make contracts and borrow money,) with liability limited to the amount invested by the shareholders

COST   the amount of money, labor and other expenses involved in producing or obtaining goods or services

CRAFT   (members of) a trade requiring special skills, such as printers

CRASH   sudden failure of a business or decline in market values of shares in a business

CREDIT   based on a person's economic standing, the money he is allowed to borrow and repay at a later date

CREDITOR   someone to whom money is owed

CURRENCY   money such as coin or bank notes which is in circulation in a country

CUSTOMS   duty or tax levied by a government on imported and, in some instances, exported goods

CYCLE   in business, a sequence of events that occurs and recurs in a given order involving boom, downturn, depression or recession, and recovery

DEBENTURE   certificate or bond signifying that a debt is owed by the signer who may be an individual or a corporation

DEBT   an obligation of an individual or corporation to pay something to a creditor

DEFICIT   the amount by which a corporation's or a government's debts are greater than its credits or assets (in government, for example, where expenditures are greater than taxes collected)

DEFLATION   fall in prices brought about by a decrease in the amount of spending

DEMAND   desire and ability to pay for certain goods and services, usually within a given price range at a given time

DEPLETION   using up of natural resources such as oil and timber

DEPRESSION   period of low business activity, wide unemployment, and falling prices

DEPOSIT   money put in a bank or given in partial payment for something purchased

DEPRECIATION   decrease in value of business property or equipment through "wear and tear"; money set aside as a reserve to meet the cost of repairing or replacing this equipment

DEVALUATION   lowering of the exchange value of one currency with respect to another by lowering the amount of gold backing it

DIRECTORATE   board chosen to run the affairs of a corporation

DISCOUNT   amount deducted from the original price of something sold; amount of interest deducted in advance in a business transaction; the rate of interest charged in a transaction

DISTRIBUTION   the process of making goods and services available to consumers as well as the promotion of the buying and selling of these goods and services

ENTREPRENEUR   a person who enters into business and risks his skills, time and money for the sake of earning a profit

EXCISE   tax on the production, sale or use of certain commodities within a country, for example tobacco and liquor

EXPORT   refers to goods sold by one country to another

FEATHERBEDDING   limiting of work or hiring of more employees than are necessary to prevent or limit unemployment in an industry

FISCAL   having to do with taxes, public revenues, or public debt

FISCAL YEAR   refers to an accounting period of twelve months, (for the United States, the year ending June 30)

FRINGE   refers to a benefit given by an employer that is not paid directly as wages but has a cost to him nonetheless

GOODS   merchandise

HOLDING   refers to a company organized to control other companies by holding their stocks and bonds

IMPORT   goods brought in, usually by purchase, by one country from another

INCOME   money received by a person or a business organization for work or services or from investment or property; refers to a tax on these receipts or earnings, usually levied by the government or a division of it such as a state

INDUSTRY   businesses as a group which are engaged in manufacturing

INFLATION   rise in prices brought about by an increase in the amount of money in circulation or by an increase in the amount of spending

INSTALLMENT   a system of credit in which goods purchased are paid for over a period of time by partial payments

INTEREST   charge for money borrowed, usually expressed as a percentage of the money lent; also money paid to a depositor for money left in a bank for a stated period

INTERLOCKING   refers to boards of directors (directorates) of several corporations which have some directors in common with the result that they control the corporations involved

INVESTMENT   money put into a business or property in the hope of receiving income or earning a profit

LABOR   workers considered as an economic group who work for wages; the work done by these wage-earners

LAISSEZ-FAIRE   economic policy which provides

for little or no interference by government in the affairs of business which is allowed to operate under its own regulations

LEVY   tax imposed or collected by a government or other authority

LIABILITY   debt owed by a business, corporation, or an individual

LOCKOUT   prevention by an employer of his workers from working by shutting down the business partly or completely until the workers settle a dispute on his terms

LOSS   amount by which the cost of an article sold is greater than the selling price

MACROECONOMICS   branch of economics developed about 1930 which deals with the economic activity of a nation as a whole as distinct from that of individual businesses

MANAGEMENT   those who direct the affairs of a business or industry considered as a group

MARGIN   the smallest return which allows a business to continue to operate profitably; the difference between the cost and the selling price of a product

MARKET   the buying and selling of goods or property; the location where the buying and selling takes place

MEDIATION   the entry into a dispute between management and labor with the intention of settling it fairly

MERCANTILISM   economic policy which prevailed from the 16th to the 18th century which put the economic welfare of the nation above that of the individual citizen and in which a nation sought to accumulate gold by having greater exports than imports

MERGER   combination of two or more businesses or corporations in which one of them ends by controlling the other(s)

MICROECONOMICS   the study of individual businesses within a national economy with emphasis on the determination of prices and the distribution of income

MONETARY   having to do with the money of a country

MONOPOLY exclusive control of a product or service in a market through group action, legal authority, or cornering of supply so that prices for the product or service can be fixed and competition eliminated

NEGOTIABLE refers to something that can be transferred legally from one person to another in return for something of equal value, usually through the use of such instruments as checks or notes

NOTE written promise to pay a debt, such as a promissory note

OBSOLESCENCE the process by which the plant and equipment of a business become outdated and cannot be used efficiently to produce the goods needed today

OVERHEAD the cost involved in running a business, such as rent, electricity, etc.

PARITY the farmer's current purchasing power as compared with that of a selected earlier period used to determine the degree of the government's support of farm prices; the equivalent value of money in one currency as compared with that of another

PARTNERSHIP form of business organization in which two or more people put money or property into a business and share the profits or losses

POVERTY extreme lack of the things necessary to sustain life, as food, shelter, and clothing

PREFERRED refers to stock on which dividends must be paid before they can be paid on common stock; holders of this stock also receive preference when a company's assets are distributed

PRODUCER one who produces goods and services for consumers

PRODUCTION creation of economic value by making goods and services available to meet the needs of consumers

PROFIT amount by which the selling price of an article sold is greater than the cost

PROLETARIAT the working class, especially the workers in industrial jobs

PROPERTY possessions which may be personal (movable), land or real estate, or securities (stocks and bonds)

PROPRIETORSHIP legal and exclusive right to ownership of some property or business

PROSPERITY condition in which the economy of a country and/or its business enjoys a state of well-being

PROTECTIONISM the practice of protecting the manufacturers of goods produced at home by taxing goods imported from abroad

RECESSION period of temporarily reduced business activity

REGRESSIVE refers to a tax whose rate decreases as the amount taxed increases

RENT income received by a land or property owner for the use of his land or property

RESERVE money or other assets kept available by a bank or other business to meet possible demands

REVENUE income that a country or a political subdivision of it receives from taxes and other sources so that it is available for use on behalf of the public

SAVINGS total money saved by an individual or a nation; bank whose principal business it is to receive savings and pay interest for the use of these savings from income it earns

SCAB a worker who works during a strike

SCARCITY condition of short supply in particular goods and services

SECURITIES documents, usually bonds or stock certificates, which are evidence of either indebtedness (bonds) or ownership (stocks)

SHOP if open, a business establishment where workers are employed regardless of union membership; if union, one in which labor and management agree that only employees who are union members or who join the union may continue to work there

SLUM highly crowded area in which housing is rundown, sanitary conditions are poor, and poverty is widespread

SPECIE   money in coin as distinguished from paper money

SPECULATION   use of capital to buy and sell stocks, property, commodities, and businesses where above average risk is taken in the hope of above average gains

STOCK   shares held by an individual in a corporation which give him an interest in its earnings and assets and the right to vote on matters concerning it

STRIKE   work stoppage carried out by workers to force the employer to improve working conditions and benefits and to increase wages

SUBSIDY   sum of money given by a government to a private individual or business in the public interest

SUPPLY   amount of goods and services available for sale usually within a given price range at a given time

SURPLUS   amount of goods over and above what is needed; the amount that the assets of a business are greater than its liabilities

SURTAX   a tax which is added on to an already existing tax

TAX   sum which an individual or corporation is required by the government to pay on income or property or an object purchased

TECHNOLOGY   use of scientific knowledge in industry and commerce

TENDER   something which is generally acceptable to be offered as payment

TRADE   the buying and selling of economic goods; an occupation involving skilled work, manual or mechanical

TRUST   combination of corporations in an industry to control prices and eliminate competition

UNDERWRITER   one who guarantees the purchase of stocks and bonds made available to the public in an offering

UNEMPLOYMENT   the condition of being out of work; the level at which this condition exists for workers generally

UNION   organization of workers which seeks to protect and advance the interests of its members with respect to working conditions and wages, usually through collective bargaining

UTILITY   usefulness; a company providing such necessary public services as gas, electricity, and water

WAGES   money paid to an employee, for work done; the share of industrial production which goes to labor in general

WELFARE   refers to a state or nation in which government rather than private organizations assumes the primary responsibility for the well-being of its citizens

WILDCAT   refers to a strike which takes place without the permission of the union representing the striking workers

Passages from the field of social studies at a high school level of difficulty are presented in this test. Background information in world and American history and civics is tested indirectly; but the answers to the questions following each reading passage can be found by close and careful reading of the passage itself.

A WORD OF ADVICE: Don't hesitate to go back to the passage several times if necessary to find the answer to a specific question. Refer to the Eight Hints for Handling Reading Comprehension Passages in Chapter 1.
    The twenty-one reading selections which have been chosen for you in this section start with the relatively easy and include several difficult passages as well.

TIME TO PRACTICE:

21 SELECTIONS

Directions: Read each of the following selections carefully. After each selection there are questions to be answered or statements to be completed. Select the *best* answer and underline it. Then blacken the appropriate space in the answer column to the right.

Selection 1

Every panic, or depression, has been preceded by feverish business activity, rising prices, rising profits and a rapid extension of credit. Each depression has been accompanied by a lack of business activity, falling prices and a very rapid increase in unemployment. In the past each has brought financial ruin to many banks and business concerns and to countless families. As long as these depressions come, we can not have an economy of plenty for any great length of time. Progressive leaders are trying to increase the buying power of the masses of our people and to induce them to save so that they may furnish an adequate market for the products of farm and factory.

1. The title below that best expresses the ideas of this passage is:
   (1) The Causes of Depressions   (2) A Possible Cure for Depressions
   (3) Price Fluctuations   (4) An Analysis of Buying Power   (5) Business Activity Preceding Depressions

2. Progressive economists feel that the best preventive of depressions rests with
   (1) farmers   (2) factory workers   (3) consumers   (4) big business   (5) educators

3. Prior to depressions business has been characterized by
   (1) increasing profits   (2) falling prices   (3) failure of banks   (4) the cutting down of credit   (5) balanced business activities

Selection 2

The American Revolution is the only one in modern history which, rather than devouring the intellectuals who prepared it, carried them to power. Most of the signatories of the Declaration of Independence were intellectuals. This tradition is ingrained in America, whose greatest statesmen have been intel-

The veto power is not used sparingly. Every year, in that hectic 30-day period, the Governor's staff and the State departments work diligently to muster the facts upon which to give him advice. But the score is still impressive; more than one out of four bills falls to the deadly stroke of the executive pen.

21. The passage indicates that the Governor
(1) vetoes about one-fourth of the bills   (2) vetoes about three-fourths of the bills   (3) vetoes all bills during the legislative session   (4) vetoes no bills during the legislative session   (5) uses the veto power very sparingly

21. 1 2 3 4 5
     || || || || ||

22. The passage deals with all of the following *except*
(1) the veto power of the Governor   (2) the procedure for a bill to become law despite a veto   (3) the veto power possessed by the Governor but not the President   (4) the frequency with which the veto is used   (5) how the President vetoes a bill

22. 1 2 3 4 5
     || || || || ||

23. The "30-day" rule applies to
(1) the time limit for exercising the veto   (2) the pocket veto   (3) the amount of time in which to appeal the Governor's action   (4) bills passed within the last ten days of a legislative session   (5) the limitation in which to pass a law over the Governor's veto

23. 1 2 3 4 5
     || || || || ||

24. The Governor's veto power is greater than that of the President in his ability to
(1) take as much time as he wishes before signing a bill   (2) veto a bill in less than ten days   (3) ignore all bills during the last month of the Legislature   (4) veto single items of the budget bill   (5) override the two-thirds vote of the Legislature

24. 1 2 3 4 5
     || || || || ||

25. A bill may become law under the following two conditions:
(1) the Governor fails to sign it within ten days—or if one-half of the Legislature votes against his veto   (2) the Governor signs it—or the Legislature vetoes it   (3) the Governor fails to sign it within ten days—or if two-thirds of the Legislature votes against his veto   (4) the Governor fails to sign it within ten days—or if one-fourth of the Legislature votes against his veto   (5) the Governor vetoes it—or the Legislature withdraws it from executive consideration

25. 1 2 3 4 5
     || || || || ||

Selection 7

I have been the more particular in this description of my journey, and shall be so of my first entry into that city, that you may in your mind compare such unlikely beginnings with the figure I have since made there. I was in my working dress, my best clothes being to come round by sea. I was dirty from my journey; my pockets were stuffed out with shirts and stockings, and I knew no soul nor where to look for lodging. I was fatigued with traveling, rowing, and want of rest; I was very hungry; and my whole stock of cash consisted of a Dutch dollar and about a shilling in copper. The latter I gave the people of the boat for my passage, who at first refused it, on account of my rowing; but I insisted on their taking it. A man being sometimes more generous when he has but a little money than when he has plenty, perhaps through fear of being thought to have but little.

Then I walked up the street, gazing about till near the market house I met a boy with bread. I had made many a meal on bread, and, inquiring where he got it, I went immediately to the baker's he directed me to, in Second Street, and asked for biscuit, intending such as we had in Boston; but they, it seems, were not made in Philadelphia. Then I asked for a threepenny loaf, and was told they had none such. So not considering or knowing the difference of money, and the greater cheapness nor the names of his bread, I bade him give me threepenny-worth of any sort. He gave me, accordingly, three great puffy rolls. I was surprised at the quantity, but took it, and having no room in my pockets, walked off with a roll under each arm, and eating the other. Thus I went up Market Street as far as Fourth Street, passing by the door of Mr. Read, my future wife's father; when she, standing at the door, saw me, and thought I made, as I certainly did, a most awkward, ridiculous appearance. Then I turned and went down Chestnut Street and part of Walnut Street, eating my roll all the way, and, coming round, found myself again at Market Street wharf, near the boat I came in, to which I went for a draught of the river water; and, being filled with one of my rolls, gave the other two to a woman and her child that came down the river in the boat with us, and were waiting to go farther.

Thus refreshed, I walked again up the street, which by this time had many clean-dressed people in it, who were all walking the same way. I joined them, and thereby was led into the great meeting house of the Quakers near the market. I sat down among them, and, after looking round awhile and hearing nothing said, being very drowsy through labor and want of rest the preceding night, I fell fast asleep, and continued so till the meeting broke up, when one was kind enough to rouse me. This was, therefore, the first house I was in, or slept in, in Philadelphia.

—Benjamin Franklin

26. Franklin states that the main purpose of his description of his entrance into Philadelphia is to
(1) recall his first meeting with future wife   (2) make a sentimental journey into the past   (3) contrast his arrival with his later achievement   (4) contrast Philadelphia with Boston   (5) emphasize his generosity

26. 1 2 3 4 5
     || || || || ||

27. Benjamin Franklin indicates he was *all* of the following EXCEPT
(1) tired   (2) hungry   (3) dirty   (4) generous   (5) prosperous

27. 1 2 3 4 5
     || || || || ||

28. In Philadelphia, Franklin did *all* of the following EXCEPT
(1) give away two of his rolls   (2) sleep in the Quaker meeting house   (3) return to his boat for a drink of water   (4) see his future wife   (5) wear his best clothes

28. 1 2 3 4 5
     || || || || ||

29. The street which was along the water was
(1) Second Street   (2) Fourth Street   (3) Chestnut Street   (4) Walnut Street   (5) Market Street

29. 1 2 3 4 5
     || || || || ||

30. Franklin's account indicates he did *all* of the following EXCEPT
(1) change his dollar   (2) follow the Quakers   (3) speak with a boy he met   (4) eat a biscuit   (5) pay for his boat trip

30. 1 2 3 4 5
     || || || || ||

Selection 8

It beats the Dutch was an expression often used by our ancestors. Perhaps such a saying arose from the facts that so often the Dutch excelled in one way or another. Indeed, they brought to the New World habits of thrift, industry and stability that have characterized them to this day, even though they were at times ridiculed by writers such as Washington Irving. Yet in the sixteenth and seventeenth centuries these people were struggling for their very existence.

The Low Countries, the Netherlands, as they were called, were located at the crossroads of the maritime world. Sea traffic from all the coasts of Europe touched at the ports there or was harbored in the sheltered waters—the zees of Holland. From France, Spain and Portugal to the south—and even from the Mediterranean—and from England, the Baltic ports, Russia and Scandinavia to the north, came traders, sailors, merchants, fishermen and travelers of all kinds. The herring fisheries alone provided a thriving business, especially when the Dutch learned a better way to preserve the fish. The prosperity of these hard-working people soon became the envy of their neighbors.

Commonly called the Spanish Netherlands, these territories were part of the vast empire of Emperor Charles V and then of Philip II of Spain. The latter, it will be remembered, was a fanatical defender of the Catholic faith and he was disturbed by the fact that the Netherlands became an asylum for religious dissenters. The religious wars had displaced many people from the realms of France and the Germanies, and even from England. Some were French Huguenots; others were Calvinists from Geneva; and there were also the Jews from Portugal and Spain. Like all refugees they sought not only asylum, but a means of livelihood; and in the prosperity of the Netherlands there were places for them. The Flemish weavers were famous in their day; Jews, forbidden to enter craft guilds, engaged in trade.

31. An appropriate title for this selection is:
(1) Contributions of Spain to the Growth of Holland   (2) The Lazy Dutch   (3) The Reign of Philip II of the Netherlands   (4) The Netherlands in the Sixteenth and Seventeenth Centuries   (5) The Catholic Stronghold in the Netherlands

32. According to the author, the expression, "It beats the Dutch," was used by our ancestors to indicate that
(1) they ridiculed the Dutch   (2) they were thriftier than the Dutch   (3) they beat the Dutch in war   (4) the Dutch did not bring habits of industry to the New World   (5) the Dutch excelled in various ways

33. The Low Countries were
(1) also known as the Baltic ports   (2) ideally located for trade   (3) shunned by most European ships   (4) located too far from the zees to have useful harbors   (5) lacking in herring fisheries

34. In the Netherlands, religious freedom was
(1) forbidden   (2) granted only to Catholics   (3) practiced by all   (4) restricted only to the Huguenots   (5) rare

35. Prosperity in the Netherlands was
(1) denied to the Flemish weavers   (2) denied to the Calvinists   (3) available to the refugees of many countries   (4) available only to the Dutch   (5) available only to the Spaniards

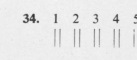

Selection 9

The Capitol Building in Washington, D.C. is more than just the home of the legislative branch of the federal government. It is an awe-inspiring edifice, symbolizing the strength and majesty of the United States of America.

From the Capitol's conception, the architect Major Pierre Charles L'Enfant envisioned the site atop Jenkins Hill, where the building now stands, as a perfect "pedestal waiting for a monument." The actual design of the Capitol evolved as a result of a public competition proposed by President Washington and Secretary of State Jefferson. The winning design, selected by Washington himself, was by Dr. William Thornton, an amateur architect. His plans provided for a square central section topped by a low dome and two attached rectangular buildings.

Construction was begun in 1793 after Congress, in one of its prime functions, appropriated the funds. Based on the award-winning design, construction was completed in three stages:

1. The north wing, now known as the Supreme Court section, was started in 1793 and completed in 1800. It was in this small building that the legislative and judicial branches of government met.

2. The southern wing, now known as Statuary Hall, was occupied in 1807 by the House of Representatives, but it was not completed until four years later.

3. The central rotunda was completed in 1827 under the direction of Architect Charles Bullfinch. Its low wooden dome capped with copper was not put into place until 1859.

When the Houses soon outgrew their quarters, Congress decided in 1850 to construct two entirely new chambers designed by Thomas Walter, an architect from Philadelphia. The House wing was finished in 1857 and the Senate wing was completed in 1859.

But before work on the new wings had progressed very far, it was realized that the two massive marble extensions on either side of the central dome were going to dwarf it, so under Walter's direction, the copper one was removed to make way for the enormous iron dome that is the symbol of the Capitol today. This immense, impressive structure weighs over nine million pounds and is 108 feet high and 96 feet in diameter. In December 1863, the dome was topped by the Statue of Freedom, almost 20 feet high and weighing 14,985 pounds.

36. The design for the Capitol was
(1) suggested by Thomas Jefferson   (2) prepared by Dr. William Thornton
(3) selected by Major Pierre Charles L'Enfant   (4) improved by President Washington   (5) vetoed by Thomas Walter

37. All of the following are true about the construction of the Capitol, *except*
(1) construction was begun in 1793   (2) construction of the original building was completed in three stages   (3) funds were appropriated by Congress   (4) additional sections were added in 1857–1859   (5) the dome was installed in 1800

38. The Capitol is the home of the
(1) executive branch of the federal government   (2) judicial branch   (3) military branch   (4) majestic branch   (5) legislative branch

39. Two new chambers were planned by Congress in
(1) 1807   (2) 1800   (3) 1850   (4) 1814   (5) 1863

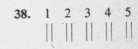

40. The chief symbol of the Capitol is its
(1) iron dome   (2) copper dome   (3) wooden dome capped with copper
(4) south wing   (5) north wing

40. 1 2 3 4 5

Selection 10

Fourscore and seven years ago our fathers brought forth on this continent a new nation, conceived in liberty, and dedicated to the proposition that all men are created equal.

Now we are engaged in a great civil war, testing whether that nation, or any nation so conceived and so dedicated, can long endure. We are met on a great battlefield of that war. We have come to dedicate a portion of that field as a final resting-place for those who here gave their lives that that nation might live. It is altogether fitting and proper that we should do this.

(1) But, in a larger sense, we cannot dedicate—we cannot consecrate—we cannot hallow—this ground. (2) The brave men, living and dead, who struggled here, have consecrated it far above our poor power to add or detract. (3) The world will little note nor long remember what we say here, but it can never forget what they did here. (4) It is for us, the living, rather, to be dedicated here to the unfinished work which they who fought here have thus far so nobly advanced. (5) It is rather for us to be here dedicated to the great task remaining before us—that from these honored dead we take increased devotion to that cause for which they gave the last full measure of devotion; that we here highly resolve that these dead shall not have died in vain; that this nation, under God, shall have a new birth of freedom; and that government of the people, by the people, for the people, shall not perish from the earth.

41. This speech was delivered at
(1) Washington, D.C.   (2) Gettysburg, Pa.   (3) Boston, Mass.   (4) Appomattox Court House   (5) Springfield, Ill.

42. The speaker was
(1) George Washington   (2) Thomas Jefferson   (3) Abraham Lincoln
(4) Ulysses S. Grant   (5) Franklin D. Roosevelt

43. In the first paragraph, the speaker refers to
(1) the Declaration of Independence   (2) the Articles of Confederation
(3) the United States Constitution   (4) the Northwest Ordinance   (5) the Monroe Doctrine

44. The purpose of the speech was to
(1) commemorate a battle   (2) remember the founding of our nation   (3) dedicate a cemetery   (4) deplore civil war   (5) seek political support in an election

45. The sentence in paragraph three which represents an incorrect prediction is
(1) sentence #1   (2) sentence #2   (3) sentence #3   (4) sentence #4   (5) sentence #5

Selection 11

Under such conditions, the *Half Moon* set sail from Amsterdam and left the Texel, an island barrier of the Zuider Zee, April 6, 1609. She went northward, according to the sailing orders and passed the North Cape on May 5. For nearly a week Hudson skirted the northern shores toward Nova Zembla. But there were several considerations that brought about a change of course. Our only record of this momentous decision is given by Van Metern of The Hague, writing in 1614:

> This circumstance (the sea full of ice), and the cold which some of his men who had been in the East Indies could not bear, caused quarrels among the crew, they being partly English, partly Dutch; upon which the captain, Henry Hudson, laid before them two propositions: the first of these was, to go to the coast of America to the latitude of 40°. The other proposition was to direct their search to Davis's Straits. This meeting with general approval, they sailed on the 14th of May, and arrived with a good wind at the Faroe Islands. After leaving the islands, they sailed on till, on the 18th of July, they reached the coast of Nova Francia, under 44°.

Juet's more detailed log of the transatlantic passage describes some of the rigors of the voyage. The rocky shores of the Faroe Islands north of the British Isles made the landing there hazardous; and storms with heavy seas were responsible for the loss of the foremast and other damage to the tiny vessel. Also, the sighting of a "sayle" on June 25 must go down as a hazard, in the days when any strange ship was assumed to be hostile, until proven to the contrary. Truly, it must have been a relief when Hudson made a landfall at Newfoundland. In fact, the men were able to take 118 cod in five hours.

Although the crew in deciding to turn west were reported to favor Davis Strait, their course was directed farther south, indicating that they (or at least some who preferred the warmer climes of the Indies) were hoping to reach Virginia. Thus their coasting trip went southward, while their interest in the lands and their wealth, as well as in the Indians, suggests that Hudson may have been as anxious to explore these shores as he was to gain a new route to the East.

46. An appropriate title for this selection is
(1) The voyage of Henry Hudson   (2) Half a league onward   (3) The discovery of the New World   (4) The discovery of Newfoundland
(5) Perfect sailing conditions

47. The *Half Moon* started from
(1) Nova Francia   (2) Nova Zembla   (3) Faroe Islands   (4) Amsterdam
(5) The Hague

48. The sea voyage took place between
(1) May and July   (2) July and December   (3) June 25th and July 18th
(4) April and July 18   (5) April and May 4

49. The crew
(1) came entirely from the East Indies   (2) was partly English, partly Indian   (3) was partly Dutch, partly Indian   (4) was partly English, partly Dutch   (5) was entirely English

50. The chief aims of the voyage were to
(1) explore the new lands and to chart the icebergs   (2) find a new route to the East and to find a source of codfish   (3) find a new route to the East and to explore the new lands   (4) become acquainted with the Indians and to see how far north they could go   (5) discover the Hudson River, and to reach Virginia

Selection 12

This is hardly the place for portraying the mental features of the Indians. The same picture, slightly changed in shade and coloring, would serve with very few exceptions for all the tribes north of the Mexican territories. But with this similarity in their modes of thought, the tribes of the lake and ocean shores, of the forests and of the plains, differ greatly in their manner of life. Having been domesticated for several weeks among one of the wildest of the hordes that roam over the remote prairies, I had unusual opportunities of observing them and flatter myself that a sketch of the scenes that passed daily before my eyes may not be devoid of interest.

They were thorough savages. Neither their manners nor their ideas were in the slightest degree modified by contact with civilization. They knew nothing of the power and real character of the white men, and their children would scream in terror when they saw me. Their religion, superstitions, and prejudices were the same handed down to them from immemorial time. They fought with the weapons that their fathers fought with, and wore the same garments of skins. They were living representatives of the "stone age"; for though their lances and arrows were tipped with iron procured from the traders, they still used the rude stone mallet of the primeval world.

Great changes are at hand in that region. With the stream of emigration to Oregon and California, the buffalo will dwindle away and the large wandering communities who depend on them for support must be broken and scattered. The Indians will soon be abased by whisky and overawed by military posts; so that within a few years the traveler may pass in tolerable security through their country. Its danger and its charm will have disappeared together.

—Francis Parkman

51. The author considers himself qualified to write about the Indians because
    (1) he is impartial   (2) he is a trained historian   (3) he lived among them
    (4) he heard about them from travelers   (5) he read widely about them

51. 1 2 3 4 5
     || || || || ||

52. Parkman emphasizes concerning the Indian tribes their
    (1) sameness of manner of thought and in manner of living   (2) sameness of manner of thought and difference in manner of living   (3) difference in manner of thought and sameness of manner of living   (4) difference in manner of thought and in manner of living   (5) lack of evidence regarding manner of thought and manner of living

52. 1 2 3 4 5
     || || || || ||

53. Parkman indicates *all* of the following as evidence of lack of civilization among the Indians EXCEPT
    (1) their primitive implements   (2) their unchanging superstitions   (3) their ignorance of the white men   (4) their dress   (5) their extreme cruelty

53. 1 2 3 4 5
     || || || || ||

54. The changes affecting the Indians as indicated in this passage include *all* the following EXCEPT
    (1) improved intellect   (2) decreased food supply   (3) increased military control   (4) decreased unity   (5) increased alcoholism

54. 1 2 3 4 5
     || || || || ||

55. Parkman's attitude with regard to the changes as they will affect the traveler is one of
    (1) approval   (2) suspicion   (3) regret   (4) doubt   (5) apprehension

55. 1 2 3 4 5
     || || || || ||

Selection 13

Membership in the United Nations is open to all peace-loving countries which accept the obligations of the Charter and are considered able and willing to carry out these obligations. The United Nations is founded on these basic principles: All Member States are sovereign and equal. All are pledged to fulfill their obligations under the Charter in good faith. All are pledged to settle their disputes by peaceful means and in such manner as not to endanger peace, security and justice.

In its international relations, no Member shall use or threaten force against the territory and political independence of any state, or behave in a manner inconsistent with the purposes of the United Nations. All are pledged to give every assistance to the United Nations when, in accordance with the Charter, it takes any action, and also not to give assistance to any state against which the United Nations is taking action to preserve or restore peace. The United Nations shall not intervene in matters which are essentially within the domestic jurisdiction of any state except when it is acting to enforce peace.

The United Nations functions through six principal organs, each charged with specific responsibilities. These organs are: The General Assembly, the Security Council, the Economic and Social Council, the Trusteeship Council, the International Court of Justice, and the Secretariat. The headquarters of the United Nations are in New York City, on an 18-acre plot of land which is international territory. Certain activities of the UN, however, are centered elsewhere, particularly in Geneva, Switzerland and The Hague in the Netherlands.

The General Assembly is the main deliberative organ of the United Nations. It meets once each year and normally remains in session for three months. It elects a President and Vice Presidents for each annual session. Each country which is a member of the UN is represented. Each country has one vote but may have as many as five representatives. Ordinarily the Assembly reaches its decisions on the basis of a simple majority of those voting; on especially important matters a two-thirds majority is required.

56. All of the following statements about the United Nations are true *except* (1) all member states are sovereign and equal   (2) the United Nations may not interfere in matters which are within the domestic jurisdiction of any country   (3) all members are pledged to settle their disputes by peaceful means   (4) it is a world government   (5) membership is open to all peace-loving nations

57. Although the headquarters of the UN are in New York City, some of its activities are also centered in
(1) Geneva, Switzerland   (2) Rome, Italy   (3) Lucerne, Switzerland   (4) Amsterdam, the Netherlands   (5) Moscow, U.S.S.R.

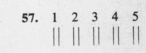

58. All of the following are organs of the United Nations, *except* the
(1) Secretariat   (2) Economic and Social Council   (3) Trusteeship Council   (4) International Court of Justice   (5) League of Nations

59. The President of the General Assembly
(1) is a permanent official   (2) serves for one year   (3) is elected every three months   (4) serves as Vice-President, on occasion   (5) must come from a neutral country, outside of the UN

60. In the General Assembly, each member country
    (1) has only one vote   (2) has five votes   (3) has only one representative
    (4) has five representatives   (5) votes only on matters requiring a two-
    thirds majority

Selection 14

Every Hindu is born into a caste from which he must take his wife and which often determines how he shall earn a living. For instance those belonging to a certain caste will be water-carriers by occupation and their sons, as a rule, will continue to carry water. In modern times members of such a caste will go into other occupations without losing their place as a member of that caste. All together there are some 2,000 castes and subcastes.

Originally, there were four main caste groups: the Brahmans, or priests; the Kshatriya, or warrior group; the Vaisya, or merchants; and the Sudras, who were the farmers. Within these main groups, innumerable subcastes developed until the main group itself became all but forgotten.

Today, as the highest caste, the Brahmans stand at the top of the social ladder. They often are the priests and the scholars of Hindu society. Brahmans may carry the honorary title of Pandit (learned man), as Pandit Nehru, from which our term pundit (meaning heavy-duty thinker) derives. Brahmans also are found in many other occupations, ranging from farming to accountancy. Many are messengers in government service, while others are cooks. Brahmans are especially desirable as cooks since food prepared by them, under the caste rules, can be eaten by members of any caste or subcaste. Otherwise Hindus may only eat food prepared by one of equal or superior caste standing. No matter what his occupation, the Brahman is still a member of the elite class.

The present caste system is by no means fixed. There are many subdivisions within each caste and new ones are constantly being formed. For instance, a former regiment of the Indian Army known as the Queen's Own Sappers and Miners used to recruit its men from Indians living near Madras in south India. It is reported that among these there is a special and highly superior caste growing up known as Queensap, made up of those who have served or descended from those who have served in the Queens Own Sappers and Miners.

Getting back to the Brahmans, you will see them everywhere wearing a sacred thread over the left shoulder as insignia of their rank. All Brahmans are vegetarian, as are most Hindus of the higher castes. To them killing any animal, even for food, is a sin.

With the growth of industrial development and modern living conditions in the cities, there has been some break-down in rigid caste rules. You may see Indians of different castes eating together in Calcutta or Bombay. But the rules are strictly observed in villages in rural India, particularly in the south.

There are a large number of Hindus who are outside the caste structure. They are called the "Untouchables" or in official documents the "Depressed Classes" and are often pitifully poor. In rural villages the section in which the Untouchables live is sometimes set off several hundred yards from the rest of the houses. Many of India's present leaders have worked to improve their miserable conditions of life, but progress has been slow.

61. The best title for this selection is
(1) The Brahman Elite   (2) The New Caste Groups   (3) The "Untouchables"   (4) Indian Food Habits   (5) The Hindu Caste System

62. At the top and bottom respectively of the social ladder in India are
(1) the Queensaps and the Pandits   (2) the Kshatriyas and the Sudras
(3) the Brahmans and the Depressed Classes   (4) the priests and the cooks
(5) the Sappers and the Miners

63. According to the article, Brahmans may be *all* of the following EXCEPT
(1) priests   (2) scholars   (3) vegetarians   (4) "Untouchables"   (5) messengers

64. A sacred thread over the left shoulder may have been worn by
(1) a former regiment of the Indian Army   (2) the "Untouchables"   (3) those outside the caste structure   (4) the four main caste groups   (5) Pandit Nehru

65. The *first* item mentioned is the *cause* of the *second* in which of the following pairs:
(1) modern city life—more flexibility in caste rules   (2) Brahmans—killing animals   (3) Vaisya—merchants   (4) cooks—highest caste   (5) two thousand subcastes—four main castes

Selection 15

The beaches of Normandy were chosen for the assault after long study of the strength of German coastal defenses and the disposition of German divisions. The absence of large ports in the area was a serious obstacle, but it was offset in some measure by the relative weakness of the German defenses and elaborate construction in Britain of two artificial harbors to be emplaced off the beaches.

The selection of target dates and hours for the assault required an accurate forecast of the optimum combination of favorable weather, tide, and light conditions. Moonlight was desirable for the airborne operations. D-day was scheduled for June 5; this date was changed to June 6 because of unfavorable but clearing weather. Hundreds of craft, en route from distant ports on the west coast of England, were already approaching the invasion area; they had to backtrack or seek shelter in the overcrowded harbors on the south coast. The final forecast for the attack day predicted high winds; the sea was still rough, but rather than accept a delay of several weeks until tide and moon provided another favorable moment, General Eisenhower made the fateful decision to go ahead.

At 0200 hours on June 6, 1944, the American 82d and 101st Airborne Divisions, as well as British airborne troops, were dropped in vital areas in the rear of German coastal defenses guarding the Normandy beaches from Cherbourg to Caen.

The seaborne assault under the over-all command of Field Marshal Montgomery was made on a broad front; British and Canadian forces commanded by Lieutenant General Sir Miles C. Dempsey and American forces commanded by Lieutenant General Omar N. Bradley deployed against 50 miles of coast line. Aerial bombardment of beach defenses along the coast began at 0314, preliminary naval bombardment at 0550, shortly after sunrise. At 0630 the first waves of assault infantry and tanks landed on the invasion beaches.

—George C. Marshall

66. The best title for this selection is
(1) The Beaches of Normandy   (2) Commanders of the Invading Forces
(3) The Allies Cooperate   (4) The Invasion of Normandy   (5) The Fifth of June

66. 1 2 3 4 5
|| || || || ||

67. The order of attack was
(1) parachutist landings, air bombardment, naval bombardment, infantry and tank landings   (2) air bombardment, parachutist landings, naval bombardment, infantry and tank landings   (3) parachutist landings, naval bombardment, air bombardment, infantry and tank landings   (4) parachutist landings, infantry and tank landings, air bombardment, naval bombardment   (5) air bombardment, naval bombardment, parachutist landings, infantry and tank landings

67. 1 2 3 4 5
|| || || || ||

68. The period of time between the first and last actions mentioned was
(1) one hour and 14 minutes   (2) two hours and 36 minutes   (3) three hours and 16 minutes   (4) three hours and 50 minutes   (5) four hours and 30 minutes

68. 1 2 3 4 5
|| || || || ||

69. All of the following are mentioned as obstacles to the landings EXCEPT
(1) high winds   (2) rough seas   (3) weak German coastal defenses   (4) lack of port facilities   (5) overcrowded English ports

69. 1 2 3 4 5
|| || || || ||

70. Highest in authority of the military leaders mentioned was
(1) Eisenhower   (2) Montgomery   (3) Dempsey   (4) Bradley   (5) the team of Dempsey and Bradley

70. 1 2 3 4 5
|| || || || ||

Selection 16

On December 9, 1948, after two years of preliminary debate in various committees, the United Nations General Assembly unanimously adopted the Convention on the Prevention and Punishment of the Crime of Genocide.

A United Nations convention, expressing the moral concern of the world organization, is also an international treaty, legally binding on those countries which ratify it.

The term "genocide," joining together the Greek *genos*, meaning race or tribe, and the Latin suffix *cide*, or killing, was coined in 1946 by the distinguished international legal scholar, Professor Raphael Lemkin.

The mass murder of six million Jews by the Nazis was the most vivid, violent and tragic expression of genocide. But this century alone has seen others—Armenians, Gypsies, Chinese, Slavs. Some 20 million people have been sacrificed to a moloch because of their racial, religious or ethnic backgrounds.

In the language of the Convention, *genocide* means certain specifically defined acts "*committed with intent to destroy, in whole or in part, a national, ethnical, racial or religious group, as such.*" The specified acts are:

- Killing members of the group.
- Causing serious bodily or mental harm to members of the group.
- Deliberately inflicting on the group conditions of life calculated to bring about its physical destruction in whole or in part.
- Imposing measures intended to prevent births within the group.
- Forcibly transferring children of the group to another group.

Since its adoption, the convention has been ratified by 67 nations, including the Federal Republic of Germany and the Communist states of Eastern Europe. Few European or Latin American states have failed to ratify (although only a small number of African countries have done so). The most prominent abstainers: the United States and Great Britain.

71. A convention as used in this passage is a
    (1) meeting of a world organization   (2) law adopted by an assembly   (3) treaty   (4) term coined by Professor Lemkin   (5) custom adhered to by many

71. 1 2 3 4 5

72. The word "genocide" literally means
    (1) mass murder   (2) race killing   (3) moloch   (4) convention   (5) ratification

72. 1 2 3 4 5

73. Genocide involves intent to destroy, according to this passage, *all* of the following EXCEPT
    (1) nations   (2) races   (3) ethnical groups   (4) political groups   (5) religious groups

73. 1 2 3 4 5

74. All of the following have been subjected to genocide EXCEPT
    (1) Jews   (2) Nazis   (3) Slavs   (4) Gypsies   (5) Chinese

74. 1 2 3 4 5

75. The convention has been ratified by *all* of the following EXCEPT
    (1) the United States   (2) West Germany   (3) most European countries   (4) most Latin American countries   (5) the Communist states of Eastern Europe

75. 1 2 3 4 5

Selection 17

We come then to the question presented: Does segregation of children in public schools solely on the basis of race, even though the physical facilities and other "tangible" factors may be equal, deprive the children of the minority group of equal educational opportunities? We believe that it does.

In *Sweatt* v. *Painter*, *supra*, in finding that a segregated law school for Negroes could not provide them equal educational opportunities, this Court relied in large part on "these equalities which are incapable of objective measurement but which make for greatness in a law school." In *McLaurin* v. *Oklahoma State Regents*, *supra*, the Court, in requiring that a Negro admitted to a white graduate school be treated like all other students, again resorted to intangible considerations: ". . . his ability to study, to engage in discussions and exchange views with other students, and, in general, to learn his profession."

Such considerations apply with added force to children in grade and high schools. To separate them from others of similar age and qualifications solely because of their race generates a feeling of inferiority as to their status in the community that may affect their hearts and minds in a way unlikely ever to be undone. The effect of this separation on their educational opportunities was well stated by a finding in the Kansas case by a court which nevertheless felt compelled to rule against the Negro plaintiffs:

"Segregation of white and colored children in public schools has a detrimental effect upon the colored children. The impact is greater when it has the sanction of the law; for the policy of separating the races is usually interpreted as denoting the inferiority of the negro group. A sense of inferiority affects the motivation of a child to learn. Segregation with the sanction of law, therefore has a tendency to [retard] the educational and mental development of negro children and to deprive them of some of the benefits they would receive in a racial[ly] integrated school system."

Whatever may have been the extent of psychological knowledge at the time of *Plessy* v. *Ferguson*, this finding is amply supported by modern authority. Any language in *Plessy* v. *Ferguson* contrary to this finding is rejected. We conclude that in the field of public education the doctrine of "separate but equal" has no place. Separate educational facilities are inherently unequal. Therefore, we hold that the plaintiffs and others similarly situated for whom the actions have been brought are, by reason of the segregation complained of, deprived of the equal protection of the laws guaranteed by the Fourteenth Amendment.

—Brown v. Board of Education of Topeka

76. "We" (line 1 and line 4) refers to
(1) Brown   (2) Topeka Board of Education   (3) the Congress   (4) the Supreme Court   (5) Plessy and Ferguson

76. 1 2 3 4 5
     || || || || ||

77. It can be inferred that the decision goes contrary to
(1) Sweatt v. Painter   (2) McLaurin v. Oklahoma State Regents   (3) Plessy v. Ferguson   (4) the 14th Amendment   (5) the Due Process Clause

77. 1 2 3 4 5
     || || || || ||

78. All of the following are correctly paired EXCEPT
(1) Sweatt v. Painter: desegregated law school   (2) McLaurin v. Oklahoma: desegregated graduate school   (3) Plessy v. Ferguson: "separate but equal"   (4) 14th Amendment: equal protection of the laws   (5) Due Process Clause: segregation with the sanction of law

78. 1 2 3 4 5
     || || || || ||

79. Segregation of children in grade or high school is rejected for
(1) historical reasons   (2) political reasons   (3) physical reasons   (4) psychological reasons   (5) economic reasons

79. 1 2 3 4 5
     || || || || ||

80. All of the following are reasons given for ending segregation EXCEPT
(1) effect on the motivation to learn   (2) educational retardation of colored children   (3) retardation of mental development of colored children   (4) benefits of integration   (5) the doctrine of "separate but equal"

80. 1 2 3 4 5
     || || || || ||

Selection 18

In spirit New York ceased to be a colony with the signing of the Declaration of Independence in 1776. That document, read aloud from the steps of the courthouse in White Plains on July 11th and at many other public gatherings, was received both exultantly and with foreboding. And well it might be. It was a grave document. It severed old and established political relations.

It declared revolution and set man against his brother, each against his kin. Nowhere so much as in New York was difference of opinion on the wisdom of this move so pronounced. And perhaps nowhere in the colonies did it usher in so much hardship and difficulty. One-third of the Revolutionary battles were fought on New York soil; its frontier settlements suffered unspeakable privations—they were burned, sacked and massacred. Communities were divided and Tory fought Rebel with Indians as allies.

Governmentally, there was little order. Throughout the Revolution New York City was run by the British army. Elsewhere loose political organizations sought to pass and enforce laws. The British colonial government had passed, and, in response to a suggestion from the Continental Congress, a committee had begun to draft a constitution. The document, patterned closely on what had gone before, was adopted as the first constitution on April 20, 1777. Characteristic of the times was the fact that the first Governor, General George Clinton, leading his troops, was not able to take his oath at Kingston until July 30, 1777.

Nor was the document the sort of blueprint of government one would expect from a reading of the Declaration of Independence. A chosen class of property owners picked the lower house of the legislature; a more highly selected group elected the governor and the upper chamber. Even the right of local self-government was severely compromised. Yet the Constitution of 1777 served the State of New York not only through the trials of war but for 45 years.

81. All of the following statements about New York State during the Revolutionary War are true *except*
(1) there was much hardship   (2) one-third of the battles were fought on its soil   (3) all the people were united   (4) the frontier settlements were in danger   (5) the Indians were allies of the Tories

82. New York ceased being a colony in spirit
(1) when the British army left   (2) when its constitution was adopted   (3) on July 30, 1777   (4) on April 20, 1777   (5) when the Declaration of Independence was signed

83. During the Revolution, New York City
(1) was governed by Governor George Clinton   (2) was ruled by the British army   (3) was the scene of Indian massacres   (4) was the place of the inauguration of the first Governor   (5) was the site of the reading of the Declaration of Independence on July 11, 1776.

84. The formation of the State Constitution was
(1) begun by the British colonial government   (2) announced in White Plains on July 11, 1776   (3) announced at Kingston on July 30, 1777   (4) suggested by the Continental Congress   (5) finally approved in 1776.

85. All of the following statements about the State Constitution are true *except*   85. 1 2 3 4 5
(1) it served the State for 45 years   (2) it served the State during the
Revolutionary War   (3) it was based entirely on the principles of the Declaration of Independence   (4) the Governor was not elected by a popular
vote of the people   (5) the legislature was picked by property owners

Selection 19

We must pursue a course designed not merely to reduce the number of delinquents. We must increase the chances for such young people to lead productive
lives.
For these delinquent and potentially delinquent youth, we must offer a New
Start. We must insure that the special resources and skills essential for their
treatment and rehabilitation are available. Because many of these young men
and women live in broken families, burdened with financial and psychological
problems, a successful rehabilitation program must include family counseling,
vocational guidance, education and health services. It must strengthen the family
and the schools. It must offer courts an alternative to placing young delinquents
in penal institutions.
I recommend the Juvenile Delinquency Prevention Act of 1967.
This act would be administered by the Secretary of Health, Education and
Welfare. It would provide:
90 per cent Federal matching grants to assist states and local communities to
develop plans to improve their juvenile courts and correction systems.
50 per cent Federal matching grants for the construction of short-term detention
and treatment facilities for youthful offenders in or near their communities.
Flexible Federal matching grants to assist local communities to operate special
diagnostic and treatment programs for juvenile delinquents and potential
delinquents.
Federal support for research and experimental projects in juvenile delinquency.
States and communities must be encouraged to develop comprehensive strate-
gies for coping with these problems. The facilities they build should be modern
and innovating, like the "half-way" houses already proven successful in practice.
These facilities should provide a wide range of community-based treatment and
rehabilitation services for youth offenders.
New methods of rehabilitation—establishing new ties between the correctional
institution, the job market and the supporting services a delinquent youth needs
when he returns to the community—should be tested.

—Lyndon B. Johnson

86. The emphasis in President Johnson's speech is on   86. 1 2 3 4 5
(1) diagnosis and research   (2) prevention and rehabilitation   (3) rehabilitation and research   (4) treatment and diagnosis   (5) research and
diagnosis

87. A "halfway house" is a link between   87. 1 2 3 4 5
(1) home and school   (2) the courts and a job   (3) correctional institution
and community   (4) local public agencies and local private agencies   (5)
research and rehabilitation

88. The new start for delinquent youth includes *all* of the following EXCEPT
(1) court placement in penal institutions   (2) educational services   (3) family counseling   (4) health services   (5) vocational guidance

88. 1   2   3   4   5
     || || || || ||

89. The proposals of President Johnson to combat juvenile delinquency would provide federal financial aid for *all* of the following EXCEPT
(1) research projects   (2) diagnostic programs   (3) temporary detention centers   (4) improvement of juvenile courts   (5) a National Crime Commission

89. 1   2   3   4   5
     || || || || ||

90. The Juvenile Delinquency Act of 1967 would be administered by
(1) local agencies   (2) the States   (3) Congress   (4) the Department of Health, Education and Welfare   (5) the courts

90. 1   2   3   4   5
     || || || || ||

Selection 20

"After all, sir, we must submit to this idea, that the true principle of a republic is, that the people should choose whom they please to govern them. Representation is imperfect in proportion as the current of popular favor is checked. This great source of free government, popular election, should be perfectly pure, and the most unbounded liberty allowed. Where this principle is adhered to; where, in the organization of the government, the legislative, executive, and judicial branches are rendered distinct; where, again, the legislature is divided into separate houses, and the operations of each are controlled by various checks and balances, and, above all, by the vigilance and weight of the state governments,—to talk of tyranny, and the subversion of our liberties, is to speak the language of enthusiasm. This balance between the national and state governments ought to be dwelt on with peculiar attention, as it is of the utmost importance. It forms a double security to the people. If one encroaches on their rights, they will find a powerful protection in the other. Indeed, they will both be prevented from overpassing their constitutional limits, by a certain rivalship which will ever subsist between them. I am persuaded that a firm union is as necessary to perpetuate our liberties as it is to make us respectable; and experience will probably prove that the national government will be as natural a guardian of our freedom as the state legislature(s) themselves."

—Alexander Hamilton

— — —

"An honorable gentleman from New York has remarked that the idea of *danger to state governments* can originate in a distempered fancy: he stated that they were necessary component parts of the system, and informed us how the President and senators were to be elected; his conclusion is, that the liberties of the people can not be endangered. I shall only observe, that, however fanciful these apprehensions may appear to him, they have made serious impressions upon some of the greatest and best men. Our fears arise from the experience of all ages and our knowledge of the dispositions of mankind. I believe the gentleman can not point out an instance of the rights of the people remaining for a long period inviolate. . . . Sir, wherever the revenues and the military force are, there will rest the power: the members or the head will prevail, as one or the other possesses these advantages. . . . Sir, if you do not give the state governments a power to protect themselves, if you leave them no other check upon Congress than the power of appointing senators, they will certainly be overcome, like the barons of whom the gentleman has spoken. Neither our civil nor militia officers will afford many advantages of opposition against the national government: if they have any powers, it will ever be difficult to concentrate them, or give them a uniform direction. Their influence will hardly be felt, while the greater number of lucrative and honorable places, in the gift of the United States, will establish an influence which will prevail in every part of the continent."

—John Lansing

91. Which one of the groups (1–5) listed below indicates statements that are consistent with Mr. Hamilton's arguments for establishing a centralized government?

   a. A centralized government would increase the nation's prestige.

   b. A centralized government would provide a double security for individual liberty.

   c. The rivalry between Federal and state governments would lead to friction between the states.

   d. The state governments would have even more influence in checking the power of the national government than would the system of checks and balances.

   e. The maintenance of a standing army would promote centralized power.

   (1) *a, b, c, d*　(2) *a, b, d*　(3) *a, b, e*　(4) *b, c, d*　(5) *c, d, e*

91. 1 2 3 4 5

92. Which one of the groups (1–5) listed below indicates Mr. Lansing's reasons for believing the Federal government would overshadow the state governments?

   a. control of patronage

   b. feeling of nationalism

   c. power of the civil officers

   d. power to raise an army

   e. power to tax

   (1) *a, b, c*　(2) *a, b, d*　(3) *a, d, e*　(4) *b, c, d*　(5) *b, c, e*

92. 1 2 3 4 5

93. Which one of the groups (1–5) listed below indicates topics on which Mr. Hamilton and Mr. Lansing disagree?

   a. ability of the states to check national power

   b. dangers to individual rights in a Federal system

   c. faith in the state rather than in the national government

   d. method of appointing senators

   e. necessity for a Federal union

   (1) *a, b, c*　(2) *a, c, e*　(3) *b, c, d*　(4) *b, d, e*　(5) *c, d, e*

93. 1 2 3 4 5

94. According to the passage, which one of the following did Mr. Hamilton believe?

(1) States should determine voting qualifications.　(2) Suffrage should be granted to all adult males.　(3) Suffrage should be limited.　(4) Suffrage should be unrestricted.　(5) United States Senators should be appointed by the state legislatures.

94. 1 2 3 4 5

95. On which one of the following topics did John Lansing base his arguments for state sovereignty?
(1) antipathy toward Hamilton (2) danger of excessive Federal taxation (3) distrust of contemporary leaders (4) examples from past history (5) personal experience under the Articles of Confederation

95. 1 2 3 4 5

Selection 21

The political party organization is designed to influence voters to support its candidates. Its base of direct operations is therefore the voting district where approximately 700 citizens cast their ballots. The entire State—metropolitan, urban and rural—is divided into such small areas, not so much because people could not conveniently vote in a few central locations, but because they could not be canvassed by party workers so effectively.

Ordinarily, the enrolled party members choose two committeemen at the annual fall primary in September except that in the presidential election year the action is taken at the spring primary in June. The county committee may by rule, however, set the term at two years; it may demand equal representation of the sexes so that there will be one committeeman and one committeewoman in each district; it can provide for as many as four committee members from a large district as long as the representation is proportional. The important point is that the primary is for each party an election for its own officers.

The names of the candidates for committeeman are placed on the ballot only when a petition is filed with the board of elections signed by 5 percent of the party members. Anyone aspiring to the position may have his name put on the ballot. But in practice the individual who has been handling party affairs, who has the blessing of the county committee and its endorsement, is difficult to beat. This situation is the result of the small turnout for primary elections. In rural areas particularly, write-in votes for precinct committeeman are, however, relatively common.

96. A prime purpose for limiting the size of the voting district to approximately 700 citizens is
(1) to allow better canvassing by party workers (2) because people could not conveniently vote in a few central locations (3) to influence the voters to consider candidates of the other parties (4) to reduce the number of political parties (5) to give rural areas the same power as the cities

96. 1 2 3 4 5

97. All of the following statements about committeemen are true EXCEPT
(1) two are chosen at the September primary (2) the elections take place at the June primary during a presidential election year (3) the term of office may be set at two years by the county committee (4) a large district may have four committee members (5) women may not serve on the committee

97. 1 2 3 4 5

98. The best title for this selection is
(1) The Presidential Election Year (2) The Designation of Electors (3) District Committeemen (4) Power of the Political Party (5) The Rural Vote

98. 1 2 3 4 5

99. The purpose of the primary election is
(1) to designate the primary candidate   (2) to insure proportional representation   (3) to equalize the vote of the sexes   (4) for each party to elect its own officers   (5) for the nomination of four committeemen per district

99. 1 2 3 4 5

100. All of the following statements about the candidates for committeeman are true EXCEPT
(1) the designee of the county committee is usually elected   (2) anyone is eligible to have his name put on the ballot   (3) the individual who has been handling party affairs is automatically elected   (4) write-in votes are relatively common in rural areas   (5) a name is placed on the ballot if it is supported by a petition of 5 percent of the party members

100. 1 2 3 4 5

ANSWERS TO *Reading Selections in the Social Studies*

1. 2	11. 3	21. 1	31. 4	41. 2	51. 3	61. 5	71. 3	81. 3	91. 2
2. 3	12. 5	22. 5	32. 5	42. 3	52. 2	62. 3	72. 2	82. 5	92. 3
3. 1	13. 1	23. 4	33. 2	43. 1	53. 5	63. 4	73. 4	83. 2	93. 1
4. 3	14. 2	24. 4	34. 3	44. 3	54. 1	64. 5	74. 2	84. 4	94. 4
5. 3	15. 1	25. 3	35. 3	45. 3	55. 3	65. 1	75. 1	85. 3	95. 4
6. 4	16. 4	26. 3	36. 2	46. 1	56. 4	66. 4	76. 4	86. 2	96. 1
7. 4	17. 2	27. 5	37. 5	47. 4	57. 1	67. 1	77. 3	87. 3	97. 5
8. 5	18. 2	28. 5	38. 5	48. 4	58. 5	68. 5	78. 5	88. 1	98. 3
9. 2	19. 4	29. 5	39. 3	49. 4	59. 2	69. 3	79. 4	89. 5	99. 4
10. 5	20. 1	30. 4	40. 1	50. 3	60. 1	70. 1	80. 5	90. 4	100. 3

What's your score?

_____ right, _____ wrong

Excellent	90–100
Good	80–89
Fair	65–79

If your score was low, the explanation of the correct answers which follows will help you. Analyze your errors. Reread the 8 Hints for Handling Reading Comprehension in Chapter 1.

ANSWERS EXPLAINED

1. Ans. 2 The selection deals with various aspects of depressions. The latter portion indicates that a possible cure for depressions may lie in the increased buying power of the masses, and the importance of savings. This will provide a market for the products of farm and factory.

2. Ans. 3 If consumers save, they will have buying power to furnish an adequate market for the products of farm and factory.

3. Ans. 1 The introductory sentence of the passage states that there are certain characteristics of business prior to depressions, such as rising prices, rising profits and a rapid expansion of credit.

4. Ans. 3 The theme of the passage is expressed in the fourth sentence. The American statesmen are described as not only performing their political function, but also as expressing a more universal responsibility. This is the basis of American political philosophy.

5. Ans. 3 The opening words of the passage indicate that the intellectuals who lead the way for a revolution are usually devoured, or destroyed, by the forces which are unleashed.

6. Ans. 4 The middle part of the passage states that American political science is the only one perfectly adapted to the emergencies of the contemporary world.

7. Ans. 4 The passage indicates that Lincoln had learned the art of storytelling to illustrate his point. This technique has been used by the peddler, the traveling salesman, the storekeeper, lawyer and politician. Lincoln expressed himself in a masterful way throughout his experience, whether he was floating a raft down the river, or speaking as President.

8. Ans. 5 The only occupation, of those mentioned in the question, that Lincoln practiced, was that of President of the United States.

9. Ans. 2 He drew his homely anecdotes from backwoods experience to make a point, not merely to amuse others.

10. Ans. 5 The author shows much insight into the qualities that made Lincoln so successful. He would have to be a student of Lincoln's life to know so much about his development.

11. Ans. 3 The passage indicates that although times have changed, the Mideast itself has not changed. This idea is stated in the last sentence of the second paragraph.

12. Ans. 5 The last paragraph states that man has dominated the stage of the turbulent Middle East through such weaknesses as his emotions, his ignorance, and his wars.

13. Ans. 1 The second and fourth paragraphs contain references to man's unchanging nature through the ages.

14. Ans. 2 The monuments and ancient relics mentioned in the first and third paragraphs were created as grandiose efforts by vain men.

15. Ans. 1 The final part of the second paragraph refers to man's existence centuries before Christ.

16. Ans. 4 In the middle part of the passage, there is a description of the steps taken to alleviate the suffering of the people after the great fire, i.e., opening the Imperial gardens to the multitude, erecting temporary buildings, and distributing food at a very moderate price.

17. Ans. 2 There is reference to the prudence and humanity of Nero in providing for the people after the fire. The charges against him are mentioned as being rumors.

18. Ans. 2 In the third sentence, it is mentioned that only four of the fourteen regions into which Rome was divided remained unaffected by the devastation. The remaining ten sections were ruined. This is almost three-quarters of the total city.

19. Ans. 4 The passage states that the government regulated the disposition of the streets, along with all the other steps it took to improve the situation.

20. Ans. 1 The author points out that Nero was under popular suspicion as the assassin of his mother and wife, as being capable of the most extravagant folly, as being responsible for setting the fire, and for singing to his lyre during the blaze.

21. Ans. 1 The last paragraph of the passage states clearly that the Governor's veto power is not used sparingly, and that more than one out of four bills fails to receive approval.

22. Ans. 5 From the content of the passage, it should be understood that it deals primarily with the veto power of the Governor, and how a bill becomes law. The veto power of the President is barely mentioned.

23. Ans. 4 The reader is referrred to the fourth paragraph of the selection, which deals with the "30-day" rule. The first sentence of this paragraph states that all bills passed within the last ten days of the legislative session are covered by this rule.

24. Ans. 4 The first sentence of the third paragraph states that the Governor has the power to veto single items of the budget bill. This is an authority not possessed by the President of the United States.

25. Ans. 3 This question requires that two conditions be mentioned that are correct. The only choice that fulfills this requirement is number 3. As is indicated at the beginning of the second paragraph, failure of the Governor to sign the bill within ten days (not counting Sundays) results in it becoming law. The first paragraph contains the statement that two-thirds of the members elected to each house may approve a bill that he has vetoed, and make it law.

26. Ans. 3 At the beginning of the passage, Franklin states that he has been particular to give a detailed account of his entry into Philadelphia, in order to compare this beginning with his later achievement.

27. Ans. 5 He states that he was tired, hungry and dirty. Also, that his whole stock of cash consisted of a Dutch dollar and about a shilling. He was also generous, in giving the shilling for his boat passage, and two of his rolls to a woman and her child on the boat.

28. Ans. 5 He did not have his best clothes with him, inasmuch as they were being delivered by sea. This information occurs in the first paragraph.

29. Ans. 5 In describing his stroll, he states that he walked back to the Market Street wharf, near the boat on which he had arrived.

30. Ans. 4 Although he asked for a biscuit, with the intention of buying one, he was only able to purchase three great puffy rolls, instead.

31. Ans. 4 The selection deals with conditions in the Netherlands in the sixteenth and seventeenth centuries. There is an exact reference to this period at the end of the first paragraph.

32. Ans. 5 The introductory part of the passage discusses the meaning of the expression, and mentions that the Dutch excelled in one way or another.

33. Ans. 2 The Low Countries, or the Netherlands, were located at the crossroads of maritime trade. The second paragraph describes the great sea traffic that took place there.

34. Ans. 3 The Netherlands became an asylum for religious dissenters at a time when the ruler of the vast empire that included Spain and this country was a fanatical defender of the Catholic faith. This point is made in the third paragraph.

35. Ans. 3 The latter part of the third paragraph states that there were places for refugees in the prosperity of the Netherlands.

36. Ans. 2 Although there were various people involved in the planning and construction of the Capitol, the design itself was prepared by Dr. William Thornton, an amateur architect. See the second paragraph.

37. Ans. 5 The low wooden dome capped with copper was not put into place until 1859. This was the last section of the Capitol as originally planned.

38. Ans. 5 As the first paragraph indicates, the Capitol is the home of the legislative branch of the federal government, consisting of the House of Representatives and the Senate.

39. Ans. 3 When the two Houses of Congress outgrew their quarters, Congress decided in 1850 to build two entirely new chambers. These were designed by Thomas U. Walter.

40. Ans. 1 The enormous iron dome is the symbol of the Capitol today. The last paragraph describes its appearance, and its characteristics.

41. Ans. 2 This is the famous Gettysburg Address, one of the most famous speeches ever delivered. It is notable not only for its remarkable conciseness, but also for the loftiness of its expression and for the almost poetic phrasing of its words. The occasion was the commemoration of the cemetery at Gettysburg, following the bloody battle fought there during the Civil War. The speaker, of course, was President Abraham Lincoln.

42. Ans. 3 See the explanation for the answer to the preceding question.

43. Ans. 1 The Gettysburg Address was delivered in 1863. Fourscore and seven years earlier, that is, 87 years earlier, the Declaration of Independence had been signed. It declared the liberty of the thirteen colonies and stated that all men are created equal.

44. Ans. 3 As was explained in the answer to question 41, the speech was delivered at the Gettysburg Cemetery. In the second paragraph, Lincoln states that this is the purpose of the occasion.

45. Ans. 3 Lincoln thought that his words would not be remembered very long after the dedication of the cemetery. This was an incorrect prediction because his speech has endured through the years.

46. Ans. 1 The passage deals with the voyage of the *Half Moon* under the direction of Henry Hudson, in 1609. The New World had been discovered by Columbus in 1492. The passage refers to the fact that Hudson landed at Newfoundland, but does not claim that he discovered it.

47. Ans. 4 The opening sentence of the passage states that the *Half Moon* set sail from Amsterdam.

48. Ans. 4 The date of the start of the trip is given in the first sentence, as April 6. In Van Metern's record, the last sentence indicates that they reached the coast of Nova Francia on the 18th of July.

49. Ans. 4 The makeup of the crew is discussed in the first sentence of Van Metern's report.

50. Ans. 3 Although Hudson was primarily interested in gaining a new route to the East, the last sentence of the passage indicates that he was also interested in exploring the new lands that he visited.

51. Ans. 3 The author states that he lived among the Indians. In fact, he declares that they were so ignorant that their children screamed in terror when they saw him.

52. Ans. 2 In the third sentence, the author points out that although there was a similarity in their modes of thought, the Indians of the lake, ocean, forest and plains regions differed in their manner of life.

53. Ans. 5 The author refers to their stone age implements, their superstitions, ignorance of the white man, and their garments of skins; but he does not mention their extreme cruelty.

54. Ans. 1 In the last paragraph, the author mentions the great changes that are at hand for the Indians, including the restrictions of decreased food supply, the presence of military posts, and the influence of whiskey. He does not mention that there would be an improvement in the intellect of the Indians.

55. Ans. 3 In the last sentences, Parkman seems to regret the disappearance of the charm, as well as the danger of the West, as a result of the changes that are to take place.

56. Ans. 4 Although there are now at least 121 member countries in the United Nations, it does not include every nation on earth, and does not constitute a world government.

57. Ans. 1 The end of the third paragraph contains the statement that certain activities of the UN are centered outside of the New York City headquarters, particularly in Geneva, Switzerland and The Hague in The Netherlands.

58. Ans. 5 The United Nations is the successor to the old League of Nations that was organized after World War I. The six principal organs of the United Nations are mentioned in the third paragraph.

59. Ans. 2 The final paragraph of the passage contains the statement that the President of the General Assembly is elected for each annual session. He therefore serves for one year.

60. Ans. 1 Regardless of its size, each member country is entitled to only one vote in the General Assembly. On the other hand, it may have as many as five representatives, depending on its size.

61. Ans. 5 Since the selection deals with a description of the caste system in India, the last choice would serve as the best title.

62. Ans. 3 The third paragraph indicates that the Brahmans stand at the top of the social ladder in India. The "Untouchables," or the "Depressed Classes" are described in the last paragraph.

63. Ans. 4 The third paragraph describes the status of the Brahman caste. As the highest caste, Brahmans are well above the "Untouchables," who are the lowest.

64. Ans. 5 As an insignia of their rank, Brahmans may carry a sacred thread over their left shoulder, as is mentioned in the fifth paragraph. Pandit Nehru was a Brahman (see third paragraph).

65. Ans. 1 The seventh paragraph indicates that the growth of industrial development and modern living conditions in the cities has been the cause of a break-down in the rigid caste rules.

66. Ans. 4 The selection deals specifically with the invasion of Normandy on June 6, 1944. The reasons for the selection of the beaches of Normandy are mentioned, as well as the cooperation of the Allies, when the fateful decision was made to go ahead with the attack. All of these details were part of the overall invasion plans.

67. Ans. 1 The last two paragraphs describe the order of events in the attack, starting with the dropping of airborne troops, or parachutists, to the first waves of infantry and tank assaults.

68. Ans. 5 The action started at 0200 hours, and four hours and 30 minutes later, or at 0630, the first waves of infantry and tanks landed on the invasion beaches.

69. Ans. 3 One of the reasons for selecting the beaches was the relative weakness of the German defenses, mentioned in the first paragraph. There were a number of obstacles to be overcome, however, such as the high winds and the rough seas. Two artificial harbors were constructed in Britain because of the lack of port facilities. Another obstacle mentioned in the second paragraph was the overcrowded harbors on the south coast.

70. Ans. 1 The end of the second paragraph refers to the fact that General Eisenhower made the fateful decision to go ahead. This indicates that he was the highest in authority, and all other actions flowed from his command.

71. Ans. 3 As mentioned in the second paragraph, a United Nations convention is also an international treaty.

72. Ans. 2 As indicated in the third paragraph, the word genocide is the joining together of the Greek *genos*, meaning race or tribe, with the Latin suffix *cide*, meaning killing.

73. Ans. 4 The fifth paragraph gives the scope of the term genocide, as including the intent to destroy a national, ethnical, racial, or religious group. It does not refer to political groups, as such.

74. Ans. 2 Genocide was practiced on a large scale by the Nazis in the destruction of six million Jews. Other groups that have been subjected to genocide, as is mentioned in the fourth paragraph, are Armenians, Gypsies and Chinese.

75. Ans. 1 The last sentence of the passage indicates that the United States has abstained from ratifying the convention.

76. Ans. 4 This obviously is a ruling of a court. Of the choices given, only that dealing with the Supreme Court would be correct. Incidentally, this selection is part of the important decision of the Supreme Court on the subject of desegregation of schools.

77. Ans. 3 The last paragraph states that the Court is rejecting the *Plessy* v. *Ferguson* decision. The other two decisions of the Court are used to substantiate its position. The Fourteenth Amendment is cited as guaranteeing protection. The Constitution prevents a person from losing his rights without due process of law.

78. Ans. 5 The last choice is not correct, because the Due Process Clause does not provide for segregation within the framework of the law. All the other choices are correctly stated throughout the passage.

79. Ans. 4 The passage indicates that to separate children in grade and high schools solely because of race is to generate a feeling of inferiority that may affect their hearts and minds. These are psychological reasons for rejecting segregation, since they deal with effects on the mind and the emotions.

80. Ans. 5 The last paragraph of the selection states that the Court rejects the doctrine of "separate but equal." It holds that separate educational facilities are inherently unequal.

81. Ans. 3 The point is made in the second paragraph that there was much difference of opinion on the wisdom of independence. Families were split on the matter, and communities were divided.

82. Ans. 5 With the signing of the Declaration of Independence, the thirteen colonies severed their relations with England. The first sentence of the selection declares that New York ceased to be a colony in spirit at that time, and with the reading of the document at various places throughout the area.

83. Ans. 2 The third paragraph states that New York City was under the domination of the British army during the Revolution.

84. Ans. 4 During those early days, there was little governmental order. A committee began to draft the constitution in response to a suggestion from the Continental Congress. These points are made in the third paragraph.

85. Ans. 3 The new constitution was hardly based on the principles of the Declaration of Independence. The last paragraph of the selection indicates that it was not the sort of document to be expected from a reading of the Declaration. The legislature and the governor were not elected by a vote of all the people, but instead, were chosen by a group of property owners.

86. Ans. 2 The purpose of President Johnson's speech is to help troubled young people lead productive lives. In dealing with delinquent and potentially delinquent youth, he is concerned about preventing them from getting into trouble; and then, if they do, in helping them to become useful citizens. These ideas are stated in the first two paragraphs, and in the rest of the selection.

87. Ans. 3 As indicated, near the end of the selection, the purpose of the half-way house is to rehabilitate youthful offenders in such a way that they are ready to return to the community through the job market.

88. Ans. 1 The steps in the New Start are described in the second paragraph. The last sentence states that they are an alternative to placing young delinquents in penal institutions.

89. Ans. 5 In stating the provisions of the Juvenile Delinquency Prevention Act of 1967, President Johnson gives the details of the federally financed program. These details are stated in the section following the third paragraph. Since the purpose is prevention and rehabilitation, there is no reference to a National Crime Commission.

90. Ans. 4 The fourth paragraph contains the statement that the act would be administered by the Secretary of Health, Education and Welfare.

91. Ans. 2 In the last sentence, Hamilton refers to the importance of a national government in making us respectable, or in increasing the nation's prestige. In the sixth sentence, he refers to a double security for the people arising out of a balance between a centralized government and a state government. He also refers, earlier in the selection, to the vigilance and weight of the state governments in checking the national government.

92. Ans. 3 In the last sentence, Lansing refers to the control of patronage, through the "number of lucrative and honorable places," that would be placed in the hands of the national government. In the middle of the passage, he mentions the power residing in the revenues and the military forces.

93. Ans. 1 Hamilton believes that the states can check national power, while Lansing fears the dangers of centralizing too much power in the national government. The latter makes the statement, in the last part of his selection, that the state governments would be overcome by Congress. Hamilton believes that individual rights would be protected in a federal system, through the system of "double security." Lansing claims that the rights of the people would not remain inviolate. Lansing refers to the dangers to state governments, in his opening sentence, while Hamilton mentions the importance of a national government in his last sentence.

94. Ans. 4 Hamilton believes in unrestricted suffrage, or voting ability, on the part of the people, as stated in his opening sentence.

95. Ans. 4 In the third sentence of his statement, Lansing refers to the experience of all ages in proving his point.

96. Ans. 1 As the end of the first paragraph indicates, the reason for limiting the size of the voting district is to bring the election to the citizen's neighborhood. Thus, it creates a constituency in which the party workers can operate effectively. The party workers can get to know all the voters in the district.

97. Ans. 5 Women are permitted to serve. In fact, as the middle of the second paragraph shows, the county committee may require equal representation of the sexes in each district.

98. Ans. 3 The selection deals with the subject of district committeemen, how they are nominated, and their term of office.

99. Ans. 4 The end of the second paragraph contains the statement giving the purpose of the primary.

100. Ans. 3 This statement is almost, but not entirely, true. The third paragraph indicates that the individual who has been handling party affairs is difficult to beat. This does not mean that he is automatically elected. He must go through the same process as all other candidates before he can be considered elected.

For Further Reading

Barron's Preparation for the High School Equivalency Examination—Reading Interpretation Tests, by Eugene J. Farley, provides extensive practice material and drill in this area.

6

The Test of Interpretation of Reading Materials in the Natural Sciences

This chapter will help you prepare for the science part of the High School Equivalency Examination. This test stresses logical reasoning, the ability to pay close attention to detail, and the ability to interpret the science content of various selections. It may also demand certain background information of high school general science dealing with some of the important scientific topics, generalizations, and developments. The reading selections, however, are not really "technical" in nature, and do not require the memorization of countless detailed facts.

HOW THIS CHAPTER CAN HELP YOU

The Glossary of Scientific Terms will help you to understand the reading passages because it explains many scientific terms which are referred to in the reading. Don't try to memorize the terms. Use this glossary for reference and information.

The question-by-question analysis of the sample selection which precedes the practice section will help you to understand the reasons for the choice of the correct answer. As you read the various passages, place a check mark alongside the most important ideas. Then, as you answer the questions, you will find it easy to locate these important points. If you are not sure of an answer, leave the question and come back to it after you have finished the others. This will allow you credit for what you know, and time to answer the more difficult question afterward.

A WORD OF ADVICE

In the examination room, you will probably not be pressed for time. However, it usually takes about two hours to do all the selections given on the Test of Interpretation of Reading Materials in Natural Sciences. In the practice exercises in this section, do not attempt to answer more than five or six selections at one sitting. Check your answers with those furnished at the end of the chapter. If an error is not obvious to you, refer to the explanation of the answers. Also check on the method explained in the sample analysis, and the tips for improving reading comprehension in Chapter 1.

TIME TO STUDY:

GLOSSARY OF SCIENTIFIC TERMS

ABDOMEN   posterior part of the body in higher animals

ABIOGENESIS   belief that living things may develop from lifeless matter

ABSOLUTE HUMIDITY   the amount of water vapor actually contained in a given quantity of air

ABSORPTION   the passage of digested food through the walls of the villi of the small intestine into the surrounding lymph and blood vessels

ACCELERATION   the change in speed when something is made to go faster

ACCRETION   increase in size of nonliving things by the addition of molecules around a center

ACETYLCHOLINE   one of the substances secreted by the end brushes of many neurons at certain synapses and nerve endings

ACID   a compound that dissociates in water to produce hydrogen ions and is usually sour

ACTH   (Adreno-Corticotropic Hormone), a hormone produced by the anterior lobe of the pituitary gland, the master gland of the body; stimulates the adrenal glands to secrete a hormone known as cortisone

ACTIVE TRANSPORT   process by which a cell uses metabolic energy to move substances through its membrane

ADIPOSE TISSUE   tissue in which fat or oil is stored

ADRENAL CORTEX   outer part of the adrenal glands

ADRENAL MEDULLA   core of the adrenal glands, which secretes adrenalin

ADRENALIN   hormone of the adrenal gland which functions in emergencies

AGAR   a gelatin-like substance obtained from seaweed; used in making culture medium for growing microorganisms

AGGLUTININ   plasma protein which reacts with a corresponding agglutinogen in clumping blood

AGONIC LINE   a line connecting locations of zero magnetic variation

AILERON   a flap in the edge of the wings of an airplane which controls its course

AIR MASS   a large body of air having the same temperature, pressure, and humidity

AIR SAC   microscopic structure in the lungs where gas exchange takes place

ALBINISM   hereditary trait in which there is a lack of pigment in the skin, hair, and eyes

ALGA (ALGAE)   one of a group of simple chlorophyll-containing plants

ALKALI   a soluble base (containing the OH radical)

ALLERGY   tendency to develop antibodies against otherwise harmless substances

ALLOY   a substance composed of two or more metals

ALTERNATING CURRENT   an electric current that changes its direction in regular cycles

ALTIMETER   an instrument used to measure height above the earth's surface

ALVEOLUS   an air sac in the lungs

AMBER   fossilized material from trees often containing fossil insects

AMEBA   a type of protozoan which has no definite shape

AMINO ACIDS   the end products of protein digestion; the inorganic building blocks of protoplasm

AMNION   liquid-filled membranous sac protecting the embryo in higher vertebrates

AMORPHOUS   without definite shape

AMPERE   the unit for measuring the intensity of an electric current

AMPHIBIANS   class of vertebrates that includes the frogs and salamanders

AMPLIFIER a device in a radio set that makes weak electric currents stronger

AMPLITUDE refers to the height of a wave (for instance, a sound wave) produced by a vibrating object

AMYLASE any enzyme which digests starch

ANAEROBIC RESPIRATION fermentation, or respiration in the absence of oxygen

ANATOMY branch of biology that studies the structure of organisms

ANEMIA condition in which the blood has insufficient red blood cells

ANEMOMETER an instrument used for measuring the velocity of the wind

ANEROID BAROMETER a type of barometer which does not use mercury or any other liquid

ANNULAR ECLIPSE a partial eclipse of the sun in which a ring of the sun appears around the black disk of the moon

ANOPHELES MOSQUITO a mosquito that carries the protozoan cause of malaria

ANTHER the part of the flower in which the pollen is produced

ANTIBIOTIC any substance made by a microorganism that destroys germs

ANTIBODY a substance, usually in the blood of an organism, which serves to counteract the effects of disease-producing bacteria

ANTICLINE the crest or upfold of a rock fold

ANTICYCLONE known as a "high"; a large mass of high pressure air with winds moving out from it clockwise

ANTIGEN a foreign substance that stimulates the body to produce antibodies

ANTISEPTIC a substance that prevents the growth or activity of germs

ANTITOXIN any substance in the body that neutralizes toxins

AORTA the largest artery which carries blood from the left ventrical of the heart to all the body except the lungs

APHELION the point on the earth's orbit farthest from the sun

APOGEE the position of a satellite at the point in its orbit when it is farthest from the earth

APPENDIX a wormlike, narrow part of the alimentary canal, in the lower righthand part of the abdomen of man

AQUA REGIA mixture of nitric acid and hydrochloric acid

ARCHIMEDES' PRINCIPLE a law which states that an object is buoyed upward by a force equal to the weight of the displaced liquid or gas

ARMATURE a piece of metal or a coil of wire that moves back and forth, or rotates, in a magnetic field

ARTERY vessel which carries blood from the heart

ARTERIOSCLEROSIS hardening of the arteries

ARTIFACTS man-made implements or structures

ASCORBIC ACID vitamin C; found in citrus fruits, tomatoes, and green vegetables

ASEPTIC free of live germs

ASEXUAL REPRODUCTION producing offspring by one parent

ASSIMILATION process by which digested food is utilized by the body to build up or repair cells

ASTEROID one of a group of "minor planets" between Mars and Jupiter, of which about 1,500 are known

ATMOSPHERE the whole mass of air surrounding the earth

ATOLL a circular coral reef which encloses a lagoon

ATOM the smallest quantity of an element that may exist and still have the properties of that element

ATOMIC FISSION the breaking down of an atom, especially its nucleus, into two or more parts, with a great release of energy

ATOMIC FUSION the joining of deuterium (heavy hydrogen) and tritium (another form of heavy hydrogen) to make helium

ATOMIC PILE a mass of uranium rods, imbedded in pure carbon, that produces a chain reaction and releases atomic energy

ATOMIC WEIGHT   the weight of an atom of any element compared with the weight of an atom of oxygen

ATP   (adenosine triphosphate), a substance that acts as a storehouse for respiration energy

AUREOMYCIN   an antibiotic produced by certain soil bacteria

AURICLE   a chamber of the heart which receives blood from the veins

AUXIN   a plant hormone

AXIS   an imaginary line through the earth's poles

AXON   the part of a nerve cell that carries impulses away from the cyton (cell body)

BACILLUS   rod-shaped bacteria

BACTERIA   microscopic, one-celled organisms depending on living or dead food material

BALANCE IN NATURE   the interdependence of all plants and animals with their environment

BANDING   practice of attaching a band or tag to an animal (usually a bird) to study its travel habits

BAROGRAPH   an instrument which measures and records changes in air pressure

BAROMETER   an instrument for measuring air pressure

BASAL METABOLISM   the rate of the body's activities when it is at rest

BEDROCK   the weathered solid rock of the earth's crust

BENIGN TUMOR   a growth which though abnormal, does not spread, but remains localized and does no particular harm unless it presses upon a vital organ

BERIBERI   a disease caused by a diet lacking vitamin B_1 (thiamine)

BETA PARTICLES   high-speed electrons

BILE   a fluid which is secreted by the liver and passes into the small intestine, where it aids in the digestion of fats

BINARY FISSION   equal division of nucleus and cytoplasm in one-celled organisms

BIOME   a community of plants and animals

BIOPSY   the removal of a small part of living tissue for microscopic examination to see if it is malignant

BLOOD BANK   a place in which whole blood may be kept for future use in transfusions

BLOOD PLATELET   cell which assists in clotting of blood

BRAIN   the main center of the human nervous system, made up of a cerebrum, cerebellum, and medulla

BREEDER REACTOR   a nuclear reactor in which more atomic fuel is made than is used up

BRONCHIAL TUBE   one of the two branches of the windpipe

BUDDING   a form of asexual reproduction in which a small part of the organism develops into a new individual

BUFFER   a substance which tends to keep the pH (hydrogen-ion concentration) constant

CALCIUM   a chemical found in many vegetables and in milk; important in building healthy bones and teeth

CALORIE   a unit of measure of the energy obtainable from food

CALORIMETER   an instrument which measures the heat energy released by the oxidation of food

CAMBIUM   the actively growing layer of cells in the stems of higher plants

CANCER   an abnormal growth, which if not detected early and removed or destroyed, will usually, in time, spread widely throughout the body and ultimately cause death

CAPACITOR   another term for condenser

CAPILLARY   a thin-walled tube; one of the tiny blood vessels in the network connecting the arteries and the veins

CARBOHYDRATE   a compound made up of carbon, hydrogen, and oxygen (ex. starch, sugar)

CARBON DIOXIDE   a colorless, odorless gas present in the air in small amounts; breathed out from the lungs

CARBON MONOXIDE   a poisonous gas that prevents oxygen from entering the red blood cells; produced when gasoline is not completely burned

CARNIVORE a flesh-eating mammal with long eye teeth and sharp claws, like the cat, lion, and dog

CAROTENE a yellow substance that is changed to vitamin A in the human body

CARTILAGE an elastic, yet hard, tissue composing most of the skeleton of the very young of all vertebrates and breastbone of adults

CAST IRON brittle iron that is usually cast in molds

CATABOLISM the life processes which break down protoplasm for the release of energy

CATALYST a substance which affects the rate of a chemical reaction without any change to itself

CELL the basic unit of plant and animal life, consisting of a small mass of protoplasm, including a nucleus, surrounded by a semipermeable membrane

CELL MEMBRANE the thin outer layer of cytoplasm acting as a cell boundary

CELLULOSE a complex carbohydrate found in the wall of plant cells

CENTIGRADE THERMOMETER a thermometer that has 100 degrees or divisions between the freezing and boiling points of water; 0°C. is the freezing point, and 100°C. is the boiling point

CENTROSOMES structures found in the cytoplasm of animal cells and form asters during mitosis

CEREBELLUM the part of the brain lying behind and below the cerebrum; controls muscular coordination

CEREBRUM the part of the brain concerned with thought and judgment

CHAIN REACTION the reaction in which the splitting of one atom causes other atoms to undergo fission

CHEMICAL CHANGE a reaction during which substances lose their identity and change their composition

CHEMOTHERAPY treatment by chemicals (drugs)

CHEMISTRY the science that deals with the make-up of substances and how they are changed into other substances

CHLORINATION the treatment of water with chlorine to kill germs

CHLOROPHYLL a green substance that enables green plants to make glucose by the process of photosynthesis

CHLOROPLAST a small green body which contains chlorophyll

CHORION outermost membrane protecting the embryo in higher vertebrates; in mammals, helps form the placenta

CHROMATIN a network of fibrils within the nucleus, which carry the genes in inheritance

CHROMOSOME one of several small more or less rod-shaped bodies in the nucleus of a cell; contain the hereditary factors (genes)

CHRONOMETER an extremely accurate clock used in navigation

CHRYSALIS the pupa of the butterfly

CILIUM one of many microscopic, waving, hairlike structures projecting from a cell

CIRRUS CLOUD a white, filmy type of cloud, usually formed at high altitudes, generally consisting of ice crystals

CLAY finely ground quartz, feldspar, and mica resulting from the erosion of rocks

CLEAVAGE repeated division of an embryo's cells, without an increase in the total mass; also, the splitting of a mineral

CLIMAX COMMUNITY final stable stage in a succession within a particular area

CLOUD SEEDING artificial method of producing precipitation from clouds

COBALT 60 radioactive cobalt used mainly for the treatment of internal cancers

COCCUS a spherical bacterium

COCHLEA a coil-like structure in the inner ear

COENZYME substance which together with enzymes controls the chemical reactions of protoplasm

COLCHICINE chemical applied to plant tissue which causes doubling of number of chromosomes, often producing new varieties

COLLOID a state of matter between true solution and suspension

COLD FRONT   the boundary between a mass of advancing cool air and a mass of warm air

COMBUSTION   rapid oxidation caused by the chemical union of a substance with oxygen

COMET   a heavenly body with a head and tail, traveling in a long, oval orbit around the sun

COMPOUND   a substance composed of two or more elements chemically united

CONCAVE LENS   a lens which makes light rays spread apart

CONDENSATION   the process of forming a liquid or solid from a vapor or gas

CONDENSER   a device for the storage of electrical energy

CONDITIONED REFLEX   an acquired automatic response

CONDUCTOR   a material, such as a copper wire, which carries a flow of electrons (electricity)

CONJUGATION   a type of sexual reproduction in which the two similar cells unite

CONSERVATION   the wise and careful use of our natural resources

CONSTELLATION   any one of the groups of stars and the area of the sky in its vicinity to which a definite name has been given such as Ursa Major, the Great Bear

CONTOUR INTERVAL   the difference in elevation between two successive contour lines

CONTOUR PLOWING   plowing in which the furrows go around the hill instead of up and down

CONVECTION CURRENT   the circulation of air as warm air moves upward and cool air moves in to replace it

CONVEX LENS   a lens which makes light rays come together at a point (focus)

COPROLITES   fossil excrement

CORNEA   the transparent tissue in front of the iris and the pupil of the eye

CORONA   a bright white light which appears to surround the sun in an eclipse of the moon

CORONARY   pertaining to the heart muscle

CORPUSCLES   red cells, found in the blood

COSMIC RAY   a ray that apparently comes from beyond the earth's atmosphere and is made up in part of particles that move with the speed of light

CRACKING   a process by which the petroleum oils of different boiling points are separated from one another and from other petroleum compounds

CRETIN   a child showing physical and mental retardation due to improper functioning of thyroid gland at birth

CREVASSE   a deep crack in a glacier

CROSS POLLINATION   the transfer of pollen from the anther of one blossom to the stigma of another flower

CRYOGENICS   the branch of physics dealing with the production of very low temperature.

CUMULUS CLOUD   a type of cloud between 5,000 and 15,000 feet above the earth, having a flat base and rounded masses piled up like mountains

CUTTING   a piece of a root, stem or leaf which can be planted to produce a new plant

CYTOPLASM   that part of the cell that lies outside the nucleus; carries on all life activities except reproduction

CYCLONE   winds blowing counterclockwise about a nearly circular region of low air pressure in the Northern Hemisphere over an area covering thousands of square miles

CYCLOTRON   an instrument used to study the properties of atoms by increasing the speed of atomic particles

DECIBEL   a unit of measuring intensity of sound (loudness)

DENDRITE   fine branches of a nerve cell

DENTINE   material under the enamel of the tooth

DEHYDRATION   the loss of water

DELTA   a deposit of silt at the mouth of a river

DEUTERIUM   heavy hydrogen, with an atomic weight of 2

DEW   moisture condensed on the surfaces of cool bodies, especially at night

DEW POINT temperature at which the air becomes saturated with moisture

DEXTROSE a substance chemically similar to glucose

DIABETES a disease in which the body cannot utilize sugar because of lack of insulin

DIAPHRAGM a sheet of muscle which separates the chest cavity from the abdomen and by its movement helps in breathing; the name also used for the vibrating disk of metal in a telephone

DICK TEST used to determine immunity to scarlet fever

DICUMAROL a drug used to retard blood clotting

DIESEL ENGINE a form of internal-combustion engine, using heavy oil instead of gasoline as fuel

DIFFUSION the process whereby the molecules of substances tend to intermingle, as when two gases or solutions are brought into contact

DIGESTION a process of chemical change that prepares food for absorption by breaking down complex molecules into simpler ones

DNA (Deoxyribonucleic acid) a material found in the nucleus of cells that controls the genetic code

DIRECT CURRENT an electric current flowing in one direction only (as contrasted with alternating current)

DISINFECTANT a chemical that kills microbes

DISTILLATION the process of heating a substance until it turns into a gas, and of condensing this gas by cooling

DOLDRUMS a belt of calms near the equator

DRAG the force exerted to reduce the forward motion of an airplane

DUCTLESS GLAND an endocrine gland which has no tube or duct to carry away its secretion; therefore the secretion (hormone) goes directly into the blood stream

DUODENUM the part of the small intestine immediately past the stomach

DYNAMO a mechanical device used to produce an electric current by rotating an armature coil in a magnetic field

EARTHSHINE illumination of the darker portion of the moon by reflection of light from the earth

EBB TIDE the outgoing tide

ECLIPSE cutting off of light from one celestial body by another

ECOLOGY the study of the relations of living things with each other and with their environment

EFFICIENCY the amount of useful work done by a machine compared with the work put into it

EGG a female sex cell which may be fertilized by a sperm

ELECTRIC CIRCUIT a complete path in which electricity travels from its source out into a wire and back to its source

ELECTRIC CURRENT a flow of electrons from one place to another

ELECTRIC MOTOR a device that transforms electric energy into mechanical work

ELECTROLYSIS a chemical reaction in which an electric current is passed through a liquid

ELECTROLYTE a substance which when dissolved in water will conduct electricity

ELECTROMAGNET a core of soft iron surrounded by a coil of wire through which an electric current passes, thus magnetizing the core

ELECTRON MICROSCOPE an optical instrument using a beam of electrons directed through an object to produce an enlarged image of about 100,000 magnification on a fluorescent screen or photographic plate

ELECTROPLATING the process by which electricity is used to deposit metal ions on a substance

ELEVATOR the movable part of an airplane, attached to the stabilizer controlling climbing and diving

EMULSION a mixture of liquids that are not soluble in each other

ENAMEL the hard outer covering of the crown of a tooth

ENDOCRINE GLAND a ductless gland which secretes its hormone directly into the blood stream

ENERGY   the ability to do work

ENTOMOLOGY   the study of insects

ENZYME   an organic substance which speeds up the reaction of chemicals without itself being changed

EQUINOX   a moment, occurring twice each year on or about March 21 and September 23, when the sun appears to cross the celestial equator

EROSION   the wearing away of the earth's surface by water, ice and winds

ESOPHAGUS   (gullet) tube which connects mouth with stomach

ESTROGEN   hormone secreted by the ovaries

EVOLUTION   change of one species of living thing into other and different species from simple to complex forms

EXHAUST STROKE   the stroke of an engine in which the piston pushes the burned gases out of the cylinder

EXFOLIATION   the splitting off of scales or flakes of rock as a result of weathering

EXHALATION   the phase of breathing that expels air out of the lungs

EXTERNAL-COMBUSTION ENGINE   an engine in which the fuel is burned outside the engine

FAHRENHEIT SCALE   a scale on a thermometer graduated so that the freezing point of water is at 32° above zero, and the boiling point is at 212° above zero

FALL-OUT   radioactive particles that fall to earth as the result of an atomic or hydrogen bomb explosion

FARSIGHTEDNESS   a defect of the eye which forms sharper images of objects at a distance than of things nearby

FATTY ACIDS   the end-products of fat digestion

FAULTING   vertical or horizontal movements between great masses of bedrock

FAUNA   animal life typical for a particular region

FERMENTATION   a chemical change brought about by enzymes produced by microbes; in the making of beer or wine, yeasts ferment sugars into alcohol and carbon dioxide

FERTILIZATION   sexual reproduction in which the gametes, a sperm and an egg, unite

FIBRIN   threadlike protein which forms the meshwork of a blood clot

FIBRINOGEN   the part of blood plasma that helps to clot the blood

FILAMENT   the fine wire inside an electric light bulb that gives off light and heat when electricity is passed through

FILTRATE   the fluid which has passed through a filter

FILTRATION BEDS   layers of sand and gravel which catch soil and other particles as water passes through

FIORD   a drowned glacial valley

FLOWER   reproductive organ of seed plant

FLUORESCENT   an object which gives off light when struck by electrons or by visible or ultraviolet light

FOCUS   the point at which light rays are brought together, or seem to be brought together by a lens or mirror

FOG   a cloud of condensed water vapor formed on or near the ground

FOLIC ACID   one of the B-complex vitamins

FOOD CHAIN   a number of kinds of living things depending upon one another for food

FOOD WEB   the complex feeding relationships within a biological community

FOOT-POUND   a measurement of work done; the product of the number of feet an object is moved by the weight (in pounds) of the object

FORCE   a push or a pull on an object

FOSSIL   remains or impression of a living thing preserved in rock or amber

FRICTION   the resistance of two surfaces sliding over one another

FRONT   boundary between two air masses

FROST   a deposit of ice crystals which forms on objects that are colder than the freezing point of water

FRUIT   ripened seed-containing structure formed from the ovary of a flower

FULCRUM the point of rest upon which a lever turns in moving an object

FUNGUS a plant of simple structure which lacks chlorophyll and therefore cannot make its own food

FUSE a device to break an electric circuit that is overloaded

FUSELAGE the body of an airplane which holds the engine, passengers, cargo

GALAXY a large group of billions of stars

GALL BLADDER sac attached to the liver, which stores bile

GALVANIZE to coat iron with zinc to protect the surface of the iron

GAMETE sex cell which unites with another gamete in sexual reproduction

GAMMA GLOBULIN a protein in blood plasma which protects against diseases such as polio

GAMMA RAYS rays similar to X rays given off by exploding atoms

GASOLINE ENGINE an internal-combustion engine which uses the heat energy of gasoline for its operation

GASTRIC JUICE the acid digestive fluid given off by the glands in the walls of the stomach

GEIGER COUNTER an instrument that detects the presence of radioactive material by giving off clicks when radioactive particles strike its tube

GENE one of the particles of the chromosome that determines heredity

GENERATOR a machine that changes mechanical energy into electrical energy by cutting magnetic lines of force with coils of wire

GERM any one of the harmful bacteria, viruses, or protozoa

GLACIER a slow-moving mass of ice

GLAND a part of the body which makes secretions such as enzymes or hormones

GLUCOSE a simple, soluble sugar oxidized in the body to give energy

GLUTATHIONE substance released by an injured animal that stimulates a Portuguese man-of-war to eat it

GOITER an enlargement of the thyroid gland

GRAFTING joining the cut branch of one plant to that of a rooted plant which supplies water and minerals

GRAVITY the force that holds everything to the earth; the attraction between any two masses of matter

GULLET region of the alimentary canal that connects the mouth and the stomach

HABIT an acquired type of behavior resulting from practice until it is done automatically

HALF-LIFE time required for half of the atoms in a radioactive specimen to change to stable end products

HARD WATER water containing a large quantity of dissolved mineral salts

HEAVY WATER water in which the hydrogen is twice as heavy as in ordinary water

HEMOGLOBIN an iron-rich chemical found in the red blood cells, which unites with oxygen

HEMOPHILIA physical condition in which blood fails to clot properly; inherited by sons from mothers who are carriers

HEREDITY the passing of traits from parents to offspring through the genes in sperms and eggs

HIBERNATION the act of sleeping throughout some or all of the winter season

HORMONE chemical messenger produced by an endocrine gland; helps in controlling and coordinating the activities of the body

HORSE LATITUDE a belt of calm air under greater pressure, about 35° north or south of the equator

HORSEPOWER a unit for measuring rate of work, equal to 550 foot-pounds per second

HOST a plant or animal on which a parasite grows

HUMIDITY the amount of water vapor in the air

HUMUS dead and decaying organic matter found in the soil

HURRICANE a tropical storm that originates in the West Indies

HYDROGEN BOMB   a bomb consisting of deuterium and tritium (forms of heavy hydrogen) which are fused into helium releasing a great deal of energy

HYDROLYSIS   reaction between salt and water, in which an acid and a base are formed

HYDROMETER   an instrument used to measure the density (specific gravity) of a liquid

HYDROPONICS   soilless growth of plants

HYGROMETER   an instrument used to measure relative humidity

HYPOTHESIS   a theory or principle taken for granted as a basis for further investigation or research

IGNEOUS ROCK   formed by the cooling and hardening of hot molten rock

IMMUNITY   the body's ability to resist or overcome infection

IMPULSE   message that travels along nerve cells or fibers

INERTIA   the property of a body at rest remaining at rest, or a body in motion remaining in motion

INFECTION   invasion of the body by a foreign microbe

INFECTIOUS DISEASE   illness caused by microorganisms

INGESTION   the taking in of food

INHALATION   the phase of breathing that draws air into the lungs

INORGANIC COMPOUND   substance which contains any combination of elements except carbon

INSOLATION   the total energy received by the earth from the radiation of the sun

INSTINCT   complex inborn pattern of involuntary responses

INSULATION   any material used to reduce the transfer of heat or to shield a conductor of electricity

INSULIN   hormone secreted by the pancreas which enables cells to use glucose

INTERNAL-COMBUSTION ENGINE   an engine in which the fuel is burned inside the cylinders

INTERNATIONAL DATE LINE   a map boundary between west and east longitude, which lies on or near the 180th meridian

INTESTINE   a section of the digestive system below the stomach in which digestion and absorption of substances take place

INVERTEBRATES   animals without a backbone

ION   electrically charged atom or group of atoms

IONOSPHERE   that part of the atmosphere, 40 to 300 miles above the Earth

IRIS   muscular, colored part of the eye, surrounding the pupil

IRRIGATION   supplying land with water by means of canals and ditches

IRRITABILITY   the ability to respond to stimuli of the environment

ISLANDS OF LANGERHANS   clusters of cells in the pancreas which secrete the hormone insulin

ISOBAR   a line on a weather map connecting observatories reporting the same barometric pressure

ISOGONIC LINE   a line connecting locations of equal magnetic variation

ISOTHERM   a line on a weather map connecting places having the same temperature

ISOTOPE   forms of the same element differing from each other in the number of neutrons within the nucleus, and therefore in atomic mass

JEJUNUM   in mammals part of the small intestine between the duodenum and the ileum

JET STREAMS   swift, high-altitude winds at heights of about 35,000 feet

KAME   a mound of stratified drift deposited by streams running off a glacier

KETTLE   a depression remaining after the melting of large blocks of ice buried in glacial drift

KIDNEY   one of a pair of bean-shaped glands, in the back part of the abdomen that collect the wastes which form the urine, which then passes to the bladder

KILOWATT-HOUR a unit of energy equal to 1,000 watts of electric power used in one hour

KINDLING TEMPERATURE the temperature to which a substance must be raised before it will burst into flame

KINETIC ENERGY energy which is actively causing something to move

KOCH'S POSTULATES rules used to prove that a particular organism causes a certain disease

LACTATION producing milk by the mammary glands

LACTEAL one of the small vessels in the villi of the small intestine which absorb digested fats

LAGOON the body of quiet water between a bar and the mainland

LARVA the young, usually wormlike stage of an invertebrate

LARYNX the voice box, located in the upper part of the windpipe in which the vocal cords are found

LATEX a milky substance from which rubber is made

LATITUDE the distance due north or south from the equator, measured in degrees and marked by an imaginary line parallel to the equator

LAVA liquid rock material that flows out on the surface of the earth from underground sources

LEACHING process by which too much water washes dissolved minerals from the soil

LEGUME a member of the pea family; peas, beans, clover, alfalfa; roots contain nodules with nitrogen-fixing bacteria

LENTICELS openings in the stems of plants for passage of air

LEUKEMIA a disease of the blood-forming organs, bone, lymph glands, spleen, etc., characterized by uncontrolled multiplication of white blood cells

LEVEE the raised bank of a stream

LEVER a bar used to move some object with the use of a fulcrum

LICHEN a simple plant that is a combination of algae and fungi

LIFT air pressure under the wing of a plane

LIGAMENT tissue joining two or more bones

LIGHT-YEAR the distance which light, traveling at about 186,000 miles each second, travels in one year

LIMESTONE a type of sedimentary rock rich in lime

LINES OF FORCE lines in a field of force of any magnet that show the amount and direction of the field

LIPASE any fat-digesting enzyme

LIQUID AIR air that has been made into a liquid by cooling it to $-312°F$

LITER unit of liquid measure roughly the same as a quart

LIVER the largest gland in the body; makes bile, stores extra sugar as glycogen

LOADSTONE a natural rock magnet occurring in the earth

LOAM ordinary garden soil, a loose soil made up mainly of clay and sand and a small amount of humus

LONGITUDE distance on the earth's surface measured in degrees east or west of the meridian of Greenwich

LOW an area of low air pressure (in the center of a cyclone or hurricane)

LUNAR ECLIPSE an eclipse which occurs when the full moon crosses the plane of the earth's umbra

LYMPH a nearly colorless liquid containing proteins, found in the lymphatic vessels of the body

LYMPHOCYTE type of white blood cell involved in immunity

LYSIN an antibody which dissolves the cells of a pathogenic microorganism

MACHINE any device which transmits force

MAGGOT larva of a fly

MAGMA molten material from which igneous rocks are derived

MAGNETIC FIELD an area in the vicinity of a magnet or an electric current in which magnetic lines of force can be noted

MAGNETISM   the property of attracting other sub-stances

MAGNETO   a generator which uses permanent magnets

MAIZE   the Indian name for corn

MALARIA   a disease of the blood caused by a proto-zoan; transmitted by the female anopheles mosquito

MALIGNANT   in tumors, a cancerous growth

MAMMAL   one of the class of vertebrates that suckle their young

MANOMETER   an instrument used to measure the pres-sure of gas

MARINE   relating to salt-water environments

MARSUPIALS   mammals whose young continue devel-opment in a pouch after birth

MASS   quantity of matter in a substance, compared by weighing

MATTER   any substance that occupies space

MEDULLA   the part at the bottom of the brain, which connects the brain to the spinal cord; controls breathing and circulation

MEGACYCLE   one million waves, as in radio waves

MEMBRANE   a thin sheet of tissue; also the outer edge of the cytoplasm of a living cell

MERIDIAN   a line running north and south on a map, numbered according to its degree of longitude

MESODERM   middle tissue layer of an animal embryo, and all tissues derived from it

MESOZOIC ERA   of the age of reptiles

METABOLISM   the chemical reactions in an organism that provide and use energy

METAMORPHIC ROCK   rock formed by heat and pres-sure from igneous or sedimentary rock

METAMORPHOSIS   the change from larval to adult form, as in insect and amphibian development

METEOR   a small heavenly body which glows for a moment as it passes through the atmosphere; a "shooting star"

METEORITE   a meteor that has struck the earth's surface

METER   a unit of length in the metric system equal to 39.37 inches

MICROBE (MICROORGANISM)   any simple organism, mi-croscopic in size

MILT   the material produced by the testes of male fish; sperm cells

MINERAL   any chemical element or compound occur-ring free or in rocks

MITOSIS   process by which the nucleus duplicates dur-ing cell division

MIXTURE   two or more substances mixed together in no definite proportions and not chemically united

MOLD   a fungus

MOLECULE   the smallest part of any substance that possesses its properties

MOLLUSK   a soft-bodied invertebrate; usually has a shell outside the body; includes the snail, the octo-pus, and the clam

MOLTING   the process by which an animal sheds its shell, skin, feathers or other outer covering and grows a new one

MOMENTUM   motion product of velocity and mass

MONSOON   seasonal wind that is more pronounced over large continental areas near the equator

MUSCLE TISSUE   animal tissue with the ability to con-tract

MUTATION   permanent change in a gene, transmitted to the offspring

NARCOTICS   habit-forming drugs which relieve pain and produce sleep or stupor

NATURAL IMMUNITY   inborn resistance to a disease

NATURAL SELECTION   survival of certain organisms through their offspring, in competition with other related members

NEANDERTHAL   a type of prehistoric man who had heavy, bony ridges over the eyes and a slanting forehead; lived in Europe in the Stone Age

NEAP TIDE   a tide having small range, and occurring between spring tides

NEMATOCYST   poison cells located on the tentacles of members of the jellyfish group

NEARSIGHTEDNESS   a defect of the eye which forms sharper images of things nearby than of things at a distance

NERVE   bundle of nerve fibers held together by connective tissue

NERVE CELL   an animal cell which is sensitive to a stimulus and which carries an impulse

NERVE FIBER   a threadlike band of tissue which carries impulses

NEURON   nerve cell

NEUTRALIZATION   reaction between an acid and a base, producing a salt and water

NEUTRON   uncharged particle found in the nucleus of the atom

NIACIN   a member of the B-complex vitamins which prevents pellagra

NIGHT BLINDNESS   a condition in which a person does not see well in dim light; cured by eating foods rich in vitamin A

NIMBUS CLOUDS   group of clouds usually producing precipitation

NITROGEN   an element which makes up 80 per cent of the air

NITROGEN CYCLE   the cycle in which nitrogen passes from the air through organisms and soil and back to the air

NITROGEN-FIXING BACTERIA   bacteria (usually found in the roots of peas, clover, and alfalfa) which can take in nitrogen and change it to a form useful to green plants

NOVA   a star which suddenly becomes brighter than normal

NUCLEAR REACTOR   a device for splitting the atom so that it can be made to produce useful energy or valuable radioactive materials

NUCLEUS   a specialized chromosome-containing portion of the protoplasm of cells; coordinates the many cell activities

NUTRIENT   one of a group of substances in food used in nourishing and repairing body tissue

NYMPH   an immature stage of certain insects resembling the adult

OPTIC NERVE   the nerve that carries impulses from the eye to the brain

ORBIT   path of a revolving object

ORE   a rock from which one or more minerals can be extracted

ORGAN   any group of tissues performing a special function in a plant or in an animal

ORGANIC COMPOUND   compound containing carbon and hydrogen

ORGANISM   any individual, living animal or plant

OSCILLATOR   anything that vibrates rapidly, particularly a radio transmitter which sends out radio waves

OSCILLOSCOPE   an instrument that makes sound waves appear as waves of light on a screen similar to a small television screen

OSMOSIS   diffusion of water through a semipermeable membrane between solutions of different concentrations

OVARY   an egg-producing organ in a female

OVIDUCT   a tube through which eggs pass from the ovary

OVULE   the part containing the egg nucleus in flowering plants; after fertilization, each ovule develops into a seed

OXIDATION   union of oxygen with some other substance; a reaction involving loss of electrons from an atom

OXYGEN   a colorless, odorless gas that makes up 20 per cent of the air; needed by cells to burn food for energy

PALEONTOLOGY   the study of fossils

PALEOZOIC ERA   age of ancient or marine life

PANCREAS   a digestive gland, near the beginning of the small intestine, which makes the pancreatic juice; also produces the hormone insulin in the cells of the islands of Langerhans

PARAMECIUM   a common protozoan found in ponds; moves by means of cilia

PARASITE   an animal or plant that obtains its food by living inside or on another living thing; includes the tapeworm, hookworm, louse, ringworm, and many harmful bacteria

PARATHYROIDS   four small ductless glands in the neck; produce a hormone that regulates the amount of calcium and phosphorus in the blood

PARTHENOGENESIS   development of an unfertilized egg

PARTIAL ECLIPSE   the incomplete darkening of one body in space by another

PASTEURIZATION   process of heating to kill pathogenic microorganisms

PATHOGEN   any organism that causes an infectious or parasitic disease

PAY LOAD   the contents of an earth satellite or rocket useful in gathering information

PELLAGRA   a deficiency disease caused by the lack of the vitamin niacin

PENDULUM   an object suspended from a fixed point so that it may swing back and forth

PENICILLIN   an antibiotic obtained from a type of mold; used effectively in the treatment of many diseases, such as pneumonia

PENUMBRA   the lighter portion of a shadow

PEPSIN   an enzyme, found in the gastric juice, which helps break down proteins into simpler proteins

PEPTONE   an intermediate product in the digestion of proteins to amino acids

PERIGEE   the position of an earth satellite at the point in its orbit when it is nearest to the earth

PERISTALSIS   waves of muscular contraction which move food through the digestive tract

PERITONEUM   a serous membrane which lines the abdominal walls and the contained organs

PETALS   the colored parts of a flower which help to attract insects

PETRIFIED   plant or animal remains that have become like stone

PHAGOCYTE   a type of white blood corpuscle, capable of engulfing bacteria

PHARYNX   the throat—common passageway for air and food

PHLOEM   the part of the fibrovascular bundle of a plant that conducts food downward

PHOSPHOR   a chemical which gives off visible light when struck by electrons, ultraviolet light, or another invisible radiation

PHOSPHORESCENCE   the capacity of a substance to emit visible light when stimulated by electrons

PHOSPHORUS   an element important in making proteins, bones, and teeth

PHOTOSYNTHESIS   the process by which a green plant makes sugar, in the presence of light, from water and carbon dioxide

PHYSICAL CHANGE   a change in which the original properties of a substance are not destroyed

PHYSIOLOGY   the branch of biology concerned with the study of functions or life processes of living things

PIG IRON   iron that is made in a blast furnace

PISTIL   the female reproductive organ of a flower, which has in it an ovary with its ovules

PITCH   a certain number of vibrations of sound waves per second (frequency) which produces a high or a low sound

PITUITARY GLAND   endocrine gland located in the middle of the head, called the master gland

PLACEBO   an inactive substance given to patients in controlled evaluation of drugs

PLACENTA   structure by means of which the young are nourished in the body of a mammal

PLANET   one of the nine bodies circling around the sun; the earth is one

PLANETOID   one of the many small bodies between the orbits of the planets Mars and Jupiter

PLANKTON   minute floating organisms found in water, which serve as food for larger animals

PLASMA   the liquid part of the blood; contains antibodies, hormones, and digested foods

PLASTIC a man-made substance capable of being molded, such as cellophane

PLATELETS tiny particles in the blood which help the blood to clot

PLEURA tissue covering the lungs and lining the chest cavity

PLUTONIUM a man-made element produced from uranium in an atomic pile

POLIO a virus disease that injures the nerve cells in the brain or spinal cord; may result in paralysis of the diaphragm or other muscles

POLLEN GRAIN in a flower, a structure which develops in the anther of the stamen

POLLINATION transfer of pollen from the stamen of a flower to a pistil

POLLUTION accumulation of harmful substances in air or water

POLYMER a giant molecule formed by smaller molecules joining together

POTENTIAL ENERGY stored energy

PORTUGUESE MAN-OF-WAR member of the jellyfish group with specialized organs

POWER the rate of doing work, that is, how long it takes to do a certain amount of work

PRECIPITATION all forms of moisture falling from the sky; hail, snow, rain, and sleet

PREVAILING WIND a wind which blows almost always from one direction

PRIMATES order of mammals that includes lemurs, monkeys, apes, and man

PROTEIN one of a group of nitrogen-containing organic compounds of large molecular size; important constituents of protoplasm

PROTON positively charged particle found in the nuclei of all atoms

PROTOPLASM the semi-solid, jelly-like material of all living cells, including the nucleus, cytoplasm, and the membrane of cells

PROTOZOA one-celled animals

PSYCHIATRIST a medical doctor who specializes in mental illnesses.

PSYCHOLOGY the study of behavior and learning

PSYCHROMETER an instrument used to determine relative humidity

PTOMAINE poisonous substance formed by the action of certain bacteria

PULLEY a wheel with a grooved rim, used with a rope or chain to change the direction of a pulling force; a simple machine

PULMONARY CIRCULATION circulation of blood from the heart through the lungs and back to the heart

PULSE the regular beat of an artery

PUPA the young stage of an insect which is enclosed in a protective covering

PURE CULTURE growth of one type of microbe

PUS yellowish-white matter made of dead tissue, white blood cells, and bacteria, present in an abscess or boil

QUARANTINE isolation of an individual carrying a contagious disease

QUININE a drug used in preventing and treating malaria

RABIES a dangerous disease of the nervous system caused by a virus; transmitted in the saliva of infected dogs, foxes, and similar animals when they bite a victim

RADAR abbreviation for *radio detection and ranging*, the device which is used for the detection of objects by radio waves

RADIANT ENERGY energy in the form of light or other kind of radiation

RADIANT HEATING a heating system in which hot water or steam pipes set in floors or walls send out heat into rooms

RADIATION the process by which energy is transferred in space

RADIOACTIVITY the property, possessed by certain elements, of naturally sending forth radiant energy through breaking up of atoms

RADIOSONDE a radio transmitter attached to a balloon and sent aloft by observers seeking information about weather conditions in the upper atmosphere

RADIUM an intensely radioactive metallic element found in minute quantities in pitchblende and other uranium minerals

RECEPTORS the endings of nerves; sensitive to touch, chemicals, taste, sound, temperature, and other stimuli

RECESSIVE TRAIT a trait that does not show up in a hybrid; hidden by the dominant trait

RECTUM the lowest part of the intestine, from which solid food wastes leave the body

REFLECTED LIGHT light that is cast back or returned by an object

REFLEX an inborn immediate response to a stimulus; done without thinking

REFRIGERANT a liquid, such as ammonia which evaporates easily and therefore is useful in the cooling coils of a refrigerator

RELATIVE HUMIDITY the ratio of the amount of water vapor present in the air to the greatest amount which would be possible at a given temperature

REPRODUCTION the process by which an organism produces others like itself

REPTILES class of scaly-skinned vertebrates that includes snakes and turtles

RESISTANCE the weight to be lifted or moved by a simple machine; also, the physical condition in which a person is able to fight off infection

RESONANCE an object is said to be in resonance with another when both vibrate with the same frequency

RESPIRATION the process by which the energy stored in food is released

RESPIRATORY SYSTEM the breathing system

RESPONSE any action or reaction of an organism resulting from a stimulus

RETINA light-sensitive layer of the eye which enables us to see

REVOLUTION a single cycle of a body in space about another body in space; for example, the earth's yearly revolution about the sun

RH FACTOR a blood type found in most people which sometimes causes damage to the blood of babies

RIBOFLAVIN vitamin B_2; found in milk, lean meat, eggs, and many vegetables; necessary for normal growth

RICKETS a condition caused by lack of vitamin D; results in a softening of the bones

RICKETTSIA disease germs intermediate in size and structure between bacteria and viruses

RNA (RIBONUCLEIC ACID) a nucleic acid found in ribosomes; transfers information from DNA to enzyme proteins

ROCKET projectile propelled by recoil from burning gases escaping at one end of the rocket

ROD CELL modified sensory neuron in the retina, adapted for vision in dim light and for detecting motion

ROOT HAIR a root cell from which a hairlike extension grows; it increases absorption of water and minerals

ROTATING CROPS a farming method in which different plants are sown in the same soil in succeeding years

ROUGHAGE the parts of foods that cannot be digested; adds bulk to the diet and prevents constipation

RUDDER a flat piece of fabric-covered wood or a piece of metal hinged to the vertical fin of an airplane to control its direction to the right or left

RUNOFF surface water which runs to the sea without entering the underground water supply

RUST a fungus, related to the smuts, different forms of which cause plant diseases such as wheat rust

SALIVA a secretion made by three pairs of glands near the tongue; contains an enzyme that changes starch into sugar

SALK VACCINE a vaccine made of polio viruses grown on living cells and killed by chemicals

SANCTUARY a haven for wild animals, where hunting is prohibited or regulated

SANDSTONE a type of sedimentary rock formed from sand under great pressure

SAPROPHYTE plant which feeds on dead organic matter

SATELLITE natural or artificial body circling the earth or some other planet

SATURATED SOLUTION   a solution containing the maximum amount of dissolved material

SCHICK TEST   a test to determine if a person is immune to diphtheria

SCURVY   a condition caused by lack of vitamin C

SEDIMENTARY ROCK   rock layers which were formed from sediment under great pressure

SEED   a developed ovule consisting of a protective coat, stored food, and an embryo plant

SEISMOGRAPH   a sensitive instrument used to record vibrations of the earth's crust and to detect earthquakes

SELECTION   process of choosing certain desired organisms for breeding

SELECTIVE PERMEABILITY   ability of a membrane to allow certain kinds of particles to diffuse through it more easily than other kinds

SENSE ORGAN   a part of the body which senses, or receives, stimuli coming from the surroundings

SENSORY NEURON   nerve cell that carries signals from sense organs toward the nerve centers

SEPALS   the tiny, green, leaf-like parts found below the petals

SERUM   blood plasma from which certain factors necessary for clotting have been removed

SERUM ALBUMIN   a protein substance making up a large part of blood plasma, used to treat shock and severe burns

SEXUAL REPRODUCTION   production of a new organism from the union of two cells

SHORT CIRCUIT   a condition resulting when two bare wires carrying electricity touch each other

SILT   soil particles intermediate in size between clay particles and sand grain

SLOW OXIDATION   the slow burning of a substance, or the burning of food which takes place in cells; rusting of iron

SMOG   a layer of fog which contains smoke and irritating gases

SMALL INTESTINE   longest region of the food tube, where most digestion and absorption take place

SOFT COAL   bituminous coal that yields illuminating gas, coal tar, and coke upon being heated without air

SOFT WATER   water that is relatively free from mineral salts

SOLAR SYSTEM   the sun with the group of bodies in space which, held by its attraction, revolve around it

SOLSTICE   a time when the sun seems to reverse its apparent movement north or south of the equator

SOLUBLE   capable of being dissolved

SOLUTION   a mixture in which a substance is dissolved in another

SOLVENT   the part of a solution in which the substance is dissolved

SONAR   the detection apparatus that can locate objects under water by sound waves

SOUND BARRIER   the shock waves caused by air particles piling up against a plane flying at the speed of sound

SPAWNING   the shedding of eggs and milt into the water during the reproductive process of fish

SPECIES   group of similar, related organisms

SPECTRUM   an arrangement of rays of light or other forms of radiant energy according to wave length

SPERM CELLS   the sex cells produced in the testis of the male; sperms are microscopic and are able to swim and unite with the egg

SPINAL CORD   a mass of nerve cells and their fibers running down a canal in the backbone and acts as a center for reflexes

SPINDLE FIBER   one of the threads attached to chromosomes during mitosis

SPIRACLES   breathing openings in the bodies of insects

SPIRILLUM   a type of bacterium, so named because of its spiral shape

SPLEEN   a small organ near the stomach in which red blood cells are stored

SPONGE   one of a group of invertebrate animals

SPONTANEOUS COMBUSTION   the bursting into flame of a substance due to the accumulated heat of slow oxidation

SPONTANEOUS GENERATION   belief in development of organisms from lifeless materials

SPORE   heavy-walled structure, probable protective, that forms within certain bacteria; also, an asexual reproductive cell

SPRING TIDE   the highest of high tides and the lowest of low tides

STAMEN   the male organ of the flower, in which the pollen is made

STAPHYLOCOCCI   spherical bacteria that grow in clusters

STARCH   complex, insoluble carbohydrate compound

STATIC ELECTRICITY   charges of electricity produced by friction

STEEL   iron to which enough carbon, manganese, silicon, etc., have been added to give it hardness and strength

STERILITY   complete absence of microscopic life; or inability to have offspring

STIGMA   the part of the pistil of a flower upon which the pollen germinates

STIMULUS   any form of energy to which protoplasm is sensitive

STOMACH   muscular region of the food tube which stores food and begins the digestion of proteins

STOMATE   pore in the leaf epidermis of a seed plant through which gases diffuse

STORAGE BATTERY   a battery which stores electricity on plates of different chemical composition

STRATOSPHERE   the middle region of the atmosphere between the troposphere and the ionosphere

STRATUM   layer of rock

STRATUS CLOUD   a cloud that extends horizontally over a large area and is at low altitude

STREPTOCOCCI   spherical bacteria that grow in chains

STREPTOMYCIN   an antibiotic used to combat infections such as tuberculosis

STRIP CROPPING   alternation of crops in narrow strips along land contours to protect the soil from erosion

SULFA DRUGS   synthetic drugs used to combat certain bacterial infections

SUSPENSION   an insoluble solid in a liquid

SWEAT GLAND   a gland in the skin which excretes a fluid made of water, salts, and urea onto the skin surface

SYMBIOSIS   beneficial relationship between organisms living closely together

SYNAPSE   space between the end brush of one neuron and the dendrites of the next, across which the nerve impulse travels

SYNTHESIS   the building up of compounds from simpler compounds or elements

SYSTEM   group of organs in an organism which deal with the same function

TADPOLE   the fish-like embryonic form of a frog, toad, or salamander

TAGGED ATOMS   radioactive atoms that may be detected by a Geiger counter

TENDON   tough tissue binding muscles to bones

TERRACING   a method of farming used on steep hillsides; reduces erosion by catching water in ditches

TESTIS   structure which produces sperm cells

THALLOPHYTE   one of the group of simplest plants; an alga or fungus

THEORY   a scientific principle that is more or less acceptable, which is offered in explanation of observed facts

THERMOGRAPH   a device used to make an automatic and continuous record of temperature changes

THERMOMETER   an instrument for measuring the temperature

THERMOSTAT   a device on a heating system which automatically controls temperature

THIAMIN   the chemical name for vitamin B_1

THORAX   the chest region of the body

THRUST   the forward motion given to an airplane by its propeller or jet engine

THUNDER   the sound following a flash of lightning due to the sudden expansion of air in the path of the discharge

THYROID   a large, ductless or endocrine gland in front of and on either side of the trachea in the lower part of the neck

THYROXIN   the hormone made by the thyroid gland; rich in iodine

TISSUE   a group of similar cells and intercellular material which perform similar work

TOPSOIL   the upper fertile layer of soil, containing humus, which is necessary to plant life

TORNADO   one of the most violent of windstorms, noted for its funnel-shaped clouds, high-speed winds, and great destructiveness over a short path and a small area

TOTAL ECLIPSE   the complete hiding of one heavenly body by another or by the umbra of the shadow cast by another

TOXIN   any poisonous substance of microbic origin

TOXOID   a chemically treated toxin; injected to make a person form antitoxin against a disease

TRACHEA   tube through which air passes from the throat or pharynx toward the lungs (windpipe)

TRADE WINDS   winds which blow toward the equator

TRAIT   a distinguishing quality of a person or thing

TRANSFORMER   a device for transforming high voltage to low voltage, or low voltage to high voltage

TRANSISTOR   an electronic device that controls the flow of electrons

TRANSPIRATION   the process by which water evaporates through the stomates of a leaf

TRICHINOSIS   a disease caused by a parasitic roundworm in the muscles of animals, usually those of hogs

TRITIUM   a form of hydrogen whose atoms are three times heavier than atoms of ordinary hydrogen

TROPICAL HURRICANE   a violent storm originating in the tropics, often called a cyclone or typhoon

TROPOSPHERE   the lowest portion of the atmosphere, the part in which we live

TUMOR   an abnormal swelling or enlargement, either benign or malignant

TUNDRA   far-northern type of ecological community; water soaked, with permanently frozen ground, bogs, and low plants

TURBINE   a rotary engine moved by steam, water or gas

ULTRASONIC SOUND   refers to high-pitched sound above the range of human hearing

ULTRAVIOLET RAY   an invisible ray which lies beyond the violet end of the spectrum; such a ray is given off by very hot bodies

UMBILICAL CORD   structure which connects a mammal embryo with the placenta

UMBRA   the darker portion of a shadow

URANIUM   a heavy, radioactive element occurring in an ore called pitchblende

UREA   a compound containing nitrogen; the chief part of urine

URETER   tube connecting each kidney with the bladder

URETHRA   tube connecting the bladder with the outside of the body

URINE   a liquid containing wastes removed from the blood by the kidneys

UTERUS   the organ of female mammals inside which the embryo develops

VACCINATE   to inoculate with dead or weakened germs, causing a light attack of a disease in order to prevent a serious attack of the same disease, as in smallpox

VACCINE   a substance consisting of dead or weakened bacteria or viruses; used to produce immunity

VACUOLE   a tiny cavity inside a plant or animal cell; filled with liquid

VALVES   flap-like structures in the heart and large veins that keep the blood flowing in one direction

VELOCITY   the rate of time in which a distance is covered in a specific direction

VEGETATIVE REPRODUCTION   reproduction by means of vegetative organs that are usually concerned with nutrition

VEIN   vessel which carries blood to the heart

VENA CAVA   the large vein that returns blood from the body to the right auricle of the heart

VENEREAL DISEASE   disease transmitted through the reproductive organs

VENTRICLE   one of the two muscular chambers of the heart which pump blood to parts of the body

VERTEBRATE   an animal having a backbone .

VIBRATION   movement due to the effect of waves on a membrane; caused by sound waves, among others

VILLUS   one of the many tiny tubelike structures on the inside wall of the small intestine which serve to absorb food

VIRULENT   any agent harmful or destructive to tissues

VIRUS   a tiny living particle, perhaps a protein molecule, which causes such diseases as smallpox

VITAMIN   a chemical found in foods and needed in small quantities for special body functioning

VOLCANO   an opening in the earth's crust from which molten rock, steam, are thrown forth

VOLT   a unit for measuring electric pressure

VOLTAIC CELL   an arrangement for generating electricity by the action of a chemical upon two unlike metals

VOLTMETER   a meter for measuring pressure (voltage) of an electric current

VULCANIZATION   process by which raw rubber is mixed with other substances to improve its properties

WARM FRONT   the boundary between a mass of advancing warm air and a retreating mass of relatively cooler air

WATER CYCLE   path through which water moves from the atmosphere, to the surface of the earth, and back to the atmosphere

WATERSHED   area from which a river or lake draws its water

WATER TABLE   the level below which the soil is saturated with water

WATT   the unit for measuring electric power

WAVE LENGTH   the distance from any point on a wave to the corresponding point on the next wave

WEATHERING   the gradual destruction of material exposed to the weather

WEIGHT   measure of the pull of gravity on an object

WEIGHTLESSNESS   absence of the effects of gravity

WHITE BLOOD CELL   blood cell that helps destroy bacteria and other foreign particles that enter the body

WIDAL TEST   used to determine whether a person has typhoid fever

WILSON CLOUD CHAMBER   a device used to study the path of nuclear particles

WORK   the product of a force times the distance the force moves a body, measured in foot-pounds

XEROPHTHALMIA   a dried eye condition due to lack of vitamin A

XEROPHYTE   a plant that can survive in an environment with a scanty available supply of water

XYLEM   the part of the fibrovascular bundle of a plant that conducts water from the root upward

YEASTS   single-celled microscopic plants lacking in chlorophyll; reproduce by budding; carry on fermentation of sugars

YOLK   the supply of food found inside the egg cells of animals

ZENITH   the point in the sky directly above the observer

ZYGOTE   cell formed by the union of two gametes; capable of developing into an adult organism

A WORD ABOUT REVIEW: Don't be alarmed at all the review material in this chapter. We've included much more than you will probably need simply because we didn't want to omit anything that might be useful to you. Remember that the High School Equivalency Tests examine background, not classroom or book learning. They test the kind of information you've acquired from reading newspapers and magazines, from T.V. and radio, from working at a job or running a home. They test experience and common sense. The review section simply organizes knowledge in this field, reminds you of some things you may have forgotten, fills in some gaps you may have in your background.

ANALYSIS OF SAMPLE SELECTION

Directions: Read each of the following selections carefully. After each selection there are questions to be answered or statements to be completed. Select the *best* answer and underline it. Then blacken the appropriate space in the answer column to the right.

Photosynthesis is a complex process with many intermediate steps. Ideas differ greatly as to the details of these steps, but the general nature of the process and its outcome are well established. Water, usually from the soil, is conducted through the xylem of root, stem and leaf to the chlorophyl-containing cells of a leaf. In consequence of the abundance of water within the latter cells, their walls are saturated with water. Carbon dioxide, diffusing from the air through the stomata and into the intercellular spaces of the leaf, comes into contact with the water in the walls of the cells which adjoin the intercellular spaces. The carbon dioxide becomes dissolved in the water in these walls, and in solution diffuses through the walls and the plasma membranes into the cells. By the agency of chlorophyl in the chloroplasts of the cells, the energy of light is transformed into the chemical energy. This chemical energy is used to decompose the carbon dioxide and water, and the products of their decomposition are recombined into a new compound. The compound first formed is successively built up into more and more complex substances until finally a sugar is produced and oxygen is given off as a by-product of the process.

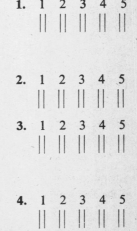

1. Synthesis of carbohydrates takes place
   (1) in the stomata   (2) in the xylem of leaf stems   (3) outside the walls of plant cells   (4) within the plasma membranes of all plant cells   (5) within plant cells that contain chloroplasts

   1. 1 2 3 4 5

2. Water is conducted to the leaf through the
   (1) chlorophyl   (2) stomata   (3) xylem   (4) phloem   (5) chloroplasts

   2. 1 2 3 4 5

3. Chemical energy is needed in photosynthesis to
   (1) bring water to the leaf   (2) decompose chlorophyl   (3) decompose water   (4) change the form of light energy   (5) recombine the products of photosynthesis

   3. 1 2 3 4 5

4. In the process of photosynthesis the chemical elements of the sugar come from
   (1) carbon dioxide alone   (2) water alone   (3) either the carbon dioxide or the water   (4) both the carbon dioxide and the water   (5) neither the carbon dioxide nor the water

   4. 1 2 3 4 5

5. According to this passage, in the process of photosynthesis, chlorophyl is (1) a carbohydrate   (2) the source of carbon dioxide   (3) responsible for changing light energy to chemical energy   (4) a source of chemical energy (5) the plasma membrane

5.   1   2   3   4   5
    || || || || ||

6. According to this author, scientists are still in doubt in regard to the phase of photosynthesis that involves (1) source of solar energy   (2) products formed   (3) rate of chlorophyl (4) raw materials needed   (5) details of the intermediate steps of the process

6.   1   2   3   4   5
    || || || || ||

7. Besides food manufacture, another useful result of photosynthesis is that it (1) aids in removing poisonous gases from the air   (2) helps to maintain the existing proportion of gases in the air   (3) changes complex compounds into simpler compounds   (4) changes certain waste products into carbohydrates   (5) changes chlorophyl into useful substances

7.   1   2   3   4   5
    || || || || ||

8. Carbon dioxide enters the plant through the (1) roots   (2) xylem   (3) plasma membrane   (4) stomata   (5) intercellular spaces

8.   1   2   3   4   5
    || || || || ||

ANSWERS

1. 5	**4.** 4	**7.** 2
2. 3	**5.** 3	**8.** 4
3. 3	**6.** 5	

ANALYSIS OF ANSWERS

Having read the passage carefully you should have obtained some definite ideas about photosynthesis. Water from the soil and carbon dioxide from the air are broken down by energy of light with the aid of chlorophyl. These new substances are built up (synthesized) into sugar. While this passage states that the details of this process are not well-established you may read elsewhere how scientists have attempted to solve this mystery. However, in answering the questions here you should confine yourself to the ideas expressed in this passage.

1. The answer is 5. This question requires one bit of background information—sugar is a carbohydrate. There are two clues to the correct answer. In the early part of the passage, it states that water which is necessary for the process, is delivered to the chlorophyl-containing cells of a leaf. Later in the passage, the author mentions the role of chlorophyl in the chloroplasts of the cells.

2. The answer is 3. The passage states, "Water, usually from the soil, is conducted through the xylem. . . ."

3. The answer is 3. The author states that the chemical energy is needed to decompose both carbon dioxide and water.

4. The answer is 4. Near the close of the passage it states that the products of the decomposed carbon dioxide and water are successively built up into sugar.

5. The answer is 3. The passage states, "By the agency of chlorophyl in the chloroplasts of the cells, the energy of light is transformed into chemical energy."

6. The answer is 5. Read the second sentence of the passage.

7. The answer is 2. The passage mentions that carbon dioxide is taken from the air by green plants, and that oxygen is given off into the air as a by-product. Since animals breathe in oxygen, and give off carbon dioxide, the balance of these gases in the air is maintained by the process of photosynthesis.

8. The answer is 4. The passage mentions, "Carbon dioxide, diffusing from the air through the stomata. . . ."

TIME TO PRACTICE:

28 SELECTIONS

Selection 1

Atomic clocks are accurate to a fraction of a second in several thousand years. How can you measure time with an atom? Remember, all you need to keep tabs on time is a device that has a continuous, regular motion—like the swing of a pendulum, or the thump of your heart. The faster the motion, the more accurate the measurement. Time determined by the movement of the tides, for example, is not as exact as time ticked out by a clock. The fastest motion available for timekeeping purposes is the vibration in the core, or *nucleus* of the atom. Atomic clocks count these ultrarapid back-and-forth movements in the center of the atom.

The Earth, too, is a clock. The movements of the Earth, of course, determine two natural divisions of time—the day and the year. These units may seem eternal. But the lengths of the day and year are changing. For, like many other clocks, the Earth is running down. The speed with which it turns on its axis is decreasing. The day on which you read this story is a second shorter than the day on which your remote ancestors awakened 100,000 years ago.

—*Science World* Sept. 16, 1965†

† Selections from *Science World* and *Senior Science* reprinted by permission. Copyright © 1963, 1964, 1965, 1966 by Scholastic Magazines, Inc.

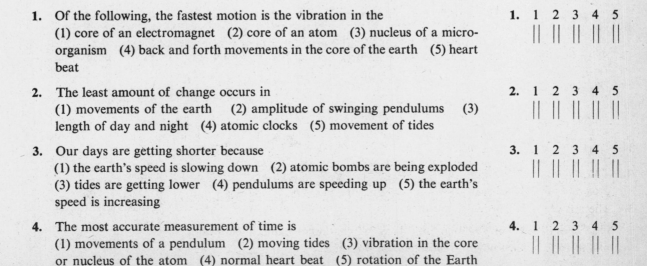

1. Of the following, the fastest motion is the vibration in the
(1) core of an electromagnet   (2) core of an atom   (3) nucleus of a microorganism   (4) back and forth movements in the core of the earth   (5) heart beat

    1. 1 2 3 4 5

2. The least amount of change occurs in
(1) movements of the earth   (2) amplitude of swinging pendulums   (3) length of day and night   (4) atomic clocks   (5) movement of tides

    2. 1 2 3 4 5

3. Our days are getting shorter because
(1) the earth's speed is slowing down   (2) atomic bombs are being exploded   (3) tides are getting lower   (4) pendulums are speeding up   (5) the earth's speed is increasing

    3. 1 2 3 4 5

4. The most accurate measurement of time is
(1) movements of a pendulum   (2) moving tides   (3) vibration in the core or nucleus of the atom   (4) normal heart beat   (5) rotation of the Earth

    4. 1 2 3 4 5

Selection 2

Mercury flows like water. Bismuth shatters like glass. Sodium is grey and lusterless. Lead is a poor conductor of electricity. Yet all these substances have something in common: all are metals. It is hard to see how such ill-assorted substances all made the same team—especially when most metals are hard, lustrous, capable of being rolled into sheets and drawn into wires, and able to conduct electricity.

That's not the only mystery. Carbon and silicon are considered to be non-metals, though carbon, in the form of graphite, is a good conductor of electricity, and crystals of silicon are hard and shiny.

The explanation for this confusion is that the word "metal" came into use before the elements had been scientifically classified according to their atomic structure. We must look at these elements at the atomic level to understand what gives them "metallic" properties.

The metal scissors you cut with, the metal girders that hold up your school roof, the metal foil in which your lunch is wrapped—all are composed of tiny *crystals*—regular, geometric arrangements of atoms. Such a regular array of atoms is called a *lattice*. A lattice is actually a stack of atomic building blocks, or *unit cells*. Iron, for example, has a cubic unit cell, made up of nine atoms— one in the middle of the cube surrounded by eight other atoms at the corners of the cube. Zinc has a hexagonal (six-sided) unit cell which has one atom surrounded by twelve others. For an idea of the size of these building blocks, think of the fact that one gram of copper contains 2,370,000,000,000,000,000,000 unit cells.

—Senior Science April 7, 1965

5. All of the following are metals except
    (1) sodium   (2) mercury   (3) zinc   (4) graphite   (5) bismuth

6. The regular array of atoms in all metals may be correctly stated to be
    (1) a lattice   (2) hexagonal   (3) cubic   (4) unchangeable   (5) irregular

7. The passage mentions exceptions to general properties of metals and non-metals. All of the following are illustrations cited except
    (1) bismuth lacks strength   (2) mercury is a liquid at ordinary conditions
    (3) graphite conducts electricity   (4) silicon crystals are hard   (5) sodium is lustrous

8. Scientifically, a chemical element is classified as a metal because of its
    (1) luster   (2) strength   (3) atomic structure   (4) conductivity   (5) physical state

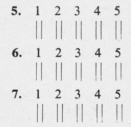

Selection 3

How many planets are there? If you answer "nine," you're wrong. There are more than 50,000 planets orbiting the middle-sized star we call the sun.

The leading actors of this mob scene in space are, of course, the "big nine" —Mercury, Venus, Earth, Mars, Jupiter, Saturn, Uranus, Neptune, and Pluto. These are the major planets.

What about the other 49,991 or so? They are the minor planets, chunks of metal and rock better known as *planetoids* or *asteroids*.

Most asteroids clutter a broad region of space between the orbits of Mars and Jupiter. This interplanetary junkyard covers a belt over 300 million miles from inner edge to outer edge.

A few asteroids, however, veer away from the main swarm. Their orbits swerve close to Earth or, for some, out toward Saturn.

What are the asteroids? Skywatchers have long pondered two possibilities. Could these objects be mere rubbish, a scrap heap left over from the formation of the solar system?

Or, as some imaginative scholars have speculated, are asteroids the dreary remains of a lost planet—a grim inheritance from an exploded world?

—*Science World* Feb. 18, 1966

9. Asteroids are best described as
(1) lost planets   (2) remains of planetoids   (3) products of activity of the sun   (4) minor planets   (5) middle-sized stars

10. Which of the following are planets?
(1) Mars and Jupiter   (2) Jupiter and Pluto   (3) Earth and Venus   (4) Pluto and Neptune   (5) all of these

11. According to the passage the actual number of planets may be expressed as
(1) the big nine   (2) the number of major planets and their satellites   (3) the planets and planetoids or asteroids   (4) the sum total of the remains of the formation of the solar system   (5) 49,991

12. Which statement, if any, is false?
(1) there are at least 1,000 planetoids   (2) all planetoids revolve in an orbit between the orbits of Mars and Jupiter   (3) planetoids are small bodies that revolve about the sun   (4) a planetoid is an asteroid   (5) none of these

Selection 4

On a grander scale, the concept of evolution does for the life sciences what Newton's theories did for the physical sciences. Within the concept of evolution, scientists have been able to relate many areas of otherwise loosely organized observations and ideas: The great age of the Earth (not always so obvious), and the prehistoric record of fossils and fossil layers embedded in the rocks of the Earth's crust. The convenient categories of Linnaeus which provided a workable system for keeping track of the million-and-a-half different kinds of living creatures—categories which also pointed to their important similarities. The famous voyage of Charles Darwin aboard H.M.S. *Beagle* during which he continually found new evidence of relations among living things. And finally, Darwin's theory of evolution and natural selection.

—*Science World* Oct. 11, 1963

13. Charles Darwin is best known as
(1) a sea captain   (2) a breeder of large dogs   (3) an evolutionist   (4) a fossil hunter   (5) a geologist

14. Taxonomy, the science of classifying living things, was founded by
(1) I. Newton   (2) C. Linnaeus   (3) H. Beagle   (4) C. Darwin   (5) H. Morgan

15. According to this passage the importance of evolution is that it
(1) gives a workable basis for classifying in the physical sciences   (2) clarifies Newton's theories   (3) initiated the work of Linnaeus   (4) explains relationships that exist among living things   (5) gives evidence of existence of fossils in the Earth's crust

Selection 5

There are four major oceans: the Pacific, Atlantic, Indian and Arctic. Together these bodies of water hold 97% of all water on the earth. A sea may be part of one of the larger oceans.

	AREA Sq. miles	DEPTH feet		AREA Sq. miles	DEPTH feet
Pacific Ocean	64,186,300	13,739	Hudson Bay	281,900	305
Atlantic Ocean	33,420,000	12,257	East China Sea	256,000	620
Indian Ocean	28,350,500	12,704	Andaman Sea	218,100	3,667
Arctic Ocean	3,662,200	4,362	Black Sea	196,100	3,906
South China Sea	1,148,500	4,802	Red Sea	174,900	1,764
Caribbean Sea	971,400	8,448	North Sea	164,900	308
Mediterranean Sea	909,100	4,926	Baltic Sea	147,500	180
Bering Sea	873,000	4,893	Yellow Sea	113,500	121
Gulf of Mexico	582,100	5,297	Gulf of California	59,100	2,375
Sea of Okhotsk	537,500	3,192	Persian Gulf	88,800	328
Sea of Japan	391,100	5,468			

16. All of the following statements are false except
(1) the Atlantic Ocean accounts for 5½ million square miles   (2) the Arctic ocean is 29 million square miles   (3) oceans account for 3 per cent of all water on earth   (4) the Pacific Ocean covers approximately 65 million square miles   (5) the Gulf of Mexico accounts for 33½ million square miles

17. Which of the following has an average depth greater than the Bering Sea?
(1) Black Sea   (2) Sea of Japan   (3) South China Sea   (4) Sea of Okhotsk   (5) Andaman Sea

18. All of the following statements are true except
(1) the Sea of Japan is smaller than the Sea of Okhotsk   (2) the Indian Ocean has a depth almost equal to the depth of the Atlantic Ocean   (3) the largest of our oceans is the Atlantic Ocean   (4) the Arctic Ocean is the smallest of the oceans   (5) the larger oceans are the deeper ones

Selection 6

Physicians have successfully operated on patients with diseased brains by freezing the affected cells with liquid nitrogen. The freezing is almost instantaneous, leaves the rest of the brain intact, and permits the surgeon to work very rapidly. Other physicians have performed delicate eye operations and destroyed cancerous growths with cold probes—instruments that direct a flow of ultracold liquid gas to a tiny area.

Liquid hydrogen and liquid oxygen fuel many of our mighty rockets.

Fruits and vegetables can be frozen so fast with liquefied gases that ice crystals don't have time to form within them. In food frozen by ordinary means, ice crystals develop within the plant cells. When the fruit or vegetable thaws, the ice melts and ruptures the cell wall. The result is "mushiness" and loss of flavor. But a tomato dipped in liquid nitrogen will freeze rock-hard in seconds, stay that way for a month, and be undamaged when it is thawed.

Recent experiments have revealed what may be the most important use yet of cryogenics. Human blood normally deteriorates in a few weeks under normal refrigeration. But it apparently can be kept indefinitely at very low temperatures. Our ever-growing need for emergency reserves of blood may be met at last.

—Senior Science Sept. 16, 1965

19. Freezing tissues is a useful procedure in medicine because it
(1) can be done instantaneously   (2) allows the surgeon to work quickly
(3) is a method of keeping blood stored indefinitely   (4) is all of the above
(5) is none of these

19. 1 2 3 4 5

20. Freezing with vegetables liquid gases is preferable to ordinary methods because
(1) ice crystals develop within plant cells   (2) ice crystals do not develop within plant cells   (3) freezing is gradual   (4) thawing is more rapid   (5) freezing is gradual and thawing is gradual

20. 1 2 3 4 5

21. Tomatoes frozen by ordinary methods are not readily available to consumers because
(1) the process involves liquid air   (2) they take a long time to thaw   (3) They lose flavor when they thaw   (4) they freeze too fast to hold the flavor   (5) ice crystals do not form in ordinary freezing

21. 1 2 3 4 5

22. This passage deals mainly with
(1) cryogenics   (2) fuels for rockets   (3) life in outer space   (4) improving frozen foods   (5) modern medicine

22. 1 2 3 4 5

Selection 7

The ellipsoidal shape of the Earth was finally confirmed after Sir Isaac Newton published his law of universal gravitation in 1687. According to Newton's law, the pull of gravity becomes weaker with increasing distance from the earth's center. By measuring the gravitational pull on the surface, variations in the distance to the center of the Earth can be calculated. Thus, the pull of gravity is weaker at the top of a mountain than in a valley.

How is the pull of gravity measured? One way is with a pendulum. The speed of a pendulum's swing depends on the strength of the gravitational force acting on it. The stronger the pull, the faster the swing. Experiments with pendulums have confirmed that gravity is indeed strongest near the Earth's poles and weakest near the Equator. Therefore, the surface near the poles must be closer to the Earth's center.

—Science World Sept. 16, 1965

23. According to Newton's law the pull of gravity becomes stronger with
(1) decreasing distance from the Earth's center   (2) increasing distance from the Earth's center   (3) increasing distance from the Earth's crust
(4) decreasing distance from the Earth's crust   (5) nearness to the equator

23. 1 2 3 4 5

24. A comparison of the Earth's surface near the poles with that of the equator shows that the poles
(1) are closer to the center of the Earth   (2) have a greater gravitational pull   (3) cause a pendulum to swing faster   (4) all of the above   (5) none of the above

24. 1 2 3 4 5

25. The shape of the Earth is best described as
(1) round (2) spherical (3) ellipsoidal (4) changeable (5) gravitational

25. 1 2 3 4 5

26. The speed of a pendulum's swing increases as the
(1) length of the pendulum increases   (2) distance from the poles increases   (3) gravitational force increases   (4) gravitational force decreases   (5) distance approaches the equator

26. 1 2 3 4 5

Selection 8

Virologists have developed ingenious new tools to study—and to use—viruses. For example, new laboratory techniques are available to separate and analyze complex chemical mixtures. Radioactive tracers can now be employed to follow individual elements through long series of chemical reactions. These developments have enabled scientists to discover just what bacteriophages and other viruses are made of. By checking on the flow of various materials into and out of infected cells, biologists have also found out how viruses act on their hosts. And, although bacteriophages are much too small to be seen with ordinary light microscopes (which can magnify things only about 2,000 times at the most), biologists are now taking much closer looks at these tiny particles with electron microscopes. These provide magnifications up to 100,000 times.

—*Science World* Nov. 25, 1964

27. How many times more is the possible magnification of an electron microscope as compared with a microscope using ordinary light?
(1) 50 (2) 500 (3) 2,000 (4) 100,000 (5) more than 100,000

27. 1 2 3 4 5

28. A virologist would be most interested in
(1) ingenious laboratory equipment   (2) bacteriophages   (3) tracers   (4) microscopes using ordinary light   (5) all of the above

28. 1 2 3 4 5

29. Research with microorganisms has been aided greatly by the introduction of
(1) viruses   (2) bacteriophages   (3) radioactive iodine   (4) electron microscopy   (5) complex chemical mixtures

29. 1 2 3 4 5

30. Individual elements can be followed through long series of chemical reactions through the use of
(1) viruses   (2) bacteriophage   (3) the light microscope   (4) radioactive tracers   (5) chemical mixtures

30. 1 2 3 4 5

Selection 9

On March 27, 1964 one of the mightiest quakes of our time rocked Alaska. One month later more than 500 aftershocks had been recorded. In fact, the catastrophe was one of the Earth's most extensively documented rumbles. Yet observations are one thing, explanations quite another. Most scientists agree that the immediate source of a tremor is the sudden release of energy which has gradually accumulated in a strained portion of the Earth's crust. But there is little agreement on the mechanism that causes or releases the stress, so that the understanding of earthquakes is an important part of the unfinished business of science.

—*Senior Science* March 3, 1965

31. Which of the following do scientists understand least?
(1) the mechanism causing the sudden release of energy trapped in the Earth's crust   (2) why earthquakes occur in Alaska   (3) the immediate source of a tremor   (4) location of areas where earthquakes occur   (5) what causes aftershocks

31. 1 2 3 4 5

32. The great Alaskan earthquake occurred
(1) in the Ice Age   (2) after 500 aftershocks occurred   (3) after 1964 aftershocks occurred   (4) in 1964   (5) in April, 1965

32. 1 2 3 4 5

33. A strained part of the Earth's crust may lead to
(1) changes in climate   (2) an accumulation of the mechanism of science   (3) an unfinished earthquake   (4) a tremor   (5) the elimination of an earthquake

33. 1 2 3 4 5

Selection 10

All animals, with the exception of primitive forms, move and respond to stimuli because a network of nerves and nerve cells transmit electrical impulses to and from the brain. If a muscle-stimulating (*motor*) impulse is blocked in its journey from brain to muscle, the muscle will be paralyzed. If a sense-stimulating (*sensory*) impulse is stopped in its journey from, say, your eye to your brain, you will not see.

Since you are not plugged into an electrical outlet, your body produces its own "electric current" to transmit nerve impulses. Of course, your body contains no Grand Coulee Dam or other hydroelectric power plant. However, like a battery, your tissues are packed with chemical compounds. Some of these compounds trigger temporary changes in electrical potential across cell membranes—chemical energy is transformed into electrical energy and a "current" is produced. In this way a nerve impulse travels from a nerve cell to a muscle cell.

—*Science World* Nov. 25, 1964

34. This passage deals with the topic of
(1) static electricity   (2) hydroelectric power   (3) impulse transfer   (4) conversion of energy   (5) sources of energy

34. 1 2 3 4 5

35. According to this passage which of the following statements is false?
(1) lower forms of life cannot respond in any way to stimuli   (2) paralysis may be due to lack of communication to the motor nerve cell   (3) sensory neurons are sensitive to stimuli   (4) the transfer of a nerve impulse requires energy   (5) living tissues are packed with chemical compounds

35. 1 2 3 4 5

36. Which of the following statements is made by the author of this passage? (1) we use our brains when we see (2) the living cell cannot convert chemical energy to electrical energy (3) the motor neuron picks up impulses from muscles (4) sensory impulses travel from the brain to the eye (5) primitive forms of life respond to stimuli by using a network of nerves and nerve cells

36. 1 2 3 4 5
|| || || || ||

37. The body tissues contain chemical compounds that start temporary changes (1) in the electrical content of an impulse (2) in electrical potential across cell membranes (3) across paralyzed muscles (4) in blind people (5) in the batteries of a muscle cell

37. 1 2 3 4 5
|| || || || ||

Selection 11

Water has a natural tendency to contract its surface. This phenomenon is triggered by the attraction that water molecules hold for one another. For example, each H_2O molecule in a drop of water is attracted to every other H_2O molecule in the drop. Since there are more molecules within the drop than at its surface, there is an unbalanced inward pull on the *surface* molecules. Some of these molecules are drawn into the drop by this unbalanced force. The reduction in the number of surface molecules causes the surface *area* of the water drop to shrink until it reaches a minimum (limited by the existing conditions). According to the laws of mathematics, a sphere has the least surface area for its *volume*. Hence, a water drop tends to assume the shape of a sphere. It is this tendency that keeps water from spreading out across a greasy or waxed surface.

But what has this surface tension of water to do with detergency? A simple observation brings home the point.

Place a spherical rubber ball on a table top. You can easily see that the amount of table surface the ball rests on is very small. Similarly, a drop of water resting on a soiled piece of cloth will not be in contact with much of the cloth's surface. It will not *wet* the cloth well. If it will not wet the cloth, it can not come in contact with many insoluble "dirt" particles, such as grease and oils, that adhere to the surface of the cloth.

Clearly then, water alone cannot be a good detergent—as you know if you have ever attempted to wash grease or oil from your hands using only water. Water becomes an efficient cleaning agent only when detergent molecules are dissolved in it. Why? Because the surface tension of the water is reduced—yes. But that is only part of the answer.

The mystery of how detergents reduce surface tension, and perform other fantastic feats, is locked in the startling and unusual structure of their molecules. The structure of a detergent molecule endows it with the incredible characteristic of being both *hydrophilic* (*water loving*) and *hydrophobic* (*water hating*).

—*Science World* Oct. 11, 1963

38. Detergents are effective because they are (1) neither hydrophilic nor hydrophobic (2) hydrophilic but not hydrophobic (3) hydrophobic but not hydrophilic (4) both hydrophilic and hydrophobic (5) sometimes hydrophilic and sometimes hydrophobic

38. 1 2 3 4 5
|| || || || ||

39. A soapy water will penetrate and clean fabrics much better than water alone because
(1) hot soapsuds wash cleaner than cold suds   (2) the surface tension of the water is reduced   (3) the cohesive forces among the molecules of water are greater than among molecules of other liquids   (4) water molecules attract water molecules with greater force   (5) the surface tension of the water is increased

39. 1 2 3 4 5
|| || || || ||

40. Which of the following has the least surface area for its volume?
(1) cube   (2) circle   (3) sphere   (4) square   (5) rectangle

40. 1 2 3 4 5
|| || || || ||

Selection 12

Crystals differ from other forms of matter not in *what* they are made of but in *how* they are put together. The arrangement of particles inside crystals is *orderly*. Each atom vibrates about a fixed position, and these positions are arranged in a regular pattern in space. Moreover, this pattern is a repetitive one. Think of a stack of window screens. The wire mesh represents a regular pattern of intersections and open spaces. But if the screens lie jumbled on the ground every which way, this pattern is not repeated throughout the pile of screens.

Now stack the screens so that their edges align and the spaces separating them are equal. Presto—an ordered, repetitive arrangement: crystalline structure.

We can now begin to see why a crystal cleaves along straight lines. The forces binding the crystal—the forces between the atoms—are weakest along the cleavage planes. Why are these forces weaker? Sometimes the planes themselves are farther apart than the atoms within the planes. Therefore the planes are bound less tightly. Sometimes the arrangement of electrical charges leaves a plane that permits cleavage.

The atoms in a diamond are arranged in planes, like our pile of window screens. Obviously, it would be much easier to separate one screen from another than to saw the pile in half. When we cleave a diamond, we are actually slicing parallel to such planes, forcing them apart.

—*Science World* Oct. 25, 1963

41. Crystals may be defined as
(1) solids with repetitive arrangement of screens   (2) solids with a natural geometric form   (3) substances composed of atoms that vibrate in variable patterns   (4) substances with strong cleavage planes   (5) forms of matter with vibrating atoms

41. 1 2 3 4 5
|| || || || ||

42. Which statement best describes cleavage of a mineral?
(1) a tendency of a mineral to be held together so that smooth surfaces are produced in one or more directions   (2) weakening of forces that bind the crystal   (3) strengthening of the electrical charges along the cleavage planes   (4) geometric arrangement of atoms in a mineral   (5) breaking the jumbled repetitive pattern of crystals

42. 1 2 3 4 5
|| || || || ||

43. It can be inferred that diamond cutters are regarded as skilled mechanics because it is difficult to
(1) work with small screen meshes   (2) understand the formation of crystals   (3) cut parallel to a cleavage plane   (4) break electrical charges of attraction between planes   (5) work with small crystals

43. 1 2 3 4 5
|| || || || ||

Selection 13

Most solutions with which you are familiar consist of a solid dissolved in a liquid. But solid solutions also exist. Copper and silver, when ground together, melted, and cooled, form such a solution. Many metallic alloys such as brass, bronze, and pewter are solid solutions. Liquids can also dissolve other liquids. Water and ethyl alcohol is one example. And air, free of dust, is a solution of many gases dissolved in nitrogen. Many combinations of liquid, gas, and solid can form a solution.

Now let's see whether we can determine why a universal solvent may never be synthesized. To do this, we have to discover why substances do or do not form solutions with one another.

—Senior Science Dec. 9, 1966

44. Which of the following is not a metallic alloy?
(1) copper   (2) brass   (3) bronze   (4) pewter   (5) all of these

44. 1 2 3 4 5

45. The solvent of the solution of the gases in the air is
(1) dust   (2) nitrogen   (3) water   (4) oxygen   (5) alcohol

45. 1 2 3 4 5

46. A solution can be formed by combinations of
(1) liquid and gas   (2) solid and liquid   (3) solid and solid   (4) any of these combinations   (5) substances other than those mentioned in 1, 2, and 3

46. 1 2 3 4 5

47. A universal solvent
(1) exists in free form   (2) exists in solution   (3) exists because all substances form solutions   (4) may never be synthesized   (5) is easily synthesized

47. 1 2 3 4 5

Selection 14

Pollutants classified as *organic* include proteins, fats, soaps, carbohydrates, resins, coal, oils, tars, and synthetic detergents; *inorganic* pollutants include acids, alkalies, salts of heavy metals, and soluble salts. If present in excessive quantities, any of these substances can disrupt the natural water environment.

Not that water was ever entirely "pure." From the time it arrives as rain, water picks up, transports, and disperses all sorts of impurities. Ordinarily microbes in the water feed on and digest waste products, transforming them into harmless by-products. But recently, the load of waste has been far beyond the amount that microbes can naturally process.

Large cities and heavy industries are the chief offenders in the pollution of water resources. According to one estimate, the Hudson River is so contaminated by both sources that even if not another quart of sewage were dumped in, it would take ten years for the river to return to its original unpolluted state.

—Science World May 12, 1965

48. Which of the following is inorganic?
(1) coal   (2) carbohydrates   (3) proteins   (4) sulfuric acid   (5) olive oil

48. 1 2 3 4 5

49. The natural scavenger action in contaminated water is carried on by
(1) pollutants   (2) man   (3) microbes   (4) sewage   (5) large industries

50. Water is never "pure" except
(1) as rain   (2) in rivers   (3) in large cities   (4) when it contains microbes
(5) in pollutants

51. Water pollution is caused mainly by
(1) man   (2) organic pollutants deposited by microbes   (3) inorganic
pollutants deposited by microbes   (4) rivers   (5) natural environment

Selection 15

Researchers have long known that when an animal is injured it releases a substance called *glutathione*. Since glutathione is soluble in water, some biologists believed this chemical might "travel" from wounded animals trapped in man-of-war tentacles to the gastrozooids. The gastrozooids might contain cells sensitive to glutathione—cells able to recognize the substance as a sort of chemical "call to dinner."

In order to test this hypothesis, experimenters isolated gastrozooids from the rest of a man-of-war colony. They then exposed the gastrozooids to an extremely weak solution of glutathione—only 0.0003 per cent. The gastrozooids responded violently; some even turned themselves inside out.

The key to food gathering, of course, is hidden in the functions and chemistry of the tentacles and their poison cells, the nematocysts. In order to deliver a choice tidbit to the gastrozooids, a 100-foot-long tentacle must be able to retract. Muscle fibers that run the length of each tentacle accomplish this feat—a man-of-war can "reel in" a captured fish in only a few seconds; in the process it may shorten a tentacle from many feet to a few inches.

—*Senior Science* March 24, 1965

52. Special cells in a "Man-of-War" called gastrozooids are very sensitive to
(1) a substance released by injured animals   (2) touch of an experimenter
(3) heat of the water   (4) cold of the water   (5) all of the above

53. Glutathione may cause
(1) tentacles to expand   (2) nematocysts to expand   (3) nematocysts to turn inside out   (4) gastrozooids to turn inside out   (5) tentacles to turn inside out

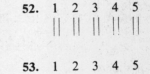

Selection 16

Man's newest "pesticides" make use of the insect's own sense of smell. Using electronic instruments, scientists have been able to analyze the minute quantities of odor given off by insects. Once the chemicals of an *insect attractant* are known, the odor can be copied. The success of the method has been amazing. By discovering what smell was irresistible to the oriental fruit fly, an entire island in the Pacific Ocean was rid of this pest. In the future, many harmful insects now attacked by chemical sprays will be "lured" into traps by their own sense of smell.

—*Science World* Sept 30, 1964

54. The oriental fruit fly was eliminated from the island in the Pacific by (1) research in regard to breeding habits   (2) use of insecticides   (3) producing chemicals to imitate scents   (4) use of repellants   (5) use of electronic shocks

54. 1 2 3 4 5
     || || || || ||

55. Which is the most suitable title for this paragraph? (1) Pest and Pesticides   (2) Freeing the Farmer from Pests   (3) Science in the Pacific   (4) Lures vs. Sprays   (5) Electronic Control of Insects

55. 1 2 3 4 5
     || || || || ||

Selection 17

During a threat of danger, the stomach, intestines, and other parts of the digestive system are almost useless—they are not weapons against attack. Therefore, the blood, which normally carries raw materials (including oxygen and sugar) to all parts of the body, is shifted away from these "non-fighting" organs to the "combat" organs—the heart, the brain and central nervous system, and the muscles. This process provides a greater supply of oxygen and sugar where the body needs it most.

Yet, the body is not satisfied simply to deliver to the "front lines" oxygen and sugar that is *available* in the blood. It also increases the quantity, or *concentration*, of these substances in the blood.

More oxygen is forced into the bloodstream by more rapid and deeper breathing. However, this oxygen will not reach its destination unless its means of transportation is increased. This is the function of red blood cells. Hence, the *spleen* (a glandlike organ near the stomach) releases its reserve store of red cells.

Now that adequate transportation is available for the oxygen, the remaining task is to get the oxygen to the body in a hurry. The heart beats more rapidly, increasing blood pressure. Thus, red blood cells move in and out of the tiny vessels in the lungs at an increased rate. The oxygen-laden blood cells are sent speeding to the brain, spinal cord, heart, and muscles.

Since blood also picks up the waste products of cells, organs, and tissues, its increased flow helps to remove the great quantities of waste produced when the body goes into "high gear."

Two "jobs" remain to be done. First, the increased supply of oxygen is all but useless unless its fuel, sugar, is available in equivalently great quantities. And, second, the body must be prepared for injury.

—*Science World* March 10, 1965

56. In times of danger, blood is shifted away from the (1) brain   (2) intestines   (3) heart   (4) voluntary muscles   (5) central nervous system

56. 1 2 3 4 5
     || || || || ||

57. Stored red blood cells are released by the (1) spleen   (2) heart   (3) brain   (4) muscles   (5) central nervous system

57. 1 2 3 4 5
     || || || || ||

58. Preparing the body for danger involves
(1) decreased concentration of blood cells (2) decrease in blood pressure
(3) decrease in rate of breathing (4) increased blood pressure and rate of
breathing (5) increased blood supply to the stomach

Selection 18

If modern biologists were polled, a majority might agree that science is con-
verging, at last, on a useful definition of life. For many, that definition would
involve the property known as *replication*. Replication means the ability of a
living organism to reproduce exactly its own vastly complicated structure out of
much less complicated ones. It also reproduces all its functions and thus passes
the ability to replicate on to its offspring.

The problem is *how*. The individual substances that make up the cell, complicated as each is, seem to lack this property of self-duplication and inheritance.
But if the building blocks of a cell are not alive, how does the cell live?

Two answers are being considered. Either life arises from the fact that the
cell's separate components are reacting together, or there really is a "living molecule" that can duplicate itself.

Some biologists think that such a "living molecule" has been found—*deoxyribonucleic acid* (DNA). DNA is a complex substance found in the nucleus of
the cell. It is believed to control biological inheritance through a "code" derived
from its own structure.

Other biologists dispute the theory that DNA can replicate. Said one recently,
"It is not that DNA is the secret of life, but that *life* is the secret of DNA."

Whatever the answer, the puzzle of life's nature is likely to be with us for a
long time to come. So that even if men find a mysterious *something* on some other
planet one day, they may still have to wonder: "Is this life?"

—*Senior Science* Sept 18, 1965

59. In an animal cell, DNA is present in greatest abundance in the
(1) vacuoles (2) cytoplasm (3) nucleus (4) centrosome (5) organism

59. 1 2 3 4 5
|| || || || !!

60. The chief importance of DNA is that
(1) its code is derived from molecules (2) it is present in non-living things
(3) it is unimportant for life (4) it seems to control inheritance (5) it is
present on other planets

60. 1 2 3 4 5
|| || || || ||

61. Replication is best described as
(1) life (2) cell division (3) exact duplication (4) a living molecule (5)
DNA

61. 1 2 3 4 5
|| || || || ||

Selection 19

Sodium chloride, being by far the largest constituent of the mineral matter
of the blood, assumes special significance in the regulation of water exchanges
in the organism. And, as Cannon has emphasized repeatedly, these latter are
more extensive and more important than may at first thought appear. He points
out "there are a number of circulations of the fluid out of the body and back
again, without loss." Thus, for example, it is estimated that from a quart to a
quart and one-half of water daily "leaves the body" when it enters the mouth as

saliva; another one or two quarts are passed out as gastric juice; and perhaps the same amount is contained in the bile and the secretions of the pancreas and the intestinal wall. This large volume of water enters the digestive processes; and practically all of it is reabsorbed through the intestinal wall, where it performs the equally important function of carrying in the digested foodstuffs. These and other instances of what Cannon calls "the conservative use of water in our bodies" involve essentially osmotic pressure relationship in which the concentration of sodium chloride plays an important part.

62. This passage implies that
(1) substances can pass through the intestinal wall in only one direction
(2) water can not be absorbed by the body unless it contains sodium chloride (3) every particle of water ingested is used over and over again
(4) sodium chloride does not actually enter the body (5) regulation of water exchanges in the organism is controlled by the concentration of sodium chloride

63. According to this passage, which of the following processes requires most water?
(1) the absorption of digested foods (2) the secretion of gastric juice (3) the secretion of saliva (4) the production of bile (5) the concentration of sodium chloride solution

64. The conservative use of water in our bodies depends on the concentration of sodium chloride because
(1) it is present in saliva (2) it is passed out with gastric juice (3) it is contained in bile (4) it regulates the water exchanges in the organism (5) it passes through the intestinal wall

65. Sodium chloride is an important constituent of
(1) gastric juice (2) bile (3) pancreatic juice (4) intestinal juice (5) blood

66. The importance of water in the intestine is its ability to
(1) form saliva (2) dilute the gastric juice (3) form bile (4) act as a vehicle for digested food (5) dissolve sodium chloride

Selection 20

A student floated a lighted candle on a cork in a shallow pan of water. He carefully inverted a bottle over the burning candle. He measured the time required for the candle to stop burning. He then removed the bottle, relit the candle, filled the bottle with exhaled air, and again inverted it over the candle. When the candle went out, he repeated this second part of his demonstration, but before filling the bottle with exhaled air, he ran 100 yards at top speed.

67. The probable purpose of this demonstration was to show that
(1) inhaled and exhaled air differ in composition (2) exhaled air contains less carbon dioxide than inhaled air (3) combustion releases heat (4) respiration produces heat (5) combustion produces carbon dioxide

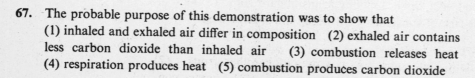

68. One observation which the student would make is that the candle went out
(1) most quickly in the first trial   (2) most quickly in the last trial   (3) at
the same time in all three trials   (4) only in the first trial   (5) as soon as
the inverted bottle was placed over the candle

68. 1 2 3 4 5
     || || || || ||

69. As a result of the demonstration, the student might be justified in concluding that exhaled air
(1) contains carbon dioxide   (2) contains no oxygen   (3) has less carbon
dioxide than inhaled air   (4) has less oxygen than inhaled air   (5) contains
as much oxygen as inhaled air

69. 1 2 3 4 5
     || || || || ||

70. As a result of this demonstration, the student might also be justified in
concluding that
(1) activity results in a higher percentage of oxygen in exhaled air
(2) activity results in a higher percentage of carbon dioxide in exhaled air
(3) respiration is similar to burning   (4) respiration produces more
carbon dioxide than burning   (5) rate of respiration remains constant

70. 1 2 3 4 5
     || || || || ||

Selection 21

In the days of sailing ships, when voyages were long and uncertain, provisions
for many months were stored without refrigeration in the holds of the ships.
Naturally no fresh or perishable foods could be included. Toward the end of
particularly long voyages the crews of such ships became ill and often many died
from scurvy. Many men, both scientific and otherwise, tried to devise a cure for
scurvy. Among the latter was John Hall, a son-in-law of William Shakespeare,
who cured some cases of scurvy by administering a sour brew made from scurvy
grass and water cress.

The next step was the suggestion of William Harvey that scurvy could be prevented by giving the men lemon juice. He thought that the beneficial substance
was the acid contained in the fruit.

The third step was taken by Dr. James Lind, an English naval surgeon, who
performed the following experiment with 12 sailors all of whom were sick with
scurvy: Each was given the same diet, except that four of the men received small
amounts of dilute sulfuric acid, four others were given vinegar and the remaining
four were given lemons. Only those who received the fruit recovered.

71. Credit for solving the problem described in the passage belongs to
(1) Hall, because he first devised a cure for scurvy   (2) Harvey, because
he first proposed a solution of the problem   (3) Lind, because he proved
the solution by means of an experiment   (4) both Harvey and Lind, because they found that lemons are more effective than scurvy grass or water
cress   (5) all three men, because each made some contribution

71. 1 2 3 4 5
     || || || || ||

72. The fatalities among sailors could be attributed to
(1) spoilage of food   (2) absence of physicians aboard ship   (3) lack of
adequate diet   (4) lack of sunshine   (5) vinegar and sulfuric acid

72. 1 2 3 4 5
     || || || || ||

73. The hypothesis tested by Lind was:
(1) Lemons contain some substance not present in other fruits.   (2)
Citric acid is the most effective treatment for scurvy.   (3) Lemons con-

73. 1 2 3 4 5
     || || || || ||

tain some unknown acid that will cure scurvy. (4) Some specific substance, rather than acids in general, is needed to cure scurvy. (5) The substance needed to cure scurvy is found only in lemons.

74. A problem that Lind's experiment did NOT solve was:
(1) Can scurvy be cured? (2) Will lemons cure scurvy? (3) Will either sulfuric acid or vinegar cure scurvy? (4) Are all citrus fruits equally effective as a treatment for scurvy? (5) Are lemons more effective than either vinegar or sulfuric acid in the treatment of scurvy?

74. 1 2 3 4 5

Selection 22

Asepsis refers to a technique which avoids the introduction of viable microorganisms. Sterilization and disinfection are processes which eliminate viable microbes; the terms are essentially synonymous, but the latter is usually limited to the use of chemicals which render infectious organisms non-viable. Antibacterial effects are divided into bacteriostasis, or reversible inhibition of the multiplication of bacteria, and irreversible bactericidal action which "kills" them. The terms disinfectant, germicide, and bactericide are synonymous for bactericidal agents. Antiseptics are antibacterial substances which can be applied to body surfaces, cavities, or wounds to prevent or combat bacterial infection; these compounds do not necessarily completely sterilize the treated surface. Chemotherapeutics are antibacterial (or, more generally, antimicrobial) substances which are sufficiently non-toxic within the tissues as well as on body surfaces.

75. Which term is best applicable in describing the bactericidal action of chemicals?
(1) asepsis (2) chemotherapy (3) disinfection (4) sepsis (5) antimicrobial

75. 1 2 3 4 5

76. Which of the following statements is best supported by the paragraph?
(1) All antiseptic substances are compounds. (2) Bacteriostasis kills bacteria rather than inhibiting them. (3) Chemotherapeutic substances are non-toxic, both within the tissues as well as on the body surfaces. (4) Reversible inhibition of bacterial growth is caused by chemotherapeutical agents. (5) antibacterial substances are toxic to living tissue.

76. 1 2 3 4 5

Selection 23

An object at rest tends to remain at rest, and an object in motion tends to keep on moving at the same speed and in the same direction. This in essence, is a statement of Newton's first law of motion. The concept of inertia, the tendency of mattern not to change its motion, was also explained by Newton. Actually when we speak of mass of matter we are dealing with the inertia of a body. The mass of matter is a measure of the inertia of a body. The more the mass an object has, the greater the inertia. To illustrate Newton's first law of motion, picture yourself standing in the aisle of a train. As it starts suddenly you find yourself falling backward because the inertia of your body has a tendency to keep you at rest as your feet move forward with the movement of the train. If the train should come to a sudden stop while you are standing in the aisle, you will tend to move forward because your body continues in a forward motion as the train stops moving.

Strictly speaking, speed and velocity are not the same. *Speed* indicates how fast an object is moving and how far it will travel in a given length of time. This may be expressed by the formula

$$(r)\ (t) = d$$

where *r* is the speed, expressed in distance for unit of time, such as miles per hour or feet per second, *t* is the time elapsed and *d* is the distance covered. For example, a car going at 40 miles, traveling for an hour and a half will cover 60 miles. *Velocity* includes direction as well as speed. Therefore, a change in velocity may refer to change in speed, or direction or both. The motion of a body is said to be *uniform* when its velocity is constant. If you ride your bicycle at 15 miles per hour along a straight level road the motion is uniform. When you change the speed or direction of the bicycle, the velocity is no longer constant, and the motion is no longer uniform.

It is quite unusual to drive an automobile with constant velocity. As you change the velocity, either by going faster or by slowing down, you are accelerating the car. *Acceleration* is a change in velocity per unit of time. Slowing down is negative acceleration or deceleration. Acceleration may be expressed by the formula

$$A = \frac{V_2 - V_1}{T}$$

where A is the acceleration, V_1 is the initial velocity, V_2 is the final velocity, and T is the time elapsed. Thus, if an automobile moving on a straight, level road, goes from 25 miles per hour to 45 miles per hour in 10 seconds, we will find that the acceleration is 2 miles per hour per second. Substituting these values in the formula above,

$$A = \frac{45\ \text{MPH} - 25\ \text{MPH}}{10\ \text{seconds}} \quad \text{or} \quad \frac{20\ \text{MPH}}{10\ \text{seconds}} \quad \text{or} \quad \frac{2\ \text{MPH}}{1\ \text{second}}$$

Negative acceleration or deceleration could be illustrated by a rolling ball moving at 6 feet per second on a level surface and comes to rest 3 seconds later. Using the same formula, we find that the deceleration is 2 feet per second per second, or 2 feet per second^2.

$$A = \frac{\text{zero} - 6\ \text{feet per second}}{3\ \text{seconds}} \quad \text{or} \quad \frac{2\ \text{feet per second}}{1\ \text{second}}$$

Newton's second law of motion describes the effect of force and mass on acceleration. Needless to say, it takes more force for a baseball pitcher to throw a fast ball than to pitch a slow ball. Likewise, it takes more force to throw a large stone than to throw a small pebble. It also requires less force to accelerate a small compact car than it does to accelerate a large truck. Stopping your car by applying the brakes also illustrates this law. The force of friction on the brakes causes deceleration. The speed with which you can slow down or come to a complete stop depends upon the speed with which the car was traveling as well as the weight of the car. Advice on highway safety in regard to excessive speeding or the matter of safe distances between cars takes this law into account.

Newton's third law of motion, often referred to as the law of interaction, states that when an object exerts a force on a second object, the second object exerts an equal and opposite force on the first. In other words, for any action there is an equal but opposite reaction. Rowing a boat illustrates this law. The oars give a mass of water some momentum toward the rear, giving the boat an equal forward momentum. Likewise, the jet plane or rocket is one mass and the exhaust gas fired from the rear is the other mass.

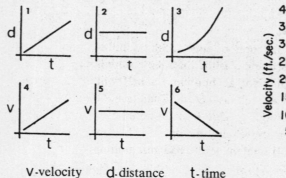
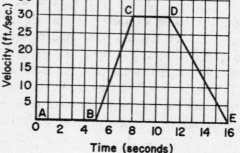

V-velocity   d-distance   t-time

The graphs labelled (1) to (6) refer to an experiment on motion with an automobile traveling along a straight, level road. The graphs show the various relationships of velocity, time, and distance traveled.

Questions 77 to 81 refer to these graphs.

77. The graph which shows decreasing velocity is
    (1) 1   (2) 3   (3) 4   (4) 5   (5) 6

    77. 1 2 3 4 5
         || || || || ||

78. The two graphs which show increasing velocity are
    (1) 1 and 2   (2) 2 and 3   (3) 2 and 4   (4) 5 and 6   (5) 3 and 4

    78. 1 2 3 4 5
         || || || || ||

79. The graph that shows no motion is
    (1) 1   (2) 2   (3) 3   (4) 4   (5) 6

    79. 1 2 3 4 5
         || || || || ||

80. The graphs that show accelerated motion are
    (1) 3 and 4 only   (2) 3 and 6 only   (3) 4 and 6 only
    (4) 3, 4, 5, and 6   (5) 3, 4, and 6

    80. 1 2 3 4 5
         || || || || ||

81. The graphs that show constant velocity are
    (1) 1 and 2 only   (2) 1 and 5 only   (3) 2 and 5 only
    (4) 1, 2, and 5   (5) 1, 4, and 5

    81. 1 2 3 4 5
         || || || || ||

Graph ABCDE represents the motion of an object. Velocity is plotted against time. Questions 82 to 86 refer to this graph.

82. In which section of the graph is the shortest distance covered?
    (1) A - B   (2) B - C   (3) C - D   (4) D - E   (5) B - E

    82. 1 2 3 4 5
         || || || || ||

83. In which section of the graph is the average velocity the greatest?
    (1) A - B   (2) B - C   (3) C - D   (4) D - E   (5) B - E

    83. 1 2 3 4 5
         || || || || ||

84. In which section or sections of the graph is the greatest distance covered?
    (1) A - B   (2) B - C   (3) C - D   (4) D - E   (5) B - C or D - E

    84. 1 2 3 4 5
         || || || || ||

85. In which section of the graph is the acceleration of deceleration the greatest?
    (1) A - B   (2) B - C   (3) C - D   (4) D - E   (5) B - E

    85. 1 2 3 4 5
         || || || || ||

86. In how many sections of the graph is the acceleration zero?
(1) one   (2) two   (3) three   (4) four   (5) five

86. 1 2 3 4 5

87. The sharp recoil when a gun is fired is an illustration of
(1) constant velocity   (2) acceleration   (3) Newton's first law of motion   (4) Newton's second law of motion   (5) Newton's third law of motion

87. 1 2 3 4 5

88. Of the following, which object is NOT being accelerated?
(1) a pendulum swinging with a constant period   (2) a satellite in a constant orbit   (3) a freely falling stone   (4) a car with constant velocity   (5) a football thrown into the air

88. 1 2 3 4 5

89. The time rate of change of velocity is known as
(1) speed   (2) moment   (3) mass   (4) final velocity   (5) acceleration

89. 1 2 3 4 5

90. A uniformly accelerated car, starting from rest, coasts down a hill. At the end of 2 seconds its velocity is 20 feet per second. Its acceleration (in feet per second^2) is
(1) 5   (2) 10   (3) 15   (4) 20   (5) 40

90. 1 2 3 4 5

Selection 24

Scientists have recently indicated considerable concern for the discovery of great amounts of chemical debris fouling vast areas of the Atlantic Ocean. They found that at least 665,000 square miles of this water from Cape Cod to the Caribbean is covered by floating oil, tar, and plastics. One group of scientists reported that small fish that eat this plastic material may die from blocked intestines. Several researchers said they were not clear about the effect of petroleum wastes on fish. Others are testing the possibility that crude oil, but not refined petroleum products, might act as nutrient to marine plant life.

Needless to say, the study of ecology, the branch of biology that deals with the interrelations between living things and their environment, is most important today. The environment of living things must be considered from the point of view of the physical factors such as temperature, soil, and water and the biotic factors which are the effects of other living things.

Fig. 1

Ecologists organize groups of living things into populations, communities, ecological systems, and the biosphere. A *population* consists of organisms of the same species living together in a given location, such as all the oak trees in a forest, or all the frogs of the same species in a pond. A *community* consists of populations of different species, living together and interacting with each other. The accompanying diagram illustrates a simple community. It pictures a large bottle with a layer of mud on the bottom. The bottle was filled with pond water and several fish and some green plants were added. The bottle was then made airtight.

An *ecological system* (or *ecosystem*) consists of the living community of a region and its nonliving environment. The *biosphere* is that part of the earth in which ecosystems function. This therefore excludes molten portions of our planet and regions at high altitudes where life does not exist.

Ecologists study the transfer of food energy through a series of organisms with emphasis on the possible effects of artificially changing the steps in the food chain in nature. The steps that may occur in such a food chain are: producer, primary consumer, secondary consumer, and decomposer. Green plants use the sun's energy to produce food from raw material. Any herbivorous animal such as the cow is a primary consumer since such an animal feeds directly upon the producer. Man who gets his food from the cow is a secondary consumer. Decomposers are organisms that live on dead organic material. Bacteria of decay and molds are decomposers.

The following diagram represents some of the relationships in a marine community.

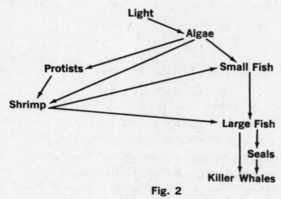

Fig. 2

Feeding relationships within a community are often described as a *food web*. The accidental or planned destruction of a single member of a food web may cause unexpected results. Killing off the coyotes, wolves, and pumas that preyed on deer in the Grand Canyon caused a rapid increase of the deer population. The lack of sufficient food for them caused starvation and the population of deer in the range was greatly reduced. Another example is the extensive killing of owls because they prey on chickens with the result that there is a sudden increase in the number of such animals as rabbits and mice which normally would be held in check by the owls.

The food energy in a food chain may be transferred by predators, scavengers, or symbionts. A *predator* kills his prey and then eats it. *Scavengers* live on dead animals or plants. Many bacteria, yeasts and molds live on dead organic material. They are known as saprophytes as contrasted with parasites that live on living things. A *symbiont* is a member of a nutritive relationship (symbiosis) in which neither partner causes harm to the other. The lichen, often seen growing on a rock is actually two plants- an alga and a fungus. The alga carries on photosynthesis giving food and is protected from drying out by the fungus. Such a type of symbiotic relationship is known as mutuaism. Where only one member benefits with no harm to the other member of the symbiotic relationship the term commensalism is applied. The remora fish can attach itself to a shark and pick up floating scraps of food discarded by the shark. This does not affect the shark in any way.

Man must be made aware of the importance of ecology. Polluting the air or his waters disturbs the balance of nature. Introducing new pesticides may destroy natural enemies that control ideal populations.

91. Of the following which are primary consumers?
    (1) spiders   (2) cows   (3) algae   (4) hemlock seedlings   (5) lichens

92. Which consists of a single species?
    (1) biosphere   (2) a community   (3) an ectosystem   (4) a biome
    (5) a population

93. In Figure 1 the living and nonliving contents of the bottle constitute
    (1) an ecosystem   (2) a population   (3) a biome   (4) a species

    (5) a genus

94. The fish in this bottle (Figure 1) most likely represent
    (1) symbionts   (2) producers   (3) decomposers   (4) saprophytes
    (5) herbivores

95. When one fish dies, the nitrogen from its body is released through the action of
    (1) viruses   (2) bacteria   (3) multicellular green plants   (4) green algae   (5) mud

96. In order to insure that the organisms in the bottle will survive for a period of time, the bottle must be
    (1) kept in darkness   (2) placed in water   (3) kept in a cool room
    (4) placed in a well-ventilated room   (5) exposed to light

97. A type of nutritional relationship in which both symbionts benefit from the association is
    (1) commensalism   (2) autotrophism   (3) parasitism   (4) saprophytism   (5) mutualism

98. In a lake containing algae, frogs, minnows, trout, and small crustaceans, which organism would probably be present in largest numbers?
    (1) minnows   (2) small crustaceans   (3) algae   (4) trout   (5) frogs

99. The earliest stage in an ecological succession from a bare rock is characterized by the presence of
    (1) trees   (2) mosses   (3) lichens   (4) grasses   (5) ferns

100. Although man has been successful in modifying his environment, many of his modifications have seriously upset the balance of nature. This can be attributed to his lack of realization that
     (1) man is supreme in power   (2) man can adapt to more environmental conditions than any other species   (3) man's abilities are superior in all areas   (4) man not only influences the balance of nature, but is influenced by it   (5) man is dependent upon the green plant for food

91. 1 2 3 4 5
92. 1 2 3 4 5
93. 1 2 3 4 5
94. 1 2 3 4 5
95. 1 2 3 4 5
96. 1 2 3 4 5
97. 1 2 3 4 5
98. 1 2 3 4 5
99. 1 2 3 4 5
100. 1 2 3 4 5

101. Which pair of organisms exhibit the type of symbiosis known as commensalism?
(1) remora and shark   (2) alga and fungus in a lichen   (3) athlete's foot fungus and man   (4) lamprey eel and trout   (5) maggots on diseased tissue

101. 1 2 3 4 5

102. The least ecologically damaging method of controlling the spread of malaria is by
(1) draining swamps where mosquitoes breed   (2) spraying swamps with DDT   (3) spreading oil over swamps   (4) introducing fish to the swamps where mosquitoes breed   (5) using chlodane

102. 1 2 3 4 5

NOTE: Questions 103 to 106 refer to Figure 2

103. Most of the energy in the body of the whales can be traced to
(1) biotic factor   (2) oxygen in the water   (3) minerals in the water
(4) temperature of the water   (5) light

103. 1 2 3 4 5

104. Of the organisms constituting this community, the least numerous would probably be   the
(1) killer whales   (2) seals   (3) large fish   (4) shrimp   (5) small fish

104. 1 2 3 4 5

105. Which is the major group of producer organisms in this community?
(1) algae   (2) shrimp   (3) killer whales   (4) seals   (5) fish

105. 1 2 3 4 5

106. The information from the chart most strongly supports the concept that, if killer whales were eliminated from this community, it might be expected that initially there would be
(1) destruction of all other animals   (2) an increase in the number of shrimp   (3) an increase in the number of small fish   (4) a decrease in the number of seals   (5) an increase in the number of seals

106. 1 2 3 4 5

ANSWERS   *Reading Selections in the Natural Sciences*

1. 2	12. 2	23. 1	34. 3	45. 2	56. 2	67. 1	78. 5	89. 5	100. 4
2. 4	13. 3	24. 4	35. 1	46. 4	57. 1	68. 2	79. 2	90. 2	101. 1
3. 1	14. 2	25. 3	36. 1	47. 4	58. 4	69. 4	80. 5	91. 2	102. 4
4. 3	15. 4	26. 3	37. 2	48. 4	59. 3	70. 2	81. 4	92. 5	103. 5
5. 4	16. 4	27. 1	38. 4	49. 3	60. 4	71. 5	82. 1	93. 1	104. 1
6. 1	17. 2	28. 2	39. 2	50. 1	61. 3	72. 3	83. 3	94. 5	105. 1
7. 5	18. 3	29. 4	40. 3	51. 1	62. 5	73. 4	84. 3	95. 2	106. 5
8. 3	19. 4	30. 4	41. 2	52. 1	63. 1	74. 4	85. 2	96. 5	
9. 4	20. 2	31. 1	42. 2	53. 4	64. 4	75. 3	86. 2	97. 5	
10. 5	21. 3	32. 4	43. 3	54. 3	65. 5	76. 3	87. 5	98. 3	
11. 3	22. 1	33. 4	44. 1	55. 4	66. 4	77. 5	88. 4	99. 3	

What's your score?

_____right, _____wrong

Excellent	99–106
Good	88–98
Fair	80–87

If your score is low, don't get discouraged. Perhaps science is a difficult subject for you. Try to find out why you failed. The analysis of correct answers which follows will help you to pinpoint your errors. If your mistake was lack of information, turn to the glossary of scientific terms and look up the meaning of the words you did not understand. If it was a mistake in interpretation, review the analysis of the question. Perhaps it would help to refresh your remembrance of the 8 Hints for Handling Reading Comprehension in Chapter 1.

ANSWERS EXPLAINED

1. Ans. 2 The passage refers to the vibrations in the core of the atom, or the nucleus of the atom, as having the fastest motion available for timekeeping purposes.

2. Ans. 4 According to the passage, the faster the motion, the more accurate the measurement. Therefore, since the atom nucleus has the fastest motion, it has the least change.

3. Ans. 1 The passage states that like many other clocks, the Earth is running down.

4. Ans. 3 The passage states that the fastest motion available for timekeeping purposes is the vibration in the core or the nucleus of the atom.

5. Ans. 4 Graphite is made of carbon, which is a nonmetal.

6. Ans. 1 Metals are composed of atoms which are arranged in a stack. These atomic building blocks form a lattice.

7. Ans. 5 The passage mentions that sodium is grey and lusterless.

8. Ans. 3 The metals were named before they had been scientifically classified according to their atomic structure. By examining these elements at the atomic level, we can understand what gives them their "metallic" properties.

9. Ans. 4 They may be considered minor planets because they travel around the sun.

10. Ans. 5 As mentioned in the second paragraph, all of these are planets.

11. Ans. 3 The actual number of planets would include the "big nine" mentioned in the second paragraph, as well as the planetoids or asteroids.

12. Ans. 2 The fourth paragraph indicates that most asteroids, or planetoids, occur in the space between the orbits of Mars and Jupiter. However, in the next paragraph, it is stated that some occur close to Earth, or out toward Saturn.

13. Ans. 3 Charles Darwin devloped the theory of evolution by natural selection. The passage states that he continually found evidence of relationships among living things during his voyage on the *Beagle*.

14. Ans. 2 Carolus Linnaeus gave us a workable system of classifying living things according to their structure.

15. Ans. 4 The theory of evolution explains many areas of otherwise loosely organized observations and ideas, including the relationships among living things.

16. Ans. 4 The first item of the chart indicates that the area of the Pacific Ocean is more than 64 million miles.

17. Ans. 2 The Bering Sea has an average depth of 4,893 feet. The Sea of Japan has an average depth of 5,468 feet.

18. Ans. 3 The chart confirms information in all choices except #3. The largest of our oceans is the Pacific not the Atlantic.

19. Ans. 4 The freezing is almost instantaneous, and permits the surgeon to work very rapidly. At very low temperatures, blood does not deteriorate, but can be stored indefinitely.

20. Ans. 2 In foods frozen by ordinary means, ice crystals develop within the plant cells. Then, when the fruit or vegetable thaws, the ice melts and ruptures the cell wall. With liquid gases, ice crystals do not form.

21. Ans. 3 When the tomatoes are frozen, ice crystals form. Upon being thawed, the ice melts, causing the cell walls to rupture. This results in a loss of flavor, and "mushiness."

22. Ans. 1 Cryogenics deals with the study of extremely low temperatures, such as those of liquid gases.

23. Ans. 1 In the second sentence of the selection, the statement is made that the pull of gravity becomes weaker with increasing distance from the Earth's center. In other words, the pull of gravity becomes stronger with decreasing distance from the earth's center.

24. Ans. 4 The passage mentions experiments with pendulums that confirmed that gravity is strongest near the Earth's poles. At the poles, the Earth is somewhat flattened, so that they are closer to the center of the Earth than at the equator.

25. Ans. 3 The opening statement of the passage refers to the ellipsoidal shape of the Earth. In other words, the shape is not exactly round, but somewhat oval.

26. Ans. 3 The stronger the pull of gravitation, the faster the swing of a pendulum.

27. Ans. 1 The electron microscope magnifies up to 100,000 times, while the ordinary light microscope magnifies up to 2,000 times. By dividing 100,000 by 2,000, we find that the electron microscope magnifies 50 times more than the light microscope.

28. Ans. 2 A virologist studies viruses. A bacteriophage is a type of virus that attacks bacterial cells.

29. Ans. 4 Since the electron microscope magnifies up to 100,000 times, research with microorganisms that previously could not be seen with the light microscope, has been greatly advanced.

30. Ans. 4 The third sentence of the passage mentions the use of radioactive tracers in following elements through chemical reactions.

31. Ans. 1 There is little agreement among scientists on the mechanism that causes or releases the stress that has gradually accumulated in a portion of the Earth's crust. This statement is made in the last sentence of the passage.

32. Ans. 4 The introductory words of the passage state that the great Alaskan earthquake occurred on March 27, 1964.

33. Ans. 4 As stated in the next to the last sentence, the immediate source of a tremor is the sudden release of energy which has gradually accumulated in a strained portion of the Earth's crust.

34. Ans. 3 In the first sentence of the second paragraph, the transfer of a nerve impulse is shown to be electrical in nature.

35. Ans. 1 Lower forms of life contain protoplasm, as do other living things. All protoplasm has the ability to respond to stimuli.

36. Ans. 1 At the end of the first paragraph, the author states that sense-stimulating impulses are sent from the eye to the brain. If these sensory impulses are stopped, we cannot see.

37. Ans. 2 The last sentence of the passage refers to the fact that these compounds trigger temporary changes in electrical potential across cell membranes.

38. Ans. 4 The last sentence of the passage states that the detergent molecule has the characteristic of being both hydrophilic and hydrophobic.

39. Ans. 2 By reducing the surface tension of the water, soap helps water wet the fabrics to a greater extent.

40. Ans. 3 The first paragraph states that according to the laws of mathematics, a sphere has the least surface area for its volume.

41. Ans. 2 The arrangement of particles within a crystal is orderly, with each atom vibrating about a fixed position. These positions are arranged in a regular pattern in space.

42. Ans. 2 A crystal cleaves, or splits, along straight lines. The forces between the atoms of the crystal are weakest along the cleavage planes. These forces are weaker because the planes may be farther apart than the atoms within the planes, or because of the arrangement of electrical charges.

43. Ans. 3 When diamond cutters cleave a diamond, they are actually slicing parallel to the cleavage planes, forcing them apart.

44. Ans. 1 Copper is an element. When it is melted with other elements, it produces an alloy. For example, silver coins are alloys of copper and silver. Brass is an alloy of copper and zinc. Bronze is an alloy of copper, tin and zinc. Pewter is an alloy of copper, lead, antimony and tin.

45. Ans. 2 The passage indicates that air is a solution of many gases dissolved in nitrogen. Nitrogen is therefore the solvent of the solution in which the gases are dissolved.

46. Ans. 4 The last sentence of the first paragraph states that many combinations of liquid, gas and solid can form a solution.

47. Ans. 4 A universal solvent would dissolve all substances. As the first part of the second paragraph intimates, there are reasons why a universal solvent may never be synthesized.

48. Ans. 4 The passage (first paragraph) refers to inorganic pollutants as including acids; sulfuric acid is an example of an acid.

49. Ans. 3 The second paragraph indicates that microbes ordinarily feed on and digest waste products, transforming them into harmless by-products.

50. Ans. 1 When water falls as rain, it is free of any contaminants; then, from the moment it lands, it picks up, transports and disperses all sorts of impurities.

51. Ans. 1 The third paragraph indicates that large cities and heavy industries are the chief offenders in the pollution of water. There may be organic or inorganic pollutants, which are deposited in rivers and interfere with the natural environment.

52. Ans. 1 The gastrozooids are very sensitive to the chemical (glutathione) released by injured animals.

53. Ans. 4 When gastrozooids were isolated and exposed to a weak solution of glutathione they responded so violently that some even turned themselves inside out.

54. Ans. 3 By analyzing the minute quantities of odor given off by insects, scientists copied the smell that was irresistible to this particular insect, and eliminated it from the island where it was a pest.

55. Ans. 4 The passage specifically deals with the use of chemicals to lure insects, instead of spraying them with pesticides.

56. Ans. 2 The introductory part of the passage states that blood is shifted away from the "non-fighting" organs, such as the stomach, intestines and other parts of the digestive system. An increased supply of blood is available to the "combat" organs—the heart, brain, central nervous system and muscles.

57. Ans. 1 There is a reserve supply of red blood cells in the spleen which is released during an emergency.

58. Ans. 4 During a threat of danger, there is an increase in the heart beat, increasing the blood pressure. There is also an increase in the rate of breathing, which sends the red blood cells through the lungs at a faster rate.

59. Ans. 3 The fourth paragraph contains the statement that DNA is found in the nucleus of the cell. Vacuoles are found in the liquid part of the cell, the cytoplasm, which store substances. An organism is a living thing.

60. Ans. 4 Much evidence points to the importance of DNA in controlling biological inheritance through a "code" derived from its own structure.

61. Ans. 3 In the first paragraph, the statement is made that replication refers to the exact duplication of the vastly complicated structure of a living organism.

62. Ans. 5 The very first sentence indicates that sodium chloride assumes special significance in the regulation of water exchange in the organism.

63. Ans. 1 Although much water is involved in the secretion of saliva, in gastric juice, bile, and the secretions of the pancreas and the intestinal wall, practically all of the water is reabsorbed through the intestinal wall with the absorption of digested food.

64. Ans. 4 The last part of the passage indicates that the concentration of sodium chloride plays an important part in the osmotic pressure relationships, that is, in the passage of water through the membranes of the body by osmosis.

65. Ans. 5 The opening sentence of the passage states that sodium chloride is the largest constituent of the mineral matter of the blood.

66. Ans. 4 The digested food is dissolved in water and is absorbed through the intestinal wall with it.

67. Ans. 1 The first trial used ordinary air, which is the same as inhaled air. In the second and third trials, he used exhaled air. He compared the time necessary for the candle to go out in each case. The difference was due to the difference in composition of the inhaled and exhaled air.

68. Ans. 2 In the last trial, the candle would go out most quickly because the exhaled air would contain the least amount of oxygen. The act of running required the use of more oxygen for the cells of the body.

69. Ans. 4 Since the candle would not burn as long in exhaled air, it is obvious that it contained less oxygen than inhaled air.

70. Ans. 2 As a result of respiration, carbon dioxide is given off. With strenuous exertion, a higher percentage of carbon dioxide would be produced, and would be excreted in the exhaled air.

71. Ans. 5 In scientific advances, scientists build on the investigations performed by other scientists. Credit therefore does not belong solely to the last scientist who comes up with a solution, but to all the others on whose work his discoveries were based. In this case, all the men mentioned made some contribution to the problem.

72. Ans. 3 Since there was a lack of fresh food on long voyages, these men did not have an adequate diet. It is now known that they were lacking vitamin C, which is found in fresh fruits and vegetables.

73. Ans. 4 Since he supplied acid of some type to all the men, and since dilute sulfuric acid and vinegar (a mild form of acetic acid) were not effective, there must have been some other specific substance present in the lemons that was needed.

74. Ans. 4 The experiment dealt specifically with three substances that were acid in nature, namely sulfuric acid, vinegar, and lemon. It did not include enough fruits to be able to come to the generalization that all citrus fruits are equally effective as a treatment for scurvy.

75. Ans. 3 The first part of the passage refers to the difference between sterilization and disinfection; it states that the latter is usually limited to the use of chemicals which render infectious organisms non-viable.

76. Ans. 3 The last sentence of the passage refers to chemotherapeutic agents as being non-toxic to the body tissues and surfaces.

77. Ans. 5 Graph #6 shows that as time increases velocity decreases.

78. Ans. 5 Graph #3 shows that the distance is increasing as time increases. However, the curve indicates that the distance is increasing more rapidly as time goes on. This is acceleration. Graph #4 shows an increase of velocity with time. This is uniform or constant acceleration.

79. Ans. 2 In graph #2 the distance remains the same as time goes on. The automobile has not changed its position. In other words there is no motion.

80. Ans. 5 See explanations for previous questions.

81. Ans. 4 Graph #1 shows that the distance traveled is directly proportional to the time elapsed. This means that the velocity is changing. In graph #2 the automobile is not in motion so that the velocity is always zero. In graph #5 the velocity is the same value at any period of time.

82. Ans. 1 In section A - B of the graph the velocity is zero. It is not moving. It is not covering distance.

83. Ans. 3 In section C - D the velocity is 30 feet per second at all times. In A - B the velocity is zero. For B - C the average velocity is $\frac{0 + 30}{2}$ or 15 feet per second. For D - E the average velocity is $\frac{30 + 0}{2}$ or 15 feet per second.

84. Ans. 3 Using the formula in the passage: $(r)(t) = d$, for section A - B the velocity is zero therefore the distance is zero. For B - C the velocity is 15 feet per second and the time is $8 - 5 = 3$ seconds, therefore the distance is 45 feet. For section C - D the velocity is 30 feet per second, the time is $11 - 8$ or 3 seconds, therefore the distance is 90 feet. In section D - E the velocity is 15 feet per second, the time is $16 - 11$ or 5 seconds, therefore the distance is 75 feet. The velocity for B - E is zero, therefore the distance is zero.

85. Ans. 2 In section A - B the velocity is constant and the acceleration is zero. In section B - C the velocity change is from zero to 30 feet per second for 3 seconds. The acceleration is 10 feet per second[2]. In section C - D there is no acceleration since the velocity is uniform (30 feet per second). In section D - E the velocity change is from 30 to zero or —30 feet per second over a period of 16 - 11 or 5 seconds. The acceleration is —6 feet per second^2. In section B - E the velocity is constant and the acceleration is zero.

86. Ans. 2 The acceleration is zero for a period when the velocity remains the same during that period. This true for sections A - B and C - D.

87. Ans. 5 This is an illustration for the law of interaction.

88. Ans. 4 Since the velocity of the car is constant, there is no change of velocity and therefore there is no acceleration. In case of the freely falling stone, the velocity increases as it falls to the ground. The velocity of a swinging pendulum changes in magnitude and direction. The velocity of a satelite in orbit changes in direction. A football thrown in the air changes velocity and direction.

89. Ans. 5 By definition.

90. Ans. 2 Apply the formula given in the passage.

$$A = \frac{V_2 - V_1}{T}$$

$$A = \frac{20 \text{ feet per second} - \text{zero}}{2 \text{ seconds}} \quad \text{or} \quad 10 \text{ feet per second per second}$$

91. Ans. 2 The passage cites cows as primary consumers with the definition.

92. Ans. 5 A population is defined in the passage as a group of organisms of the same species living together in a given location.

93. Ans. 1 The passage defines an ecosystem as the living community of a region and its nonliving environment.

94. Ans. 5 Herbivores are animals that eat plants.

95. Ans. 2 Bacteria of decay break down dead organic material into simple compounds. Nitrates (nitrogen compounds) are one of the substances thus produced.

96. Ans. 5 Photosynthesis requires light. The algae in this bottle are the only organisms in the bottle capable of carrying on this process. The other living things in the container depend on the green plants directly or indirectly for food.

97. Ans. 5 By definition.

98. Ans. 3 See explanation for #109.

99. Ans. 3 Lichens can establish themselves on bare rock and ultimately erode the rock.

100. Ans. 4 The modern problem of air and water pollution shows that man has upset the balance of nature.

101. Ans. 1 The relationship between the remora fish and the shark is described in the passage.

102. Ans. 4 The fish would eat the mosquito larvae and thus reduce the population of adult mosquitoes which carry the causative agent of malaria.

103. Ans. 5 See explanation for #109.

104. Ans. 1 Whales are the largest, most complicated of all the organisms here.

105. Ans. 1 See explanation for #109.

106. Ans. 5 Since the whales eat the seals there would be an increase in the number of seals if the whales were eliminated.

A WORD ABOUT TESTS: Do you consider yourself a person who "goes to pieces" on tests? Cheer up! Psychologists claim that more than ninety per cent of us think we don't perform well on tests *of any kind*. Nobody likes tests. But more than 80% of the people who have taken the High School Equivalency Tests in the New York area, for example, have passed them. They must be doing something right. And so can you—with the right attitude and careful preparation.

For Further Reading

Barron's Preparation for the High School Equivalency Examination—Reading Interpretation Tests, by Eugene J. Farley, provides extensive practice material and drill in this area.

7

The Test of General Mathematical Ability

This chapter is designed to prepare you for the mathematics part of the High School Equivalency Test. It covers arithmetic, some of the main concepts of algebra and geometry, and such special topics as insurance, taxation, installment buying, and graphs.

HOW TO USE THIS CHAPTER

In the review section and practice exercises there is much material that would lend itself to classroom study. It will, of course, be completely adaptable to self-study.

The final portion of this chapter contains five typical mathematics tests with both answers and explanations of answers.

ARITHMETIC

TIME TO STUDY:

Sets

We often have occasion to talk about sets of objects. For example, we have a set of dishes, a group of people, a bunch of bananas, and a deck of cards. In mathematics, we often work with sets of numbers. The set of numbers used in counting is an important set of numbers in mathematics. A set is simply a collection of objects.

The objects that belong to a set are called *members* or *elements* of the set. When we talk about a set in mathematics we must be sure that we know which objects are members of the set and which objects are not members of the set. There are two main methods of describing a set. We may describe a set in words or we may list the members of the set inside braces. For example,

WORD DESCRIPTION	LISTING
1. The set of the days of the week	{Monday,Tuesday,Wednesday, Thursday,Friday,Saturday,Sunday}.

2. The set of counting numbers
   less than 6 $\{1,2,3,4,5\}$.

We usually think of a set as having several members. In mathematics, a set may contain as few as two members, or one member, or even no members. A set which contains no members is called "the empty set". The symbol used to describe the empty set is "$\{\}$". For example,

WORD DESCRIPTION	LISTING
1. The set of countries bordering the United States.	$\{$Canada, Mexico$\}$
2. The set of capitals of the United States.	$\{$Washington, D.C.$\}$
3. The set of counting numbers less than 2.	$\{1\}$
4. The set of months of the year having 40 days.	$\{\ \}$
5. The set of counting numbers less than 1.	$\{\ \}$

When a set has many members it is not convenient to describe the set by listing. In such a case, we write the first few members of the set, followed by three dots, and then the last members of the set. For example,

WORD DESCRIPTION	LISTING
1. The set of letters of the alphabet	$\{a,b,c,\ldots,z\}$
2. The set consisting of the first 50 counting numbers	$\{1,2,3,\ldots,50\}$

A set whose members may be counted with the counting coming to an end is called a *finite set*. For example, the set of people living in California is a finite set since the set may be counted with the counting coming to an end. In fact, this is done every time a census is taken. However, there are sets whose members may be counted but the counting will never end. Consider the set of even numbers.

$$\{2,4,6,\ldots\}$$

Such a set is an example of an *infinite set* since the listing of its elements will never come to an end. The following are examples of infinite set.

WORD DESCRIPTION	LISTING
1. The set of odd numbers	$\{1,3,5,\ldots\}$
2. The set of counting numbers	$\{1,2,3,\ldots\}$

Consider the set of counting numbers $\{1,2,3,\ldots\}$. If we multiply each number of the set of counting numbers by 5 we have the set $\{5,10,15,\ldots\}$. We may describe the set $\{5,10,15,\ldots\}$ as the set of multiples of 5. In the same way

WORD DESCRIPTION		LISTING
1.	Set of multiples of 3	{3,6,9, . . .}
2.	Set of multiples of 4	{4,8,12, . . .}
3.	Set of multiples of 6	{6,12,18, . . .}

TIME TO PRACTICE:

Directions: **Solve the following problems and blacken the space at the right under the number which corresponds to the one you have selected as the correct answer.**

1. The listing which describes the set whose members are the first three counting numbers is
(1) {3}   (2) {0,1,2}   (3) {1,2,3}   (4) {3,6,9}   (5) {0,3}

2. The set consisting of the first four multiples of 10 is
(1) {0,1,10,20}   (2) {10,20,30,40}   (3) {5,10,15,20}
(4) {10,50,80,90}   (5) {0,10,20,30}

3. An example of the empty set is
(1) the set of months of the year
(2) the set of governors of the state of Illinois
(3) the set of women doctors
(4) the set of counting numbers greater than 1
(5) the set of counting numbers between 4 and 5

4. An example of an infinite set is
(1) the set of people living in Los Angeles.
(2) the set of TV sets in use in the United States.
(3) the set of multiples of 9.
(4) the set of sailors in the United States Navy.
(5) The set of counting numbers less than 875.

5. The symbol used to describe the empty set is
(1) 0   (2) ∪   (3) 1   (4) {}   (5) 0,1,2, . . .

6. The set of multiples of 9 is
(1) {9,18,27, . . .}   (2) {1,9,18, . . .}   (3) {0,9,18, . . .}
(4) {9,18,24, . . .}   (5) {9,15,18, . . .}

ANSWERS:

1. 3   **3.** 5   **5.** 4
2. 2   **4.** 3   **6.** 1

TIME TO STUDY:

Subsets

While shopping a woman is shown a blue dress, a green dress, and a yellow dress. She likes all three dresses and thinks about buying some of them. Here are the possible ways in which she can make a choice.

She can buy all three dresses

{Blue,Green,Yellow}

She can buy any two of the dresses

{Blue,Green}   {Green,Yellow}   {Blue,Yellow}

She can buy just one of the dresses

{Blue}   {Green}   {Yellow}

She can buy none of the dresses   { }

All eight of the woman's choices represent subsets of the set {Blue,Green, Yellow}. Notice, in particular, that the set {Blue,Green,Yellow} is considered a subset of itself and that the empty set, { }, is considered a subset of the set {Blue,Green,Yellow}. The following is a definition of a subset of a set.

DEFINITION: A subset of a given set is a set which contains all, some, or none of the members of a given set.

EXAMPLE: Write all the subsets of the set   {a,b,c,d}.
The subset which contains four members is   {a,b,c,d}.
The subsets which contain three numbers are
{a,b,c},   {a,b,d},   {a,c,d},   {b,c,d}.
The subsets which contain two members are
{a,b},   {a,c},   {a,d},   {b,c},   {b,d},   {c,d}.
The subsets which contain one member are
{a},   {b},   {c},   {d}.
The subset which contains no members is   { }.

TIME TO PRACTICE:

Directions: **Solve the following problems and blacken the space at the right under the number which corresponds to the one you have selected as the correct answer.**

1.   A subset of the set {2,4,6,8,10} is
     (1) {0,2,4,6,8}   (2) {2,4,6,7,8}   (3) {2,4,8,10,12}
     (4) {2,4,6,8,10}   (5) {0,2,4,8}

2.   A subset of every set is
     (1) the set of counting numbers
     (2) { }
     (3) an infinite set
     (4) the set of even numbers
     (5) the set of multiples of the numbers in the given set.

3.   All the subsets of the set {x,y,z} which contain two members are
     (1) {x,y}, {x,z}   (2) {x,y,z}   (3) {x,y}, {x,z}, {y,z},
     (4) { }   (5) {x}, {y}, {z}

4.   A subset of the set whose members are the first 10 counting numbers is
     (1) {10,20,30}   (2) {5,10,15}   (3) {2,4,6,8,10,12}
     (4) {5,7,9,11}   (5) {1,3,5}

5.   Which one of the following statements is correct?
     (1) Some sets have no subsets.
     (2) If a set has 4 members then it has 4 subsets.

(3) A set has more members than any of its subsets.

(4) A subset of a given set contains fewer members than the number of members in the given set.

(5) The empty set, { }, is a subset of every set.

ANSWERS:

1. 4 **2.** 2 **3.** 3 **4.** 5 **5.** 5

TIME TO STUDY:

The Number Line

It is often useful to pair numbers and sets of numbers with points on a line. Here is how this is done. We draw a straight line and on it take a point which we label "0". This starting point is called the origin. Next, we take a point to the right of the zero-point and label it "1", as follows. The arrows on the line indicate that the line extends infinitely in either direction.

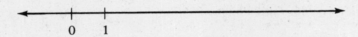

Now, we use the distance between 0 and 1 as a unit and mark off the next few counting numbers, as follows.

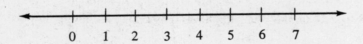

The number that is paired with a point is called the *coordinate* of that point. For example, the coordinate of point A on the number line below is 2.

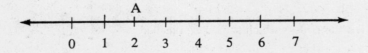

We may use the number line to draw the graph of a set of numbers. In drawing the graph of a set of numbers we draw the number line, find the members of the set on the number line, and darken the points paired with the numbers.

EXAMPLE: Draw the graph of the set {0,1,3,5} on the number line

TIME TO PRACTICE:

Directions: **Solve the following problems and blacken the space at the right under the number which corresponds to the one you have selected as the correct answer.**

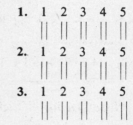

1. The number paired with the origin on the number line is
    (1) 1   (2) 0   (3) 2   (4) 5   (5) 3

2. The coordinate of a point is
    (1) a number   (2) a point   (3) a letter   (4) a line   (5) an arrow

3. The set whose graph is shown below is

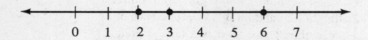

    (1) {0,2,3,6}   (2) {1,2,3,6}   (3) {2,3,4,5,6}   (4) {0,1,2,3,6}
    (5) {2,3,6}

4. The set whose graph is shown below is

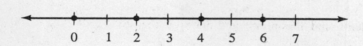

    (1) {0,1,2,4}   (2) {0,2,4,6}   (3) {1,2,4,6}   (4) {0,1,2,4,6}
    (5) {0,1,2,3,6}

    ANSWERS:

1. 2   **2.** 1   **3.** 5   **4.** 2

Whole Numbers

The process of division involves some ideas which should be recalled.

When we divide 18 by 3, we have $18 \div 3 = 6$. In this case, 18 is called the *dividend*, 3 is called the *divisor* and 6 is called the *quotient*.

When we divide 27 by 4, we have $27 \div 4 = 6\frac{3}{4}$. In this case, 27 is the dividend, 4 is the divisor, 6 is called the quotient, and 3 is called the *remainder*.

If we wish to check the answer to a division example we multiply the divisor by the quotient and add the remainder to obtain the dividend.

EXAMPLE: Divide 897 by 36 and check the result.

$$
\begin{array}{r}
24 \rightarrow \text{quotient} \\
\text{divisor} \leftarrow 36\overline{)897} \rightarrow \text{dividend} \\
72 \\
\hline
177 \\
144 \\
\hline
33 \rightarrow \text{remainder}
\end{array}
$$

TIME TO PRACTICE:

Addition:

1. 307	**2.** 49	**3.** 1069	**4.** $685.17
58	26	3205	48.09
129	7	467	103.15
984	38	5180	234.68
+ 236	+ 92	+ 2073	+ 580.80

Subtraction:

5. From 805 take 196   **5.**_____

6. Subtract 69 from 204   **6.**_____

7. Find the difference between 817 and 349   **7.**_____

8. Subtract 107 from 315   **8.**_____

Find the products:

9. 4327	**10.** 3092	**11.** 283	**12.** 409
× 39	× 45	× 97	× 307

Divide and check your results:

13. Divide 986 by 29   **13.**_____

14. Divide 29,040 by 48   **14.**_____

15. Divide 1,035 by 37   **15.**_____

16. Divide 47,039 by 126   **16.**_____

ANSWERS

1. 1,714	5. 609	9. 168,753	13. 34
2. 212	6. 135	10. 139,140	14. 605
3. 11,994	7. 468	11. 27,451	15. $27\frac{36}{37}$
4. $1,651.89	8. 208	12. 125,563	16. $373\frac{41}{126}$

TIME TO STUDY:

Rational Numbers

A number obtained when we divide a counting number or 0 by a counting number is called a *rational number*. For example, $\frac{2}{3}$, $\frac{9}{7}$, and $\frac{5}{1}$, or 5 are rational numbers. 0 is also a rational number since 0 may be written as $\frac{0}{6}$.

A fraction is a form in which a rational number may be written. That is, $\frac{2}{3}$ is a rational number in fractional form. But 4 is a rational number which is not in fractional form. A fraction is a form which has a numerator and a denominator. Every rational number has a fractional name. For example, the rational number 5 has the fractional name $\frac{10}{2}$.

All counting numbers and 0 are rational numbers. Thus, the set of counting numbers is a subset of the set of rational numbers. Rational numbers may be located on the number lines, as shown below.

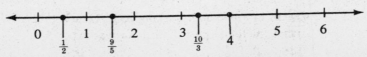

Fractions

In counting we need only whole numbers. However, when we measure we frequently have parts and we need fractions. For example, consider the circle below. The circle is divided into four equal parts and each part is $\frac{1}{4}$ of the circle.

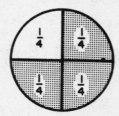

Since the shaded portion contains three of these parts, we say that the shaded portion is $\frac{3}{4}$ of the circle. In this case, the number 4 tells us that the circle is divided into 4 equal parts and is called the *denominator*. The number 3 tells us that we are considering 3 of these parts and is called the *numerator*. In this section, we will obtain some practice in understanding the meaning of fraction.

EXAMPLE: A baseball team won 37 games and lost 15 games. What fractional part of the games played did the team win?

The required fraction is

$$\frac{\text{number of games won}}{\text{total number of games played}} = \frac{37}{37 + 15} = \frac{37}{52}.$$

EXAMPLE: A certain school has an enrollment of 500 students. Of these students, x are girls. What fractional part of the enrollment consists of boys?

Since the total enrollment is 500 and x students are girls, the number of boys is obtained by subtracting the number x from 500. Thus, the number of boys enrolled in the school is $500 - x$.

The required fraction is

$$\frac{\text{number of boys}}{\text{total enrollment}} = \frac{500 - x}{500}.$$

TIME TO PRACTICE:

Directions: Solve the following problems and blacken the space at the right under the number which corresponds to the one you have selected as the correct answer.

1. The Star Movie Theatre has 650 seats. At one performance 67 seats were unoccupied. What fractional part of the theatre seats were occupied?
   (1) $\frac{67}{650}$ (2) $\frac{583}{650}$ (3) $\frac{67}{583}$ (4) $\frac{67}{717}$ (5) $\frac{583}{717}$

   1.   1   2   3   4   5
        || || || || ||

2. Mr. Davis parked his car at 2:45 P.M. in a one-hour parking zone. If he drove away at 3:08 P.M., during what fractional part of an hour was his car parked?
   (1) $\frac{63}{100}$ (2) $\frac{53}{60}$ (3) $\frac{45}{60}$ (4) $\frac{8}{60}$ (5) $\frac{23}{60}$

   2.   1   2   3   4   5
        || || || || ||

3. Mr. Barnes spent a dollars for a jacket and \$18 for a pair of slacks. What fractional part of the money spent, was spent for the jacket?

(1) $\dfrac{a}{18}$ (2) $\dfrac{18}{a}$ (3) $\dfrac{18}{a+18}$ (4) $\dfrac{a}{a+18}$ (5) $\dfrac{a+18}{a}$

4. Mr. Stern planned to drive a distance of x miles. After driving 120 miles, Mr. Stern stopped for gas. What fractional part of the trip had Mr. Stern covered when he stopped?

(1) $\dfrac{x}{120}$ (2) $\dfrac{120}{x}$ (3) $\dfrac{x}{x+120}$ (4) $\dfrac{120}{x+120}$ (5) $\dfrac{x+120}{x}$

5. On a test taken by 80 students, y students failed. What fractional part of the students passed the test?

(1) $\dfrac{80-y}{80}$ (2) $\dfrac{y}{80}$ (3) $\dfrac{80}{y}$ (4) $\dfrac{y-80}{80}$ (5) $\dfrac{80}{80-y}$

6. A dealer bought a shipment of 150 suits. Of these, 67 were blue, 39 were brown, and the rest were gray. What fractional part of the shipment was made up of gray suits?

(1) $\frac{67}{150}$ (2) $\frac{106}{150}$ (3) $\frac{39}{150}$ (4) $\frac{44}{150}$ (5) $\frac{83}{150}$

7. A carpenter cut strips x inches wide from a board 16 inches wide. After he had cut 5 strips, what fractional part of the board was left? Do not allow for waste.

(1) $\dfrac{5x}{16}$ (2) $\dfrac{16-5x}{16}$ (3) $\dfrac{5}{16-x}$ (4) $\dfrac{5}{16x}$ (5) $\dfrac{5}{16}$

8. A class has 35 students. If y pupils were absent what fractional part of the class was present?

(1) $\dfrac{y}{35}$ (2) $\dfrac{35}{y}$ (3) $\dfrac{35-y}{35}$ (4) $\dfrac{y-35}{35}$ (5) $\dfrac{y}{35+y}$

9. A family spent a dollars for food, b dollars for rent, and c dollars for all other expenses. What fractional part of money spent was spent for food?

(1) $\dfrac{a+b+c}{a}$ (2) $\dfrac{a}{a+b+c}$ (3) $\dfrac{a}{a+b}$ (4) $\dfrac{b}{a+c}$ (5) $\dfrac{a+c}{a+b+c}$

10. An electrical contractor used 6 men on a job. The men worked 5 days each at a salary of \$30 per day. In addition, the contractor spent \$573 for materials. What fractional part of the total cost of the job was spent for labor?

(1) $\frac{180}{1473}$ (2) $\frac{150}{1473}$ (3) $\frac{210}{1473}$ (4) $\frac{180}{1473}$ (5) $\frac{900}{1473}$

11. A table and four chairs cost \$735. If the cost of each chair was z dollars, what fractional part of the total cost was spent for chairs?

(1) $\dfrac{z}{735}$ (2) $\dfrac{735}{z}$ (3) $\dfrac{4z}{735}$ (4) $\dfrac{735}{4z}$ (5) $\dfrac{735-4z}{4z}$

12. A hockey team won 8 games, lost 3 games, and tied x games. What fractional part of the games played were won?

(1) $\dfrac{8}{11+x}$ (2) $\dfrac{3}{11+x}$ (3) $\dfrac{8}{11}$ (4) $\dfrac{8}{11x}$ (5) $\dfrac{x}{11+x}$

ANSWERS

1. 2	4. 2	7. 2	10. 5
2. 5	5. 1	8. 3	11. 3
3. 4	6. 4	9. 2	12. 1

TIME TO STUDY:

OPERATIONS WITH FRACTIONS

In order to be able to work with fractions we must know how to perform operations with fractions. We will first explain the meanings of *improper fraction* and *mixed numbers* and then show how to reduce a fraction to lowest terms.

An *improper fraction* is a fraction in which the numerator is equal to or greater than the denominator. For example, $\frac{7}{3}$ and $\frac{8}{5}$ are improper fractions.

A *mixed number* consists of the sum of a whole number and a fraction.

In working with fractions we will frequently use the *multiplication property of 1*. That is, when a number is multiplied by 1 the value of the number remains unchanged.

CHANGING AN IMPROPER FRACTION TO A MIXED NUMBER

It is sometimes necessary to change an improper fraction to a mixed number.

EXAMPLE: Change $\frac{17}{5}$ to a mixed number.

$$\frac{17}{5} = \frac{2 + 15}{5} = \frac{2}{5} + \frac{15}{5} = 3\frac{2}{5}$$

We may obtain the same result by dividing the numerator 17 by the denominator 5.

$$\begin{array}{r} 3\frac{2}{5} \\ 5\overline{)17} \end{array}$$

CHANGING A MIXED NUMBER TO AN IMPROPER FRACTION

The example below shows how a mixed number may be changed to an improper fraction.

EXAMPLE: Change $2\frac{3}{7}$ to an improper fraction

$$2\frac{3}{7} = 2 + \frac{3}{7}$$
$$2 = \frac{14}{7}$$
$$2\frac{3}{7} = \frac{14}{7} + \frac{3}{7} = \frac{17}{7}$$

The same result may be obtained by multiplying the whole number 2 by the denominator 7, and adding 3, to obtain the numerator. The denominator is unchanged.

$$2\frac{3}{7} = 2 \times 7 + 3 = 17 \rightarrow \text{numerator}$$
$$2\frac{3}{7} = \frac{17}{7}$$

REDUCING A FRACTION TO LOWEST TERMS

We may use the multiplication property of 1 to reduce a fraction to lowest terms.

EXAMPLE: Reduce $\frac{21}{28}$ to lowest terms

$$\frac{21}{28} = \frac{3 \times 7}{4 \times 7} = \frac{3}{4} \times \frac{7}{7} = \frac{3}{4} \times 1 = \frac{3}{4}$$

The same result may be obtained by dividing the numerator and denominator of the fraction by the same number, 7.

$$\frac{21}{28} = \frac{21 \div 7}{28 \div 7} = \frac{3}{4}$$

TIME TO PRACTICE:

Change the following improper fractions to mixed numbers.

1. $\frac{8}{5}$		**3.** $\frac{22}{7}$		**5.** $\frac{17}{3}$		**7.** $\frac{29}{4}$
2. $\frac{9}{8}$		**4.** $\frac{26}{9}$		**6.** $\frac{11}{10}$		**8.** $\frac{17}{8}$

Change the following mixed numbers to improper fractions.

9. $1\frac{2}{3}$		**11.** $2\frac{7}{10}$		**13.** $3\frac{1}{2}$		**15.** $6\frac{1}{4}$
10. $5\frac{3}{7}$		**12.** $3\frac{5}{7}$		**14.** $4\frac{5}{8}$		**16.** $8\frac{3}{4}$

Reduce the following fractions to lowest terms

17. $\frac{4}{6}$		**19.** $\frac{12}{32}$		**21.** $\frac{6}{12}$		**23.** $\frac{42}{63}$
18. $\frac{16}{18}$		**20.** $\frac{36}{64}$		**22.** $\frac{15}{20}$		**24.** $\frac{76}{114}$

ANSWERS

1. $1\frac{3}{5}$	7. $7\frac{1}{4}$	13. $\frac{7}{2}$	19. $\frac{3}{8}$
2. $1\frac{1}{8}$	8. $2\frac{1}{8}$	14. $\frac{37}{8}$	20. $\frac{9}{16}$
3. $3\frac{1}{7}$	9. $\frac{5}{3}$	15. $\frac{25}{4}$	21. $\frac{1}{2}$
4. $2\frac{8}{9}$	10. $\frac{38}{7}$	16. $\frac{35}{4}$	22. $\frac{3}{4}$
5. $5\frac{2}{3}$	11. $\frac{27}{10}$	17. $\frac{2}{3}$	23. $\frac{2}{3}$
6. $1\frac{1}{10}$	12. $\frac{26}{7}$	18. $\frac{8}{9}$	24. $\frac{2}{3}$

TIME TO STUDY:

MULTIPLYING FRACTIONS

To multiply two or more fractions we multiply the numerators to obtain the numerator of the product and the denominators to obtain the denominator of the product.

EXAMPLE: Multiply $\frac{4}{7}$ by $\frac{3}{5}$

$$\frac{4}{7} \times \frac{3}{5} = \frac{4 \times 3}{7 \times 5} = \frac{12}{35}$$

Sometimes, the process of multiplying fractions may be simplified by reducing to lowest terms before performing the multiplication.

EXAMPLE: Multiply $\frac{8}{15}$ by $\frac{5}{12}$

$$\frac{8}{15} \times \frac{5}{12}$$

Since 8 and 12 can both be divided by 4 we can simplify our result by performing this division before multiplying. Similarly, 5 and 15 can both be divided by 5.

$$\frac{\overset{2}{\cancel{8}}}{\underset{3}{\cancel{15}}} \times \frac{\overset{1}{\cancel{5}}}{\underset{3}{\cancel{12}}} = \frac{2 \times 1}{3 \times 3} = \frac{2}{9}$$

If we are required to multiply a whole number by a fraction we may write the whole number in fractional form with denominator 1 and proceed as before.

EXAMPLE: Multiply 12 by $\frac{5}{9}$

$$12 \times \frac{5}{9} = \frac{12}{1} \times \frac{5}{9} = \frac{\overset{4}{\cancel{12}}}{1} \times \frac{5}{\underset{3}{\cancel{9}}} = \frac{4 \times 5}{1 \times 3} = \frac{20}{3}.$$

If we are required to multiply two mixed numbers we convert the mixed numbers to improper fractions and proceed as before.

EXAMPLE: Multiply $3\frac{2}{3}$ by $1\frac{1}{5}$

$$3\frac{2}{3} = \frac{11}{3} \quad \text{and} \quad 1\frac{1}{5} = \frac{6}{5}$$

$$\frac{11}{3} \times \frac{6}{5} = \frac{11}{\underset{1}{\cancel{3}}} \times \frac{\overset{2}{\cancel{6}}}{5} = \frac{11 \times 2}{1 \times 5} = \frac{22}{5}.$$

TIME TO PRACTICE:

Perform the following multiplications:

1. $\frac{2}{3} \times \frac{5}{7}$
2. $\frac{1}{4} \times \frac{3}{10}$
3. $\frac{1}{6} \times \frac{4}{5}$
4. $\frac{3}{8} \times \frac{5}{12}$
5. $15 \times \frac{2}{3}$

6. $\frac{5}{6} \times \frac{9}{10}$
7. $12 \times \frac{5}{6}$
8. $\frac{5}{8} \times 24$
9. $3 \times 2\frac{2}{5}$
10. $8 \times 1\frac{3}{4}$

11. $2 \times 3\frac{5}{8}$
12. $1\frac{1}{3} \times 2\frac{1}{2}$
13. $1\frac{5}{8} \times 3\frac{1}{3}$
14. $2\frac{3}{4} \times 3\frac{1}{5}$
15. $4\frac{1}{8} \times 3\frac{1}{3}$

ANSWERS

1. $\frac{10}{21}$
2. $\frac{3}{40}$
3. $\frac{2}{15}$
4. $\frac{5}{32}$
5. 10

6. $\frac{3}{4}$
7. 10
8. 15
9. $\frac{36}{5}$
10. 14

11. $\frac{23}{3}$
12. $\frac{10}{3}$
13. $\frac{65}{12}$
14. $\frac{44}{5}$
15. $\frac{55}{4}$

TIME TO STUDY:

DIVIDING FRACTIONS

Suppose we wish to divide $\frac{2}{5}$ by $\frac{3}{4}$. We may write this operation as $\dfrac{\frac{2}{5}}{\frac{3}{4}}$.

Recall that we may multiply the numerator and denominator of a fraction by the same number. Notice what happens when we multiply the numerator and denominator of the above fraction by $\frac{4}{3}$.

$$\frac{\frac{2}{5} \times \frac{4}{3}}{\frac{3}{4} \times \frac{4}{3}} = \frac{\frac{8}{15}}{1} = \frac{8}{15}.$$

We see that the final result was obtained by multiplying the dividend $\frac{2}{5}$ by the divisor inverted, $\frac{4}{3}$. This gives us a method for dividing one fraction by another.

To divide one fraction by another invert the divisor and multiply the resulting fractions.

EXAMPLE: Divide $\frac{2}{3}$ by $\frac{5}{6}$

$$\frac{2}{3} \div \frac{5}{6} = \frac{2}{3} \times \frac{6}{5}$$

$$\frac{2}{\cancel{3}} \times \frac{\cancel{6}^{2}}{5} = \frac{4}{5}$$

EXAMPLE: Divide 8 by $\frac{6}{7}$

We write 8 in fractional form as $\frac{8}{1}$ and proceed as before

$$8 \div \frac{6}{7} = \frac{8}{1} \times \frac{7}{6}$$

$$\frac{\cancel{8}^{4}}{1} \times \frac{7}{\cancel{6}_{3}} = \frac{28}{3}$$

EXAMPLE: Divide $3\frac{3}{5}$ by $2\frac{1}{10}$

$$3\frac{3}{5} = \frac{18}{5}, \quad \text{and} \quad 2\frac{1}{10} = \frac{21}{10}$$

$$\frac{18}{5} \div \frac{21}{10} = \frac{18}{5} \times \frac{10}{21}$$

$$\frac{\cancel{18}^{6}}{\cancel{5}_{1}} \times \frac{\cancel{10}^{2}}{\cancel{21}_{7}} = \frac{12}{7}$$

TIME TO PRACTICE:

Perform the following divisions:

1. $\frac{1}{3} \div \frac{1}{2}$
2. $\frac{2}{7} \div \frac{2}{3}$
3. $\frac{3}{4} \div \frac{5}{8}$
4. $\frac{7}{10} \div \frac{1}{5}$
5. $\frac{7}{8} \div \frac{9}{16}$

6. $5 \div \frac{1}{2}$
7. $4 \div \frac{2}{5}$
8. $1\frac{1}{8} \div \frac{9}{20}$
9. $\frac{5}{8} \div 1\frac{1}{4}$
10. $\frac{7}{8} \div 5\frac{1}{4}$

11. $2\frac{2}{5} \div 3\frac{3}{10}$
12. $2\frac{3}{4} \div 3\frac{1}{7}$
13. $3\frac{1}{3} \div 4\frac{1}{8}$
14. $3\frac{3}{4} \div 2\frac{2}{8}$
15. $5\frac{5}{8} \div 2\frac{5}{8}$

ANSWERS

1. $\frac{2}{3}$	4. $\frac{7}{2}$	7. 10	10. $\frac{1}{6}$	13. $\frac{4}{5}$
2. $\frac{3}{7}$	5. $\frac{14}{9}$	8. $\frac{5}{2}$	11. $\frac{8}{11}$	14. $\frac{27}{16}$
3. $\frac{6}{5}$	6. 10	9. $\frac{2}{3}$	12. $\frac{7}{8}$	15. $\frac{20}{9}$

TIME TO STUDY:

ADDING FRACTIONS

Two fractions may be added directly if they have the same denominator. For example,

$$\frac{1}{5} + \frac{2}{5} = \frac{1+2}{5} = \frac{3}{5}$$

The diagram below shows why this is true

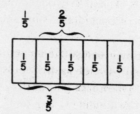

Next, let us consider the addition of two fractions with different denominators. For example, let us add $\frac{1}{2}$ and $\frac{1}{3}$ using the diagram below to help us

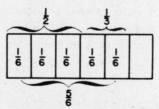

Thus, we see that $\frac{1}{2} + \frac{1}{3} = \frac{5}{6}$. Now, let us see how we may obtain the same result without the use of a diagram. Actually, we convert both $\frac{1}{2}$ and $\frac{1}{3}$ to equivalent fractions whose denominators are 6 by using the multiplication property of 1.

$$\frac{1}{2} = \frac{1}{2} \times \frac{3}{3} = \frac{3}{6}$$

$$\frac{1}{3} = \frac{1}{3} \times \frac{2}{2} = \frac{2}{6}$$

$$\frac{2}{6} + \frac{3}{6} = \frac{2+3}{6} = \frac{5}{6}$$

The denominator, 6, which was used above is called the Least Common Denominator, or the *L.C.D.* for short. It is the smallest number into which each of the denominators of the fractions to be added can be divided evenly. For example, if we wish to add $\frac{3}{10}$ and $\frac{8}{15}$, the *L.C.D.* is 30. Since finding the *L.C.D.* is most important we will get some practice in this process.

We may use sets of multiples to find the *L.C.D.* Study the following examples.

EXAMPLE: Find the *L.C.D.* used in adding the fractions $\frac{2}{3}$ and $\frac{5}{7}$. We write the sets of multiples of the denominators of the two fractions.

   The set of multiples of 3 is $\{3, 6, 9, 12, 15, 18, 21, 24, 27, \ldots\}$

   The set of multiples of 7 is $\{7, 14, 21, \ldots\}$

The first number which is a multiple of both the denominators, 3 and 7, is the *L.C.D.* In this case, the *L.C.D.* is 21.

EXAMPLE: Find the *L.C.D.* used in adding the fractions $\frac{3}{8}$ and $\frac{7}{10}$.

   The set of multiples of 8 is $\{8, 16, 24, 32, 40, 48, 56, \ldots\}$

   The set of multiples of 10 is $\{10, 20, 30, 40, \ldots\}$

The *L.C.D.* is 40.

TIME TO PRACTICE:

In each case, find the *L.C.D.*

1. $\frac{2}{3} + \frac{1}{4}$	6. $\frac{1}{5} + \frac{7}{10}$	11. $\frac{1}{4} + \frac{5}{8}$
2. $\frac{1}{6} + \frac{1}{3}$	7. $\frac{1}{4} + \frac{5}{8}$	12. $\frac{3}{8} + \frac{1}{12}$
3. $\frac{5}{6} + \frac{3}{8}$	8. $\frac{5}{9} + \frac{1}{12}$	13. $\frac{3}{10} + \frac{7}{15}$
4. $\frac{1}{9} + \frac{1}{6}$	9. $\frac{1}{3} + \frac{2}{11}$	14. $\frac{5}{6} + \frac{1}{10}$
5. $\frac{3}{4} + \frac{7}{18}$	10. $\frac{2}{7} + \frac{1}{4}$	15. $\frac{7}{10} + \frac{1}{12}$

ANSWERS

1. 12	6. 10	11. 8
2. 6	7. 12	12. 24
3. 24	8. 36	13. 30
4. 18	9. 33	14. 30
5. 36	10. 28	15. 60

TIME TO STUDY:

ADDING FRACTIONS WITH UNLIKE DENOMINATORS

We are now ready to get some practice in adding fractions with unlike denominators.

EXAMPLE: Add $\frac{7}{8}$ and $\frac{5}{6}$

   The *L.C.D.* is 24

$$\frac{7}{8} = \frac{7}{8} \times \frac{3}{3} = \frac{21}{24}$$

$$\frac{5}{6} = \frac{5}{6} \times \frac{4}{4} = \frac{20}{24}$$

$$\frac{21 + 20}{24} = \frac{41}{24}, \text{ or } 1\frac{17}{24}$$

In adding mixed numbers we add the whole numbers and the fractions separately and then combine the results.

EXAMPLE: Add $3\frac{5}{8}$ and $2\frac{3}{4}$
The *L.C.D.* is 12

$$\frac{5}{6} = \frac{5}{6} \times \frac{2}{2} = \frac{10}{12}$$

$$\frac{3}{4} = \frac{3}{4} \times \frac{3}{3} = \frac{9}{12}$$

$$\frac{10 + 9}{12} = \frac{19}{12}$$

The result is $5\frac{19}{12}$ which can be written as $5 + 1 + \frac{7}{12}$, or $6\frac{7}{12}$.

TIME TO PRACTICE:

Add the following:

1. $\frac{1}{12} + \frac{5}{12}$ 6. $\frac{2}{9} + \frac{2}{3}$ 11. $2\frac{3}{8} + 3\frac{1}{2}$ 16. $\frac{1}{2} + \frac{1}{3} + \frac{1}{4}$

2. $\frac{3}{10} + \frac{1}{2}$ 7. $\frac{3}{10} + \frac{1}{5}$ 12. $2\frac{7}{10} + \frac{1}{6}$ 17. $\frac{2}{3} + \frac{1}{4} + \frac{5}{6}$

3. $\frac{7}{8} + \frac{2}{3}$ 8. $\frac{5}{6} + \frac{3}{8}$ 13. $4\frac{1}{3} + 2\frac{2}{5}$ 18. $\frac{3}{5} + \frac{1}{6} + \frac{7}{10}$

4. $\frac{5}{6} + \frac{1}{3}$ 9. $\frac{3}{7} + \frac{1}{2}$ 14. $1\frac{5}{6} + 2\frac{1}{2}$

5. $\frac{3}{4} + \frac{1}{6}$ 10. $1\frac{4}{9} + \frac{5}{6}$ 15. $2\frac{5}{12} + 3\frac{1}{9}$

ANSWERS

1. $\frac{6}{12} = \frac{1}{2}$ 6. $\frac{8}{9}$ 11. $5\frac{7}{8}$ 16. $\frac{13}{12} = 1\frac{1}{12}$

2. $\frac{8}{10} = \frac{4}{5}$ 7. $\frac{5}{10} = \frac{1}{2}$ 12. $2\frac{26}{30} = 2\frac{13}{15}$ 17. $\frac{21}{12} = 1\frac{3}{4}$

3. $\frac{37}{24} = 1\frac{13}{24}$ 8. $\frac{29}{24} = 1\frac{5}{24}$ 13. $6\frac{11}{15}$ 18. $\frac{44}{30} = 1\frac{7}{15}$

4. $\frac{7}{6} = 1\frac{1}{6}$ 9. $\frac{13}{14}$ 14. $4\frac{1}{3}$

5. $\frac{11}{12}$ 10. $2\frac{5}{18}$ 15. $5\frac{19}{36}$

TIME TO STUDY:

SUBTRACTING FRACTIONS

To subtract fractions which have the same denominator we subtract the numerators and retain the denominator.

EXAMPLE: From $\frac{6}{7}$ subtract $\frac{2}{7}$

$$\frac{6}{7} - \frac{2}{7} = \frac{6 - 2}{7} = \frac{4}{7}$$

To subtract fractions which have different denominators we find the *L.C.D.*, convert the fractions to fractions which have the same denominator, and then perform the subtraction as we did in the last example.

EXAMPLE: From $\frac{8}{9}$ subtract $\frac{1}{6}$
The *L.C.D.* is 18

$$\frac{8}{9} = \frac{8}{9} \times \frac{2}{2} = \frac{16}{18}$$
$$\frac{1}{6} = \frac{1}{6} \times \frac{3}{3} = \frac{3}{18}$$
$$\text{Difference} = \frac{13}{18}$$

When mixed numbers are involved in subtraction it is sometimes necessary to borrow, as in the example below.

EXAMPLE: From $4\frac{1}{8}$ subtract $1\frac{5}{12}$

The *L.C.D.* is 24

$$4\frac{1}{8} = 4\frac{3}{24}$$
$$1\frac{5}{12} = 1\frac{10}{24}$$

Since we cannot subtract $\frac{10}{24}$ from $\frac{3}{24}$ we write $4\frac{3}{24}$ as $3 + 1 + \frac{3}{24} = 3 + \frac{24}{24} + \frac{3}{24} = 3\frac{27}{24}$

$$3\frac{27}{24}$$
$$1\frac{10}{24}$$
$$\text{Difference} = 2\frac{17}{24}$$

TIME TO PRACTICE:

Perform the following subtractions:

1. $\frac{5}{9} - \frac{1}{9}$
2. $\frac{11}{12} - \frac{7}{12}$
3. $\frac{2}{3} - \frac{1}{6}$
4. $\frac{3}{4} - \frac{1}{3}$
5. $\frac{5}{6} - \frac{1}{4}$

6. $\frac{7}{10} - \frac{3}{5}$
7. $\frac{5}{8} - \frac{1}{6}$
8. $\frac{2}{3} - \frac{1}{2}$
9. $\frac{4}{5} - \frac{2}{3}$
10. $\frac{8}{9} - \frac{5}{6}$

11. $\frac{9}{10} - \frac{5}{6}$
12. $3\frac{1}{2} - 1\frac{1}{3}$
13. $4\frac{5}{6} - 2\frac{3}{4}$
14. $3\frac{1}{8} - 1\frac{1}{4}$
15. $5\frac{4}{9} - 2\frac{5}{6}$

ANSWERS

1. $\frac{4}{9}$
2. $\frac{4}{12} = \frac{1}{3}$
3. $\frac{3}{6} = \frac{1}{2}$
4. $\frac{5}{12}$
5. $\frac{7}{12}$

6. $\frac{1}{10}$
7. $\frac{11}{24}$
8. $\frac{1}{6}$
9. $\frac{2}{15}$
10. $\frac{1}{18}$

11. $\frac{2}{30} = \frac{1}{15}$
12. $1\frac{3}{6} = 2\frac{1}{6}$
13. $\frac{25}{12} = 2\frac{1}{12}$
14. $1\frac{5}{8} = 1\frac{7}{8}$
15. $\frac{47}{18} = 2\frac{11}{18}$

TIME TO STUDY:

PROBLEMS INVOLVING FRACTIONS

In general, there are three types of problems involving fractions.

1. To find a number that is a fractional part of a given number.

   EXAMPLE: A dealer sold 70 TV sets one month. If $\frac{2}{5}$ of the sets sold were color sets, how many color sets were sold?

   The word "of" indicates that we are to multiply 70 by $\frac{2}{5}$.

$$\frac{70}{1} \times \frac{2}{5} = \frac{\overset{14}{\cancel{70}}}{1} \times \frac{2}{\cancel{5}} = 28$$

The dealer sold 28 color TV sets.

2.   To find what fractional part one number is of another.

>   EXAMPLE: A hotel has 70 guests rooms. Of these, 15 are single rooms. What fractional part of the total number of rooms are the single rooms?
>   We form a fraction as follows
>
> $$\frac{\text{number of single rooms}}{\text{total number of rooms}} = \frac{15}{70}, \quad \text{or} \quad \frac{3}{14}$$

3.   To find a number when a fractional part of the number is known.

>   EXAMPLE: In a town election only $\frac{2}{3}$ of the registered voters cast ballots. If there were 1,620 votes cast, how many voters were there?
>   We know that $\frac{2}{3}$ of the voters amount to 1,620
>
> $$\frac{2}{3} \text{ of voters} = 1,620$$
>
> $$\frac{1}{3} \text{ of voters} = \frac{1,620}{2} = 810$$

Then, $\frac{3}{3}$ or the total number of voters = 810 × 3 = 2,430
There were 2,430 registered voters.

TIME TO PRACTICE:

Directions: Solve the following problems and blacken the space at the right under the number which corresponds to the one you have selected as the correct answer.

1.   The Globe Theatre has 600 seats. At one performance $\frac{4}{5}$ of the seats were occupied. How many seats were occupied?
     (1) 400   (2) 420   (3) 450   (4) 480   (5) 750

1.   1 2 3 4 5

2.   At a sale Mr. Morse bought a suit for $72. This was $\frac{3}{4}$ of the regular price of the suit. The regular price of the suit was
     (1) $100   (2) $96   (3) $88   (4) $54   (5) $75

2.   1 2 3 4 5

3.   An oil tank contains 640 gallons. When it is $\frac{3}{8}$ full the number of gallons in the tank is
     (1) 240   (2) 320   (3) 350   (4) 400   (5) 450

3.   1 2 3 4 5

4.   A football team scored 35 points in a football game. If the team scored 21 points in the first half, the fractional part of the total scored in the second half was
     (1) $\frac{3}{5}$ (2) $\frac{7}{12}$ (3) $\frac{1}{5}$ (4) $\frac{2}{5}$ (5) $\frac{3}{7}$

4.   1 2 3 4 5

5.   The Star Company employs 17 engineers. If this is $\frac{1}{3}$ of the total work force, the number of employees of the Star Company is
     (1) 20   (2) 41   (3) 47   (4) 23   (5) 51

5.   1 2 3 4 5

6.   The Mills family saves n dollars per year. The number of dollars saved in 5 months is
     (1) $5n$ (2) $\frac{5}{12}n$ (3) $12n$ (4) $n + 5$ (5) $\frac{5}{12}$

6.   1 2 3 4 5

7. A plane contains 5 times as many second class seats as first class seats. The fractional part of second class seats on the plane is
(1) $\frac{1}{6}$ (2) $\frac{1}{5}$ (3) $\frac{5}{6}$ (4) $\frac{3}{5}$ (5) $\frac{1}{3}$

7. 1 2 3 4 5
    || || || || ||

8. A baseball player hit 90 singles in one season. If this was $\frac{3}{5}$ of his total number of hits, the number of hits the player made that season was
(1) 54   (2) 150   (3) 540   (4) 144   (5) 154

8. 1 2 3 4 5
    || || || || ||

9. During a sale on radios, $\frac{1}{4}$ of the stock was sold the first day. The next day $\frac{2}{3}$ of the remaining sets were sold. The fractional part of the total stock sold during the second day was
(1) $\frac{2}{3}$ (2) $\frac{1}{4}$ (3) $\frac{1}{6}$ (4) $\frac{1}{2}$ (5) $\frac{1}{12}$

9. 1 2 3 4 5
    || || || || ||

10. It takes a man n hours to complete a job. The fractional part of the job that he can complete in 3 hours is
(1) $3n$ (2) $\frac{3}{n}$ (3) $\frac{n}{3}$ (4) $3 + n$ (5) $\frac{1}{n + 3}$

10. 1 2 3 4 5
    || || || || ||

11. The regular price for hats is x dollars each. If they are reduced by $\frac{1}{5}$ of the regular price, the new price is
(1) $\frac{1}{5}x$ (2) $x + \frac{1}{5}$ (3) $\frac{4}{5}x$ (4) $x + \frac{4}{5}$ (5) $5x$

11. 1 2 3 4 5
    || || ||| || ||

12. On a motor trip Mr. Andrews covers $\frac{3}{8}$ of the distance during the first day when he drove 300 miles. The total distance to be covered by Mr. Andrews is
(1) 624 miles   (2) 640 miles   (3) 720 miles   (4) 750 miles   (5) 800 miles

12. 1 2 3 4 5
    || || || || ||

13. The Palmer Shoe Company received a shipment of 288 pairs of shoes composed equally of black and brown shoes. If 36 pairs of the brown shoes are returned and replaced by pairs of black shoes, the fractional part of the shipment consisting of black shoes is
(1) $\frac{3}{8}$ (2) $\frac{5}{8}$ (3) $\frac{7}{12}$ (4) $\frac{1}{8}$ (5) $\frac{3}{4}$

13. 1 2 3 4 5
    || || || || ||

14. An auditorium contains 540 seats and is $\frac{4}{9}$ filled. The number of seats left unoccupied is
(1) 240   (2) 60   (3) 120   (4) 200   (5) 300

14. 1 2 3 4 5
    || || || || ||

15. At a dance, x boys and y girls attended. Of the total attendance, the fraction which represents the number of boys is
(1) $\frac{x}{y}$ (2) $\frac{y}{x}$ (3) $\frac{y}{x + y}$ (4) $\frac{x}{x + y}$ (5) $\frac{x + y}{x}$

15. 1 2 3 4 5
    || || || || ||

16. Mr. Adams paid $\frac{1}{4}$ of his total monthly income for rent. If Mr. Adams earned y dollars per month, the number of dollars remaining after he paid his rent was
(1) $\frac{1}{4}y$ (2) $y + 4$ (3) $\frac{3}{4}y$ (4) $12y$ (5) $3y$

16. 1 2 3 4 5
    || || || || ||

17. Mrs. Benson is on a diet. For breakfast and lunch she consumed $\frac{4}{9}$ of her allowable number of calories. If she still had 1,000 calories left for the day, her daily allowance in calories was
(1) 1500   (2) 1800   (3) 1200   (4) 2250   (5) $444\frac{4}{9}$

17. 1 2 3 4 5
    || || || || ||

18. In his will, Mr. Mason left $\frac{1}{2}$ of his estate to his wife, $\frac{1}{3}$ to his daughter, and the balance consisting of $12,000, to his son. The value of Mr. Mason's estate was
    (1) $24,000   (2) $60,000   (3) $14,400   (4) $65,000   (5) $72,000

18. 1 2 3 4 5
     || || || || ||

19. An oil tank is $\frac{3}{10}$ full. It takes 420 gallons more to fill the tank. The number of gallons the tank holds is
    (1) 600   (2) 480   (3) 840   (4) 1260   (5) 1,000

19. 1 2 3 4 5
     || || || || ||

20. A family spends $\frac{1}{4}$ of its income for rent and $\frac{1}{5}$ for food. The fractional part of its income left is
    (1) $\frac{9}{20}$ (2) $\frac{19}{20}$ (3) $\frac{11}{20}$ (4) $\frac{4}{5}$ (5) $\frac{8}{9}$

20. 1 2 3 4 5
     || || || || ||

ANSWERS

1. 4	6. 2	11. 3	16. 3
2. 2	7. 3	12. 5	17. 2
3. 1	8. 2	13. 2	18. 5
4. 4	9. 4	14. 5	19. 1
5. 5	10. 2	15. 4	20. 3

TIME TO STUDY:

ARRANGING FRACTIONS IN ORDER

We know that $\frac{1}{2}$ and $\frac{3}{6}$ are equivalent fractions. This fact can be checked as follows:

$$\frac{1}{2} \times\!\!\!\!\times \frac{3}{6}$$

$$1 \times 6 = 2 \times 3$$

We know that $\frac{3}{4}$ is greater than $\frac{2}{5}$. This fact can be checked as follows:

$$\frac{3}{4} \times\!\!\!\!\times \frac{2}{5}$$

$$3 \times 5 \text{ is greater than } 4 \times 2$$

The symbol ">" means "is greater than"
Thus, we may write $\frac{3}{4} > \frac{2}{5}$ because $15 > 8$.

We know that $\frac{3}{7}$ is less than $\frac{5}{6}$. This fact can be checked as follows:

$$\frac{3}{7} \times\!\!\!\!\times \frac{5}{6}$$

$$3 \times 6 \text{ is less than } 7 \times 5$$

The symbol "<" means "is less than."
Thus, we may write $\frac{3}{7} < \frac{5}{6}$ because $18 < 35$.

TIME TO PRACTICE:

In each case, use the symbol $=$, $>$, or $<$ to show the relationship between the given fractions:

1. $\frac{3}{4}$, $\frac{7}{10}$

2. $\frac{6}{9}$, $\frac{40}{60}$

3. $\frac{2}{3}$, $\frac{11}{16}$

4. $\frac{5}{8}$, $\frac{4}{7}$

5. $\frac{4}{9}$, $\frac{7}{15}$

6. $\frac{12}{20}$, $\frac{3}{5}$

7. $\frac{7}{11}$, $\frac{13}{19}$

8. $\frac{7}{9}$, $\frac{15}{17}$

9. $\frac{21}{28}$, $\frac{24}{32}$

10. $\frac{8}{13}$, $\frac{5}{8}$

11. $\frac{5}{16}$, $\frac{10}{31}$

12. $\frac{4}{11}$, $\frac{8}{21}$

13. $\frac{15}{35}$, $\frac{12}{28}$

14. $\frac{6}{13}$, $\frac{11}{20}$

15. $\frac{9}{17}$, $\frac{5}{7}$

ANSWERS

1. $\frac{3}{4} > \frac{7}{10}$

2. $\frac{6}{9} = \frac{40}{60}$

3. $\frac{2}{3} < \frac{11}{16}$

4. $\frac{5}{8} > \frac{4}{7}$

5. $\frac{4}{9} < \frac{7}{15}$

6. $\frac{12}{20} = \frac{3}{5}$

7. $\frac{7}{11} < \frac{13}{19}$

8. $\frac{7}{9} < \frac{15}{17}$

9. $\frac{21}{28} = \frac{24}{32}$

10. $\frac{8}{13} < \frac{5}{8}$

11. $\frac{5}{16} < \frac{10}{31}$

12. $\frac{4}{11} < \frac{8}{21}$

13. $\frac{15}{35} = \frac{12}{28}$

14. $\frac{6}{13} < \frac{11}{20}$

15. $\frac{9}{17} < \frac{5}{7}$

TIME TO STUDY:

Decimals

A decimal fraction, or decimal, is a fraction in which the denominator is not written. The denominator is a number which is a multiple of 10 such as 10, 100, 1,000, etc. and is shown by the way the decimal is written. For example,

Written as common fractions	Written as decimals
$\frac{3}{10}$	.3
$\frac{19}{100}$	.19
$\frac{7}{100}$	.07
$\frac{163}{1,000}$	.163

If a number consists of a whole number and a fraction, the whole number is written first and then followed by the decimal. For example,

$$8\tfrac{3}{10} = 8.3$$
$$9\tfrac{7}{100} = 9.07$$

The value of a decimal is not changed by annexing zeros to the right of the decimal. For example,

$$\tfrac{1}{2} = .5 = .50 = .500 = .5000$$

One reason for the use of decimals is that they are convenient to write and to work with. For example, it is more convenient to write that a shirt costs $3.25 rather than $3¼.

ADDITION OF DECIMALS

Mrs. Gordon bought the following items at a supermarket: bread, $.30; steak, $4.00; coffee, $.85; fish, $2.20. When she checked the total cost she arranged her work as follows:

$$\begin{array}{r} \$ \ .30 \\ 4.00 \\ .85 \\ +\ 2.20 \\ \hline \$7.35 \end{array}$$

You can see that she followed this rule:
In adding decimals, always put the decimal points under each other.

SUBTRACTION OF DECIMALS

In subtracting decimals we follow the same rule:

EXAMPLE: Subtract 9.73 from 15.58

$$\begin{array}{r} 15.58 \\ -\ 9.73 \\ \hline 5.85 \end{array}$$

MULTIPLICATION OF DECIMALS

Mr. Burns figures that it cost him about 8.4 cents per mile for the expense of his car. He drives 28.6 miles to work and back each week. How much does it cost him to do this?

In order to obtain the result we must multiply 28.6 by 8.4. Note that in this multiplication we write 8.4 cents as $.084. Before we actually multiply we can see that the answer should be roughly in the neighborhood of $2.50.

$$\begin{array}{r} 28.6 \\ \times\ .084 \\ \hline 1144 \\ 2\ 288 \\ \hline 2.4024 \end{array}$$

Do you agree that the answer should be $2.4024, or about $2.40?

The above example illustrates the following rule:

In multiplying decimals the number of decimal places in the product is the sum of the number of decimal places in the numbers being multiplied.

EXAMPLES:

$$\begin{array}{ll} .02 & \text{(2 decimal places)} \\ \times .3 & \text{(1 decimal place)} \\ \hline .006 & \text{(3 decimal places)} \end{array} \qquad \begin{array}{ll} 1.02 & \text{(2 decimal places)} \\ \times .004 & \text{(3 decimal places)} \\ \hline .00408 & \text{(5 decimal places)} \end{array}$$

DIVISION OF DECIMALS

Consider the following division $\dfrac{8.46}{.2}$. Since we may multiply the numerator and denominator of a fraction by the same number without changing the value of the fraction, we may multiply the numerator and denominator of this fraction by 10 to obtain

$$\frac{8.46}{.2} = \frac{84.6}{2}$$

This is usually written as

$$.2\overline{)8.4.6} \quad \text{or} \quad 2\overline{)84.6}$$ (quotient 42.3)

The result is 42.3

In general, in dividing decimals, we multiply both the divisor and the dividend by whatever multiple of 10 (10, 100, 1000, etc.) is necessary to make the *divisor* a whole number and then proceed with the division. The decimal point in the quotient is always in the same place as in the new dividend.

EXAMPLES:

$$6.93 \div .3 \qquad 35.75 \div .05 \qquad .08136 \div .006$$

$$.3\overline{)6.9.3} \text{ (23.1)} \qquad .05\overline{)35.75.} \text{ (7 15.)} \qquad .006\overline{)081.36} \text{ (13.56)}$$

Sometimes, there is a remainder and you are told to find the answer to the nearest tenth, nearest hundredth, etc. In such cases, carry out the division to one more place than is called for. If the digit just to the right of the desired decimal place is 5 or greater, add 1 to the desired decimal place number. Otherwise, drop the digit to the right of the desired decimal place.

EXAMPLE: Divide 3.734 by .9 and express the answer to the nearest tenth.

$$.9\overline{)3.7.34} \text{ (4.14)} - \text{The answer is 4.1}$$

EXAMPLE: Divide 2.4853 by .7 and express the answer to the nearest hundredth

$$.7\overline{)2.4.981} \text{ (3.568)} - \text{The answer is 3.57}$$

CONVERTING FRACTIONS TO DECIMALS

It is sometimes necessary to change a fraction to a decimal fraction. To do this we divide the numerator by the denominator, adding zeros after the decimal point in the numerator when they are needed.

EXAMPLE: Change $\frac{3}{8}$ to a decimal

$$8\overline{)3.000} \text{ (.375)}$$

$$\frac{3}{8} = .375$$

EXAMPLE: Change $\frac{5}{12}$ to a decimal

$$12\overline{)5.0000} \text{ (.4166}\frac{2}{3}\text{)}$$

To the nearest tenth, $\frac{5}{12} = .4$

To the nearest hundredth, $\frac{5}{12} = .42$

To the nearest thousandth, $\frac{5}{12} = .417$

A WORD ABOUT REVIEW: There is a great deal of review in this chapter— more, perhaps, than you actually need for the examination. Use it to *your* best advantage. If there are certain topics you are sure of, you might want to skip them. If there are some that need special attention, concentrate your studying on those.

TIME TO PRACTICE:

1. Add $38.52 + 7.096 + 92.5 + .837$ **1.**_____

2. Add $2.8 + .7 + .09 + 153 + .078$ **2.**_____

3. From 1.9 subtract .023   **3.**_____

4. Take 3.794 from 12.82   **4.**_____

5. Multiply 5.683 by 2.9   **5.**_____

6. Multiply 3.14 by .015   **6.**_____

7. Divide 1.6357 by .37 and express the result to the nearest hundredth.   **7.**

_____

8. Divide .32277 by 5.3   **8.**_____

9. Convert $\frac{17}{20}$ to a decimal   **9.**_____

10. Convert $\frac{8}{15}$ to a decimal to the nearest hundredth   **10.**_____

ANSWERS

1. 138.953
2. 156.668
3. 1.877
4. 9.026
5. 16.4807

6. .0471
7. 4.42
8. .0609
9. .85
10. .53

TIME TO STUDY:

Per Cent

We have seen that rational numbers may be expressed as fractions or as decimals. A rational number may also be expressed as a per cent. In this section, we will learn how to work with per cents.

On a motor trip of 100 miles, 73 miles were on a parkway. If we wish to indicate the part of the trip taken on a parkway we may say that $\frac{73}{100}$ of the trip was on a parkway. Another way of stating the same fact is to say that .73 of the trip was taken on a parkway. A third way to express the same idea is to say that 73% of the trip was taken on a parkway. Per cent is just another way of writing a fraction in which the denominator is 100. The % sign is used instead of writing the denominator 100. In short, 73% means $\frac{73}{100}$ or .73.

It is a simple matter to change a per cent to a decimal or a fraction.

EXAMPLE: Change 45% to (a) a decimal (b) a fraction

$$45\% = .45$$
$$45\% = \tfrac{45}{100}, \quad \text{or} \quad \tfrac{9}{20}$$

Similarly, a decimal or a fraction may be changed to a per cent.

EXAMPLES: Change .37 to a per cent

$$.37 = \tfrac{37}{100} = 37\%$$

Change .025 to a per cent

$$.025 = \frac{2.5}{100} = 2.5\%, \quad \text{or} \quad 2\tfrac{1}{2}\%.$$

Change $\tfrac{3}{4}$ to a per cent

We first change $\tfrac{3}{4}$ to a decimal and then to a per cent

$$4\overline{)3.00} = .75$$

$$\tfrac{3}{4} = .75 = 75\%$$

Change $\tfrac{5}{19}$ to a per cent

We first change $\tfrac{5}{19}$ to a decimal and then to a per cent

$$19\overline{)5.00}$$
$$\underline{3\,8}$$
$$1\,2\,0$$
$$\underline{1\,1\,4}$$
$$6$$

$$\tfrac{5}{19} = .26\tfrac{6}{19} = 26\tfrac{6}{19}\%.$$

TIME TO PRACTICE:

Fill in the blank spaces in the table below

	FRACTION	DECIMAL	PER CENT
1.	$\tfrac{1}{2}$	——	——
2.	—	.35	——
3.	—	—	36%
4.	$\tfrac{3}{7}$	——	——
5.	—	.24	——
6.	—	—	$4\tfrac{1}{2}\%$
7.	$\tfrac{5}{9}$	——	——

8.	—	$.37\frac{1}{2}$	____
9.	__	____	$83\frac{1}{3}\%$
10.	$1\frac{1}{5}$	____	____

ANSWERS

FRACTION	DECIMAL	PER CENT
1. $\frac{1}{2}$	.50	50%
2. $\frac{35}{100} = \frac{7}{20}$	.35	35%
3. $\frac{36}{100} = \frac{9}{25}$	.36	36%
4. $\frac{3}{7}$	$.42\frac{6}{7}$	$42\frac{6}{7}\%$
5. $\frac{6}{25}$	.24	24%
6. $\frac{4\frac{1}{2}}{100} = \frac{9}{200}$	$.04\frac{1}{2} = .045$	$4\frac{1}{2}\%$
7. $\frac{5}{9}$	$.55\frac{5}{9}$	$55\frac{5}{9}\%$
8. $\frac{37\frac{1}{2}}{100} = \frac{75}{200} = \frac{3}{8}$	$.37\frac{1}{2}$	$37\frac{1}{2}\%$
9. $\frac{83\frac{1}{3}}{100} = \frac{250}{300} = \frac{5}{6}$	$.83\frac{1}{3}$	$83\frac{1}{3}\%$
10. $1\frac{1}{5}$	1.2	120%

Certain fractions and the equivalent per cents are used frequently. It is helpful to memorize these equivalents

$\frac{1}{2} = 50\%$	$\frac{3}{4} = 75\%$	$\frac{4}{5} = 80\%$	$\frac{3}{8} = 37\frac{1}{2}\%$
$\frac{1}{3} = 33\frac{1}{3}\%$	$\frac{1}{5} = 20\%$	$\frac{1}{6} = 16\frac{2}{3}\%$	$\frac{5}{8} = 62\frac{1}{2}\%$
$\frac{2}{3} = 66\frac{2}{3}\%$	$\frac{2}{5} = 40\%$	$\frac{5}{6} = 83\frac{1}{3}\%$	$\frac{7}{8} = 87\frac{1}{2}\%$
$\frac{1}{4} = 25\%$	$\frac{3}{5} = 60\%$	$\frac{1}{8} = 12\frac{1}{2}\%$	

TIME TO STUDY:

Problems on Per Cents

Since per cents are fractions in another form, problems involving per cents are similar to problems in fractions.

1. To find a per cent of a given number

> EXAMPLE: In a factory, 4,775 machine parts were manufactured. When these were tested, 4% of them were found to be defective. How many parts were defective?

> In this case, the word "of" indicates that we are to multiply 4,775 by 4%. Since 4% = .04, we have

$$\begin{array}{r} 4775 \text{ parts manufactured} \\ \times\,.04 \text{ per cent defective} \\ \hline 191.00 \text{ number of parts defective} \end{array}$$

191 machine parts were defective.

2. To find what per cent one number is of another

> **EXAMPLE:** During the season a professional basketball player tried 108 foul shots and made 81 of them. What per cent of the shots tried were made?

We form a fraction as follows

$$\frac{\text{number of shots made}}{\text{total number of shots tried}} = \frac{81}{108}$$

This fraction may be expressed as a per cent by changing $\frac{81}{108}$ to a decimal and then to a per cent

$$
\begin{array}{r}
.75 \\
108\overline{)81.00} \\
75\,6 \\
\hline
5\,40 \\
5\,40 \\
\hline
\end{array}
$$

$$\frac{81}{108} = .75 = 75\%$$

The player made 75% of his shots.

3. To find a number when a per cent of it is given

> **EXAMPLE:** A business man decided to spend 16% of his expense budget for advertising. If he spent $2,400, what was his total expense?

We know that 16% or $\frac{16}{100}$ of his expenses amount to $2,400

$$\frac{16}{100} \text{ of expense} = 2,400$$

$$\frac{1}{100} \text{ of expense} = \frac{2,400}{16} = 150$$

Then $\frac{100}{100}$, or total expense $= 150 \times 100 = \$15,000$

TIME TO PRACTICE:

Directions: **Solve the following problems and blacken the space at the right under the number which corresponds to the one you have selected as the right answer.**

1. Of $500 spent by the Jones family one month, $150 was spent for clothing. The per cent spent for clothing was
(1) $33\frac{1}{3}\%$ (2) 40% (3) 30% (4) 12% (5) 20%

1. 1 2 3 4 5
    || || || || ||

2. Mr. Frank bought a jacket for $48 and a pair of slacks for $12.50. If there was a sales tax of 3% added to his bill the amount of the tax was
(1) $18 (2) $1.82 (3) $.63 (4) $.18 (5) $.36

2. 1 2 3 4 5
    || || || || ||

3. A TV dealer made 20% of his annual sales during the month before Christmas. If he sold 130 sets during this month, the number of sets he sold during the year was
    (1) 650   (2) 260   (3) 1,300   (4) 520   (5) 390

3.   1 2 3 4 5
|| || || || ||

4. Of 600 students in a high school graduating class 85% plan to go on to college. The number of students planning to go on to college is
    (1) 5,100   (2) 51   (3) 540   (4) 500   (5) 510

4.   1 2 3 4 5
|| || || || ||

5. A motorist planned a trip covering 720 miles. After he had covered 600 miles, the per cent of the mileage he had planned to cover was
    (1) 80%   (2) $83\frac{1}{3}$%   (3) 60%   (4) $16\frac{2}{3}$%   (5) 85%

5.   1 2 3 4 5
|| || || || ||

6. A school library contained 3,200 books. Of these, 48% were books of fiction. The number of books of fiction that the library contained was
    (1) 1,200   (2) 1,208   (3) 1,536   (4) 1,380   (5) 1,300

6.   1 2 3 4 5
|| || || || ||

7. A homeowner figured that 60% of his expenses were taxes. If his tax bill was $900 the total expense of running his house was
    (1) $540   (2) $5,400   (3) $1,800   (4) $1,500   (5) $2,000

7.   1 2 3 4 5
|| || || || ||

8. The value of a new car decreases 35% during the first year. Mr. Ames paid $4,000 for a new car. The value of the car at the end of the first year was
    (1) $1,400   (2) $1,600   (3) $2,400   (4) $2,500   (5) $2,600

8.   1 2 3 4 5
|| || || || ||

9. In a large housing development there were 1,250 apartments. Of these, 250 were three-room apartments. The per cent of three-room apartments in the development was
    (1) $16\frac{2}{3}$%   (2) 25%   (3) 20%   (4) 24%   (5) 30%

9.   1 2 3 4 5
|| || || || ||

10. Mrs. Breen bought a dining room suite for $800. She agreed to pay 25% down and the rest in installments. Her down payment was
    (1) $400   (2) $200   (3) $150   (4) $100   (5) $250

10.   1 2 3 4 5
|| || || || ||

11. An oil tank contains 560 gallons. After 210 gallons were used the per cent of oil left in the tank was
    (1) $37\frac{1}{2}$%   (2) 40%   (3) 60%   (4) $62\frac{1}{2}$%   (5) 58%

11.   1 2 3 4 5
|| || || || ||

12. When Mrs. Green had paid $600 for her fur coat she had paid 40% of the total cost. The total cost of her fur coat was
    (1) $1,000   (2) $1,200   (3) $1,500   (4) $2,400   (5) $1,800

12.   1 2 3 4 5
|| || || || ||

13. Mrs. Miller received a bill for electricity for $7.50. She was allowed a discount of 2% for early payment. If Mrs. Miller paid promptly her payment was
    (1) $.15   (2) $7.45   (3) $7.05   (4) $7.35   (5) $7.25

13.   1 2 3 4 5
|| || || || ||

14. A table usually sells for $72. Because it was slightly shopworn it sold for $60. The per cent of reduction was
    (1) 20%   (2) $16\frac{2}{3}$%   (3) 80%   (4) 30%   (5) $12\frac{1}{2}$%

14.   1 2 3 4 5
|| || || || ||

15. The sales tax on a lawn mower was $2.40. If the tax rate is 3%, the selling price of the mower was
    (1) $7.20   (2) $72   (3) $800   (4) $80   (5) $72.50

15.   1 2 3 4 5
|| || || || ||

16. A bookstore sold 800 copies of a popular cook book at $5 each. If the dealer makes a profit of 40% on each sale, his total profit on the sale of the cook books was

    (1) $160   (2) $960   (3) $240   (4) $1,200   (5) $1,600

16. 1 2 3 4 5 || || || || ||

17. At an evening performance, $83\frac{1}{3}\%$ of the seats in a movie house were occupied. If 500 people attended this performance the seating capacity of the movie house was

    (1) 600   (2) 500   (3) 583   (4) 650   (5) 750

17. 1 2 3 4 5 || || || || ||

18. A food store made sales of $9,000 during one week. If 5% of the sales amount was profit, the profit for the week was

    (1) $45   (2) $4,500   (3) $450   (4) $544.42   (5) $434.42

18. 1 2 3 4 5 || || || || ||

19. The Blue Sox baseball team won 56 games and lost 28 games. The per cent of the games won by the Blue Sox was

    (1) 50%   (2) $66\frac{2}{3}\%$ (3) $33\frac{1}{3}\%$ (4) 40%   (5) 36%

19. 1 2 3 4 5 || || || || ||

20. The Star Motel had 60 rooms occupied one night. This was 80% of the total number of rooms. The total number of rooms in the motel was

    (1) 80   (2) 48   (3) 140   (4) 75   (5) 100

20. 1 2 3 4 5 || || || || ||

ANSWERS

1. 3	**6.** 3	**11.** 4	**16.** 5
2. 2	**7.** 4	**12.** 3	**17.** 1
3. 1	**8.** 5	**13.** 4	**18.** 3
4. 5	**9.** 3	**14.** 2	**19.** 2
5. 2	**10.** 2	**15.** 4	**20.** 4

TIME TO STUDY:

Business Applications of Percentages

Manufacturers will frequently suggest a price for which an article is to be sold. This is called the *list price*. Dealers will often reduce the price in order to meet competition. The amount by which the price is reduced is called the *discount*. And the reduced price is called the *net price* or *selling price*.

    EXAMPLE: In a department store, a chair was marked as follows: "List Price $45. For sale at $31.50." What was the rate of discount?

The discount is $45.00 − $31.50 = $13.50
To find the rate of discount we use the fraction

$$\frac{\text{Discount}}{\text{List Price}} = \frac{13.50}{45.00}$$

$$= \frac{135}{450}$$

$$= \frac{3}{10} = 30\%$$

The rate of discount was 30%.

1. The list price of an overcoat was $120. Mr. Barr bought the coat at a discount of 10%. The net price of the coat was
    (1) $132 (2) $12.00 (3) $108   (4) $118   (5) $100

2. A men's store advertises a shirt that usually sells for $8.00 at a special price of $6.00. The rate of discount was
    (1) $33\frac{1}{3}$% (2) 25% (3) 20% (4) 40% (5) 35%

3. A radio set is sold at a discount of $12\frac{1}{2}$%. If the discount amounts to $6, the list price of the radio set is
    (1) $42 (2) $45 (3) $54 (4) $50 (5) $48

4. An electric toaster has a list price of $21.00. If it is sold at a discount of $33\frac{1}{3}$% the net price is
    (1) $7.00 (2) $28.00 (3) $14.00 (4) $25.00 (5) $16.00

5. The net price of a watch was $40.00 at a discount of 20%. The list price of the watch was
    (1) $50.00 (2) $30.00 (3) $48.00 (4) $35.20 (5) $45.00

	1	2	3	4	5
1.	‖	‖	‖	‖	‖
2.	‖	‖	‖	‖	‖
3.	‖	‖	‖	‖	‖
4.	‖	‖	‖	‖	‖
5.	‖	‖	‖	‖	‖

ANSWERS

1. 3   **2.** 2   **3.** 5   **4.** 3   **5.** 1

TIME TO STUDY:

Sometimes, a manufacturer will allow a trade discount and an additional discount on top of the trade discount. Two or more discounts are called *successive discounts*.

>   EXAMPLE: Mr. Boyd bought a table from a dealer. The list price was $180 and he was allowed a discount of 15%. In addition, he received a 2% discount for payment within 10 days. How much did Mr. Boyd pay for the table?

$180 list price
×.15 rate of discount
900
180
$27.00 amount of discount
180.00
−27.00
$153.00 cost price

When we compute the second discount, we base it on the price after the first discount is taken off.

$153.00 cost price
$\times$ .02 rate of discount
$ 3.06 discount for early payment
$153.00
$-$ 3.06
$149.94 actual payment

TIME TO PRACTICE:

1. Mr. Mack bought a TV set. The list price was $400. He was allowed successive discounts of 10% and 5%. How much did Mr. Mack actually pay for the TV set?
(1) $340.00 (2) $350.00 (3) $352.00 (4) $342.00 (5) $324.00

1. 1 2 3 4 5
    || || || || ||

2. Mr. Drew bought a shipment of books. The list price of the books was $180. If Mr. Drew was allowed discounts of 15% and 5%, how much did he actually pay for the books?
(1) $153.00 (2) $171.00 (3) $144.00 (4) $150.00 (5) $145.35

2. 1 2 3 4 5
    || || || || ||

3. On a purchase of $500, how much is saved by taking discounts of 20% and 10%, rather than discounts of 10% and 15%?
(1) $40.00 (2) $23.50 (3) $22.50 (4) $32.50 (5) $35.00

3. 1 2 3 4 5
    || || || || ||

4. Mr. Benson bought a boat which had a list price of $120. He was allowed a $12\frac{1}{2}$% discount and an additional 2% discount for cash. How much did Mr. Benson pay for the boat?
(1) $102.90 (2) $103.90 (3) $112.90 (4) $98.90 (5) $105.00

4. 1 2 3 4 5
    || || || || ||

ANSWERS

1. 4   2. 5   3. 3   4. 1

TIME TO STUDY:

When a business man decides upon the price at which to sell an article he must consider a number of items. First, the cost of the article is noted. Then the business man must consider such items as rent, sales help, and other expenses. This is called *overhead*. Then he must add on the profit. Thus, we have

$$\text{Selling Price} = \text{Cost} + \text{Overhead} + \text{Profit}$$

EXAMPLE: One week the Town Shoe Shop's receipts amounted to $1,590. The merchandise sold cost $820 and the overhead was 20% of the sales. What was the profit?

The overhead was $1{,}590 \times .20 = \$318$

To obtain the profit we must subtract the cost and the overhead from the profit.

$$
\begin{array}{rl}
\$ \ 820 & \text{cost of merchandise} \\
+ \ 318 & \text{overhead} \\
\hline
1{,}138 & \text{cost} + \text{overhead}
\end{array}
$$

$$
\begin{array}{rl}
1{,}590 & \text{selling price} \\
-1{,}138 & \text{cost} + \text{overhead} \\
\hline
\$ \ 452 & \text{profit}
\end{array}
$$

The profit was $452.

TIME TO PRACTICE:

1. The cost of a desk is $68. The overhead is $10.00 and the profit is $18.00. The selling price is
   (1) $77.50   (2) $86.50   (3) $95   (4) $96   (5) $92

   1.   1   2   3   4   5

2. A merchant buys lawn mowers at $43.50. He sells them at retail for $75. If his overhead is 12% of the selling price his profit was
   (1) $9   (2) $22.50   (3) $23.50   (4) $61.50   (5) $31.50

   2.   1   2   3   4   5

3. A merchant bought a shipment of cameras at a cost of $1,600 and sold the shipment for $2,500. If his profit was 25% of the cost of the shipment, his overhead expenses were
   (1) $900   (2) $400   (3) $650   (4) $500   (5) $4,100

   3.   1   2   3   4   5

4. Raincoats cost a dealer $12 each. He plans to sell the raincoats at a profit of 30%. If his overhead on each sale is $2, the selling price of the raincoats is
   (1) $15.60   (2) $14   (3) $17.60   (4) $17.00   (5) $19.00

   4.   1   2   3   4   5

5. The receipts of the Village Cafeteria for one week were $2,850. The cost of merchandise sold was $970 and the overhead was 34% of the receipts. The profit was
   (1) $969   (2) $911   (3) $1939   (4) $1,011   (5) $1,881

   5.   1   2   3   4   5

ANSWERS

1. 4   2. 2   3. 4   4. 3   5. 2

TIME TO STUDY:

We are often interested in finding the per cent of increase or decrease.

EXAMPLE: The price of a bus ride was increased from $1.20 to $1.35. What was the per cent of increase?

$1.35 new fare
— 1.20 original fare
$ .15 increase in fare

To find the per cent of increase we form the following fraction

$$\frac{.15}{1.20} \quad \frac{\text{increase in fare}}{\text{original fare}}$$

We now change this fraction to a percent, as follows

$$\frac{.15}{1.20} = \frac{15}{120} = \frac{3}{24} = \frac{1}{8}$$

$$\begin{array}{r} .125 \\ 8\,)\overline{1.000} \end{array}$$

The per cent of increase was $12\frac{1}{2}\%$.

EXAMPLE: During the past ten years the population of a small town decreased from 1,250 to 1,000. What was the per cent of decrease?

1,250 original population
— 1,000 population after decrease
250 actual decrease

To find the per cent of decrease we form the following fraction

$$\frac{250}{1250} \quad \frac{\text{actual decrease}}{\text{original population}}$$

We now change this fraction to a per cent, as follows:

$$\begin{array}{r} .20 \\ 1250\,)\overline{250.00} \\ \underline{250\ 0} \\ 0 \end{array}$$

The per cent of decrease was 20%

Sometimes, we have occasion to work with per cents greater than 100%.

EXAMPLE: The profit of the X Corporation this year was 108% of its profit last year. If its profit last year was $250,000, what is its profit this year?

$$\begin{array}{r} 250,000 \text{ profit last year} \\ \times\ 1.08 \text{ percentage this year} \\ \hline 20\ 000\ 00 \\ 250\ 000\ 0 \\ \hline \$270,000.00 \end{array}$$

Its profit this year is $270,000

EXAMPLE: Mr. Fowler bought some stock at $40 per share. Three years later Mr. Fowler sold the stock at $90 per share. What per cent of profit did Mr. Fowler make?

$90 selling price of stock per share
— $40 cost of stock per share
$50 profit per share

$$\frac{50}{40} \quad \frac{\text{profit per share}}{\text{original cost per share}}$$

$$\begin{array}{r} 1.25 \\ 40\overline{)50.0} \\ \underline{40} \\ 10\,0 \\ \underline{8\,0} \\ 2\,00 \\ \underline{2\,00} \end{array}$$

Mr. Fowler made a profit of 125%

TIME TO PRACTICE:

1. A man bought a house for $15,000. Eight years later he sold the house for $24,000. What per cent of profit did he make?
   (1) 40% (2) 37½% (3) 50% (4) 60% (5) 75%

   1. 1 2 3 4 5

2. During a sale, an overcoat was reduced from $80 to $68. What was the per cent of reduction?
   (1) 18% (2) 15% (3) 20% (4) 12% (5) 16%

   2. 1 2 3 4 5

3. A dealer sold a watch at 130% of his cost. If the sale price was $39.00, what did the watch cost the dealer?
   (1) $5.70 (2) $11.70 (3) $16.50 (4) $30.00 (5) $250.00

   3. 1 2 3 4 5

4. The price of tomatoes increased from $.16 per pound in season to $.40 per pound out of season. What was the per cent of increase?
   (1) 250% (2) 150% (3) 125% (4) 140% (5) 200%

   4. 1 2 3 4 5

5. Mr. Thorne's salary was $140 per week. He received a promotion and his salary rose to $250 per week. The per cent of increase of his salary, to the nearest per cent, is
   (1) 79% (2) 80% (3) 78% (4) 179% (5) 178%

   5. 1 2 3 4 5

6. 137½% of what number is 55?
   (1) 50 (2) 39 (3) 40 (4) 45 (5) 42

   6. 1 2 3 4 5

ANSWERS

1. 4   2. 2   3. 4   4. 2   5. 1   6. 3

TIME TO STUDY:

Insurance

The amount of money paid for insurance is called the *premium*. It is usually paid annually. On many types of insurance the premium rate is stated as so many dollars per $100 or per $1,000 of insurance purchased.

There are several types of life insurance sold. The ordinary life policy provides that the person buying the insurance continues to pay a premium for many years to come although dividends may reduce the premium as time goes on. The twenty-payment life policy provides that the person insured will pay the premium over a period of 20 years. The endowment policy provides that a person will pay premiums for a stated number of years. At the end of the period he will receive a lump sum. During the period of the policy he is protected by insurance. The rates are determined by the insurance company and are given to the agent in tabular form. For example, the figures below are a portion of such a table.

AGE IN YEARS	ORDINARY LIFE PREMIUM PER $1,000 OF INSURANCE	TWENTY-PAYMENT LIFE PREMIUM PER $1,000 OF INSURANCE	ENDOWMENT PREMIUM PER $1,000 OF INSURANCE
20	$17.50	$23.40	$26.50
25	19.75	25.60	29.10
30	22.60	29.80	34.40
35	25.40	34.75	38.50
40	30.20	40.50	43.10

EXAMPLE: At the age of 30, a man takes out a twenty-payment life policy for $7,500. What is his annual premium?

At age 30, the table indicates that the rate is $29.80 per $1,000. In 7,500 there are 7.5 thousands. His annual premium is 7.5 × $29.80 = $223.50.

TIME TO PRACTICE:

1. The annual premium rate on $6,500 worth of an ordinary life insurance policy is $28.24 per $1,000. The annual premium is
   (1) $18.35 (2) $173.55 (3) $183.56 (4) $1,835.50 (5) $184.55

1. 1 2 3 4 5

2. A house is insured against fire for 70% of its value. If the house has a value of $24,000 and the premium rate is $.23 per $100, the annual premium is
   (1) $386.40 (2) $38.64 (3) $37.64 (4) $38.54 (5) $37.54

2. 1 2 3 4 5

3. A car is insured for fire and theft for $2,850. If the annual premium rate is $1.04 per $100 the annual premium is
   (1) $29.64 (2) $39.90 (3) $29.12 (4) $30.16 (5) $39.64

3. 1 2 3 4 5

4. The annual premium rate for a twenty-payment life policy is $36.40 per $1,000. The total amount paid in premiums over a twenty year period for a $6,500 policy is
   (1) $236.60 (2) $573.20 (3) $4,532 (4) $6,532 (5) $4,732

4. 1 2 3 4 5

5. The annual premium on a fire insurance policy for $12,000 is $22.80. The premium rate per $100 is
   (1) $1.90 (2) $3.74 (3) $.19 (4) $37.46 (5) $.29

5. 1 2 3 4 5

ANSWERS

1. 3   **2.** 2   **3.** 1   **4.** 5   **5.** 3

TIME TO STUDY:

Investments

The most common investment is the placement of money in a savings bank where it draws interest. In order to compute interest we use the following formula *Interest = Principal × Rate × Time* which is often written

$$I = P \times R \times T \quad \text{or} \quad I = PRT$$

The principal is the amount invested, the annual rate is the per cent of the principal given the investor each year, and the time is stated in years.

EXAMPLE: What is the interest on $1,200 at $4\frac{1}{2}\%$ for 9 months?

$$I = PRT$$

In this case, $P = 1200$, $R = \dfrac{4\frac{1}{2}}{100}$, and $T = \dfrac{9}{12}$ or $\dfrac{3}{4}$

$$I = 1200 \times \frac{4\frac{1}{2}}{100} \times \frac{3}{4}$$

If we multiply the numerator and denominator of $\dfrac{4\frac{1}{2}}{100}$ by 2 we have $\dfrac{9}{200}$.

$$I = 1200 \times \frac{9}{200} \times \frac{3}{4}$$

$$I = 1200 \times \frac{9}{200} \times \frac{3}{4} = \frac{81}{2}, \quad \text{or} \quad 40\frac{1}{2}.$$

The interest is $40.50

If the interest is added to the principal we have the *amount*. In this case, the amount is $1200 + 40.50, or $1240.50.

Many banks compound interest every three months. That is, they add the interest to the principal at the end of three months. Then they compute interest for the next three months on an increased principal. This computation is made from tables. Interest that is not compounded is called *simple interest*.

A corporation is owned by stockholders who own *shares of stock*. Many such shares are traded on a stock exchange and are listed in the newspapers with current prices. For example,

American Telephone—$52\frac{1}{8}$
United States Steel   —$46\frac{1}{4}$

Stocks such as these pay dividends based upon the prosperity of the company.

A corporation may borrow money by selling *bonds* to the public. Bonds carry a fixed rate of interest and are issued for a certain number of years. At the *maturity date* of the bond the corporation pays back the borrowed amount to the bond-holder. Thus, a shareholder is a part owner of a company but a bondholder is a creditor.

EXAMPLE: Mr. Black owns 45 shares of stock in company A. The stock pays an annual dividend of $1.60 per share. How much does Mr. Black receive in dividends per year?

To obtain the amount of dividends we multiply 45 by $1.60.

$$45 \times 1.60 = \$72.00$$

Mr. Black receives $72 in dividends.

EXAMPLE: Mr. Glenn owns six $1,000 bonds that pay $5\frac{1}{2}\%$ interest each year. How much interest does Mr. Glenn receive each year?

This is a problem in computing simple interest. The principal is $6 \times \$1,000$, or $6,000, the rate is $5\frac{1}{2}\%$, and the period is 1 year.

$$\text{Interest} = 6000 \times \frac{5\frac{1}{2}}{100} \times 1$$

$$= 6000 \times \frac{11}{200} \times 1$$

$$= \overset{30}{\cancel{6000}} \times \frac{11}{\underset{1}{\cancel{200}}} \times 1 = 330$$

Mr. Glenn receives $330 in interest.

TIME TO PRACTICE:

1. Simple interest on $2,400 at $4\frac{1}{2}\%$ for 3 years is
   (1) $288.00   (2) $32.40   (3) $3,240.00   (4) $324.00   (5) 314.00

   1. 1 2 3 4 5
      ‖ ‖ ‖ ‖ ‖

2. Mr. Payne borrowed $5,200 from a friend for 1 year and 3 months. He agreed to pay $5\frac{1}{2}\%$ simple interest on the loan. The amount of money that he paid back to his friend at the end of the loan period was
   (1) $5,553.50   (2) $357.50   (3) $5,557.50   (4) $4,842.50   (5) $5,000.00

   2. 1 2 3 4 5
      ‖ ‖ ‖ ‖ ‖

3. Mrs. Holden kept $3,800.00 in a savings bank for 9 months at 5% simple interest. The interest on her money was
   (1) $142.50   (2) $285.00   (3) $3,942.50   (4) $1.43   (5) $1,425.00

   3. 1 2 3 4 5
      ‖ ‖ ‖ ‖ ‖

4. Mr. Moss bought 80 shares of X Corporation at $28\frac{3}{4}$ and sold the shares a year later at $31\frac{1}{2}$. His profit, before paying commission, was
   (1) $22.00   (2) $220.00   (3) $140.00   (4) $180.00   (5) $242.00

   4. 1 2 3 4 5
      ‖ ‖ ‖ ‖ ‖

5. Mr. Kern owns 120 shares of Y Corporation. The corporation declared a dividend of $1.35 per share. The amount Mr. Kern received in dividends was
   (1) $16.20   (2) $121.35   (3) $135.00   (4) $162.00   (5) $1,620.00

   5. 1 2 3 4 5
      ‖ ‖ ‖ ‖ ‖

6. Mr. Cooper owns 280 shares of Z Corporation. The corporation pays a quarterly dividend of $.35 per share. The amount Mr. Cooper receives in dividends for the year is
   (1) $98.00   (2) $9.80   (3) $392.00   (4) $196.00   (5) $280.00

6.   1   2   3   4   5

7. Mr. Ross owns eight $1,000 bonds that pay $6\frac{1}{2}\%$ interest each year. The amount of interest Mr. Ross receives each year is
   (1) $65   (2) $520   (3) $106   (4) $130   (5) $260

7.   1   2   3   4   5

8. Mr. Dolan borrows $960 at $5\frac{1}{2}\%$ for 3 months. The total amount that he will have to repay is
   (1) $13.20   (2) $132.00   (3) $1,092.00   (4) $973.20   (5) $946.80

8.   1   2   3   4   5

ANSWERS

1. 4	5. 4
2. 3	6. 3
3. 1	7. 2
4. 2	8. 4

A WORD ABOUT REVIEW: Don't be alarmed at all the review material in this chapter. We've included much more than you will probably need simply because we didn't want to omit anything that might be useful to you. Remember that the High School Equivalency Tests examine background, not classroom or book learning. They test the kind of information you've acquired from reading newspapers and magazines, from T.V. and radio, from working at a job or running a home. They test experience and common sense. The review section simply organizes knowledge in this field, reminds you of some things you may have forgotten, fills in some gaps you may have in your background.

TIME TO STUDY:

Taxation

We ordinarily pay many kinds of taxes. In this section we will consider the more common types of taxes.

Many states in the United States have a *sales tax* on articles bought at retail. This may be 2%, 3%, or 4% of the retail price of an article.

> EXAMPLE: Mrs. Horn buys a small rug for $39.95. If she has to pay a sales tax of 3%, what is the total cost of the rug?
>
> 3% of $39.95 = .03 × $39.95 = $1.1985
>
> In a case such as this the amount of tax is rounded off to the nearest penny. In this case, the tax is $1.20. Mrs. Horn must pay $39.95 + $1.20, or $41.15.

A home owner must pay a real estate tax. This tax is based upon the assessed valuation of the home. The assessed valuation of a home is determined by town or city authorities. The tax rate may be expressed as a per cent or in the form "$4.70 per $100." In many localities, there is a separate school tax which is also based on the assessed valuation of the home.

EXAMPLE: Mr. Martin's home is assessed at $23,500. His realty tax is $3.89 per $100 and his school tax is $1.27 per $100. What is Mr. Martin's total tax on his home?

We note that there are 235 hundreds in $23,500 since 23,500 = 235 × 100.

The realty tax is 235 × 3.89 = $914.15
The school tax is 235 × 1.27 = +$298.45
Total tax = $1,212.60

The federal government and most state governments levy an income tax. Every person or business with an income above a certain minimum amount must file a tax return. The tax is based upon taxable income which is obtained after certain allowable deductions are taken off the gross income. For federal income taxes and some state income taxes employers are required to withhold part of wages. Employers are also required to deduct a certain amount for social security taxes. After all deductions are made, the amount the employee gets is called "take-home pay."

EXAMPLE: Mr. Dean's weekly salary is $125. Each week his employer deducts 4.4% of his salary for social security. He also deducts $5.70 for his federal withholding tax. What is Mr. Dean's weekly take-home pay?

4.4% of $125 = .044 × 125 = $5.50
Total deductions = 5.70 + 5.50 = $11.20
Mr. Dean's take-home pay is $125 − $11.20 = $113.80

EXAMPLE: Mr. Stark earns $12,500 per year. In paying his tax he has allowable deductions of $3,750. On his state tax he pays 2% on the first $3,000 of taxable income, 3% on the next $3,000 of taxable income and 4% on the balance of his taxable income. What is his state tax?

Mr. Stark's taxable income is $12,500 − $3,750 = $8,750

Tax on the first $3,000 is 2% of $3,000 = $60.00
Tax on the next $3,000 is 3% of $3,000 = $90.00
Balance is $8,750 − $6,000 = $2,750
Tax on $2,750 is 4% of $2,750   = + $110.00
Total Tax = $260.00

TIME TO PRACTICE:

1. Mr. Minor buys an overcoat for $98.50. If he must pay a sales tax of 3%, the total cost of the coat is
(1) $2.96 (2) $101.46 (3) $99.45 (4) $127.55 (5) $100.46

1. 1 2 3 4 5

2. On a purchase of a table for $64, Mr. Morton paid a sales tax of $2.56. The rate of sales tax was
  (1) 3% (2) 3½% (3) 2% (4) 2½% (5) 4%

                         2. 1 2 3 4 5

3. Mr. Powell's home is assessed at $16,500. The realty tax rate is $3.97 per $100. Mr. Powell's realty tax is
  (1) $645.05 (2) $65.50 (3) $655.05 (4) $654.05 (5) $644.05

                         3. 1 2 3 4 5

4. Mr. Olson bought a house for $32,000. It was assessed at 80% of his purchase price. If the school tax is $1.93 per $100, Mr. Olson's school tax was
  (1) $494.08 (2) $617.60 (3) $61.76 (4) $49.41 (5) $515.28

                         4. 1 2 3 4 5

5. Mr. Emerson sets aside $60 per month to cover his realty and school taxes. His home is assessed at $19,400. His realty tax is $3.14 per $100 and his school tax is $1.19 per $100. The amount he must add at the end of the year to cover both taxes is
  (1) $840.02 (2) $720.00 (3) $110.02 (4) $120.02 (5) $20.02

                         5. 1 2 3 4 5

6. Mr. Howe has a gross income of $9,800.00 per year. His deductions amount to $3,650.00. He pays state income taxes at the rate of 2% on the first $1,000 of taxable income, 3% on the next $2,000 of taxable income, and 4% on the balance. His total tax is
  (1) $146.00 (2) $126.00 (3) $206.00 (4) $140.00 (5) $137.50

                         6. 1 2 3 4 5

7. Mr. Robinson earns $135 per week. Each week his employer deducts 4.4% of his salary for social security. He also deducts $6.85 for his federal withholding tax. Mr. Robinson's weekly take-home pay is
  (1) $130.27 (2) $122.21 (3) $128.15 (4) $11.58 (5) $124.42

                         7. 1 2 3 4 5

8. Mr. Tobin's taxable income is $8,900. On this, he must pay 2% on the first $3,000, 3% on the next $3,000, and 4% on the balance for state income tax. During the year his employer had withheld $4.50 per week. To settle his tax bill at the end of the year, Mr. Tobin had to pay an additional
  (1) $32.00 (2) $31.00 (3) $59.00 (4) $226.00 (5) $225.00

                         8. 1 2 3 4 5

ANSWERS

1. 2	3. 3	5. 4	7. 2
2. 5	4. 1	6. 3	8. 1

ALGEBRA

TIME TO STUDY:

Fundamentals

As we have seen earlier, we frequently use letters to represent numbers in algebra. For example, in the formula

$$I = P \times R \times T$$

I represents interest, *P* represents principal, *R* represents rate, and *T* represents time. This is done because it enables us to solve many kinds of problems. That is, *P* may be $5,000 in one problem and $786 in another problem. In indicating multiplication in arithmetic we always use the $\times$ sign. For example, 5×6. In indicating multiplication in algebra three methods are used

1. Use the multiplication symbol. For example, $P \times R$
2. Use a raised dot. For example, $P \cdot R$
3. Place the numbers and letters next to each other.

For example, $7a$ means $7 \times a$ or $7 \cdot a$; bc means $b \times c$ or $b \cdot c$. For other operations we use the same symbols as are used in arithmetic.

In order to use algebra effectively we must learn how to translate from ordinary language into symbols and letters.

EXAMPLE: John is x years old. How old will he be 7 years from now?
ANSWER: $x + 7$

EXAMPLE: An apple costs a cents. What is the cost of 6 apples?
ANSWER: $6 \times a$, or $6 \cdot a$, or $6a$ ($6a$ is preferred)

EXAMPLE: Alice weighed y pounds a year ago. Since then she has lost 9 pounds. What is her present weight?
ANSWER: $y - 9$

EXAMPLE: Take a number z. Increase it by 2. Multiply the result by 6.
ANSWER: $6(z + 2)$. Notice that the number represented by $(z + 2)$ is to be multiplied by 6. The answer might also be written $(z + 2)6$.

TIME TO PRACTICE:

---

1. A sweater costs $18. The cost of c sweaters is
   (1) $18 + c$ (2) $18 \div c$ (3) $c \div 18$ (4) $18c$ (5) $c - 18$

2. Fred is x years old. Bill is 4 years younger. Bill's age is
   (1) $x + 4$ (2) $x - 4$ (3) $4 - x$ (4) $4x$ (5) $4x - 4$

3. A car travels y miles per hour. The distance covered by the car in z hours is
   (1) $y + z$ (2) $y - z$ (3) yz (4) $y \div z$ (5) $z \div y$

4. Bob had $15 and spent x dollars. The amount he had left was
   (1) $x - 15$ (2) $15x$ (3) $15 \div x$ (4) $x \div 15$ (5) $15 - x$

5. If 12 eggs cost a cents, the cost of one egg is
   (1) $12a$ (2) $\dfrac{12}{a}$ (3) $\dfrac{a}{12}$ (4) $12 + a$ (5) $a - 12$

6. Paul bought 3 ties at x dollars each. The change that he received, in dollars, from a $20 bill was
   (1) $3x$ (2) $20 + 3x$ (3) $3x - 20$ (4) $20 - 3x$ (5) $3x \div 20$

7. Mr. Barry bought a suit for y dollars. The sales tax rate on the purchase was 3%. The sales tax was
   (1) $.03y$ (2) $3y$ (3) $.03 + y$ (4) $y \div 3$ (5) $y + .03y$

1. 1 2 3 4 5
2. 1 2 3 4 5
3. 1 2 3 4 5
4. 1 2 3 4 5
5. 1 2 3 4 5
6. 1 2 3 4 5
7. 1 2 3 4 5

8. Bill had y dollars. He bought a articles at b dollars each. The amount of money Bill had left was

   (1) $ab - y$ (2) $ab + y$ (3) $y - ab$ (4) $\dfrac{y}{ab}$ (5) aby

ANSWERS

1. 4	**3.** 3	**5.** 3	**7.** 1
2. 2	**4.** 5	**6.** 4	**8.** 3

TIME TO STUDY:

Exponents and Evaluations

There are times when we wish to multiply a number by itself. Of course, if we wish to multiply 7 by itself we can write 7×7. However, in modern science where we may have occasion to multiply a number by itself many times it becomes awkward to write such numbers as $7 \times 7 \times 7 \times 7 \times 7 \times 7 \times 7 \times 7 \times 7$. Instead, we use a short cut and write the product of nine sevens as 7^9. In this case, 9 is known as an *exponent* and 7 is called the *base*.

> EXAMPLES: 6^3 means $6 \times 6 \times 6$
> a^5 means $a \times a \times a \times a \times a$
> $3b^4$ means $3 \times b \times b \times b \times b$

We often wish to find the numerical value of an algebraic expression when we know the numerical value assigned to each number. The examples below show how this is done.

> EXAMPLE: Find the numerical value of $5x + 3y - 7z$ when $x = 6$, $y = 4$, and $z = 1$.
>
> $5x + 3y - 7z = 5 \cdot 6 + 3 \cdot 4 - 7 \cdot 1 = 30 + 12 - 7 = 35$
>
> EXAMPLE: Find the value of $4a^3 - 2b + 9c^2$ when $a = 5$, $b = 3$, and $c = 2$.
>
> $4a^3 - 2b + 9c^2 = 4 \cdot 5^3 - 2 \cdot 3 + 9 \cdot 2^2 = 500 - 6 + 36 = 530$
>
> EXAMPLE: Find the value of $5(x^3 - 2y^2)$ when $x = 4$ and $y = 3$.
>
> $5(x^3 - 2y^2) = 5(4^3 - 2 \cdot 3^2) = 5(64 - 18)$
> $= 5 \cdot 46 = 230$

TIME TO PRACTICE:

In the following examples $x = 5$, $y = 4$, $z = 3$, $a = 2$; and $b = 1$.

1. The value of $2x^2 + 3y$ is
   (1) 112   (2) 32   (3) 47   (4) 62   (5) 98

2. The value of $3x + 5a - 7b$ is
   (1) 18   (2) 17   (3) 15   (4) 20   (5) 37

3. The value of $3ab + x^2y$ is
    (1) 9 (2) 32 (3) 11 (4) 15 (5) 106

4. The value of $2x^2 - y^2 + 5ab$
    (1) 54 (2) 94 (3) 44 (4) 92 (5) 78

5. The value of $3x^2y^3z$ is
    (1) 8,100 (2) 14,400 (3) 96 (4) 900 (5) 1,800

6. The value of $\dfrac{y^2}{a^2}$ is

    (1) 8 (2) 2 (3) 16 (4) 4 (5) 36

7. The value of $\dfrac{a^3}{y} + 2xz$ is

    (1) 23 (2) 31 (3) 9 (4) 32 (5) 54

8. The value of $\dfrac{4x^2}{5a} + 3y^2 - z^3$ is

    (1) 21 (2) 29 (3) 32 (4) 46 (5) 31

ANSWERS

1. 4	**3.** 5	**5.** 2	**7.** 4
2. 1	**4.** 3	**6.** 4	**8.** 5

Formulas

Mr. Wells had a garden 60 feet long and 40 feet wide. He wished to fence in the garden. How many feet of fencing did he need?

We can see that he needed two lengths of 60 feet each and two widths of 40 feet each. Thus, he needed $2 \times 60 + 2 \times 40$, or $120 + 80 = 200$ feet.

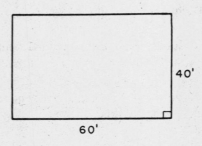

Now, suppose we wish to find a formula to find the distance around (called the "perimeter") the rectangle. A rectangle is a figure having four sides and four right angles. If we represent the perimeter by P, the length by l, and the width by w,

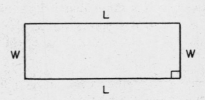

$$P = l + w + l + w$$
$$\text{or} \quad P = 2l + 2w$$

We can write this as $P = 2(l + w)$.

$P = 2l + 2w$, or $P = 2(l + w)$ is an example of a *formula* in mathematics.

EXAMPLE: The formula $C = 25 + 5(n - 3)$ gives the cost of borrowing a book from a circulating library. The minimum number of days is 3 and the minimum cost is 25 cents. In this formula,

C = cost, in cents, and n = number of days for which the book is borrowed. What is the cost of borrowing a book for 7 days?

$$C = 25 + 5(7 - 3)$$
$$C = 25 + 5(4)$$
$$C = 25 + 20 = \$.45$$

TIME TO PRACTICE:

1. Mr. Dale wishes to fence in a rectangular lawn which is 60 feet long and 30 feet wide. He uses the formula $P = 2(l + w)$ to obtain the result. The perimeter is
(1) 90 (2) 120 (3) 150 (4) 180 (5) 200

1. 1 2 3 4 5

2. The formula $A = \dfrac{a + b + c}{3}$ is used to find the average (A) of three numbers a, b, and c. The average of 95, 109, and 114 is
(1) 108 (2) 106 (3) 160 (4) $104\frac{2}{3}$ (5) 110

2. 1 2 3 4 5

3. The formula $C = 50 + 10(n - 4)$ is used to find the cost, C, of a taxi ride where n represents the number of $\frac{1}{4}$ miles of the ride. The cost of a taxi ride of $2\frac{3}{4}$ miles is
(1) $1.00 (2) $.90 (3) $1.50 (4) $1.20 (5) $1.30

3. 1 2 3 4 5

4. The formula $C = 32m + 18h$ is used to find the daily labor cost, in dollars, of a job in carpentry. m represents the number of master carpenters and h represents the number of helpers.

On a certain job, 6 master carpenters are used and 4 helpers are used. The daily labor cost is
(1) $192 (2) $104 (3) $50 (4) $236 (5) $264

4. 1 2 3 4 5

5. The formula for the length and width of a certain flag is $L = 1.8W$, where L = the length of the flag and W = the width of the flag. A flag has a width of 5 feet. Its length is
(1) 2.3 feet (2) 9 feet (3) 90 feet (4) 1.3 feet (5) 8 feet

5. 1 2 3 4 5

6. The weight of an adult is given by the formula $W = \frac{1}{2}(h - 60) + 110$ where W = weight in pounds and h = height in inches. If Mr. Conrad is 68 inches tall he should weigh
(1) 144 (2) 164 (3) 154 (4) 174 (5) 184

6. 1 2 3 4 5

ANSWERS

1. 4
2. 2

3. 4
4. 5

5. 2
6. 3

TIME TO STUDY:

Solving Equations

The ability to solve equations is important because it enables us to solve many different types of problems. In this section we will learn how to solve some of the simpler kinds of equations. In a later section we will apply these skills in problem solving.

An equation states that two quantities are equal. Consider the equation

$$3x + 2 = 20$$

This tells us that $3x + 2$ and 20 name the same number. If this is so, then x must represent the number 6 since

$$3 \times 6 + 2 = 20$$

And 6 is the only number which will replace x and make $3x + 2$ equal to 20. The number, 6, which makes the statement $3x + 2 = 20$ true is called the *root* of the equation and is said to *satisfy* the equation.

TIME TO PRACTICE:

In each case, select the root of the equation.

1. $x + 2 = 9$
    (1) 5 (2) 9 (3) 7 (4) 3 (5) 10

2. $x - 3 = 5$
    (1) 5 (2) 3 (3) 2 (4) 10 (5) 8

3. $2x = 10$
    (1) 8 (2) 5 (3) 20 (4) $\frac{1}{5}$ (5) 9

4. $\frac{x}{3} = 4$
    (1) 12 (2) $\frac{4}{3}$ (3) $\frac{3}{4}$ (4) 1 (5) 6

5. $2x + 1 = 7$
    (1) 4 (2) $3\frac{1}{2}$ (3) 5 (4) 3 (5) 6

6. $2x - 1 = 9$
    (1) 10 (2) 8 (3) 5 (4) 4 (5) 3

7. $\frac{x}{2} + 3 = 7$
    (1) 4 (2) 8 (3) $1\frac{1}{2}$ (4) $2\frac{1}{2}$ (5) 20

8. $\frac{x}{3} - 1 = 5$
    (1) 18 (2) 12 (3) 2 (4) 6 (5) 15

	1	2	3	4	5
1.	‖	‖	‖	‖	‖
2.	‖	‖	‖	‖	‖
3.	‖	‖	‖	‖	‖
4.	‖	‖	‖	‖	‖
5.	‖	‖	‖	‖	‖
6.	‖	‖	‖	‖	‖
7.	‖	‖	‖	‖	‖
8.	‖	‖	‖	‖	‖

9. $\dfrac{2x}{5} + 1 = 9$

    (1) 8 (2) 50 (3) 20 (4) 6 (5) 4

10. $\dfrac{3x}{4} - 2 = 1$

    (1) 5 (2) 6 (3) 12 (4) 4 (5) 9

11. $2x + 3 = 10$

    (1) 4 (2) $6\frac{1}{2}$ (3) $3\frac{1}{2}$ (4) $7\frac{1}{2}$ (5) 5

12. $3x - 4 = 6$

    (1) $3\frac{1}{3}$ (2) $\frac{2}{3}$ (3) 2 (4) $3\frac{1}{2}$ (5) 7

9. 1 2 3 4 5 || || || || ||

10. 1 2 3 4 5 || || || || ||

11. 1 2 3 4 5 || || || || ||

12. 1 2 3 4 5 || || || || ||

ANSWERS

1. 3	**3.** 2	**5.** 4	**7.** 2	**9.** 3	**11.** 3
2. 5	**4.** 1	**6.** 3	**8.** 1	**10.** 4	**12.** 1

TIME TO STUDY:

We will now study systematic methods of finding the root of an equation.

Consider the equation $x + 2 = 5$. This tells us that a certain number added to 2 will give us a result of 5. We can see that $x = 3$. Now, how can we get from

$$x + 2 = 5$$
$$\text{to} \qquad x = 3?$$

To get from $x + 2$ to x we need only to subtract 2 from $x + 2$. Thus, $x + 2 - 2 = x$. Since $x + 2$ and 5 name the same number we may subtract the same number from $x + 2$ and from 5 and obtain equal results

$$x + 2 - 2 = 5 - 2$$
$$\text{or} \qquad x = 3$$

Consider the equation $x - 1 = 5$. In order to obtain x on the left side of the equation we add 1 to $x - 1$. Since $x - 1$ and 5 name the same number we may add 1 to both $x - 1$ and 5 to obtain equal results

$$x - 1 + 1 = 5 + 1$$
$$\text{or} \qquad x = 6$$

Consider the equation $2x = 12$. In order to obtain x on the left side of the equation we must divide $2x$, or twice x, by 2. Since $2x$ and 12 name the same number, we divide both $2x$ and 12 by 2 to obtain equal results

$$2x = 12$$
$$\tfrac{2}{2}x = \tfrac{12}{2}$$
$$1x, \quad \text{or} \quad x = 6$$

Consider the equation $\frac{y}{3} = 4$. In order to obtain y on the left side of the equation we must multiply $\frac{y}{3}$, or $\frac{1}{3}$ of y, by 3. Since $\frac{y}{3}$ and 4 name the same number, we multiply both $\frac{y}{3}$ and 4 to obtain equal results.

$$\frac{y}{3} = 4$$

$$3 \times \frac{y}{3} = 3 \times 4$$

$$y = 12$$

The above procedures may be remembered if we note that

1. We subtract when we have a sum $x + 2 - 2 = 5 - 2$
2. We add when we have a difference $x - 1 + 1 = 5 - 1$
3. We divide when we have a product $\frac{2x}{2} = \frac{12}{2}$

4. We multiply when we have a quotient $3 \times \frac{y}{3} = 3 \times 4$

TIME TO PRACTICE:

Solve the following equations:

1. $x + 1 = 3$	**6.** $x - 3 = 4$	**11.** $x - 2 = 9$	**16.** $x - 1 = 5$
2. $x - 2 = 4$	**7.** $5x = 10$	**12.** $x + 4 = 7$	**17.** $3x = 21$
3. $3x = 12$	**8.** $\frac{x}{4} = 2$	**13.** $\frac{x}{5} = 2$	**18.** $x + 4 = 7$
4. $\frac{x}{2} = 5$	**9.** $x + 2 = 9$	**14.** $3x = 18$	**19.** $\frac{x}{4} = 3$
5. $x + 5 = 7$	**10.** $5x = 15$	**15.** $x + 9 = 11$	**20.** $x - 5 = 11$

ANSWERS

1. 2	6. 7	11. 11	16. 6
2. 6	7. 2	12. 3	17. 7
3. 4	8. 8	13. 10	18. 3
4. 10	9. 7	14. 6	19. 12
5. 2	10. 3	15. 2	20. 16

TIME TO STUDY:

Solving More Difficult Equations

In order to solve interesting problems it is necessary to be able to solve more difficult equations.

    EXAMPLE: Solve the equation

$$5x + 2x = 28$$

Since $5x + 2x = 7x$, we have

$$7x = 28$$
$$x = \frac{28}{7}$$
$$x = 4$$

    EXAMPLE: Solve the equation

$$\tfrac{2}{3}x = 16$$

In order to obtain x on the left side we must multiply $\tfrac{2}{3}x$ by $\tfrac{3}{2}$. Since $\tfrac{2}{3}x$ and 16 name the same number we multiply both $\tfrac{2}{3}x$ and 16 to obtain equal results.

$$\tfrac{3}{2} \cdot \tfrac{2}{3}x = \tfrac{3}{2} \cdot 16$$
$$x = 24$$

    EXAMPLE: Solve the equation $2x + 3 = 15$

$$2x + 3 = 15$$
$$2x + 3 - 3 = 15 - 3$$
$$2x = 12$$
$$\frac{2x}{2} = \frac{12}{2}$$
$$x = 6$$

    EXAMPLE: Solve the equation $\tfrac{3}{5}x - 1 = 8$

$$\tfrac{3}{5}x - 1 = 8$$
$$\tfrac{3}{5}x - 1 + 1 = 8 + 1$$
$$\tfrac{3}{5}x = 9$$
$$\tfrac{5}{3} \cdot \tfrac{3}{5}x = \tfrac{5}{3} \cdot 9$$
$$x = 15$$

TIME TO PRACTICE:

Solve the following equations:

1. $2x + 3x = 40$
2. $\tfrac{2}{3}x = 12$
3. $4x - 1 = 27$
4. $\dfrac{x}{5} + 4 = 6$

5. $3x - 5 = 16$
6. $3x + 7 = 37$
7. $4x - 2 = 22$
8. $\dfrac{x}{2} - 3 = 5$

9. $2x + x + 5 = 17$
10. $\frac{1}{5}x + 2 = 30$
11. $\frac{2}{3}x + 5 = 7$
12. $5x - 2x + 4 = 31$

13. $\frac{x}{7} + 5 = 6$
14. $3x + 2x + 1 = 21$
15. $2x + x - 3 = 12$
16. $\frac{3}{4}x - 7 = 8$

ANSWERS

1. 8
2. 18
3. 7
1. 10

5 7
6. 10
7. 6
8. 16

9. 4
10. 35
11. 3
12. 9

13. 7
14. 4
15. 5
16. 20

TIME TO STUDY:

Solving Problems

We may use equations to solve problems such as the following.

EXAMPLE: A plumber must cut a pipe 50 inches long into two pieces so that one piece shall be 12 inches longer than the other piece. Find the length of each piece.

Let x = the length of one piece

And $x + 12$ = the length of the other piece

Since the sum of the two pieces is 50 inches we have

$$x + x + 12 = 50$$
$$2x + 12 = 50$$
$$2x + 12 - 12 = 50 - 12$$
$$2x = 38$$
$$\frac{2x}{2} = \frac{38}{2}$$
$$x = 19$$

One piece is 19 inches and the other piece is 31 inches.

EXAMPLE: Divide an estate of $46,000 among three sons so that the second son gets $6,000 more than the youngest, and the eldest three times as much as the youngest.

Let x = amount the youngest son gets

And $x + 6,000$ = amount the second son gets

And $3x$ = amount the eldest son gets

$$x + x + 6{,}000 + 3x = 46{,}000$$
$$5x + 6{,}000 = 46{,}000$$
$$5x + 6{,}000 - 6{,}000 = 46{,}000 - 6{,}000$$
$$5x = 40{,}000$$
$$\frac{5}{5}x = \frac{40{,}000}{5}$$
$$x = 8{,}000$$

The youngest son gets $8,000.
The second son gets $8,000 + $6,000 = $14,000.
The eldest son gets 3 × $8,000 = $24,000.

EXAMPLE: Eighteen coins, consisting of nickels and dimes, have a total value of $1.25. How many dimes are there?
Let x = the number of dimes
And $18 - x$ = the number of nickels
$10x$ = the value of the dimes
$5(18 - x)$ = the value of the nickels

$$10x + 5(18 - x) = 125$$
$$10x + 90 - 5x = 125$$
$$5x + 90 = 125$$
$$5x + 90 - 90 = 125 - 90$$
$$5x = 35$$
$$x = \tfrac{35}{5} = 7$$

There are 7 dimes.

EXAMPLE: A dealer has some candy worth 75 cents per pound and some candy worth 55 cents per pound. He wishes to make a mixture of 80 pounds that will sell for 60 cents per pound. How many pounds of each type of candy should he use?
Let x = the number of pounds of 75-cent candy
And $80 - x$ = the number of pounds of 55-cent candy
$75x$ = value of 75-cent candy
$55(80 - x)$ = value of 55-cent candy
80×60, or 4800 = value of mixture

$$75x + 55(80 - x) = 4800$$
$$75x + 4400 - 55x = 4800$$
$$20x + 4400 = 4800$$
$$20x + 4400 - 4400 = 4800 - 4400$$
$$20x = 400$$
$$x = \tfrac{400}{20} = 20$$

The dealer uses 20 pounds of the 75-cent candy and 60 pounds of the 55-cent candy.

EXAMPLE: An investment of $2,700, part at 4% and part at 3%, earns a yearly income of $93. Find the amount invested at each rate.
Let x = the amount invested at 4%
And $2700 - x$ = the amount invested at 3%
$.04x$ = income on 4% investment
$.03(2700 - x)$ = income on 3% investment

$$.04x + .03(2700 - x) = 93$$
$$.04x + 81 - .03x = 93$$
$$.01x + 81 = 93$$
$$.01x + 81 - 81 = 93 - 81$$
$$.01x = 12$$
$$\tfrac{1}{100}x = 12$$
$$100(\tfrac{1}{100}x) = 100 \times 12$$
$$x = 1200$$

He invested $1,200 at 4% and $1,500 at 3%.

EXAMPLE: Two cars start at the same time from two cities which are 480 miles apart and travel toward each other. One car averages 35 miles per hour and the other car averages 45 miles per hour. In how many hours will the two cars meet?

Let x = the number of hours it takes cars to meet

In problems involving motion it is convenient to collect our information as shown below.

RATE × TIME = DISTANCE

FIRST CAR	35	x	$35x$
SECOND CAR	45	x	$45x$

Since the sum of the two distances covered is 480 miles, we have

$$35x + 45x = 480$$
$$80x = 480$$
$$x = \frac{480}{80} = 6$$

The cars will meet in 6 hours.

TIME TO PRACTICE:

Solve the following problems:

1. Two partners in a business earn $60,000 one year. If the senior partner's share is 3 times that of the junior partner, what is the junior partner's share?

2. A wooden beam is 58 inches long. A carpenter must cut the beam so that the longer part is 8 inches longer than the shorter part. How long is the shorter part?

3. A certain kind of concrete contains five times as much gravel as cement. How many cubic feet of each of these materials will there be in 426 cubic feet of the concrete?

4. The length of a field is 3 times its width. If the perimeter (distance around the field) of the field is 312 feet, what is the width of the field?

5. A master carpenter earns $3 per hour more than his helper. Together they earn $91 for a 7-hour job. How much does the helper earn per hour?

6. A boy has $3.75 in nickels and dimes. If he has 6 more dimes than nickels, how many dimes does he have?

7. Mr. Dale asked his son to deposit $495 in the bank for him. There were exactly 70 bills, consisting of 10-dollar and 5-dollar bills. Find the number of 10-dollar bills he had to deposit.

8. The perimeter of a triangle is 27 inches. One side is 3 inches longer than the shortest side and the longest side is twice the length of the shortest side. What is the length of the shortest side?

9. The sum of two numbers is 50. If the larger one is 5 more than twice the smaller, what is the smaller number?

10. A dealer wishes to mix candy worth $.90 per pound with candy worth $.65 per pound in order to obtain 40 pounds of candy which can be sold at $.75 per pound. How many pounds of the 90-cent candy should he use?

11. Mr. Charles invests $20,000, part at 5% and the rest at 4%. If he obtains an annual income of $920, how much does he invest at each rate?

12. Tickets at a movie house cost $2 for adults and $1 for children. For a matinee performance, 800 tickets were sold and the receipts were $1150. How many adult tickets were sold?

13. At a sale, some radio sets were sold for $50 each and the rest for $35 each. If 175 sets were sold and the receipts were $7250, how many $50 sets were sold?

14. Mr. Carter invested a sum of money at 4%. He invested a second sum, $400 more than the first sum, at 6%. If the total annual income was $184, how much did he invest at each rate?

15. In basketball a foul basket counts 1 point and a field basket counts 2 points. A team scored 73 points, making 8 more field baskets than foul baskets. How many foul baskets did they make?

16. A sofa was marked for sale at $270. This was a discount of 25% on the original sale price. What was the original sale price?

17. The sum of the ages of a father and son is 62. If the father is 11 years more than twice the age of the son, how old is the son?

18. A boy has $4.35 in nickels and dimes. If he has 12 more dimes than nickels, how many nickels does he have?

19. The perimeter of a rectangular field is 204 feet. If the length is 3 feet less than 4 times the width, what is the width of the field?

20. A grocer wishes to mix coffee selling for $.88 per pound with coffee selling for $.80 per pound to produce a mixture of 20 pounds that will sell for $.86 per pound. How many pounds of $.88 coffee should he use?

21. Two cars start at the same time to travel toward each other from points 440 miles apart. If the first car averages 42 miles per hour and the second car averages 46 miles per hour, in how many hours will they meet?

22. Two trains start at the same time and travel in opposite directions. The first train averages 32 miles per hour and the second train averages 34 miles per hour. In how many hours are they 462 miles apart?

23. Two trains are 800 miles apart. They start at 9:00 A.M. traveling toward each other. One train travels at an average rate of 45 miles per hour and the other train travels at the rate of 55 miles per hour. At what time do they meet?

24. Two motor boats start at the same time from the same place and travel in opposite directions. If their rates are 12 miles per hour and 16 miles per hour respectively, in how many hours are they 140 miles apart?

ANSWERS

1. $15,000	**9.** 15	**16.** $360
2. 25 inches	**10.** 16	**17.** 17
3. 71 cu. ft. of cement	**11.** $12,000 at 5%	**18.** 21
355 cu. ft. of gravel	$8,000 at 4%	**19.** 21 feet
4. 39 feet	**12.** 350	**20.** 15
5. $5.00	**13.** 75	**21.** 5 hours
6. 27	**14.** $1,600 at 4%	**22.** 7 hours
7. 29	$2,000 at 6%	**23.** 5:00 P.M.
8. 6 inches	**15.** 19	**24.** 5 hours

TIME TO STUDY:

Ratio and Proportion

We may compare two quantities by subtraction or by division. For example, Mr. Carson earns $24 per day and Mr. Burns earns $16 per day. We may say that Mr. Carson earns $8 more per day than Mr. Burns. Or, we may say that the ratio of Mr. Carson's earnings per day to Mr. Burns' earnings per day is $\frac{24}{16}$. We may reduce $\frac{24}{16}$ to $\frac{3}{2}$ which indicates that Mr. Carson earns $1\frac{1}{2}$ times as much per day as Mr. Burns.

The comparison of the two pay rates may be written as $\frac{24}{16}$ or as $24:16$. In general, the ratio of a number a to a number b (b cannot be zero) is $\frac{a}{b}$ or $a:b$.

> EXAMPLE: At a party there are 12 men and 8 women. What is the ratio of men to women?
> The ratio is $\frac{12}{8}$ or $12:8$. In simplest form, this is $\frac{3}{2}$ or $3:2$.
> What is the ratio of women to men?
> The ratio is $\frac{8}{12}$ or $8:12$. In simplest form, this is $\frac{2}{3}$ or $2:3$.
> What is the ratio of men to the number of people at the party?
> The ratio is $\frac{12}{20}$ or $12:20$. In simplest form, this is $\frac{3}{5}$ or $3:5$.

Consider the following problem.

A baseball team wins 15 games out of 30 games played. If the team continues to win at the same rate, how many games will it win out of 40 games played?

Let n = number of games it will win in 40 games played

The ratio of games won to games played is $\frac{15}{30}$. It is also $\frac{n}{40}$. These ratios may be written as $15:30$ and $n:40$.

Thus, $\frac{15}{30} = \frac{n}{40}$. Such a statement which tells us that one ratio is equal to another is called a *proportion*. Of course, in this case, we know that $n = 20$ since the team wins $\frac{1}{2}$ of the games it plays.

Proportions have a very useful property which we will investigate. Consider the proportion

$$\frac{1}{3} = \frac{2}{6}, \quad \text{or} \quad 1:3 = 2:6$$

The two inside terms, 3 and 2, are called the *means* of the proportion and the two outside terms, 1 and 6, are called the *extremes* of the proportion. Notice that if we multiply the two means we obtain $3 \times 2 = 6$. Also, if we multiply the two extremes we obtain $1 \times 6 = 6$. This illustrates the following property of proportions.

In a proportion, the product of the means is equal to the product of the extremes.

This property is very helpful in solving problems.

EXAMPLE: The ratio of alcohol to water in a certain type of antifreeze is 3:4. If a tank contains 24 quarts of alcohol, how many quarts of water must be added to make the antifreeze mixture?

Let x = the number of quarts needed

$$\frac{\text{alcohol}}{\text{water}} \frac{3}{4} = \frac{24}{x}$$

Now, we may use the property of proportions to find x.

$$3:4 = 24:x$$

$3x = 4 \times 24,$ $3x = 96,$ $x = 32$ quarts of water.

We may use the same property in the form

$$\frac{3}{4} \diagdown \frac{24}{x}$$

$3x = 4 \times 24,$ $3x = 96,$ $x = 32$ quarts of water

The following examples will indicate how we may use ratio and proportion.

EXAMPLE: If 3 ties cost $8.37 what is the cost of 5 ties at the same rate?

Let y = cost of 5 ties

We form the proportion

$$3:8.37 = 5:y$$
$$3y = 5 \times 8.37$$
$$3y = 41.85$$
$$y = \frac{41.85}{3} = 13.95$$

5 ties cost $13.95 at the same rate.

EXAMPLE: The scale on a map is 1 inch to 60 miles. If the distance between two cities is $2\frac{3}{4}$ inches, what is the actual distance between the cities?

Let d = the actual distance between the cities

$$1:60 = 2\tfrac{3}{4}:d$$
$$1 \times d = 60 \times 2\tfrac{3}{4}$$
$$d = 60 \times \tfrac{11}{4} = 165$$

The actual distance is 165 miles.

EXAMPLE: Two numbers are in the ratio 9:5. Their difference is 28. Find the numbers.

Let $9x$ = the larger number

And $5x$ = the smaller number

Then $9x - 5x = 28$
$$4x = 28$$
$$x = \tfrac{28}{4} = 7$$

The larger number is $9x$, or $9 \cdot 7 = 63$.
The smaller number is $5x$, or $5 \cdot 7 = 35$.

EXAMPLE: The numerator and denominator of a fraction are in the ratio $3:7$. If 2 is added to both numerator and denominator, the ratio becomes $1:2$. Find the original fraction.
Let $3n$ = numerator of the fraction
And $7n$ = denominator of the fraction
If we add 2 to both numerator and denominator, the numerator becomes $3n + 2$ and the denominator becomes $7n + 2$. Thus, we have

$$\frac{3n + 2}{7n + 2} = \frac{1}{2}$$
$$1(7n + 2) = 2(3n + 2)$$
$$7n + 2 = 6n + 4$$
$$7n + 2 - 2 = 6n + 4 - 2$$
$$7n = 6n + 2$$
$$7n - 6n = 6n - 6n + 2$$
$$n = 2$$

The original numerator was $3n$, or $3 \times 2 = 6$.
The original denominator was $7n$, or $7 \times 2 = 14$.
The original fraction was $\frac{6}{14}$.

TIME TO PRACTICE:

---

1. At a dance, the ratio of the number of boys to the number of girls is $4:3$. If there are 32 boys present, the number of girls present is
(1) 36 (2) 40 (3) 20 (4) 24 (5) 28

1. 1 2 3 4 5

2. John earned \$75 one week and spent \$60. The ratio of the amount John saved to the amount John spent is
(1) 1:5 (2) 1:4 (3) 4:1 (4) 4:5 (5) 5:4

2. 1 2 3 4 5

3. On a trip, a motorist drove x miles on a local road and y miles on a parkway. The ratio of the number of miles driven on parkway to the total number of miles driven was
(1) $\dfrac{y}{x}$ (2) $\dfrac{x}{y}$ (3) $\dfrac{y}{x+y}$ (4) $\dfrac{x}{x+y}$ (5) $\dfrac{x+y}{y}$

3. 1 2 3 4 5

4. A picture measures 2 inches by $1\frac{1}{2}$ inches. If the picture is enlarged so that the 2 inch dimension becomes $3\frac{1}{2}$ inches, the other dimension becomes
(1) $2\frac{5}{8}$ inches (2) $2\frac{1}{2}$ inches (3) $10\frac{1}{2}$ inches (4) $2\frac{1}{4}$ inches (5) $2\frac{3}{8}$ inches

4. 1 2 3 4 5

5. The ratio of a father's age to his son's age is $9:2$. If the son's age is 12 years, the age of the father, in years, is
(1) 45 (2) 36 (3) 63 (4) 50 (5) 54

5. 1 2 3 4 5

6. If 3 shirts cost \$14, the cost of a dozen shirts at the same rate is
   (1) \$42 (2) \$56 (3) \$35 (4) \$48.50 (5) \$60

6. 1 2 3 4 5

7. On a map, the scale is $1''$ to 80 miles. The actual distance between two cities is 200 miles. The distance between the cities, on the map, is
   (1) 2 inches (2) 3 inches (3) $3\frac{1}{2}$ inches (4) $2\frac{1}{2}$ inches (5) 4 inches

7. 1 2 3 4 5

8. A certain recipe that will yield 4 portions calls for $1\frac{1}{2}$ cups of sugar. If the recipe is used to yield 6 portions then the amount of sugar needed is
   (1) $2\frac{1}{2}$ cups (2) $2\frac{3}{4}$ cups (3) $2\frac{1}{4}$ cups (4) 2 cups (5) 3 cups

8. 1 2 3 4 5

9. It takes a train c hours to cover d miles. If the train travels k miles at the same rate, the number of hours it takes is
   (1) cdk (2) $\dfrac{ck}{d}$ (3) $\dfrac{d}{ck}$ (4) $\dfrac{dc}{k}$ (5) $\dfrac{dk}{c}$

9. 1 2 3 4 5

10. A gallon of paint covers 240 square feet of surface. If a living room contains 906 square feet of paintable surface and a kitchen contains 334 square feet of surface; the number of gallons of paint needed for the living room and kitchen is
    (1) 6 (2) $4\frac{1}{2}$ (3) $5\frac{1}{6}$ (4) $5\frac{1}{2}$ (5) $6\frac{1}{2}$

10. 1 2 3 4 5

11. A recipe for hot chocolate calls for 2 ounces of chocolate, 4 cups of milk, and 4 tablespoons of sugar. If only 3 cups of milk are available the number of ounces of chocolate to be used is
    (1) 3 (2) $\frac{2}{3}$ (3) $1\frac{1}{2}$ (4) 6 (5) $\frac{3}{4}$

11. 1 2 3 4 5

12. Mr. Ash finds that it costs him \$47.50 for each 1,000 miles that he drives his car. One month he drives his car 1,800 miles. His cost for the car that month is
    (1) \$855 (2) \$95.00 (3) \$82.50 (4) \$85.50 (5) \$8.55

12. 1 2 3 4 5

13. An artist finds that he obtains the most pleasing result when the ratio of the length of a picture to its width is 8:5. If the length of a picture is 2 feet 8 inches, then its width should be
    (1) 2 feet (2) 1 foot 8 inches (3) 2 feet 8 inches (4) 3 feet (5) 2 feet 5 inches

13. 1 2 3 4 5

14. A recipe for chocolate fudge calls for $\frac{3}{4}$ cup of corn syrup and $\frac{1}{2}$ teaspoon of salt. If 1 cup of corn syrup is used, the number of teaspoons of salt to be used is
    (1) $\frac{2}{3}$ (2) $1\frac{1}{3}$ (3) $\frac{3}{8}$ (4) $2\frac{2}{3}$ (5) $\frac{3}{4}$

14. 1 2 3 4 5

15. Mr. Donovan finds that his car covers 17 miles per gallon of gas on the open road. The number of gallons of gas he uses in driving x miles is
    (1) $17x$ (2) $\dfrac{17}{x}$ (3) $17 + x$ (4) $\dfrac{x}{17}$ (5) $x - 17$

15. 1 2 3 4 5

16. A man finds that he spends a total of y dollars per month for heating oil during 7 months of cold weather. If he wishes to prorate this cost over a 12-month period, the cost per month is
    (1) $\dfrac{12}{7y}$ (2) $\dfrac{y}{12}$ (3) $\dfrac{12y}{7}$ (4) $\dfrac{y+7}{12}$ (5) $84y$

16. 1 2 3 4 5

17. A 25-acre field yields 375 bushels of wheat. How many acres should be planted to yield 525 bushels of wheat?
(1) 33 (2) 32 (3) 45 (4) 35 (5) 75

17. 1 2 3 4 5

18. A house which is assessed at $15,000 is taxed $585. At the same rate the tax on a house which is assessed for $20,000 is
(1) $446.25 (2) $78 (3) $780 (4) $1170 (5) $680

18. 1 2 3 4 5

19. A family consumes q quarts of milk each week. The number of quarts this family consumes in 10 days is
(1) $\frac{7q}{10}$ (2) $\frac{10q}{7}$ (3) $\frac{70}{q}$ (4) $\frac{10}{7q}$ (5) $\frac{q}{70}$

19. 1 2 3 4 5

20. In making a certain type of concrete, the ratio of cement to sand used is 1:4. In making x barrels of this concrete, the number of barrels of cement used is
(1) $\frac{x}{5}$ (2) $\frac{x}{4}$ (3) x (4) $4x$ (5) $\frac{1}{5x}$

20. 1 2 3 4 5

ANSWERS

1. 4	6. 2	11. 3	16. 2
2. 2	7. 4	12. 4	17. 4
3. 3	8. 3	13. 2	18. 3
4. 1	9. 2	14. 1	19. 2
5. 5	10. 3	15. 4	20. 1

TIME TO STUDY:

Signed Numbers

On a very cold day it is announced on the radio that the temperature is 5 degrees below zero. In the weather report printed in the newspaper the temperature is listed as $-5°$. We often have occasion to talk about quantities that have opposite meanings. For example,

Profit of $5 = +5$, or 5	Loss of $5 = -5$
Gain of 3 pounds $= +3$, or 3	Loss of 3 pounds $= -3$
50 miles north $= +50$, or 50	50 miles south $= -50$

The numbers -5, -3, and -50 are called *negative numbers*. We will consider problems involving *signed numbers* or integers. The *negative* or *minus* sign must always appear. The *positive* or *plus* sign may be omitted.

In working with the number line we have paired points to the right of 0 with numbers. May we pair points to the left of 0 with numbers? Yes, we pair points to the left of 0 with negative numbers, as shown below.

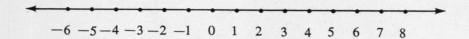

$$-6\ -5\ -4\ -3\ -2\ -1\ \ 0\ \ 1\ \ 2\ \ 3\ \ 4\ \ 5\ \ 6\ \ 7\ \ 8$$

The set {. . . , —5, —4, —3, —2, —1, 0, 1, 2, 3, 4, 5, . . .} is called the set of integers, or the set of signed numbers. Notice that the set of positive integers {1, 2, 3, 4, 5, . . . } is an infinite set. Also, the set of negative integers {. . . , —5, —4, —3, —2, —1} is an infinite set.

EXAMPLE: A woman who weighed 167 pounds went on a diet. The changes in her weight for five monthly periods were —3, +1, —5, +2, and —7. What was her weight at the end of the five-month period? She gained 1 pound and 2 pounds, or 3 pounds

She lost 3 pounds, 5 pounds, and 7 pounds, or 15 pounds
Her net loss was 12 pounds.
Her weight at the end of the five months was
$$167 - 12 = 155 \text{ pounds}$$

TIME TO PRACTICE:

1. Mr. Egan's bank balance was $1,247. It changed as follows over a four month period

$$-\$152, +\$384, -\$516, +\$217$$

His bank balance at the end of the four month period was
(1) $67   (2) $601   (3) $459   (4) $1180   (5) $1269

2. At 8 o'clock one morning the temperature was 12° above zero. The following changes took place during that day

| noon | +8° | 8 P.M. | —9° |
| 4 P.M. | +5° | 12 midnight | —7° |

The temperature at midnight was
(1) 15°   (2) —9°   (3) 9°   (4) 15°   (5) 0°

3. Mr. Dunn bought some stock in the *XYZ* Corporation at $41\frac{1}{8}$. During the next week it changed in market price as follows:

$$-\tfrac{3}{4}, +\tfrac{1}{2}, -\tfrac{3}{8}, -\tfrac{7}{8}, +1$$

The price at the end of the week was
(1) $40\frac{5}{8}$ (2) $39\frac{7}{8}$ (3) $41\frac{1}{2}$ (4) $41\frac{1}{4}$ (5) $41\frac{5}{8}$

4. In a football game, a team had the ball on its 30 yard line. Its gain or loss on a series of 3 plays is shown below.

$$+3, -7, +9$$

1. 1 2 3 4 5

2. 1 2 3 4 5

3. 1 2 3 4 5

4. 1 2 3 4 5

The position of the ball after this series of plays was
(1) 26 yard line   (2) 32 yard line   (3) 34 yard line   (4) 35 yard line   (5) 37 yard line

5. A plane reached an altitude of 6,742 feet. Its movement after that is given by the following signed numbers.

$$-1,050, +2,873, -469$$

The altitude of the plane after these changes was
(1) 5,388   (2) 5,692   (3) 8,096   (4) 8,261   (5) 9,034

5. 1 2 3 4 5
    || || || || ||

ANSWERS

1. 4   **2.** 3   **3.** 1   **4.** 4   **5.** 3

GEOMETRY

TIME TO STUDY:

Points, Lines and Space

By a point in geometry we mean a definite location in space. A point has no length, or width, or thickness. We usually name a point by a capital letter of the alphabet.

When we use the world "line" in geometry we always mean a straight line. Moreover, a line extends infinitely in either direction. For this reason arrows are usually shown on a line, as follows.

We can think of a line as a special set of points. A line is usually named by naming two points on the line with a double-arrowed symbol. For example, the line above may be named $\overleftrightarrow{AB}$.

We often have occasion to deal with a definite part of a line. Such a part of a line is called a *segment*. We can think of a segment as two points on a line together with the set of points between the two points. The two points are called the endpoints of the line. We usually name a segment by naming the endpoints and placing a bar above. For example, the segment below is called $\overline{CD}$.

C   D

By a ray in geometry we mean the set of points A and all the points on a straight line through A that are on one side of A. Point A is called the endpoint of the ray. We name a ray by naming its endpoint and another point on the ray with an arrow symbol. For example, the ray shown below is called $\overrightarrow{AE}$.

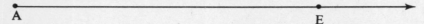

We can think of a plane in geometry as a set of points making up a perfectly flat surface. A plane is suggested by the floor of a room or the cover of a book.

By space in geometry we mean the set of all points.

Geometric Figures

Geometric figures may be classified in two groups, plane figures and solid figures. If all the points of a figure lie in the same plane it is called a plane figure. By a plane we mean a perfectly flat surface. If the points of a figure lie in more than one plane it is called a solid figure. Below we have diagrams of some important plane and solid figures.

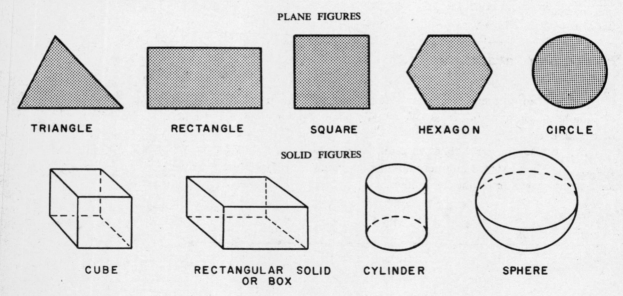

PLANE FIGURES

TRIANGLE   RECTANGLE   SQUARE   HEXAGON   CIRCLE

SOLID FIGURES

CUBE   RECTANGULAR SOLID   CYLINDER   SPHERE
                OR BOX

Geometric Concepts and Relationships

An angle is a set of points consisting of two rays having the same endpoint. For example, the rays $\overrightarrow{AB}$ and $\overrightarrow{AC}$ having the same endpoint, A, form the

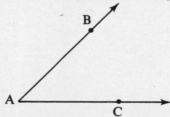

angle shown. We name an angle by naming a point on one ray, then the common endpoint, and finally a point on the other ray. The symbol for angle is $\angle$. The angle shown may be called $\angle BAC$, or $\angle CAB$.

An angle may be measured by using a protractor. As shown in the figure the measure of ∠AOB is 70°.

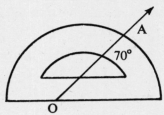

The following types of angles are important.

∠RST is an acute angle. An acute angle is an angle whose measure is less than 90°.

∠VWX is a right angle. A right angle is an angle whose measure is 90°.

∠OFG is an obtuse angle. An obtuse angle is an angle whose measure is greater than 90° and less than 180°.

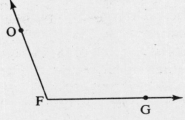

∠LOC is a straight angle. A straight angle is an angle whose measure is 180°.

When two lines meet to form right angles we say that the lines are perpendicular to each other. The symbol "⊥" is used to indicate perpendicular lines. In the diagram, $\overleftrightarrow{DE}$ is perpendicular to $\overleftrightarrow{BC}$ ($\overleftrightarrow{DE} \perp \overleftrightarrow{BC}$). The four right angles formed are ∠DAB, ∠DAC, ∠EAB, and ∠EAC.

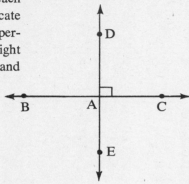

When two lines in the same plane do not meet, no matter how far they are extended in either direction the lines are said to be parallel to each other.

The symbol "||" is used to indicate parallel lines. Another way of saying that two lines are paralled is to say that their intersection is the empty set. In the diagram, $\overleftrightarrow{RS} \parallel \overleftrightarrow{PQ}$.

There are some important terms associated with the circle.

A *radius* of a circle is a line segment from the center of the circle to any point on the circle. $\overline{OA}$ is a radius.

A *diameter* of a circle is a line segment that passes through the center of the circle and has its two endpoints on the circle. $\overline{CD}$ is a diameter. The length of the diameter of a circle is twice the length of the radius of the circle.

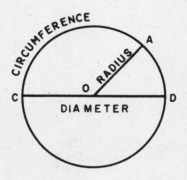

The *circumference* of a circle is the length of the curved line forming the circle. It is measured in units of length such as inches or feet.

If the number of units in the circumference of a circle is divided by the number of units in the diameter of the circle the result is π (pi). The numerical value of π is approximately equal to 3.14, or $\frac{22}{7}$. The formula for the circumference of a circle is $C = 2 \times \pi \times r$, or $C = 2\pi r$ where r is the radius of the circle.

EXAMPLE: The diameter of a circle is 12 inches. Find the circumference of the circle. (Use $\pi = 3.14$.)

Since the diameter is 12 inches, the radius is 6 inches.

$$C = 2\pi r$$
$$C = 2 \times 3.14 \times 6 = 37.68 \text{ inches}$$

TIME TO PRACTICE:

---

1. In the figure, $\overleftrightarrow{EB} \perp \overleftrightarrow{AC}$. A right angle is
   (1) $\angle FBA$ (2) $\angle DBF$ (3) $\angle CBE$ (4) $\angle EBD$ (5) $\angle ABC$

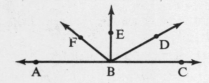

   1. 1 2 3 4 5
       || || ||| || ||

2. An obtuse angle is
   (1) $\angle EBA$ (2) $\angle DBE$ (3) $\angle CBA$ (4) $\angle FBC$ (5) $\angle EBC$

   2. 1 2 3 4 5
       || || || ||| ||

3. The diameter of a circle is 30 inches. The radius of the circle is
   (1) 60 inches (2) 60π inches (3) 15 inches (4) 15π inches (5) $7\frac{1}{2}$ inches

   3. 1 2 3 4 5
       || || ||| || ||

4. The diameter of a circle is 20 inches. If $\pi = 3.14$, then the circumference of the circle is
   (1) 3.14 (2) 62.8 (3) 314 (4) 6.28 (5) 31.4

   4. 1 2 3 4 5
       || ||| || || ||

5. The distance around a circular garden bed is 22 feet. If $\pi = \frac{22}{7}$, the radius of the garden bed is
   (1) 7 feet (2) 14 feet (3) 11 feet (4) 22 feet (5) $3\frac{1}{2}$ feet

   5. 1 2 3 4 5
       || || || |||

ANSWERS

1. 3   **2.** 4   **3.** 3   **4.** 2   **5.** 5

TIME TO STUDY:

One of the basic figures in the study of geometry is the triangle. Because it is a rigid figure, that is, a figure that is firm, it is used for braces and supports. There are three kinds of triangles which are important because they occur frequently.

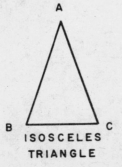

ISOSCELES TRIANGLE

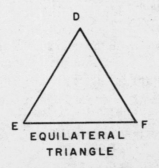

EQUILATERAL TRIANGLE

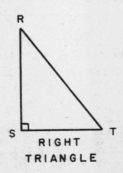

RIGHT TRIANGLE

An *isosceles triangle* is a triangle which has two sides of equal length. △*ABC* is isosceles.

An *equilateral triangle* is a triangle which has three sides of equal length. △*DEF* is equilateral.

A *right triangle* is a triangle which has one right angle. The longest side is called the *hypotenuse*.

The following facts about triangles are useful.

The sum of the measures of the angles of a triangle is 180°.

In an isosceles triangle, the angles opposite the equal sides have equal measures. Or, base angles of an isosceles triangle have equal measures.

In an equilateral triangle, the angles have equal measures and the measure of each angle is 60°

EXAMPLE: Each base angle of an isosceles triangle contains *x*°. How many degrees does the third angle of the triangle contain?

The sum of the two base angles is 2*x*°. Since the sum of all three angles is 180°, we may obtain the value of the third angle by subtracting 2*x* from 180. The third angle contains (180 − 2*x*).

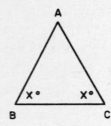

TIME TO PRACTICE:

---

1. If two angles of a triangle measure 65° and 79°, the third angle of the triangle contains
    (1) 56° (2) 144° (3) 115° (4) 36° (5) 101°

    1. 1 2 3 4 5

2. One acute angle of a right triangle contains *n*°. The other acute angle contains
    (1) 2*n*° (2) (90° − *n*)° (3) 90° (4) (90° + *n*)° (5) (180° − *n*)°

    2. 1 2 3 4 5

3. One angle of an isosceles triangle contains 102°. Each of the other angles contains
    (1) 78° (2) 34° (3) 39° (4) 49° (5) 35°

    3. 1 2 3 4 5

4. The measures of two acute angles of a right triangle are in the ratio 2:3. The smallest angle of the triangle contains
    (1) 36° (2) 54° (3) 30° (4) 70° (5) 24°

    4. 1 2 3 4 5

5. The measures of the angles of a triangle are in the ratio 1:2:3. The largest angle of the triangle contains
    (1) 60° (2) 90° (3) 120° (4) 100° (5) 80°

    5. 1 2 3 4 5

ANSWERS

1. 4   2. 2   3. 3   4. 1   5. 2

TIME TO STUDY:

Indirect Measurement

If we wish to measure a length we ordinarily use a ruler. However, this would not be practical if we wish to find the height of a mountain or the distance across a river. Such measurements are made indirectly. In this section, we will learn some of the methods of indirect measurement.

Consider the following problem:

A boy scout troop hikes 8 miles east and then 6 miles north. How many miles is the troop from its starting point?

If we look at the diagram we see that the triangle formed is a right triangle. We will make use of a well-known property of right triangles called the Pythagorean Theorem.

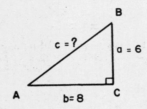

PYTHAGOREAN THEOREM—In a right triangle, the square of the hypotenuse is equal to the sum of the squares of the other two sides.

Thus, in the diagram shown,

$$c^2 = a^2 + b^2$$
$$c^2 = (6)^2 + (8)^2$$
$$c^2 = 36 + 64$$
$$c^2 = 100$$

The equation $c^2 = 100$ asks the question, "What number multiplied by itself is equal to 100?" The number that makes this statement true is $c = 10$. Thus, the boy scout troop is 10 miles from the starting point.

In the same example, suppose that the scout troop had hiked 7 miles east and then 5 miles north. How many miles would the troop be from the starting point?

According to the Pythagorean Theorem,

$$c^2 = a^2 + b^2$$
$$c^2 = (7)^2 + (5)^2$$
$$c^2 = 49 + 25$$
$$c^2 = 74$$

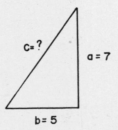

We must now find the number which, when multiplied by itself, is equal to 74. We write this number as $\sqrt{74}$ and we can estimate that the required number is between 8 and 9 since

$$8^2 = 64 \quad \text{and} \quad 9^2 = 81.$$

$\sqrt{74}$ is an *irrational number*. That is, it cannot be written exactly in fraction or in decimal form but we can find its value correct to the nearest tenth, the nearest hundredth, etc.

$\sqrt{74} = 8.6$ correct to the nearest tenth. Note that $(8.6)^2 = 73.96$.

The following is a method for finding the square root of a number. It is sometimes called "the divide and average method."

FINDING THE SQUARE ROOT OF A NUMBER

EXAMPLE 1: Find $\sqrt{196}$

We first estimate the answer. Suppose we estimate that the answer is 12. We divide 12 into 196

$$
\begin{array}{r}
16 \text{ quotient} \\
12\overline{)196} \\
\underline{12} \\
76 \\
\underline{72}
\end{array}
$$

If 12 had been our answer we would have obtained a quotient of 12. Since we did not, we get the average of the divisor (12) and the quotient (16).

$$\text{Average} = \frac{12 + 16}{2} = \frac{28}{2} = 14$$

Next, we use 14 as the divisor

$$
\begin{array}{r}
14 \\
14\overline{)196} \\
\underline{14} \\
56 \\
\underline{56}
\end{array}
$$

Thus, $\sqrt{196} = 14$

EXAMPLE 2: Find $\sqrt{74}$ to the nearest tenth

Our first estimate is 8.2 since we wish to find the result to the nearest tenth. Next, we divide

$$
\begin{array}{r}
9. \\
8.2\overline{)74.0} \\
\underline{738} \\
2
\end{array}
$$

Our quotient is 9 and we average

$$\frac{8.2 + 9}{2} = \frac{17.2}{2} = 8.6$$

$$
\begin{array}{r}
8.6 \\
8.6\overline{)74.0} \\
\underline{68\ 8} \\
5\ 20 \\
\underline{5\ 16} \\
4
\end{array}
$$

Since the divisor and the quotient are identical we have our result correct to the nearest tenth.

Irrational numbers are clearly different from rational numbers. Rational numbers may be expressed in fractional form with the numerator an integer and the denominator an integer other than 0. Irrational numbers cannot be expressed in this way. However, irrational numbers may be paired with points

on the number line. For example,

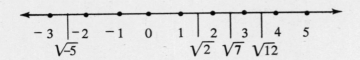

The set of rational numbers together with the set of irrational numbers is called the set of *real numbers*. We can think of a real number as a number which can be paired with a point on the number line.

TIME TO PRACTICE:

1. Find the square roots of each of the following:

   a. 169   c. 289   e. 841
   b. 225   d. 1156   f. 1369

2. Find the square roots of each of the following correct to the nearest tenth:

   a. 59   c. 42   e. 112
   b. 30   d. 85   f. 97

3. A ladder leans against a building and just reaches the ledge of a window 20 feet above the ground. If the foot of the ladder is 15 feet from the foot of the building, what is the length of the ladder?

4. A wire stretches from the top of a pole 15 feet high to a stake in the ground which is 8 feet from the pole. Find the length of the wire.

5. A plot of ground is 48 feet long and 20 feet wide. A path extends diagonally across the plot of ground. What is the length of this path?

6. What is the length of the ramp in the figure at the right?

7. A baseball infield is a square, 90 feet on each side. Find, correct to the nearest tenth of a foot, the distance from home plate to second base.

8. Find, correct to the nearest foot, the diameter of a round table which can be taken through a doorway which measures 5 feet in width and 8 feet in height.

ANSWERS

1.		2.		3.	25 feet
a.	13	a.	7.7	4.	17 feet
b.	15	b.	5.5	5.	52 feet
c.	17	c.	6.5	6.	34 feet
d.	34	d.	9.2	7.	127.3 feet
e.	29	e.	10.6	8.	9 feet
f.	37	f.	9.8		

TIME TO STUDY:

Congruence and Similarity

Two geometric figures are said to be *congruent* if they have exactly the same size and shape. The symbol for congruence is ≅. The two triangles shown in the diagram are congruent. That is, $\triangle ABC \cong \triangle DEF$. Since congruent triangles can be made to fit if one is

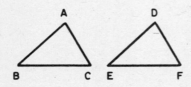

placed on top of the other, corresponding sides have the same length. For example, in the figure, $AB = DE$, $AC = DF$, and $BC = EF$. Congruent triangles can be used to make measurements indirectly.

> **EXAMPLE:** We find the distance (DE) across the river shown in the diagram as follows.

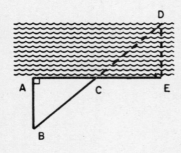

> At point E sight a point D on the other bank of the river. Measure EA at right angles to ED. At C the midpoint of EA set a stake. Then mark off distance AB so that $\angle A$ is a right angle and point B lines up with points

C and D. It can be shown that $\triangle ABC \cong \triangle DEC$ and that AB and DE are corresponding sides. Thus, distance AB, which can be measured, is equal to DE, the distance across the river.

Two geometric figures are said to be *similar* if they have the same shape. Because similar figures have the same shape their corresponding angles are equal and their corresponding sides are in proportion. The symbol for similarity is ∼. The two triangles shown in the

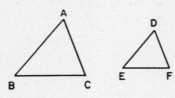

diagram are similar. That is, $\triangle ABC \sim \triangle DEF$. Since corresponding sides of similar triangles are in proportion, we have

$$\frac{AB}{DE} = \frac{AC}{DF} = \frac{BC}{EF}$$

Similar triangles can be used to make measurements indirectly.

> **EXAMPLE:** At a certain hour, a tree casts a shadow 24 feet long. At the same time, a post 5 feet high casts a shadow 2 feet long. What is the height of the tree?
>
> Since the triangles are similar, their corresponding sides are in proportion. That is,

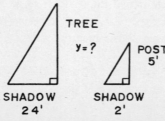

$$\frac{y}{5} = \frac{24}{2}$$
$$2y = 120$$
$$y = 60$$

The tree is 60 feet high.

TIME TO PRACTICE:
---

1. An example of congruent figures is
   (1) a right triangle and an equilateral triangle   (2) a room and a blue-print of the room   (3) two of your shirts   (4) a ship and a model of the ship   (5) a man and his photograph

2. An example of similar figures is
   (1) a square and a triangle   (2) a picture and an enlargement of the same picture   (3) a man and his dog   (4) a house and a garage   (5) a tennis ball and a tennis racket

3. If $\triangle ABC \cong \triangle DEF$, then $x =$
   (1) 7   (2) 8   (3) 15   (4) 9   (5) 17

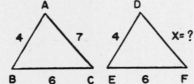

4. If $\triangle KLP \sim \triangle RST$, then $y =$
   (1) 5   (2) 7   (3) 8   (4) 12   (5) 3

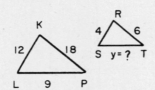

5. A tower casts a shadow of 48 feet. At the same time a pole 6 feet high casts a shadow of 4 feet. The height of the tower, in feet, is
   (1) 32   (2) 96   (3) 100   (4) 72   (5) 84

ANSWERS

1. 3   2. 2   3. 1   4. 5   5. 4

TIME TO STUDY:

Areas

We have seen that the perimeter of a geometric figure is a measure of its outside boundary. For example, the perimeter of the rectangle at the right is $3 + 8 + 3 + 8$, or 22 feet. In the case of a circle, the perimeter is called the circumference and is measured by using the formula $C = 2\pi r$.

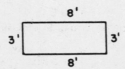

If we wish to find the amount of carpeting needed to cover a floor, we have a problem of finding the surface *area* of the floor. In finding a length we use units such as 1 inch, 1 foot, 1 yard, or 1 mile. In finding the area of a floor, our unit of measure is 1 square foot, or 1 square yard. Below are diagrams of 1 square foot and 1 square yard

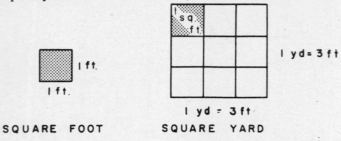

SQUARE FOOT   SQUARE YARD

If we wish to find the number of square feet in a floor we must find the number of square feet units that will fit on the floor. Similarly, if we wish to find the number of square yards in the floor, we must find the number of square yard units that will fit on the floor. Let us see how this works in the following example:

EXAMPLE: A wooden board measures 6 feet by 9 feet. What is the area of the board (a) in square feet (b) in square yards?

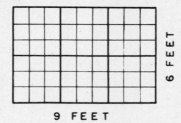

(a) Since there are 9 feet along the length and 6 feet along the width, the area of the board is 54 square feet.

(b) Since there are 3 yards along the length and 2 yards along the width, the area of the board is 6 square yards.

You can see that there are 9 square feet in 1 square yard.

We will be concerned with the areas of the following figures:

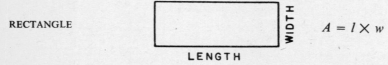

RECTANGLE $A = l \times w$

The area of a rectangle is found by multiplying the number of units in the length by the number of units in the width.

TRIANGLE $A = 1/2\ bh$

The area of a triangle is equal to one-half the product of its base and altitude.

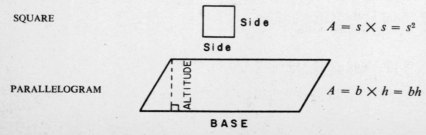

SQUARE $A = s \times s = s^2$

PARALLELOGRAM $A = b \times h = bh$

A parallelogram is a quadrilateral (4 sided figure) whose opposite sides are parallel.

The area of a parallelogram is equal to the product of its base and altitude. The altitude is a line drawn from a vertex perpendicular to the opposite side (called the base)

TRAPEZOID

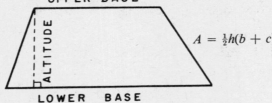

$A = \frac{1}{2}h(b + c)$

A trapezoid is a quadrilateral having two and only two sides parallel.

The area of a trapezoid is equal to one-half the altitude multiplied by the sum of the bases.

EXAMPLE: Find the area of a trapezoid whose altitude is 8 inches and whose bases are 12 inches and 7 inches.

$$A = \frac{1}{2}h(b + c)$$

In this case, $h = 8$, $b = 12$, and $c = 7$

$$A = \frac{1}{2} \cdot 8(12 + 7)$$
$$A = 4(19) = 76 \text{ square inches.}$$

CIRCLE

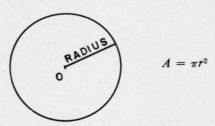

$A = \pi r^2$

The area of a circle is equal to the product of π and the square of the radius

EXAMPLE: Find the area of a circle whose radius is 14 inches.

$$A = \pi r^2$$
$$A = \pi \times 14 \times 14 = 196\pi$$

If we wish to obtain a more useful answer, we must take an approximate numerical value for π. The approximate values of π usually used are $\frac{22}{7}$ and 3.14.

If $\pi = \frac{22}{7}$, we have

$$\text{Area} = 196 \times \frac{22}{7} = \overset{28}{\cancel{196}} \times \frac{22}{\cancel{7}} = 616 \text{ square inches}$$

If $\pi = 3.14$, we have

$$\text{Area} = 196 \times 3.14 = 615.44 \text{ square inches}$$

The answers differ slightly because the approximations for π are slightly different.

TIME TO PRACTICE:

1. The perimeter of a square is 24 inches. The area of the square is
    (1) 576 sq. in.   (2) 16 sq. in.   (3) 64 sq. in.   (4) 36 sq. in.   (5) 100 sq. in.

    1.   1   2   3   4   5
        || || || || ||

2. A metal sheet is in the form of a trapezoid whose bases are 20″ and 15″ and whose altitude is 8″. The area of the sheet is
    (1) 420 sq. in.   (2) 270 sq. in.   (3) 140 sq. in.   (4) 110 sq. in.   (5) 47 sq. in.

    2.   1   2   3   4   5
        || || || || ||

3. A rectangle and a square have equal areas. The length of the rectangle is 20 inches and its width is 5 inches. A side of the square is
    (1) 100 inches   (2) 10 inches   (3) 20 inches   (4) 40 inches   (5) 12 inches

    3.   1   2   3   4   5
        || || || || ||

4. A circular mirror has a diameter of 14 inches. The area of the mirror is [use $\pi = \frac{22}{7}$]
    (1) 154 sq. in.   (2) 144 sq. in.   (3) 616 sq. in.   (4) 308 sq. in.   (5) 88 sq. in.

    4.   1   2   3   4   5
        || || || || ||

5. A machine part is cut according to the diagram. The area of the machine part is [use $\pi = \frac{22}{7}$]
    (1) 231 sq. in.   (2) 432 sq. in.   (3) 576 sq. in.   (4) 462 sq. in.   (5) 154 sq. in.

    5.   1   2   3   4   5
        || || || || ||

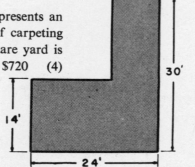

6. The diagram at the right represents an L-shaped room. The cost of carpeting this room at $10.50 per square yard is
    (1) $5,040   (2) $864   (3) $720   (4) $650   (5) $560

    6.   1   2   3   4   5
        || || || || ||

7. The diagram at the right is a cross-section of a pipe. If the radius of the outer circle is 10 inches and the radius of the inner circle is 6 inches, the area of the cross-section is [use $\pi = 3.14$]
    (1) 314 sq. in.   (2) 200.96 sq. in.   (3) 110.04 sq. in.   (4) 157 sq. in.   (5) 220.08 sq. in.

    7.   1   2   3   4   5
        || || || || ||

8. Mr. Ross has a lawn 40 feet long and 32 feet wide. He builds a cement walk around the lawn 4 feet in width. The area of the cement walk is
    (1) 1920 sq. ft.   (2) 16 sq. ft.   (3) 1124 sq. ft.   (4) 640 sq. ft.   (5) 500 sq. ft.

    8.   1   2   3   4   5
        || || || || ||

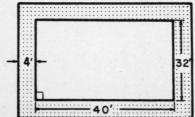

9. A wheel is 7 feet in diameter. The number of revolutions the wheel makes in covering a mile is [use $\pi = \frac{22}{7}$]
(1) 2400   (2) 240   (3) 480   (4) 570   (5) 720

10. The area of the figure at the right, in square inches, is
(1) 96   (2) 48   (3) 72   (4) 66   (5) 90

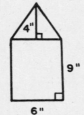

11. A square is 8 inches on a side. If its length is increased by 4 inches and its width decreased by 3 inches, then the area of the square is decreased by
(1) 7 sq. in.   (2) 1 sq. in.   (3) 9 sq. in.   (4) 4 sq. in.   (5) 5 sq. in.

12. The design on the right is a square with quarter-circles drawn at each vertex. The area of the shaded portion, in square inches, is
(1) $36 - 6\pi$ (2) $36 - 9\pi$ (3) $36 - 4\pi$ (4) $36 + 9\pi$
(5) $36 + 4\pi$

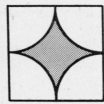

ANSWERS

1. 4	**4.** 1	**7.** 2	**10.** 4
2. 3	**5.** 4	**8.** 4	**11.** 4
3. 2	**6.** 5	**9.** 2	**12.** 2

TIME TO STUDY:

Volumes

If we wish to find the amount of material that can be fitted into the box shown at the right we have a problem in finding the *volume* of the box. In finding a length we use units such as 1 inch, 1 foot, etc. In finding an area we use units such as 1 square inch, 1 square foot, etc. In finding volume we use units such as cubic inches, cubic feet, etc. Below is a sketch of a cubic inch. It is a cube whose length, width, and height are each 1 inch. Thus, if we wish to find the number of cubic

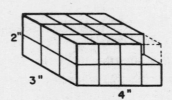

inches in the box shown we must find the number of cubes that can be fitted into the box. In this case, we can fit 4 cubes along the length and 3 cubes along

the width. We can therefore fit 12 cubes in one layer. Since we can place 2 layers in the box, the volume of the box is $2 \times 12 = 24$ cubic inches. In general, the volume of a box (called a rectangular solid) is obtained by multiplying the number of units in the length by the number of units in the width by the number of units in the height. The formula for the volume of a rectangular solid is

$$V = l \times w \times h, \quad \text{or} \quad V = lwh$$

If we wish to find the volume of a cube, we note that, in a cube, the length, width, and height are equal. If we let each dimension of a cube be represented by s, we have for the volume of a cube

$$V = s \times s \times s, \quad \text{or} \quad V = s^3$$

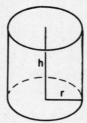

An important solid figure which we find in constant use is the *cylinder*. In a cylinder, the upper and lower bases are circles. The volume of a cylinder is obtained by multiplying the area of the base by the altitude. Thus, the formula for the volume of a cylinder is

$$V = \pi r^2 \times h, \quad \text{or} \quad V = \pi r^2 h$$

EXAMPLE: A coal bin is in the form of a rectangular solid. The bin is 14 feet long, 10 feet wide, and 6 feet high. If the bin is two-thirds full, how many tons of coal are there in the bin? One tone of coal occupies 35 cubic feet of space.

Volume of bin $= lwh = 14 \times 10 \times 6 = 840$ cubic feet

Since the bin is two-thirds full, the number of cubic feet in the bin is $\frac{2}{3} \times 840 = 560$ cubic feet.

To find the number of tons in the bin we divide 560 by 35.

$$\begin{array}{r} 16 \\ 35\overline{)560} \\ 35 \\ \hline 210 \\ 210 \\ \hline \end{array}$$

The bin contains 16 tons of coal

EXAMPLE: A storage oil tank in the form of a cylinder is three-fourths full. The radius of the base of the tank is 14 feet and the height of the tank is 12 feet. Find the number of gallons of oil in the tank if each cubic foot of space holds $7\frac{1}{2}$ gallons of oil [Use $\pi = \frac{22}{7}$]

Volume of cylinder $= \pi r^2 h$
$$= \tfrac{22}{7} \times 14 \times 14 \times 12$$
$$= 7392 \text{ cubic feet}$$

Since the tank is three-fourths full, we have

$$\tfrac{3}{4} \times 7392 = 5544 \text{ cubic feet of oil}$$

To find the number of gallons of oil we multiply 5544 by 7.5.
The tank contains 41,580 gallons of oil.

TIME TO PRACTICE:

1. A water tank in the form of a rectangular solid is 8 feet long, 6 feet wide, and 9 feet high. If 1 cubic foot contains $7\frac{1}{2}$ gallons, the number of gallons of water that the tank holds when it is two-thirds full is
    (1) $38\frac{2}{5}$ (2) 2,060 (3) 412 (4) 2,160 (5) 824

1. 1 2 3 4 5
    || || || || ||

2. The foundation of a house is in the form of a rectangular solid. The length of the foundation is 20 feet, the width is 18 feet, and the height is 6 feet. The number of loads of soil to be carted away from the foundation, if each load contains 60 cubic feet, is
    (1) 57,600   (2) 36   (3) 27   (4) 30   (5) 48

2. 1 2 3 4 5
    || || || || ||

3. An aquarium is in the form of a cube. Each side of the cube is 21 inches. If 1 gallon of water is contained in 231 cubic inches, the number of gallons of water in the aquarium when full, is
    (1) $4\frac{1}{11}$ (2) $400\frac{1}{11}$ (3) $40\frac{1}{11}$ (4) 42   (5) 75

3. 1 2 3 4 5
    || || || || ||

4. A food can in the form of a cylinder has a base radius of 5 inches and a height of 7 inches. The number of cubic inches in the can is [use $\pi = \frac{22}{7}$]
    (1) 550   (2) 280   (3) 2,200   (4) 320   (5) 575

4. 1 2 3 4 5
    || || || || ||

5. A large cylindrical tank is used for storing water. The radius of the base of the tank is 14 feet and the height of the tank is 20 feet. If 1 cubic foot holds 7.5 gallons of water, the number of gallons of water in the tank when it is $\frac{7}{8}$ full is
    (1) 1,403   (2) 8,570   (3) 8,850   (4) 4,420   (5) 80,850

5. 1 2 3 4 5
    || || || || ||

ANSWERS

1. 4   2. 2   3. 3   4. 1   5. 5

TIME TO STUDY:

Areas of Solids

We are sometimes interested in the area of a solid figure. For example, a room is in the form of a rectangular solid. If we wish to paint the room, we would be interested in the area of the walls and ceiling. Also, the label on a can covers only the area on the side of the can.

We can see that the area of the rectangular solid in the diagram is obtained by adding *lw* (bottom) + *lw* (top) + *wh* (side) + *wh* (side) + *lh* (front) + *lh* (back). As a formula, we have

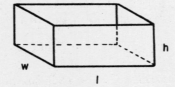

$$A = 2lw + 2wh + 2lh$$

The formula for the side area of a cylinder, called the *lateral area*, is

$$A = 2\pi rh$$

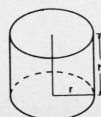

EXAMPLE: Find the number of square feet of cardboard used in making a carton 4 feet long, 3 feet wide, and 2 feet high.

We use the formula

$$A = 2lw + 2wh + 2lh$$

In this case, $l = 4$, $w = 3$, and $h = 2$.

$$A = 2 \times 4 \times 3 + 2 \times 3 \times 2 + 2 \times 4 \times 2$$

$$A = 24 + 12 + 16 = 52$$

52 square feet of cardboard are used.

EXAMPLE: A can has a radius of $3\frac{1}{2}$ inches and is 5 inches high. What is the area of the label used on the can? [Use $\pi = \frac{22}{7}$]

Lateral Area of cylinder $= 2\pi rh$

$$= 2 \cdot \frac{22}{7} \times \frac{7}{2} \times 5$$

$$= 110$$

110 square inches of paper are used on the label.

TIME TO PRACTICE:

---

1. A room is 20 feet long, 12 feet wide, and 8 feet high. The number of square feet of wallpaper needed to paper the walls of this room is

   HINT: We do not include the floor and ceiling. Thus, the formula we use is $A = 2wh + 2lh$

   (1) 992   (2) 800   (3) 1824   (4) 512   (5) 1,920

   1. 1 2 3 4 5
       || || || || ||

2. A safe in the form of a rectangular solid is made of steel. The safe measures 30 inches in length, 18 inches in width, and 16 inches in height. The number of square inches of steel used to make the safe is

   (1) 8,640   (2) 17,280   (3) 2,616   (4) 1,308   (5) 3,192

   2. 1 2 3 4 5
       || || || || ||

3. A room is 24 feet long, 15 feet wide, and 9 feet high. If the walls and ceiling are to be painted, the number of square feet to be covered is

   (1) 1,062   (2) 1,402   (3) 3,240   (4) 1,186   (5) 1,132

   3. 1 2 3 4 5
       || || || || ||

4. A cylindrical stove-pipe has a radius of 7 inches and is 48 inches long. Its area is [use $\pi = \frac{22}{7}$]

   (1) 2,002 sq. in.   (2) 1,056 sq. in.   (3) 956 sq. in.   (4) 2,112 sq. in.   (5) 1,006 sq. in.

   4. 1 2 3 4 5
       || || || || ||

5. An open cylindrical pail has a metal base and plastic sides. The radius of the pail is 14 inches and its height is 40 inches. The number of square inches of plastic used in making the pail is [use $\pi = \frac{22}{7}$]

   (1) 1,760   (2) 3,520   (3) 7,040   (4) 6,160   (5) 3,420

   5. 1 2 3 4 5
       || || || || ||

ANSWERS

1. 4   2. 3   3. 1   4. 4   5. 2

GRAPHS

Pictures or graphs are often used in reports, magazines, and newspapers to present a set of numerical facts. This enables the viewer to make comparisons and to draw quick conclusions. In this section, we will learn how to interpret pictographs, bar graphs, line graphs, and circle graphs.

TIME TO STUDY:

Pictographs

A pictograph is a graph in which objects are used to represent numbers

EXAMPLE:

POPULATION OF VARIOUS CITIES IN A CERTAIN STATE

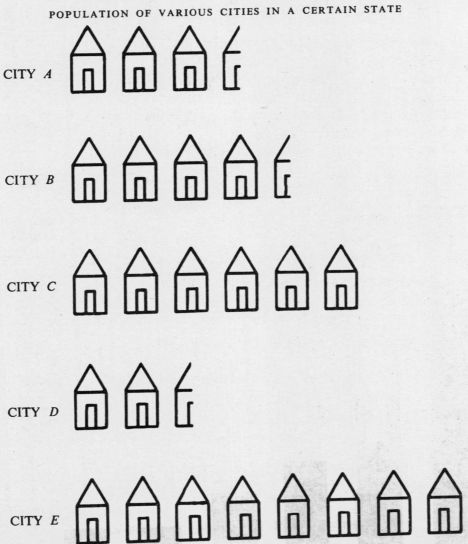

EACH HOUSE SYMBOL REPRESENTS 10,000 PEOPLE

b. Approximately how many times as many motor vehicles were registered in 1955 as in 1925?

ANSWER—Registered in 1955—250,000
Registered in 1925—50,000

There were 5 times as many motor vehicles registered in 1955 as in 1925.

c. What per cent of increase in registration took place between 1935 and 1965?

ANSWER—Registered in 1935—50,000
Registered in 1965—300,000
Increase in registration—250,000

$$Per\ cent\ of\ increase = \frac{Increase}{Original} = \frac{250,000}{50,000} = \frac{5}{1}, \quad or \quad 500\%$$

d. Between what two periods shown was the increase the greatest?

ANSWER—Between 1945 and 1950. This is shown on the graph by the sharpest rise in the line.

e. Between what two periods shown was there no increase?

ANSWER—Between 1940 and 1945. This is shown by the flat line between 1940 and 1945.

Circle Graphs

A circle graph is used when a quantity is divided into parts and we wish to make a comparison of the parts. Recall that a complete revolution is divided into 360°. Thus, if we wish to mark off one-quarter of the circle, the angle at the center must be $\frac{1}{4} \times 360°$, or 90°. For the same reason, a part of the circle with an angle at the center of 60° will be $\frac{60}{360}$, or $\frac{1}{6}$ of the circle.

EXAMPLE: The circle graph below shows how the wage earners in a certain city earned their living in a certain year.

WHAT WAGE EARNERS DID

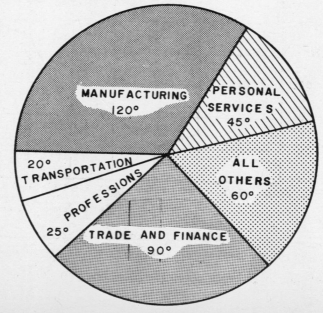

a. What fractional part of the labor force works in professions?

ANSWER—$\frac{25}{360} = \frac{5}{72}$

b. What fractional part of the labor force works in personal services?

ANSWER—$\frac{45}{360} = \frac{1}{8}$

c. If there were 180,000 workers in the city, how many are engaged in manufacturing?

ANSWER—The fractional part of the workers engaged in manufacturing was $\frac{120}{360} = \frac{1}{3}$.

$\frac{1}{3}$ of 180,000 = 60,000 workers in manufacturing

d. What is the ratio of the number of workers in transportation to the number of workers in personal services?

ANSWER—The ratio is 20:45, or more simply 4:9.

e. What per cent of the workers are in trade and finance?

ANSWER—The fractional part of the total number of workers in trade and finance is $\frac{90}{360} = \frac{1}{4}$. The fraction $\frac{1}{4}$ written as a per cent is 25%.

Formula Graphs

In working with a formula we may have occasion to obtain a number of bits of information. Instead of using the formula each time it may be easier to work from a graph of the formula.

In most parts of Europe and in all scientific work the scale used to measure temperature is the Centigrade scale. In the United States, the Fahrenheit scale is used. We sometimes find it necessary to convert from one scale to the other. The graph below shows how the scales are related.

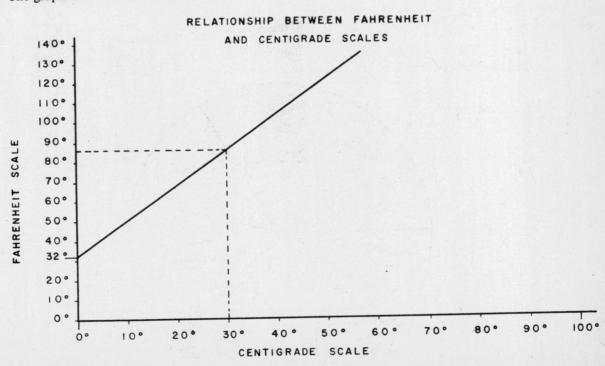

RELATIONSHIP BETWEEN FAHRENHEIT AND CENTIGRADE SCALES

a. A weather report in Paris indicated that the temperature was 30° Centigrade. What was the corresponding Fahrenheit temperature?

ANSWER—Locate 30° on the Centigrade scale (the horizontal scale). At this point draw a line so that it is perpendicular to the Centigrade scale line (as shown in the diagram). You can read the corresponding Fahrenheit temperature by drawing a line perpendicular to the Fahrenheit scale line from the point where the first line cuts the graph. The answer is 86°.

b. What Centigrade reading corresponds to a Fahrenheit reading of 77°?

ANSWER— 25°

c. During one day the temperature rose from 41° to 68° Fahrenheit. What was the corresponding rise in the temperature on the Centigrade scale?

ANSWER—The Centigrade temperature rose from 5° to 20°.

TIME TO PRACTICE:

The bar graph below shows the average monthly rainfall, in inches, for the first six months of a year in a certain city.

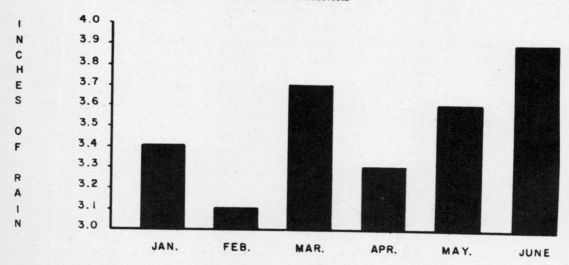

AVERAGE MONTHLY RAINFALL FOR 6 MONTHS

1. The month with the greatest rainfall was
   (1) February   (2) March   (3) May   (4) June   (5) January

   1. 1 2 3 4 5

2. The total rainfall for the six months was
   (1) 20 inches   (2) 19 inches   (3) 19.6 inches   (4) 21 inches   (5) 18.5 inches

   2. 1 2 3 4 5

3. The average monthly rainfall for the 6 month period was
   (1) 3 inches   (2) $3\frac{1}{2}$ inches   (3) $3\frac{1}{6}$ inches   (4) $3\frac{5}{6}$ inches   (5) $3\frac{1}{3}$ inches

   3. 1 2 3 4 5

The graph below shows the record of profits of the Beacon Co. for a period of 8 years.

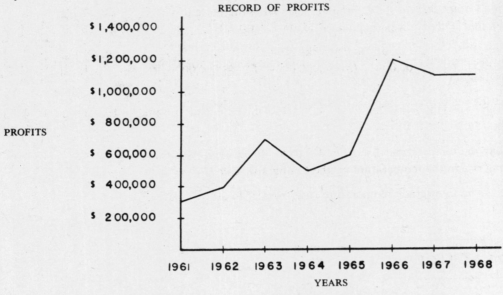

RECORD OF PROFITS

PROFITS

YEARS

4. The profits of the Beacon Co. rose most sharply between the years
(1) 1962–1963   (2) 1965–1966   (3) 1966–1967   (4) 1963–1964   (5) 1961–1962

4. 1 2 3 4 5

5. The year when the profits of the Beacon Co. were about $700,000 was
(1) 1965 (2) 1968 (3) 1964 (4) 1963 (5) 1966

5. 1 2 3 4 5

6. The profits of the Beacon Co. dropped most sharply between the years
(1) 1967–1968   (2) 1964–1965   (3) 1963–1964   (4) 1961–1962   (5) 1966–1967

6. 1 2 3 4 5

7. In a large city the breakdown of the $30,000,000 raised by means of real estate taxes for all purposes, except schools, is shown in the graph below. To raise this sum, the tax rate was set at $21.95 per $1,000 of assessed valuation.

TAXES RAISED

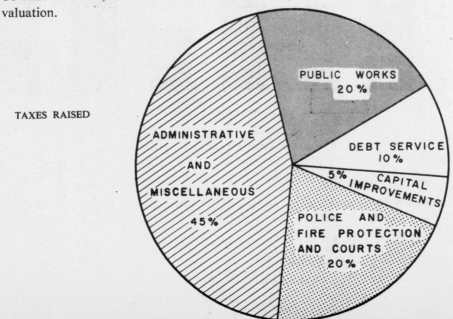

The angle at the center of the public works sector is
(1) 90° (2) 72° (3) 100° (4) 80° (5) 75°

8. Mr. Mitchell's home is assessed at $18,000. His real estate tax bill is
(1) $385.10 (2) $394.10 (3) $3,951 (4) $395.10 (5) $375

8. 1 2 3 4 5
|| || || || ||

9. The amount of money spent for public works is
(1) $5,000,000 (2) $1,500,000 (3) $6,000,000 (4) $3,000,000 (5) $2,500,000

9. 1 2 3 4 5
|| || || || ||

10. The ratio of money spent for administrative and miscellaneous to the money spent for public works is
(1) 9:4 (2) 4:9 (3) 9:5 (4) 5:9 (5) 2:1

10. 1 2 3 4 5
|| || || || ||

11. Mr. Jones and Mr. Crane are salesmen. They kept a record of their sales over a 10-month period. The solid line on the graph below represents Mr. Jones' volume of sales and the broken line represents Mr. Crane's volume of sales.

COMPARISON OF SALES VOLUME—MR. JONES AND MR. CRANE

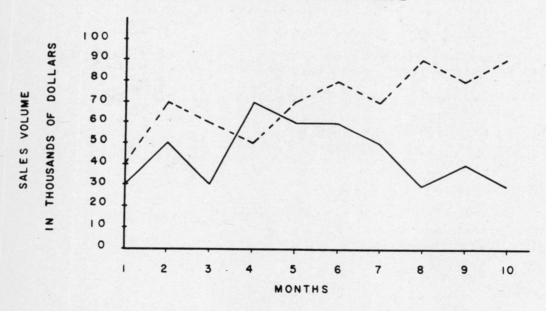

Mr. Jones' greatest sales volume for the 10-month period occurred on the month numbered
(1) 3 (2) 4 (3) 7 (4) 6 (5) 9

11. 1 2 3 4 5
|| || || || ||

12. How much greater volume was Mr. Crane's best month over Mr. Jones' best month?
(1) 10 (2) 30 (3) 50 (4) 90 (5) 20

12. 1 2 3 4 5
|| || || || ||

13. How much greater was Mr. Crane's average for the 10 months than Mr. Jones' average for this period?
(1) 44 (2) 70 (3) 25 (4) 36 (5) 16

13. 1 2 3 4 5
|| || || || ||

The graphs below were published by the federal government to show where the tax dollar comes from and where it goes.

WHERE THE TAX DOLLAR COMES FROM   WHERE THE TAX DOLLAR GOES TO

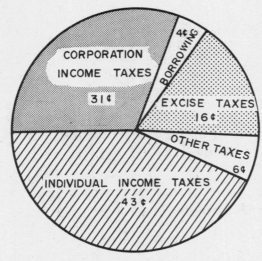
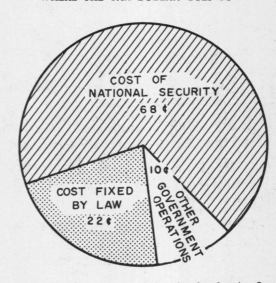

14. The per cent spent on national security was
(1) 78%   (2) 90%   (3) 68%   (4) 10%   (5) 32%

15. The per cent more money obtained from individual income taxes than from corporation income taxes was
(1) 6%   (2) 12%   (3) 43%   (4) 31%   (5) 22%

16. The angle at the center of the sector for "Cost of Other Government Operations" is
(1) 10°   (2) 20°   (3) 40°   (4) 36°   (5) 80°

17. The per cent of income derived from both corporation income taxes and individual income taxes is
(1) 84%   (2) 12%   (3) 75%   (4) 82%   (5) 74%

ANSWERS

1. 4	5. 4	9. 3	13. 3	17. 5
2. 4	6. 3	10. 1	14. 3	
3. 2	7. 2	11. 2	15. 2	
4. 2	8. 4	12. 5	16. 4	

MEASURES

TIME TO STUDY:

Length

The most common measures of length are

        12 inches = 1 foot   5,280 feet = 1 mile
          3 feet = 1 yard   1,760 yards = 1 mile

EXAMPLE: A plumber has a pipe $\frac{3}{4}$ yard in length. If he cuts off a piece 23 inches long, how much pipe does he have left?

$$\frac{3}{4} \text{ yard} = \frac{3}{4} \times 36 = 27 \text{ inches}$$

The plumber has 4 inches of pipe left.

TIME TO PRACTICE:

1. A plane flies at a height of 23,760 feet. In miles, this is
   (1) 4   (2) $4\frac{2}{3}$ (3) $4\frac{1}{4}$ (4) $4\frac{1}{2}$ (5) $4\frac{3}{4}$

2. Mrs. Bryant buys 6 yards of linen. The number of towels 27 inches in length that she can cut is
   (1) 8   (2) 6   (3) 12   (4) 9   (5) 15

3. A room is 18 feet long and 12 feet wide. The number of rubber tiles measuring 8 inches by 8 inches needed to cover the floor is
   (1) 45   (2) 27   (3) 486   (4) 286   (5) 45

4. A lecture room is 50 feet wide. On each side of the room there is an aisle 40 inches wide. The number of seats, 20 inches wide, that can be fitted across the room is
   (1) 20   (2) 26   (3) 40   (4) 30   (5) 35

5. A long distance race covers $6\frac{3}{4}$ miles. The number of yards covered is
   (1) 10,560   (2) 12,000   (3) 11,000   (4) 11,880   (5) 14,350

1.   1   2   3   4   5

2.   1   2   3   4   5

3.   1   2   3   4   5

4.   1   2   3   4   5

5.   1   2   3   4   5

ANSWERS

1. 4   2. 1   3. 3   4. 2   5. 4

TIME TO STUDY:

Time

The most common measures of time are

60 seconds = 1 minute	12 months = 1 year
60 minutes = 1 hour	365 days = 1 year

EXAMPLE: A man works from 9:45 A.M. until 1:30 P.M. How many hours does he work?

From 9:45 A.M. to 10:00 A.M. is 15 minutes, or $\frac{1}{4}$ hour
From 10:00 A.M. to 1:00 P.M. is 3 hours
From 1:00 P.M. to 1:30 P.M. is 30 minutes, or $\frac{1}{2}$ hour
The time the man worked is $\frac{1}{4} + 3 + \frac{1}{2} = 3\frac{3}{4}$ hours

TIME TO PRACTICE:

1. A man is paid $2.50 per hour. He works from 10:45 A.M. until 3:15 P.M. He earns
   (1) $10.00 (2) $12.50 (3) $11.25 (4) $11.75 (5) $12.25

   1. 1 2 3 4 5
   || || || || ||

2. A bell rings every 45 minutes. The number of times the bell rings in 15 hours is
   (1) 18 (2) 20 (3) 11 (4) 12 (5) 25

   2. 1 2 3 4 5
   || || || || ||

3. A man leaves New York on a plane at 10:40 A.M. bound for Los Angeles. If he gains 3 hours in time and the trip takes 5 hours and 50 minutes, he arrives at Los Angeles at
   (1) 1:30 P.M. (2) 2:30 P.M. (3) 3:30 P.M. (4) 3:10 P.M. (5) 2:50 P.M.

   3. 1 2 3 4 5
   || || || || ||

4. In flight, a plane covers 1 mile in 1 second. At the same rate of speed the mileage the plane covers in 1 hour is
   (1) 100 (2) 400 (3) 720 (4) 3000 (5) 3600

   4. 1 2 3 4 5
   || || || || ||

5. On March 5, a man borrows $900 from a bank for 90 days. He must repay the loan on
   (1) June 1 (2) June 5 (3) June 3 (4) June 8 (5) June 9

   5. 1 2 3 4 5
   || || || || ||

   ANSWERS

1. 3   **2.** 2   **3.** 1   **4.** 5   **5.** 3

TIME TO STUDY:

Weight

The most commonly used measures of weight are

16 ounces = 1 pound   2,000 pounds = 1 ton

EXAMPLE: How many 2-ounce portions of candy can be obtained from a 10-pound box?

Since there are 16 ounces in 1 pound, each pound of candy will yield $\frac{16}{2}$, or 8 portions. Therefore, 10 pounds of candy will yield 8 × 10, or 80 portions.

TIME TO PRACTICE:

1. Bread sells for $.32 per pound. The cost of a bread weighing 3 pounds 6 ounces is
   (1) $.98 (2) $1.08 (3) $1.12 (4) $.78 (5) $1.15

   1. 1 2 3 4 5
   || || || || ||

2. A 12-ounce package of cheese costs $.69. What is the cost of one pound of the same cheese?
(1) $.78 (2) $.95 (3) $.96 (4) $.92 (5) $1.04

  2. 1 2 3 4 5

3. A shipment of coal weighs 9,500 pounds. What is the cost of the shipment if 1 ton of coal costs $24.60?
(1) $116.85 (2) $106.85 (3) $110.70 (4) $104.55 (5) $112.60

  3. 1 2 3 4 5

4. Steak sells for $1.18 per pound. What is the cost of a steak that weighs 1 pound 13 ounces?
(1) $2.05 (2) $1.98 (3) $2.20 (4) $1.92 (5) $2.14

  4. 1 2 3 4 5

5. A truckload of steel bars weighs $3\frac{1}{4}$ tons. If each bar weighs 26 pounds, the number of bars on the truck is
(1) 25 (2) 2,500 (3) 240 (4) 250 (5) 270

  5. 1 2 3 4 5

ANSWERS

1. 2   2. 4   3. 1   4. 5   5. 4

TIME TO STUDY:

Liquid Measure

The most commonly used liquid measures are

  16 fluid ounces = 1 pint   2 measuring cups = 1 pint
    2 pints = 1 quart   4 quarts = 1 gallon

EXAMPLE: A snack bar sells half-pint bottles of milk at 10 cents a bottle. If 3 gallons of milk are sold one morning, how much money is taken in?

Since half-pint bottles sell for 10 cents, a full pint is sold for 20 cents. Thus, 1 quart would sell for 40 cents and 1 gallon would sell for $1.60. And, 3 gallons would sell for 3 × $1.60, or $4.80.

TIME TO PRACTICE:

1. The number of measuring cups of milk in a 5-gallon can is
(1) 40 (2) 60 (3) 80 (4) 100 (5) 160

  1. 1 2 3 4 5

2. A can of orange juice contains 36 ounces. The number of pints of orange juice is
(1) 2 (2) $2\frac{1}{2}$ (3) $1\frac{1}{4}$ (4) $2\frac{1}{4}$ (5) 3

  2. 1 2 3 4 5

3. A punchbowl contains $3\frac{1}{2}$ gallons of punch. The number of 4-ounce portions that can be obtained from the punchbowl is
(1) 102 (2) 112 (3) 204 (4) 115 (5) 156

  3. 1 2 3 4 5

4. A restaurant cook uses 150 measuring cups of milk in one day. The cost of the milk at $.32 per quart is
   (1) $12.00   (2) $19.20   (3) $182.00   (4) $18.20   (5) $19.50

   4. 1 2 3 4 5

5. The number of fluid ounces in 1 gallon is
   (1) 64   (2) 48   (3) 100   (4) 96   (5) 128

   5. 1 2 3 4 5

ANSWERS

1. 3   **2.** 4   **3.** 2   **4.** 1   **5.** 5

Dry Measure

Such commodities as berries, apples, and potatoes are often sold by the quart or bushel. The most commonly used dry measures are

2 pints = 1 quart;   8 quarts = 1 peck;   4 pecks = 1 bushel

EXAMPLE: A dealer received a shipment of 60 bags of apples, each bag containing 1 peck. If a bushel of the apples weighed 48 pounds and the dealer sold them at a price of 3 pounds for 35 cents, how much did he receive?

The dealer received 60 pecks of apples. This is $\frac{60}{4}$, or 15 bushels.

Since each bushel weighed 48 pounds the total weight of the shipment was 15 × 48, or 720 pounds.

At 3 pounds for 35 cents, the dealer received $\frac{720}{3}$ × .35, or 240 × .35, or $84.00.

TIME TO PRACTICE:

1. A storekeeper paid $2.80 for a bushel of potatoes. If 1 peck of potatoes weighs 15 pounds and the storekeeper sold the potatoes in 5 pound bags at $.43 per bag, his profit on the deal was
   (1) $3.36   (2) $2.26   (3) $2.36   (4) $2.16   (5) $5.16

   1. 1 2 3 4 5

2. If a bushel of coal weighs 80 pounds and coal sells for $24.00 per ton, the cost of a bushel of coal is
   (1) $1.00   (2) $.98   (3) $2.00   (4) $.96   (5) $1.02

   2. 1 2 3 4 5

3. A fruiterer received a truckload of berries containing 15 bushels. If he sold the berries at $.28 per pint, the amount he received for the berries was
   (1) $268.80   (2) $134.40   (3) $26.88   (4) $168.80   (5) $16.88

   3. 1 2 3 4 5

4. A fruiterer paid $9.60 for 2 bushels of apples. If he sold the apples for $1.80 per peck his profit was
   (1) $3.80   (2) $4.40   (3) $4.50   (4) $4.80   (5) $5.80

   4. 1 2 3 4 5

ANSWERS

1. 3   **2.** 4   **3.** 1   **4.** 4

The Metric System

The metric system of measures is used in most scientific work and in most European countries. It is especially useful because its units are related by multiples of 10. In this section, we will consider the most frequently used metric measures.

The important unit of length in the metric system is the *meter*. The meter is a little bigger than 1 yard. In fact,

1 meter = 39.37 inches, approximately

The *kilometer*, or 1,000 meters, is used for measuring large distances, like the distance between two cities.

1 kilometer = $\frac{5}{8}$ mile, approximately

The important unit of liquid measure in the metric system is the *liter*.

1 liter = 1.1 liquid quarts, approximately

The basic unit of weight in the metric system is the *gram*. The gram is used extensively in the scientific laboratory. In practice, the kilogram, or 1,000 grams, is used extensively in weighing foods and other merchandise.

1 kilogram = 2.2 pounds, approximately

To sum up, the following equivalents are important.

1 meter = 39.37 inches, approximately
1 kilometer = $\frac{5}{8}$ mile, approximately
1 liter = 1.1 liquid quarts, approximately
1 kilogram = 2.2 pounds, approximately

EXAMPLE: In traveling on a European road an American motorist notes that the speed limit is 70 kilometers per hour. How fast is this in miles per hour, approximately?

Since 1 kilometer = $\frac{5}{8}$ mile, approximately

$$\frac{5}{8} \times 70 = \frac{350}{8} = 43\tfrac{3}{4}$$

This is approximately $43\tfrac{3}{4}$ miles per hour

TIME TO PRACTICE:

1. A package from Europe is marked to contain $3\tfrac{1}{2}$ kilograms. In pounds, this is
    (1) 77   (2) 770   (3) 7.7   (4) 6.6   (5) 14

    1. 1 2 3 4 5
            ‖ ‖ ‖ ‖ ‖

2. If you weigh 160 pounds, your weight in kilograms, to the nearest kilogram, is
    (1) 72   (2) 73   (3) 352   (4) 35.2   (5) 70

    2. 1 2 3 4 5
            ‖ ‖ ‖ ‖ ‖

3. A motorist bought 50 liters of gasoline. The number of gallons bought, to the nearest gallon, is
(1) 14 (2) 13 (3) 11 (4) 12 (5) 15

3. 1 2 3 4 5
|| || || || ||

4. If a plane is flying at the rate 760 kilometers per hour, its rate of speed in miles per hour is
(1) 1,216 (2) 1,200 (3) 675 (4) 455 (5) 475

4. 1 2 3 4 5
|| || || || ||

5. A building lot, rectangular in shape, is 35 meters in length and 15 meters in width. Its perimeter, in feet, to the nearest foot, is
(1) 3,937 (2) 328 (3) 109 (4) 984 (5) 394

5. 1 2 3 4 5
|| || || || ||

6. The distance between two European cities is 440 kilometers. At an average speed of 50 miles per hour, the number of hours it would take a motorist to cover this distance is
(1) 5 (2) 8⅘ (3) 10 (4) 5½ (5) 6

6. 1 2 3 4 5
|| || || || ||

ANSWERS

1. 3   2. 2   3. 1   4. 5   5. 2   6. 4

TIME TO STUDY:

Operations with Measures

It is often necessary to add, subtract, multiply, and divide with measures. The examples below indicate how this is done.

EXAMPLE: A woman bought 2 lb. 14 oz. of steak and 3 lb. 6 oz. of lamb. What was the total weight of her purchase?

$$2 \text{ lb. } 14 \text{ oz.}$$
$$\underline{3 \text{ lb. } 6 \text{ oz.}}$$
$$5 \text{ lb. } 20 \text{ oz.}$$

Since there are 16 ounces in 1 pound, we have

5 lb. 20 oz. = 5 lb. + 1 lb. + 4 oz. = 6 lb. 4 oz.

EXAMPLE: A plumber had a piece of pipe 6 ft. 3 in. long. If he cut off a piece 2 ft. 7 in. in length, what was the size of the pipe that was left?

6 ft. 3 in. = 5 ft. + 1 ft. + 3 in. = 5 ft. 15 in.
2 ft. 7 in. = 2 ft. 7 in.   = 2 ft. 7 in.
                                         3 ft. 8 in.

The piece of pipe that was left was 3 ft. 8 in.

EXAMPLE: A butcher cuts steaks each of which weighs 1 lb. 9 oz. What is the weight of 5 such steaks?

$$1 \text{ lb. } 9 \text{ oz.}$$
$$\underline{\times 5}$$
$$5 \text{ lb. } 45 \text{ oz.} = 5 \text{ lb. } + 32 \text{ oz.} + 13 \text{ oz.} = 7 \text{ lb. } 13 \text{ oz.}$$

EXAMPLE: Mrs. Gordon buys a bolt of cloth 21 ft. 8 in. in length. She cuts the bolt into four equal pieces to make drapes. What is the length of each drape?

$$4\overline{)21 \text{ ft. } 8 \text{ in.}} = 4\overline{)20 \text{ ft. } + 1 \text{ ft. } + 8 \text{ in.}}$$
$$= 4\overline{)20 \text{ ft. } 20 \text{ in.}}$$
$$= 5 \text{ ft. } 5 \text{ in.}$$

Each drape is 5 ft. 5 in.

TIME TO PRACTICE:

1. A picture frame is 2 ft. 6 in. long and 1 ft. 8 in. wide. The perimeter of the frame is
   (1) 4 ft. 2 in.   (2) 8 ft. 8 in.   (3) 8 ft. 6 in.   (4) 8 ft.   (5) 8 ft. 4 in.

2. A movie show lasts 2 hr. 15 min. A movie house has 5 such shows daily. The time consumed by the 5 shows is
   (1) 11 hrs.   (2) 11 hrs. 15 min.   (3) 10 hrs. 15 min.   (4) 12 hrs. 30 min.
   (5) 12 hrs.

3. On a certain day the sun rises at 6:48 A.M. and sets at 7:03 P.M. The time from sunrise to sunset is
   (1) 12 hrs. 15 min.   (2) 12 hrs. 5 min.   (3) 11 hrs. 45 min.   (4) 12 hrs. 25 min.   (5) 10 hrs. 15 min.

4. If 6 cans of orange juice weigh 15 lb. 6 oz., the weight of 1 can of orange juice is
   (1) 2 lb. 6 oz.   (2) 2 lb. 7 oz.   (3) 2 lb. 1 oz.   (4) 2 lb. 9 oz.   (5) 2 lb. 3 oz.

5. A jug contains 2 gallons 3 quarts of milk. The number of 8 oz. glasses that can be filled from this jug is
   (1) 24   (2) 32   (3) 44   (4) 36   (5) 40

6. A carpenter has a board 5 ft. 3 in. in length. He cuts off a piece 2 ft. 7 in. in length. The length of the piece that is left is
   (1) 3 ft. 6 in.   (2) 2 ft. 6 in.   (3) 2 ft. 3 in.   (4) 2 ft. 8 in.   (5) 2 ft. 5 in.

7. A set of books weighs 7 lb. 10 oz. The weight of 4 such sets is
   (1) 28 lb. 4 oz.   (2) 30 lb. 8 oz.   (3) 29 lb. 8 oz.   (4) 29 lb. 10 oz.   (5) 29 lb. 12 oz.

8. A store sold 6 gal. 2 qt. of ice cream on one day and 7 gal. 3 qt. the next day. The amount of ice cream sold on both days was
   (1) 15 gal. 2 qt.   (2) 14 gal. 3 qt.   (3) 14 gal. 1 qt.   (4) 15 gal. 1 qt.   (5) 13 gal. 2 qt.

1. 1 2 3 4 5
2. 1 2 3 4 5
3. 1 2 3 4 5
4. 1 2 3 4 5
5. 1 2 3 4 5
6. 1 2 3 4 5
7. 1 2 3 4 5
8. 1 2 3 4 5

ANSWERS

1. 5   3. 1   5. 3   7. 2
2. 2   4. 4   6. 4   8. 3

SAMPLE TESTS

This section is designed to give you practice in taking the mathematics section of the High School Equivalency Test. In taking each of these practice tests try to give yourself the benefit of good conditions. Select a quiet place and allow yourself two hours. You may be able to complete the test in less time.

After you have completed the test check your answers. Then use the answers to find your score. It is wise to study the solutions and explanations. You may discover new ways to attack problems. Also, you will obtain help on the questions that you could not answer and you will be able to correct any errors that you made. Remember that you do not have to get a perfect score to pass the test. If you find that you are weak on a certain topic you may review the material in the text on that topic.

A WORD ABOUT TESTS: Do you consider yourself a person who "goes to pieces" on tests? Cheer up! Psychologists claim that more than ninety per cent of us think we don't perform well on tests *of any kind*. Nobody likes tests. But more than 80 % of the people who have taken the High School Equivalency Tests in the New York area, for example, have passed them. They must be doing something right. And so can you—with the right attitude and careful preparation.

TIME TO PRACTICE:

TEST 1

1. Mrs. Parker purchased a dinette set which was marked $400. Since she bought the dinette set on the installment plan, she had to make a down payment of 25% of the marked price plus 12 monthly payments of $30. How much more than the marked price did Mrs. Parker pay?
   (1) $25   (2) $50   (3) $60   (4) $460

    1. 1 2 3 4

2. Mr. Black had an L-shaped lawn, as shown in the figure. He decided to use fertilizer on the lawn at $4 per bag. If 1 bag was needed for every 2,000 square feet of lawn, how much did he spend for fertilizer?
   (1) $4   (2) $16   (3) $24   (4) $48

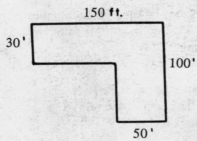

    2. 1 2 3 4

3. The inside dimensions of rectangular storage bin are 10 feet long, 6 feet wide, and 8 feet deep. When the bin is filled to a depth of 3 feet, how many packages of wheat does it contain if one package occupies 2 cubic feet?
   (1) 90   (2) 360   (3) 480   (4) 960

    3. 1 2 3 4

4. A man's taxable income is $4,200. The tax instructions tell him to pay 2% on the first $1,000 of his taxable income, 3% on each of the second and third $1,000, and 4% on the remainder. Find the total amount of income tax which he must pay.
    (1) $88   (2) $98   (3) $128   (4) $168

    4. 1 2 3 4

5. A family has an income of $800 per month. The graph shows what part is allotted for each purpose. Which of the following statements is *incorrect?*
    (1) Food and rent account for more than one-half the income.   (2) If $25 per month is paid for insurance the family saves $39 per month.   (3) The number of degrees at the center of the sector used to represent operating expenses is 10°.   (4) The monthly cost of clothing is $104.

    5. 1 2 3 4

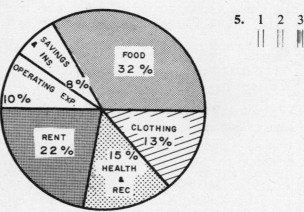

6. The side of a square is x inches. What is the perimeter of a square whose side is 3 inches shorter?
    (1) $4x$ (2) $x - 12$ (3) $4x - 3$ (4) $4(x - 3)$

    6. 1 2 3 4

7. A man left $24,000 to his wife and son. The ratio of the wife's share to the son's share was 5:3. How much did the wife receive?
    (1) $9,000   (2) $12,000   (3) $15,000   (4) $18,000

    7. 1 2 3 4

8. The diameter of a bicycle wheel is 28 inches. How many inches does the bicycle move when the wheel makes one complete revolution. [use $\pi = \frac{22}{7}$]
    (1) 22   (2) 88   (3) 176   (4) 200

    8. 1 2 3 4

9. If $a = 5$, $b = 3$, and $c = 4$, the numerical value of $6a^2 - bc^2$ is
    (1) 2   (2) 52   (3) 102   (4) 852

    9. 1 2 3 4

10. A snapshot 8 inches long and 6 inches wide is to be enlarged so that its length will be 12 inches. How many inches wide will the enlarged snapshot be?
    (1) $8   (2) $6   (3) $7   (4) $10

    10. 1 2 3 4

11. A salesman earns a salary of $300 per month plus a 10% commission on all sales above $6,000. One month his sales were $15,000. How much did he earn that month?
    (1) $300   (2) $900   (3) $1,000   (4) $1,200

    11. 1 2 3 4

12. Corner *AFE* is cut from the rectangle as shown in the figure. The area of the remaining figure in square inches is
    (1) 29   (2) 68   (3) 78   (4) 88

    12. 1 2 3 4

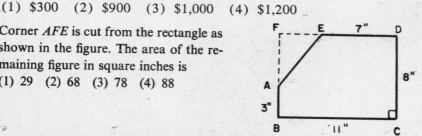

13. A guy wire reaches from the top of a vertical telephone pole 20 feet high to a point on level ground 15 feet from the base of the pole. What is the length of the guy wire?
    (1) 25 feet   (2) $27\frac{1}{2}$ feet   (3) 28 feet   (4) 30 feet

    13. 1 2 3 4

14. In the figure at the right the radius of the large circle is R and the radius of each small circle is r. Write a formula that can be used to find the area, A, of the shaded portion.
(1) $A = \pi R^2 - \pi r^2$ (2) $A = 2\pi R - 2\pi r$ (3) $A = \pi R^2 - 3\pi r^2$ (4) $A = \pi R - \pi r$

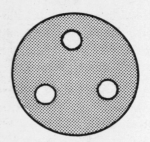

14.   1   2   3   4

15. An experimenter planted 120 seeds, of which 90 sprouted. What per cent of the seeds failed to sprout?
(1) 25%   (2) 24%   (3) 30%   (4) 75%

15.   1   2   3   4

16. A flask contains an acid solution of 40 pints which is 20% pure acid. If 10 pints of pure acid are added to flask the per cent of acid in the new mixture is
(1) 18%   (2) 24%   (3) 30%   (4) 36%

16.   1   2   3   4

17. The graph below shows the lengths of some famous rivers correct to the nearest hundred miles.

LENGTHS OF FAMOUS RIVERS

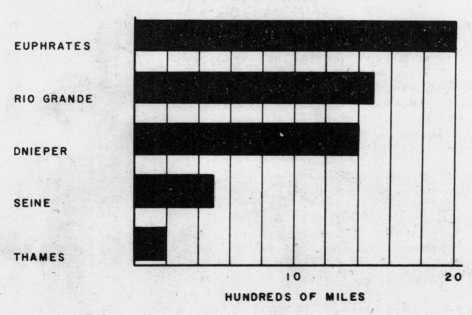

EUPHRATES
RIO GRANDE
DNIEPER
SEINE
THAMES

10   20
HUNDREDS OF MILES

Which one of the following statements is correct?
(1) The Thames is more than one-half as long as the Seine.   (2) The Dnieper is 1,200 miles long.   (3) The Euphrates is about 250 miles longer than the Rio Grande.   (4) The Rio Grande is about 1,000 miles longer than the Seine.

17.   1   2   3   4

18. Eight barrels of oil are needed to sprinkle ½ mile of roadway. How many barrels of oil are needed to sprinkle 3½ miles of roadway?
(1) 7   (2) 15   (3) 50   (4) 56

18.   1   2   3   4

19. Mr. Brown asked his son to deposit $100 in the bank for him. There were exactly 12 bills consisting of 10-dollar and 5-dollar bills. How many 10-dollar bills did he deposit?

   (1) 4   (2) 6   (3) 8   (4) none of these

20. An airplane traveled 1,000 miles in 2 hours and 30 minutes. What was the average rate of speed, in miles per hour, for this trip?

   (1) 200   (2) 300   (3) 400   (4) 600

21. In an isosceles triangle the measure of the vertex angle is 30° more than each of the base angles. Find the measure, in degrees, of the largest angle of the triangle.

   (1) 50°   (2) 60°   (3) 70°   (4) 80°

22. An example of congruent figures is

   (1) Any two neckties.   (2) A floor and a wall of the same room.   (3) Any two pages of a book.   (4) A state of the United States and a map of this state.

23. Mr. Robinson purchases an ordinary life insurance policy whose face value is $10,000. At his age, the premium is $24.00 per thousand. How much does he pay for this policy semi-annually?

   (1) $100   (2) $120   (3) $240   (4) $400

24. A stone pillar in the form of a cylinder is 7 feet tall and 4 feet in diameter. What is the weight of the pillar if 1 cubic foot of the stone weighs 200 pounds? [use $\pi = \frac{22}{7}$]

   (1) 1,760 lb.   (2) 16,000 lb.   (3) 16,600 lb.   (4) 17,600 lb.

25. A professional basketball team scored 25% of its points in the first quarter, 15% in the second quarter, and 40% in the third quarter. If the team scored 20 points in the fourth quarter, how many points did the team score during the game?

   (1) 80   (2) 92   (3) 100   (4) 120

26. A ship sails x miles the first day, y miles the second day, and z miles the third day. The average distance covered per day is

   (1) $\frac{xyz}{3}$ (2) $\frac{x+y+z}{3}$ (3) $3xyz$ (4) none of these

27. If 6 is subtracted from 3 times a certain number, the result is 84. Find the number.

   (1) 20   (2) 24   (3) 28   (4) 30

28. Mr. Barnes bought a car for $4,000. The car's depreciation for the first year was 25%. After the second year the depreciation was 20% of its value at the beginning of that year. What was the value of the car after two years?

   (1) $2,000   (2) $2,200   (3) $2,400   (4) $3,000

29. A recipe calls for $2\frac{1}{2}$ ounces of chocolate and $\frac{1}{2}$ cup of corn syrup. If only 2 ounces of chocolate are available the amount of corn syrup that should be used is

   (1) $\frac{1}{5}$ cup   (2) $\frac{2}{5}$ cup   (3) $\frac{2}{5}$ cup   (4) $\frac{4}{5}$ cup

30. Mr. Hart made a cedar chest, 4 ft. long, 2 ft. 6 in. wide, and 3 ft. high. How many square feet of lumber did he use?

   (1) 30   (2) 49   (3) 56   (4) 59

	1	2	3	4
19.			‖	
20.			‖	
21.	‖	‖	‖	‖
22.	‖	‖	‖	‖
23.	‖	‖	‖	‖
24.	‖	‖	‖	‖
25.	‖	‖	‖	‖
26.	‖	‖	‖	‖
27.	‖	‖	‖	‖
28.	‖	‖	‖	‖
29.	‖	‖	‖	‖
30.	‖	‖	‖	‖

ANSWERS TO *Test 1*

1. 3	**7.** 3	**13.** 1	**19.** 3	**25.** 3
2. 2	**8.** 2	**14.** 3	**20.** 3	**26.** 2
3. 1	**9.** 3	**15.** 1	**21.** 4	**27.** 4
4. 3	**10.** 3	**16.** 4	**22.** 3	**28.** 3
5. 3	**11.** 4	**17.** 4	**23.** 2	**29.** 3
6. 4	**12.** 3	**18.** 4	**24.** 4	**30.** 4

What's your score?

_____right, _____wrong

Excellent	27–30
Good	24–26
Fair	21–23

Refer to page 376 where these answers are explained.

TEST **2**

1. Mr. Benton insured his building against fire for $30,000 at the annual rate of $.34 per $100. After he rebuilt the wooden section of the building with fireproof material, he found that his insurance rate was reduced to $.29 per $100 annually. How much did Mr. Benton save yearly by making the repair?
(1) $12   (2) $15   (3) $150   (4) $180

2. The figure formed by two rays with a common endpoint is
(1) a point   (2) a triangle   (3) a segment   (4) an angle

3. In five years, the population of a town increased from 2,800 to 3,500. The per cent of increase was
(1) 20%   (2) 25%   (3) 30%   (4) 40%

4. If p pounds of oranges can be bought for c cents, how many pounds can be bought for 98 cents?
(1) $\dfrac{98c}{p}$ (2) $98cp$ (3) $\dfrac{cp}{98}$ (4) $\dfrac{98p}{c}$

5. A man invests $6,000 at 5% annual interest. How much more must he invest at 6% annual interest so that his annual income from both investments is $900?
(1) $3,000   (2) $5,000   (3) $8,000   (4) $10,000

6. A coal bin is 10 ft. long, 5 ft. wide, and 4 ft. 6 in. high. It is loaded with soft coal to a height of 4 feet. If soft coal weighs 80 lb. per cubic foot, how many tons of soft coal are there in the bin?
(1) 6   (2) 8   (3) 9½   (4) 12

7. Mr. Dobbs bought a car or which he made a down payment of $1,600 and $100 per month for 24 months. He could have saved 10% of the price he paid had he paid cash. What was the cash price of the car?
(1) $3,600   (2) $4,000   (3) $4,200   (4) $4,800

7. 1 2 3 4
    || || || ||

8. Two wholesalers, *A* and *B*, sell identical products for the prices and discounts given below:
   A: $750 with 20% discount, plus additional 2% discount for cash
   B: $800 with 25% discount, plus additional 5% discount for cash
Which wholesaler makes the better offer to a cash buyer and by how much?
(1) *B* by $18   (2) *A* by $25   (3) *B* by $64   (4) *A* by $60

8. 1 2 3 4
    || || || ||

9. Mr. Burns wishes to cover the floor of his finished basement, pictured in the figure at the right, with linoleum. If the linoleum sells for $1.00 per square foot, what will the cost be?
(1) $250   (2) $264   (3) $274
(4) $300

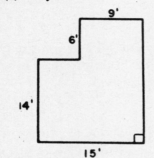

9. 1 2 3 4
    || || || ||

10. At the right, there is a graph of the way a man spends his day. Which of the following statements is correct?
(1) The man works 8 hours per day.   (2) The man spends 1 hour more on meals than he does on travel.   (3) The man sleeps 7 hours per day.   (4) The man spends half his time on work and travel.

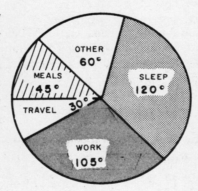

10. 1 2 3 4
     || || || ||

11. A man earns *x* dollars per month and spends *y* dollars per month. How many dollars will he save in 1 year?
(1) $12xy$ (2) $12x - y$ (3) $12(x - y)$ (4) $x - 12y$

11. 1 2 3 4
     || || || ||

12. In a theatre audience of 500 people, 80% were adults. How many children were in the audience?
(1) 20   (2) 50   (3) 80   (4) 100

12. 1 2 3 4
     || || || ||

13. A basket of tomatoes weighing 20 pounds costs $8.00. At the same rate, what should a 15 pound basket cost?
(1) $6.00   (2) $7.00   (3) $7.50   (4) $10.00

13. 1 2 3 4
     || || || ||

14. A ship sails 8 miles east and 15 miles north. How far is it from its starting point?
(1) 12 miles   (2) 17 miles   (3) 19 miles   (4) 20 miles

14. 1 2 3 4
     || || || ||

15. The scale on a map is 1 inch to 50 miles. On the map two cities are $2\frac{1}{2}$ inches apart. The actual distance between the cities in miles is
(1) 75   (2) 100   (3) 125   (4) 250

16. A semicircle surmounts a rectangle whose length is 2a and whose width is a. A formula for finding A, the area of the whole figure, is
(1) $A = 2a^2 + \dfrac{\pi a^2}{2}$ (2) $A = 2\pi a^2$ (3) $A = 3\pi a^2$ (4) $A = 2a^2 + \pi a^2$

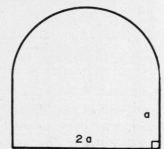

17. A painter and a helper spend 5 days in painting a house. The painter receives twice as much as the helper. If the two men receive $375 for the job, how much does the painter receive?
(1) $175   (2) $200   (3) $225   (4) $250

18. Mr. Frank bought a suit for $160 after it had been marked down 20%. What was the original cost of the suit?
(1) $128   (2) $150   (3) $200   (4) $250

19. A man bought 100 shares of X stock at $25 per share and sold the stock a year later at $30 per share. On both purchase and sale the commission and other expenses were $50. What was the per cent of profit on the deal?
(1) 16%   (2) 20%   (3) 25%   (4) 18%

20. The following table gives the annual premium payable for a life insurance policy taken out a various ages.

AGE IN YEARS	PREMIUM PER $1,000
22	$18
30	$22
38	$28
46	$38

If the policy is fully paid up after 20 years, how much is saved by taking out a $1,000 policy at age 30 rather than at age 46?
(1) $16.   (2) $32.   (3) $320. $400

21. A shipment of 2,200 pounds of fertilizer is packed in 10 kilogram bags. How many bags are needed for the shipment?
(1) 10   (2) 20   (3) 50   (4) 100

22. In a right triangle the ratio of the two acute angles is 3:2. The number of degrees in the larger acute angle is
(1) 36°   (2) 54°   (3) 72°   (4) 90°

23. The graph below shows the temperatures on a March day in a certain town.

READINGS DURING ONE MARCH DAY

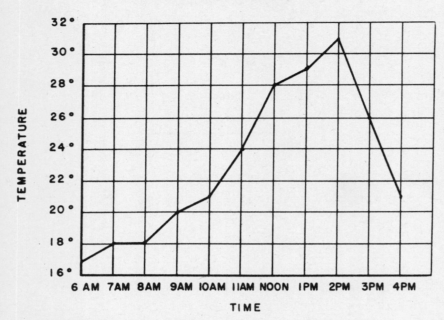

Which of the following is incorrect?
(1) The change in temperature between noon and 4 P.M. was −7°.   (2) The highest temperature reached was 31°.   (3) The change in temperature between 8 A.M. and noon was −10°.   (4) The average temperature for the day was about 23°.

24. Find the width of the pipe shown if the diameter of the outer circle is $7\frac{1}{4}''$ and the diameter of the inner circle is $4\frac{1}{2}''$.
(1) $2\frac{3}{4}''$ (2) $1\frac{3}{8}''$ (3) $5\frac{7}{8}''$ (4) $11\frac{3}{4}''$

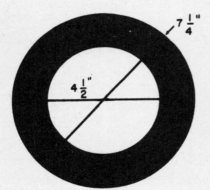

25. An example of two similar figures is
(1) A table and a chair.   (2) A pen and a pencil.   (3) A snapshot and an enlargement of the snapshot.   (4) A motorcycle and a car.

26. A toy bank contained $6.20 in quarters and dimes. If there were 8 more quarters than dimes, how many dimes were in the bank?
(1) 12   (2) 15   (3) 20   (4) 32

27. Find the numerical value of $5a^2b - 3ab^2$ if $a = 7$ and $b = 4$.
(1) 56   (2) 224   (3) 644   (4) 654

28. A man's taxable income is $2,500. The directions on the tax form instruct him to pay $400 plus 20% of the taxable amount over $2,000. How much tax must he pay?
(1) $450   (2) $500   (3) $900   (4) $1,000

28. 1 2 3 4

29. A metal alloy contains 48% iron, 34% brass, and the rest copper. In 50 pounds of this alloy the number of pounds of copper is
(1) 19   (2) 6   (3) 9   (4) 8.4

29. 1 2 3 4

30. The value of x in the equation $4x - 7 = 18$ is
(1) 6   (2) $2\frac{3}{4}$ (3) $6\frac{1}{4}$ (4) 7

30. 1 2 3 4

ANSWERS TO *Test 2*

1. 2	**9.** 2	**17.** 4	**25.** 3
2. 4	**10.** 2	**18.** 3	**26.** 1
3. 2	**11.** 3	**19.** 2	**27.** 3
4. 4	**12.** 4	**20.** 3	**28.** 2
5. 4	**13.** 1	**21.** 4	**29.** 3
6. 2	**14.** 2	**22.** 2	**30.** 3
7. 1	**15.** 3	**23.** 3	
8. 1	**16.** 1	**24.** 2	

What's your score?

_____right, _____wrong

Excellent   27–30
Good   24–26
Fair   21–23

Refer to page 380 where these answers are explained.

TEST **3**

1. A TV set priced at $400 was reduced 25% in price just before a new model came out. In addition, a 10% discount for cash was allowed. What was the actual cash price the buyer paid for this TV set?
(1) $130   (2) $260   (3) $270   (4) $320 ·

1. 1 2 3 4

2. A man is planning to remake his lawn next fall. The lawn, which is level and in the shape of a rectangle 90 feet long and 30 feet wide, is to be covered with topsoil to a depth of 4 inches. The man carts the topsoil in a small truck which holds 15 cubic feet. How many full loads will he need?
(1) 30   (2) 40   (3) 45   (4) 60

2. 1 2 3 4

3. The drawing at the right is part of a bar graph showing the population of a small town. How many people lived in the town in 1967?
(1) 2,500   (2) 2,000   (3) 250,000   (4) 3,000

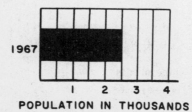

POPULATION IN THOUSANDS

3. 1 2 3 4

4. The description which best fits congruent figures is that they have (1) the same shape but not the same size   (2) the same size but not the same shape   (3) the same size and the same shape   (4) none of these

4. 1 2 3 4

5. A motorist left on a trip at 9:00 A.M. and stopped driving at 3:30 P.M. If his average speed for the trip was 50 miles per hour, how many miles did he cover?
(1) 325   (2) 350   (3) 400   (4) 425

5. 1 2 3 4

6. If 1 pound 8 ounces of meat costs $1.80, what is the cost of the meat per pound?
(1) $.85   (2) $1.00   (3) $1.20   (4) $1.50

6. 1 2 3 4

7. In a store, four clerks each receive $150 per week, and two stock boys each receive $75 per week. What is the average salary for the 6 workers in the store.
(1) $100   (2) $120   (3) $125   (4) $130

7. 1 2 3 4

8. A bookcase has three shelves. Two of the shelves have x books each and the third shelf has y books. What is the total number of books in the bookcase?
(1) $2xy$ (2) $x + 2y$ (3) $2x + y$ (4) $2(x + y)$

8. 1 2 3 4

9. A front lawn measures 25 ft. in length and 15 ft. in width. The back lawn of the same house measures 50 ft. in length and 30 ft. in width. What is the ratio of the area of the front lawn to the area of the back lawn?
(1) 1:4   (2) 1:2   (3) 2:3   (4) 3:4

9. 1 2 3 4

10. How many 6-ounce portions of milk may be obtained from 12 one-gallon cans?
(1) 64   (2) 128   (3) 256   (4) 512

10. 1 2 3 4

11. A farmer is making a rectangular gate 5 ft. high and 12 ft. wide. How long is the diagonal piece which he uses to strengthen the gate?
(1) 13 ft.   (2) 15 ft.   (3) 16 ft.   (4) 17 ft.

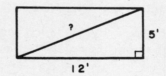

11. 1 2 3 4

12. In the figure at the right a circle is fitted inside a square. If the diameter of the circle is 6 in., what is the area of the shaded portion in square inches?
(1) 9π (2) $36 - 9\pi$ (3) $36 + 9\pi$ (4) $36 - 36\pi$

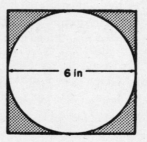

6 in

12. 1 2 3 4

13. What is the value of $3a^2 - 2a + 5$ when $a = 4$?
(1) 43   (2) 45   (3) 61   (4) 141

13. 1 2 3 4

14. If $3x - 5 = 16$ the value of x is
(1) $3\frac{2}{3}$ (2) 5   (3) 7   (4) $26\frac{2}{3}$

14. 1 2 3 4

15. The circle graph at the right shows the **BUDGET** budget of the James family. Which of the following is incorrect?
(1) If the James family has a monthly income of $720 their allowance for rent is $180.   (2) More than half the James family budget is spent on rent and food. (3) The angle at the center of the clothing sector is 44°.   (4) The amount of the budget set aside for clothing and savings is more than one-third of the income.

15. 1 2 3 4

16. A flask is full of lemonade. At lunch, $\frac{1}{3}$ of the flask is emptied. At dinner, $\frac{3}{4}$ of the remainder is used. What fractional part of the lemonade is left?
(1) none   (2) $\frac{1}{6}$ (3) $\frac{1}{5}$ (4) $\frac{1}{12}$

16. 1 2 3 4

17. Mr. Kane bought a new living room suite that was marked $800. He made a down payment of 25% of the marked price and agreed to pay the balance in 20 installments of $35 each. How much could he have saved by paying cash?
(1) $10   (2) $50   (3) $100   (4) $150

17. 1 2 3 4

18. Mr. Conner is a salesman. He receives a salary of $5,000 a year and a certain per cent on yearly sales above $10,000. One year his total salary amounted to $15,000 on sales of $110,000. What was his rate of commission on all sales above $10,000?
(1) 5%   (2) 6%   (3) 8%   (4) 10%

18. 1 2 3 4

19. The perimeter of a rectangle is 40 feet. If its length is 15 feet 6 inches, what is the width of the rectangle?
(1) 4 feet 6 inches   (2) 5 feet   (3) 9 feet   (4) 9 feet 6 inches

19. 1 2 3 4

20. A telephone pole throws a shadow 48 feet long. At the same time, a fence post 3 feet high throws a shadow 4 feet long. How high is the telephone pole?
(1) 30 ft.   (2) 36 ft.   (3) 64 ft.   (4) 60 ft.

20. 1 2 3 4

21. A European visitor to the United States is told that the airline distance between New York and Los Angeles is 2,500 miles. When he converts this distance to kilometers, what result does he obtain?
(1) 1,550   (2) 3,000   (3) 4,000   (4) 4,500

21. 1 2 3 4

22. At the age of 30, Mr. Green takes out a 20-year endowment policy for $10,000. His annual premium is $50 per $1,000 of insurance. How much does he pay over the 20-year period?
(1) $10,000   (2) $12,000   (3) $12,500   (4) $20,000

22. 1 2 3 4

23. In a triangle, the measure of the largest angle is three times the measure of the smallest, and the measure of the other angle is twice the measure of the smallest. What is the measure of the largest angle of the triangle.
(1) 60°   (2) 75°   (3) 80°   (4) 90°

23. 1 2 3 4

24. The price of a car was increased from $4,000 to $4,800. What was the percent of increase?
(1) 5%   (2) 10%   (3) 20%   (4) 25%

24. 1 2 3 4

25. On May 15 an electric meter read 5472 kilowatt-hours. The following month, on June 15, the meter read 5542 kilowatt-hours. Following are the rates:

    For the first 10 kilowatt-hours or less $.82
    For the next 45 kilowatt-hours $.05 per kilowatt-hour
    For the next 55 kilowatt-hours $.03 per kilowatt-hour
    For all over 110 kilowatt-hours $.02 per kilowatt-hour

What was the total charge for the kilowatt-hours consumed during the month from May 15 to June 15?
(1) $3.82 (2) $3.92 (3) $3.52 (4) $4.68

25. 1 2 3 4
     || || || ||

26. During a community chest drive $105,000 was raised. This amounted to 105% of the quota. What was that quota?
(1) $90,000 (2) $100,000 (3) $110,000 (4) $120,000

26. 1 2 3 4
     || || || ||

27. A family spent $\frac{1}{5}$ of its income on rent and $\frac{1}{4}$ of its income on food. It then had $99 left for other expenses. What was the weekly income of the family?
(1) $165 (2) $180 (3) $200 (4) $220

27. 1 2 3 4
     || || || ||

28. What is the area of the machine part on the right? Each end curve is a semi-circle. Use $\pi = \frac{22}{7}$.
(1) $38\frac{1}{2}$ sq. in. (2) $66\frac{1}{2}$ sq. in. (3) 105 sq. in. (4) 98 sq. in.

28. 1 2 3 4
     || || || ||

29. If $S = \frac{1}{2}gt^2$ find the value of S if $g = 32$ and $t = 8$.
(1) 128 (2) 256 (3) 512 (4) 1,024

29. 1 2 3 4
     || || || ||

30. Two numbers are in the ratio 7:2. Their difference is 45. What is the larger of the two numbers?
(1) 9 (2) 18 (3) 63 (4) 90

30. 1 2 3 4
     || || || ||

ANSWERS TO *Test 3*

1. 3	**9.** 1	**17.** 3	**25.** 3
2. 4	**10.** 3	**18.** 4	**26.** 2
3. 1	**11.** 1	**19.** 1	**27.** 2
4. 3	**12.** 2	**20.** 2	**28.** 2
5. 1	**13.** 2	**21.** 3	**29.** 4
6. 3	**14.** 3	**22.** 1	**30.** 3
7. 3	**15.** 3	**23.** 4	
8. 3	**16.** 2	**24.** 3	

What's your score?

_____right, _____wrong

Excellent   27–30
Good   24–26
Fair   21–23

Refer to page 385 where these answers are explained.

TEST **4**

1. A man looked at the gauge (measuring device) on the oil tank in his home on November first. The gauge showed that the tank was $\frac{7}{8}$ full. On December first he checked again and found that the tank was $\frac{1}{4}$ full. The tank holds 320 gallons when full. At $.20 cents per gallon, what was the cost of the oil used during the month of November?
    (1) $30   (2) $36   (3) $40   (4) $50

    1.   1   2   3   4
         || || || ||

2. The description which fits similar figures is
    (1) they have the same area   (2) they have the same perimeter   (3) they have the same volume   (4) they have the same shape

    2.   1   2   3   4
         || || || ||

3. The circle at the right represents a family's total income. The shaded section shows the part of the income that is saved. If the family income is $8,400 per year the amount saved per year is
    (1) $524   (2) $1,400   (3) $2,800   (4) $1,500

    3.   1   2   3   4
         || || || ||

4. A man drove for 2 hours at the average rate of 45 miles per hour. During the next 3 hours he covered 140 miles. His average speed for the entire trip in miles per hour was
    (1) 45   (2) 46   (3) 56   (4) 70

    4.   1   2   3   4
         || || || ||

5. The graph shows food expenditures in the United States for each five-year period between 1930 and 1950 inclusive. During which five-year period did food expenditures remain about the same?
    (1) 1930–1935   (2) 1935–1940   (3) 1940–1945   (4) 1945–1950

    FOOD EXPENDITURES
    1930–1950

    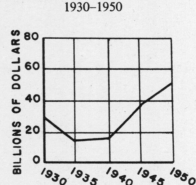

    5.   1   2   3   4
         || || || ||

6. If the measures of two angles of a triangle are 40° and 70° then the triangle is
    (1) equilateral   (2) right   (3) isosceles   (4) none of these

    6.   1   2   3   4
         || || || ||

7. A man wishes to buy a set of tools for his workshop. Dealer X lists the tools at $440 with a 25% discount. Dealer Y lists the same make of tools for $400, subject to discounts of 10% and 5%. How much does the man save by taking the better offer?
    (1) $10   (2) $12   (3) $15   (4) $18

    7.   1   2   3   4
         || || || ||

8. The area of the figure at the right is
    (1) $xy + 2a^2$ (2) $xy + a^2$ (3) $xy - 2a^2$
    (4) $xy - a^2$

    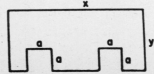

    8.   1   2   3   4
         || || || ||

9. In basketball a foul basket counts 1 point and a field basket counts 2 points. A team scored 103 points making 8 more field baskets than foul baskets. How many field baskets did the team make?
    (1) 29   (2) 32   (3) 39   (4) 37

    9. 1 2 3 4
        ‖ ‖ ‖ ‖

10. A brick wall is 50 ft. long, 6 ft. high, and 6 in. thick. What is the weight of the wall if 1 cu. ft. of brick weighs 120 lb.?
    (1) 9 tons   (2) 12 tons   (3) 15 tons   (4) 18 tons

    10. 1 2 3 4
        ‖ ‖ ‖ ‖

11. Two motorists start out from towns 420 miles apart and travel toward each other at the rate of 30 and 40 miles per hour respectively. In how many hours will they meet?
    (1) 2   (2) 6   (3) 7   (4) 10

    11. 1 2 3 4
        ‖ ‖ ‖ ‖

12. Find the cost of 5 ft. 3 in. of plastic slipcover material at $4.00 per foot.
    (1) $7.00   (2) $21.00   (3) $23.00   (4) $21.12

    12. 1 2 3 4
        ‖ ‖ ‖ ‖

13. An auditorium contains x rows with y seats in each row. The number of seats in the auditorium is
    (1) $x + y$ (2) xy (3) $x - y$ (4) $x \div y$

    13. 1 2 3 4
        ‖ ‖ ‖ ‖

14. A rectangle and a square have the same perimeter. The length of the rectangle is 2 feet greater than the side of the square and the width of the rectangle is 2 feet less than a side of the square. Which statement is true?
    (1) The rectangle and the square have the same area.   (2) The area of the rectangle is greater than the area of the square.   (3) The area of the square is 4 square feet greater than the area of the rectangle.   (4) The area of the rectangle is twice the area of the square.

    14. 1 2 3 4
        ‖ ‖ ‖ ‖

15. In a mixture of water and turpentine containing 21 ounces, there are 7 ounces of turpentine. If 4 ounces of water are added, the per cent of turpentine in the mixture is
    (1) 25%   (2) 28%   (3) 30%   (4) $33\frac{1}{3}$%

    15. 1 2 3 4
        ‖ ‖ ‖ ‖

16. A rectangular swimming pool is 80 feet long and 60 feet wide. What is the diagonal distance across the pool?
    (1) 70 ft.   (2) 90 ft.   (3) 100 ft.   (4) 140 ft.

    16. 1 2 3 4
        ‖ ‖ ‖ ‖

17. The measure of the smallest angle of a triangle is 20° less than the measure of the second angle and 40° less than the measure of the third angle of the triangle. What is the measure of the smallest angle of the triangle, in degrees?
    (1) 40°   (2) 45°   (3) 50°   (4) 60°

    17. 1 2 3 4
        ‖ ‖ ‖ ‖

18. A scale drawing of a building plot has a scale of 1″ to 40 feet. How many inches on the drawing represent a distance of 175 feet on the plot?
    (1) $4\frac{1}{8}$ (2) $4\frac{3}{8}$ (3) $4\frac{1}{2}$ (4) $4\frac{3}{4}$

    18. 1 2 3 4
        ‖ ‖ ‖ ‖

19. A rectangular piece of metal is 30 inches long and 18 inches wide. At each corner, a square 4 inches on a side is cut off and the edges are turned up to form an open box. The volume of this box is
    (1) 880 cu. in.   (2) 1,200 cu. in.   (3) 1,456 cu. in.   (4) 2,160 cu. in.

    19. 1 2 3 4
        ‖ ‖ ‖ ‖

20. There are 42 coins consisting of half-dollars and quarters. The value of the coins is $16.00. How many half-dollars are there?
    (1) 18   (2) 20   (3) 22   (4) 24

    20. 1 2 3 4
        ‖ ‖ ‖ ‖

21. It takes an electrician x hours to wire a house. What part of the job does he do in 2 hours?

   (1) $\frac{2}{x}$ (2) $2x$ (3) $\frac{x}{2}$ (4) none of these

22. Find the value of $8y^2 - 7y - 1$ if $y = 5$.
   (1) 164   (2) 165   (3) 1564   (4) 1565

23. A family spends 20% of its monthly income on rent, 23% on food, 42% on other expenses, and saves the balance. If the family saves $150, what is its monthly income?
   (1) $100   (2) $1,000   (3) $1,200   (4) $10,000

24. If 4 apples sell for 29 cents, what is the cost of 2 dozen apples at the same rate?
   (1) $1.34   (2) $1.54   (3) $1.74   (4) $1.94

25. If $2x + 7 = 19$ then the value of x is
   (1) 5   (2) 6   (3) 7   (4) 13

26. The ratio of the measures of the two acute angles of a right triangle is 2:3. The measure of the smallest angle of the triangle is
   (1) 18°   (2) 24°   (3) 30°   (4) 36°

27. A salesman was offered a monthly salary of $1,500 or a commission of 10% on sales. He accepted the commission basis and sold $198,000 worth of goods for the year. How much did he gain that year by taking the commission basis over the salary basis?
   (1) $800   (2) $1,000   (3) $1,600   (4) $1,800

28. Below is a table for premiums on ordinary life insurance.

IF TAKEN OUT AT AGE	ANNUAL PREMIUM PER $1,000 OF INSURANCE
20	$18
25	$20
30	$24
35	$28
40	$33

   A man took out four of these insurance policies as follows: $1,000 at age 20; $2,000 at age 25; $2,000 at age 30; $5,000 at age 35.
   Find the total premium he pays per year on the four policies.
   (1) $246   (2) $256   (3) $268   (4) $276

29. The roof of a house is in the form of a square measuring 40 feet on a side. It costs $800 to replace this roof. At the same rate, the cost of replacing the roof of another house in the form of a square measuring 80 feet on a side is
   (1) $1,600   (2) $2,000   (3) $2,400   (4) $3,200

30. The perimeter of a rectangle is 84 feet. If the length of the rectangle is 24 feet, what is its width?

(1) 18 feet   (2) 30 feet   (3) 36 feet   (4) 60 feet

30. 1 2 3 4
     || || || ||

ANSWERS TO *Test 4*

1. 3	**9.** 4	**17.** 1	**25.** 2
2. 4	**10.** 1	**18.** 2	**26.** 4
3. 2	**11.** 2	**19.** 1	**27.** 4
4. 2	**12.** 2	**20.** 3	**28.** 1
5. 2	**13.** 2	**21.** 1	**29.** 4
6. 3	**14.** 3	**22.** 1	**30.** 1
7. 2	**15.** 2	**23.** 2	
8. 3	**16.** 3	**24.** 3	

What's your score?

_____right, _____wrong

Excellent   27–30
Good   24–26
Fair   21–23

Refer to page 388 where these answers are explained.

TEST 5

1. Mr. Martin bought a new car for $5,000. He could either pay cash or make a down payment of 20% of the price of the car and pay 24 monthly installments of $200 each. How much did he save by paying cash?

(1) $400   (2) $500   (3) $600   (4) $800

1. 1 2 3 4
    || || || ||

2. A circle graph is drawn in which the angle at the center for one of the sectors is 72°. This sector represents what part of the circle?

(1) $\frac{1}{10}$ (2) $\frac{1}{5}$ (3) $\frac{3}{10}$ (4) .72

2. 1 2 3 4
    || || || ||

3. The area of the figure at the right is

(1) 200 sq. ft.   (2) 240 sq. ft.   (3) 260 sq. ft.
(4) 320 sq. ft.

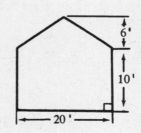

3. 1 2 3 4
    || || || ||

4. The wholesale list price of a watch is $50. A dealer bought a shipment of watches at a discount of 20% and sold the watches at 10% above the wholesale list price. What was his profit on each watch?

(1) $8   (2) $10   (3) $12   (4) $15

4. 1 2 3 4
    || || || ||

5. A man's will provided that his wife receive $\frac{1}{2}$ of his estate, and his three sons divide the rest equally. If each son's share was $8,000, what was the value of the estate?

(1) $24,000   (2) $32,000   (3) $40,000   (4) $48,000

6. In a store where the selling price is 40% above cost, how much did the store pay for an article that was marked to sell for $28?

(1) $16   (2) $20   (3) $22   (4) $24

7. On a cold day, the following temperature readings were taken:

6:00 A.M. $-12°$
7:00 A.M. $-7°$
8:00 A.M. $-2°$
9:00 A.M. $0°$
10:00 A.M. $+6°$

What is the average of these temperature readings?

(1) $0°$ (2) $2°$ (3) $-3°$ (4) $3°$

8. What is the cost of digging a cellar 30 feet long, 24 feet wide, and 9 feet deep, at $2.00 per cubic yard?

(1) $126   (2) $480   (3) $500   (4) $113,560

9. It takes 20 men 36 days to do a certain job. How long would it take 24 men to do the same job?

(1) 25 days   (2) 30 days   (3) 32 days   (4) $43\frac{1}{5}$ days

10. A rectangular garden plot is 28 feet long and 21 feet wide. What is the length of a walk that is placed diagonally across the plot?

(1) 25 feet   (2) 30 feet   (3) 32 feet   (4) 35 feet

11. How many $4'' \times 8''$ bricks are needed to build a walk $6'$ wide and $30'$ long?

(1) 73   (2) 126   (3) 810   (4) 960

12. The radius of an apple pie is 5 inches. The radius of a larger apple pie is 10 inches. What is the ratio of the surface area of the smaller pie to the surface area of the larger pie?

(1) 1:2   (2) 1:4   (3) 1:8   (4) none of these

13. A recipe calls for $\frac{1}{2}$ lb. of sugar for 2 lb. of rhubarb. If 5 lb. of rhubarb are used, how many pounds of sugar are needed?

(1) $1\frac{1}{8}$ (2) $1\frac{1}{4}$ (3) $1\frac{1}{2}$ (4) $1\frac{3}{4}$

14. On a trip from Madrid to Rome an airline charges $2.50 per kilogram for excess baggage. An American traveler has 22 pounds of excess baggage. How much does he have to pay?

(1) $20   (2) $25   (3) $50   (4) $60

15. Which of the following represents a scale ratio of 1:12?

(1) $\frac{1}{4}$ in. to 1 ft.   (2) 2 ft. to 24 yd.   (3) 1 in. to $\frac{1}{4}$ mile   (4) 1 ft. to 4 yd.

16. In the figure at the right, the length of the side of the square is 10 inches. The curves are quarter circles. What is the area of the shaded portion?
(1) $100 - 100\pi$ (2) $100 - 50\pi$ (3) $100 - 25\pi$
(4) $100 - 10\pi$

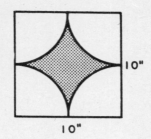

16.   1   2   3   4
    || || || ||

17. A man buys x gallons of gasoline at 38 cents a gallon. He gives the attendant a 10-dollar bill. How much does he receive in change?
(1) $10 - 38x$ (2) $38x + 10$ (3) $10x + 38$ (4) $1000 - 38x$

17.   1   2   3   4
    || || || ||

18. Find the value of $3y^2 + 2(y - 1)$ if $y = 5$.
(1) 83   (2) 84   (3) 233   (4) 234

18.   1   2   3   4
    || || || ||

19. After the price of a sofa was raised 20% its price was $180. What was the price before the increase?
(1) $150   (2) $160   (3) $175   (4) $216

19.   1   2   3   4
    || || || ||

20. The difference between $\frac{1}{4}$ of a number and $\frac{1}{5}$ of the same number is 7. The number is
(1) 20   (2) 35   (3) 120   (4) 140

20.   1   2   3   4
    || || || ||

21. A certain store advertised: "All stock reduced 25%. No down payment. Pay $\frac{1}{2}$ on February 10, $\frac{1}{3}$ on March 10, and the balance on April 10." Mr. Hill bought a coat which was marked $200 before the sale. What was his payment on April 10?
(1) $15   (2) $20   (3) $25   (4) $30

21.   1   2   3   4
    || || || ||

22. The graph below shows the receipts and expenses for a certain town for the years shown. The receipts are designated by shaded bars and the expenses by unshaded bars.

22.   1   2   3   4
    || || || ||

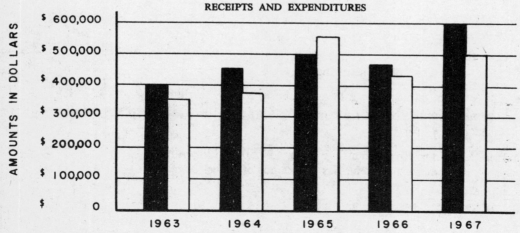

RECEIPTS AND EXPENDITURES

The year in which receipts exceeded expenses by about $100,000 was
(1) 1964   (2) 1965   (3) 1966   (4) 1967

23. A church spire casts a shadow 29 feet long when a pole 6 feet high casts a shadow 2 feet long. Find the height of the spire.
(1) $9\frac{2}{3}$ feet (2) 58 feet (3) 85 feet (4) 87 feet

24. How much longer does it take a motorist to travel one mile at 20 miles per hour than at 60 miles per hour?
(1) 1 minute (2) 2 minutes (3) 3 minutes (4) 5 minutes

25. A woman paid $1.75 for 1 lb. 12 oz. of meat. The cost of the meat per pound was
(1) $.75 (2) $.80 (3) $.95 (4) $1.00

26. A jug contains 10 quarts of a mixture of water and wine that is 40% wine. If 10 quarts of water are added to the jug, what per cent of the resulting mixture is wine?
(1) 4% (2) 20% (3) 25% (4) 40%

27. Which of the following is the best buy? Assume that the quality of the product is the same.
(1) 8 oz. of butter for $.34 (2) 10 oz. of butter for $.39 (3) 6 oz. of butter for $.27 (4) 9 oz. of butter for $.42

28. A salesman receives a base salary of $100 per week and a commission of 2% on sales. What were his sales for a week when he earned $240?
(1) $700 (2) $6,000 (3) $7,000 (4) $70,000

29. A basketball team has won 32 games out of 43 played. How many of its remaining 21 games must it win so that it will end the season winning 75% of its games?
(1) 15 (2) 16 (3) 17 (4) 18

30. If $x = \frac{1}{2}$, $y = \frac{1}{3}$, and $z = \frac{1}{4}$, find the value of $\dfrac{x + 6y + 12z}{4}$.
(1) $1\frac{1}{4}$ (2) $1\frac{3}{8}$ (3) $1\frac{5}{8}$ (4) $5\frac{1}{2}$

ANSWERS TO *Test 5*

1. 2 4	**9.** 2	**17.** 4	**25.** 4
2. 3 2	**10.** 4	**18.** 1	**26.** 2
3. 4 3	**11.** 3	**19.** 1	**27.** 2
4. 1 4	**12.** 2	**20.** 4	**28.** 3
5. 2 4	**13.** 2	**21.** 3	**29.** 2
6. 4 2	**14.** 2	**22.** 4	**30.** 2
7. 3	**15.** 4	**23.** 4	
8. 2	**16.** 3	**24.** 2	

What's your score?

_____right, _____wrong

Excellent	27–30
Good	24–26
Fair	21–23

Refer to page 393 where these answers are explained.

ANSWERS EXPLAINED

TEST **1**

1. Ans. 3 The down payment was $\frac{1}{4}$ of 100, or $100.

The sum of the 12 monthly payments was 12 × 30, or $360.

The total cost on the installment plan was 100 + 360, or $460.

2. Ans. 2 We must find the area of the lawn. There are two simple ways to do this.

METHOD 1

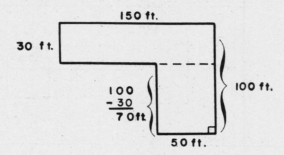

We draw a line to cut the figure into two rectangles and find the area of each rectangle.

$$50 \times 70 = \quad 3,500$$
$$30 \times 150 = +4,500$$
$$\text{Total area} = \quad 8,000 \text{ sq. ft.}$$

Since 1 bag covers 2,000 sq. ft. of lawn, 4 bags are needed.

$$4 \times 4 = \$16$$

METHOD 2

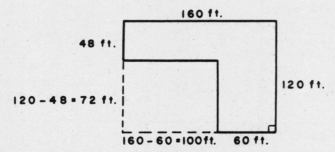

We draw two lines to obtain a large rectangle. We will find the area of the lawn by subtracting the area of the rectangle wiht two dotted sides from the area of the large rectangle.

$$\text{Area of large rectangle} = 150 \times 100 = \quad 15,000 \text{ sq. ft.}$$
$$\text{Area of dotted rectangle} = 100 \times \quad 70 = -7,000 \text{ sq. ft.}$$
$$\text{Area of lawn} \qquad\qquad = \quad 8,000 \text{ sq. ft.}$$

4 bags are needed at $4 per bag.

$$4 \times 4 = \$16$$

3. Ans. 1 The volume of the wheat in the bin = length × width × height

$$\text{Volume} = 10 \times 6 \times 3 = 180 \text{ cu. ft.}$$

Since each package occupies 2 cubic feet, the number of packages is

$$180 \div 2 = 90$$

Since the bin is 6 feet deep and is filled to a depth of 3 feet, it is half full.

$$\frac{416}{2} = 208 \text{ cubic feet of wheat}$$

Since each bushel occupies $1\frac{1}{3}$ cubic feet, the number of bushels is $208 \div 1\frac{1}{3}$, $208 \div \frac{4}{3}$, $208 \times \frac{3}{4} = 156$.

4. Ans. 3 2% of $1,000 = 1,000 \times .02 = \$20$
3% of $2,000 = 2,000 \times .03 = \$60$
4% of $1,200 = 1,200 \times .04 = \$48$
Total tax $= \$128$

5. Ans. 3 Operating expenses are 10% of the total. To find the number of degrees at the center of the sector used to represent operating expenses we find 10% of 360, or $.10 \times 360 = 36°$.

6. Ans. 4 The side of the square which is 3 inches shorter than the original square is $x - 3$. The perimeter of the smaller square is $4(x - 3)$.

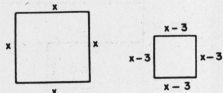

7. Ans. 3 Let $5x =$ mother's share
and $3x =$ son's share

$$5x + 3x = 24,000$$
$$8x = 24,000$$
$$x = \frac{24,000}{8} = 3,000$$

Since the mother's share is $5x$ it is $5 \times 3,000 = \$15,000$.

8. Ans. 2 The radius of the wheel is $\frac{28}{2} = 14$ inches. When the wheel makes one complete revolution, the bicycle moves the length of the circumference of the wheel.

$$\text{Circumference} = 2\pi r = 2 \times \frac{22}{2} \times 14 = 88 \text{ inches}$$

To find the number of revolutions the wheel makes in traveling one mile, we must divide 1 mile, or the number of inches in one mile, by 88. Since there are 5,280 feet in 1 mile, there are $5,280 \times 12$ inches in 1 mile.

$$\frac{5,280 \times 12}{88} = \frac{\overset{60}{\cancel{5280}} \times 12}{\underset{1}{\cancel{88}}} = 720$$

The wheel makes 720 revolutions in traveling 1 mile.

9. Ans. 3 $6a^2 = 6 \times 5 \times 5 = 150$
$bc^2 = 3 \times 4 \times 4 = 48$
$6a^2 - bc^2 = 150 - 48 = 102$

10. Ans. 3 Since the picture and its enlargement are similar, the lengths have the same ratio as the widths, or

$$\frac{\text{length of picture}}{\text{length of enlargement}} = \frac{\text{width of picture}}{\text{width of enlargement}}$$

$$\frac{8}{12} = \frac{6}{\text{width of enlargement}}$$

$$8 \times \text{width of enlargement} = 12 \times 6 = 72$$

$$\text{width of enlargement} = \frac{72}{8} = 9$$

The width of the enlargement is 9 inches.

11. Ans. 4 Sales above \$6,000 were 15,000 — 6,000 = \$9,000
Commission was 10% of 9,000 = .1 × 9,000 = \$900
Total salary was 300 + 900 = \$1,200

12. Ans. 3 We will find the area of the rectangle *BCDF* and subtract from this the area of triangle *AEF*.

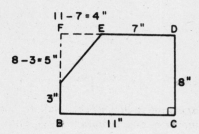

Area of rectangle $BCDF = BC \times CD$
$$= 11 \times 8 = 88$$
$AF = 8 - 3 = 5'',\ FE = 11 - 7 = 4''$
Area of triangle $AEF = \frac{1}{2}(AF \times FE)$
$$= \frac{1}{2}(5)(4) = 10$$

The area of the remaining figure is 88 — 10 = 78 square inches.

13. Ans. 2 Since $\triangle ABC$ is a right triangle, we may use the Pythagorean Rule.

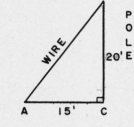

$$(AB)^2 = (AC)^2 + (BC)^2$$
$$(AB)^2 = (15)^2 + (20)^2$$
$$(AB)^2 = 225 + 400 = 625$$
$$AB = \sqrt{625} = 25$$

14. Ans. 3 To find a formula for the area of the shaded portion we find the area of the large circle and subtract from this result the sum of the areas of the small circles.

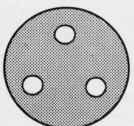

Area of large circle $= \pi R^2$
Area of each small circle $= \pi r^2$
Sum of areas of 3 small circles $= 3\pi r^2$
Area of shaded portion $= \pi R^2 - 3\pi r^2$

15. Ans. 1 The number of seeds that failed to sprout was 120 — 90 = 30 seeds
The fraction representing the part of the seeds that failed to sprout is $\frac{30}{120}$.
$$\frac{30}{120} = \frac{1}{4} \text{ and } \frac{1}{4} = 25\%$$

16. Ans. 4 20% of 40 = .2 × 40 = 8.00
The fraction representing the part of the solution that was acid originally is
$$\frac{\text{acid}}{\text{mixture}} = \frac{8}{40}$$
When 10 pints of acid are added we have
$$\frac{\text{acid}}{\text{mixture}} = \frac{8 + 10}{40 + 10} = \frac{18}{50}$$
$$\frac{18}{50} \times \frac{2}{2} = \frac{36}{100} = 36\%$$

The new mixture contains 36% acid.

17. Ans. 4 Note that each subdivision line on the horizontal axis represents 200 miles.

The Rio Grande is about 1,500 miles long.
The Seine is about 500 miles.
The Rio Grande is about 1,000 miles longer than the Seine.

18. Ans. 4 Since 8 barrels are needed to sprinkle $\frac{1}{2}$ mile of roadway, 16 barrels are needed to sprinkle 1 mile of roadway.
To sprinkle $3\frac{1}{2}$ miles of roadway we need $3\frac{1}{2} \times 16$ barrels.
$$3\frac{1}{2} = \frac{7}{2}$$
$$\frac{7}{2} \times 16 = 56$$
56 barrels of oil are needed.

19. Ans. 1 Let x = the number of 10-dollar bills
and $12 - x$ = the number of 5-dollar bills
$10x$ = the value of the 10-dollar bills
$5(12 - x)$ = the value of the 5-dollar bills

$$10x + 5(12 - x) = 100$$
$$10x + 60 - 5x = 100$$
$$5x + 60 = 100$$
$$5x + 60 - 60 = 100 - 60$$
$$5x = 40$$
$$x = 8$$

He deposited 5 10-dollar bills.

20. Ans. 3 To find the average rate of speed we divide the distance covered by the time consumed.

2 hours and 30 minutes = $2\frac{1}{2}$ hours

$$\frac{1000}{2\frac{1}{2}} = \frac{1000}{\frac{5}{2}} = 1000 \times \frac{2}{5} = 400$$

The average speed was 400 miles per hour.

21. Ans. 4 In $\triangle ABC$, let each base angle be $x°$. Then the vertex angle is $(x + 30)°$.
Since the sum of the angles of a triangle is 180°, we have

$$x + x + x + 30 = 180$$
$$3x + 30 = 180$$
$$3x + 30 - 30 = 180 - 30$$
$$3x = 150$$

$$x = \frac{150}{3} = 50$$

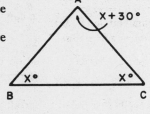

Thus, each base angle is 50° and the vertex angle is 50 + 30, or 80°.
The largest angle is 80°.

22. Ans. 3 Congruent figures are figures which have the same shape and the same size.

23. Ans. 2 Mr. Robinson's annual payment is $24 \times 10 = \$240$.
His semi-annual payment is $\frac{1}{2}$ of 240, or \$120.

24. Ans. 4 To find the volume of the pillar we use the formula

$$V = \pi r^2 h$$

In this case, $\pi = \frac{22}{7}$, $r = 2$, and $h = 7$

$$V = \frac{22}{7} \times 2 \times 2 \times 7 = 88 \text{ cubic feet}$$

Since each cubic foot weighs 200 pounds, the weight of the pillar is $88 \times 200 =$ 17,600 pounds.

25. Ans. 3 In the first three quarters the team scored $25 + 15 + 40 = 80\%$ of its total. In the fourth quarter, the team scored $100 - 80 = 20\%$ of its total.

$$20\% \text{ of its total was } 20 \text{ points}$$
$$1\% \text{ of its total was } 1 \text{ point}$$
$$100\%, \text{ or its full total was } 100 \times 1 = 100$$

The team scored 100 points in the game.

26. Ans. 2 To find the average of three numbers we add the three numbers and divide the result by 3. The correct answer is $\dfrac{x + y + z}{3}$.

27. Ans. 4 Let $x = $ the number

$$3x - 6 = 84$$
$$3x - 6 + 6 = 84 + 6$$
$$3x = 90$$
$$x = 30$$

The number is 30.

28. Ans. 3 The first year's depreciation was $.25 \times 4{,}000 = \$1{,}000$.
The car was worth $4{,}000 - 1{,}000 = \$3{,}000$ at end of first year.
The second year's depreciation was $.20 \times 3{,}000 = \$600$.
The car was worth $\$3{,}000 - \$600 = \$2{,}400$ at the end of the second year.

29. Ans. 2 Since $\dfrac{2}{2\frac{1}{2}}$ of the needed amount of chocolate was available we will need $\dfrac{2}{2\frac{1}{2}}$ of the amount of corn syrup in the recipe

$$\frac{2}{2\frac{1}{2}} = \frac{2}{\frac{5}{2}} = 2 \times \frac{2}{5} = \frac{4}{5}$$

Thus, we need only $\frac{4}{5}$ of $\frac{1}{2}$ cup of corn syrup.

$$\tfrac{4}{5} \times \tfrac{1}{2} = \tfrac{4}{10} = \tfrac{2}{5} \text{ of a cup.}$$

30. Ans. 4 To find the amount of lumber needed we use the formula

$$A = 2lw + 2lh + 2wh$$

In this case, $l = 4$, $w = 2\frac{1}{2}$, and $h = 3$

$$A = 2(4)(\tfrac{5}{2}) + 2(4)(3) + 2(\tfrac{5}{2})(3)$$
$$A = 20 + 24 + 15$$
$$A = 59$$

ANSWERS EXPLAINED

TEST 2

1. Ans. 2 There are 300 hundreds in 30,000

At \$.34 per \$100 Mr. Benton paid $.34 \times 300 = \$102$
At \$.29 per \$100 Mr. Benton paid $.29 \times 300 = \$87$
Mr. Benton saved $102 - 87 = \$15$ per year

ALTERNATE METHOD

> Mr. Benton saved $.05 per $100.
> .05 × 300 = $15.00
> Mr. Benton saved $15.

2. Ans. 4 The figure formed by two rays with a common endpoint is an angle.

3. Ans. 2 The numerical increase was 3,500 — 2,800 = 700

The fraction which indicates the increase is

Reduced to lowest terms $\frac{700}{2800} = \frac{7}{28} = \frac{1}{4}$

$$\frac{1}{4} = 25\%$$

4. Ans. 4 The student will find this type of problem easier to solve if he rewrites it, using numbers for letters. In this case, we might say

If 5 pounds of oranges can be bought for $.30, how many pounds can be bought for $.98?

The cost of one pound may be obtained by dividing 5 into .30. Thus, 1 pound of oranges can be bought for $.06. To find the number of pounds that can be bought for $.98, we divide 6 into $.98.

Now, let us follow the same procedure with letters. If p pounds of oranges can be bought for c cents, one pound can be bought for $\frac{c}{p}$ cents. Next, we must divide $\frac{c}{p}$ into 98.

$$\frac{98}{\frac{c}{p}} = 98 \div \frac{c}{p} = 98 \times \frac{p}{c} = \frac{98p}{c}$$

5. Ans. 4 If a man invests $6,000 at 5% annual interests his annual income is 6,000 × .05 = $300. Thus, he must invest a sum which will give him 900 — 300 = $600 more.

> 6% of sum needed is $600
> 1% of sum needed is $100
> 100%, or the full amount = 100 × 100 = $10,000.

6. Ans. 2 To obtain the volume of coal in the bin we use the formula $V = lwh$. In this case, $l = 10$, $w = 5$, and $h = 4$.

$$V = 10 \times 5 \times 4 = 200 \text{ cu. ft.}$$

Since 1 cubic foot of coal weighs 80 pounds, the weight of the coal in the bin, expressed in pounds, is 200 × 80 = 16,000 pounds.

In order to find the number of tons in this weight we must divide 16,000 by 2,000. The weight of the coal in the bin is 8 tons.

7. Ans. 1 Mr. Dobbs paid 1,600 + 24 (100) = 1,600 + 2,400 = $4,000
He could have saved 10% of 4,000 = $\frac{1}{10}$ of 4,000 = $400 for cash.
The cash price of the car was 4,000 — 400 = $3,600.

8. Ans. 1 Net price on *A*'s proposition

$750 − .20 × $750, or $750 − $150 = $600
Additional discount of 2% = 600 × .02 = $12
Net price on *A*'s proposition is $600 − $12, or $588.

Net price on *B*'s proposition

$800 − .25 × $800, or $800 − $200 = $600
Additional discount of 5% = 600 × .05 = $30
Net price on *B*'s proposition is $600 − $30 = $570
B's proposition is better by $18.

9. Ans. 2 We divide the figure into two rectangles by drawing the dotted line.
   The area of the upper rectangle is 6 × 9 = 54 square feet.
   The area of the lower rectangle is 14 × 15 = 210 square feet.
   The total area is 54 + 210 = 264 square feet.
   The cost of the linoleum is 264 × 1 = $264.

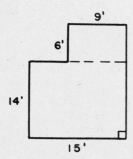

10. Ans. 2   Time spent on meals = $\frac{45}{360}$ × 24 = 3 hours
                    Time spent on travel = $\frac{30}{360}$ × 24 = 2 hours

11. Ans. 3 If he earns *x* dollars per month and spends *y* dollars per month he saves *x* − *y* dollars in 1 month. In one year, he saves 12(*x* − *y*) dollars.

12. Ans. 4 Since 80% of the audience were adults then 100 − 80 = 20% of the audience were children.

20% = $\frac{1}{5}$ and $\frac{1}{5}$ of 500 = 100

13. Ans. 1 If 20 pounds of tomatoes cost $8.00 then 1 pound of tomatoes cost 8.00 ÷ 20 = $.40.
   If 1 pound of tomatoes cost $.40 then 15 pounds of tomatoes cost 15 × .40 = $6.00.

14. Ans. 4 In the right triangle *ABC*, we use the Pythagorean Rule.

$(AB)^2 = (AC)^2 + (BC)^2$
$(AB)^2 = (8)^2 + (15)^2$
$(AB)^2 = 64 + 225 = 289$
$AB = \sqrt{289} = 17$

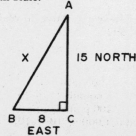

15. Ans. 3 If two cities are $2\frac{1}{2}$ inches apart, the actual distance between them is $2\frac{1}{2} \times 50$.

$$2\frac{1}{2} = \frac{5}{2} \ , \ \ \frac{5}{2} \times 50 = 125$$

The actual distance is 125 miles.

16. Ans. 1 The figure is composed of a semi-circle and a rectangle.

The diameter of the semi-circle is $2a$ and the radius is a. The area of the semi-circle is $\frac{1}{2}\pi a^2$.

The area of the rectangle is $2a^2$. The combined area is $2a^2 + \dfrac{\pi a^2}{2}$.

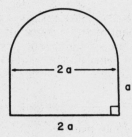

17. Ans. 4 Let x = pay of helper
And $2x$ = pay of painter

$$x + 2x = 375$$
$$3x = 375$$
$$x = 125$$

The painter receives $2x$, or $250.

18. Ans. 3 $20\% = \frac{1}{5}$. After the suit has been marked down 20% it was priced at 80%, or $\frac{4}{5}$ of the original price.

$\frac{4}{5}$ of the original price was $160
$\frac{1}{5}$ of the original price was $40
$\frac{5}{5}$, or the complete original price, was $200.

19. Ans. 1 Since commissions and other expenses were $47 on both purchase and sale we can disregard this factor in finding the per cent of profit.

The cost of the stock was 25×100 = $2,500
The selling price of the stock was 30×100 = $3,000
The profit was $3,000 - 2,500$ = $500
The fraction which represents the profit is $\dfrac{500}{2,500}$

When reduced to lowest terms $\dfrac{500}{2,500} = \dfrac{5}{25} = \dfrac{1}{5}$

$$\frac{1}{5} = 20\%.$$

20. Ans. 3 At age 30, the premium is $22 yearly. After 20 years one pays 20×22 = $440.

At age 46, the premium is $38 yearly. After 20 years one pays 20×38 = $760. The saving is $760 - 440 = 320$.

21. Ans. 4   1 kilogram = 2.2 pounds
      10 kilograms = 22 pounds
  1000 kilograms = 2200 pounds
The number of bags needed is $1,000 \div 10 = 100$.

22. Ans. 2 In a right triangle, one angle is 90° and the sum of the other two angles is 90°.

Let $3x$ = the larger acute angle
And $2x$ = the smaller acute angle

$$3x + 2x = 90$$
$$5x = 90$$
$$x = \tfrac{90}{5} = 18$$

The larger angle is 3×18, or 54°.

23. Ans. 3 The temperature at 8 A.M. was 18°
The temperature at noon was 28°
This represented an *increase* of 10°.

24. Ans. 2 The width of the pipe can be found by subtracting the radius of the smaller circle from the radius of the larger circle.

Diameter of larger circle = $7\tfrac{1}{4}''$, or $\tfrac{29}{4}''$
Radius of larger circle = $\tfrac{1}{2} \times \tfrac{29}{4}$, or $\tfrac{29}{8}''$
Diameter of smaller circle = $4\tfrac{1}{2}''$, or $\tfrac{9}{2}''$
Radius of smaller circle = $\tfrac{1}{2} \times \tfrac{9}{2}$, or $\tfrac{9}{4}''$
$$\tfrac{29}{8} - \tfrac{9}{4} = \tfrac{29}{8} - \tfrac{18}{8} = \tfrac{11}{8}$$

Width of the pipe is $1\tfrac{3}{8}$ inches.

25. Ans. 3 Similar figures are figures which have the same shape.
(3) is the correct choice since a snapshot and its enlargement have exactly the same shape.

26. Ans. 1

Let x = number of dimes
And $x + 8$ = number of quarters
Then $10x$ = value of dimes
And $25(x + 8)$ = number of quarters
$$10x + 25(x + 8) = 620$$
$$10x + 25x + 200 = 620$$
$$35x + 200 = 620$$
$$35x + 200 - 200 = 620 - 200$$
$$35x = 420$$
$$x = \tfrac{420}{35} = 12$$

27. Ans. 3

$$5a^2b = 5 \times 7 \times 7 \times 4 = 980$$
$$3ab^2 = 3 \times 7 \times 4 \times 4 = 336$$
$$5a^2b - 3ab^2 = 980 - 336 = 644$$

28. Ans. 2 He must pay $400 + .20 ($500)
$$.20 (\$500) = \$100$$

Total payment is $400 + 100 = \$500$.

29. Ans. 3 The per cent of copper in the alloy is 100% — (48% + 34%). The per cent of copper in the alloy is 100% — 82% = 18%.

$$18\% \text{ of } 50 = .18 \times 50 = 9$$

30. Ans. 3

$$4x - 7 = 18$$
$$4x - 7 + 7 = 18 + 7$$
$$4x = 25$$
$$x = \tfrac{25}{4} = 6\tfrac{1}{4}$$

ANSWERS EXPLAINED

TEST **3**

1. Ans. 3 25% of 400 $= \frac{1}{4}$ of 400 $=$ \$100.
The new price was 400 — 100 $=$ \$300.
The discount for cash was 10%, or $\frac{1}{10}$.

$$\frac{1}{10} \text{ of } 300 = \$30$$

The cash price was 300 — 30 $=$ \$270.

2. Ans. 4 The volume of topsoil to be carted is obtained by using the formula $V = l \times w \times h$.

In this case, $l = 90$, $w = 30$, and $h = \frac{4}{12}$ or $\frac{1}{3}$.
$$V = 90 \times 30 \times \frac{1}{3} = 900 \text{ cubic feet}$$

The number of full loads is $\frac{900}{15} = 60$.

3. Ans. 1 Note that the solid bar ends midway between the 2 and the 3. That is, the population is 2.5 thousands. Thus, the population is 2,500.

4. Ans. 3 Congruent figures are figures that can be made to fit exactly. Thus, congruent figures have the same size and the same shape.

5. Ans. 1 The motorist traveled $6\frac{1}{2}$ hours. Since his average speed was 50 miles per hour, the distance he covered was $6\frac{1}{2} \times 50$.

$$6\frac{1}{2} = \frac{13}{2}, \quad \frac{13}{2} \times 50 = 325$$

6. Ans. 3 1 pound 8 ounces $=$ 1 pound $+ \frac{8}{16}$ pound $= 1\frac{1}{2}$ pounds.
$$1\frac{1}{2} = \frac{3}{2}$$
Since $\frac{3}{2}$ pounds cost \$1.80
$\frac{1}{2}$ pound costs \$.60

$\frac{2}{2}$ or 1 pound costs \$1.20

7. Ans. 3 To find the average we must find the total wages and divide this total by the number of wage earners.
The clerks earned $4 \times 150 = \$600$

The clerks earned $4 \times 150 = \$600$
The stock boys earned $2 \times 75 = \$150$
Total wages $= 600 + 150 = \$750$

Since there were 6 wage earners the average is $750 \div 6 = \$125$.

8. Ans. 3 If the problem had indicated that each of the first two shelves contains 100 books and the third shelf 50 books, we would have had $100 + 100 + 50 = 250$ books.
We follow the same procedure with x and y books

$$x + x + y = 2x + y \text{ books}$$

9. Ans. 1 The area of the front lawn is $25 \times 15 = 375$ square feet.
The area of the back lawn is $50 \times 30 = 1500$ square feet.
The ratio of the area of the front lawn to the area of the back lawn is $375:1500$, or in simplified form, the ratio is $1:4$.
Note that when we double both length and width of a rectangle we obtain a new rectangle which has 4 times the area of the original triangle. This is always true regardless of the dimensions of the rectangle.

10. Ans. 3 32 fluid ounces = 1 quart
     128 fluid ounces = 4 quarts, or 1 gallon
     12 gallons = 128 × 12 = 1536 fluid ounces

The number of portions of milk is 1536 ÷ 6 = 256.

11. Ans. 3 In the diagram, $\triangle ABC$ is a right triangle. To find side AB we may use the Pythagorean Rule.

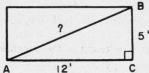

$$(AB)^2 = (AC)^2 + (BC)^2$$
$$(AB)^2 = (12)^2 + (5)^2$$
$$(AB)^2 = 144 + 25 = 169$$
$$AB = \sqrt{169}$$
$$AB = 13$$

12. Ans. 2 An examination of the diagram indicates that each side of the square is 6 inches long. Thus, the area of the square is 36 square inches.

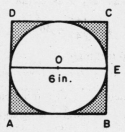

 To find the area of the shaded portion we must subtract the area of the circle from the area of the square. Since the diameter of the circle is 6 inches, the radius of the circle is 3 inches. To find the area of the circle we use the formula $A = \pi r^2$. In this case, $A = \pi \times 3 \times 3 = 9\pi$.
 The area of the shaded portion is $36 - 9\pi$.

13. Ans. 2 $3a^2 - 2a + 5$ means $3 \times a \times a - 2 \times a + 5$
When $a = 4$ we have

$$3 \times 4 \times 4 - 2 \times 4 + 5 = 48 - 8 + 5 = 45$$

14. Ans. 3 $3x - 5 = 16$
$$3x - 5 + 5 = 16 + 5$$
$$3x = 21$$
$$x = \tfrac{21}{3} = 7$$

15. Ans. 3 The clothing expense is 22% of the budget. Thus, the angle at the center is .22 × 360 = 79.2° and not 44°.

16. Ans. 2 After lunch, the flask is $\frac{2}{3}$ full. At dinner $\frac{3}{4}$ of this $\frac{2}{3}$ is used.

$$\tfrac{3}{4} \times \tfrac{2}{3} = \tfrac{1}{2}$$

Thus, at lunch $\frac{1}{3}$ of the flask is used and at dinner $\frac{1}{2}$ of the flask is used.

$$\tfrac{1}{3} + \tfrac{1}{2} = \tfrac{2}{6} + \tfrac{3}{6} = \tfrac{5}{6}$$

At both meals, $\frac{5}{6}$ of the flask is used.
Thus, $\frac{1}{6}$ of the flask remains.

17. Ans. 3 25% = $\frac{1}{4}$, $\frac{1}{4}$ of 800 = 200

     The down payment was $200
    20 installments at $35 = 20 × 35 = $700
     Total payment was 200 + 700 = $900

    Savings by paying cash = 900 — 800 = $100

18. Ans. 4 The commission part of his salary was

$$15,000 - 5,000 = \$10,000$$
Sales above $10,000 were
$$110,000 - 10,000 = 100,000$$

Thus, he received a commission of $10,000 on $100,000 of sales. His rate of commission, axpressed as a fraction, was $\frac{10000}{100000} = \frac{1}{10}$, $\frac{1}{10} = 10\%$

19. Ans. 1 The sum of two lengths of the rectangle is $15'6'' + 15'6'' = 31'$.

Since the perimeter is 40 feet the sum of the two widths is $40 - 31 = 9$ feet.

Each width is $\frac{1}{2}$ of 9 feet, or $4\frac{1}{2}$ feet, or 4 feet 6 inches.

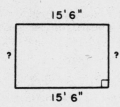

20. Ans. 2 The ratio of the pole to its shadow is equal to the ratio of the fence post to its shadow.

Let $x = $ height of the telephone pole.

$$\frac{x}{48} = \frac{3}{4}$$

$$4x = 3 \times 48 = 144$$

$$x = \frac{144}{4} = 36$$

The telephone pole is 36 feet high.

21. Ans. 3 Since 1 kilometer $= \frac{5}{8}$ of a mile, each mile $= \frac{8}{5}$ of a kilometer.

$$\frac{8}{5} \times 2,500 = 8 \times 500 = 4,000$$

22. Ans. 1 At $50 per $1,000, the annual premium for $10,000 is $50 \times 10 = \$500$. Over a 20-year period Mr. Green pays $20 \times 500 = \$10,000$.

23. Ans. 4

Let $x = $ the measure of the smallest angle.
Then $3x = $ the measure of the largest angle
And $2x = $ the measure of the third angle

$$x + 3x + 2x = 180$$
$$6x = 180$$
$$x = \frac{180}{6} = 30$$
$$3x = 3(30) = 90$$

24. Ans. 3 The increase was $4,800 - 4,000 = \$800$

The rate of increase, expressed as a fraction is $\frac{800}{4000}$.

When reduced to lowest terms $\frac{800}{4000} = \frac{1}{5}$.

$$\frac{1}{5} = 20\%$$

25. Ans. 3
$$\begin{array}{r} 5542 \\ -\ 5472 \\ \hline 70 \end{array}$$

70 kilowatt-hours of current were used
For first 10 kilowatt-hours   —$ .82
For next 45 kilowatt-hours, $.05 \times 45$—$2.25
For final 15 kilowatt-hours, $.03 \times 15$—$ .45
Total charge—$3.52

26. Ans. 2 $105\% = 105,000$

$$1\% = \frac{105,000}{105} = 1,000$$

$$100\% = 100\,(1,000) = \$100,000$$

27. Ans. 2 Rent + Food = $\frac{1}{4} + \frac{1}{5} = \frac{9}{20}$

Thus, $\frac{11}{20}$ of income was left for other expenses

$$\frac{11}{20} = 99$$
$$\frac{1}{20} = 99 \div 11 = 9$$
$$\frac{20}{20} = 20 \, (9) = \$180$$

28. Ans. 2 We may regard this figure as a rectangle with two semi-circles cut out. Or, we may regard the figure as a rectangle with one circle cut out.

Area of rectangle = $7 \times 15 = 105$ sq. in.

Area of circle = $\pi r^2 = \frac{\overset{11}{\cancel{22}}}{\cancel{7}} \times \frac{\cancel{7}}{\cancel{2}} \times \frac{7}{2} = \frac{77}{2}$

Area of circle = $\frac{77}{2}$ or $38\frac{1}{2}$ sq. in.

Area of machine part = $105 - 38\frac{1}{2} = 66\frac{1}{2}$ sq. in.

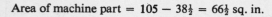

29. Ans. 4 $S = \frac{1}{2}gt^2$ means $S = \frac{1}{2} \times g \times t \times t$
$$S = \frac{1}{2} \times 32 \times 8 \times 8 = 1,024$$

30. Ans. 3 Let $7x$ = the larger number
And $2x$ = the smaller number

$$7x - 2x = 45$$
$$5x = 45$$
$$x = \frac{45}{5} = 9$$

The larger number is $7x$, or 7×9, or 63.

ANSWERS EXPLAINED

TEST **4**

1. Ans. 3 $\frac{7}{8} - \frac{1}{4} = \frac{7}{8} - \frac{2}{8} = \frac{5}{8}$

The man used $\frac{5}{8}$ of a full tank.
$$\frac{5}{8} \times 320 = 200 \text{ gallons}$$
200 gallons at \$.20 per gallon = $200 \times .2 = \$40$.

2. Ans. 4 Similar figures have the same shape.

3. Ans. 2 The angle at the center of the shaded portion is 60°. This represents $\frac{60}{360}$, or $\frac{1}{6}$ of the circle.

Since the family income is \$8,400 per year, the savings amounted to $\frac{1}{6} \times 8,400 = \$1,400$.

4. Ans. 2 To find the average speed for the trip we must divide the total distance covered by the total time.

At 45 miles per hour the man covered $45 \times 2 = 90$ miles
Total distance covered = $90 + 140 = 230$ miles
Total time = $2 + 3 = 5$ hours
Average rate of speed = $230 \div 5 = 46$ miles per hour.

5. Ans. 2 Between 1935 and 1940 the change in food expenditures was very slight.

6. Ans. 3 Since the measures of two angles are 40° and 70°, the measure of the third angle is 180° — 110° = 70°.

Since the measures of two angles of the triangle are 70°, the triangle is isosceles.

7. Ans. 2 $25\% = \frac{1}{4}$, $\frac{1}{4}$ of 440 = 110

$440 - 110 = \$330$, Dealer X offer
$10\% = \frac{1}{10}$, $5\% = \frac{1}{20}$
$\frac{1}{10}$ of 400 = 40
$440 - 40 = \$360$
$\frac{1}{20}$ of 360 = 18
$360 - 18 = \$342$, Dealer Y offer
$342 - 330 = \$12$

$12 is saved by taking Dealer X's offer.

8. Ans. 3 We are asked to find the area of a large rectangle x units long and y units wide. From this area two squares are cut out, each one a units on a side

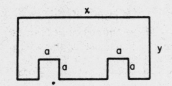

The area of the large rectangle = xy
The area of each of the small squares = a^2
The area of the figure is $xy - 2a^2$

9. Ans. 4 Let x = the number of foul baskets.
And $x + 8$ = the number of field baskets
x = the number of foul basket points
$2(x + 8)$ = the number of field basket points

$$x + 2(x + 8) = 103$$
$$x + 2x + 16 = 103$$
$$3x + 16 = 103$$
$$3x + 16 - 16 = 103 - 16$$
$$3x = 87$$
$$x = \tfrac{87}{3} = 29$$
$$x + 8 = 29 + 8 = 37$$

There were 37 field baskets.

10. Ans. 1 6 in. = $\frac{1}{2}$ foot

To find the volume of the wall we use the formula
$$V = l \times w \times h$$
In this case, $l = 50$, $w = 6$, and $h = \frac{1}{2}$
$$V = 50 \times 6 \times \tfrac{1}{2} = 150 \text{ cu. ft.}$$
Weight of wall = $150 \times 120 = 18{,}000$ pounds
Weight of wall in tons = $\frac{18000}{2000} = 9$ tons.

11. Ans. 3 Let x = the number of hours each motorist traveled.

Since the first motorist traveled at the rate of 30 miles per hour for x hours he covered $30x$ miles.

Since the second motorist traveled at the rate of 40 miles per hour for x hours he covered $40x$ miles.

	RATE	× *TIME*	= *DISTANCE*
First Motorist	30	x	$30x$
Second Motorist	40	x	$40x$

The sum of both distances is 420

$$30x + 40x = 420$$
$$70x = 420$$
$$x = \tfrac{420}{70} = 6$$

They meet in 6 hours.

12. Ans. 2 3 in. = $\frac{3}{12}$ = $\frac{1}{4}$ foot, $5\frac{1}{4}$ = $\frac{21}{4}$

$$\frac{21}{4} \times \$4.00 = \$21.00$$

13. Ans. 2 If the auditorium had contained 10 rows with 7 seats in each row we would have obtained the result by multiplying 10 by 7.
  In this case, we must multiply x by y.
  The result is xy.

14. Ans. 3 We can answer this question by taking a specific case. Suppose we let each side of the square be 10 units. Then the length of the rectangle would be 12 units and its width would be 8 units.

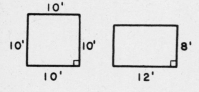

  Area of square = 10 × 10 = 100 square units
Area of rectangle = 12 × 8 = 96 square units

  The area of the square is 4 square units greater than the area of the rectangle.
  No matter what we take as the dimensions of the square, the answer will still be the same.

15. Ans. 2 The original mixture contains 7 ounces of turpentine out of a total of 21 ounces. We can express the fractional part of turpentine in the mixture as

$$\frac{7}{21} \left(\frac{\text{amount of turpentine}}{\text{amount of total mixture}} \right)$$

  If we now add 4 ounces of water, the amount of turpentine remains at 7 and the mixture is increased to 25 ounces. The fractional part of turpentine in the new mixture is

$$\frac{7}{25} \left(\frac{\text{amount of turpentine}}{\text{amount of total mixture}} \right)$$

  To convert this to a per cent we divide 7 by 25

$$\begin{array}{r} .28 \\ 25)\overline{7.0} \\ \underline{5\,0} \\ 2\,00 \\ \underline{2\,00} \end{array}$$

  The per cent of turpentine in the new mixture is 28%.

16. Ans. 3 In right triangle ABC, AB is the hypotenuse. To find AB we may use the Pythagorean Rule.

$(AB)^2 = (AC)^2 + (BC)^2$
$(AB)^2 = (80)^2 + (60)^2$
$(AB)^2 = 6400 + 3600$
$(AB)^2 = 10,000$
$AB = \sqrt{10,000}$
$AB = 100$

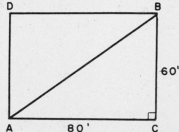

The diagonal distance is 100 feet.

17. Ans. 1 Let x = number of degrees in the smallest angle
And $x + 20°$ = number of degrees in the second angle
And $x + 40°$ = number of degrees in the third angle

$$x + x + 20 + x + 40 = 180$$
$$3x + 60 = 180$$
$$3x + 60 - 60 = 180 - 60$$
$$3x = 120$$
$$x = \tfrac{120}{3} = 40$$

The smallest angle of the triangle is 40°.

18. Ans. 2 Since $1''$ represents 40 feet, we must find the number of 40 feet units in 175 feet.

$$\begin{array}{r} 4 \\ 40)\overline{175} \\ \underline{160} \\ 15 \end{array}$$

Thus, we have $4\tfrac{15}{40}$, or $4\tfrac{3}{8}$ inches.

19. Ans. 1 If 4 inches are cut off on each side of the length, the length of the resulting box is $30 - 8 = 22$ inches.

If 4 inches are cut off on each side of the width, the width of the resulting box is $22 - 8 = 14$ inches.

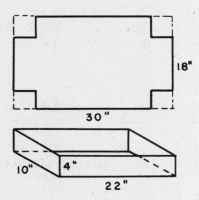

The height of the box = 4 inches
The *Volume* of the box = lwh
$$= 22 \times 10 \times 4 = 880$$

Volume = 880 cu. in.

20. Ans. 3

Let x = number of half-dollars
And $42 - x$ = number of quarters
$50x$ = value of half-dollars
$25(42 - x)$ = value of quarters
$$50x + 25(42 - x) = 1600$$
$$50x + 1050 - 25x = 1600$$
$$25x + 1050 = 1600$$
$$25x + 1050 - 1050 = 1600 - 1050$$
$$25x = 550$$
$$x = \tfrac{550}{25} = 22$$

15% of income is $150
1% of income is $150 \div 15 = \$10$
100% of income is $100 \times 10 = \$1,000$

21. Ans. 1 If it takes a man 10 hours to do a job, he can do $\tfrac{1}{10}$ of it in 1 hour, $\tfrac{2}{10}$ in 2 hours, etc.

If it takes an electrician x hours to wire a house, he can do $\dfrac{1}{x}$ of it in 1 hour, and $\dfrac{2}{x}$ in 2 hours.

22. Ans. 3 $8y^2 - 7y - 1$ means $8 \times y \times y - 7xy - 1$.
When $y = 5$, we have
$$8 \times 5 \times 5 - 7 \times 5 - 1 = 200 - 35 - 1 = 164$$

23. Ans. 2 The total expenditure is $20\% + 23\% + 42\% = 85\%$. The family saves $100\% - 85\% = 15\%$.

$$15\% \text{ of income} = \$150$$
$$1\% \text{ of income} = 150 \div 15 = \$10$$
$$100\%, \text{ or total income} = 100 \times 10 = \$1,000$$

24. Ans. 3 If 4 apples cost 29 cents, then one apple costs $\frac{29}{4}$.
Two dozen apples cost $24 \times \frac{29}{4} = 174$, or $1.74.

ALTERNATE METHOD

We may also obtain the result by using a proportion.
Let x = cost of 2 dozen apples

$$\frac{29}{4} = \frac{x}{24}$$

$$4x = 696$$

$$x = \frac{696}{4} = 174, \text{ or } \$1.74$$

25. Ans. 2 $2x + 7 = 19$
$$2x + 7 - 7 = 19 - 7$$
$$2x = 12$$
$$x = \tfrac{12}{2} = 6$$

26. Ans. 4 Let $2x$ = measure of the smallest angle of the triangle
And $3x$ = measure of the larger acute angle of the triangle
Since the sum of the measures of the angles of a triangle is $180°$, the sum of the measures of the acute angles of a triangle is $90°$.

$$2x + 3x = 90$$
$$5x = 90$$
$$x = \tfrac{90}{5} = 18$$
$$2x = 36$$

The measure of the smallest angle of the triangle is $36°$.

27. Ans. 4 At $1,500 per month the salesman earned $12 \times 1,500 = \$18,000$ per year.
At 10% of sales, the salesman earned $.1 \times 198,000 = 19,800$ per year.
He gained $19,800 - 18,000 = \$1,800$ by taking the commission basis.

28. Ans. 1

Policy	Premium
$1,000 at age 20	$18
$2,000 at age 25	$40
$2,000 at age 30	$48
$5,000 at age 35	$140
Total	$246

29. Ans. 4 The area of the smaller roof = $40 \times 40 = 1,600$ square feet.
The area of the larger roof = $80 \times 80 = 6,400$ square feet.
Since $6,400 = 4 \times 1,600$ the area of the larger roof is 8 times as great as the area of the smaller roof.

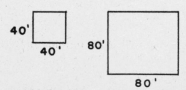

Thus, the cost of the larger roof = $4 \times 800 = \$3,200$.

30. Ans. 3 Let x = width of rectangle

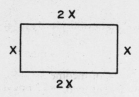

$$x + 24 + x + 24 = 84$$
$$2x + 48 = 84$$
$$2x + 48 - 48 = 84 - 48$$
$$2x = 36$$
$$x = \tfrac{36}{2} = 18 \text{ feet}$$

ANSWERS EXPLAINED

TEST 5

1. Ans. 4 $20\% = \tfrac{1}{5}$, $\tfrac{1}{5}$ of 5,000 = \$1,000 down payment
24 installments at \$200 each = $24 \times 200 = \$4,800$
$1,000 + 4,800 = \$5,800$ paid by buying on the installment plan.
$5,800 - 5,000 = \$800$ saved by paying cash.

2. Ans. 2 Since the measure of an angle that describes a complete revolution is 360°, we have

$$\tfrac{72}{360} = \tfrac{1}{5}$$

3. Ans. 3 We can find the total area by finding the area of the rectangle and adding to it the area of the triangle.

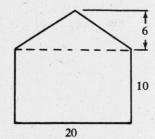

Area of rectangle = $20 \times 10 = 200$
Area of triangle = $\tfrac{1}{2}bh = \tfrac{1}{2}(20)(6) = 60$
Total area = $200 + 60 = 260$ sq. ft.

4. Ans. 4 20% of $50 = \tfrac{1}{5} \times 50 = 10$

$50 - 10 = \$40$, Cost to dealer
10% of $50 = \tfrac{1}{10} \times 50 = 5$
$50 + 5 = \$55$, Selling price of watch
$55 - 40 = \$15$ Profit

5. Ans. 4 Each son received $\tfrac{1}{3}$ of $\tfrac{1}{2}$, or $\tfrac{1}{3} \times \tfrac{1}{2}$, or $\tfrac{1}{6}$ of estate.

$\tfrac{1}{6}$ of estate = \$8,000
$\tfrac{6}{6}$, or total estate = $6 \times 8,000 = \$48,000$

6. Ans. 2 140% of cost = 28
1% of cost = $\tfrac{28}{140}$
100%, or full cost = $\tfrac{28}{140} \times 100 = \tfrac{2800}{140} = \$20$

7. Ans. 3 Readings: $-12°$
$-7°$
$-2°$
Change: $-21° + 6° = -15°$

To obtain the average we divide -15 by 5 to get the result $-3°$.

8. Ans. 2 30 feet =   = 10 yards
24 feet =   = 8 yards
9 feet =   = 3 yards

To find the volume of the cellar we use the formula
$$V = l \times w \times h$$

In this case, $l = 10$, $w = 8$, and $h = 3$
$$V = 10 \times 8 \times 3 = 240 \text{ cubic yards}$$
$$240 \times 2 = \$480, \text{ cost of digging cellar}$$

9. Ans. 2 If it takes 20 men 36 days to do a job, the total amount of work is $20 \times 36 = 720$ man-days.

Let x = number of days it would take 24 men

$$24x = 720$$
$$x = \tfrac{720}{24} = 30 \text{ days}$$

It would take 24 men 30 days.

10. Ans. 1 In the right triangle ABC, we use the Pythagorean Rule

$$(AB)^2 = (AC)^2 + (BC)^2$$
$$(AB)^2 = (28)^2 + (21)^2$$
$$(AB)^2 = 784 + 441 = 1225$$
$$AB = \sqrt{1225} = 35$$

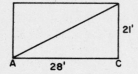

11. Ans. 3 Each brick covers an area $4''$ by $8''$ or 32 square inches.

It is necessary to cover an area 6 feet by 30 feet, or 72 inches by 360 inches. Area to be covered is $72 \times 360 = 25,920$ square inches. To obtain the number of bricks needed we divide 25,920 by 32

$$\begin{array}{r} 810 \\ 32\overline{)25920} \\ \underline{256} \\ 32 \\ \underline{32} \end{array}$$

810 bricks are needed.

12. Ans. 2 The area of the smaller pie = $5 \times 5 \times \pi = 25\pi$ square inches
The area of the larger pie = $10 \times 10 \times \pi = 100\pi$ square inches
The ratio of the area of the smaller pie to the larger pie is $25\pi : 100\pi$, or $1:4$.

13. Ans. 3 Since $\tfrac{5}{2}$ as much rhubarb is used as is needed we must use $\tfrac{5}{2}$ as much sugar as was called for in the recipe

$$\tfrac{5}{2} \times \tfrac{1}{2} = \tfrac{5}{4}, \text{ or } 1\tfrac{1}{4} \text{ lb.}$$

14. Ans. 1   1 kilogram = 2.2 pounds
10 kilograms = 22 pounds

Since the traveler has 22 pounds, or 10 kilograms, in excess baggage he must pay 10×2.50, or \$25.

15. Ans. 4 1 ft = 12 inches
4 yd = $4 \times 36 = 144$ inches

The scale 1 ft to 4 yds means

12 inches to 144 inches

Thus 1 ft to 4 yds represents a scale ratio $1:12$.

16. Ans. 3 To obtain the area of the shaded portion we find the area of the square and subtract from it the area of the 4 quarter-circles.

Area of square = $10 \times 10 = 100$ square inches

Area of 4 quarter-circles is the same as the area of one complete circle. Since the radius of each quarter-circle is 5 the area of the 4 quarter-circles is πr^2, or $\pi \times 5 \times 5 = 25\pi$.

The area of the shaded portion is $100 - 25\pi$.

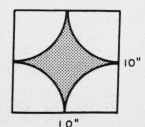

17. Ans. **4** If a man buys x gallons of gas at 38 cents a gallon he pays $38x$ cents. A 10-dollar bill contains 1,000 cents. Thus, the result is $1000 - 38x$ cents. Note that we subtract a number of cents, $38x$, from a number of cents, 1,000.

18. Ans. **1** $3y^2 + 2(y - 1)$ means $3 \times y \times y + 2 \times (y - 1)$.
If $y = 5$, we have

$$3 \times 5 \times 5 + 2(5 - 1) = 75 + 2 \times 4$$
$$= 75 + 8 = 83$$

19. Ans. **1** $20\% = \frac{1}{5}$. After the price was raised by 20% the new price was $\frac{6}{5}$ of the old price.

$$\frac{6}{5} \text{ of price} = \$180$$
$$\frac{1}{5} \text{ of price} = \$30$$
$$\frac{5}{5} \text{ of price} = \$150$$

20. Ans. **4** Let n = the number

$$\frac{1}{4}n = \frac{5}{20}n$$
$$\frac{1}{5}n = \frac{4}{20}n$$
$$\frac{1}{4}n - \frac{1}{5}n = \frac{5}{20}n - \frac{4}{20}n = \frac{1}{20}n$$
$$\frac{1}{20}n = 7$$
$$\frac{20}{20}n = 20 \times 7 = 140$$

21. Ans. **3** $25\% = \frac{1}{4}$

$$\frac{1}{4} \text{ of } \$200 = \$50$$
$$200 - 50 = \$150, \text{ cost of coat}$$
$$\frac{1}{2} = \frac{3}{6}, \frac{1}{3} = \frac{2}{6}$$
$$\frac{1}{2} + \frac{1}{3} = \frac{3}{6} + \frac{2}{6} = \frac{5}{6}$$
$$\frac{6}{6} - \frac{5}{6} = \frac{1}{6}$$

Thus, Mr. Hill had to pay $\frac{1}{6}$ of the cost of the coat on April 10.
$$\frac{1}{6} \text{ of } \$150 = \frac{1}{6} \times 150 = \$25$$

22. Ans. **4** In 1967, the receipts were \$600,000 and the expenses were \$500,000. In 1967, the excess of receipts over expenses was \$100,000.

23. Ans. **4** The ratio of the pole to its shadow is 6 : 2, or 3 : 1. That is, the pole was three times as long as its shadow.
The spire is also three times as long as its shadow. And $3 \times 29 = 87$ feet, height of spire.

ALTERNATE METHOD

Let x = height of spire

$$\frac{x}{29} = \frac{6}{2}$$
$$2x = 174$$
$$x = 87$$

24. Ans. **2** At 20 miles per hour, the car covers 20 miles in 60 minutes. Therefore, the motorist covers 1 mile in 3 minutes.
At 60 miles per hour, the car covers 60 miles in 60 minutes. Therefore, the motorist covers 1 mile in 1 minute.

$$3 \text{ minutes} - 1 \text{ minute} = 2 \text{ minutes}$$

25. Ans. 4   12 oz. $= \frac{12}{16} = \frac{3}{4}$ of a pound.

$1\frac{3}{4}$ pounds of meat cost \$1.75

$\frac{7}{4}$ pounds of meat cost \$1.75

$\frac{1}{4}$ pound of meat costs   .25

$\frac{4}{4}$, or 1 pound of meat, costs $4 \times .25 = \$1.00$

26. Ans. 2 $40\% = \frac{4}{100} = \frac{2}{5}$

$$\frac{2}{5} \times 10 = 4$$

The jug contains 4 quarts of wine.

If 10 quarts of water are added to the jug, the jug contains 20 quarts. Since no wine is added the jug still contains 4 quarts of wine.

Thus, the mixture in the jug is $\frac{4}{20}$, or 20%, wine.

27. Ans. 2   If we examine the choices we see that the cost of 1 ounce of butter is
(1) more than \$.04
(2) less than \$.04
(3) more than \$.04
(4) more than \$.04
Thus, (2) is the best buy.

28. Ans. 3   As commission, the salesman received $240 - 100 = \$140$.

2% of sales $= \$140$
1% of sales $= \$70$
100% of sales $= 100 \times 70 = \$7,000$

29. Ans. 2   We represent the fraction of games won over total number of games as

$$\frac{\text{games won}}{\text{games played}} = \frac{32}{43}$$

The team plays 21 more games. Thus, the team plays a total of $43 + 21$, or 64 games. If the team is to win 75%, or $\frac{3}{4}$, of its games it must win $\frac{3}{4} \times 64$; or 48 games. Thus, the team must win $48 - 32$, or 16 more games.

30. Ans. 2 $\dfrac{x + 6y + 12z}{4} = \dfrac{\frac{1}{2} + 6 \times \frac{1}{3} + 12 \times \frac{1}{4}}{4}$

$$= \frac{\frac{1}{2} + 2 + 3}{4} = \frac{5\frac{1}{2}}{4}$$

$$= \frac{11}{2} \div 4 = \frac{11}{2} \times \frac{1}{4} = \frac{11}{8}$$

$$\frac{11}{8} = 1\frac{3}{8}.$$

PART THREE

8

Test A

TEST YOURSELF

Now that you have completed your study of the materials we have prepared and the exercises which were included to give you practice, you may wish to test yourself on materials similar to those used in the actual examination. The correct answers are included so that you can see where you made any mistakes. If you locate any, go back to the question and try to find the reason for your error.

SUB-TEST **1.**

Correctness and Effectiveness of Expression

Directions **(1-20):**   **Choose the *one* misspelled word in each of the following numbered groups.**

1. (1) license   (2) misstep   (3) analysis   (4) solemn   (5) libarian

2. (1) immediate   (2) challenging   (3) indispensable   (4) exaggerate
   (5) campain

3. (1) feirce   (2) conductor   (3) spiritual   (4) faucet   (5) rabbit

4. (1) durable   (2) exquisite   (3) nuetral   (4) traitorous
   (5) promptness

5. (1) circulate   (2) utility   (3) contradict   (4) interupt
   (5) compliment

6. (1) cemetery   (2) medical   (3) legality   (4) stingy   (5) apparant

7. (1) purity   (2) commentator   (3) discouragment   (4) sergeant
   (5) conscience

8. (1) temporary   (2) scandel   (3) subtract   (4) implication
   (5) noodle

8.   1 2 3 4 5

9. (1) biscuit   (2) original   (3) forehead   (4) doggedly   (5) keeness

9.   1 2 3 4 5

10. (1) elementary   (2) mortgage   (3) desireous   (4) occupancy
    (5) illiterate

10. 1 2 3 4 5

11. (1) travel   (2) conductor   (3) equiping   (4) proposal
    (5) twofold

11. 1 2 3 4 5

12. (1) philosopher   (2) minority   (3) managment   (4) emergency
    (5) bibliography

12. 1 2 3 4 5

13. (1) constructive   (2) employee   (3) stalwart   (4) masterpeice
    (5) theoretical

13. 1 2 3 4 5

14. (1) dissappoint   (2) volcanic   (3) illiterate   (4) myth
    (5) superficial

14. 1 2 3 4 5

15. (1) totally   (2) penninsula   (3) sandwich   (4) ripening
    (5) salvation

15. 1 2 3 4 5

16. (1) pastel   (2) aisle   (3) primarly   (4) journalistic
    (5) diminished

16. 1 2 3 4 5

17. (1) warrier   (2) unification   (3) enamel   (4) defendant
    (5) sustained

17. 1 2 3 4 5

18. (1) incidental   (2) lubricent   (3) conversion   (4) jurisdiction
    (5) diminished

18. 1 2 3 4 5

19. (1) auxilary   (2) boundaries   (3) session   (4) fabric   (5) ceiling

19. 1 2 3 4 5

20. (1) imperious   (2) deprecate   (3) rebutal   (4) wharf   (5) giddy

20. 1 2 3 4 5

Directions (21-30):   Each of the sentences contains an underlined expression. Below each sentence are four suggested answers. Choose the one that will make a correct sentence.

21. The chairman of the board, with ten of the directors, was elected for another term.   (1) Correct as is   (2) directors, were   (3) directors were   (4) directors was

   21. 1 2 3 4 5

22. While walking along the road, a car nearly struck me.   (1) Correct as is   (2) Walking along the road,   (3) While I was walking along the road,   (4) When walking along the road,

   22. 1 2 3 4 5

23. "I believe," the man said, "That you are wrong."   (1) Correct as is   (2) said, "that   (3) said; "That   (4) said; "that

   23. 1 2 3 4 5

24. There were all sorts of games for us to play: tennis, soccer, baseball, and golf.   (1) Correct as is   (2) play; tennis   (3) play, tennis,   (4) play tennis,

   24. 1 2 3 4 5

25. There have been many an argument about it's proper usage.   (1) Correct as is   (2) There have been many an argument about its   (3) There has been many an argument about it's   (4) There has been many an argument about its

   25. 1 2 3 4 5

26. "The wise man," said a famous writer, "reads both books and life itself."   (1) Correct as is   (2) writer "reads   (3) writer "Reads   (4) writer, "Reads

   26. 1 2 3 4 5

27. The book must be old, for it's cover is torn.   (1) Correct as is   (2) its' cover is torn   (3) it's cover is tore   (4) its cover is torn

   27. 1 2 3 4 5

28. William Faulkner's great themes are the following; courage, pride, pity.   (1) Correct as is   (2) following   (3) following,   (4) following:

   28. 1 2 3 4 5

29. My edition is more recent then yours.   (1) Correct as is   (2) than yours   (3) than your's   (4) then yours'

   29. 1 2 3 4 5

30. Because of the bad weather, the newspapers have lain there in the shipping room since morning.   (1) Correct as is   (2) have lain their   (3) have laid there   (4) have laid their

   30. 1 2 3 4 5

Directions (31-42):   In each of the following sets of sentences, only one sentence contains an error in grammar, usage, spelling, punctuation, etc. Choose the sentence which has this error.

31. (1) Is this hers or theirs?
    (2) Having been recognized, Frank took the floor.
    (3) Alex invited Sue; Paul, Marion; and Dan, Helen.
    (4) If I were able to do the task, you can be sure that I'd do it.
    (5) Stamp collecting, or philately as it is otherwise called is truly an international hobby.

   31. 1 2 3 4 5

32. (1) He has proved himself to be reliable.
(2) The fisherman had arisen before the sun.
(3) By the time the truck arrived, I had put out the blaze.
(4) The doctor with his colleagues were engaged in consultation.
(5) I chose to try out a new method, but in spite of my efforts it failed.

32. 1 2 3 4 5
     ‖ ‖ ‖ ‖ ‖

33. (1) He has drunk too much iced tea.
(2) I appreciated him doing that job for me.
(3) The royal family fled, but they were retaken.
(4) The secretary and the treasurer were both present on Friday.
(5) Iago protested his honesty, yet he continued to plot against Desdemona.

33. 1 2 3 4 5
     ‖ ‖ ‖ ‖ ‖

34. (1) The family were all together at Easter.
(2) It is altogether too fine a day for us to stay indoors.
(3) However much you dislike him, you should treat him fairly.
(4) The judges were already there when the contestants arrived.
(5) The boy's mother reported that he was alright again after the accident.

34. 1 2 3 4 5
     ‖ ‖ ‖ ‖ ‖

35. (1) Ham and eggs is a substantial breakfast.
(2) By the end of the week the pond had frozen.
(3) I should appreciate any assistance you could offer me.
(4) Being that tomorrow is Sunday, we expect to close early.
(5) If he were to win the medal, I for one would be disturbed.

35. 1 2 3 4 5
     ‖ ‖ ‖ ‖ ‖

36. (1) Give the letter to whoever comes for it.
(2) He feels bad, but his sister is the one who looks sicker.
(3) He had an unbelievable large capacity for hard physical work.
(4) Earth has nothing more beautiful to offer than the autumn colors of this section of the country.
(5) Happily we all have hopes that the future will soon bring forth the fruits of a lasting peace.

36. 1 2 3 4 5
     ‖ ‖ ‖ ‖ ‖

37. (1) This kind of apples is my favorite.
(2) Either of the players is capable of performing ably.
(3) Though trying my best to be calm, the choice was not an easy one for me.
(4) The nearest star is not several light years away; it is only 93,000,000 miles away.
(5) There were two things I still wished to do — to see the Lincoln Memorial and to climb up the Washington Monument.

37. 1 2 3 4 5
     ‖ ‖ ‖ ‖ ‖

38. (1) It is I who is to blame.
(2) That dress looks very good on Jane.
(3) People often take my brother to be me.
(4) I could but think she had deceived me.
(5) He himself told us that the story was true.

38. 1 2 3 4 5
     ‖ ‖ ‖ ‖ ‖

39. (1) They all went but Mabel and me.
    (2) Has he ever swum across the river?
    (3) We have a dozen other suggestions besides these.
    (4) The Jones's are going to visit their friends in Chicago.
    (5) The ideal that Arthur and his knights were in quest of was a better world order.

39.   1   2   3   4   5

40. (1) Would I were able to be there with you!
    (2) Whomever he desires to see should be admitted.
    (3) It is not for such as we to follow fashion blindly.
    (4) His causing the confusion seemed to affect him not at all.
    (5) Please notify all those whom you think should have this information.

40.   1   2   3   4   5

41. (1) She was not only competent but also friendly in nature.
    (2) Not only must we visualize the play we are reading; we must actually hear it.
    (3) The firm was not only acquiring a bad reputation but also indulging in illegal practices.
    (4) The bank was not only uncooperative but also was indifferent to new business offered them.
    (5) I know that a conscious effort was made not only to guard the material but also to keep it from being used.

41.   1   2   3   4   5

42. (1) How old shall you be on your next birthday?
    (2) I am sure that he has been here and did what was expected of him.
    (3) Near to the bank of the river, stood, secluded and still, the house of the hermit.
    (4) Because of its efficacy in treating many ailments, penicillin has become an important addition to the druggist's stock.
    (5) *Robinson Crusoe*, which is a fairy tale to the child, is a work of social philosophy to the mature thinker.

42.   1   2   3   4   5

Directions (43-60):   Choose the number of the word or expression that most nearly expresses the meaning of the capitalized word.

43. GHASTLY   (1) hasty   (2) furious   (3) breathless   (4) deathlike (5) spiritual

43.   1   2   3   4   5

44. BELLIGERENT   (1) worldly   (2) warlike   (3) loud-mouthed   (4) furious   (5) artistic

44.   1   2   3   4   5

45. PROFICIENCY   (1) wisdom   (2) oversupply   (3) expertness   (4) advancement   (5) sincerity

45.   1   2   3   4   5

46. COMPASSION   (1) rage   (2) strength of character   (3) forcefulness (4) sympathy   (5) uniformity

46.   1   2   3   4   5

47. DISSENSION   (1) treatise   (2) pretense   (3) fear   (4) lineage   (5) discord

47.   1   2   3   4   5
|| || || || ||

48. INTIMATE   (1) charm   (2) hint   (3) disguise   (4) frighten   (5) hum

48.   1   2   3   4   5
|| || || || ||

49. BERATE   (1) classify   (2) scold   (3) underestimate   (4) take one's time   (5) evaluate

49.   1   2   3   4   5
|| || || || ||

50. DEARTH   (1) scarcity   (2) width   (3) affection   (4) wealth   (5) warmth

50.   1   2   3   4   5
|| || || || ||

51. MEDITATE   (1) rest   (2) stare   (3) doze   (4) make peace   (5) reflect

51.   1   2   3   4   5
|| || || || ||

52. TAUNT   (1) jeer at   (2) tighten   (3) rescue   (4) interest   (5) ward off

52.   1   2   3   4   5
|| || || || ||

53. DEITY   (1) renown   (2) divinity   (3) delicacy   (4) destiny   (5) futility

53.   1   2   3   4   5
|| || || || ||

54. GRAVITY   (1) displeasure   (2) thankfulness   (3) suffering   (4) roughness   (5) seriousness

54.   1   2   3   4   5
|| || || || ||

55. CONTEMPTUOUS   (1) thoughtful   (2) soiled   (3) dishonorable   (4) scornful   (5) self-satisfied

55.   1   2   3   4   5
|| || || || ||

56. WAIVE   (1) exercise   (2) swing   (3) claim   (4) give up   (5) wear out

56.   1   2   3   4   5
|| || || || ||

57. ASPIRE   (1) fade away   (2) excite   (3) desire earnestly   (4) breathe heavily   (5) roughen

57.   1   2   3   4   5
|| || || || ||

58. PERTINENT   (1) related   (2) saucy   (3) quick   (4) impatient   (5) excited

58.   1   2   3   4   5
|| || || || ||

59. DEVASTATION   (1) desolation   (2) displeasure   (3) dishonor   (4) neglect   (5) religious fervor

59.   1   2   3   4   5
|| || || || ||

60. IMMINENT   (1) sudden   (2) important   (3) delayed   (4) threatening   (5) forceful

60. 1 2 3 4 5

ANSWERS TO SUB-TEST 1 *Correctness and Effectiveness of Expression*

1. 5	7. 3	13. 4	19. 1	25. 4	31. 5	37. 3	43. 4	49. 2	55. 4
2. 5	8. 2	14. 1	20. 3	26. 1	32. 4	38. 1	44. 2	50. 1	56. 4
3. 1	9. 5	15. 2	21. 1	27. 4	33. 2	39. 4	45. 3	51. 5	57. 3
4. 3	10. 3	16. 3	22. 3	28. 4	34. 5	40. 5	46. 4	52. 1	58. 1
5. 4	11. 3	17. 1	23. 2	29. 2	35. 4	41. 4	47. 5	53. 2	59. 1
6. 5	12. 3	18. 2	24. 1	30. 1	36. 3	42. 2	48. 2	54. 5	60. 4

What's your score?

If you got at least 50 correct you are prepared to take the test which will earn you a high school equivalency diploma.

SUB-TEST **2**

Interpretation of Literary Materials

Directions: **Read each of the following passages carefully. Then select the answer to each of the numbered questions which in your opinion best completes the statement or question.**

Passage I

The crooked crosses overhead proclaim
High homage to the god-of-living-rooms;
As silently as Pharaohs in their tombs
Men sit before the sacrificial flame.

The incense from the king-size cigarettes
Is wafted idly toward the altar box
Where current ministers harangue their flocks
With tired wit and lively murder threats.

Tonight I shall not play the pious role
Nor join the dead who once had been so quick;
But I shall try to walk, strange heretic,
Among neglected precincts of my soul.

1. The "crooked crosses" (line 1) are (1) church towers   (2) ceiling beams   (3) telephone poles   (4) television antennae   (5) altar decorations

1. 1 2 3 4 5

2. The poet implies that most television viewers are (1) amused   (2) belligerent   (3) hypnotized   (4) enthusiastic   (5) indifferent

2. 1 2 3 4 5

3. The poet criticizes television programs in (1) line 4   (2) line 6   (3) line 8
(4) line 10   (5) line 12

3.   1   2   3   4   5

4. The poet has decided not to watch television, but to devote the evening
to (1) prayer   (2) repentance   (3) self-education   (4) self-contempla-
tion   (5) physical conditioning

4.   1   2   3   4   5

5. From the poem it can be inferred that the poet is probably (1) a radio
listener rather than a television viewer   (2) a person well informed about
television   (3) not an owner of a television set (4) an employee of a
television studio   (5) a busy man who has very little time to devote to
entertainment.

5.   1   2   3   4   5

Passage II

John Greenleaf Whittier was the "Quaker-Puritan" scion of Massachusetts
farmers. For this frail young man, however, farm life was too tough an existence. His early interest in books and legends led him toward journalism, with
poetry as a pleasant side line. He became a Quaker firebrand and agitator, the
politician among abolitionists, and a gadfly to New England Congressmen during the original "Great Debate." His impassioned prose and poetry against
slavery were often directed at a clergy whose acceptance of it he fought as a
Quaker and a Christian.

Only after the Civil War, when emancipation had been at least nominally
won, did the aging Whittier emerge as the genial, easygoing "folkbard" remembered today. Until recently the prominence given this last phase of his literary
life by scholarly circles has obscured his earlier contributions to American
literature and political freedom and tolerance.

6. The author of this passage indicates that Whittier's   (1) lifetime was one
of invalidism   (2) nature caused him to detest farm life   (3) early
writings were overlooked for some time   (4) ideas are similar to Robert
Frost's   (5) chief desire was to lead the quiet life of the Quakers

6.   1   2   3   4   5

7. The passage implies that Whittier showed a kind of personal courage
when he   (1) fought in the Civil War   (2) attacked men in high places
with his writings   (3) worked on the family farm in spite of his dislike
for farming   (4) toned down his style because of his Quaker background
(5) gave up poetry to write political tracts

7.   1   2   3   4   5

8. From reading the passage, we may infer that if Whittier were alive today
he would most probably take up his pen in support of   (1) segregation
(2) politicians   (3) the United Nations   (4) desegregation   (5) folk
literature

8.   1   2   3   4   5

Passage III

Some scraps of evidence bear out those who hold a very high opinion of
the average level of culture among the Athenians of the great age. The funeral
speech of Pericles is the most famous indication from Athenian literature that

its level was indeed high. Pericles was, however, a politician, and he may have been flattering his audience. We know that thousands of Athenians sat hour after hour in the theater listening to the plays of the great Greek dramatists. These plays, especially the tragedies, are at very high intellectual level throughout. There are no letdowns, no concessions to the lowbrows or to the demands of "realism," such as the scene of the gravediggers in *Hamlet*. The music and dancing woven into these plays are almost certainly at an equally high level. Our opera—not Italian opera, not even Wagner, but the restrained, difficult opera of the 18th century—is probably the best modern parallel. The comparison is no doubt dangerous, but can you imagine almost the entire population of an American city (in suitable installments, of course) sitting through performances of Mozart's *Don Giovanni* or Gluck's *Orpheus*? Perhaps the Athenian masses went to these plays because of a lack of other amusements. They could at least understand something of what went on, since the subjects were part of their folklore. For the American people, the subjects of grand opera are not part of their folklore.

9. The title that best expresses the ideas of this passage is: (1) Advantages of Greek Culture (2) Music and Dancing in Greek plays (3) The Great Age of Greek Culture (4) The Influence of Greek Drama on Opera (5) The Inspired Greeks

9. 1 2 3 4 5

10. The author seems to question the sincerity of (1) politicians (2) playwrights (3) opera goers (4) "low brows" (5) gravediggers

10. 1 2 3 4 5

11. The author implies that the average American (1) enjoys *Hamlet* (2) loves folklore (3) does not understand grand opera (4) seeks a high cultural level (5) lacks entertainment

11. 1 2 3 4 5

12. The author's attitude toward Greek plays is one of (1) qualified approval (2) grudging admiration (3) studied indifference (4) partial hostility (5) great respect

12. 1 2 3 4 5

13. The author suggests that Greek plays (1) made great demands upon their actors (2) flattered their audiences (3) were written for a limited audience (4) were dominated by music and dancing (5) stimulated their audiences

13. 1 2 3 4 5

Passage IV

Stone-cutters fighting time with marble, you foredefeated
Challengers of oblivion,
Eat cynical earnings, knowing rock splits, records fall down,
The square-limbed Roman letters
Scale in the thaws, wear in the rain.   The poet as well
Builds his monument mockingly;
For man will be blotted out, the blithe earth die, the brave sun
Die blind and blacken to the heart:
Yet stones have stood for a thousand years, and pained thoughts found
The honey of peace in old poems.

14. The phrase "fighting time with marble" means that the stone-cutters (1) despair of completing their work in a lifetime (2) look for recognition in the future rather than in the present (3) consider marble the most challenging substance to work with (4) take pride in working slowly and carefully (5) aspire to produce an imperishable monument

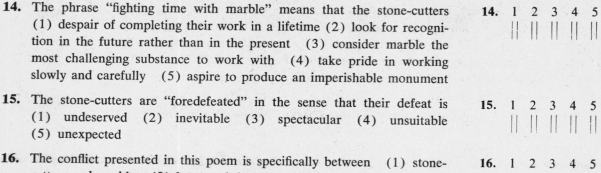

14. 1 2 3 4 5

15. The stone-cutters are "foredefeated" in the sense that their defeat is (1) undeserved (2) inevitable (3) spectacular (4) unsuitable (5) unexpected

15. 1 2 3 4 5

16. The conflict presented in this poem is specifically between (1) stone-cutters and marble (2) hope and despair (3) poets and stone-cutters (4) man's creations and time (5) challenge and achievement

16. 1 2 3 4 5

Passage V

I pray to be the tool which to your hand
Long use has shaped and moulded till it be
Apt for your need, and, unconsideringly,
You take it for its service. I demand
To be forgotten in the woven strand
Which grows the multicoloured tapestry
Of your bright life, and through its tissues lie
A hidden, strong, sustaining, grey-toned band.
I wish to dwell around your daylight dreams
The railing to the stairway of the clouds
To guard your steps securely up, where streams
A faery moonshine washing pale the crowds
Of pointed stars. Remember not whereby
You mount, protected, to the far-flung sky.

17. In this poem, the poet addresses himself to (1) anyone who reads the poem (2) a carpenter, a weaver, or a dreamer (3) a loved one (4) a very unhappy person (5) an artist

17. 1 2 3 4 5

18. In lines 4 through 8, the poet conveys his desire to (1) be appreciated by others (2) become a source of strength (3) live in contentment (4) create something beautiful (5) brighten the life of a friend

18. 1 2 3 4 5

19. In lines 9 through 11, the poet implies that the person whom he addresses (1) may need assistance (2) distrusts his dreams (3) is very troubled (4) wastes time daydreaming (5) bathes in "faery moonshine"

19. 1 2 3 4 5

20. In this poem, the attitude of the poet is one of (1) indifference (2) derision (3) resentment (4) despair (5) unselfishness

20. 1 2 3 4 5

Passage VI

If a serious literary critic were to write a favorable, full-length review of *How Could I Tell Mother She Frightened My Boy Friends Away,* Grace Plumbuster's new story, his startled readers would assume either that he had gone mad or that Grace Plumbuster was his editor's wife. If the review was unfavorable, they would probably be even more astonished; they would wonder why on earth he had squandered so much energy on attacking something that nobody in his right mind would dream of defending. Animadversions on the use of sledge hammers to crack nuts would be bandied about, and the reviewer's reputation would be gravely imperiled. The point is that serious literary critics are not expected to waste their time on pulp fiction. The elaborate demolition of ephemera is no part of their province. They can pick and choose, and when they elect to knock, fair play demands that they should take on someone more or less their own size.

21. The title that best expresses the ideas of this passage is: (1) The Task of the Critic (2) The Problem of the Pulps (3) The Critic's Readers (4) Why Critics Succeed (5) The Critic's Responsibility to the Editor

22. The writer of this passage most probably intended us to assume that the book *How Could I Tell Mother She Frightened My Boy Friends Away* is (1) satirical (2) autobiographical (3) serious (4) sincere (5) imaginary

23. According to the passage, the serious literary critic is expected to (1) dispute with his editor (2) favorably review pulp fiction, if he so desires (3) demand fair play from his readers (4) ignore insignificant writing (5) dispute the public

24. As used in this passage, the word "ephemera" (line 11) most nearly means (1) important works (2) literary reputations (3) trivial writing (4) selected authors (5) editors' opinions

21. 1 2 3 4 5

22. 1 2 3 4 5

23. 1 2 3 4 5

24. 1 2 3 4 5

Passage VII

It is here, perhaps, that poetry may best act nowadays as corrective and complementary to science. When science tells us that the galaxy to which our solar system belongs is so enormous that light, traveling at 186,000 miles per second, takes between 60,000 and 100,000 years to cross from one rim to the other of the galaxy, we laymen accept the statement but find it meaningless—beyond the comprehension of heart or mind. When science tells us that the human eye has about 137 million separate "seeing" elements, we are no less paralyzed, intellectually and emotionally. Man is appalled by the immensities and the minuteness which science has disclosed for him. They are indeed unimaginable. But may not poetry be a possible way of mediating them to our imagination? of scaling them down to imaginative comprehension? Let us remember Perseus, who could not look directly at the nightmare Gorgon without being turned to stone, but could look at her image reflected in the shield the goddess of wisdom lent him.

25. The title that best expresses the ideas of this passage is (1) Poetry and Imagination (2) A Modern Gorgon (3) Poetry as a Mediator (4) The Vastness of the Universe (5) Imaginative Man

25. 1 2 3 4 5

26. According to the passage, the average man   (1) should have a better memory   (2) is impatient with science   (3) cannot trust the scientists   (4) is overwhelmed by the discoveries of science   (5) does not understand either science or poetry

26. 1 2 3 4 5
  ‖ ‖ ‖ ‖ ‖

27. Perseus was most probably   (1) a scientist   (2) a legendary hero   (3) an early poet   (4) a horrible creature   (5) a minor god

27. 1 2 3 4 5
  ‖ ‖ ‖ ‖ ‖

28. This passage is chiefly developed by means of   (1) examples   (2) cause and effect   (3) narration   (4) definition   (5) anecdotes

28. 1 2 3 4 5
  ‖ ‖ ‖ ‖ ‖

ANSWERS TO SUB-TEST 2   *Interpretation of Literary Material*

1. 4	**6.** 3	**11.** 3	**16.** 4	**21.** 1	**26.** 4
2. 3	**7.** 2	**12.** 5	**17.** 3	**22.** 5	**27.** 2
3. 3	**8.** 4	**13.** 5	**18.** 2	**23.** 4	**28.** 1
4. 4	**9.** 3	**14.** 5	**19.** 1	**24.** 3	
5. 2	**10.** 1	**15.** 2	**20.** 5	**25.** 3	

What's your score?

If you got at least 21 correct you are prepared to take the test which will earn you a high school equivalency diploma.

SUB-TEST **3.**

Intrepretation of Reading Materials in the Social Studies

Directions: **Read each of the following passages carefully. Then select the answer to each of the numbered questions which in your opinion best completes the statement or question.**

Passage I

The whole question of industrialism is a complex one. For laborers, it means that greater skills are required, and, in the last analysis, that the work may prove more difficult than in the past, where the time element had less importance. The positive benefits, however, outweigh these considerations. The laborer today has greater leisure, is less provincial, and enjoys the fruits of his labors to a far greater degree than was hitherto possible. In a way we may say that we have reached the end of the Industrial Revolution. We may call it today a technological revolution, in that science has found ways to utilize the efforts of a man beyond the dreams of yesteryear. The dawn of the Atomic Age presages further benefits for all of us. Some have called the dawning age the Power-Metal Age. The term is significant, for in these two elements our country is rich and, if not self-sufficient, at least we have shown ourselves alert in exploiting these two elements to a degree hitherto unseen in the world.

1. The author's chief purpose in writing this passage seems to be to (1) point out the difficulties of industrialism (2) defend the work of scientists (3) explain why modern man has considerable leisure time (4) explain why the Industrial Revolution came to an end (5) describe certain manifestations of industrialism

2. The author implies that the laborer of tomorrow will (1) enjoy greater benefits (2) have fewer opportunities for employment (3) grow more provincial (4) be destroyed by automation (5) be required to work more slowly

3. The author implies that the future strength of his country will be found in its (1) vast numbers of laborers (2) skilled technicians (3) plentiful sources of power and metal (4) more effective use of leisure time (5) mobile labor force

4. When the author states that "work may prove more difficult than in the past" (line 3), he implies that (1) back-breaking physical labor is going to return (2) running the machines of the future will be an exacting task (3) wartime conditions will make work difficult (4) the laborer is going to have to spend more time on the job (5) many laborers are going to be out of jobs

5. The first positive proof that the author has a specific country in mind is in line (1) 1 (2) 6 (3) 7 (4) 12 (5) 5

Passage II

Many harsh allegations were made against Woodrow Wilson by his enemies, and some still survive in the folklore of today. It was said, for example, that he wanted only flattery from his associates, that he did not take kindly to frankness or dissent. It was said that he was a cold, distant, arrogant man who reached his decisions, not by rational processes, but by intuition, and formed his conclusions in isolation.

To me these allegations seem completely preposterous. They do not fit in with any experience I ever had with him, although admittedly my contacts were limited. That he was a man of steely determination who allowed no compromise on what he regarded as a matter of principle is transparently true. Equally true is the fact that he had too little appreciation of "human lubricants": the need of explanation, conference, and team play, the ability to keep differences of opinion on an impersonal level. He did not suffer fools gladly—neither fools nor people with untidy minds. There was an element of intellectual impatience in his makeup, and more than a dash of volatile temper. It was not easy for him to forget or forgive. In other words, he was a human being, and he had his temperamental and physical limitations.

6. In the author's experience, Wilson had little patience with people who (1) attempted to flatter him (2) questioned his motives (3) did not think clearly (4) played practical jokes (5) were too outspoken

7. The author evidently admires Wilson for his   (1) self-control   (2) personal integrity   (3) dignified manner   (4) powers of intuition   (5) objective outlook

7.   1   2   3   4   5

8. The statement, ". . . he had too little appreciation of 'human lubricants,' " suggests that Wilson   (1) lacked a sense of humor   (2) enjoyed controversy for its own sake   (3) found it difficult to express gratitude   (4) was not at ease in social gatherings   (5) did not always consider others' ideas and feelings

8.   1   2   3   4   5

9. The author admits that in his experience Wilson   (1) had a quick temper   (2) was haughty in manner   (3) reached irrational decisions   (4) refused to consult his advisers   (5) relied heavily on intuition

9.   1   2   3   4   5

10. In the second paragraph, the author indicates that Wilson   (1) was disliked by those who knew him intimately   (2) allowed his physical condition to affect his judgment   (3) was hurt by the accusations of his enemies   (4) possessed characteristics that caused him to be misunderstood   (5) enjoyed little happiness in his personal life

10.   1   2   3   4   5

11. The author accepts Wilson's shortcomings because he (the author) (1) never observed them in his association with Wilson   (2) hopes they will soon be forgotten   (3) realizes that Wilson often suffered physical pain   (4) believes that Wilson displayed no more than human weaknesses   (5) feels that Wilson has been treated fairly by his critics

11.   1   2   3   4   5

Passage III

Disregard for odds and complete confidence in one's self have produced many of our great successes. But every young man who wants to go into business for himself should appraise himself as a candidate for the one percent to survive. What has he to offer that is new or better? Has he special talents, special know-how, a new invention or service, or more capital than the average competitor? Has he the most important qualification of all, a willingness to work harder than anyone else? A man who is working for himself without limitation of hours or personal sacrifice can run circles around any operation that relies on paid help. But he must forget the eight-hour day, the forty-hour week, and the annual vacation. When he stops work, his income stops unless he hires a substitute. Most small operations have their busiest day on Saturday, and the owner uses Sunday to catch up on his correspondence, bookkeeping, inventorying, and maintenance chores. The successful self-employed man invariably works harder and worries more than the man on a salary. His wife and children make corresponding sacrifices of family unity and continuity; they never know whether their man will be home or in a mood to enjoy family activities.

12. The title that best expresses the ideas of this passage is   (1) Overcoming Obstacles   (2) Running One's Own Business   (3) How to Become a Millionaire   (4) Young Men in Industry   (5) Why Small Businesses Fail

12.   1   2   3   4   5

13. This passage suggests that (1) small businesses are the ones that last (2) salaried workers are untrustworthy (3) a willingness to work will overcome loss of income (4) small business failures cause depressions (5) working for one's self may lead to success

14. The author of this passage would most likely believe in (1) individual initiative (2) socialism (3) corporations (4) government aid to small business (5) nonunion labor

Passage IV

The Greek language is a member of the Aryan or Indo-European family and its various dialects constitute the Hellenic group. It was probably spoken in Europe and Asia at least 1,500 years before the Christian Era by Greeks with classical learning. Later it was a universal language among the cultured classes, just as Latin afterward became the medium of international communication. During the Dark Ages Greek was little known to Western Europe, except in monasteries, although it remained the language of the Byzantine Empire. The emigration of the Greeks to Italy after the fall of Constantinople, and during the century preceding, gave a new impetus to the study of the Greek language, and the revival of learning gave it the place it has ever since occupied.

15. The title that best expresses the ideas of this passage is (1) The Greek Language (2) Greece, Past and Present (3) Importance of the Greek Dialects (4) Greek, the Universal Language (5) An Interesting Language

16. A result of Greece's being the center of classical learning was that (1) it built great schools (2) its citizens were all cultured (3) Greek was the universal language among the cultured classes (4) Greek was not important during the Dark Ages (5) Greek displaced Latin

17. The Greek language (1) was probably spoken in Europe as early as 1500 B.C. (2) was introduced into Europe by way of Constantinople (3) was responsible for the revival of learning (4) became dominant in Italy (5) had more dialects than Latin

Passage V

The problems we face in conserving natural resources are laborious and complex. The preservation of even small bits of marshlands or woods representing the last stands of irreplaceable biotic communities is interwoven with the red tape of law, conflicting local interests, the overlapping jurisdiction of governmental and private conservation bodies, and an intricate tangle of economic and social considerations. During the time spent in resolving these factors, it often happens that the area to be preserved is swallowed up. Even more formidable is the broad-scale conservation problem raised by the spread of urban belts in such places as the northeastern part of the United States. The pressures of human growth are so acute in such instances that they raise issues which would tax the wisdom of Solomon.

18. The title that best expresses the ideas of this passage is   (1) Conservation's Last Stand   (2) The Encroaching Suburbs   (3) Hindrances to Conservation   (4) How to Preserve our Resources   (5) An Insoluble Problem

18.   1   2   3   4   5

19. The most perplexing problem of conservationists is the one involving (1) population growth   (2) public indifference   (3) favorable legislation   (4) division of authority   (5) increased taxes

19.   1   2   3   4   5

20. The author's attitude toward the situation he describes is   (1) optimistic (2) realistic   (3) apathetic   (4) illogical   (5) combative

20.   1   2   3   4   5

Passage VI

One man's productivity, however, varies greatly from country to country. It depends on the amount of assistance the average worker is given in the form of machinery—that is to say, on the horsepower per head. It depends also—and this may be a point of growing importance—on the spirit and stamina of the workers. The industrial workers of certain countries have been working under heavy strain for many years. During that time they have been badly fed. Moreover, the countries referred to have become dependent in a significant degree on slave labor, the inefficiency of which is notorious.

21. The title that best expresses the ideas of this passage is   (1) Machinery Makes the Difference   (2) Horsepower per Head   (3) Worker Productivity   (4) Countries and Workers   (5) The Importance of Spirit and Stamina

21.   1   2   3   4   5

22. The author implies that   (1) workers have neglected their health (2) slaves are weak   (3) machinery adds one horsepower to each worker   (4) working under strain reduces output   (5) one man counts little

22.   1   2   3   4   5

Passage VII

A legendary island in the Atlantic Ocean beyond the Pillars of Hercules was first mentioned by Plato in the *Timaeus*. Atlantis was a fabulously beautiful and prosperous land, the seat of an empire nine thousand years before Solon. Its inhabitants overran part of Europe and Africa, Athens alone being able to defy them. Because of the impiety of its people, the island was destroyed by an earthquake and inundation. The legend may have existed before Plato and may have sprung from the concept of Homer's Elysium. The possibility that such an island once existed has caused much speculation, resulting in a theory that pre-Columbian civilizations in America were established by colonists from the lost island.

23. The title that best expresses the ideas of this passage is (1) A Persistent Myth (2) Geography according to Plato (3) The First Discoverers of America (4) Buried Civilizations (5) A Labor of Hercules

23. 1 2 3 4 5
‖ ‖ ‖ ‖ ‖

24. According to the passage, we may most safely conclude that the inhabitants of Atlantis (1) were known personally to Homer (2) were ruled by Plato (3) were a religious and superstitious people (4) used the name Columbia for America (5) left no recorded evidence of their existence

24. 1 2 3 4 5
‖ ‖ ‖ ‖ ‖

25. According to legend, Atlantis was destroyed because the inhabitants (1) failed to obtain an adequate food supply (2) failed to conquer Greece (3) failed to respect their gods (4) believed in Homer's Elysium (5) had become too prosperous

25. 1 2 3 4 5
‖ ‖ ‖ ‖ ‖

Passage VIII

History is a fable agreed upon. At best, it is only a part-told tale. The conquerors tell their own story. The stagehands never get the spotlight. The janitor and the night watchman remain in darkness. The names of the kings and caudillos monopolize attention.

When Jerusalem fell, who wielded the hammer and trowel to raise its walls again? Who actually watered the Hanging Gardens of Babylon? Were there no cooks and foot soldiers and ditch diggers and road makers in the conquering armies of the Caesars? Who taught Shakespeare the alphabet? Who thinks of the unknown heroes who created the alphabet itself and gave signs to sounds and made possible the memory of mankind in our libraries? The Presidents we know; the peasants are anonymous.

The locomotive engineer and the bus driver do their job to get us where we want to go—all unknown soldiers unless accident and death break the journey. Who ever thinks of the man in the front cab of the subway train unless a sudden jerk reminds us that he is human too? Can we spell out the debt we owe to those who give as well as get and put necessities and luxury within our reach? At least we should remember sometimes our collective debt to those who work in obscurity.

26. The title that best expresses the ideas of this passage is (1) Heroes of History (2) A Look at the Past (3) Anonymous Makers of History (4) The Debts We Owe (5) Our Unknown Soldiers

26. 1 2 3 4 5
‖ ‖ ‖ ‖ ‖

27. The author indicates that (1) man has a long memory (2) most people do not know their history very well (3) those who serve others are important to the world (4) it is useless to expect recognition for one's work (5) it is too bad that people have neglected historical records so shamefully

27. 1 2 3 4 5
‖ ‖ ‖ ‖ ‖

28. This passage was probably written in observance of (1) Thanksgiving Day (2) Veterans Day (3) Father's Day (4) Independence Day (5) Labor Day

28. 1 2 3 4 5
‖ ‖ ‖ ‖ ‖

ANSWERS TO SUB-TEST 3   *Interpretation of Reading Materials in the Social Studies*

1. 5	6. 3	11. 4	16. 3	21. 3	26. 3
2. 1	7. 2	12. 2	17. 1	22. 4	27. 3
3. 3	8. 5	13. 5	18. 3	23. 1	28. 5
4. 2	9. 1	14. 1	19. 1	24. 5	
5. 4	10. 4	15. 1	20. 2	25. 3	

What's your score?

If you got at least 20 correct you are prepared to take the test which will earn you a high school equivalency diploma.

SUB-TEST 4.

Interpretation of Reading Materials in the Natural Sciences

Directions: **Read each of the following selections carefully. Then select the answer to each of the numbered questions which in your opinion best completes the statement or question.**

Selection A

When a new individual is produced from a single parent cell or from two parent cells, the process of reproduction occurs. This life function differs from all the other life processes in that it preserves the species rather than insuring the survival of the individual. To understand how a cell divides, one must consider the behavior of the nuclear material and the cytoplasmic division. Mitosis is the process by which the hereditary material of the nucleus is doubled and then distributed into the daughter cells. This is accompanied by the division of the cytoplasmic material so that, as a result of cell division, normally two cells similar to the parent cells are produced. This is the basis of all forms of asexual reproduction where a single parent is involved, as is the case in binary fission in single-celled organisms such as amoeba, paramecia, and bacteria, or in the process of budding in yeast cells or sporulation in bread mold.

A moving picture of an animal cell undergoing mitotic division would show the orderliness of this process with the result that each daughter cell receives an exact copy of the hereditary material of the parent cell. If we were to stop the motion picture from time to time we could examine carefully some significant changes, and arrive at stages to which biologists have assigned specific names. We would first see the interphase, then the prophase, the metaphase, the anaphase, and finally the telophase.

If we examine a plant cell we would find the process basically similar. However, we would find that the plant cell does not have centrioles, does not form astral rays but does have the problem of forming a thick cell plate in the center of the spindle.

The process of mitosis has been studied very carefully. Scientists hope some light will be shed on the abnormal cell division that occurs in malignancies by observing the normal process of cell division. Also, research in mitosis is important to the science of genetics. The chromosomes—long, thin strands— are carriers of nucleoprotein which is made up of DNA molecules. Chromosomes are visible only when the cell is undergoing division. Biologists have observed that the number of chromosomes counted during mitosis is characteristic of the species. For example, in the fruit fly, this number is 8 except in the sex cells or gametes. Only 4 chromosomes are found in the egg cell or sperm cell of the fruit fly. However during the union of these cells in fertilization the normal, characteristic number is restored.

Scientists may be guilty of errors. However, they are constantly checking and make revisions where necessary. It was long believed that the normal number of chromosomes in man is 48. Recent research on tissue culture has made it necessary to revise this figure to 46.

Tissue culture is the technique by which cells can be grown artificially outside the body. By special procedures, human dividing cells were permitted to reach the metaphase but prevented from developing further. The material with many metaphase cells were squashed, the cells were spread out and the chromosomes photographed through a microscope. The photographs showed 23 pairs of chromosomes in each cell. Today we refer to the normal number of chromosomes in man as 46.

1. Which of the following terms does not belong with the others?
   (1) sporulation   (2) sexual reproduction   (3) binary fission   (4) budding   (5) asexual reproduction

2. It can be inferred that which of the following is the correct number of chromosomes found in the human egg cell?
   (1) 8   (2) 23   (3) 24   (4) 46   (5) 48

3. The number of chromosomes in the body cells is (?) as many as that of the reproductive cells.
   (1) ½   (2) ⅛   (3) ¼   (4) twice   (5) the same

4. The process by which cells normally divide is called
   (1) mitosis   (2) fertilization   (3) gamete-formation
   (4) tissue culture   (5) chromosomes

5. Abnormal cell division is most important for research in
   (1) plants   (2) chromosome composition   (3) cancer   (4) DNA
   (5) fruit flies

6. Centrosomes are found only in
   (1) animal cells   (2) plant cells   (3) dividing plant cells   (4) cells of small animals   (5) living cells

1. 1 2 3 4 5

2. 1 2 3 4 5

3. 1 2 3 4 5

4. 1 2 3 4 5

5. 1 2 3 4 5

6. 1 2 3 4 5

7. The life process essential to the survival of the species but not to the individual is
(1) growth   (2) movement   (3) food manufacture   (4) reproduction   (5) protection

7. 1 2 3 4 5

8. The bread mold reproduces by
(1) spore-formation   (2) budding   (3) binary fission   (4) amitosis   (5) regeneration

8. 1 2 3 4 5

9. Which of the following terms includes all the others?
(1) binary fission   (2) asexual reproduction   (3) sporulation   (4) budding   (5) mitosis

9. 1 2 3 4 5

10. The stages of mitosis prevented from forming in order to count chromosomes in tissue culture technique are
(1) metaphase and anaphase   (2) interphase and prophase   (3) anaphase and telophase   (4) telophase and interphase   (5) prophase and metaphase

10. 1 2 3 4 5

11. The union of sex cells is called the process of
(1) reduction division   (2) mitosis   (3) amitosis   (4) fertilization   (5) gamete formation

11. 1 2 3 4 5

12. Budding of yeast is a form of
(1) sexual reproduction   (2) fertilization   (3) gamete   (4) cutting   (5) asexual reproduction

12. 1 2 3 4 5

Selection B

All living things need proper temperature. Our body stays at 98.6° F. in good health. To survive in cold or hot climates special protection is required. The same is true for plants and animals. Roses will not grow in the icelands while polar bears cannot thrive near the equator.

Temperatures vary. In Antarctica temperatures colder than 100° F. below zero have been recorded. A temperature of above 149° F. has been recorded in Death Valley, California. Even greater variations have been recorded in the laboratory and in industry. The lowest possible temperature is 459° F. below zero.

These low temperatures are of interest to the scientist who specializes in cryogenics. Cyrogenic temperatures start at the point where oxygen liquefies (–297° F.) and go down to the lowest temperature possible according to scientists. This point, known as absolute zero, is almost –460° F. or 273° below zero on the centigrade scale. Physicists are approaching this temperature by modern methods of removing most heat out of solids. At low temperatures, atoms and molecules move slowly. It is as though one is watching a slow-motion replay of a football game which offers an ideal way of analyzing a specific occurrence. Scientists have thus found many clues to the nature of atoms and molecules. From the physicist's point of view, temperature is a measure of the average kinetic energy, or energy of motion, of these particles.

At high temperatures atoms and molecules move faster and thus turn into liquids or gases. The human body cannot survive high temperatures partly because the proteins in our protoplasm would coagulate.

13. Absolute zero is at
    (1) 0° Centigrade   (2) 0° Fahrenheit   (3) −460° Centigrade   (4) −273° Fahrenheit   (5) −460° Fahrenheit

    13. 1 2 3 4 5
         ‖ ‖ ‖ ‖ ‖

14. The lowest temperature recorded outside the laboratory is
    (1) −100° F.   (2) 149° F.   (3) −459° F.   (4) −297° F.   (5) 100° F.

    14. 1 2 3 4 5
         ‖ ‖ ‖ ‖ ‖

15. Oxygen liquefies at a temperature of minus
    (1) 297° F.   (2) 459° F.   (3) 149° F.   (4) 100° F.   (5) 100° C.

    15. 1 2 3 4 5
         ‖ ‖ ‖ ‖ ‖

16. It can be inferred that Death Valley is not suitable for constant, successful human existence because of its effect on the
    (1) shape of atoms   (2) number of molecules   (3) protoplasm   (4) sweat glands   (5) liquids

    16. 1 2 3 4 5
         ‖ ‖ ‖ ‖ ‖

17. Liquefying air requires
    (1) adding heat   (2) adding pressure and heat   (3) reducing pressure and adding heat   (4) decreasing the movement of atoms   (5) removing the heat

    17. 1 2 3 4 5
         ‖ ‖ ‖ ‖ ‖

18. Cryogenics may be described as
    (1) the supercold world   (2) the science of atomic structure   (3) crystallography   (4) the study of Centigrade and Fahrenheit   (5) physical chemistry

    18. 1 2 3 4 5
         ‖ ‖ ‖ ‖ ‖

19. Temperature may be defined as the
    (1) maximum energy of motion of atoms and molecules   (2) minimum energy of motion of atoms and molecules   (3) maximum kinetic energy of particles   (4) average kinetic energy of atoms and molecules   (5) average possible potential energy of particles.

    19. 1 2 3 4 5
         ‖ ‖ ‖ ‖ ‖

Selection C

Without interference by man, nature has its own way of purifying water. These may be physical, chemical, or biological.

As streams flow they become purer. This process is open to question since some dangerous components may remain. Communities that wish to use water from "self-purified" streams now use added precautions including filtration and chlorination.

Aeration, which may be accompanied by wind action, turbulent flow, and waterfalls, causes an exchange of gases between the atmosphere and the water. Hydrogen sulphide, carbon dioxide, and methane are liberated from the water and oxygen is absorbed from the atmosphere.

Light has an important effect on water. Light stimulates photosynthesis in aquatic plant life by which carbon dioxide is absorbed and oxygen is liberated. Furthermore this plant life utilizes organic material that may be dissolved in the water for its own maintenance and thus removes substances from the water. Also, light has a germicidal effect on the surface of the water though its effect on water below the immediate surface is slight.

Sedimentation of suspended particles removes organic bacterial food from the water. This process, caused by gravity, is most effective in quiet waters.

Oxidation and reduction are two important chemical processes by which water is naturally purified. Some bacteria oxidize organic material thus converting it to mineral substances. In the absence of oxygen, other organisms, known as anaerobic bacteria, can split organic compounds and prepare the way for subsequent oxidation. These anaerobic bacteria thrive at the bottom of bodies of water where there is a great deal of concentrated pollution.

Biological cycles also purify water. Protozoa, one-celled animals, thrive on bacteria. As these are reduced in the population, green algae appear. They in turn consume carbon dioxide, nitrates, and ammonia and produce oxygen. Large invertebrate animals such as worms and mollusks appear and feed on the deposits at the bottom. All of these reduce the bacteria population.

20. Streams would purify themselves if it were not for
(1) man   (2) evaporation   (3) condensation   (4) filtration
(5) chlorination

20.   1   2   3   4   5

21. Aeration of water accomplishes a
(1) loss of oxygen   (2) loss of methane   (3) gain of carbon dioxide
(4) gain of hydrogen   (5) gain of carbon dioxide and loss of oxygen

21.   1   2   3   4   5

22. Sedimentation is the result of
(1) wind action   (2) bacterial residue   (3) turbulent water   (4) gravity
(5) organic material

22.   1   2   3   4   5

23. Which of the following statements correctly refers to the process of photosynthesis?
(1) It is carried on by all protozoa.   (2) Oxygen is necessary for the process to occur.   (3) Light is necessary for the process to occur.   (4) Carbon dioxide is given off during this process.   (5) The process has a germicidal effect on deep stagnant water.

23.   1   2   3   4   5

24. Wastes at the bottom of ponds may best be removed by the action of
(1) fish   (2) aerobic bacteria   (3) green plants   (4) anaerobic bacteria
(5) algae

24.   1   2   3   4   5

25. All of the following tend to purify water except
(1) oxidation   (2) reduction   (3) light   (4) aquatic plants   (5) bacteria

25.   1   2   3   4   5

Selection D

Almost ninety per cent of all the species of the animal kingdom are classified as members of the phylum Arthropoda. It is estimated that about one million species belong to this group. Its name is derived from the Greek stems arthro (jointed) and poda (legs). Within this phylum the members are grouped into classes which include the centipedes, millipedes, lobsters, crabs, barnacles, shrimp, spiders, and insects.

The largest class of the arthropods are the insects of which entomologists tell us about 625,000 different species have been studied. Basically, all insects have three pairs of legs and three distinct body parts—head, thorax, and abdomen. Spiders are unlike insects in this regard as they have two body parts—the cephalothorax (a fusion of the head and thorax) and an abdomen. Many other differences between spiders and insects justify classifying spiders together with the scorpions as arachnids. The breathing apparatus of insects consists of a system of tracheae or tubes with external openings called spiracles while most members of the arachnida class breathe through gills or "book lungs."

Insects have many representatives on the earth for several reasons, including successful reproduction and an ability to adapt to a changing environment. The egg of the insect undergoes a remarkable transformation in body form. The egg usually changes into a larva, then to a pupa, and finally emerges as an adult. Zoologists refer to these changes as metamorphosis. The grasshopper is an exception, and scientists call the process an incomplete metamorphosis because the young grasshopper, called a nymph, resembles the adult except for size. After a series of molting, in which the exoskeleton is split and discarded, increase in size results and the adult stage is reached.

The life history stages of insects with complete metamorphosis often have specific names and demonstrate special economic importance. The larval stage of the house fly is called a maggot while this stage of a developing moth or butterfly is called a caterpillar, and in the case of the mosquito it is called a wriggler. In controlling mosquitoes, the breathing habits of the wriggler are important. This explains why pouring oil over stagnant water will help eliminate mosquitoes in a given locality. The apple worm is not a worm at all. It is the larval stage of the codling moth which feeds on the apple blossoms. The clothes moth does its damage on woolens in its larval stage, so that spraying the clothes closet with insecticide when the adult clothes moth is detected may very well be a case of protection after "the horse is stolen." The pupa state of the moth is called a cocoon while chrysalis is the correct term for the pupa state of a butterfly.

Taxonomists group the insect world into about twenty different orders according to wing number and structure, mouth parts, and metamorphosis. The termites belong to the Isoptera, a group with chewing mouth parts and wings not always present. The grasshoppers, roaches, and crickets are grouped together in the order Orthoptera. The wings in this group are straight back against the body. The forewings are leathery and the hindwings are used for flying. The Hemiptera have forewings which are thickened at the base or are sometimes absent. The bedbug belongs to this group. The largest order of insects is the Coleoptera which includes the beetles with their horny forewings which meet in a straight line down the back. The moths and butterflies with their broad wings, covered with tiny scales and sucking mouth parts belong to the Lepidoptera order. Flies and mosquitoes are classified as Diptera. Members of this group have one pair of wings, with the hind wings reduced to organs of balance. Bees, wasps, and ants with their membranous wings are grouped together in the order Hymenoptera.

26. Which of the following does not possess jointed appendages?   26. 1 2 3 4 5
    (1) lobster (2) crab (3) starfish (4) spider (5) butterfly

27. Which of the following would the entomologist regard as most unlike the others?
    (1) spider   (2) mosquito   (3) house fly   (4) butterfly   (5) grasshopper

27. 1   2   3   4   5

28. Which of the following is an arachnid?
    (1) grasshopper   (2) scorpion   (3) centipede   (4) shrimp   (5) crab

28. 1   2   3   4   5

29. The breathing apparatus of the grasshopper consists of
    (1) external lungs   (2) gills   (3) slits   (4) spiracles   (5) tentacles

29. 1   2   3   4   5

30. The grasshopper goes through incomplete metamorphosis because it
    (1) molts   (2) forms a larva   (3) does not produce larvae and pupae
    (4) produces nymphs from cocoons   (5) produces nymphs that are larger than adults

30. 1   2   3   4   5

31. Wrigglers are to mosquitoes as maggots are to
    (1) larvae   (2) pupae   (3) mosquitoes   (4) flies   (5) adults

31. 1   2   3   4   5

32. Larvae of the codling moth destroy
    (1) clothing   (2) mosquitoes   (3) apples   (4) tomato roots
    (5) leaves of cherry trees

32. 1   2   3   4   5

33. Which of the following is not a characteristic of insects?
    (1) three distinct body parts   (2) breathing apparatus consisting of tracheae   (3) cephalothorax   (4) six legs   (5) jointed antennae

33. 1   2   3   4   5

34. Which of the following is most closely related to the roach?
    (1) house fly   (2) ant   (3) beetle   (4) bedbug   (5) grasshopper

34. 1   2   3   4   5

35. The possession of a membranous wing is characteristic of the
    (1) Hymenoptera   (2) Coleoptera   (3) Diptera   (4) Orthoptera
    (5) Isoptera

35. 1   2   3   4   5

36. The order of insects having the greatest number of different representatives includes the
    (1) moths and butterflies   (2) beetles   (3) wasps and ants   (4) grasshoppers   (5) true bugs

36. 1   2   3   4   5

Selection E

PRIMATES, *pri-ma'tez:* name given by Linnæus to the first order of Mammalia in his system, and which he placed first, because he ranked man among them, and accounted them highest in the scale of nature. He assigned as the characters of the order, incisor teeth in the front of the mouth, four in the upper jaw, in one row; mammæ two, pectoral. In this order he placed four genera, *Homo* (in which he included man and the orang-outang), *Simia, Lemur,* and *Vespertilio*; corresponding to the *Bimana* (Man alone), *Quadrumana,* and *Cheiroptera* of Cuvier. That many of the P. of Linnæus really occupy a higher place, either as to organization or as to intelligence, than many other Mammalia, is more than doubtful.

37. This passage is most probably an excerpt from a (an)
    (3) modern collegiate dictionary   (2) old botanical reference book
    (3) eighteenth century encyclopedia   (4) children's wonderland of knowledge   (5) British dictionary

37. 1   2   3   4   5

38. Linnæus was a Swedish scientist who

(1) studied primates   (2) studied the anatomy of mammals   (3) devised a system of identifying higher animals   (5) devised a system of classifying and assigning names to living things

38. 1 2 3 4 5

39. As a basis for reclassification of higher forms, Linnæus used

(1) tooth structure   (2) size   (3) body weight   (4) behavior (5) internal organs

39. 1 2 3 4 5

40. Cuvier's classification differed from that of Linnæus in that Cuvier

(1) grouped man with the orang-outang   (2) based his findings on the work of Linnæus   (3) placed man in the group Homo   (4) placed all primates in one group   (5) placed man in group by himself

40. 1 2 3 4 5

Selection F

Fractional distillation is the physical separation of the components of a liquid mixture that have different boiling points, by controlled vaporization and condensation. The most volatile component will boil off first. It may then be condensed and collected in a separate container. As the temperature is raised, other components boil off at their respective boiling points and are then condensed separately. An excellent example of fractional distillation is its application to the refining of petroleum. The most volatile liquid component of petroleum is gasoline. In the fractional distillation of petroleum, the gasoline boils off first and is condensed. As the temperature is gradually raised, kerosene, fuel oil, lubricating oil, vaseline, and paraffin are boiled off and condensed in that order.

41. Which of the following correctly describes what is meant by "the most volatile component of a liquid mixture"?

(1) the most explosive component   (2) the part of the mixture which can be condensed and collected   (3) the component of the mixture that has the lowest boiling point   (4) the component of the mixture that boils off last   (5) the most industrially useful component

41. 1 2 3 4 5

42. According to this passage, if you had a liquid mixture of fuel oil, lubricating oil, vaseline, kerosene, and paraffin, the first product of fractional distillation would be

(1) paraffin   (2) vaseline   (3) lubricating oil   (4) fuel oil (5) kerosene

42. 1 2 3 4 5

43. Which of the following statements is true?

(1) Fractional distillation depends upon the chemical properties of a substance.   (2) Condensation precedes vaporization in fractional distillation.   (3) In fractional distillation the mixture is boiled, separated into components, and then condensed.   (4) In fractional distillation the mixture is boiled, condensed, and separated.   (5) In the refining of petroleum, the less valuable oils are boiled off first and then premium gasoline is condensed.

43. 1 2 3 4 5

Selection G

The human body has three types of muscle—smooth (without striations) which are generally the involuntary muscles such as those of the alimentary canal and the iris of the eye, skeletal or striated muscles which are the voluntary muscles, and the cardiac muscle which is found only in the heart.

There is unfortunately no definite rule regarding the nomenclature of muscles. Muscles derive their name (1) from their situation—e.g., the temporal, pectorals, gluteals, etc.; or (2) from their direction—e.g., the rectus, obliquus, etc., of which there may be several pairs—e.g., rectus femoris, rectus abdominalis, rectus capitis, etc.; or (3) from their uses—e.g., the masseter, the various flexors, extensors; or (4) from their shape—e.g., the deltoid, trapezius, rhomboid, etc.; or (5) from the number of their divisions—e.g., the biceps and triceps; or (6) from their points of attachment—e.g., the sterno-cleido-mastoid, the genio-hyo-glossus, the sterno-thyroid, etc. In the description of a muscle, its points of attachment are denoted by the words *origin* and *insertion*; the former applied to the more fixed point or that toward which the motion is directed, the latter to the more movable point. The application of these terms is, however, in many cases arbitrary, as many muscles pull equally toward both attachments. Muscles opposed in action are termed *antagonists*, this antagonism being in most cases required by the necessity that exists for an active moving power in opposite directions. Thus, by one set of muscles, the *flexors*, the limbs are bent; while by a contrary set, the *extensors*, they are straightened. One set, termed the muscles of mastication, closes the jaws, while another set opens them; and probably every muscle in the body has its antagonists in one or more other muscles.

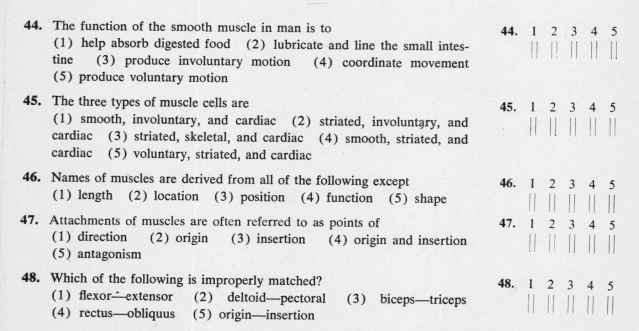

44. The function of the smooth muscle in man is to
(1) help absorb digested food   (2) lubricate and line the small intestine   (3) produce involuntary motion   (4) coordinate movement
(5) produce voluntary motion

44. 1 2 3 4 5

45. The three types of muscle cells are
(1) smooth, involuntary, and cardiac   (2) striated, involuntary, and cardiac   (3) striated, skeletal, and cardiac   (4) smooth, striated, and cardiac   (5) voluntary, striated, and cardiac

45. 1 2 3 4 5

46. Names of muscles are derived from all of the following except
(1) length   (2) location   (3) position   (4) function   (5) shape

46. 1 2 3 4 5

47. Attachments of muscles are often referred to as points of
(1) direction   (2) origin   (3) insertion   (4) origin and insertion
(5) antagonism

47. 1 2 3 4 5

48. Which of the following is improperly matched?
(1) flexor—extensor   (2) deltoid—pectoral   (3) biceps—triceps
(4) rectus—obliquus   (5) origin—insertion

48. 1 2 3 4 5

ANSWERS TO SUB-TEST 4 *Interpretation of Reading Materials in the Natural Sciences*

1. 2	**9.** 5	**17.** 5	**25.** 5	**33.** 3	**41.** 3
2. 2	**10.** 3	**18.** 1	**26.** 3	**34.** 5	**42.** 5
3. 4	**11.** 4	**19.** 4	**27.** 1	**35.** 1	**43.** 4
4. 1	**12.** 5	**20.** 1	**28.** 2	**36.** 2	**44.** 3
5. 3	**13.** 5	**21.** 2	**29.** 4	**37.** 3	**45.** 4
6. 1	**14.** 1	**22.** 4	**30.** 3	**38.** 5	**46.** 1
7. 4	**15.** 1	**23.** 3	**31.** 4	**39.** 1	**47.** 4
8. 1	**16.** 3	**24.** 4	**32.** 3	**40.** 5	**48.** 2

ANSWERS EXPLAINED *page 423-424*

What's your score?

If you got at least 35 correct you are prepared to take the test which will earn you a high school equivalency diploma.

ANSWERS EXPLAINED

1. Ans. 2 All other choices are asexual.

2. Ans. 2 Since the normal number of chromosomes in the body cells of man is now considered to be 46, the number of chromosomes in the sperms and eggs would be one-half that number.

3. Ans. 4 Body cells have twice the number of chromosomes as sex cells. In fertilization (union of sex cells) the normal number of chromosomes is restored.

4. Ans. 1 By definition.

5. Ans. 3 The passage refers to malignancies as illustrations of abnormal cell division.

6. Ans. 1 The third paragraph refers to differences between plant and animal mitotic division.

7. Ans. 4 See sentence 2.

8. Ans. 1 The last sentence of the first paragraph cites this illustration.

9. Ans. 5 Mitosis is the basis for the normal division of a single cell. Asexual reproduction and the illustrations of this process are all examples of mitosis.

10. Ans. 3 Observe the correct order of stages of mitosis as stated in the second paragraph.

11. Ans. 4 By definition.

12. Ans. 5 The last sentence of the first paragraph cites this illustration.

13. Ans. 5 See second paragraph where it is referred to as −460° F.

14. Ans. 1 Observe temperature recorded for Antarctica.

15. Ans. 1 The passage mentions the point at which cryogenic temperatures start.

16. Ans. 3 Proteins of protoplasm coagulate at very high temperatures.

17. Ans. 5 Removing heat from substance causes molecules to move more slowly. States of matter (solid, liquid, gas) depend on this factor.

18. Ans. 1 Cryogenic temperatures are 297° Fahrenheit below zero.

19. Ans. 4 Refer to the sentence describing the physicist's point of view.

20. Ans. 1 Man is responsible for many forms of water pollution, including industrial processes.

21. Ans. 2 During aeration of water, methane and carbon dioxides are liberated, and oxygen is absorbed from the air.

22. Ans. 4 Objects heavier than water will drop to the bottom of the water. This is an effect of gravity.

23. Ans. 3 Green plants absorb carbon dioxide and liberate oxygen during photosynthesis. Light is needed by the plant in order to carry on the process.

24. Ans. 4 Anaerobic bacteria thrive in environments that do not have oxygen.

25. Ans. 5 While bacteria of decay may at times decompose organic wastes as in #24, in this question the other four choices are definite methods of water purification. Another justification for this choice is that bacteria may be pathogenic.

26. Ans. 3 The starfish is not an arthropod.

27. Ans. 1 The spider is an arachnid, the others listed are true insects.

28. Ans. 2 The scorpion is an arachnid, the others listed are other arthropods.

29. Ans. 4 Refer to the second paragraph.

30. Ans. 3 Complete metamorphosis involves changes from egg to larva to pupa before the adult stage.

31. Ans. 4 Larvae of mosquitoes are called wrigglers, while larvae of flies are called maggots.

32. Ans. 3 Consult the fourth paragraph.

33. Ans. 3 The arachnid group, unlike the insects, have a fused head and thorax region called a cephalothorax.

34. Ans. Ans. 5 The grasshopper and the roach are members of the orthoptera order.

35. Ans. 1. Refer to sentence relating to bees, wasps, and ants.

36. Ans. 2 Refer to sentence relating to coleoptera.

37. Ans. 3 The language of the passage rules out its usefulness for children. Its scientific, technical nature rules out the dictionary. A botanical reference would confine its discussion to plants.

38. Ans. 5 Linnaeus was a taxonomist who classified living things and assigned scientific names to them.

39. Ans. 1 Consult second sentence.

40. Ans. 5 Linnaeus put man and the orang-outang in the group Homo. Cuvier put man alone in the group Bimana.

41. Ans. 3 A substance with a low boiling point will begin to evaporate before a substance with a higher boiling point.

42. Ans. 5 Refer to the last sentence of the passage.

43. Ans. 4 Refer to the next to the last sentence of the passage.

44. Ans. 3 The first two choices refer to epithelial cells. Coordination is a function of the nervous system.

45. Ans. 4 By definition.

46. Ans. 1 Muscles do vary in length but this is not a criterion for naming muscles according to this passage.

47. Ans. 4 Points of attachment are denoted by origin and insertion.

48. Ans. 2 Deltoid refers to shape of muscles while pectoral refers to location.

SUB-TEST **5.**

General Mathematical Ability

Directions: **Solve the following problems.**

1. Calculate the cost of 3,000 pounds of coal at $24 per ton. (1 ton=2,000 pounds)
(1) $30   (2) $36   (3) $38   (4) $40   (5) $48

1. 1 2 3 4 5

2. Parking meters in Cambridge read: "12 minutes for 1¢. Maximum deposit 10¢." What is the maximum time allowed for a driver to be legally parked at one of these meters?
(1) 12 minutes   (2) 1.2 hours   (3) 1 hour 12 minutes   (4) 2 hours
(5) 100 minutes

2. 1 2 3 4 5

3. On five successive days a deliveryman listed his mileage as follows: 64; 138; 92; 28; 56. If his truck averaged 14 miles per gallon of gasoline, how many gallons should he have used during these five days?
(1) 26   (2) 27   (3) 28   (4) 37.8   (5) 75.6

3. 1 2 3 4 5

4. How many two gallon containers can hold the same amount of paint as six three gallon containers?
(1) ½   (2) 3   (3) 6   (4) 9   (5) 12

4. 1 2 3 4 5

5. Which of the following has the largest value?
(1) $\dfrac{1}{.04}$ (2) $\dfrac{1}{.4}$ (3) $\dfrac{.1}{4}$ (4) $\dfrac{.1}{.4}$ (5) .4

5. 1 2 3 4 5

6. A student desires an average of 88% for five tests during a semester. His marks thus far are: 84%, 92% 96%, and 85%. What mark must he get on his next test?
(1) 83%   (2) 84%   (3) 85%   (4) 88%   (5) 90%

6. 1 2 3 4 5

7. Cast iron weighs 450 pounds per cubic foot. How many cubic feet are there in a casting that weighs 405,000 pounds?
(1) 90   (2) 100   (3) 900   (4) 1000   (5) 9,000

7. 1 2 3 4 5

8. A. B. Carpet cleaners do rug cleaning at 12½¢ a square foot. To clean a rug 8 feet by 10 feet it will cost
(1) $9.60   (2) $10.00   (3) $10.50   (4) $10.60   (5) $11.00

8. 1 2 3 4 5

9. If I mix 20 pounds of candy, which cost me 65¢ a pound, with 30 pounds of candy, which cost me 85¢ a pound, the average cost per pound of this mixture is
(1) 38.5¢   (2) 70¢   (3) 77¢   (4) 75¢   (5) 76¢

9. 1 2 3 4 5

10. The difference between the $\sqrt{100}$ and 3^2 is
(1) 0   (2) 1   (3) 89   (4) 91   (5) 97

10. 1 2 3 4 5

11. In planning the available space along a wall 27 feet long the following allowances must be made for equipment and work space: $5\frac{1}{4}$ feet; 3 feet 2 inches; $7\frac{2}{3}$ feet; 4 feet 6 inches. How many feet of space would remain unused?
(1) 6.5   (2) $6\frac{5}{12}$ (3) $6\frac{7}{12}$ (4) 7.4   (5) $7\frac{7}{12}$

11. 1 2 3 4 5

12. A hockey team won w games, lost l games and tied t games. What part of the games played were won?

(1) $\dfrac{w}{w + l + t}$ (2) $\dfrac{w}{wlt}$ (3) $\dfrac{w}{wl}$ (4) $\dfrac{w}{w + l}$ (5) $\dfrac{l}{w + l + t}$

12. 1 2 3 4 5

13. One-half the pupils at Madison High School walk to school. One-fourth of the remainder go to school by bicycle. What part of the school population travels by some other means?

(1) $\frac{1}{8}$ (2) $\frac{3}{8}$ (3) $\frac{3}{4}$ (4) $\frac{1}{4}$ (5) $\frac{5}{8}$

13. 1 2 3 4 5

14. Which one of the following has the smallest value?

(1) $\frac{2}{3}$ (2) 0.6 (3) $62\frac{1}{2}\%$ (4) $\sqrt{3.6}$ (5) $(.6)^2$

14. 1 2 3 4 5

15. By buying a dress at a clearance sale Florence saved $12, which was a saving of 25% on the original price. The original price was

(1) $36 (2) $40 (3) $48 (4) $54 (5) $60.

15. 1 2 3 4 5

16. School enrollment increased from 300 to 1200. The percentage of increase in enrollment was

(1) 25% (2) 75% (3) 90% (4) 300% (5) 400%

16. 1 2 3 4 5

17. The average of 89.3%, 72.8%, 94.5%, and 88.6% is

(1) 85% (2) 85.3% (3) 85.6% (4) 86% (5) 86.3%

17. 1 2 3 4 5

18. When 72 is increased by $12\frac{1}{2}\%$ of itself the result is

(1) $72\frac{1}{8}$ (2) 73 (3) 80 (4) 81 (5) $83\frac{1}{2}$

18. 1 2 3 4 5

19. Find $\frac{1}{4}\%$ of 556.

(1) .139 (2) 1.39 (3) 13.9 (4) 2.78 (5) 5.56

19. 1 2 3 4 5

20. You may correctly write $3\frac{1}{2}\%$ as

(1) .0035 (2) .035 (3) .35 (4) 3.5 (5) 35

20. 1 2 3 4 5

21. Which of the following is most closely equal to 5% of 2,980?

(1) 75 (2) 90 (3) 150 (4) 198 (5) 300

21. 1 2 3 4 5

22. What percent of the circles in the box at the right are shaded?

(1) 7 (2) 14 (3) 21 (4) 35 (5) 65
(6) 70

22. 1 2 3 4 5

23. The rise in a commutation ticket from $5.50 to $7.70 represents a per cent increase of

(1) 22% (2) 28.7% (3) 30% (4) 40% (5) 32%

23. 1 2 3 4 5

24. An article which formerly sold for $80 is now offered at a discount of 25%. Since it is not attractive to customers the dealer wishes to offer an additional discount to reduce the present price to $48. What per cent should he now offer?

(1) 5% (2) $14\frac{2}{7}\%$ (3) 20% (4) $28\frac{4}{7}\%$ (5) 41%

24. 1 2 3 4 5

25. The simple interest on a $600 loan at 5% for 3 months is

(1) $7.50 (2) $10. (3) $12.50 (4) $15.00 (5) $30.

25. 1 2 3 4 5

26. Sara is paid a weekly salary of $35 plus a commission of 5% on her sales. What were her total earnings during a week when her sales amounted to $325?
(1) $19.   (2) $16.25   (3) $41.25   (4) $51.25   (5) $61.25

26. 1 2 3 4 5

27. A refrigerator is offered on the installment plan at a cost of $360. If 30% of the cost must be paid on delivery plus 12 equal monthly payments, what amount will be required for each monthly payment?
(1) $21.00   (2) $25.20   (3) $30   (4) $108   (5) $252

27. 1 2 3 4 5

28. A library contains 60 books of biography. If this number is 5% of the total number of books on the shelves, how many books are there in the library?
(1) 57   (2) 63   (3) 120   (4) 300   (5) 1200

28. 1 2 3 4 5

29. A real estate broker sold a lot for Mr. Morgan for $9,600 and received a 5% commission. What will Mr. Morgan receive as the net proceeds of the sale?
(1) $480   (2) $4800   (3) $9000   (4) $9120   (5) $10,080

29. 1 2 3 4 5

30. Mr. Sturm insured his house for 3 years for $15,000. The rate for the entire 3 year policy is 75¢ per $100. The average annual cost of this policy is
(1) $22.50   (2) $30.00   (3) $37.50   (4) $75.00   (5) $112.50

30. 1 2 3 4 5

31. According to the schedule shown below, Michael (age 24) decides to make quarterly payments for a $1000 policy, while Philip (age 25) will make semi-annual payments on his $1000 policy. Which of the following statements is correct?

(1) Philip will pay $18.95 more each year.   (2) Michael will pay the same amount as Phillip.   (3) Philip will pay 18¢ more than Michael each year.   (4) Michael will pay 18¢ more than Philip each year.   (5) Philip will pay $9.36 more each year than Michael.

31. 1 2 3 4 5

ANNUAL PREMIUM AND INSTALLMENT PAYMENTS
PER $1,000 ON ORDINARY LIFE INSURANCE
AT AGES FROM 21 THROUGH 25

Age	Annual Premium	Semiannual installment	Quarterly Installment
21	$16.62	$8.48	$4.32
22	17.08	8.71	4.44
23	17.55	8.95	4.56
24	18.04	9.20	4.69
25	18.56	9.47	4.83

32. A $1000 bond earns interest at the annual rate of 5%, payable quarterly. What is the amount of interest earned on six of these bonds each quarter?
(1) $12.50   (2) $50   (3) $75   (4) $150   (5) $300

32. 1 2 3 4 5

33. The tax rate for Stocktown is 0.029 of assessed valuation. This may be expressed as $29 per

(1) $1.00   (2) $10.00   (3) $100.00   (4) $1000.00
(5) $10,000.00

34. Town A has a real estate tax of $31.25 per $1000. Town B has a real estate tax of $3.45 per $100. How much more (per $100) is the tax greater in one town than the other?

(1) $32\frac{1}{2}¢$ (2) $2.28   (3) $3.25   (4) $22.80   (5) $32.50

35. At noon the temperature at Iceberg City was 2° below zero. The following expresses the temperature changes as signed numbers:
1 p.m. −2; 2 p.m. −4; 3 p.m. +3; 4 p.m. −6
The temperature at 4 p.m. was

(1) −7°   (2) −9°   (3) −11°   (4) −13°   (5) −17°

36. The National Football Allstars received the ball on the 20-yard line. The gain or loss of yardage for the next three plays is expressed as signed numbers as follows: +9 yards, −5 yards, +6 yards. After this series of plays the ball is on the (?) yard. (?) equals

(1) 10   (2) 15   (3) 28   (4) 30   (5) 40

37. What is the difference between $11x$ and $-4x$?
(1) $+7x$ (2) $-7x$ (3) 7   (4) 15   (5) $15x$

38. If one pencil costs c¢, then 6 pencils will cost
(1) $6c$ (2) $c/6$ (3) $6/c$ (4) $3c$ (5) $9c$

39. One fifth of $5x^2 + 20$ equals
(1) $x^2 + 20$ (2) $x^2 + 4$ (3) $x^2 + 5$ (4) $5x^2 + 4$
(5) $25x^2 + 100$

40. If $x = -3$ then $3x^2$ equals
(1) −27   (2) 9   (3) 18   (4) +27   (5) ±27

41. What is the value of $3ab + x^2y$ if $a = 4, b = 5, y = 3$, and $x = 2$?
(1) 27   (2) 34   (3) 48   (4) 67   (5) 72

42. If $3x = 21$, then $21x$ equals
(1) 3   (2) 7   (3) 14   (4) 63   (5) 147

43. The width of a field is three times its length. If the perimeter (the distance around the field) is 72 feet, then the length of the field is
(1) 9 feet   (2) 12 feet   (3) 18 feet   (4) 27 feet   (5) 36 feet

44. If the airplane completes its flight of 1365 miles in 7 hours and 30 minutes, the average speed (in miles per hour) is
(1) 180   (2) 181   (3) 182   (4) 185   (5) 187

45. Bill is twice as old as Jim. The sum of their ages is 39. Bill's age is
(1) 10   (2) 13   (3) 19   (4) 20   (5) 26

45. 1 2 3 4 5

46. The sum of two numbers is 19. The larger is 5 less than twice the smaller. The smaller number is
(1) 8   (2) 9   (3) 10   (4) 11   (5) 12

46. 1 2 3 4 5

47. What is the ratio of 800 pounds to 2 tons? (1 ton = 2000 pounds)
(1) 1:5   (2) 1:4   (3) 40:1   (4) 5:1   (5) 4:1

47. 1 2 3 4 5

48. If p pencils cost c cents, at that price n pencils will cost

(1) $\dfrac{pc}{n}\phi$ (2) $\dfrac{cn}{p}\phi$ (3) $npc\,\phi$ (4) $\dfrac{np}{c}\phi$ (5) $pc\,\phi$

48. 1 2 3 4 5

49. The ratio of men to women in attendance at a meeting is 9:2. If there are 12 women in the audience, what is the total attendance?
(1) 33   (2) 44   (3) 54   (4) 66   (5) 77

49. 1 2 3 4 5

50. Thirty feet of a certain type of wire weighs 4 pounds. How many feet of wire will weigh 6 pounds?
(1) 24   (2) 30   (3) 40   (4) 45   (5) 77

50. 1 2 3 4 5

51. A distance of 25 miles is represented on a map by $2\frac{1}{2}$ inches. On this map, how many miles are represented by 1 inch?
(1) 7.5   (2) 8   (3) 10   (4) 11   (5) 12.5

51. 1 2 3 4 5

52. To convert temperature from the Centigrade scale to the Fahrenheit scale we use the formula $F = \dfrac{9}{5}C + 32$. Convert 5° C. to a Fahrenheit reading
(1) 21°   (2) 33°   (3) 35°   (4) 37°   (5) 41°

52. 1 2 3 4 5

53. In the formula $S = 6e^2$, $e = 3$ then S equals
(1) 18   (2) 30   (3) 36   (4) 54   (5) 324

53. 1 2 3 4 5

54. If $x = 5$ and $y = 4$ the value of $x^2 - 2y$ equals
(1) 2   (2) 6   (3) 17   (4) 18   (5) 33

54. 1 2 3 4 5

55. If $x - 3 = 4$, then $7x$ equals
(1) 1   (2) 7   (3) 14   (4) 28   (5) 49

55. 1 2 3 4 5

56. Mr. Lyons has filed a petition for bankruptcy. His liabilities amount to $5000. His assets consist of cash amounting to $1500. How much can a creditor with a claim of $500 expect to receive?
(1) $50   (2) $100   (3) $125   (4) $150   (5) $250

56. 1 2 3 4 5

57. One angle of an isosceles triangle contains 100°. The other two must each contain
(1) 20°   (2) 40°   (3) 60°   (4) 80°   (5) 90°

57. 1 2 3 4 5

58. If the perimeter of a square is 16 feet, its area (in square feet) is
(1) 4   (2) 8   (3) 16   (4) 64   (5) 256

58. 1 2 3 4 5

59. If the area of a square is 25 square yards its perimeter is

    (1) 5 yards   (2) 10 yards   (3) 15 yards   (4) 20 yards

    (5) 25 yards

The circle graph (right) shows how 180,000 wage earners in a certain city earned their living during a given period. Using the degrees indicated, answer questions 60 and 61.

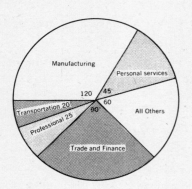

60. The number of persons engaged in transportation in this city during this period was

    (1) 3600   (2) 9000   (3) 10,000   (4) 18,000   (5) 36,000

61. If the number of persons in trade and finance is represented as M, then the number in manufacturing is represented as

    (1) M/3   (2) M + 3   (3) 30M   (4) 4M/3   (5) 3M/4

The graph (below) shows the average rainfall for a six-month period in a certain city. Use this information to answer questions 62 and 63.

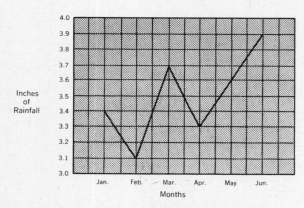

62. The total number of inches of rainfall for this period was

    (1) 19.1   (2) 19.2   (3) 19.4   (4) 20.6   (5) 21

63. How many more inches fell in March than in February?

    (1) $\frac{1}{6}$ (2) $\frac{1}{2}$ (3) .6   (4) 1   (5) 6

64. Martin has a piece of lumber 9 feet 8 inches long. He wishes to cut it into four equal lengths. How far from the edge should he make for the first cut?

    (1) 2.5 feet   (2) 2 feet 5 inches   (3) 2.9 feet   (4) 29 feet

    (5) 116 inches

65. How much longer (in yards) is a 100-meter dash than a 100 yard dash, if 1 meter equals 1.09 yards?

(1) .09   (2) 0.9   (3) 9.0   (4) 9.9   (5) 99

EXPLANATION OF ANSWERS *page 433-437*

ANSWERS AND ANALYSIS TO SUB-TEST 5   *General Mathematical Ability*

This page supplies the correct answers and helps you with an analysis of your performance on this practice test. The number in parenthesis after the correct choice refers to the topic covered by that particular question. In the Outline of Topics below you will find the page on which this topic is explained. In addition, on page *433* you will find the explanations for the answers of this sub-test.

1. 2 (1.1)	**12.** 1 (1.2)	**23.** 4 (1.4)	**34.** 1 (1.7)	**45.** 5 (2.5)	**56.** 4 (2.6)
2. 4 (1.1)	**13.** 2 (1.2)	**24.** 3 (1.4)	**35.** 3 (2.1)	**46.** 1 (2.5)	**57.** 2 (3.2)
3. 2 (1.1)	**14.** 5 (1.3, 1.4)	**25.** 1 (1.4)	**36.** 4 (2.1)	**47.** 1 (2.6)	**58.** 3 (3.2)
4. 4 (1.1)	**15.** 3 (1.4)	**26.** 4 (1.4)	**37.** 5 (2.1)	**48.** 2 (2.6)	**59.** 4 (3.2)
5. 1 (1.2, 1.3)	**16.** 4 (1.4)	**27.** 1 (1.4)	**38.** 1 (2.1)	**49.** 4 (2.6)	**60.** 3 (4)
6. 1 (1.1, 1.4)	**17.** 5 (1.4)	**28.** 5 (1.4)	**39.** 2 (2.1)	**50.** 4 (2.6)	**61.** 4 (4)
7. 3 (1.1)	**18.** 4 (1.4)	**29.** 4 (1.4)	**40.** 4 (2.2)	**51.** 3 (2.6)	**62.** 5 (4)
8. 2 (1.1)	**19.** 2 (1.4)	**30.** 3 (1.5)	**41.** 5 (2.2)	**52.** 5 (2.3)	**63.** 3 (4)
9. 3 (1.1)	**20.** 2 (1.3, 1.4)	**31.** 3 (1.5)	**42.** 5 (2.4)	**53.** 4 (2.3)	**64.** 2 (5)
10. 2 (1.1)	**21.** 3 (1.4)	**32.** 3 (1.6)	**43.** 1 (2.5)	**54.** 3 (2.2)	**65.** 3 (5)
11. 2 (1.2)	**22.** 4 (1.4)	**33.** 4 (1.7)	**44.** 3 (1.2, 2.3)	**55.** 5 (2.4)	

OUTLINE OF TOPICS

1. Arithmetic
    1.1 Whole Numbers p. 270
    1.2 Fractions p. 272
    1.3 Decimals p. 285
    1.4 Percent p. 288
    1.5 Insurance p. 298
    1.6 Investment p. 300
    1.7 Taxation p. 302

2. Algebra
    2.1 Fundamentals p. 304
    2.2 Exponents and Evaluation p. 306
    2.3 Formulas p. 307
    2.4 Solving Equations p. 309
    2.5 Solving Problems p. 313
    2.6 Ratio and Proportion p. 317
    2.7 Signed Numbers p. 321

3. Geometry
    3.1 Geometric Figures p. 324
    3.2 Geometric Concepts and Relationships p. 324
    3.3 Indirect Measurements p. 329
    3.4 Congruence and Similarity p. 332
    3.5 Areas p. 333
    3.6 Volumes p. 337
    3.7 Areas of Solids p. 339

4. Graphs and Interpretation of Data p. 341

5. Measures p. 349

> *What's your score?*

If you got at least 46 correct you are prepared to take the test which will earn you a high school equivalency diploma.

ANSWERS EXPLAINED TO SUB-TEST 5 *General Mathematical Ability*

1. Ans. 2 2000 pounds = 1 ton
   3000 pounds = 1½ tons
   ($24) (1½) = $36

2. Ans. 4 (10¢) will pay for (12 minutes) (10) = 120 minutes or 2 hours

3. Ans. 2 Total mileage for this period = 378 miles
   $378 \div 14 = 27$

4. Ans. 4 Six 3-gallon containers = 18 gallons
   Nine 2-gallon containers = 18 gallons
   or (6) (3) = (9) (2)

5. Ans. 1 (1) $\dfrac{1}{.04} = \dfrac{100}{4} = 25$ (2) $\dfrac{1}{.4} = \dfrac{10}{4} = 2.5$ (3) $\dfrac{.1}{4} = \dfrac{1}{40} = .0205$
   (4) $\dfrac{.1}{.4} = \dfrac{1}{4} = .25$ (5) = .4

6. Ans. 1 To obtain an average of 88% on 5 tests, the sum of the marks must be (88) (5) or 440%. Since the sum of 4 tests is 357%, 440% — 357% = 83%

7. Ans. 3 450 pounds = weight of 1 cubic foot, then 405,000 pounds = 405,000 ÷ 450 pounds = 900 cubic feet.

8. Ans. 2 Area of rug = 8′ × 10′ = 80 square feet
   (12½ ¢) (80 square feet) = $10.

9. Ans. 3 20 pounds @ .65   = $13.00
   30 pounds @ .85   =$25.50
   total cost (50 pounds) = $38.50
   $38.50 ÷ 50 pounds = 77¢ per pound

10. Ans. 2 $\sqrt{100} = 10$ and $3^2 = 9$ then 10 — 9 = 1

11. Ans. 2 $5\frac{1}{4} = 5\frac{3}{12}$ $3\frac{1}{6} = 3\frac{2}{12}$ $7\frac{2}{3} = 7\frac{8}{12}$
    Sum = $19\frac{19}{12}$ = $20\frac{7}{12}$ feet
    27 feet — $20\frac{7}{12}$ feet = $6\frac{5}{12}$ feet

12. Ans. 1 Number of games played was $w + l + t$
    Number of games won was w
    $\dfrac{\text{Number of games won}}{\text{Number of games played}} = \dfrac{w}{w + l + t}$ is part won

13. Ans. 2 ½ do not walk to school. Since ¼ of ½ use bicycles then ¾ of that ½ (¾) (½) or ⅜ must travel by some other means.

14. Ans. 5 $\frac{2}{3} = .66+$
    $.6 = .60$
    $62\frac{1}{2}\% = .625$
    $\sqrt{3.6} = 1+$
    $(.6)^2 = .36$

15. Ans. 3 If \$12 = 25% or $\frac{1}{4}$ of the original price, then \$48 equal $\frac{4}{4}$ or the original price.

16. Ans. 4 Increase of enrollment was 1200 — 300 or 900

$$\frac{\text{Increase}}{\text{Original}} = \frac{900}{300} = 3. = 300\%$$

17. Ans. 5 Sum of 89.3%, 72.8%, 94.5%, 88.6% = 345.2%

$$\frac{\text{Sum}}{\text{Number of Cases}} = \text{Average} \qquad 345.2 \div 4 = 86.3\%$$

18. Ans. 4 $12\frac{1}{2}\% = \frac{1}{8}$ $\qquad (\frac{1}{8})(72) = 9 \qquad 72 + 9 = 81$

19. Ans. 2 1% of 556 = 5.56 $\qquad \frac{1}{4}$% of 556 = 5.56 $\div$ 4 or 1.39

20. Ans. 2 $3\frac{1}{2}\% = 3.5\% = \frac{3.5}{100} = \frac{35}{1000} = .035$

21. Ans. 3 $10\% = \frac{1}{10} = .1$

$(10\%)(2980) = (.1)(2980) = 298$

5% of 2980 = 298 $\div$ 2 or 149. The closest answer is 150.

22. Ans. 4 There are 20 circles of which 7 are shaded.

$$\frac{7}{20} = \frac{35}{100} = 35\%$$

23. Ans. 4 \$7.70 — \$5.50 = \$2.20 (amount of increase)

$$\frac{\text{Amount of increase}}{\text{Original Price}} = \frac{\$2.20}{\$5.50} = \frac{2}{5} = 40\%$$

24. Ans. 3 Original list price (\$80) less 25% (\$20) = \$60

New price = \$48 $\qquad$ New reduction = \$60 — \$48 or \$12

$$\frac{\$12}{\$60} = \frac{1}{5} = 20\%$$

25. Ans. 1 Interest = Principal $\times$ Rate $\times$ Time (years)

Interest = $\$600 \times \frac{5}{100} \times \frac{3}{2}$

Interest = \$7.50

26. Ans. 4 Commission was 5% of \$325 or \$16.25

(Salary) \$35 + \$16.25 = \$51.25 (total earnings)

27. Ans. 1 30% of \$360 = \$108 (down payment)

\$360 (cost) — \$108 (down payment) = \$252

\$252 divided by 12 = \$21

28. Ans. 5 $5\% = \frac{5}{100}$ or $\frac{1}{20}$ If $\frac{1}{20} = 60$, then $\frac{20}{20} = 1200$

29. Ans. 4 (5%) of (\$9600) = (.05)(\$9600) = \$480.00

\$9600 — \$480 = \$9120 (net proceeds)

30. Ans. 3 $\frac{75\cancel{c}}{\$100} = \frac{\$7.50}{\$1000}$ or $\frac{\$75.00}{\$10,000}$ or $\frac{\$112.50}{\$15,000}$

\$112.50 = premium for 3 years

\$37.50 = premium for 1 year

31. Ans. 3 Michael will pay (4) (\$4.69) or \$18.76 each year.

Philip will pay (2) (\$9.47) or \$18.94 each year.

Philip will pay \$18.94 — \$18.76 or 18$\cancel{c}$ more each year.

32. Ans. 3 5% or (.05)(\$1000) = \$50 (annual interest on bond)

Quarterly interest = \$50 $\div$ 4 = \$12.50 (each bond)

6 bonds will yield (6)(\$12.50) or \$75.

33. Ans. 4 $.029 = \frac{29}{1000}$ or $\frac{\$29}{\$1000}$ or \$29 per \$1000

34. Ans. 1 Town A with a rate of $31.25 per $1000 is equivalent to $3.125 per $100. Town B has a rate of $3.45 per $100. Difference is $3.45 — $3.125 or 32½¢.

35. Ans. 3 The sum of —2, —4, and —6 = —12 and since, —12 + 3 = —9 the temperature dropped a total of 9 degrees from the noon temperature of —2°. Therefore the temperature at 4 p.m. was —11°.

36. Ans. 4 $+9 - 5 + 6 = +10$

The ball was advanced from the 20-yard line to the 30-yard line.

37. Ans. 5 $11x - (-4x) = 11x + 4x = 15x$

38. Ans. 1 $\dfrac{\text{pencils}}{¢}$ $\qquad \dfrac{1}{c} = \dfrac{6}{?}$

$? = 6c$

39. Ans. 2 $\dfrac{5x^2 + 20}{5} = \dfrac{5x^2}{5} + \dfrac{20}{5}$

or $\dfrac{\cancel{5}x^2}{\cancel{5}} + \dfrac{\overset{4}{\cancel{20}}}{\cancel{5}}$ or $x^2 + 4$

40. Ans. 4 $3x^2 = (3)(-3)(-3) = +27$

41. Ans. 5 $3ab + x^2y$

$(3)(4)(5) + (2)(2)(3)$

$\qquad 60 \quad + \quad 12 \qquad$ equals 72

42. Ans. 5 $3x = 21$

$\qquad x = 7$

$21x = (21)(7)$

$21x = 147$

43. Ans. 1 Let x = length, then $3x$ = width

The perimeter $= x + x + 3x + 3x +$ or $8x$

$8x = 72$ feet

$\quad x = \;\; 9$ feet

44. Ans. 3 $\dfrac{\text{Distance}}{\text{Time}}$ = Average speed $= \dfrac{1365 \text{ miles}}{7.5 \text{ hours}} = 182$ miles per hour

45. Ans. 5 Let x = Jim's age, then Bill's age is $2x$

$x + 2x = 39$

$\quad 3x = 39$

$\qquad x = 13$ (Jim's age) and $2x = 26$ (Bill's age)

46. Ans. 1 Let x = the smaller number, then $2x - 5$ is the larger number

$3x - 5$ = sum of the numbers

$3x - 5 = 19$

$\quad 3x = 24$

$\qquad x = 8$

47. Ans. 1 $\dfrac{800 \text{ pounds}}{2 \text{ tons}} = \dfrac{800 \text{ pounds}}{4000 \text{ pounds}} = \dfrac{\overset{1}{\cancel{800}} \text{ pounds}}{\underset{5}{\cancel{4000}} \text{ pounds}}$

48. Ans. 2 Let x = price of n number of pencils

$\dfrac{p \text{ pencils}}{c \text{ cents}} = \dfrac{n}{x}$

By cross-multiplication: $px = c\,n$

and $x = \dfrac{c\,n}{p}$

49. Ans. 4 If the ratio is 9:2 $\left(\dfrac{9}{2} \right)$ then $\dfrac{\text{number men}}{\text{number women}} = \dfrac{9}{2} = \dfrac{?}{12}$

$? = 54$ men

Attendance $= 54 + 12 = 66$

50. Ans. 3   Let x = number of feet with weight of 6 pounds

$$\frac{30 \text{ feet}}{4 \text{ pounds}} = \frac{x}{6}$$
$$4x = 180$$
$$x = 45 \text{ feet}$$

51. Ans. 3 $25 \div 2\frac{1}{2} = 25 \div \frac{5}{2}$ or $(25)\dfrac{2}{5} = 10$ miles

52. Ans. 5 $F = \dfrac{9}{5} C + 32°$

$$F = \frac{9}{5} (5°) + 32°$$
$$F = 9° + 32° = 41°$$

53. Ans. 4 $S = 6e^2$
$$S = (6)(3)^2$$
$$S = (6)(9) \text{ or } 54$$

54. Ans. 3 $x^2 - 2y$
$$(5)^2 - 2(4)$$
$$25 - 8 = 17$$

55. Ans. 5 $x - 3 = 4$
$$x = 7$$
$$7x = (7)(7) = 49$$

56. Ans. 4 $\dfrac{\text{Available Cash}}{\text{Debts Owed}} = \dfrac{\$1500}{\$5000} = .3$

Therefore Mr. Lyons can pay only (.3) of his debts. A creditor with a claim of $500 will receive (.3)($500) or $150.

57. Ans. 2   The sum of the angles of a triangle equals 180°. If one angle equals 100°, the sum of the other two angles equals 80°. Since this is an isosceles triangle, each of the other two angles contains ½ of 80° or 40°.

58. Ans. 3   Perimeter of square = 4(side) = 16 feet
Let x = side, $4x$ = the perimeter
$$4x = 16$$
$$x = 4 \text{ feet}$$
Area of square = (side)^2
Area of square = (4)^2 or 16 square feet

59. Ans. 4   Area of square = (side)^2
Let x = side
Area = x^2 = 25 square yards
Then x = 5 yards
Perimeter of square equals 4(side) or (4)(5) = 20 yards

60. Ans. 3 $\dfrac{20°}{360°} = \dfrac{1}{18}$ $\dfrac{1}{18}$ of 180,000 = 10,000

6 . Ans. 4   If 90° = M
$$\frac{90°}{M} = \frac{120°}{?}$$
By cross-multiplication: $90? = 120M$
$$? = \frac{120M}{90}$$
$$? = \frac{4M}{3}$$

62. Ans. 5   The sum of 3.4, 3.1, 3.7, 3.3, 3.6, and 3.9 is 21

63. Ans. 3   According to the graph,
March had 3.7 inches and February had 3.1 inches.
Difference = 0.6 inches

64. Ans. 2   9 feet 8 inches = 116 inches

$116 \div 4 = 29$ inches or 2 feet 5 inches

65. Ans. 3   100 meters = (1.09 yards) (100) = 109 yards

$109 - 100 = 9$ yards

9

Test B

SUB-TEST **1.**

Correctness and Effectiveness of Expression

Directions **(1-20):** **Choose the *one* misspelled word in each of the follow-ing numbered groups.**

1. (1) luxuries (2) fourteen (3) morale (4) excellant (5) proprietor

    1. 1 2 3 4 5

2. (1) windsheild (2) presentable (3) preamble (4) nibble (5) dogged

    2. 1 2 3 4 5

3. (1) sensitive (2) imprisionment (3) ignorance (4) evaporate
   (5) advantageous

    3. 1 2 3 4 5

4. (1) rebeled (2) occasional (3) druggist (4) novelty (5) counselor

    4. 1 2 3 4 5

5. (1) surrender (2) nuisance (3) principally (4) perspire (5) garantee

    5. 1 2 3 4 5

6. (1) vegetate (2) devout (3) misinterpeted (4) amendment (5) hesitant

    6. 1 2 3 4 5

7. (1) involvment (2) recipient (3) internal (4) affluent (5) dutiful

    7. 1 2 3 4 5

8. (1) lease (2) stitches (3) thrust (4) eligable (6) verse

    8. 1 2 3 4 5

9. (1) quizes (2) bulletin (3) strictly (4) superb (5) entitled

    9. 1 2 3 4 5

10. (1) noticable (2) merchandise (3) shrieked (4) antidote (5) apologize

    10. 1 2 3 4 5

11. (1) khaki   (2) survival   (3) laboratory   (4) intensefied   (5) stature

    11. 1 2 3 4 5

12. (1) diesel   (2) cocoa   (3) alphabettical   (4) visible   (5) overlaid

    12. 1 2 3 4 5

13. (1) neutral   (2) ballot   (3) parallysis   (4) enterprise   (5) abnormal

    13. 1 2 3 4 5

14. (1) ironical   (2) mountainous   (3) permissible   (4) carburetor (5) blizard

    14. 1 2 3 4 5

15. (1) penalty   (2) affidavit   (3) document   (4) notery   (5) valid

    15. 1 2 3 4 5

16. (1) provocative   (2) apparition   (3) forfiet   (4) procedure   (5) requisite

    16. 1 2 3 4 5

17. (1) terrifying   (2) museum   (3) minimum   (4) competitors   (5) efficincy

    17. 1 2 3 4 5

18. (1) hangar   (2) spokesman   (3) mustache   (4) cathederal (5) pumpkin

    18. 1 2 3 4 5

19. (1) guidance   (2) until   (3) usage   (4) loyalist   (5) prarie

    19. 1 2 3 4 5

20. (1) renewel   (2) charitable   (3) abrupt   (4) humankind   (5) strengthen

    20. 1 2 3 4 5

Directions (21-30): **Each of the sentences contains an underlined expression. Below each sentence are four suggested answers. Choose the one that will make a correct sentence.**

21. Her salary is lower than a typist.   (1) Correct as is   (2) lower than a typist's   (3) lower then a typist's   (4) lower than a typist

    21. 1 2 3 4 5

22. However hard John works, he is not pleased.   (1) Correct as is   (2) However, hard John works,   (3) However hard, John works   (4) However hard, John works,

    22. 1 2 3 4 5

23. Not one of the children have ever sang in public before.   (1) Correct as is   (2) have ever sung   (3) has ever sang   (4) has ever sung

    23. 1 2 3 4 5

24. Which of the men who are here are you looking for?   (1) Correct as is   (2) who is here are you looking for   (3) whom are here are you looking for   (4) for whom you are looking for is here

    24. 1 2 3 4 5

25. Each of the winners happily excepted complementary tickets to the performance. (1) Correct as is (2) accepted complementary tickets (3) accepted complimentary tickets (4) excepted complimentary tickets

26. In my opinion I think that Jane's is the best suggestion. (1) Correct as is (2) In my opinion, Jane's (3) In my opinion I think, that Jane's (4) In my opinion I think, that Jane's

27. The following officers were elected at our class meeting: John president, Larry vice president, Elaine Secretary. (1) Correct as is (2) : John, president, Larry, vice president, Elaine, secretary (3) ; John president; Larry vice president; Elaine secretary (4) : John, president; Larry, vice president; Elaine, secretary

28. Mother becomes very tired whenever one of us children were sick. (1) Correct as is (2) was (3) is (4) are

29. Are you certain that your books are different than our's? (1) Correct as is (2) different from our's? (3) different than ours'? (4) different from ours?

30. The prizes were distributed among James, him, and me. (1) Correct as is (2) him, and I. (3) he, and me. (4) he, and I.

Directions (31-42): **Each of the following questions contains four sentences in which words or expressions are incorrectly used. Choose the sentence which does *not* have any of these errors.**

31. (1) It is always a pleasure for we boys to visit a firehouse.
(2) The magician waved his hands so skillful that the audience was completely mystified.
(3) Do not hand in the report until your certain that it is complete.
(4) I fear that it is you who are mistaken.
(5) Mailing a letter a few days early is better than to run the risk of its arriving late.

32. (1) My clothes are correct to the occasion.
(2) When that program is over, the children know its time for bed.
(3) John, where is the party at?
(4) The committee consisted of John, Henry, Tom, and me.
(5) Irregardless of what you believe, your answer is incorrect.

33. (1) The letters were intended for we two only.
(2) There is sometimes only one course possible.
(3) It's plan is similar to the plan of our house.
(4) Being that he was the best qualified person, he received the appointment.
(5) If he would have studied harder, he would have received a passing grade.

34. (1) I was surprised to learn that he has not always spoke English fluently.

(2) The lawyer promised to notify my mother and I of his plans for a new trial.

(3) The most important feature of the series of swimming lessons were the large number of strokes taught.

(4) That the prize proved to be beyond her reach did not surprise him.

(5) I am not all together in agreement with the author's point of view.

35. (1) If only we had began before it was too late!

(2) Lets evaluate our semester's work.

(3) This is a club with which I wouldn't want to be associated with.

(4) The enemy fled in many directions, leaving there weapons on the battlefield.

(5) I hoped that John could effect a compromise between the opposing forces.

36. (1) Here, Mr. Chairman, is all the reports of the executive committee.

(2) At the school picnic the childrens lunches disappeared.

(3) "Whom can you send to help us?" inquired Aunt May.

(4) Food prepared in this manner tastes more deliciously.

(5) What have been the principal affects of the serum?

37. (1) After the vocalist had sang his final number, he spoke briefly to the group.

(2) Do you mind my borrowing a book from John?

(3) The general lead his troops into battle.

(4) He is one of those persons which deserve great credit for perseverance.

(5) Although he had excepted the invitation, John failed to appear at the party.

38. (1) If you had been more patient you might not have tore it.

(2) Mother would not let Mary and I attend the hockey game.

(3) They're not the only ones to be blamed for the incident.

(4) I'm not certain that your's is the best solution.

(5) We intended to have gone before Tuesday.

39. (1) He became an authority on the theater and it's great personalities.

(2) I know of no other person in the club who is more kind-hearted than she.

(3) After George had ran the mile, he was breathless.

(4) Johnson has scarcely no equal as a quarterback.

(5) It was the worse storm that the inhabitants of the island could remember.

40. (1) Mary and Joan waited breathlessly, each girl hoping she had won the award for outstanding scholarship.

(2) It was us girls who swept the gym floor after the dance.

(3) People's efficiency are seriously affected by illness and worry.

(4) The money found on the stairs proved to be neither John's nor our's.

(5) The blue, red and yellow sweaters belong to Jean, Marie and Alice respectfully.

41. (1) He pleaded with his mother to let John and he pitch a tent in the yard.

(2) The teacher explained the principal of refrigeration.

(3) The number of votes cast in the election was very small.

(4) Try to find one that is shorter then this one.

(5) Too many commas in a passage often causes confusion in the reader's mind.

41. 1 2 3 4 5

42. (1) When I first saw the car, its steering wheel was broke.

(2) I find that an essential item for we beginners is missing.

(3) I believe that you had ought to study harder.

(4) This is John, whom, I am sure, will be glad to serve you.

(5) His father or his mother has read to him every night since he was very small.

42. 1 2 3 4 5

Directions (43-60): Choose the number of the word or expression that most nearly expresses the meaning of the capitalized word.

43. WARY   (1) dangerous (2) cautious   (3) clear   (4) warm   (5) exciting

43. 1 2 3 4 5

44. INTERLOPER   (1) alien   (2) intruder   (3) questioner   (4) magician (5) rainmaker

44. 1 2 3 4 5

45. INCONSISTENT   (1) insane   (2) senatorial   (3) undeviating   (4) contradictory   (5) faithful

45. 1 2 3 4 5

46. VULNERABLE   (1) usually harmless   (2) slyly greedy   (3) poisonous (4) deeply religious   (5) open to attack

46. 1 2 3 4 5

47. INDIGNATION   (1) poverty   (2) anger   (3) exaggeration   (4) mercy (5) publicity

47. 1 2 3 4 5

48. ABATE   (1) strike out   (2) catch   (3) diminish   (4) embarrass (5) wound

48. 1 2 3 4 5

49. SUSTENANCE   (1) nourishment   (2) overabundance   (3) anxiety (4) equality   (5) alertness

49. 1 2 3 4 5

50. BULWARK   (1) target   (2) grass   (3) safeguard   (4) tail   (5) compartment

50. 1 2 3 4 5

51. DEMEANOR (1) bearing (2) expenditure (3) irritability (4) questionnaire (5) death

51. 1 2 3 4 5

52. INFILTRATE (1) pass through (2) stop (3) consider (4) challenge openly (5) meet secretly

52. 1 2 3 4 5

53. REVOCATION (1) certificate (2) repeal (3) animation (4) license (5) plea

53. 1 2 3 4 5

54. LOQUACIOUS (1) grim (2) stern (3) talkative (4) lighthearted (5) liberty-loving

54. 1 2 3 4 5

55. APERTURE (1) basement (2) opening (3) phantom (4) protective coloring (5) light refreshment

55. 1 2 3 4 5

56. PUNGENT (1) biting (2) smooth (3) quarrelsome (4) wrong (5) proud

56. 1 2 3 4 5

57. CORROBORATE (1) deny (2) elaborate (3) confirm (4) gnaw (5) state

57. 1 2 3 4 5

58. BENEVOLENCE (1) good fortune (2) well-being (3) inheritance (4) violence (5) charitableness

58. 1 2 3 4 5

59. PETULANT (1) rotten (2) fretful (3) unrelated (4) weird (5) throbbing

59. 1 2 3 4 5

60. DERELICT (1) abandoned (2) widowed (3) faithful (4) insincere (5) hysterical

60. 1 2 3 4 5

ANSWERS TO SUB-TEST 1 *Correctness and Effectiveness of Expression*

1. 4	**7.** 1	**13.** 3	**19.** 5	**25.** 3	**31.** 4	**37.** 2	**43.** 2	**49.** 1	**55.** 2
2. 1	**8.** 4	**14.** 5	**20.** 1	**26.** 2	**32.** 4	**38.** 3	**44.** 2	**50.** 3	**56.** 1
3. 2	**9.** 1	**15.** 4	**21.** 2	**27.** 4	**33.** 2	**39.** 2	**45.** 4	**51.** 1	**57.** 3
4. 1	**10.** 1	**16.** 3	**22.** 1	**28.** 3	**34.** 4	**40.** 1	**46.** 5	**52.** 1	**58.** 5
5. 5	**11.** 4	**17.** 5	**23.** 4	**29.** 4	**35.** 5	**41.** 3	**47.** 2	**53.** 2	**59.** 2
6. 3	**12.** 3	**18.** 4	**24.** 1	**30.** 1	**36.** 3	**42.** 5	**48.** 3	**54.** 3	**60.** 1

If you got at least 50 correct you are prepared to take the test which will earn you a high school equivalency diploma.

SUB-TEST **2.**

Interpretation of Literary Materials

Directions: **Read each of the following passages carefully. Then select the answer to each of the numbered questions which in your opinion best completes the statement or question.**

Passage I

It would be difficult today to name as many as a dozen practicing essayists in this country; a half dozen would be nearer to the mark. We have article writers, novelists, poets by the thousands, but only a handful of professional writers devoted to one of the oldest of literary forms, and still, potentially at least, one of the most delightful and rewarding to read. From the time of Montaigne, who fathered it, the essay has had its roots in personality; the day may not be too far distant when articles can be produced by supermachines, and, indeed, many of them already have that flavor, for the article need be little more than a marshaling of facts, fortified perhaps by the forging of an argument for or against what the facts present. But the essay is the product of a ruminative mind, and its value depends not upon the weight of the facts assembled (it may not assemble any), but upon the character and quality of that mind—its perceptiveness, its attitudes, its sharpness, its imagination. It can take off from the most trivial incident or observation and end in the empyrean.

Why has the essay fallen into disrepute? Most magazine editors think that the essay is an outmoded form, that it has no place in our world. Of facts we have a surfeit, and we have not yet digested those of which we are already in possession. Our need is not so much for the acquisition of more, as for reflection upon those we have; not so much for arguments based upon them as for meditations on what they suggest and what they mean. For modern man, the acquisition of facts is like a habitforming drug; the more he takes, the more he craves. Like the drug, eventually they bog him down. There are few periodicals left in which an essay can find publication, though there is an abundant market for factual pieces and for critical analyses commanding higher prices. Yet neither is comparable to a first-rate essay. Still, writers, like butchers, must pay their bills.

1. The title below that best expresses the main ideas of this passage is:
(1) The Faults of the Essay   (2) The Status of the Essay   (3) More Fact than Fiction   (4) The Superiority of the Article over the Essay   (5) Characteristics of the Essay

1. 1 2 3 4 5
|| || || || ||

2. The essay is declining, the author believes, because
(1) man is writing less and less   (2) man is becoming too idea-conscious   (3) man's rapid pace allows for too little reading   (4) society is becoming too impersonal   (5) machines are replacing men in so many fields

2. 1 2 3 4 5
|| || || || ||

3. The tone of the passage suggests that the author has a feeling of
(1) optimism   (2) anger   (3) pride   (4) derision   (5) regret

3. 1 2 3 4 5
|| || || || ||

4. The passage suggests that modern man has a passion to
(1) write   (2) dream   (3) succeed   (4) consume   (5) suffer

4. 1 2 3 4 5
|| || || || ||

5. The author regards certain kinds of articles as being
(1) logical   (2) tasteless   (3) artful   (4) literary   (5) artistic

5. 1 2 3 4 5
|| || || || ||

Passage II

For all of E. E. Cummings' typographical innovations, he was an old-fashioned poet. He wrote about death and love, the graces of nature and the disgraces of civilization. He implored beautiful ladies for their favors and wittily thanked them afterwards. He distrusted power and satirized people in power. He adored Paris and said so in random lines as taking as any in English about that lovely city. He valued childhood and described its innocence with wide-open-eyed clarity. He adored puns and practiced them like an Elizabethan.

In all this he was an old-fashioned poet. Even his typography, which seemed so modern, was ancient in intention. Cummings revered Latin and Greek verse and understood that English for all its excellences, had never achieved the concision and special effects available to the interlocking syntaxes of those inflected languages. In his poems he wanted to make many things happen simultaneously. He wanted to catch action in words and yet keep it shivering. He wanted words to merge as impressions in the mind do. He wanted to reach back and forward, pulling past and future into a present instant. To do this he used punctuation like a second language. This was not an innovation so much as a thorough realization of a lost art.

6. The title that best expresses the ideas of this passage is:
(1) Fashion in Poetry   (2) The Art of E. E. Cummings' Poetry   (3) The Poetic Innovations of E. E. Cummings   (4) Poetry, a Lost Art   (5) Impressionism in Cummings' Poetry

6. 1 2 3 4 5
|| || || || ||

7. In the first paragraph the author implies that Cummings
(1) spent many years of his life in France   (2) felt more at home with children than with adults   (3) wrote parodies of Elizabethan poems   (4) used themes that have been used by other poets   (5) did not consider love a serious emotion

7. 1 2 3 4 5
|| || || || ||

8. Cummings' reverence for Greek and Latin verse helped to
   (1) give him an insight into limitation of the English language   (2) gain him a reputation as an old-fashioned poet   (3) teach him to avoid complicated syntaxes and inflections   (4) influence his choice of subject matter   (5) make him more thorough in depicting the passage of time

8. 1 2 3 4 5

9. According to the author, Cummings was an experimenter in his use of
   (1) unusual typefaces   (2) puns   (3) involved syntax   (4) punctuation   (5) sensory images

9. 1 2 3 4 5

10. From this passage one may most safely conclude that Cummings
   (1) had little respect for the poetry of his contemporaries   (2) would be critical of some present-day leaders   (3) collected watches and calendars   (4) approved of men of action   (5) wrote poetry in at least two languages

10. 1 2 3 4 5

11. In stating that Cummings was "old-fashioned", the author is using the word as a term of
   (1) suspicion   (2) compassion   (3) respect   (4) envy   (5) sarcasm

11. 1 2 3 4 5

- Passage III

Next to his towering masterpiece, *Moby Dick*, *Billy Budd* is Melville's greatest work. It has the tone of a last testament, and the manuscript was neatly tied up by his wife, Elizabeth, and kept in a trunk for some thirty years. It was not until 1924 that it was first published. Slowly it has become recognized as the remarkable work it is. *Billy Budd* has been dramatized for Broadway, done on T.V., made into an opera, and reached a highly satisfying form in Ustinov's movie.

Scholars disagree, somewhat violently, about what Melville was trying to say. He did make it pretty clear that he was recounting a duel between Good and Evil.

Several times he remarked that Billy Budd is as innocent and ignorant as Adam before the fall. His enemy is like Satan in Milton's *Paradise Lost*.

When Billy Budd destroys the letter, and is sentenced to be hanged according to the letter of the law, controversy exists as to wheher the Captain is simply a mortal man preserving order, or a Jehovah-like figure, dispensing cruel justice.

Melville, it is claimed, cleverly took pains to hide his heretical feelings. *Billy Budd* is written as if told by a pious, God-loving man.

Ironically, Melville's iconoclasm has largely misfired, for the story today is accepted as either one of simple suspense or a reverent parable of God, Satan, and Adam. Meanwhile the scholars are still arguing, and *Billy Budd* remains like a porcupine, thorny, with interesting ambiguities.

12. The phrase that best expresses the ideas of this passage is
   (1) a controversial work   (2) the dramatization of *Billy Budd*   (3) life's ambiguities   (4) the Captain's revenge   (5) the King's justice

12. 1 2 3 4 5

13. Regarding *Billy Budd*, critics seem to disagree about the book's
(1) plot (2) theme (3) mood (4) setting (5) introduction

13. 1 2 3 4 5

14. As used in this passage, the word "recounting" (line 9) most nearly means
(1) adding up (2) adding again (3) figuring (4) telling (5) complaining about

14. 1 2 3 4 5

15. The passage suggests that the character Billy Budd was
(1) satanic (2) ambiguous (3) naive (4) brutal (5) vain

15. 1 2 3 4 5

16. The author's purpose in writing this passage seems to be to
(1) point out aspects of *Billy Budd* (2) show that *Billy Budd* is well written (3) defend Melville against his critics (4) defend Melville's iconoclasm (5) describe Melville's growth as a literary artist

16. 1 2 3 4 5

17. The passage indicates that the Captain
(1) disobeyed the law (2) treated his crew very badly (3) disliked Billy intensely (4) was incapable of action (5) was responsible for discipline

17. 1 2 3 4 5

18. Certain lines in this passage suggest that Melville was
(1) Jehovah-like (2) childishly naive (3) very scholarly (4) rather shrewd (5) immune to pain

18. 1 2 3 4 5

Passage IV

I find it takes the young writer a long time to become aware of what language really is as a medium of communication. He thinks he should be able to put down his meaning at once and be done with it, and he puts it down and releases his feeling for it in language that is meaningless to anyone else. He has to learn that he can load almost any form of words with his meaning and be expressing himself but communicating nothing. He has to learn that language has grown naturally out of the human need to communicate, that it belongs to all those who use it, and its communicative capacities have developed to meet the general need, that it is most alive when it comes off the tongue supported as it always is by the look and action of the speaker, that the tongue use of it is universal but the written use of it is relatively rare. He must come to see that tongue use is filled with clichés which are the common counters best serving the general need. Words and phrases that come off his tongue made alive by the living presence of himself become on paper dead transcriptions. Somehow he must overcome the capacity of words to remain dead symbols of meaning as they are in the dictionary. He must breathe life into them as he sets them on paper.

19. The title that best expresses the ideas of this passage is:
(1) Why Clichés are Valueless (2) The Young Writer Speaks (3) How Speech Aids the Writer (4) Writing: a Universal Language (5) Why Writing is Difficult

19. 1 2 3 4 5

20. The passage indicates that when words are spoken and then written
    (1) they become more powerful   (2) they become more understandable
    (3) their effect is different   (4) their capacity for communication is in-
    creased   (5) their dictionary definitions have no value

20. 1 2 3 4 5

21. The author implies that young writers are
    (1) in too much of a hurry to have their say   (2) lacking in confidence
    (3) too critical in analyzing their own work   (4) too emotional in their
    approach to writing   (5) lacking in the ability to find topics

21. 1 2 3 4 5

22. The passage suggests that
    (1) the written word has more of a potential than the spoken word
    (2) clichés will eventually disappear   (3) books are dead symbols
    (4) words exist for a purpose   (5) words in themselves are accurate
    reflections of reality

22. 1 2 3 4 5

23. The author implies that clichés
    (1) are rarely used in writing   (2) have no place in speaking   (3) per-
    form some functions usefully   (4) have equal value for writers and speak-
    ers   (5) brand their users as lazy

23. 1 2 3 4 5

24. The passage suggests that
    (1) writing is more difficult than speaking   (2) writing requires less cre-
    ativity than speaking   (3) writing possesses distinct advantages over
    speaking   (4) the audience is not a factor for the writer as it is for the
    speaker   (5) effective writers are usually effective speakers

24. 1 2 3 4 5

Passage V

With Apples

The last leaves are down, and the iron
Trunks, solitary, say they can stand there
Seven cold months without perceptible
Change. But the green ground changes

5   Daily, so that Hallaway's old horses,
The brown one, the black one,
Nibble at next to nothing where the hoarfrost
Of hours ago gave way before the yellow and still blowing,
Blowing—some of them purple—leaves.

10 These move, head down, but listen:
Someone may be coming, even now, in the bright wind,
With apples. I am coming
Four pockets full, and extras on the hip.
Hi, there, Handsome Jerry!

15 Don't you know me, Slobbery Mack?

25. The phrase that best expresses the ideas of this poem is
(1) iron trunks (2) green ground (3) welcome visitor (4) blowing leaves (5) secret rendezvous

25. 1 2 3 4 5

26. We may most safely conclude from the passage that the narrator
(1) is very rich (2) has always coveted the horses (3) has many friends (4) knows the horses (5) is visiting Hallaway

26. 1 2 3 4 5

27. The phrase "iron trunk" refers specifically to
(1) the fence posts (2) the strength of nature (3) Hallaway's horses (4) the horse barns (5) the trees

27. 1 2 3 4 5

28. The area in which Hallaway's horses are found most probably has been
(1) recently plowed (2) thoroughly grazed (3) converted to new crops (4) hit by drought (5) abandoned for years

28. 1 2 3 4 5

29. From the passage we can most safely conclude that the horses
(1) are housed in a cold stable (2) have been put out to pasture (3) are lost in the leafy woods (4) have been abandoned (5) are trying to escape

29. 1 2 3 4 5

30. In line 10, "These" refers to the
(1) old horses (2) blowing leaves (3) cold months (4) passing hours (5) passers-by

30. 1 2 3 4 5

31. In line 11, "Someone" is most probably
(1) Hallaway (2) a casual passer-by (3) a sympathetic person (4) a stranger (5) Handsome Jerry

31. 1 2 3 4 5

32. From this poem we gain the *least* information about
(1) Hallaway's horses (2) the weather (3) the leaves (4) Hallaway (5) the land

32. 1 2 3 4 5

ANSWERS TO SUB-TEST 2 *Interpretation of Literary Material*

1. 2	**6.** 2	**11.** 3	**16.** 1	**21.** 1	**26.** 4	**31.** 3
2. 5	**7.** 4	**12.** 1	**17.** 5	**22.** 4	**27.** 5	**32.** 4
3. 5	**8.** 1	**13.** 2	**18.** 4	**23.** 3	**28.** 2	
4. 4	**9.** 4	**14.** 4	**19.** 5	**24.** 1	**29.** 2	
5. 2	**10.** 2	**15.** 3	**20.** 3	**25.** 3	**30.** 1	

What's your score?

If you got at least 23 correct you are prepared to take the test which will earn you a high school equivalency diploma.

SUB-TEST **3.**

Interpretation of Reading Materials in the Social Studies

Directions: **Read each of the following passages carefully. Then select the answer to each of the numbered questions which in your opinion best completes the statement or question.**

Passage I

The average citizen today is knowledgeable about "landmark" court decisions concerning such questions as racial segregation, legislative apportionment, prayers in the public schools, or the right of a defendant to counsel in a criminal prosecution. Too often, however, he thinks that these decisions settle matters once and for all. Actually, of course, these well-publicized court decisions are merely guideposts pointing toward a virtually endless series of vexing legal questions. It is often more difficult to determine how far the courts should travel along a road than to decide what road should be taken.

Illustrations of this difficulty exist in all areas of the law, and especially in those most familiar to the lay public. For example, this nation could hardly fail to agree that state-compelled racial segregation in the public schools is a denial of the equal protection of the laws guaranteed by the 14th amendment. The real difficulty lies in determining how desegregation shall be accomplished and how to solve the problem of de facto school segregation, perpetuated by the practical if unfortunate realities of residential patterns.

Similarly, there was substantial editorial approval of the Supreme Court's initial decision that grossly inequitable legislative apportionment was a proper matter for judicial scrutiny. The traditional democratic ideal of majority rule, it was argued, could not be subverted by apportionment schemes which at times appeared to give the rural voter twice the electoral strength of his urban counterpart. But when this principle was extended to render unlawful the composition of virtually every state legislature in the nation, the reaction to such an extension received as much attention as the apportionment decision itself.

1. According to the author, the effect of many decisions in the courts has been to (1) make citizens study the law (2) lead to more legal complications (3) contradict the Constitution (4) deny states' rights (5) provide final solutions to many problems

2. The author implies that, in so far as important court decisions are concerned, the public today is generally (1) disinterested (2) mystified (3) critical (4) well-informed (5) disapproving

3. According to the author, the Court's decision on legislative apportionment was based on the principle of (1) majority rule (2) electoral strength (3) equal protection under the law (4) legal precedents (5) judicial tradition

4. As used in the passage, the word "landmark" (line 1) most nearly means
(1) exciting   (2) just   (3) significant   (4) publicized   (5) legal

4. 1 2 3 4 5

5. Of the questions mentioned, the two that are most thoroughly discussed
are   (1) racial segregation and legislative apportionment   (2) racial segregation and prayers in the public schools   (3) legislative apportionment
and prayers in the public schools   (4) legislative apportionment and the
right of a defendant to counsel   (5) desegregation and segregation

5. 1 2 3 4 5

Passage II

The propensity of Americans to join is not new. It goes back to the ladies'
reading clubs and other cultural groups which spread on the moving frontier,
and which were the forerunners of parent-teacher associations and the civic
and forum groups of today. The jungle of voluntary associations was already
dense enough for De Tocqueville to note that "in no country in the world
has the principle of association been more unsparingly applied to a multitude
of different objects than in America." The permissiveness of the State, the
openness of the society, the newness of the surroundings, the need for inter-
weaving people from diverse ethnic groups—or conversely, their huddling
together inside the ethnic tent until they could be assimilated—all these shap-
ing forces were present from the start. What came later was the breaking up
of the rural and small-town life of America and the massing in impersonal
cities, bringing a dislocation that strengthened the impulse to join like-minded
people.

6. The phrase that best expresses the ideas of this passage is   (1) the ances-
tor of the PTA   (2) Americans as joiners   (3) the growth of organizations in cities   (4) the end of the small town   (5) associations in rural
America

6. 1 2 3 4 5

7. De Tocqueville apparently believed that Americans   (1) improved themselves by joining clubs   (2) overcame many difficulties as pioneers
(3) used the principle of association freely   (4) valued friendships greatly
(5) were greedy for many riches

7. 1 2 3 4 5

8. De Tocqueville pointed out that the associations he observed were
(1) illegal   (2) permissive   (3) varied   (4) dense   (5) large

8. 1 2 3 4 5

9. According to the passage, which statement can best be made about the
desire to join?   (1) it was fostered by laws   (2) it probably fulfilled a
need   (3) it resulted in less assimilation than ever   (4) it was basically
an autocratic, not a democratic phenomenon   (5) it caused the breakup
of rural and small-town life

9. 1 2 3 4 5

10. The author's chief purpose in writing this passage seems to be to   (1) en-
courage people to join clubs   (2) discredit De Tocqueville's viewpoint
(3) defend people's right to join clubs   (4) explain the basis for certain
groups in America   (5) indicate why ethnic groups have increased

10. 1 2 3 4 5

Passage III

Foreign propagandists have a strange misconception of our national character. They believe that we Americans must be hybrid, mongrel, undynamic; and we are called so by the enemies of democracy because, they say, so many races have been fused together in our national life. They believe we are disunited and defenseless because we argue with each other, because we engage in political campaigns, because we recognize the sacred right of the minority to disagree with the majority and to express that disagreement even loudly. It is the very mingling of races, dedicated to common ideals, which creates and recreates our vitality. In every representative American meeting there will be people with names like Jackson and Lincoln and Isaacs and Schultz and Kovacs and Sartori and Jones and Smith. These Americans with varied backgrounds are all immigrants or the descendants of immigrants. All of them are inheritors of the same stalwart tradition of unusual enterprise, of adventurousness, of courage—courage to "pull up stakes and git moving." That has been the great compelling force in our history. Our continent, our hemisphere, has been populated by people who wanted a life better than the life they had previously known. They were willing to undergo all conceivable hardships to achieve the better life. They were animated, just as we are animated today, by this compelling force. It is what makes us Americans.

11. The title below that best expresses the ideas of this selection: (1) No Common Ideals (2) America's Motivating Force (3) American Immigrants (4) The Evils of Foreign Propaganda (5) Defenseless America

12. According to the paragraph, our national character thrives because we have (1) few disagreements (2) majority groups (3) shared our wealth (4) driving ambition (5) minority rights

13. Foreign propagandists believe that Americans (1) are enemies of democracy (2) lack a common heritage (3) have a unified national character (4) refuse to argue with each other (5) are ashamed of foreign descent

13. 1 2 3 4 5

14. Foreign propagandists and the author both agree that Americans (1) are disunited (2) have no common tradition (3) come from varied backgrounds (4) have the courage of their convictions (5) are deeply religious

Passage IV

The term *factory system* is applied to the system of production which developed as a result of the Industrial Revolution. It arose in England at the end of the 18th century and spread in the 19th and 20th to other parts of the world. Under this system, goods are produced with the use of machinery rather than by hand as under the Domestic System. Machinery is cumbersome and requires many workers to operate it; hence it was no longer possible to produce goods in the home. Special buildings had to be constructed to house the machinery; these became known as factories. Workers from nearby areas gathered each day in these factories. This caused concentration of population around them and led to the rise of cities. Workers were no longer skilled artisans or craftsmen; instead, each became proficient at the particular work done by the machine which he tended. A division of labor was set up for greater speed and efficiency. Various machines were devised, each to be used for turning out some portion of the product for later assembly. No one worker, therefore, turned out the entire product. Many workers were employed in one factory, sometimes numbering hundreds, or thousands. Wage-earning workers had little or no contact with the actual owner of the factory. These were the chief characteristics of the *factory system* as it evolved.

15. The factory system is directly responsible for
    (1) the rise of suburbia in the 17th century
    (2) individual pride in the production of goods
    (3) specialization and division of labor   (4) the need for skilled craftsmen   (5) closer employer-employee relationship

15. 1 2 3 4 5
    || || || || ||

16. The factory system replaced the
    (1) Industrial Revolution   (2) domestic system   (3) worker
    (4) small farmer   (5) machine system

16. 1 2 3 4 5
    || || || || ||

17. The author of this passage would agree with all of the following statements except
    (1) The factory system is responsible for automation.
    (2) There was no need for labor unions under the domestic system.
    (3) The factory system had its beginnings in England.   (4) The guild system replaced technology.   (5) The factory system depended upon inventions of new machinery.

17. 1 2 3 4 5
    || || || || ||

Passage V

Since 1750, about the beginning of the Age of Steam, the earth's population has more than tripled. This increase has not been an evolutionary phenomenon with biological causes. Yet there was an evolution—it took place in the world's economic organization. Thus 1,500,000,000 more human beings can now remain alive on the earth's surface, can support themselves by working for others who in turn work for them. This extraordinary tripling of human population in six short generations is explained by the speeded-up economic unification which took place during the same period. Thus most of us are now kept alive by this vast cooperative unified world society. Goods are the great travelers over the earth's surface, far more than human beings. Endlessly streams of goods crisscross, as on Martian canals, with hardly an inhabited spot on the globe unvisited.

18. The title below that best expresses the ideas of this passage is: (1) Modern Phenomena   (2) The Age of Steam   (3) Increasing Population
    (4) Our Greatest Traveler   (5) Our Economic Interdependence

18. 1 2 3 4 5
    || || || || ||

19. A generation is considered to be   (1) 20 years   (2) 25 years   (3) 33 years   (4) 40 years   (5) dependent on the average age at marriage

19. 1 2 3 4 5
    || || || || ||

20. The writer considers trade necessary for   (1) travel   (2) democracy
    (3) political unity   (4) self-preservation   (5) the theory of evolution

20. 1 2 3 4 5
    || || || || ||

21. The basic change which led to the greatly increased population concerns
(1) new explorations   (2) economic factors   (3) biological factors   (4)
an increase in travel   (5) the growth of world government

Passage VI

The man in the street speaks vaguely of "the olden times," for he has but
one epithet to apply to all the ages which lie between the dawn of history and
the invention of the locomotive. If he thinks of them at all, Julius Caesar and
Queen Elizabeth are to him essentially contemporaries, and from his point of
view he is quite justified in thinking of them as such, since to one who judges
of the value of life by the comforts amidst which it is passed, it is hardly worth
while to make any distinction except that between a way of life which comes
up to the 17th century standard and one which does not. All ages except the
present were alike in being compelled to get along without the things of
which he is most proud, and what he calls "progress" did not begin until a
very short time ago.

22. The title below that best expresses the ideas of this passage is: (1) Eval-
uating One's Contemporaries   (2) The Comforts of the Past   (3) History, Short-sighted View   (4) The 19th Century   (5) The True Nature
of Progress

23. The average man's knowledge of history is   (1) limited   (2) theoretical
(3) profound   (4) scholarly   (5) wide

24. As used in the passage, the word "epithet" (line 2) most nearly means
(1) statement   (2) question   (3) reason   (4) characteristic   (5) expression

25. The author implies that the average man   (1) considers progress an outdated notion   (2) often thinks of past ages   (3) has a narrow set of
values   (4) has a historical perspective   (5) is purposely vague about
history

Passage VII

Underlying historical events which influenced two great American peoples,
citizens of Canada and of the United States, to work out their many problems
through the years with such harmony and mutual benefit constitute a story
which is both colorful and fascinating. It is a story of border disputes, questions and their solutions, for certainly the controversies and wars of the early
years of Canada and the northern colonies of what now is the United States,
and after 1783 their continuation through the War of 1812, scarcely constituted a sound foundation for international friendship. The fact too that great
numbers of Loyalists fled to Canada during the Revolutionary period, combined with the general Loyalist sentiment of the citizens of Canada, both of
French and British extraction, might well have brought about historical
antipathy between the two countries, such as often has proved unsurmountable
in similar circumstances in other parts of the world.

Yet it is a fact that solutions were found for every matter of disagreement that arose and, as it is, the two nations have been able to work out a peaceful result from the many difficulties naturally arising in connection with a long and disputed boundary line, in many cases not delineated by great natural barriers.

26. The title that best expresses the ideas of this passage is: (1) A Proud Record (2) Our Northern Neighbor (3) Cooperation with Canada (4) Our Northern Boundary Line (5) The Role of the Loyalists in Canada

26. 1 2 3 4 5

27. Disagreements between Canada and the United States (1) did not occur after 1800 (2) were solved in every case (3) constituted a basis for friendship (4) were solved principally to America's advantage (5) resulted from the presence of natural barriers

27. 1 2 3 4 5

28. The writer considers the period before 1812 (1) an insurmountable barrier (2) a time of geographical disputes (3) the definer of our differences (4) a cementer of our Canadian friendship (5) the period that settled our northern boundary

28. 1 2 3 4 5

ANSWERS TO SUB-TEST 3 *Interpretation of Reading Materials in the Social Studies*

1. 2	**5.** 1	**9.** 2	**13.** 2	**17.** 4	**21.** 2	**25.** 3
2. 4	**6.** 2	**10.** 4	**14.** 3	**18.** 5	**22.** 3	**26.** 3
3. 1	**7.** 3	**11.** 2	**15.** 3	**19.** 3	**23.** 1	**27.** 2
4. 3	**8.** 3	**12.** 4	**16.** 2	**20.** 4	**24.** 5	**28.** 2

What's your score?

If you got at least 20 correct you are prepared to take the test which will earn you a high school equivalency diploma.

SUB-TEST **4.**

Interpretation of Reading Materials in the Natural Sciences

Directions: **Read each of the following selections carefully. Then select the answer to each of the numbered questions which in your opinion best completes the statement or question.**

Selection H

Ecologists warn man that he may disappear from this planet unless he takes steps to make wiser use of the factors of his environment. It is no wonder that some speculate that the Age of Insects may replace the Age of Man.

The insect world is man's greatest competitor for the domination of Earth. Grasshoppers chew on crops. Aphids suck juices from our plants. Many insects eat gluttonously during the caterpillar stage. Termites destroy wooden structures. Many insects are carriers of the causative agents of human disease. The female anopheles mosquito transmits the protozoan that causes malaria while another species carries the virus responsible for yellow fever. The common house fly may carry an assortment of germs to our food.

Insects are so well adapted to survive that man has to modify his chemical warfare against them. Not too many years ago, dichloro-diphenyl-trichlorethane (DDT) was a potent weapon. But insects have a newly evolved immunity to DDT. Also, as a result of the criticism of the side effects of this chemical, chemists had to research for new insecticides. A good insecticide must not only destroy insects but must not have the tendency of accumulating in the bodies of the fish and birds that feed on insects. An apparently effective insecticide that protected crops was recently found to drain off into rivers where the chemical killed fish.

Insects enjoy many advantages for survival. Insects reproduce often and in large numbers. Their small size is a very definite advantage. Their food needs are small and they can easily escape detection, especially with their keen sense of sight and smell. They are not fussy about diet and can adapt to changes, as illustrated by the new forms they have reproducd that defy man's poisons. Camouflage helps many insects blend with the environment. The names assigned to such insects as the "walking stick" and the "dead leaf" are illustrations. Mimicry is another device used for protection and ultimate survival. Birds often turn down a meal of a viceroy butterfly that mimicks the unpleasant-tasting monarch butterfly.

Let us bear in mind that we do need some members of the insect world. They pollinate some of our flowers without which some fruit formation would be impossible. Our pure silk comes from the material of the cocoon of an insect. Also do not overlook the work of the honeybee.

1. Which of the following is unlike the others?
(1) house fly   (2) grasshopper   (3) mosquito   (4) malarial protozoan   (5) termite

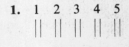

2. Ecology is basically concerned with
(1) dangers of atomic destruction   (2) life on other planets   (3) man's use of the factors of his environment   (4) destruction of insect pests (5) practical use of insecticides

3. Yellow fever is caused by a virus carried by the
(1) house fly   (2) mosquito   (3) protozoan   (4) virus (5) anopheles

4. Man must change his insecticide from time to time because
(1) insects learn to avoid old poisons   (2) DDT is no longer effective (3) insects have keen senses   (4) valuable insects are often destroyed by a particular poison   (5) insects give rise to new poison-resistant forms

5. All of the following have survival value for insects except
(1) mimicry   (2) camouflage   (3) body size   (4) metamorphosis   (5) rate of reproduction

5. 1 2 3 4 5

6. Insects are important agents of pollination
(1) when no winds prevail   (2) when seedless fruits are desired   (3) where pollen is deep-seated in the floral parts   (4) where man cannot reach into the floral parts for cross-pollination   (5) during rainy spring seasons

6. 1 2 3 4 5

7. Codling moths lay their eggs in
(1) woolens   (2) ripe apples   (3) garbage heaps   (4) apple blossoms (5) rotten apples

7. 1 2 3 4 5

8. Without insects we would not have
(1) disease   (2) fruits   (3) nylon   (4) beeswax   (5) natural syrups

8. 1 2 3 4 5

9. Insects are generally most destructive during
(1) reproductive stage   (2) caterpillar stage   (3) adult stage   (4) pupal stage   (5) mating seasons

9. 1 2 3 4 5

Selection I

Let us remember that the struggle for water has plagued man throughout history. With the flood and ebb of a river empires have tumbled. Water is necessary for life. It makes up about two-thirds of the composition of your body and helps carry food to the cells and wastes away from the cells.

A good water supply must be hygienically safe and pleasant tasting. Man needs unsalted water for home use, farming, and industry. Water containing salts would corrode machinery used in manufacturing in addition to introducing chemical impurities. Since more than ninety-five per cent of our water lies in the salty seas, man is compelled to capture water during the water cycle when water from the oceans evaporates. But here too he finds that most of the rain and snow that falls is not available for him. Plants remove a great deal of it plus the fact that some water reaches the ground and evaporates. Add to this the fact that most of the fresh water on the surface of the earth is not available for use. For example, the Antarctic ice cap, if melted would provide as much water as all our rivers supply in about 800 years.

What is involved in purifying water? Basically it involves a number of physical and chemical processes to remove undesirable constituents. These include the removal of pathogenic microorganisms and the elimination of harmful, unpalatable, and objectionable substances.

Aeration diminishes bad tastes and odors and by adding more oxygen and decreasing the carbon dioxide content, corrosiveness is decreased and iron is made insoluble. Coagulation causes the settling of lumps of iron, manganese, and bacteria. This may be accomplished by adding aluminum sulphate. These coagulated substances are then removed by sedimentation. Another physical process is filtration, often through soil by which substances including those that cause undesirable color, taste, or odor are reduced.

10. The author of this passage states that
(1) the problem of obtaining good drinking water has plagued man since the Industrial Revolution   (2) palatability is synonymous with purity of water   (3) most of the world's water is in the sea   (4) man no longer depends upon evaporation and condensation of natural waters for his water supply   (5) the removal of undesirable microorganisms from water

11. Industry must avoid salt water because
(1) water is needed for livestock   (2) crops must be considered before man-made products   (3) it is used in desalination plants   (4) it causes corrosion   (5) water makes up two-thirds of the body composition

12. The best title for this passage is
(1) The Water Cycle   (2) Fresh Water Needed   (3) Melt the Glaciers! (4) The History of Water   (5) Water Conservation

13. All of the following contribute to water purification except
(1) aeration   (2) coagulation   (3) sedimentation   (4) filtration   (5) pollution

14. Which of the following contributes to water purification?
(1) aluminum sulphate   (2) iron   (3) manganese   (4) carbon dioxide   (5) non-green plant life

Selection J

All living things exhibit responsiveness. Though plants do not have a nervous system, they do produce chemical regulators called hormones. The two types of growth hormones are auxins and gibberellins.

Auxins, which are very similar to animal hormones, are produced in one part and the chemical is transported to another part of the plant. Also, they are effective in small concentrations. Auxins are produced in the tips of stems and roots, and by young buds and leaves. They function in one of several ways. They either initiate cell division, cause an increase in rate of cell division, or cause cells to elongate. When auxins reach the area of elongation of young roots or stems they cause the cell walls to become more plastic thus permitting greater absorption of water which is necessary for elongation. Indole acetic acid is such a natural auxin. On the other hand, naphthaleneacetic acid (NAA) and 2, 4-D have been artificially produced.

Gibberellins, of which gibberellic acid is an example, cause an increase in the rate of cell division in the entire stem and thus increase the length of the stem.

Scientists can produce synthetic plant hormones. For example, NAA is used on blossoms to produce fruit without pollination. These resulting seedless fruits have great economic value. The use of 2, 4-D in killing weeds without damaging the grass on lawns is widespread. Botanists classify seed-bearing plants into dicots and monocots. Interesting enough it has been found that in certain concentrations 2, 4-D is more effective on dicots than on monocots. Actually they cause such abnormal growth that the dicot plant dies. Since most weeds are dicots and grass is a monocot, an effective chemical weed killer has been developed from our knowledge of plant hormones and taxonomy.

There was a time when we accepted the turning of leaves toward light with the explanation that it was a tropism. Research with plant hormones has now given us a scientific explanation. We now know that cells at the tip of the stem produce auxin which is transported down to the region of elongation. Since light destroys the activity of auxin, only one side of the stem has an increase of growth. This unequal rate of growth causes the stem to bend toward the light.

15. In order for blossoms to produce fruits the process normally required is
(1) pollination   (2) responsiveness   (3) tropism   (4) seed dispersal
(5) elongation

15. 1 2 3 4 5
     || || || || ||

16. The tendency of leaves to grow toward a source of light is **best** explained by
(1) need for light for photosynthesis   (2) bending of stem   (3) effect of light on auxins in the stem   (4) tropism   (5) need for hormones

16. 1 2 3 4 5
     || || || || ||

17. Responsiveness in animals is a function of
(1) auxins   (2) gibberllins   (3) bones   (4) nerves   (5) NAA

17. 1 2 3 4 5
     || || || || ||

18. The one term that does not belong with the others is
(1) NAA   (2) DDT   (3) 2, 4-D   (4) indole acetic acid   (5) gibberellic acid

18. 1 2 3 4 5
     || || || || ||

19. Which of the following terms includes all the others?
(1) naphthaleneacetic acid   (2) 2, 4-D   (3) NAA   (4) auxin   (5) indole acetic acid

19. 1 2 3 4 5
     || || || || ||

20. A plant hormone may best be described as a
(1) weed killer   (2) synthetic chemical   (3) chemical messenger   (4) tropism   (5) seedless fruit

20. 1 2 3 4 5
     || || || || ||

21. According to the author of this passage all of the following are true statements except

(1) A small amount of auxin can produce an increase of cell division
(2) Cellulose cell walls prevent absorption and loss of water.   (3) Synthetic plant hormones function in the same way as auxins   (4) Gibberellins cause an increase in the length of stems   (5) Auxins control cell division

21. 1 2 3 4 5
     || || || || ||

22. Chemical weed killers may be described as
(1) monocots   (2) dicots   (3) concentrated NAA   (4) dilute gibberellic acid   (5) concentrated auxins

22. 1 2 3 4 5
     || || || || ||

23. Hormones are distributed throughout the human body by the
(1) nerves   (2) roots   (3) bark   (4) blood   (5) muscles

23. 1 2 3 4 5
     || || || || ||

Selection K

The present-day horse is an animal whose evolution can be traced through complete series of fossil ancestors. The first horse, or dawn horse, was called *eohippus* and lived about 60,000,000 years ago. It was but a foot high, had four toes on each front foot, and three on each hind foot. Each toe had a toenail, which was a primitive hoof. The teeth were small, with little if any ridges. It had a short neck and a small skull. Descendants of this first horse include a slightly larger *mesohippus*. The mesohippus had three toes on each foot, but the middle toe was large and carried most of the weight. The teeth had well-developed ridges. A still later fossil had a foot much like the horse of today, but there were still two small side toes that were in evidence which did not touch the ground. It was still smaller than the modern horse. The modern horse has but tiny splints remaining of the two toes on the sides of the legs.

24. The best title for the above passage is
    (1) Eohippus Mesohippus   (2) Changes in Structure due to Environment   (3) Evolution of the Horse   (4) Horse Breeding   (5) Improvements in Horses

25. The author draws his facts from the study of
    (1) toes   (2) fossils   (3) teeth   (4) splints   (5) body size

26. Organisms often possess structures which are useless to the individual but are thought to have been functional in their remote ancestors. Such structures are called *vestigial*. Which of the following is a vestigial structure?

    (1) the four toes of Eohippus   (2) the toenail of Eohippus   (3) the large toe of Mesohippus   (4) the splints of modern horse   (5) the hoof of modern horse

27. Which of the following statements is true of Equus, the modern horse?
    (1) it lived 60 million years ago   (2) it has few ridges on its teeth (3) it resembles Eohippus more than Mesohippus   (4) it walks on its splints   (5) it walks on the remains of a middle toe

28. Mesohippus differs from eohippus in that
    (1) mesohippus disappeared before eohippus evolved   (2) eohippus had three toes on each foot   (3) mesohippus had two small side toes that didn't touch the ground   (4) mesohippus had more highly developed tooth structure   (5) eohippus had a larger middle toe

Selection L

The skin has several functions. An important function is the regulation of body temperature. If the body is too warm, the sweat glands of the skin will excrete water more profusely, resulting in a greater evaporation and therefore cooling. In colder weather, the smooth muscles and capillaries of the skin contract, driving the blood away from the surface, thus preventing the escape of body heat. Another important function of the skin is excretion. The sweat glands in excreting water also excrete salts and nitrogenous wastes dissolved in the water. The skin also helps to protect the body since it completely covers it and therefore prevents the entrance of injurious substances and disease bacteria. Still another function of the skin is as a sense receptor. The skin has five different types of nerve endings that respond to such stimuli as touch, pressure, cold, heat and pain. Different nerves are specific for each type of stimulus and are distributed in patterns all over the body. Impulses are sent through the nerves and through the spinal cord into the brain, setting up protective reflexes and helping the organism in general to adjust to its environment.

29. "Sense receptor" (line 10) may best be described as a
(1) receiver of stimuli   (2) receiver of responses from the spinal cord
(3) carrier of responses to the spinal cord   (4) carrier of responses to the brain   (5) carrier and receiver of responses all over the body.

30. All of the following are implied by the author, except
(1) Evaporation has a cooling effect.   (2) The skin functions very much like the human kidney.   (3) Unbroken skin is vulnerable to bacteria.
(4) Perspiration is a useful function   (5) The skin is a receptor of changes in the environment of the individual.

31. Which of the following statements is true?
(1) Any nerve ending in the skin can conduct impulses of touch, pressure, or cold.   (2) In warm weather blood is driven away from the surface of the skin to prevent excessive heating by the blood.   (3) In cold weather blood is driven to the surface of the skin to bring heat and energy.   (4) The salty taste of sweat is due to the dissolved salts and nitrogeneous substances.   (5) Sweat glands excrete more when the body is cold to aid in the retention of body heat.

Selection M

The number of species of butterflies is very great, and the arrangement of them has been found difficult, chiefly on account of the great similarity in all important respects which prevails among them all. They are divided, however, into two well-marked sections, of which the first is characterized by having only a single pair of spurs or spines on the *tibiae* (or fourth joints of the legs), placed at their lower extremity; while in the other section, the tibiae of the hinder legs have two pair of spurs, one at each extremity. The distinction, seemingly unimportant in itself, is accompanied by other differences. The second section of butterflies may be regarded as forming a sort of connecting link between butterflies and hawkmoths. A few British species belong to it, but the species are generally tropical, and some of them, found in tropical America, are remarkable for their rapidity and power of flight, and for the migrations which they perform, besides being among 'the most splendid insects in creation,' a resplendent green inimitable by art, relieving the velvet black of their wings, and varying with every change of light. The beautiful iridescence of the wings of these and many other butterflies is due to the peculiar position of the scales.

32. The tibiae are parts of the
(1) wing   (2) spine   (3) spurs   (4) leg   (5) scales

32. 1 2 3 4 5
     || || || || ||

33. Iridescence refers to the characteristic of wing in which it is
(1) velvety   (2) scaly   (3) able to change its color   (4) green
(5) able to change its position

33. 1 2 3 4 5
     || || || || ||

34. This passage most probably was written for a (an)
(1) dictionary   (2) tropical book on plant and animal life   (3) encyclopedia for children living in rural communities   (4) book describing the beauty of butterflies   (5) British book on natural history

34. 1 2 3 4 5
     || || || || ||

35. Which of the following statements is correct?
(1) Butterflies exhibit more similarities among themselves than differences
(2) Hawk-moths are butterflies   (3) All butterflies have two pair of spurs on the hind legs   (4) The wings of butterflies make up in beauty what they lack in power   (5) The colors of butterfly wings are green and black.

35. 1 2 3 4 5
     || || || || ||

Selection N

The small intestine has two basic functions: to digest food within the small intestine and to make possible the absorption of the digested food into the blood. Many juices are secreted into the small intestine to help digest food. *Pancreatic juice* digests fats, protein and starch. *Bile* emulsifies the fats. The walls of the small intestine secrete *intestinal juice* which completes the digestion of proteins and sugars. Lining the walls of the small intestine are millions of microscopic hairs called *villi*. Their job is to carry on the absorption of digested foods. The villi increase the surface area of the small intestine and thus the soluble digested food has a greater surface area through which absorption can take place. The villi are very thin-walled, and possess capillaries and lacteals within. This thinness speeds up absorption. The extreme length of the small intestine and its many folds, or convolutions, also increase the surface area and thus facilitate absorption.

36. The best title for the above passage is
(1) The Small Intestine and its Digestive Juices   (2) The Small Intestine — Digestion and Absorption   (3) The Work of the Villi   (4) The Intestines and the Pancreas   (5) The Interrelationship of Enzymes

36. 1 2 3 4 5
     || || || || ||

37. According to the passage, absorption of soluble digested food is made possible by
(1) bile   (2) intestinal juices   (3) pancreatic juice   (4) villi   (5) many juices in the intestines

37. 1 2 3 4 5
     || || || || ||

38. Which or the following is **not** true?
(1) Digestive juices in the small intestine come from other organs as well as from its own walls   (2) The small intestine is well adapted to carry on absorption of digested food   (3) Pancreatic juice contains several enzymes that can digest different nutrients   (4) Pancreatic juice emulsifies fat   (5) The food that enters the intestine from the stomach is not completely digested

38. 1 2 3 4 5
‖   ‖   ‖   ‖   ‖

ANSWERS EXPLAINED   *page 464-465*

ANSWERS TO SUB-TEST 4   *Interpretation of Reading Materials in the Natural Sciences*

1. 4	**8.** 4	**15.** 1	**22.** 5	**29.** 1	**36.** 2
2. 3	**9.** 2	**16.** 3	**23.** 4	**30.** 3	**37.** 4
3. 2	**10.** 3	**17.** 4	**24.** 3	**31.** 4	**38.** 3
4. 5	**11.** 4	**18.** 2	**25.** 2	**32.** 4	
5. 4	**12.** 2	**19.** 4	**26.** 4	**33.** 3	
6. 3	**13.** 5	**20.** 3	**27.** 5	**34.** 5	
7. 4	**14.** 1	**21.** 2	**28.** 4	**35.** 1	

What's your score?

If you got at least 27 correct you are prepared to take the test which will earn you a high school equivalency diploma.

ANSWERS EXPLAINED

1. Ans. 4 The malarial protozoan is a single-celled animal organism while the others are insects.

2. Ans. 3 By definition.

3. Ans. 2 A particular species of mosquito carries the virus causing yellow fever.

4. Ans. 5 Refer to the third paragraph.

5. Ans. 4 Metamorphosis is a form of reproduction. All the other choices given increase insect population and help them escape enemies.

6. Ans. 3 Wind pollination cannot occur where pollen is not exposed to the environment. When insects alight on flowers to suck nectar, pollen is caught in the body of the insect and may be transported to another flower of that species.

7. Ans. 4 The "worm" sometimes found in apparently undamaged apples is the larval stage of the codling moth which laid its eggs in the flower and developed as the ovary of the flower developed into a fruit. This caterpillar or its pupa would emerge from the apple as it falls off the tree, injuring the skin of the apple.

8. Ans. 4 Not all causative agents of disease are carried by insects. By wind pollination or self pollination some fruits would develop without insects. Nylon is man made. Syrups are usually products of sugar.

9. Ans. 2 Refer to the second paragraph of the passage.

10. Ans. 3 More than 95% of our water lies in the salty seas.

11. Ans. 4 Refer to the second paragraph of the passage.

12. Ans. 2 This selection deals mainly with the need for a good water supply.

13. Ans. 5 Pollution is the greatest enemy of a good water supply.

14. Ans. 1 Aluminum sulphate causes the clumping of many impurities of water. By gravity these coagulated substances are removed by sedimentation.

15. Ans. 1 Pollination is the transfer of the pollen grains containing the male sex cells to the region of the ovary where the female sex cells are located. The developing ovary, with its seeds, forms the fruit.

16. Ans. 3 The auxin in the stem is destroyed by light. If only one side of the stem is exposed to light, unequal growth will occur, causing bending.

17. Ans. 4 Nerve cells carry impulses.

18. Ans. 2 DDT is an insecticide. The others are plant hormones.

19. Ans. 4 These are auxins.

20. Ans. 3 Hormones are made in one structure and produce their effects in other parts.

21. Ans. 2 Cell walls vary in their ability to allow substances to pass in and out of the cell. If absorption were prevented entirely, the cell would have no contact with the environment.

22. Ans. 5 Auxins in certain concentrations cause plant parts to grow disproportionately so that the lack of balance between the root and the structure above ground would cause death.

23. Ans. 4 Observe that this question applies the information of the passage to humans.

24. Ans. 3 The passage traces the anatomical changes in the ancestors of the modern horse.

25. Ans. 2 Since these ancestors of Equus have long disappeared, the only evidence of structure comes from fossils.

26. Ans. 4 Refer to the last sentence of this passage.

27. Ans. 5 The horse's hoof is the toenail of a middle toe.

28. Ans. 4 Eohippus had teeth without ridges. Mesohippus had teeth with well developed ridges.

29. Ans. 1 The passage refers to the skin as a sense receptor with five different types of nerve endings that respond to stimuli.

30. Ans. 3 Skin prevents the entrance of injurious substances and bacteria. A break in skin makes this entrance possible.

31. Ans. 4 The sweat glands excrete water with the salts and nitrogenous wastes dissolved in it.

32. Ans. 4 Refer to the second sentence.

33. Ans. 3 Refer to the last sentence of the passage.

34. Ans. 5 Observe the level of vocabulary, the technical terms used and the reference to British species as they apparently are of local interest.

35. Ans. 1 Refer to the opening sentence.

36. Ans. 2 The passage refers mainly to the small intestine mentioning structures outside the intestine only as they affect the small intestine.

37. Ans. 4 Villi are described as microscopic hairs which absorb digested food.

38. Ans. 3 The passage mentions that pancreatic juice digests fats, proteins, and starch. To accomplish this chemical reaction it must contain several enzymes since enzymes are specific in their action.

SUB-TEST **5.**

General Mathematical Ability

Directions: **Solve the following problems.**

1. The charge for 4 ounces of candy sold at $1.20 per pound should be
(1) 20¢ (2) 30¢ (3) 40¢ (4) 50¢ (5) 60¢

1. 1 2 3 4 5

2. If you divide the product of 5.7 and 39.6 by 0.2 the quotient will be
(1) 11.29 (2) 45.04 (3) 1128.6 (4) 198 (5) 450.44

2. 1 2 3 4 5

3. Steel weighs approximately 0.28 pounds per cubic inch. What is the weight (in pounds) of a steel shaft that contains 123.5 cubic inches
(1) 22.3 (2) 33.58 (3) 34.58 (4) 35.6 (5) 44

3. 1 2 3 4 5

4. Last week Philip worked 40 hours at the rate of $1.40 an hour. His older brother Mark earns $1.75 an hour at his job. How many hours must Mark work in order to equal Philip's earnings?
(1) 24 (2) 30 (3) 32 (4) 34 (5) 36

4. 1 2 3 4 5

5. Balloons costing 36¢ per dozen are sold for 5¢ each. How much profit will be made by selling 14 dozen balloons?
(1) $.24 (2) $.28 (3) $1.68 (4) $3.36 (5) $8.40

5. 1 2 3 4 5

6. A refrigerator can be purchased for $450 or on the installment plan for $45 down and $28.80 a month for 15 months. The charge for installment buying is
(1) $18 (2) $27 (3) $45 (4) $53 (5) $62

6. 1 2 3 4 5

7. A salesman's report of sales follows: Monday $750. Tuesday $850. Wednesday $600. Thursday $900. What must his sales be on Friday so that he will have an average of $800 in sales for this five day week?
(1) $780 (2) $800 (3) $850 (4) $900 (5) $3100

7. 1 2 3 4 5

8. $\dfrac{\frac{1}{4} - \frac{3}{16}}{\frac{1}{8}}$ equals
(1) $-\frac{1}{16}$ (2) $+\frac{1}{16}$ (3) $\frac{3}{8}$ (4) $\frac{1}{2}$ (5) 2

8. 1 2 3 4 5

9. The gasoline gauge shows that the tank is $\frac{1}{5}$ full. Martin asks the attendant at the service station to pump enough gasoline so that the tank is half full. How much gasoline should be put into this 20-gallon tank?
(1) 4 (2) 6 (3) 8 (4) 10 (5) 16

9. 1 2 3 4 5

10. Mr. Marshall left half of his estate to his wife and $\frac{1}{4}$ of the remainder to his grandson. What part of his estate is not acounted for in this statement?
(1) $\frac{1}{8}$ (2) $\frac{5}{8}$ (3) $\frac{1}{4}$ (4) $\frac{3}{4}$ (5) $\frac{3}{8}$

10. 1 2 3 4 5

11. A class has s number of students. One day 5 students are absent. What part of the class is present?
(1) $s - 5$ (2) $\dfrac{5}{s}$ (3) $\dfrac{5}{s-5}$ (4) $\dfrac{s-5}{s}$ (5) $\dfrac{s-5}{5}$

11. 1 2 3 4 5

12. The change from the ⅔ requirement to ⅗ majority to stop filibustering is a decrease of
(1) 25%   (2) 6⅔%   (3) 33⅓%   (4) 50%   (5) 66⅔%

12. 1 2 3 4 5

13. A road 49.5 miles long had its work halted when a contractor completed 62% of it. How many miles are left to be built?
(1) 11.88   (2) 18.11   (3) 18.18   (4) 18.81   (5) 30.69

13. 1 2 3 4 5

14. An article marked $48 is sold for $40. The per cent of discount allowed is
(1) 8   (2) 12½   (3) 16⅔   (4) 20   (5) 25

14. 1 2 3 4 5

15. If bought for cash, a washer listed at $192 will be given a discount of $7.68. What is the per cent of discount offered for the cash purchase?
(1) 2.5%   (2) 4%   (3) 4.2%   (4) 25%   (5) 40%

15. 1 2 3 4 5

16. Mr. Richman earned $6469.80 this year as compared with $7890 last year. The per cent decrease was
(1) 17   (2) 18   (3) 19   (4) 20   (5) 22

16. 1 2 3 4 5

17. What is ¼ % of 400?
(1) .1   (2) 1.0   (3) 10   (4) 10.1   (5) 100

17. 1 2 3 4 5

18. When the toll charge increased from 50 cents to 60 cents it represented a per cent increase of
(1) 10%   (2) 16⅔%   (3) 20%   (4) 30%   (5) 40%

18. 1 2 3 4 5

19. Which of the following is not equal in value to the others?
(1) 1½%   (2) $\frac{15}{1000}$ (3) .15   (4) .015   (5) 1.5%

19. 1 2 3 4 5

20. A television set is marked $250 for a cash purchase or a 10% charge for installment buying. For the installment plan the store requires a down payment of $100 and monthly payments of $8.75. How many monthly payments will be required?
(1) 18   (2) 19   (3) 20   (4) 21   (5) 22

20. 1 2 3 4 5

21. A department store pays its sales clerks a salary of $42 per week plus a bonus of 2% on all sales over $300. Lucy Smith earned $53 last week. Her total sales were
(1) $530   (2) $550   (3) $825   (4) $850   (5) $900

21. 1 2 3 4 5

22. A chair listed at $81 is sold for $54 during a clearance sale. The per cent of discount allowed during the sale is
(1) 16⅔   (2) 25   (3) 33⅓   (4) $60.   (5) 66⅔

22. 1 2 3 4 5

23. When purchasing fire insurance, you discover that a three-year policy can be purchased for 2.7 times the annual rate. According to this information, how much will the three-year premium be on a fire insurance policy for $4,000 issued at an annual rate of 24 cents per $100 valuation?
(1) $2.88   (2) $9.60   (3) $25.92   (4) $28.80   (5) $38.40

23. 1 2 3 4 5

24. Mr. J.P.M. bought 100 shares of Shurshot stock at $40 per share (brokerage fees and taxes included). The stock paid a dividend of 80¢ per share quarterly. What is the annual rate of income on this investment?
(1) 2%   (2) 3.2%   (3) 5%   '(4) 8%   (5) 20%

24. 1 2 3 4 5
|| || || || ||

25. Miguel had an investment in stock of several different companies that had a total cost of $6,650. The dividends received from his stock last year amounted to: $42.40; $78; $22; $150.20. The total dividends received last year were what per cent of the cost of the stock?
(1) 4%   (2) 2.3%   (3) 4.4%   (4) 22.7%   (5) 44%

25. 1 2 3 4 5
|| || || || ||

26. In a certain city the real estate tax rate is $42.75 per $1,000 of assessed value. A house valued at $20,000 is assessed at 42% of its value. The real estate tax on this property is
(1) $336   (2) $359.10   (3) $369   (4) $840   (5) $850

26. 1 2 3 4 5
|| || || || ||

27. The sides of this figure (with a perimeter of 45 inches) are expressed algebraically in inches. The smallest side is
(1) 9 inches   (2) 11.2 inches   (3) 12 inches
(4) 35 inches   (5) 36 inches

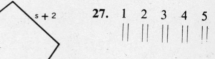

27. 1 2 3 4 5
|| || || || ||

28. The product of $(2x + 5)$ and $(x - 4)$ equals
(1) $2x^2 - 20$ (2) $2x^2 - 3x - 20$ (3) $2x^2 + 5x$ (4) $2x^2 + 13x - 20$
(5) $5x - 20$

28. 1 2 3 4 5
|| || || || ||

29. Given a, an odd integer, divide the next even integer by b and the quotient will be
(1) $\dfrac{a+1}{b}$ (2) $\dfrac{ab}{b+1}$ (3) $\dfrac{2a}{b}$ (4) $\dfrac{2a+1}{b}$ (5) $\dfrac{b}{a+1}$

29. 1 2 3 4 5
|| || || || ||

30. At 6 a.m. the temperature in Maine was 6 degrees below zero. At noon the temperature was 6 degrees above zero. During the six-hour period the temperature rose (?) degrees?
(1) 0   (2) 1   (3) 3   (4) 6   (5) 12

30. 1 2 3 4 5
|| || || || ||

31. What is the value of $\dfrac{2a + 3b}{c}$ when
$a = \dfrac{1}{2}$, $b = \dfrac{2}{3}$ and $c = \dfrac{3}{4}$?
(1) ½   (2) 2¼   (3) 2½   (4) 3   (5) 4

31. 1 2 3 4 5
|| || || || ||

32. When $a = 4$, $b = 5$, $x = 2$ and $y = 3$, the value of $(x + y)^2 - (a + b)$ is
(1) 1   (2) 5   (3) 16   (4) 34   (5) 45

32. 1 2 3 4 5
|| || || || ||

33. How far will a car travel in 3 hours and 45 minutes if its average speed is 32 miles per hour?
(1) 96 miles   (2) 98 miles   (3) 100 miles   (4) 120 miles
(5) 130 miles

33. 1 2 3 4 5
|| || || || ||

34. Given the formula: $A + B + C = 180°$. If $B = C = 45°$ then $A =$
(1) 22½°   (2) 45°   (3) 67½°   (4) 90°   (5) 135°

34. 1 2 3 4 5
|| || || || ||

35. $x^5 \div x^3 =$
    (1) 2   (2) $2x$ (3) x^8 (4) x^{-2} (5) x^2

36. If $5n - 1 = 34$, then $2\frac{1}{2}\,n$ equals
    (1) 7   (2) 14   (3) $16\frac{2}{3}$ (4) 17   (5) $17\frac{1}{2}$

37. To convert temperature from the Centigrade scale to the Fahrenheit scale we use the formula $F = \frac{9}{5}C + 32°$. Convert a reading of 25° Centigrade.
    (1) $32\frac{5}{9}$ (2) 42   (3) 45   (4) 52   (5) 77°

38. If $2x + t = 1$ then $t =$
    (1) $1 - 2x$ (2) $-x$ (3) $\frac{1}{2}x$ (4) $\frac{x}{2}$ (5) $1 + 2x$

39. For which equation is 3 a value of x?
    (1) $2x - 5 = 11$ (2) $\frac{x}{4} = 12$ (3) $3x + 1 = 10$ (4) $x^2 = 6$
    (5) $3x - 1 = 10$

40. If 5 pencils cost c cents what would be the cost of p pencils?
    (1) $\frac{5c}{p}\,\cent$ (2) $\frac{pc}{5}\,\cent$ (3) $5cp\cent$ (4) $\frac{5p}{c}\,\cent$ (5) $5c\cent$

41. The perimeter of a square whose area is 100 square feet is
    (1) 10   (2) 20   (3) 30   (4) 40   (5) 50

42. How many square yards of carpeting will be needed for the floor plan of the living room and foyer shown here?
    (1) 16.6   (2) 33.3   (3) 45   (4) 50
    (5) 450

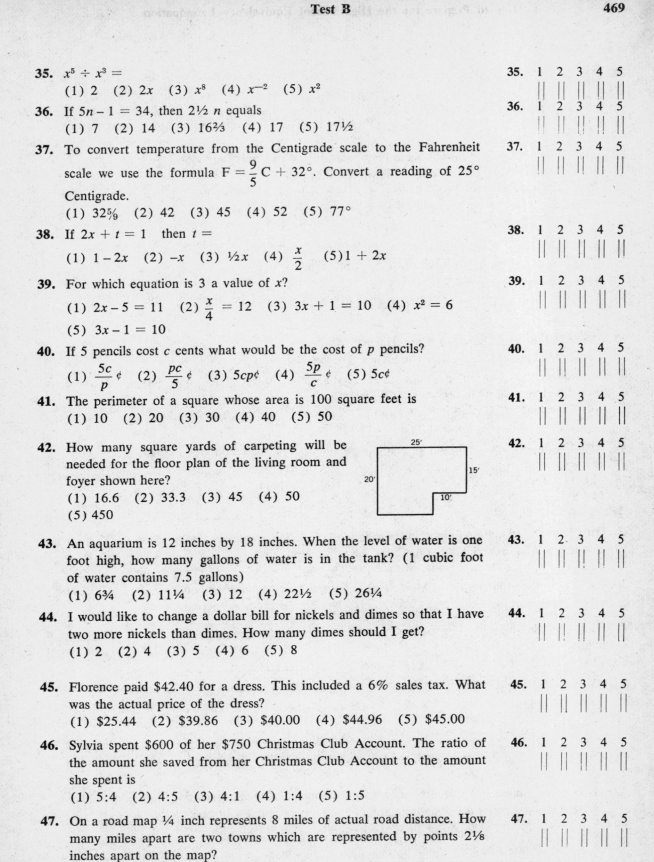

43. An aquarium is 12 inches by 18 inches. When the level of water is one foot high, how many gallons of water is in the tank? (1 cubic foot of water contains 7.5 gallons)
    (1) $6\frac{3}{4}$ (2) $11\frac{1}{4}$ (3) 12   (4) $22\frac{1}{2}$ (5) $26\frac{1}{4}$

44. I would like to change a dollar bill for nickels and dimes so that I have two more nickels than dimes. How many dimes should I get?
    (1) 2   (2) 4   (3) 5   (4) 6   (5) 8

45. Florence paid $42.40 for a dress. This included a 6% sales tax. What was the actual price of the dress?
    (1) $25.44   (2) $39.86   (3) $40.00   (4) $44.96   (5) $45.00

46. Sylvia spent $600 of her $750 Christmas Club Account. The ratio of the amount she saved from her Christmas Club Account to the amount she spent is
    (1) 5:4   (2) 4:5   (3) 4:1   (4) 1:4   (5) 1:5

47. On a road map $\frac{1}{4}$ inch represents 8 miles of actual road distance. How many miles apart are two towns which are represented by points $2\frac{1}{8}$ inches apart on the map?
    (1) 17   (2) 32   (3) 34   (4) 40   (5) 68

	1	2	3	4	5
35.	‖	‖	‖	‖	‖
36.	‖	‖	‖	‖	‖
37.	‖	‖	‖	‖	‖
38.	‖	‖	‖	‖	‖
39.	‖	‖	‖	‖	‖
40.	‖	‖	‖	‖	‖
41.	‖	‖	‖	‖	‖
42.	‖	‖	‖	‖	‖
43.	‖	‖	‖	‖	‖
44.	‖	‖	‖	‖	‖
45.	‖	‖	‖	‖	‖
46.	‖	‖	‖	‖	‖
47.	‖	‖	‖	‖	‖

48. The following is a recipe for corn meal crisps:

   1 cup yellow corn meal   ¼ teaspoon baking powder
   ½ cup sifted flour   2 tablespoons melted shortening
   ⅔ teaspoon salt   ⅓ cup milk

If Joan finds that she cannot accurately measure ⅓ cup milk and decides to use a full cup of milk then she will have to use
(1) 1 cup of sifted flour and 6 tablespoons of melted shortening   (2) 2 teaspoons of salt and 1 teaspoon of baking powder   (3) 3 tablespoons of melted shortening and ¾ teaspoon of baking powder   (4) 2 teaspoons of salt and ¾ teaspoon of baking powder   (5) 1½ cups of sifted flour and 3 teaspoons of baking powder.

48.   1   2   3   4   5

49. If one plane can carry p passengers, how many planes will be needed to carry a passengers?
(1) ap (2) $\dfrac{p}{a}$ (3) $\dfrac{a}{p}$ (4) $\dfrac{1}{ap}$ (5) $\dfrac{ap}{p}$

49.   1   2   3   4   5

50. A line one inch long on a certain graph represents $200. How long a line would be needed to represent $500 on this graph?
(1) 2.1″   (2) 2.5″   (3) 3½″   (4) 5″   (5) 5½″

50.   1   2   3   4   5

51. If two angles of a triangle are $x°$ and $y°$ then the third angle contains (?) degrees. ? =
(1) $180 + x + y$ (2) $180 + x - y$ (3) $180 + (x - y)$ (4) $x + y - 180$ (5) $180 - x - y$

51.   1   2   3   4   5

52. The angles of triangle ABC are in the ratio of 1:2:3. The smallest angle in triangle ABC contains
(1) 30°   (2) 45°   (3) 60°   (4) 70°   (5) 90°

52.   1   2   3   4   5

53. Which of the following is a pair of vertical angles?
(1) 1 and 3   (2) 5 and 8   (3) 1 and 2
(4) 5 and 4   (5) 5 and 6

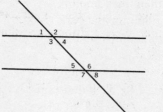

53.   1   2   3   4   5

54. Of the following, the best example of two objects that are similar but not necessarily congruent is
(1) a right triangle and a square   (2) 2 right triangles   (3) 2 isosceles triangles   (4) 2 right isosceles triangles   (5) a square and a rectangle

54.   1   2   3   4   5

55. Of the following, the best example of congruent figures is
(1) a negative and an enlargement   (2) a house and a picture of the house   (3) two of your jackets   (4) two triangles   (5) two socks

55.   1   2   3   4   5

56. The diagram (right) represents a lawn surrounding Mr. Martin's house. To calculate how much grass he needs he must calculate the area. The correct area in square feet is
(1) 4320   (2) 7680
(3) 12,000   (4) 72,000
(5) 76,000

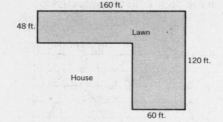

56.   1   2   3   4   5

57. This diagram (right) represents an aquarium. The volume equals (?) cubic inches
(1) 324   (2) 720   (3) 1080   (4) 12,960
(5) 16,000

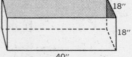

57.   1   2   3   4   5

58. How much soil (in cubic feet) must be excavated from a lot to prepare for a rectangular foundation which must be 50 feet by 100 feet by 20 feet?
(1) 10,000   (2) 20,000   (3) 33,333   (4) 100,000   (5) 200,000

58.   1   2   3   4   5

59. Refer to the graph headed "Foreign Investments in the United States." By what amount does the investment in manufacturing exceed the amount invested in petroleum?
(1) $1½ million   (2) $3½ million   (3) $0.5 billion   (4) $1½ billion   (5) $3½ billion

59.   1   2   3   4   5

60. The amount invested in finance and insurance in a previous year was 25% less than the amount indicated in the graph for the current year. The amount invested in that previous year was
(1) $½ billion   (2) $1 billion
(3) $1½ billion   (4) $2 billion
(5) $2½ billion

60.   1   2   3   4   5

"Foreign Investments in the United States."

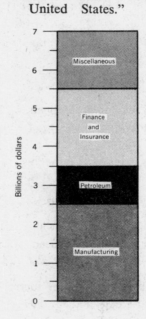

61. If you remove 3 quarts, 1 pint from 3 gallons, the remainder will be
(1) 2 gallons, 1 pint   (2) 1 pint   (3) 2 quarts, 1 pint   (4) 2 gallons, 1 quart   (5) 1 gallon, 1 pint

61.   1   2   3   4   5

62. A piece 7 yards, 2 feet, 8 inches is cut from a piece of cloth 11 yards, 1 foot, 6 inches. The length of the remaining piece of cloth is
(1) 3.1 yards   (2) 31.1 yards   (3) 3 yards, 10 feet   (4) 3 yards, 1 foot, 10 inches   (5) 3 yards, 2 feet

62.   1   2   3   4   5

Sharpee Shirt Manufacturing Co.
Production Record
1960–1970

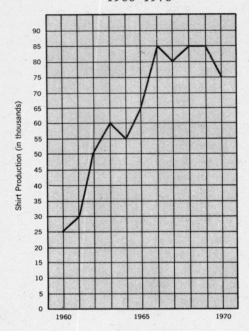

Directions: (Questions **63–65** refer to graph headed "Sharpee Shirt Manufacturing Co.")

63. The number of shirts produced in 1960 was
  (1) 2500   (2) 25,000   (3) 30,000   (4) 55,000   (5) 60,000

63. 1 2 3 4 5

64. The decrease in the number of shirts produced from 1963 to 1964 was
  (1) 500   (2) 1000   (3) 5000   (4) 15,000   (5) 1500

64. 1 2 3 4 5

65. The company plans for 1971 call for an increase of production of 33⅓ %. The number of shirts expected for 1971 is
  (1) 1000   (2) 10,000   (3) 25,000   (4) 100,000   (5) 175,000

65. 1 2 3 4 5

EXPLANATION OF ANSWERS *page 474-478*

ANSWERS AND ANALYSIS OF ERRORS SUB-TEST 5 *General Mathematical Ability*

This page supplies the correct answers and helps you with an analysis of your performance on this practice test. The number in parenthesis after the correct choice refers to the topic covered by that particular question. In the Outline of Topics below you will find the page on which this topic is explained. In addition, on page *474* you will find the explanations for the answers of this sub-test.

1. 2 (1.1)	**12.** 2 (1.2, 1.4)	**23.** 3 (1.5)	**34.** 4 (2.3)	**45.** 3 (2.5)	**56.** 3 (3.5)
2. 3 (1.1)	**13.** 4 (1.4)	**24.** 4 (1.6)	**35.** 5 (2.2)	**46.** 4 (2.6)	**57.** 4 (3.6)
3. 3 (1.1)	**14.** 3 (1.4)	**25.** 3 (1.6)	**36.** 5 (2.2)	**47.** 5 (2.6)	**58.** 4 (3.6)
4. 3 (1.1)	**15.** 2 (1.4)	**26.** 2 (1.7)	**37.** 5 (2.3)	**48.** 4 (2.6)	**59.** 4 (4)
5. 4 (1.1)	**16.** 2 (1.4)	**27.** 1 (2.1)	**38.** 1 (2.4)	**49.** 3 (2.6)	**60.** 3 (4)
6. 2 (1.1)	**17.** 2 (1.4)	**28.** 2 (2.1)	**39.** 3 (2.4)	**50.** 2 (2.6)	**61.** 1 (5)
7. 4 (1.1)	**18.** 3 (1.4)	**29.** 1 (2.1)	**40.** 2 (2.6)	**51.** 5 (3.2)	**62.** 4 (5)
8. 4 (1.2)	**19.** 3 (1.3, 1.4)	**30.** 5 (2.1)	**41.** 4 (3.5)	**52.** 1 (3.2)	**63.** 2 (5)
9. 2 (1.2)	**20.** 3 (1.4)	**31.** 5 (2.2)	**42.** 4 (3.5)	**53.** 2 (3.2)	**64.** 3 (5)
10. 5 (1.2)	**21.** 4 (1.4)	**32.** 3 (2.2)	**43.** 2 (3.6)	**54.** 4 (3.4)	**65.** 4 (5)
11. 4 (1.2)	**22.** 3 (1.4)	**33.** 4 (2.3)	**44.** 4 (2.5)	**55.** 3 (3.4)	

OUTLINE OF TOPICS

1. Arithmetic
    1.1 Whole Numbers p. 270
    1.2 Fractions p. 272
    1.3 Decimals p. 285
    1.4 Percent p. 288
    1.5 Insurance p. 298
    1.6 Investment p. 300
    1.7 Taxation p. 302

2. Algebra
    2.1 Fundamentals p. 304
    2.2 Exponents and Evaluation p. 306
    2.3 Formulas p. 307
    2.4 Solving Equations p. 309
    2.5 Solving Problems p. 313
    2.6 Ratio and Proportion p. 317
    2.7 Signed Numbers p. 321

3. Geometry
    3.1 Geometric Figures p. 324
    3.2 Geometric Concepts and Relationships p. 324
    3.3 Indirect Measurements p. 329
    3.4 Congruence and Similarity p. 332
    3.5 Areas p. 333
    3.6 Volumes p. 337
    3.7 Areas of Solids p. 339

4. Graphs and Interpretation of Data p. 341

5. Measures p. 349

What's your score?

If you get at least 46 correct you are prepared to take the test which will earn you a high school equivalency diploma.

ANSWERS EXPLAINED TO SUB-TEST 5   *General Mathematical Ability*

1. Ans. 2   4 ounces = $\frac{1}{4}$ pound
$1.20 ÷ 4 = 30¢

2. Ans. 3   Product is the result of multiplication. Quotient is the result of division.
(39.6) × (5.7) = 225.72
225.72 ÷ 0.2 = 112.86

3. Ans. 3   1 cubic inch weighs .28 pounds
123.5 cubic inches weigh (123.5)(.28) or 34.58 pounds

4. Ans. 3   Philip earned (40)($1.40) or $56.
Mark must work $\dfrac{\$56}{\$1.75}$ or 32 hours

5. Ans. 4   Cost of each = 36¢ ÷ 12 or 3¢
Profit on each = 2¢
Profit on   1 dozen = 24¢
Profit on 14 dozen = (14)(24¢) or $3.36

6. Ans. 2   ($28.80)(15) = $432.00 (monthly payments)
$\underline{\hspace{1.2em}\$ 45.00}$ (down payment)
$477.00 (installment plan price)
$450.00 (cash price)
$ 27.00 charge for installment buying

7. Ans. 4   To attain an average of $800 for five days, total sales must be (5)($800) or $4000
Sales for 4 days = $3100
$4000 − $3100 = $900

8. Ans. 4 $\dfrac{\dfrac{1}{4}-\dfrac{3}{16}}{\dfrac{1}{8}} = \left[\dfrac{1}{4}-\dfrac{3}{16}\right]÷\dfrac{1}{8}$ or, $\left[\dfrac{4}{16}-\dfrac{3}{16}\right]÷\dfrac{1}{8}$
or, $\dfrac{1}{16}÷\dfrac{1}{8}$ or $\dfrac{1}{16}\cdot\dfrac{8}{1}$ or $\dfrac{1}{2}$

9. Ans. 2   After pumping in gasoline the level will rise from $\frac{1}{5}$ to $\frac{1}{2}$ or from $\frac{2}{10}$ to $\frac{5}{10}$ which represents a rise of $\frac{3}{10}$ of the capacity of the tank. ($\frac{3}{10}$) (20 gallons) or 6 gallons

10. Ans. 5   After accounting for $\frac{1}{2}$ of the estate which the widow received, the grandson received $\frac{1}{4}$ of the one-half that remained and the part not accounted for is $\frac{3}{4}$ of this one-half or ($\frac{3}{4}$)($\frac{1}{2}$) or $\frac{3}{8}$

11. Ans. 4 $s − 5$ = number of students present
$\dfrac{s-5}{s}$ = part of entire class present

12. Ans. 2 $\frac{2}{3}$ = 66$\frac{2}{3}$%
$\frac{3}{5}$ = 60%
Difference = 6$\frac{2}{3}$%

13. Ans. 4   38% or .38 was not done
(.38)(49.5 miles) = 18.81 to be built

14. Ans. 3 $\dfrac{\text{Discount}}{\text{Marked Price}} = \dfrac{8}{48} = \dfrac{1}{6} = 16\frac{2}{3}\%$

15. Ans. 2 $\dfrac{\text{Discount}}{\text{Selling Price}} = \dfrac{\$7.68}{\$192} = .04 = 4\%$ discount

16. Ans. 2 Difference in earnings $= \$1420.20$

$\dfrac{\text{Difference}}{\text{Last year's earnings}} = \dfrac{\$1420.20}{\$7890} = .18 = 18\%$

17. Ans. 2 1% of $400 = (.01)(400) = 4$

$\tfrac{1}{4}\% = 4 \div 4 = 1$

18. Ans. 3 Rate of Increase $= \dfrac{\text{change}}{\text{original}} = \dfrac{10\cancel{c}}{50\cancel{c}} = \dfrac{1}{5} = 20\%$

19. Ans. 3 $1\tfrac{1}{2}\% = 1.5\% = \dfrac{1.5}{100} = \dfrac{15}{1000} = .015$

20. Ans. 3 Cost $= \$250 + 10\%$ of $\$250$

Cost $= \$250 + \$25 = \$275$

Down payment $= \$100$

$\$275 - \$100 = \$175$ to be paid out in monthly payments. Since $\$8.75$ is amount of each installment, $\$175 \div \$8.75 = 20$ (installments)

21. Ans. 4 Lucy earned $\$53$ of which $\$42$ was her regular salary. She must have received $\$11$ as a bonus. $\$11$ represents 2% $(.02)$ of sales over and above $\$300$. Let $x =$ sales over and above $\$300$. Then

$.02x = \$11$

$2x = \$1100$

$x = \$550$

Therefore total sales $= \$300 + \$550$ or $\$850$.

22. Ans. 3 $\$81 - \$54 = \$27$ (discount)

$\dfrac{\text{Discount}}{\text{List Price}} = \dfrac{\$27}{\$81} = \dfrac{1}{3}\ 33\tfrac{1}{3}\%$

23. Ans. 3 $\dfrac{.24}{100} = .24\% = .0024$

Annual premium $= (\$4000)(.0024) = \$9.60$

Three year policy will cost $(\$9.60)(2.7)$ or $\$25.92$

24. Ans. 4 A quarterly dividend is paid four times a year.

Annual dividend per share $= \$3.20$.

Rate of income $= \dfrac{\text{Annual dividend}}{\text{Cost of stock}} = \dfrac{\$3.20}{\$40.00} = \dfrac{8}{100} = 8\%$

25. Ans. 3 Dividends $= \$42.40 + \$78.00 + \$22.00 + \$150.20$ or $\$292.60$

$\dfrac{\text{Dividends}}{\text{Cost}} = \dfrac{\$292.60}{\$6650} = .044 = 4.4\%$

26. Ans. 2 Assessed value $= 42\%$ of $\$20,000$ or $\$8,400$

Tax rate $= \$42.75$ per $\$1000$ or,

$\dfrac{\$42.75}{\$1000} = \dfrac{4.275}{100} = 4.275\%$ or $.04275$

(assessed value) (tax rate) $=$ Tax

$(\$8400)(.04275) = \$359.10$

27. Ans. 1 Perimeter $= s + s + 2 + s + 3 + s + 4$ or $4s + 9$

$4s + 9 = 45$

$4s = 36$

$s = 9$

28. Ans. 2 $\begin{array}{r} 2x + 5 \\ x - 4 \\ \hline 2x^2 + 5x \\ -8x - 20 \\ \hline 2x^2 - 3x - 20 \end{array}$

29. Ans. 1 If a is an odd integer, then $a + 1$ is the next integer, which is an even integer. Divide by b:

$$\frac{a + 1}{b}$$

30. Ans. 5 From $-6°$ to zero $= 6$ degrees, and from zero to $+6° = 6$ degrees. Therefore, total $= 12$ degrees.

31. Ans. 5 $\dfrac{2a + 3b}{c} = \dfrac{2(\frac{1}{2}) + 3(\frac{2}{3})}{\frac{3}{4}} = \dfrac{1 + 2}{\frac{3}{4}} = \dfrac{3}{\frac{3}{4}}$

or, $3 \div \dfrac{3}{4}$ or, $(3)\dfrac{4}{3} = 4$

32. Ans. 3 $(x + y)^2 - (a + b)$
$(2 + 3)^2 - (4 + 5)$
$(5)^2 \quad - \quad (9)$
$25 \quad - \quad 9$
16

33. Ans. 4 3 hours 45 minutes $= 3\frac{45}{60}$ or $3\frac{3}{4}$ hours
Distance $= (\text{Rate})(\text{Time})$
Distance $= (32)(3\frac{3}{4}) = 120$ miles

34. Ans. 4 If $B = C = 45°$, then $B = 45°$ and $C = 45°$
Since $A + B + C = 180°$
$A + 45° + 45° = 180°$
$A + 90° = 180°$
$A = 180° - 90°$ or $90°$

35. Ans. 5 $x^5 = (x)(x)(x)(x)(x)$
$x^3 = (x)(x)(x)$
$\dfrac{(x)(x)(x)(x)(x)}{(x)(x)(x)} = x^2$

36. Ans. 5 $5n - 1 = 34$
$5n = 35$
Then, $\dfrac{5n}{2} = \dfrac{35}{2}$ or $17\frac{1}{2}$

37. Ans. 5 $F = \dfrac{9}{5} C + 32°$

$F = \left(\dfrac{9}{5}\right)(25) + 32°$

$F = 45° + 32° = 77°$

38. Ans. 1 $2x + t = 1$
$t = 1 - 2x$

39. Ans. 3 $2x - 5 = 11 \qquad\qquad \dfrac{x}{4} = 12$
$2x = 16$
$x = 8 \quad (1) \qquad x = 48 \quad (2)$

$x^2 = 6 \qquad\quad 3x + 1 = 10$
$x = \sqrt{6} \quad (4) \qquad 3x = 9$
$x = 3 \quad (3)$

$3x - 1 = 10$
$3x = 11$
$x = \dfrac{11}{3} = 3\frac{2}{3} \quad (5)$

40. Ans. 2 Let $x =$ cost of p pencils
$\dfrac{5 \text{ pencils}}{c \text{ cents}} = \dfrac{p}{x}$
$5x = pc$
$x = \dfrac{pc}{5}$

41. Ans. 4   Area $=$ (side)^2
100 ft$^2 =$ (side)^2
10 ft $=$ side
Perimeter $= 4$(side) or 4(10 feet) or 40 feet

42. Ans. 4 Divide the floor space into 2 rectangles by drawing line NM.
Area of a rectangle $=$ (length)(width)
Area of smaller rectangle is $(10)(15)$ or 150 square feet
Area of larger rectangle is $(20)(15)$ or 300 square feet
Total area of floor space equals $150 + 300$ or 450 square feet.
Since 9 square feet equals 1 square yard, 450 square feet $= 450 \div 9$ or 50 square yards.

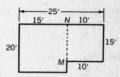

43. Ans. 2 Volume $= 12$ inches $\times 18$ inches $\times 1$ foot
Volume $= 1$ foot $\times 1.5$ feet $\times 1$ foot
Volume $= 1.5$ cubic feet
Since 1 cubic foot of water $= 7.5$ gallons
1.5 cubic feet of water $= (7.5)(1.5) = 11.25$ or $11\frac{1}{4}$

44. Ans. 4   Let $x =$ number of dimes
Then $2x =$ number of nickels
$(10)(x)\cent =$ value of the dimes
$(5)(x + 2)\cent =$ value of the nickels
$10x + 5x + 10 = 100$ cents (one dollar)
$15x = 90$
$x = 6$ (number of dimes)

45. Ans. 3   Let $x =$ price of dress
$(6\%)(x) = .06x =$ tax
$x + .06x = \$42.40$
$100x + 6x = 4240$
$106x = 4240$
$x = \$40$

46. Ans. 4 Sylvia saved $\$750 - \$600 = \$150$
Sylvia spent $\$600$
$\dfrac{\text{Amount Saved}}{\text{Amount Spent}} = \dfrac{\$150}{\$600} = \dfrac{1}{4} = 1{:}4$

47. Ans. 5   8 miles $= \frac{1}{4}$ inch
32 miles $= 1$ inch
$(32)(2\frac{1}{8}) = 68$ miles

48. Ans. 4 Since Joan is using three times as much milk, she will need: $(3)(1$ cup$)$ or 3 cups of corn meal, $(3)(\frac{1}{2}$ cup$)$ or $1\frac{1}{2}$ cups of flour, $(3)(\frac{2}{3})$ teaspoons salt, $(3)(\frac{1}{4})$ or $\frac{3}{4}$ teaspoons baking powder. and $(3)(2)$ or 6 tablespoons shortening.

49. Ans. 3 Let $x =$ number of airplanes necessary to carry a passengers
$\dfrac{1 \text{ airplane}}{p \text{ passengers}} = \dfrac{x}{a}$
$p\,x = a$
$x = \dfrac{a}{p}$

50. Ans. 2 $\dfrac{\text{one inch}}{\$200} = \dfrac{x \text{ inches}}{\$500}$
$200\,x = \$500$
$x = 2\frac{1}{2}$ inches (or 2.5 inches)

51. Ans. 5 The sum of the angles of a triangle $= 180°$
If 2 angles $= x° + y°$
Then the third angle $= 180° - (x + y)°$ or $180 - x - y$ degrees

52. Ans. 1　Let x = number of degrees in smallest angle

then $2x$ = next larger angle

and $3x$ = largest angle

$\quad 6x$ = sum of the three angles

$\quad 6x = 180°$

$\quad\ x = 30°$

53. Ans. 2　Vertical angles are the opposite angles which are formed when two straight lines intersect.

54. Ans. 4　In an isosceles right triangle the acute angles are each 45°.

55. Ans. 3　To be congruent two objects must be of the same size *and* shape.

56. Ans. 3　Draw line AB. to form 2 rectangles.

Area of rectangle = (length) (width)

(60 feet) (72 feet) = 4320 square feet

(160 feet) (48 feet) = 7680 square feet

Total = 12,000 square feet

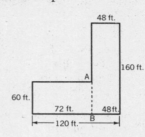

57. Ans. 4　Volume = (length) (width) (height)

Volume = (40 inches) (18 inches) (18 inches) = 12,960 cubic inches

58. Ans. 4　Volume = (length) (width) (height)

Volume = (50 feet) (100 feet) (20 feet)

Volume = 100,000 cubic feet

59. Ans. 4　Foreign investment in manufacturing　$2½ billion

Foreign investment in petroleum　　　$1　billion

$\qquad\qquad$ difference　　　　　　　$1½ billion

60. Ans. 3　Amount invested in finance and insurance= $2　billion

25% (or ¼) of $2 billion　　　　= $ ½ billion

$2 billion − $½　　　　　　　　= $1½ billion

61. Ans. 1　3 gallons = 2 gallons　3 quarts　2 pints

$\qquad\qquad\qquad\quad$ —　　　　3 quarts　1 pint

Difference = 2 gallons　　　　　　　　1 pint

62. Ans. 4　11 yards 1 foot 6 inches　= 10 yards 3 feet 18 inches

$\qquad\qquad\qquad\qquad$ — 7 yards 2 feet　8 inches

$\qquad$ difference　　　　　　3 yards 1 foot 10 inches

63. Ans. 2　Read graph

64. Ans. 3　1963 Production　60,000

1964 Production　55,000

$\qquad$ difference　　5,000

65. Ans. 4　Production in 1970　　　75,000

Increase of 33⅓% (⅓)　　25,000

Estimated for 1971　　　100,000

10

Test C

SUB-TEST 1.
Correctness and Effectiveness of Expression

Directions (1-20): Choose the *one* misspelled word in each of the following numbered groups.

1. (1) cartoon   (2) neice   (3) loyalty   (4) height   (5) rural

2. (1) bicycle   (2) poisoned   (3) flexable   (4) masquerade
   (5) remedial

3. (1) relinquish   (2) passenger   (3) occurrence   (4) aggravate
   (5) athelete

4. (1) interuption   (2) memorandum   (3) cordially   (4) precedence
   (5) philosopher

5. (1) evidently   (2) mathmatics   (3) nutritious   (4) colleague
   (5) embarrassed

6. (1) advantagous   (2) nonchalant   (3) surveyor   (4) competition
   (5) syllable

7. (1) pronunciation   (2) disobedient   (3) aniversary   (4) vengeance
   (5) sympathy

8. (1) luxurious   (2) pamphlet   (3) magician   (4) persuasion
   (5) cruelity

9. (1) extrordinary   (2) obsessed   (3) bureaucrat   (4) maneuverable
   (5) connoisseur

10. (1) appliance   (2) shepherd   (3) magnificient   (4) inaugurate
    (5) hybrid

10.   1 2 3 4 5

11. (1) verticle   (2) musician   (3) tomatoes   (4) athletic   (5) decision

11.   1 2 3 4 5

12. (1) eventually   (2) disilusioned   (3) divine   (4) inimitable
    (5) fraudulent

12.   1 2 3 4 5

13. (1) neutrality   (2) horseradish   (3) contemporaries   (4) inducement
    (5) prelimnery

13.   1 2 3 4 5

14. (1) deteryorate   (2) priority   (3) cuddle   (4) shrivel   (5) narcotic

14.   1 2 3 4 5

15. (1) obnoxious   (2) balancing   (3) squadron   (4) illicit
    (5) clearence

15.   1 2 3 4 5

16. (1) timetable   (2) gymnasium   (3) humid   (4) disolve   (5) gracious

16.   1 2 3 4 5

17. (1) spiciness   (2) bibliography   (3) injunction   (4) mediator
    (5) discriminate

17.   1 2 3 4 5

18. (1) endearing   (2) mannerism   (3) predecesser   (4) gardener
    (5) instantaneous

18.   1 2 3 4 5

19. (1) shrewdness   (2) purified   (3) acceptable   (4) uniqueness
    (5) corugated

19.   1 2 3 4 5

20. (1) baptize   (2) diversity   (3) parochial   (4) abandonning
    (5) hypnosis

20.   1 2 3 4 5

Directions (21-30):   Each of the following sentences contains an underlined expression. Below each sentence are four suggested answers. Choose
the one that will make a correct sentence.

21. This book will be of little help to either you or me.
    (1) Correct as is   (2) either you or I   (3) either you nor I   (4) either
    you nor me

21.   1 2 3 4 5

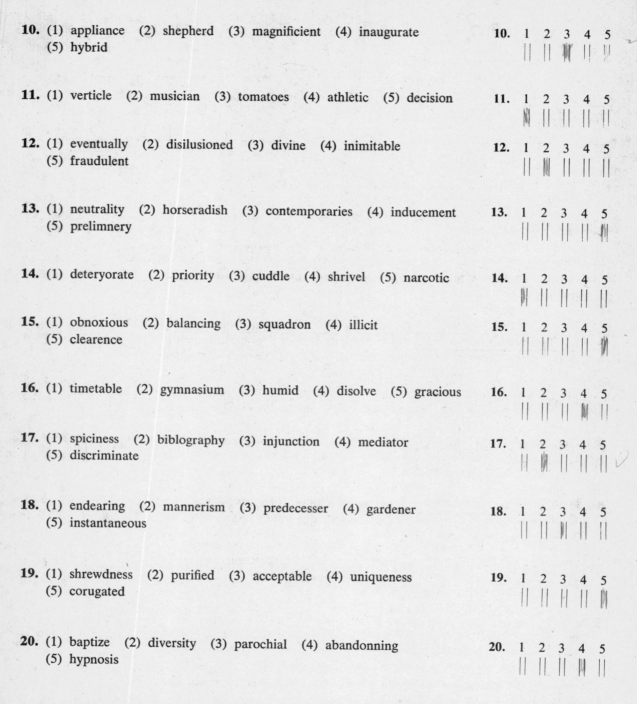

22. Jefferson is given credit <u>as to being</u> the author of the Declaration of Independence.   (1) Correct as is   '(2) as for being   (3) as for   (4) as

22. 1 2 3 4 5

23. Before you <u>were born Helen</u> we lived in Albany.   (1) Correct as is (2) were born Helen,   (3) , Helen were born   (4) were born, Helen,

23. 1 2 3 4 5

24. The mayor said that he was going to look into his own <u>cities' finances and its</u> hiring policies.   (1) Correct as is   (2) city's finances and its (3) citys' finances and its   (4) cities finances and it's

24. 1 2 3 4 5

25. All students, <u>who have a final average of 90 or better,</u> are excused from taking final exams.   (1) Correct as is   (2) who have a final average of 90 or better   (3) whom have a final average of 90 or better,   (4) that have a final average of 90 or better,

25. 1 2 3 4 5

26. They held a big feast to give thanks and <u>praying</u> for help in times to come.   (1) Correct as is   (2) having prayed   (3) to have prayed   (4) to pray

26. 1 2 3 4 5

27. The captain recognizing a few faces in the crowd, <u>jumped onto a table and had demanded silence.</u>   (1) Correct as is   (2) The captain, recognizing a few faces in the crowd, jumped onto a table and demanded silence.   (3) The captain, recognizing a few faces in the crowd jumped onto a table and demanded silence.   (4) The captain, having recognized a few faces in the crowd, jumped onto a table and had demanded silence.

27. 1 2 3 4 5

28. The roses <u>loveliness and it's life</u> are maintained by insects.   (1) Correct as is   (2) rose's loveliness and its life   (3) rose's loveliness and it's life (4) rose's loveliness and its' life

28. 1 2 3 4 5

29. Everybody <u>except Frances and me</u> remembered to bring excuses. (1) Correct as is   (2) except Frances and I   (3) accept Frances and me (4) excepting Frances and I

29. 1 2 3 4 5

30. To young people, the importance of these <u>things vary.</u>   (1) Correct as is   (2) things, vary   (3) things varies   (4) things, varies

30. 1 2 3 4 5

Directions (31-42):   **The following selection has portions underlined and numbered. At the right of this material you will find numbers corresponding to those below the underlined portions, each followed by five choices. If in your opinion the underlined portion is correct choose number 1, otherwise choose the one that will make the necessary correction.**

The use of the machine <u>produced</u> up
                        31
to the present time many outstanding changes in our modern world. One of the most significant of these changes <u>have been</u> the marked decreases in
32
the length of the working day and the

31. (1) produced   (3) has produced
    (2) produces   (4) had produced
    (5) will have produced

31. 1 2 3 4 5

32. (1) have been   (3) were
    (2) was   (4) has been
    (5) will be

32. 1 2 3 4 5

working week. The fourteen-hour day
not only has been reduced to one of
                    33
ten hours but also, in some lines of
work, one of eight or even six.

The trend toward a decrease is further evidenced in the longer weekend
already given to employes in many
  34
business establishments. There seems
also to be a trend toward shorter
working weeks and longer summer
vacations. An important feature of
this development is that leisure is no
longer the privilege of the wealthy
few, — it has become the common
        35
right of most people. Using it wisely,
                              36
leisure promotes health, efficiency and
happiness, for there is time for each

individual to live their own "more
                    37

abundant life" and having opportu-
                        38
nities for needed recreation.

Recreation, like the name implies, is
                39
a process of revitalization. In giving
expression to the play instincts of the

human race, new vigor and effectiveness are afforded by recreation to the
body and to the mind.
        40

33. (1) The fourteen-hour day not
only has been reduced
(2) Not only the fourteen - hour
day has been reduced
(3) Not the fourteen-hour day
only has been reduced
(4) The fourteen-hour day has
not only been reduced
(5) The fourteen-hour day has
been reduced not only

34. (1) already   (3) allready
(2) all ready   (4) ready
(5) all in all

35. (1) , — it   (3) ; it
(2) : it   (4) . . . it
(5) omit punctuation

36. (1) Using it wisely
(2) If used wisely
(3) Having used it wisely
(4) because of its wise use
(5) Because of usefulness

37. (1) their   (3) its   (5) your
(2) his   (4) our

38. (1) having   (3) to have
(2) having had (4) to have had
(5) had

39. (1) like
(2) since
(3) though
(4) for
(5) as

40. (1) new vigor and effectiveness
are afforded by recreation
to the body and to the
mind.
(2) recreation affords new vigor
and effectiveness to the
body and to the mind.
(3) there are afforded new vigor
and effectiveness to the
body and to the mind.
(4) by recreation the body and
mind are afforded new vigor
and effectiveness.
(5) the body and the mind afford
new vigor and effectiveness
to themselves by recreation.

33. 1 2 3 4 5

34. 1 2 3 4 5

35. 1 2 3 4 5

36. 1 2 3 4 5

37. 1 2 3 4 5

38. 1 2 3 4 5

39. 1 2 3 4 5

40. 1 2 3 4 5

Of course not all forms of amusement, <u>by no means</u>, constitute recrea-
41
tion. Furthermore, an activity that provides recreation for one person may prove exhausting for another.

Today, however, play among adults, as well as children, is regarded as a vital necessity of modern life. <u>Play being recognized</u> as an important fac-
42
tor in improving mental and physical health and thereby reducing human misery and poverty.

41. (1) by no means
(2) by those means
(3) by some means
(4) by every means
(5) by any means

42. (1) . Play being recognized as
(2) , by their recognizing play as
(3) . They recognizing play as
(4) . Recognition of it being
(5) , for play is recognized as

41. 1 2 3 4 5

42. 1 2 3 4 5

Directions (43-60): Choose the number of the word or expression that most nearly expresses the meaning of the capitalized word.

43. GIRD (1) surround (2) appeal (3) request (4) break (5) glance

43. 1 2 3 4 5

44. WANGLE (1) moan (2) mutilate (3) exasperate (4) manipulate (5) triumph

44. 1 2 3 4 5

45. PROCUREMENT (1) acquisition (2) resolution (3) healing (4) importance (5) miracle

45. 1 2 3 4 5

46. CULMINATION (1) rebellion (2) lighting system (3) climax (4) destruction (5) mystery

46. 1 2 3 4 5

47. INSUPERABLE (1) incomprehensible (2) elaborate (3) unusual (4) indigestible (5) unconquerable

47. 1 2 3 4 5

48. CLICHE (1) summary argument (2) new information (3) new hat (4) trite phrase (5) lock device

48. 1 2 3 4 5

49. CONCESSION (1) nourishment (2) plea (3) restoration (4) similarity (5) acknowledgment

49. 1 2 3 4 5

50. INSIPID (1) disrespectful (2) uninteresting (3) persistent (4) whole (5) stimulating

50. 1 2 3 4 5

51. REPRISAL (1) retaliation (2) drawing (3) capture (4) release (5) suspicion

51. 1 2 3 4 5

52. ATROCIOUS (1) brutal (2) innocent (3) shrunken (4) yellowish (5) unsound

52. 1 2 3 4 5

53. BLITHE (1) wicked (2) criminal (3) merry (4) unintelligible (5) substantial

53. 1 2 3 4 5

54. PRESTIGE (1) speed (2) influence (3) omen (4) pride (5) excuse

54. 1 2 3 4 5

55. TRITE (1) brilliant (2) unusual (3) funny (4) stiff (5) commonplace

55. 1 2 3 4 5

56. VINDICATE   (1) outrage   (2) waver   (3) enliven   (4) justify   (5) fuse

57. EXUDE   (1) accuse   (2) discharge   (3) inflect   (4) appropriate   (5) distress

58. LIVID   (1) burned   (2) patient   (3) hurt   (4) salted   (5) discolored

59. FACTION   (1) clique   (2) judgment   (3) truth   (4) type of architecture   (5) health

60. INCLEMENT   (1) merciful   (2) sloping   (3) harsh   (4) disastrous   (5) personal

24 wrong

ANSWERS TO SUB-TEST 1   *Correctness and Effectiveness of Expression*

1. 2	**7.** 3	**13.** 5	**19.** 5	**25.** 2	**31.** 3	**37.** 2	**43.** 1	**49.** 5	**55.** 5
2. 3	**8.** 5	**14.** 1	**20.** 4	**26.** 4	**32.** 4	**38.** 3	**44.** 4	**50.** 2	**56.** 4
3. 5	**9.** 1	**15.** 5	**21.** 1	**27.** 2	**33.** 5	**39.** 5	**45.** 1	**51.** 1	**57.** 2
4. 1	**10.** 3	**16.** 4	**22.** 4	**28.** 2	**34.** 1	**40.** 2	**46.** 3	**52.** 1	**58.** 5
5. 2	**11.** 1	**17.** 2	**23.** 4	**29.** 1	**35.** 3	**41.** 5	**47.** 5	**53.** 3	**59.** 1
6. 1	**12.** 2	**18.** 3	**24.** 2	**30.** 3	**36.** 2	**42.** 5	**48.** 4	**54.** 2	**60.** 3

What's your score?

If you got at least 50 correct you are prepared to take the test which will earn you a high school equivalency diploma.

SUB-TEST **2**

Interpretation of Literary Materials

Directions: **Read each of the following passages carefully. Then select the answer to each of the numbered questions which in your opinion best completes the statement or question.**

Passage I

With notes and preface and the rest
And every kind of teacher's aid
To harry schoolboys into learning
The unpremeditated verse,
Written because the heart was hot
With quite a different kind of burning.
And that is the revenge of time,
And that, they say, the workman's pay.

It may be so, I wouldn't know
I wrote it poor, in love, and young,
In indigestion and despair
And exaltation of the mind,
Not for the blind to lead the blind;
I have no quarrel with the wise,
No quarrel with the pedagogue,
And yet I wrote for none of these.

And yet these are the words, in print,
And should an obdurate old man
Remember half a dozen lines
Stuck in his mind like thistle seed,
Or if, perhaps, some idle boy
Should sometimes read a page or so
In the deep summer, to his girl,
And drop the book half finished there,
Since kissing was a better joy,
Well, I shall have been paid enough.
I'll have been paid enough indeed.

1. Lines 1 through 4 strongly imply that
    (1) schoolboys are required to study the poet's verse intensively   (2)
    unpremeditated verse has a great appeal for schoolboys   (3) a poet
    should provide his readers with explanatory notes   (4) memorizing
    poetry requires little effort   (5) the poet's verse is unpopular with
    teachers

2. The writer apparently does *not* approve of
    (1) workman's pay   (2) the way poetry often is taught   (3) unpre-
    meditated verse   (4) inspiration   (5) time's passing

3. The poem being discussed was written because the poet
    (1) desired recognition   (2) wished to avenge himself on teachers   (3)
    needed to give expression to his feelings   (4) hoped to impress people
    with his wisdom   (5) felt that he had a message for both the young
    and the old

    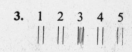

4. According to the writer, one good reason for a reader's leaving the book
    of poems half read is that
    (1) the book contains ideas that are no longer valid   (2) the book was
    written before the poet had perfected his style   (3) actual experiences
    may be more rewarding than reading   (4) poetry is boring for most
    people   (5) only a half dozen lines are worth remembering

    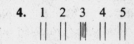

5. The poet considers that time had its revenge (line 7) in that his poem
    (1) earned him only a day laborer's pay   (2) has become a subject for
    formal study   (3) offended the wise   (4) is remembered only in part
    (5) has little appeal for young lovers

Passage II

It may be difficult to find an acceptable definition of style; every critic has his own. But every reader of great literature has come under the spell of style. Those critics who are most hostile to the habit of rapid reading are convinced that the rapid reader cannot savor style. But if the creative reader sets up the proper mental and emotional slant, he does so because he is sensitive to the writer's style. Dozens of phrases can be offered to describe style, but perhaps the best one is: "Style — it is the man." The quality that pervades a passage, the author's spirit — that is style, and no rate of reading must ever prevent the reader's savoring to the fullest degree the style of a passage. Sometimes the irresistible pull of a passage forces the reader to read rapidly. To read slowly, deliberately, would be to miss the essential quality of the passage; the words would be lifeless.

6. The title that best expresses the main idea of this passage is:
(1) The Lure of Great Writing   (2) The Meaning of Style   (3) The Attitude of Critics   (4) Dangers of Reading too Rapidly   (5) How to Improve Reading Rate

6.   1 2 3 4 5

7. Which does the author consider the most important for a reader?
(1) reading deliberately   (2) reading rapidly   (3) appreciating an author's style   (4) defining style   (5) disagreeing with critics

7.   1 2 3 4 5

8. We may most reasonably conclude that a *creative* reader is one who
(1) disregards hostile critics   (2) writes effectively himself   (3) concentrates on great literature   (4) has a feeling for the emotional content of writing   (5) resists a tendency to read rapidly

8.   1 2 3 4 5

9. As used in the passage, "savor," line 4 (note also "savoring," line 9), most nearly means
(1) enjoy the distinctive quality of   (2) interrupt the flow of   (3) understand the directness of   (4) interpret the monotonies of   (5) appreciate the difficulty of

9.   1 2 3 4 5

Passage III

Plutarch loved those who could use life for grand purposes and depart from it as grandly, but he would not pass over weaknesses and vices which marred the grandeur. His hero of heroes is Alexander the Great; he loves him above all other men, while his abomination of abominations is bad faith, dishonorable action. Nevertheless he tells with no attempt to extenuate how Alexander promised a safe conduct to a brave Persian army if they surrendered, and then, "even as they were marching away he fell upon them and put them all to the sword," "a breach of his word," Plutarch says sadly, "which is a lasting blemish to his achievements." He adds piteously, "but the only one." He hated to tell that story.

10. The author indicates that Plutarch
(1) was quick to criticize others   (2) became disillusioned easily   (3) sometimes indulged in self-pity   (4) was overimpressed by heroism   (5) could not overlook bad faith

10.   1 2 3 4 5

11. The author indicates that Plutarch, in his account of Alexander's treatment of the Persians, was speaking
(1) impulsively   (2) forgivingly   (3) reluctantly   (4) spitefully   (5) disloyally

12. Which of the following conclusions is *least* justified by the passage?
(1) Plutarch considered Alexander basically a great man.   (2) The Persians believed that Alexander was acting in good faith.   (3) The Persians withdrew from the battlefield in orderly array.   (4) The author is familiar with Plutarch's writing.   (5) The author considers Plutarch unfair to Alexander.

13. As used in this passage, the word "extenuate" (line 5) means
(1) interpret   (2) exaggerate   (3) emphasize   (4) excuse   (5) condemn

Passage IV

. . . For within the hollow crown
That rounds the mortal temples of a king
Keeps Death his Court, and there the antic sits,
Scoffing his state and grinning at his pomp,
Allowing him a breath, a little scene,
To monarchize, be fear'd and kill with looks,
Infusing him with self and vain conceit,
As if this flesh which walls about our life
Were brass impregnable, and humour'd thus
Comes at the last and with a little pin
Bores through his castle wall, and farewell king!
Cover your heads and mock not flesh and blood
With solemn reverence. Throw away respect,
Tradition, form, and ceremonious duty,
For you have but mistook me all this while:
I live with bread like you, feel want,
Taste grief, need friends. Subjected thus,
How can you say to me, I am a king?

14. In line 2 "temples" refers to the king's
(1) head   (2) ancestry   (3) reign   (4) chapel   (5) castle

15. The "antic" in line 3 is
(1) the king himself   (2) Death   (3) a madman   (4) an aged courtier
(5) the respectful citizen

16. According to the speaker, kings are lured into believing that they are
(1) beloved   (2) short-lived   (3) invulnerable   (4) amusing   (5) humble

17. The speaker wishes his listeners to understand that kings
(1) do not rule by divine right   (2) should be addressed with respect
(3) are no different from other men   (4) are suspicious of flattery   (5) find formal ceremonies boring

18. The listeners have apparently approached the king to
(1) bid him farewell   (2) pledge their loyalty   (3) admit that they were
mistaken in him   (4) scoff at him   (5) demand his abdication

18.   1 2 3 4 5
      || || || || ||

19. The speaker apparently believes that in most respects the role of king is
(1) unenviable   (2) glorious   (3) dishonorable   (4) desirable   (5) un-
changeable

19.   1 2 3 4 5
      || || || || ||

Passage V

For though the terms are often confused, obscurity is not at all the same
thing as unintelligibility. Obscurity is what happens when a writer undertakes
a theme and method for which the reader is not sufficiently prepared. Unintelligibility is what happens when the writer undertakes a theme and method for
which he himself is not sufficiently prepared.

A good creation is an enlarging experience, and the act of enlargement
must require the reader to extend himself. Only the thoroughly familiar —
which is to say, the already encompassed — may reasonably be expected to
be immediately clear. True, the surface of a poem may seem deceptively
clear, thus leading the careless reader to settle for an easy first-response as
the true total. But even in work of such surface clarity as Frost's, it will
be a foolish reader indeed who permits himself the illusion that one easy
reading will reveal all of the poem. In this sense, indeed, there can be no
great poetry without obscurity.

20. The title that best expresses the ideas of this passage is:
(1) Enlarging Experience   (2) The Cult of Unintelligibility   (3) The
Clarity of Robert Frost's Poems   (4) The Familiar in Poetry   (5) The
Careful Writer

20.   1 2 3 4 5
      || || || || ||

21. The author defines obscurity and unintelligibility in order to
(1) show his knowledge of literature   (2) please the reader   (3) set
the stage for what follows   (4) clarify his own thinking   (5) defend
unintelligibility

21.   1 2 3 4 5
      || || || || ||

22. According to this selection, good poetry
(1) has surface clarity   (2) has figurative language   (3) confuses the
reader   (4) requires more than one reading   (5) can be appreciated
only by college students

22.   1 2 3 4 5
      || || || || ||

23. Which quality would the author of this passage expect in a poet?
(1) sense of humor   (2) skill in rhyming   (3) use of the direct
approach   (4) surface clarity   (5) knowledge of subject

23.   1 2 3 4 5
      || || || || ||

24. The author of this selection implies that
(1) the understanding of literature requires effort   (2) most readers of
literature read carelessly   (3) most modern poems are unintelligible
(4) obscure poems are inevitably great poems   (5) familiar poems are
the most popular

24.   1 2 3 4 5
      || || || || ||

25. As used in the passage, the word "encompassed" (line 8) most nearly means
(1) guided   (2) expected   (3) encountered   (4) described   (5) revised

25.   1   2   3   4   5
     || || || || ||

     Passage VI

I have known the inexorable sadness of pencils,
Neat in their boxes, dolor of pad and paper-weight,
All the misery of manila folders and mucilage,
Desolation in immaculate public places,
5   Lonely reception room, lavatory, switchboard,
The unalterable pathos of basin and pitcher,
Ritual of multigraph, paper-clip, comma,
Endless duplication of lives and objects.
And I have seen dust from the walls of institutions,
10   Finer than flour, alive, more dangerous than silica,
Sift, almost invisible, through long afternoons of tedium,
Dropping a fine film on nails and delicate eyebrows,
Glazing the pale hair, the duplicate gray standard faces.

26. The phrase that best expresses the main ideas of this poem is
(1) the public place   (2) keeping up appearances   (3) why employers are miserable   (4) the look of sameness   (5) the danger of silica

26.   1   2   3   4   5
     || || || || ||

27. In the poem, the dust is compared to
(1) nails and eyebrows   (2) flour and silica   (3) hair and faces   (4) walls and afternoons   (5) lives and objects

27.   1   2   3   4   5
     || || || || ||

28. "Duplicate" in line 13 has the meaning of
(1) uniformity   (2) change   (3) authority   (4) grief   (5) foolishness

28.   1   2   3   4   5
     || || || || ||

29. The poet chooses as a reflection of modern life the world of
(1) the dead   (2) the office   (3) the movie   (4) the elementary school   (5) the dust

29.   1   2   3   4   5
     || || || || ||

ANSWERS TO SUB-TEST 2   *Interpretation of Literary Material*

1. 1	**6.** 2	**11.** 3	**16.** 3	**21.** 3	**26.** 4
2. 2	**7.** 3	**12.** 5	**17.** 3	**22.** 4	**27.** 2
3. 3	**8.** 4	**13.** 4	**18.** 2	**23.** 5	**28.** 1
4. 3	**9.** 1	**14.** 1	**19.** 1	**24.** 1	**29.** 2
5. 2	**10.** 5	**15.** 2	**20.** 1	**25.** 3	

    What's your score?

If you got at least 21 correct you are prepared to take the test which will earn you a high school equivalency diploma.

SUB-TEST 3

Interpretation of Reading Materials in the Social Studies

Directions: **Read each of the following passages carefully. Then select the answer to each of the numbered questions which in your opinion best completes the statement or question.**

Passage I

It was not a governing class that America needed—that ideal cherished by the Federalists and revived by the civil service reformers—but a people intelligent enough to use government to prosper the commonwealth, realistic enough to recognize the economic bases of politics, moderate enough to exercise self-restraint, bold enough to countenance experiments, mature enough to distinguish between statesmanship and demagoguery, far-sighted enough to plan for their children and their children's children. All this was, to be sure, a large order, and only perfectionists could be disappointed that it was not filled. Yet if Americans remained politically immature, they revealed as great a competence in the art and science of politics as any other people, and rather more than most. They were reluctant to modernize their machinery of government, yet though it needed constant care it never wholly broke down as it often did in the Old World. They tolerated corruption, yet their political standards were as high as their business standards, and the contrast between the conduct of the Civil War and the Second World War suggest some progress in political morality. They clung to the vocabulary of laissez faire, yet faithfully supplied the money and the personnel for vastly expanded governmental activities. They frightened themselves with bogies of bureaucracy, regimentation, and dictatorship, but in fact remained singularly free from bureaucracy in the Old World sense, avoided political regimentation, and never knew the meaning of dictatorship as so many people in Europe, Latin America, and the East knew it.

1. The phrase that best expresses the main idea of this passage is:
   (1) America's competence at self-government   (2) An American governing class   (3) American political morality   (4) Political maturity   (5) Intelligence in government service

   1.   1   2   3   4   5

2. Which statement is true, according to the passage?
   (1) The American political system works better than any other systems.
   (2) Americans did not fear dictatorship.   (3) Americans were constantly eager to modernize their government.   (4) Political morality degenerated after the Civil War.   (5) Government machinery never broke down in the Old World.

   2.   1   2   3   4   5

3. The author's attitude towards Americans as politicians is one of
   (1) amusement   (2) doubt   (3) suspicion   (4) approval   (5) disapproval

   3.   1   2   3   4   5

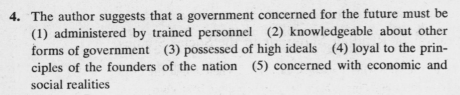

4. The author suggests that a government concerned for the future must be (1) administered by trained personnel   (2) knowledgeable about other forms of government   (3) possessed of high ideals   (4) loyal to the principles of the founders of the nation   (5) concerned with economic and social realities

5. The author suggests that Americans as politicians have been essentially (1) idealistic   (2) realistic   (3) selfish   (4) pessimistic   (5) hypocritical

Passage II

By the words *public duty* I do not necessarily mean *official* duty, although it may include that. I mean simply that constant and active practical participation in the details of politics without which, upon the part of the most intelligent citizens, the conduct of public affairs falls under the control of selfish and ignorant or crafty and venal men. I mean that personal attention—which, as it must be incessant, is often wearisome and even repulsive—to the details of politics, attendance at meetings, service upon committees, care and trouble and expense of many kinds, patient endurance of rebuffs, chagrins, ridicules, disappointments, defeats—in a word, all those duties and services which, when selfishly and meanly performed, stigmatize a man as a mere politician; but whose constant, honorable, intelligent, and vigilant performance is the gradual building, stone by stone and layer by layer, of that great temple of self-restrained liberty which all generous souls mean that our government should be.

6. The title that best expresses the ideas of the paragraph is:
(1) The Public Duty of Intelligent Men   (2) The Evils of Indifference
(3) Characteristics of the Mere Politician   (4) The Imaginary Democracy
(5) True Patriotism

7. The maintenance of the American democratic ideal depends upon
(1) a highly educated body of citizens   (2) unification of political parties
(3) absence of dissenting ideas   (4) an easily led minority   (5) alert sharing of civic responsibility

8. Which one of the following statements best expresses an idea found in the passage?
(1)Politics has never been under the control of selfish men   (2) Personal attention of officeholders insures American democratic principles   (3) Genuine public spirit demands personal sacrifice   (4) *Public duty* is synonymous with official duty   (5) American liberty is based upon constant legislation

Passage III

History has long made a point of the fact that the magnificent flowering of ancient civilization rested upon the institution of slavery, which released opportunity at the top for the art and literature which became the glory of antiquity. In a way, the mechanization of the present-day world produces the condition of the ancient in that the enormous development of labor-saving devices and of contrivances which amplify the capacities of mankind affords the base for the leisure necessary to widespread cultural pursuits. Mechanization is the present-day slave power, with the difference that in the mechanized society there is no group of the community which does not share in the benefits of its inventions.

9. The title that best expresses the ideas of this passage is:
    (1) Slavery in the Ancient World   (2) Today's Community   (3) Worthwhile Use of Leisure   (4) Ancient Culture   (5) Modern Slave Power

9. 1 2 3 4 5
    || || || || ||

10. Which factor has produced more leisure time?
    (1) the abolition of slavery   (2) the glory of antiquity   (3) the development of art and literature   (4) an increase in inventions   (5) the development of the community

10. 1 2 3 4 5
    || || || || ||

11. The flowering of any civilization has always depended on
    (1) the galley slave   (2) leisure for the workingman   (3) mechanical power   (4) leisure for cultural pursuits   (5) transportation

11. 1 2 3 4 5
    || || || || ||

12. The author's attitude toward mechanization is one of
    (1) awe   (2) acceptance   (3) distrust   (4) fear   (5) devotion

12. 1 2 3 4 5
    || || || || ||

Passage IV

The Mideast lives amid vanished glories, present prejudices and future fears. Scrabble in its soil with a hoe and you will find relics of empires long, long gone—birthplaces of civilization that have waxed and waned—and monuments to religions almost as old as recorded history.

From the Nile to the Euphrates, where transworld air routes now cover much the same trails as the plodding camel caravans of the past. Man—persistent, passionate, prejudiced—carries on the age-old plot of the human drama. All has altered, yet nothing has changed in the Middle East since centuries before Christ.

Palmyra, the caravan city of Queen Zenobia, is now a magnificent but melancholy reminder of the dreams of men long dead. Baalbek, where even the gods of yesterday have died, is but a tourist attraction, though today no tourists come. The Pyramids themselves, grandiose monuments to man's eternal hope of immortality, are scuffed and wrinkled now—cosmetically patched against the inexorability of the centuries.

Yet, essentially nothing has changed. Man and his emotions, Man and his ignorance and knowledge, man in his pride, Man at war with other men, sets the scene and dominates the stage of the turbulent Middle East.

13. The title that best expresses the ideas of this passage is:
    (1) New Discoveries in The Mideast   (2) The Appeal of the Pyramids   (3) The Unchanging Mideast   (4) New Routes to the Mideast   (5) The Birthplace of Empires

13. 1 2 3 4 5
    || || || || ||

14. According to the passage, problems in the Middle East have been due to the
(1) waning of civilization (2) lack of tourist trade (3) collapse of former civilizations (4) disappearance of belief in immortality (5) weaknesses of man

15. The passage suggests that
(1) man's nature does not change (2) man will eventually triumph over ignorance (3) man's destiny has changed (4) man's nature has improved in the last thousand years (5) man's prejudices against others will gradually disappear

16. The passage suggests that men of the ancient Middle East were
(1) irreligious (2) vain (3) melancholy (4) poor (5) unimaginative

17. The reader may conclude from the passage that ancient civilizations
(1) existed before Christianity (2) embraced one God (3) relied upon agriculture as their industry (4) were interested in the drama (5) were democratic in nature

Passage V

Despite the many categories of the historian, there are only two ages of man. The first age, the age from the beginnings of recorded time to the present, is the age of the cave man. It is the age of war. It is today. The second age, still only a prospect, is the age of civilized man. The test of civilized man will be represented by his ability to use his inventiveness for his own good by substituting world law for world anarchy. That second age is still within the reach of the individual in our time. It is not a part-time job, however. It calls for total awareness, total commitment.

18. The title that best expresses the ideas of this passage is:
(1) The Historian at Work (2) The Dangers of All-out War (3) The Power of World Anarchy (4) Mankind on the Threshold (5) The Decline of Civilization

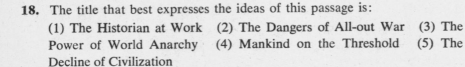

19. The author's attitude toward the possibility of man's reaching an age of civilization is one of
(1) limited hope (2) complete despair (3) marked uncertainty (4) complacency (5) anger

Passage VI

Today we have no historical work on a grand scale because of the more scientific view of evidence. The work of the quarriers and the masons has become so intricate that the architects have been compelled to limit the scale of their buildings. But I have seen one heresy relinquished. Few historians would now consent to the dogma that history is a science. It is a science but it is a great deal more. It is an art, a synthesis rather than a compilation, an interpretation as well as a chronicle. The historian, if he is to do justice to the past, must have a constructive imagination and reasonable mastery of words. The scientist must be joined to the man of letters.

20. The title that best expresses the ideas of this passage is:
(1) Building through the Ages   (2) The Function of the Historian   (3) The Influence of Science   (4) History as a Chronicle   (5) Art, a Synthesis

20. 1 2 3 4 5
|| || || || ||

21. The author implies that
(1) the work of stone masons has become complicated   (2) building has been discontinued   (3) art should take the place of history   (4) a constructive imagination is required in architecture   (5) historians are more careful of their facts today than formerly

21. 1 2 3 4 5
|| || || || ||

Passage VII

There is controversy and misunderstanding about the proper functions of juvenile courts and their probation departments. There are cries that the whole process produces delinquents rather than rehabilitates them. There are speeches by the score about "getting tough" with the kids. Another large group thinks we should be more understanding and gentle with delinquents. This distrust of the services offered can be attributed in large part to the confusion in the use of these services throughout the country.

On the one hand, the juvenile courts are tied to the criminal court system, with an obligation to decide guilt and innocence for offenses specifically stated and formally charged. On the other, they have the obligation to provide treatment, supervision and guidance to youngsters in trouble, without respect to the crimes of which they are accused. These two conflicting assignments must be carried out—quite properly—in an informal, private way, which will not stigmatize a youngster during his formative years.

And, as the courts' preoccupation with the latter task has increased, the former (that of dispensing justice) has retreated, with the result that grave injustices are bound to occur.

22. The title that best expresses the ideas of this passage is:
(1) Grave Injustices   (2) A Problem for Today's Teenagers   (3) Rehabilitating Youthful Criminals   (4) Fitting the Punishment to the Crime   (5) Justice for Juvenile Offenders

22. 1 2 3 4 5
|| || || || ||

23. The author contends that public distrust of juvenile courts is primarily the result of
(1) resentment on the part of those convicted by them   (2) the dual function of these courts   (3) lack of a sufficient number of probation officers   (4) injustices done by the courts   (5) the cost of keeping up the courts

23. 1 2 3 4 5
|| || || || ||

24. The passage suggests that the author
(1) is familiar with the problem   (2) is impatient with justice   (3) sides with those who favor leniency for juvenile offenders   (4) regards all offenses as equally important   (5) favors maximum sentences at all times

24. 1 2 3 4 5
|| || || || ||

25. The tone of this passage is
(1) highly emotional   (2) highly personal   (3) optimistic   (4) calm   (5) sarcastic

25. 1 2 3 4 5
|| || || || ||

ANSWERS TO SUB-TEST 3 *Interpretation of Reading Materials in the Social Studies*

ANSWERS TO SUB-TEST 3 *Interpretation of Reading Materials in the Social Studies*

1. 1	**6.** 1	**11.** 4	**16.** 2	**21.** 5
2. 1	**7.** 5	**12.** 2	**17.** 1	**22.** 5
3. 4	**8.** 3	**13.** 3	**18.** 4	**23.** 2
4. 5	**9.** 5	**14.** 5	**19.** 1	**24.** 1
5. 2	**10.** 4	**15.** 1	**20.** 2	**25.** 4

What's your score?

If you got at least 18 correct you are prepared to take the test which will earn you a high school equivalency diploma.

SUB-TEST 4

Interpretation of Reading Materials in the Natural Sciences

Directions: **Read each of the following selections carefully. Then select the answer to each of the numbered questions which in your opinion best completes the statement or question.**

Selection O

Scientists may differ in their explanation of the method by which evolution has occurred but there is little disagreement among them in regard to the doctrine that all living things have evolved from less complex forms. The paleontologists have studied enough fossils to justify this conclusion. In addition, evidence from other branches of science points to the fact that organic change has occurred and is still going on.

The origin of man himself has been the subject of study for many years by the anthropologist. Also, important knowledge has been added about ancient man and his civilization by the archeologist. Within the study of man, anthropologists specialize in their research. One may study the history of a language while another may devote his career to the investigation of various types of pottery. Physical anthropology makes a study of the anatomy of various vertebrates, particularly the primates which is the group of mammals that includes man, apes, monkeys, and chimpanzees. Comparisons of the anatomy of present forms are made with structures of animals of the past using information gained in the study of fossils.

How did man evolve? To answer the question, biologists who specialize in different areas contribute information. The embryologist studies the development of tissues, organs, and systems before birth. Biological inheritance has given many clues to the answer to this question. Genetics has made great strides since the days of Gregor Mendel. Research in the field of biochemistry has helped the modern geneticist explain the mechanism of heredity. In addition, the physiologist, interested in the functioning of body, uses information obtained by the biochemist and eventually presents data needed to answer questions about life.

Another question puzzling man is — How did life originate? We agree that all life comes from preexisting life but to answer this question we must consider a time when there was no life. We must seek an explanation to the origin of the complex organic compounds, since we know that our present day complex organic compounds are the results of life processes.

Any consideration of the origin of life must be concerned with the element carbon since organic substances are carbon compounds. We must also consider amino acids, the building blocks of protein and protoplasm — the living substance. One explanation tells us that simple chemical elements of the atmosphere were combined to form an amino acid which could have later been synthesized into a more complex bit of "stuff" which we now call protoplasm. The energy needed to cause this chemical synthesis, they say, might have been furnished by lightning or by the ultraviolet energy of the sun.

1. Mendel is known for his work in the field of
   (1) geology   (2) paleontology   (3) genetics   (4) anthropology   (5) anatomy

   1. 1 2 3 4 5

2. Which of the following terms includes all the others?
   (1) man   (2) primate   (3) monkey   (4) ape   (5) chimpanzee

   2. 1 2 3 4 5

3. Descent and change is a common definition of
   (1) paleontology   (2) anatomy   (3) biochemistry   (4) evolution   (5) archaeology

   3. 1 2 3 4 5

4. The most conclusive source of evidence for organic evolution comes from
   (1) the sun   (2) fossils   (3) genetics   (4) organic chemistry   (5) laboratory experiments

   4. 1 2 3 4 5

5. Which of the following terms is unlike the others?
   (1) chemist   (2) embryologist   (3) geneticist   (4) physiologist   (5) anatomist

   5. 1 2 3 4 5

6. All living matter contains the chemical element
   (1) water   (2) phosphorus   (3) carbon   (4) carbon dioxide   (5) protein

   6. 1 2 3 4 5

7. Which of the following best indicates that evolution is still taking place?
   (1) recent fossil discoveries   (2) melting of polar ice caps   (3) archaeological studies   (4) new varieties of fruit flies are appearing   (5) research by anthropologists

   7. 1 2 3 4 5

8. The problem of explaining the origin of life on the earth involves an answer to the question of the origin of
   (1) ultraviolet rays   (2) proteins   (3) atoms   (4) molecules   (5) inorganic carbon

   8. 1 2 3 4 5

9. Synthesis involves
(1) breaking down any complex compound   (2) breaking down protoplasm   (3) building up complex compounds from simpler substances
(4) conversion of one substance into another by physical means   (5) any
chemical reaction

Selection P

A popular dislike of moths notwithstanding, many naturalists enjoy observing their habits and the richness of their colors. They are distinguished from
most butterflies by their bristle-shaped antennae, tapering from base to apex.
Moths are generally nocturnal, though there are a few exceptions. They often
exhibit great richness and beauty of colors, though in brightness of color not
generally equal to butterflies. Their food is similar to that of butterflies. They
lay great numbers of eggs, which exhibit varieties of form and color as great
as those of the insects themselves. Their caterpillars are more widely various
in form and characters than those of butterflies; differing from each other in
the number of their legs, and in horns, protuberances, caudal appendages,
hairy covering, etc. Some are social both in the larva and chrysalis state;
forming, on their entering the latter state, very curious nests. The chrysalis
of a moth is never angular nor furnished with protuberances, and is generally
enveloped in a silken cocoon, close and compact; though some moth chrysalids
are found in a mere space filled with threads which cross each other in various
directions. Silk-worm moths are among the insects most useful to man; but
moths in general are regarded as injurious, the larvae of many feeding on
leaves of various kinds, and often destroying valuable crops; and the larvae
of some small species being very destructive to clothes and books.

10. Moths differ from butterflies mainly in
(1) that a large number of eggs are produced   (2) feeding habits   (3)
the complete metamorphosis from egg to larva to pupa stages   (4) the
shape of legs   (5) the shape of antennae

11. Moths do most of their damage
(1) in daytime   (2) as chrysalids   (3) in the cocoon   (4) as larvae
(5) as adults when wings are fully formed

12. The following statements regarding moths are correct except
(1) The silkworm is a moth   (2) Many moths have colorful wings
though not as bright as those of butterflies   (3) Many differences exist
in the structure of the larvae of different species of moths   (4) All
moths hide during daytime hours   (5) Moths do not have a characteristic type of cocoon

Selection Q

The natural successions of plant and animal communities refer to the
changes in animal and plant life of a region as a result of environmental
changes. The study of organisms in relation to their environment is known

as *ecology*. With changes in environment, the previous animal and plant life disappears and is succeeded by new types, adapted to new conditions. Thus, a bare rock area can support the primitive algae and lichens. Gradually, as the rock decomposes to become soil, the mosses, grasses and quick-growing weeds would appear, followed by small shrubs. As the soil becomes deeper and more porous, the larger evergreens would appear crowding out the grasses and shrubs. If these rocky, shallow soils change to deeper ones of firmer loam, the evergreens are replaced with hardwoods such as maple and beech.

A knowledge of succession is very important in tackling the problem of conservation. Thus, an exposed grassland area has no protection from wind and rain and, if the grass cover is removed, the topsoil will be gradually worn away by wind and water and conditions will revert to the more primitive rocky substance. Similarly, if a forest is destroyed, the mosses and ferns of that forest, requiring shade, and the forest animals, requiring protection and food, will disappear and be replaced by insects and other animals common to the grassland and shrub area that had preceded the forest.

Many methods of soil conservation are now in use. Planting of cover crops like clover and grass holds down the soil particles. Terracing involves the building of step-like cut-outs on the sides of hills to prevent runoff of rain water and accompanying erosion. Contour plowing is the plowing of furrows around a hill according to the land contours rather than up and down the hill. This again prevents excessive runoff of water and the accompanying erosion of the soil. In strip cropping, a close-growing crop such as alfalfa or rye is planted in alternate strips with a densely planted crop such as corn or cotton. The close-growing crops bind the soil and absorb rain runoff, preventing erosion of the land.

13. Of the following, the most appropriate title for the above passage is
(1) Living Communities   (2) Forestry   (3) Rock Decomposition
(4) Soil Conservation   (5) Plants and their Enemies

13. 1 2 3 4 5

14. Ecology may best be described as the study of
(1) methods of preventing runoff of water   (2) erosion of land   (3) the relationship between the environment and living things   (4) the effect of living things on the environment   (5) changes in plants

14. 1 2 3 4 5

15. According to this author, after a forest fire the first living things to reappear would be
(1) forest animals   (2) grasses and shrubs   (3) mosses and ferns   (4) maple and beech   (5) algae and lichens

15. 1 2 3 4 5

16. Which of the following represents the most probable order of natural succession of plants in a barren rocky area?
(1) mosses, grasses, shrubs, trees   (2) lichens, mosses, grasses, shrubs
(3) lichens, grasses, shrubs, mosses   (4) grasses, shrubs, trees, mosses
(5) mosses, lichens, grasses, shrubs

16. 1 2 3 4 5

17. All of the following are methods of soil conservation mentioned in the passage except
(1) crop rotation   (2) terracing   (3) strip cropping   (4) contour plowing   (5) use of cover crops

17. 1 2 3 4 5

18. The principal way in which forests help prevent soil erosion is by the
(1) trees that provide homes for wildlife   (2) leaves that manufacture
food   (3) leaves that take in carbon dioxide and give off oxygen   (4)
forest floors that absorb water   (5) forest shielding the soil from the
sun's heat

18. 1 2 3 4 5
    ‖ ‖ ‖ ‖ ‖

Selection R

The potato plant is one of the most important cultivated plants. From a
botanical standpoint, the fact that it stores its foods in the tuber, an underground stem, makes it useful to man. The plant is a perennial having her-
baceous stems 1-3 feet high, without thorns or prickles; pinnate leaves with
two or more pair of leaflets and an odd one, the leaflets entire at the margin;
flowers an inch or an inch and a half in breadth, the wheel-shaped corolla
white or purple, and more or less veined; followed by globular fruit of a
straw color when ripe, about three-fourths of an inch in diameter, and
containing many seeds; the roots producing tubers. The herbage has a slightly
narcotic smell, and the tender tops are used in some countries like spinach.
The tubers are, however, the only valuable part of the plant.

It has been estimated that the same area of ground which would produce
30 lbs. of wheat, would produce 1,000 lbs. of potatoes. But potatoes are not
nearly as nutritious as wheat, and an exclusive diet of them is not favorable
to development of the physical powers and of mental energy. It is calculated
that 100 lbs. of good wheat-flour, or 107 lbs. of the grain, contain as much
actual nutriment as 613 lbs. of potatoes. The inferiority of the nutritious
power is due largely to its comparatively small quantity of phosphates and
albuminoids. Hence it is most advantageously used with some very nitrogenous
article of food, e.g., animal food, or curds, or cheese. The tuber, in a fresh
state, contains 71–80 per cent. of water; 13–25 of starch, 3–7 of fibre or
woody matter, 3–4 of gum, dextrine, and sugar, and 2 of albumen, gluten,
and casein.

Besides its value as a culinary vegetable, the potato is important in other
respects. Its starch is very easily separated, and is in large proportions. It is
used largely in textile manufactories under the name *farina*, which is converted
into dextrine or British gum. In Holland and in Russia, where there is much
difficulty in keeping potatoes through the winter, large quantities of starch
are made and converted into sugar or syrup. The refuse of the starch-
manufactories is economized; it is pressed out from the water, and used either
for pig-feeding or for fertilizing. In some parts of Europe, much spirit for
drinking is made from potatoes; it is called Potato Brandy.

Propagation is nearly always effected by means of tubers, either whole or
cut in pieces each of which contains one or more 'eyes' or buds, but may be
done by means of sprouts forced early in the season.

19. Potatoes are a good source of
(1) phosphates   (2) wheat flour   (3) nitrogen   (4) starch   (5) gluten

19. 1 2 3 4 5
    ‖ ‖ ‖ ‖ ‖

20. Knowing the per cent of nitrogen in a food helps you determine its
content of
(1) potato   (2) gum   (3) protein   (4) dextrines   (5) vegetable oils

20. 1 2 3 4 5
    ‖ ‖ ‖ ‖ ‖

21. The potato is composed chiefly of
    (1) starch   (2) water   (3) sugar   (4) cellulose fiber   (5) phosphates

21. 1 2 3 4 5
    || || || || ||

22. The tuber is a (an)
    (1) farm implement   (2) aerial root   (3) underground stem   (4) poorly developed herbaceous stem   (5) highly specialized root

22. 1 2 3 4 5
    || || || || ||

23. The "eye" of a potato is a (an)
    (1) seed   (2) root bud   (3) modified stem   (4) bulb   (5) modified flower

23. 1 2 3 4 5
    || || || || ||

24. This passage is most probably an excerpt from a (an)
    (1) recent magazine article on plant life   (2) article written at least 200 years ago   (3) old botany textbook   (4) recent American encyclopedia   (5) farmer's almanac

24. 1 2 3 4 5
    || || || || ||

Selection S

Epithelium is a tissue that covers a surface. It would be a mistake, however, to think of it merely as a covering for the external surface. Some internal surfaces such as the mouth, throat, stomach, intestine and lungs are actually continuous from the outside.

Anatomists formerly used the term Mucous System to include the skin, the true glands, and the moist glandular linings of the body cavity. All of these are continuous with one another, and are essentially composed of similar parts. The mucous membranes, the moist glandular linings, and the internal membranes may be divided into the following groups: the *alimentary*, the *respiratory*, and the *genito-urinary*.

The *alimentary mucous membrane* commences at the lips, and not only forms the inner coat of the intestinal canal from the mouth to the anus, but gives off prolongations which, after lining the ducts of the various glands (the salivary glands, the liver, and the pancreas) whose products are discharged into this canal, penetrate into the innermost recesses of these glands, and constitute their true secreting element. Besides these larger offsets, there are in the stomach and small intestine an infinite series of minute tubular prolongations.

The *respiratory mucous membrane* begins at the nostrils, and under the name *schneiderian* or *pituitary membrane*, lines the nasal cavities, whence it sends on either side an upward prolongation through the lachrymal duct to form the *conjunctiva* of the eye; backward, through the posterior nares (the communication between the nose and the throat), it sends a prolongation through the Eustachian tube to the middle ear (the cavity of the tympanum), and is continuous with the pharyngeal mucous membrane (which is a portion of the alimentary tract); it then, instead of passing down the oesophagus, enters and forms a lining to the larynx, trachea, and bronchial tubes to their termination. From the continuity of these two tracts, some writers describe them as a single one, under the name of the gastro-pulmonary tract.

25. All of the following are functions of epithelial tissue except
    (1) secretion   (2) excretion   (3) protection   (4) contraction   (5) lubrication

25. 1 2 3 4 5
    || || || || ||

26. If the basic pattern of structure of the human body is regarded as a tube within a tube, then the inner tube is the
  (1) respiratory mucous membrane   (2) alimentary mucous membrane
  (3) pituitary membrane   (4) eustachian tube   (5) pharyngeal membrane

26. 1 2 3 4 5

27. The lachrymal duct is in the
  (1) eye   (2) throat   (3) ear   (4) larynx   (5) tracheae

27. 1 2 3 4 5

28. All of the following structures secrete substances into the alimentary canal except
  (1) liver   (2) pancreas   (3) salivary gland   (4) larynx   (5) stomach

28. 1 2 3 4 5

29. Which of the following is part of the alimentary tract?
  (1) bronchi   (2) larynx   (3) esophagus   (4) trachea   (5) tympanum

29. 1 2 3 4 5

Selection T

The butterfly is the common name for a group of insects belonging to the Lepidoptera group. They are distinguished from other lepidopterous insects by the brillance of coloring on the upper as well as the under side of the wings. Almost all butterflies when at rest usually hold their wings erect, the under side being thus chiefly exhibited; while the other lepidopterous insects, when at rest, hold their wings in a horizontal or somewhat inclined position, and some have them wrapped round the body. Butterflies are also the only lepidopterous insects which have no spines, bristles, or hooks on the margins of their wings, by which the second wing on each side can be attached to the first, but both when flying and at rest, have all their wings quite separate. Antennae of butterflies are generally simple, slender, and elongated, and terminated by a little club. Their caterpillars have always 16 feet. The pupa or chrysalis is angular.

Short-lived as they all are generally believed to be, some of the tropical species perform wonderful migrations; concerning which, however, nothing but the fact is yet well known.

The eggs of butterflies are deposited on the plants, the leaves of which are to supply the food of the caterpillars. In cold and temperate climates, the eggs deposited in autumn are not hatched till the following spring; but it is believed that many species produce several broods in a year, as the eggs in summer may be hatched in a few days. The caterpillars of each species are generally confined to some particular kind of plant, the leaves of which they devour; their ravages are well known, but the excessive increase of their numbers is in part restrained by many enemies, and by none more than by the ichneumons and other insects which deposit their eggs in them, and the larvae of which feed on them.

30. The ichneumon fly may best be described as a (an)
  (1) parasite   (2) lepidopteran   (3) companion of the butterfly   (4) adult hawk-moth   (5) wingless fly

30. 1 2 3 4 5

31. The following are characteristics of butterflies except
(1) brilliant wings   (2) absence of spines on the margin of wings
(3) wings are held in horizontal, inclined position when not in flight
(4) feelers are simple, elongated structures with a club-like structure at
the tip   (5) adult life is short

32. Butterflies may be described as insects which
(1) are the only member of the Lepidoptera group   (2) cannot move
in the caterpillar stage   (3) can migrate in the chrysalis stage   (4)
can produce many offspring in a single season   (5) can use any variety
of plant as a site for developing their young

33. The population of butterflies is held down by
(1) losses during migration   (2) the brilliance of their wings which
make them vulnerable as food for larger animals   (3) shortened adult
life   (4) natural enemies that feed on developing young   (5) cold
winters that destroy eggs

Selection U

Unlike most solids, gases are more soluble at lower temperatures. Thus, as the temperature of a solvent such as water decreases, the solubility of a gas, such as carbon dioxide, increases. Lowering the temperature decreases the kinetic energy of the molecules of the dissolved gas and so the molecules of the gas have a greater tendency to stay in solution. It is for this reason that carbonated beverages are kept in the refrigerator, so that the carbon dioxide gas will remain in solution.

Increasing the pressure has a negligible effect on the solubility of *solids* in liquids, since the molecules of the solid are already very close together. However, molecules of gases are very far apart with very weak attractive forces between them. An increase in pressure literally forces more of the molecules of the gas into the solvent. *Henry's Law* states that the solubility of a gas in a liquid is directly proportional to the pressure of the gas above the liquid. Thus, doubling the pressure means that twice the quantity of the gas will dissolve in the liquid. If the pressure is decreased, many of the molecules immediately escape from solution. The fizzing of carbonated beverages when the cap is removed can be explained by the decreased solubility of the carbon dioxide as a result of the decreased pressure.

34. The author's purpose in writing this passage was to
(1) describe the manufacture of beverages   (2) suggest the best method
of storing beverages   (3) explain solubility   (4) explain the difference
between solids, liquids, and gases   (5) disprove Henry's Law

35. In the third sentence of the passage "kinetic energy" refers to
(1) carbon dioxide   (2) water   (3) soda   (4) air   (5) soda water

36. According to the passage,
(1) Solids are more soluble at lower temperatures   (2) Gases are more
soluble at lower temperatures   (3) Carbonated beverages are kept
refrigerated to drive out the dissolved gas   (4) The fizzing of carbonated

beverages is the result of more gas going into solution (5) Gases are more soluble at higher temperatures

37. Which of the following statements is true?   37.   1   2   3   4   5
(1) Raising the temperature of a solvent will allow more gas to go into solution.   (2) Lowering the temperature of a solvent will allow more gas to go into solution   (3) Temperature changes have no effect on the solubility of a solid in a liquid   (4) Pressure changes have no effect on the solubility of a gas in a liquid

ANSWERS EXPLAINED   *page 503-504*

ANSWERS TO SUB-TEST 4   *Interpretation of Reading Materials in the Natural Sciences*

1. 3	**6.** 3	**11.** 4	**16.** 2	**21.** 2	**26.** 2	**31.** 3	**36.** 2
2. 2	**7.** 4	**12.** 4	**17.** 1	**22.** 3	**27.** 1	**32.** 4	**37.** 2
3. 4	**8.** 2	**13.** 4	**18.** 4	**23.** 2	**28.** 4	**33.** 4	
4. 2	**9.** 3	**14.** 3	**19.** 4	**24.** 3	**29.** 3	**34.** 3	
5. 1	**10.** 5	**15.** 2	**20.** 3	**25.** 4	**30.** 1	**35.** 1	

What's your score?

If you got at least 26 correct you are prepared to take the test which will earn you a high school equivalency diploma.

1. Ans. 3 The passage mentions that great strides have been made in genetics since the days of Mendel.

2. Ans. 2 Man, monkey, ape, and chimpanzee belong to the Primate group of mammals.

3. Ans. 4 By definition.

4. Ans. 2 Refer to the second sentence of the opening paragraph.

5. Ans. 1 All but the chemist are specialists in the field of biology.

6. Ans. 3 Water, carbon dioxide, and protein are chemical compounds. Not all living things have the chemical element phosphorus.

7. Ans. 4 The appearance of any new form—mutation—is an illustration of evolution.

8. Ans. 2 Protoplasm is a complex protein.

9. Ans. 3 By definition.

10. Ans. 5 Refer to second sentence.

11. Ans. 4 Larvae feed on leaves. The clothes moth feeds on woolens in the larval stage.

12. Ans. 4 Most, but not all moths, are nocturnal.

13. Ans. 4 This passage deals mainly with soil conservation, showing how ecological considerations must be made to tackle the problem of conservation.

14. Ans. 3 Refer to second sentence of the first paragraph.

15. Ans. 5 the first paragraph refers to natural successions of life in a forest.

16. Ans. 2 See paragraph one, sentences 4 and 5.

17. Ans. 1 This method is not treated by this author.

18. Ans. 4 The absorption of water by the roots of trees prevents flooding.   Also, the dead leaves of trees act as a sponge to hold water.

19. Ans. 4 Potatoes contain only slight amounts of nitrogen or phosphates.

20. Ans. 3 Protein compounds contain nitrogen. Carbohydrates and fats do not contain nitrogen.

21. Ans. 2 The potato cotains 71-80 per cent water.

22. Ans. 3 By definition.

23. Ans. 2 Observe closing paragraph.

24. Ans. 3 The detailed, technical descriptions of the botanical parts in addition to the economic aspects of the potato plant give the clues to this answer. While it appears to be British it is hardly a recently written excerpt. Also, it definitely has more information than a farmer would need.

25. Ans. 4 Contraction is a function of muscle.

26. Ans. 2 Refer to the third paragraph.

27. Ans. 1 The passage mentions that the lachrymal duct leads to the eye.

28. Ans. 4 Refer to the next to last sentence of this passage.

29. Ans. 3 The esophagus is another name for the gullet which connects mouth and stomach. The other choices mentioned in this passage are parts of the respiratory mucous membrane.

30. Ans. 1 Ichneumons lay their eggs in the bodies of larvae of butterflies.

31. Ans. 3 Refer to third sentence of opening paragraph.

32. Ans. 4 Moths are also lepidopterans. Locomotion is a characteristic of the caterpillar stage but not in the cocoon (chrysalis) stage. Each species of caterpillar prefers a special plant for egg laying. Some produce one generation in one season while others produce several broods in a season.

33. Ans. 4 Refer to closing sentence of the passage.

34. Ans. 3 This passage deals mainly with various factors affecting solubility.

35. Ans. 1 The dissolved gas is carbon dioxide.

36. Ans. 2 Refer to the opening sentence of this passage.

37. Ans. 2 The second sentence of the first paragraph answers this question.

SUB-TEST **5**
General Mathematical Ability

Directions: **Solve the following problems.**

1. The quotient when 285.8417 is divided by 4.009 is
  (1) zero   (2) 7.13   (3) 61.3   (4) 71.3   (5) 713

1. 1 2 3 4 5

2. Candy bars purchased at 45¢ per dozen were sold for 7¢ each at a bazaar. How much was gained if 10 dozen of these candy bars were sold?
  (1) 39¢   (2) $3.90   (3) $4.50   (4) $8.40   (5) $39.00

2. 1 2 3 4 5

3. What is two-halves of $2\frac{1}{2}$ plus $2\frac{1}{2}$?

(1) 1   (2) $2\frac{1}{2}$ (3) 4   (4) 5   (5) 6

3. 1 2 3 4 5

4. If you divide $2\frac{2}{3}$ by $1\frac{1}{3}$ the quotient will be one and

(1) $\frac{1}{4}$ (2) $\frac{1}{5}$ (3) $\frac{4}{5}$ (4) $\frac{4}{9}$ (5) $\frac{5}{9}$

4. 1 2 3 4 5

5. Which of the following should be added to $\frac{1}{4}$ to give a sum of .75?

(1) 0.5   (2) $\frac{1}{3}$ (3) 5%   (4) $\frac{3}{4}$ (5) 30%

5. 1 2 3 4 5

6. How many pieces of tubing 17 inches long can be cut from a piece of tubing which is 34 feet long?

(1) 2   (2) 12   (3) 20   (4) 22   (5) 24

6. 1 2 3 4 5

7. My electric meter showed 7921 kilowatt—hours last month. Now it shows 8215 kilowatt—hours. If the utility company charges $.04 per kilowatt, how much should I pay for this electricity?

(1) $2.94   (2) $11.76   (3) $12.16   (4) $15.76   (5) $16.14

7. 1 2 3 4 5

8. Michael is paid $150 a week for delivering milk plus 8¢ a mile for the use of his automobile. One week he traveled 102 miles in making deliveries with his automobile. How much did he receive for the use of his automobile that week?

(1) $.82   (2) $8.16   (3) $81.60   (4) $150.82   (5) $158.16

8. 1 2 3 4 5

9. A machine costs $4250 when new. After ten years use it had a trade-in value of $1160. What was the amount of the average annual depreciation on this machine?

(1) $30.90   (2) $300   (3) $309   (4) $390   (5) $3090

9. 1 2 3 4 5

10. Only $\frac{2}{7}$ of the Arena was occupied during a basketball game. The attendance figure that game was 3800. The total capacity of the Arena is

(1) 5438   (2) 5500   (3) 13,000   (4) 13,300   (5) 133,000

10. 1 2 3 4 5

11. A class has x number of boys and y number of girls. What part of the class is made up of boys?

(1) $\dfrac{x}{x+y}$ (2) $\dfrac{x}{xy}$ (3) $\dfrac{y}{xy}$ (4) $\dfrac{y}{x+y}$ (5) $\dfrac{x}{y}$

11. 1 2 3 4 5

12. A man looked at the gauge of his 280-gallon oil tank on the first of the month and found it $\frac{7}{8}$ full. At the end of the month he observed it was $\frac{1}{4}$ full. How many gallons of fuel oil were used during this particular month?

(1) 70   (2) 105   (3) 175   (4) 210   (5) 245

12. 1 2 3 4 5

13. A salesman earns $200 a week plus a 5% commission on all sales over $8000. One week his sales were $15,000. His earnings that week were

(1) $200   (2) $235   (3) $350   (4) $500   (5) $550

13. 1 2 3 4 5

14. A baseball team has won 50 games out of 75 played. It has 45 games still to play. How many of these must the team win to make its record for the season 60%?

(1) 20   (2) 21   (3) 22   (4) 25   (5) 30

14. 1 2 3 4 5

15. A fruit and vegetable dealer bought 840 bags of potatoes at $1.05 per bag which he sold during the month for a total of $992.25. His per cent of profit is

(1) 8%   (2) 10%   (3) 12½%   (4) 15%   (5) 18%

15. 1 2 3 4 5

16. What is the cost of one article which is sold at $30 per hundred less a 20% discount?

(1) 12¢   (2) 24¢   (3) 27¢   (4) 30¢   (5) 50¢

16. 1 2 3 4 5

17. House paint at $4.90 per gallon can is advertised to sell at a 10% discount for quantity buying. The cost of a 4-gallon case of this paint will cost

(1) $1.96   (2) $4.41   (3) $17.64   (4) $19.60   (5) $20.56

17. 1 2 3 4 5

18. I can buy a refrigerator on the installment plan for $360 including carrying charges. If I make a down payment of 25% and pay the balance in 8 equal monthly payments, what would be the monthly payment?

(1) $27.00   (2) $33.33   (3) $33.75   (4) $45.00   (5) $270.00

18. 1 2 3 4 5

19. A chair is marked $210. A 5% discount is allowed for a cash purchase but if purchased on the installment plan a down payment of 20% of the marked price is required, plus 12 monthly payments of $16.50 each. How much is saved for buying for cash?

(1) $40   (2) $40.50   (3) $41.00   (4) $51.00   (5) $51.50

19. 1 2 3 4 5

20. A record player listed at $50 is offered for $42.50 during a sale. The per cent of discount allowed is

(1) 5   (2) 10   (3) 15   (4) 20   (5) 25

20. 1 2 3 4 5

21. A building is insured with two companies as follows: the Bistate Insurance Company, $12,000; the Farmers Mutual Company, $8,000. What would be the Bistate Insurance Company's share of a fire loss amounting to $1,820?

(1) $364   (2) $546   (3) $728   (4) $1092   (5) $1456

21. 1 2 3 4 5

22. If you can save $5 by buying a jacket at a sale where a 25% discount is given, what was the original price?

(1) $10   (2) $15   (3) $20   (4) $25   (5) $30

22. 1 2 3 4 5

23. The enrollment in a special course increased from 150 to 180 pupils. The per cent increase was

(1) 5%   (2) 10%   (3) 16⅔%   (4) 20%   (5) 30%

23. 1 2 3 4 5

24. Which of the following does *not* have the same value as the other four?

(1) ½%   (2) .5%   (3) $\frac{1}{500}$ (4) $\frac{1}{200}$ (5) .005

24. 1 2 3 4 5

25. 104% of 68 equals

(1) 27.2   (2) 65.28   (3) 70.72   (4) 95.2   (5) 272

25. 1 2 3 4 5

26. The value 17.2% may correctly be expressed as

(1) .00172   (2) .0172   (3) .1072   (4) .172   (5) 1.72

26. 1 2 3 4 5

27. What is the sales tax on an article costing $D, if the town has a 6% sales tax?

(1) $6D   (2) $D + .6   (3) $.6D   (4) $.06D   (5) $D + .06

27. 1 2 3 4 5

28. How much money must be invested in securities paying an annual return of 6%, in order to receive an income of $1200 per year?
    (1) $2000 (2) $7200 (3) $20,000 (4) $72,000 (5) $200,000

28. 1 2 3 4 5
     ‖ ‖ ‖ ‖ ‖

29. A merchant purchased a fire insurance policy with a face value of $45,000 on his building. The annual premium rate was $.86 per $100. What premium did he pay for one year's protection under this policy?
    (1) $38.70 (2) $387 (3) $430 (4) $450 (5) $860

29. 1 2 3 4 5
     ‖ ‖ ‖ ‖ ‖

30. Joan is m years old now. Last year she was (?) years old.
    (1) $m - 1$ (2) $m + 1$ (3) $2m$ (4) $2m + 1$ (5) $2m - 1$

30. 1 2 3 4 5
     ‖ ‖ ‖ ‖ ‖

31. The sides of a triangle are $4x$, $2x - 20$, and $x - 10$. The perimeter (sum of the sides) is
    (1) $7x - 30$ (2) $5x + 10$ (3) $5x - 30$ (4) $7x + 10$ (5) $6x - 30$

31. 1 2 3 4 5
     ‖ ‖ ‖ ‖ ‖

32. The price of a dozen jumbo size eggs is j¢. At that price, the cost of 2 such eggs would be (?) cents.
    (1) $\dfrac{j}{6}$ (2) $\dfrac{j}{12}$ (3) $\dfrac{j}{2}$ (4) $3j$ (5) $6j$

32. 1 2 3 4 5
     ‖ ‖ ‖ ‖ ‖

33. A stock dropped 2 points on Monday, gained 4 points on Tuesday, dropped 6 points on Wednesday, dropped another point on Thursday, and gained 5 points on Friday. The net change during this week was
    (1) zero (2) $+ 1$ (3) $- 2$ (4) $+ 2$ (5) $- 1$

33. 1 2 3 4 5
     ‖ ‖ ‖ ‖ ‖

34. Martin drove 80 miles in 2 hours. After lunch he covered 100 miles in 3 hours. His average rate (in miles per hour) for the entire trip was
    (1) 36 (2) 37 (3) 45 (4) 77 (5) 90

34. 1 2 3 4 5
     ‖ ‖ ‖ ‖ ‖

35. The product of $- 4x^2$ and $- 2x$ is
    (1) $- 8x^3$ (2) $8x^3$ (3) $8x$ (4) $8x^2$ (5) $- 8x^2$

35. 1 2 3 4 5
     ‖ ‖ ‖ ‖ ‖

36. If $a = 4$, $b = 5$, $x = 2$, and $y = 3$ what is the value of $x^2 + 5ab - 2y^2$?
    (1) 1 (2) 78 (3) 86 (4) 99 (5) 122

36. 1 2 3 4 5
     ‖ ‖ ‖ ‖ ‖

37. $(x^2)(x^3) =$
    (1) $5x$ (2) x^5 (3) x^6 (4) $6x$ (5) $2x^5$

37. 1 2 3 4 5
     ‖ ‖ ‖ ‖ ‖

38. If $4x - 8 = 16$, then $8x$ equals
    (1) 6 (2) 16 (3) 24 (4) 32 (5) 48

38. 1 2 3 4 5
     ‖ ‖ ‖ ‖ ‖

39. If $\dfrac{x}{4} = 3$ then $4x$ equals
    (1) 1 (2) 3 (3) 12 (4) 24 (5) 48

39. 1 2 3 4 5
     ‖ ‖ ‖ ‖ ‖

40. A piece of copper pipe 75 inches long is cut so that one piece is four times longer than the other. The length of the smaller piece is
    (1) 1 foot 3 inches (2) $2\frac{1}{3}$ feet (3) $2\frac{1}{2}$ feet (4) 15 feet (5) 60 inches

40. 1 2 3 4 5
     ‖ ‖ ‖ ‖ ‖

41. Eighty is $\frac{4}{3}$ of
    (1) 60 (2) 70 (3) 80 (4) 90 (5) $106\frac{2}{3}$

41. 1 2 3 4 5
     ‖ ‖ ‖ ‖ ‖

42. If $A = \dfrac{h}{2}(b + c)$. Find the value of A when $h = 4$, $b = 5$, $c = 6$
    (1) 5.5 (2) 11 (3) 15 (4) 22 (5) 30

42. 1 2 3 4 5
     ‖ ‖ ‖ ‖ ‖

43. Using the formula $V = \dfrac{l\,w\,h}{3}$ find V if $l = 6$, $w = 2$, and $h = 5$.

    (1) 4.3   (2) 6.5   (3) 20   (4) 39   (5) 60

43. 1 2 3 4 5

44. The sum of two numbers is 12 and their difference is 4. The larger of the two numbers is

    (1) 2   (2) 4   (3) 6   (4) 8   (5) 10

44. 1 2 3 4 5

45. If an article sells for 35¢ per dozen, how much would you have to pay for 72 of these articles?

    (1) $1.40   (2) $1.65   (3) $2.04   (4) $2.10   (5) $2.36

45. 1 2 3 4 5

46. Martin can finish his term paper in 3 weeks. Sam can do his term paper in 5 days. The ratio of time required by Sam to the time required by Martin is

    (1) 3:5   (2) 5:3   (3) 5:21   (4) 4:1   (5) 21:5

46. 1 2 3 4 5

47. In an audience of x people there are w number of women. The ratio of men to women in this audience is

    (1) $\dfrac{x}{x-w}$ (2) $\dfrac{x-w}{x}$ (3) $\dfrac{w-x}{w}$ (4) $\dfrac{x-1}{w}$ (5) $\dfrac{x-w}{w}$

47. 1 2 3 4 5

48. A picture 8 inches long and 6 inches wide is to be enlarged so that its length will be 12 inches. The enlarged picture will have a width of

    (1) 9 inches   (2) 10 inches   (3) 12 inches   (4) 14 inches   (5) 16 inches

48. 1 2 3 4 5

49. I left at 7:30 a.m. for a destination 441 miles away. I arrived there that evening at six o'clock after making several rest stops totaling $1\frac{1}{2}$ hours. My average speed (miles per hour) for the entire trip was

    (1) 42   (2) 43   (3) 45   (4) 49   (5) 55

49. 1 2 3 4 5

50. If 3 pencils cost c cents, how many can be bought for 30 cents?

    (1) $10c$ (2) $90c$ (3) $\dfrac{90}{c}$ (4) $\dfrac{10}{c}$ (5) $\dfrac{c}{10}$

50. 1 2 3 4 5

51. On a map having a scale of $\frac{1}{8}$ inch $= 15$ miles what is the distance (in miles) between two cities that are $3\frac{1}{2}$ inches apart on the map?

    (1) 66   (2) 120   (3) 132   (4) 220   (5) 420

51. 1 2 3 4 5

52. A new state highway is planned along the diagonal of a rectangular town which is 12 miles long and 5 miles wide. How many miles long will the new highway be?

    (1) 7   (2) 8.5   (3) 13   (4) 17   (5) 34

52. 1 2 3 4 5

53. If the perimeter of a square is 40″ its area in inches is

    (1) 10   (2) 16   (3) 50   (4) 100   (5) 160

53. 1 2 3 4 5

54. The area (in square feet) of this figure is

    (1) 26   (2) 129   (3) 180   (4) 234   (5) 270

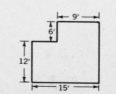

54. 1 2 3 4 5

55. What is the weight of a block of ice 2′ x 3′ x 1′6″ if a cubic foot of ice weighs 62.5 pounds?
(1) 56.25 lbs   (2) 306.25 lbs   (3) 3062.5 lbs   (4) 562.5 lbs
(5) 5625 lbs

55. 1 2 3 4 5

56. How many cubic inches of water (in terms of π) can a glass cylindrical jar hold, if the distance across the top is 6 inches and its height is 12 inches?
(1) 36π (2) 54π (3) 72π (4) 108π
(5) 432π

56. 1 2 3 4 5

57. If 2 angles of a triangle are 20° and 70°, then the triangle is
(1) equilateral   (2) isosceles   (3) scalene   (4) right   (5) obtuse

57. 1 2 3 4 5

58. From 3:40 p.m. to ten minutes before 4 o'clock the hand of a clock describes an angle of
(1) 10°   (2) 20°   (3) 40°   (4) 60°   (5) 120°

58. 1 2 3 4 5

This graph shows the sales of the various departments in a supermarket for the period September 15-20. Use this information to answer questions 59-61.

59. The total sales for all departments for this period in this store amounted to
(1) $5,600   (2) $6,800   (3) $7,400   (4) $8,360   (5) $8,400

59. 1 2 3 4 5

60. What is the amount of average daily sales in the Meat Department?
(1) $345   (2) $400   (3) $417   (4) $480   (5) $500

60. 1 2 3 4 5

61. The Dairy Department is planning a special sales promotion next week to increase their sales by 5%. The expected sales next week should be
(1) $80   (2) $1608   (3) $1650   (4) $1680   (5) $2400

61. 1 2 3 4 5

62. What amount of money was spent for labor?
(1) $4,800   (2) $9,600
(3) $96,000   (4) $48,000
(5) $960,000

DISTRIBUTION FOR SALES
OF $240,000
ACE MANUFACTURING CO.
(questions 62, 63)

62. 1 2 3 4 5

63. Next year sales are expected to increase by 8%. What should the expected sales amount to next year?
(1) $240,192   (2) $241,920
(3) $259,000   (4) $259,200
(5) $432,000

63. 1 2 3 4 5

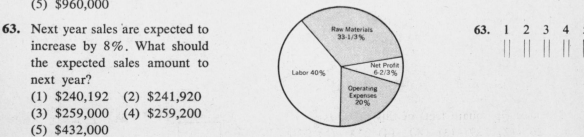

64. If 18 feet 10 inches is cut from a wire which is 25 feet 8 inches, the length of wire left will be
(1) 6 feet 2 inches   (2) 6.1 feet   (3) 6 feet 9 inches   (4) 6 feet 10 inches
(5) 7 feet 2 inches

64. 1 2 3 4 5

65. What is the maximum number of half-pint bottles that can be filled with a 10-gallon can of milk?   65. 1 2 3 4 5

(1) 40   (2) 80   (3) 100   (4) 160   (5) 320

EXPLANATION OF ANSWERS *page 511-516*

ANSWERS AND ANALYSIS TO SUB-TEST 5 *General Mathematical Ability*

This page supplies the correct answers and helps you with an analysis of your performance on this practice test. The number in parenthesis after the correct choice refers to the topic covered by that particular question. In the Outline of Topics below you will find the page on which this topic is explained. In addition, on page *508* you will find the explanations for the answers of this sub-test.

1. 4 (1.1)	**12.** 3 (1.2)	**23.** 4 1.4)	**34.** 1 (1.1, 2.3)	**45.** 4 (2.6)	**56.** 4 (3.6)
2. 2 (1.1)	**13.** 5 (1.4)	**24.** 3 (1.3, 1.4)	**35.** 2 (2.1)	**46.** 3 (2.6)	**57.** 4 (3.2)
3. 4 (1.2)	**14.** 3 (1.4)	**25.** 3 (1.4)	**36.** 3 (2.2)	**47.** 5 (2.6)	**58.** 4 (3.2)
4. 3 (1.2)	**15.** 3 (1.4)	**26.** 4 (1.3, 1.4)	**37.** 2 (2.2)	**48.** 1 (2.6)	**59.** 5 (4)
5. 1 (1.2, 1.3)	**16.** 2 (1.4)	**27.** 4 (1.4)	**38.** 5 (2.4)	**49.** 4 (1.2, 2.3)	**60.** 2 (4)
6. 5 (1.1)	**17.** 3 (1.4)	**28.** 3 (1.6)	**39.** 5 (2.4)	**50.** 3 (2.6)	**61.** 4 (4)
7. 2 (1.1)	**18.** 3 (1.4)	**29.** 2 (1.5)	**40.** 1 (2.5)	**51.** 5 (2.6)	**62.** 3 (4)
8. 2 (1.1)	**19.** 2 (1.4)	**30.** 1 (2.1)	**41.** 1 (1.2, 2.5)	**52.** 3 (3.3)	**63.** 4 (4)
9. 3 (1.1)	**20.** 3 (1.4)	**31.** 1 (2.1)	**42.** 4 (2.3)	**53.** 4 (3.2)	**64.** 4 (5)
10. 4 (1.2)	**21.** 4 (1.5)	**32.** 1 (2.1)	**43.** 3 (2.3)	**54.** 4 (3.5)	**65.** 4 (5)
11. 1 (1.2)	**22.** 3 (1.4)	**33.** 1 (2.1)	**44.** 4 (2.5)	**55.** 4 (3.6)	

OUTLINE OF TOPICS

1. Arithmetic
1.1 Whole Numbers p. 270
1.2 Fractions p. 272
1.3 Decimals p. 285
1.4 Percent p. 288
1.5 Insurance p. 298
1.6 Investment p. 300
1.7 Taxation p. 302

2. Algebra
2.1 Fundamentals p. 304
2.2 Exponents and Evaluation p. 306
2.3 Formulas p. 307
2.4 Solving Equations p. 309
2.5 Solving Problems p. 313
2.6 Ratio and Proportion p. 317
2.7 Signed Numbers p. 321

3. Geometry
3.1 Geometric Figures p. 324
3.2 Geometric Concepts and Relationships p. 324
3.3 Indirect Measurements p. 329
3.4 Congruence and Similarity p. 332
3.5 Areas p. 333
3.6 Volumes p. 337
3.7 Areas of Solids p. 339

4. Graphs and Interpretation of Data p. 341

5. Measures p. 349

> *What's your score?*

If you got at least 46 correct you are prepared to take the test which will earn you a high school equivalency diploma.

ANSWERS EXPLAINED TO SUB-TEST 5 *General Mathematical Ability*

1. Ans. 4 Quotient = Dividend   Divisor

$$
\begin{array}{r}
71.3 \\
4.009.\ \sqrt{285.841.7} \\
280\ 63 \\
\hline
5211 \\
4009 \\
\hline
12027 \\
12027 \\
\hline
\end{array}
$$

2. Ans. 2 Selling price per dozen = (7¢)(12)   = $ .84
Cost per dozen   = $ .45
Profit on sale of   1 dozen   = $ .39
Profit on sale of 10 dozen   = $3.90

3. Ans. 4 $\left(\dfrac{2}{2}\right)$ of $2\frac{1}{2} = 2\frac{1}{2}$

$2\frac{1}{2} + 2\frac{1}{2} = 5$

4. Ans. 3 $2\frac{2}{5} \div 1\frac{1}{3}$ (mixed fraction)

$\dfrac{12}{5} \div \dfrac{4}{3}$ (improper fraction)

$\dfrac{12}{5} \cdot \dfrac{3}{4}$ (invert the divisor)

$\dfrac{3}{5} \cdot \dfrac{3}{1} = \dfrac{9}{5} = 1\frac{4}{5}$

5. Ans. 1 $\dfrac{1}{4} + ? = .75$

$\dfrac{1}{4} + ? = \dfrac{3}{4}$

$\dfrac{1}{4} + \dfrac{2}{4} = \dfrac{3}{4}$

$\dfrac{2}{4} = \dfrac{1}{2} = .5$

6. Ans. 5 34 feet = (34)(12) = 408 inches
408 inches ÷17 inches = 24 pieces

7. Ans. 2 8215 − 7921 = 294 kilowatt-hours
(294) (.04) = $11.76

8. Ans. 2 (102 miles) (.08) = $8.16

9. Ans. 3 Amount of depreciation = $4250 − $1160 = $3090
$3090   ÷   10 years   = $309 (average annual depreciation)

10. Ans. 4 If $\dfrac{2}{7} = 3800$

Then, $\dfrac{1}{7} = 1900$

and, $\dfrac{7}{7} = (1900)\,(7)$ or 13,300

OR ALGEBRAICALLY

Let x = total capacity

$$\frac{2}{7}\,x = 3800$$

$$x = 13,300$$

11. Ans. 1 $\dfrac{\text{boys}}{\text{boys} + \text{girls}}$ = part of class composed of boys = $\dfrac{x}{x+y}$

12. Ans. 3   The drop was from $\dfrac{7}{8}$ to $\dfrac{1}{4}$ (or $\dfrac{2}{8}$)

$$\frac{7}{8} - \frac{2}{8} = \frac{5}{8}$$

$\dfrac{5}{8}$ of 280 gallons = 175 gallons

13. Ans. 5 $15,00 − $8000 = $7000

               5% $(7000) = $ 350

            + regular salary $ 200

                  total $ 550

14. Ans. 3   Total number of games for the entire season = 75 + 45 = 120

(60%) (120 games) = 72 games

Since the team has already won 50 games, it must still win 22 games.

15. Ans. 3   Cost = (840) ($1.05) or $882.00

Total sales for month $992.25

      Profit $110.25

$$\frac{\$110.25}{\$882} = \frac{1}{8} = 12\tfrac{1}{2}\%$$

16. Ans. 2 $30 less 20% ($\tfrac{1}{5}$) or $6 = $24 (cost per hundred)

Therefore cost of each = 24¢

17. Ans. 3   Regular price of 4 gallons = ($4.90) (4) = $19.60

10% reduction = $1.96

Cost for quantity buying is $19.60 − $1.96 = $17.64

18. Ans. 3   Cost of refrigerator = $360 less $\tfrac{1}{4}$ ($360) = $270

$270 ÷ 8 payments = $33.75

19. Ans. 2 $210 less 5% = $210 − $10.50 = $199.50 (cash price)

However, if purchased on the installment plan,

down payment = 20% of $210 or $42

installments = (12) ($16.50) = $198

total payments made when buying on the installment plan = $240. The difference between buying for cash and on the installment plan is $240 − $199.50 or $40.50

20. Ans. 3   List Price − Selling Price = Discount

$$\frac{\text{Discount}}{\text{List Price}} = \frac{\$7.50}{\$50} = .15 = 15\%$$

21. Ans. 4   Total insurance protection = $20,000

Bistate carries $\dfrac{\$12,000}{\$20,000}$ or $\tfrac{3}{5}$ of protection

Bistate is responsible for $\tfrac{3}{5}$ of loss or ($\tfrac{3}{5}$) ($1820) or $1092

22. Ans. 3   25% = $\tfrac{1}{4}$

If $5 is $\tfrac{1}{4}$ of original price

Then $20 is $\dfrac{4}{4}$ or the full original price

23. Ans. 4 $\dfrac{\text{change}}{\text{original}} = \dfrac{30}{150} = \dfrac{1}{5} = 20\%$

24. Ans. 3 $\frac{1}{2}\% = \dfrac{\frac{1}{2}}{100} = \dfrac{1}{200}$

$.5\% = \dfrac{.5}{100} = \dfrac{1}{200}$

$.005 = \dfrac{5}{1000} = \dfrac{1}{200}$

$\dfrac{1}{200} = \dfrac{1}{200}$

$\dfrac{1}{500} \neq \dfrac{1}{200}$

25. Ans. 3 100% of 68 = 68

4% (or .04) of 68 = 2.72

104% of 68 = 70.72

26. Ans. 4 % means $\dfrac{?}{100}$

$17.2\% = \dfrac{17.2}{100} = .172$

27. Ans. 4 $6\% = \dfrac{6}{100} = .06$

6% of \$D = (.06) (\$D) = \$.06D

28. Ans. 3 Principal $\times$ Rate = Interest

Principal = Interest $\div$ Rate

Principal = \$1200 $\div$ 6% or .06 = \$20,000

29. Ans. 2 $\dfrac{\$.86}{\$100} = .86\% = .0086$

(Insurance Policy) (Rate) = Premium

(\$45,000)   (.0086) = \$387

30. Ans. 1 Last year she was $(m - 1)$ or one year less than her present age (m)

31. Ans. 1 $\quad 4x$

$2x - 20$

$\underline{\quad x - 10}$

$7x - 30$ (sum)

32. Ans. 1 If   12 eggs cost $j\cent$

and 1 egg costs $\dfrac{j}{12}\cent$

and   2 eggs cost $(2)\left(\dfrac{j}{12}\right)\cent$ or $\dfrac{j}{6}\cent$

33. Ans. 1 $-2 - 6 - 1 = -9$

$+4 + 5 = +9$

$+9 - 9 = 0$

34. Ans. 1 Total distance = 180 miles

Total time   = 5 hours

$180 \div 5$ = 36 miles per hour

35. Ans. 2 $\qquad -4x^2 = (-4)(x)(x)$

$-2x = (-2)(x)$

$(-4)(-2) = +8$

$(-4x^2)(-2x) = 8x^3$

36. Ans. 3 $x^2 + 5ab - 2y^2$

$(2)(2) + (5)(4)(5) - (2)(3)(3)$

$4 \ + 100 - \ 18$

$104 - 18 = 86$

37. Ans. 2
$$x^2 = (x)(x)$$
$$x^3 = (x)(x)(x)$$
$$(x^2)(x^3) = (x)(x)(x)(x)(x) \text{ or } x^5$$

38. Ans. 5 $4x - 8 = 16$
$$4x = 16 + 8$$
THEREFORE
$8x$ equals $2(16 + 8)$
OR
$$8x = 48$$

39. Ans. 5 $\dfrac{x}{4} = 3$
$$x = 12$$
$$4x = (12)(4) \text{ or } 48$$

40. Ans. 1   Let x = shorter piece
then, $4x$ = longer piece
$$5x = 75 \text{ inches}$$
$$x = 15 \text{ inches or 1 foot 3 inches}$$

41. Ans. 1 If 80 is $\dfrac{4}{3}$ of a number

then 20 is $\dfrac{1}{3}$ of that number

and 60 is $\dfrac{3}{3}$ of that number

OR, ALGEBRAICALLY Let x = the number

then $\dfrac{4}{3} x = 80$

and $x = 60$

42. Ans. 4 $A = \dfrac{h}{2}(b + c)$

$A = \dfrac{4}{2}(5 + 6)$

$A = 2(11) = 22$

43. Ans. 3 $V = \dfrac{l\,w\,h}{3}$

$V = \dfrac{(6)(2)(5)}{(3)} = 20$

44. Ans. 4 $x + y = 12$ (1)
$x - y = 4$ (2)
Add equation (1) and (2) then,
$$2x = 16$$
$$x = 8$$

45. Ans. 4 $72 = 6$ dozen
If 35¢ is cost of 1 dozen
Then $(6)(35¢)$ or $2.10 is cost of 6 dozen

46. Ans. 3 $\dfrac{\text{Time for Sam}}{\text{Time for Martin}} = \dfrac{5 \text{ days}}{3 \text{ wks.}} = \dfrac{5 \text{ days}}{21 \text{ days}} = 5{:}21$

47. Ans. 5 If there are x people and w are women, there must be $x - w$ men in the audience.
$$\dfrac{\text{Number of men}}{\text{Number of women}} = \dfrac{x - w}{w}$$

48. Ans. 1 $\dfrac{\text{length}}{\text{width}} = \dfrac{8 \text{ inches}}{6 \text{ inches}} = \dfrac{12 \text{ inches}}{x \text{ inches}}$
$$8x = 72$$
$$x = 9 \text{ inches}$$

49. Ans. 4 From 7:30 a.m. to 6 p.m. $= 10\frac{1}{2}$ hours
Less rest periods $\underline{1\frac{1}{2}\text{ hours}}$
Time Spent Riding 9 hours
Average speed $= \dfrac{\text{Distance}}{\text{Time}} = \dfrac{441}{9} = 49$ miles per hour

50. Ans. 3 Let $x =$ number of pencils bought at 30¢
$$\frac{3 \text{ pencils}}{c \text{ cents}} = \frac{x}{30}$$
$$cx = 90$$
$$x = \frac{90}{c}$$

51. Ans. 5 Since $\frac{1}{8}$ inch $= 15$ miles, then $\frac{8}{8}$ (or 1 inch) $= (8)(15)$ or 120 miles. Therefore $3\frac{1}{2}$ inches $= (120)(3\frac{1}{2})$ or 420 miles.

52. Ans. 3 Then new road is the hypotenuse of a right triangle. Apply the *Pythagorean Principle:*
$$5^2 + 12^2 = x^2$$
$$25 + 144 = x^2$$
$$169 = x^2$$
$$13 = x$$

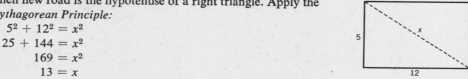

53. Ans. 4 Perimeter of square $= 4(\text{side})$
Let $x =$ side
$4x =$ perimeter
$4x = 40$ inches
$x = 10$ inches
Area of square $= (\text{side})^2 = (10)^2 = 100$

54. Ans. 4 Divide the figure (right) into two rectangles as shown.
Area of a rectangle $= (\text{base})(\text{altitude})$
Area of larger rectangle $= (15)(12) = 180$ square feet
Area of smaller rectangle $= (6)(9) = 54$ square feet
Total area $= 180 + 54$ or 234 square feet.

55. Ans. 4 Volume $= 2' \times 3' \times 1\frac{1}{2}' = 9$ cubic feet
Weight $= (62.5)(9) = 562.5$ pounds

56. Ans. 4 The distance across top $=$ the diameter $= 6$ inches
Therefore the radius $= 3$ inches
Volume $= \pi r^2 h$ where h $=$ height
Volume $= \pi(3'')(3'')(12'') = 108\pi$ cubic inches

57. Ans. 4 The sum of the angles of a triangle equals $180°$.
If 2 angles $= 70° + 20°$ or $90°$ then the third angle must equal $90°$.

58. Ans. 4 The minute hand travels $\dfrac{10 \text{ min.}}{60 \text{ min.}} = \dfrac{1}{6}$ of the way around the clock.
$\dfrac{1}{6}$ of $360° = 60°$

59. Ans. 5 $600 + $2800 + $1600 + $1000 + $2400 = $8,400$. (Total)

60. Ans. 2 Total sales in Meat Department for this six-day period (September 15-20) is $2400.
$2400 \div 6 = 400.

61. Ans. 4 Sales in Dairy Department were $1600
5% (.05) of $1600 $\underline{\$80}$ (expected increase)
$1680 (expected sales)

62. Ans. 3 40% ($\frac{2}{5}$) of $240,000 = $96,000$

63. Ans. 4   8% (.08) of $240,000 = $19,200 (expected gain)
$240,000 + $19,200 = $259,200 (expected sales next year)

64. Ans. 4   25 feet 8 inches =   24 feet 20 inches
                                 — 18 feet 10 inches
                                    6 feet 10 inches

65. Ans. 4   4 quarts = 1 gallon
               10 gallons = 40 quarts
                2 pints   = 1 quart
               10 gallons = 80 pints or 160 half-pints